Your Study of

The New Testament

Made Easier, Third Edition

Part 2

Acts through James

ISBN 13: 978-1-4621-4421-1

Published by CFI, an imprint of Cedar Fort, Inc.
2373 W. 700 S., Springville, UT 84663
Distributed by Cedar Fort, Inc., www.cedarfort.com

Library of Congress Control Number: 2022939322

Cover design by Shawnda T. Craig

Printed in the United States of America

10 9 8 7 6 5 4 3 2 1

Printed on acid-free paper

GOSPEL STUDIES SERIES

Your Study of

The New Testament

Made Easier, Third Edition

Part 2

Acts through James

David J. Ridges

CFI
An imprint of Cedar Fort, Inc.
Springville, Utah

BOOKS BY DAVID J. RIDGES

The Gospel Study Series

- *Your Study of The Book of Isaiah Made Easier, Second Edition*
- *The New Testament Made Easier, Third Edition, Part 1*
- *The New Testament Made Easier, Third Edition, Part 2*
- *The New Testament Made Easier, Third Edition, Part 3*
- *Your Study of The Book of Mormon Made Easier, Part 1*
- *Your Study of The Book of Mormon Made Easier, Part 2*
- *Your Study of The Book of Mormon Made Easier, Part 3*
- *Book of Mormon Made Easier, Family Deluxe Edition, Volumes 1 and 2*
- *Your Study of The Doctrine and Covenants Made Easier, Second Edition, Part 1*
- *Your Study of The Doctrine and Covenants Made Easier, Second Edition, Part 2*
- *Your Study of The Doctrine and Covenants Made Easier, Second Edition, Part 3*
- *The Old Testament Made Easier, Third Edition, Part 1*
- *The Old Testament Made Easier—Selections from the Old Testament, Third Edition, Part 2*
- *The Old Testament Made Easier—Selections from the Old Testament, Third Edition, Part 3*
- *The Old Testament Made Easier—Selections from the Old Testament, Third Edition, Part 4*
- *Your Study of the Pearl of Great Price Made Easier*
- *Your Study of Jeremiah Made Easier*
- *Your Study of The Book of Revelation Made Easier, Second Edition*

Our Savior's Life and Mission to Redeem and Give Hope

Mormon Beliefs and Doctrines Made Easier

The Proclamation on the Family: The Word of the Lord on More than 30 Current Issues

Using the Signs of the Times to Strengthen Your Testimony

Doctrinal Details of the Plan of Salvation: From Premortality to Exaltation

Introduction

Welcome to the third edition of Your Study of the The New Testament Made Easier. This third edition is a substantial expansion of the second edition and is a three-volume set. It contains numerous additional notes and explanations, plus many additional verses from the Joseph Smith Translation of the Bible, which were not included in the second edition.

In Part 1, we will study the life of our Savior as taught in the Four Gospels—Matthew, Mark, Luke, and John, as found in the King James version of the Bible as published and used by The Church of Jesus Christ of Latter-day Saints. (It is interesting to note that only 31 days of the Savior's life and ministry are covered in the Four Gospels.) Part 2 and a portion of Part 3 are a study of Acts through Revelation. Parts 1, 2, and 3 include every verse in the New Testament. The remainder of Part 3 consists of the book *Our Savior's Life and Mission to Redeem and Give Hope* by David J. Ridges. It is a pleasant and fairly easy read of the Savior's life and mission to cleanse, heal, and make exaltation available to us. This book makes use of Matthew, Mark, Luke, and John as it helps you better understand and appreciate the Savior's mortal mission and Atonement and how His marvelous, infinite Atonement can fill your life with richness, confidence, and peace.

Note: In Part 1, I have used bold font for many words and phrases in Matthew, Mark, and Luke as an example of ways you might highlight or mark your own scriptures and also to point things out to you for teaching purposes. Beginning with the Gospel of John, I do not use bold, except for occasional emphasis, and particularly to point out the JST changes to Bible verses. By the way, I often use "we" rather than "I" when making my comments. The reason is simple. My parents taught me to avoid "I trouble."

—David J. Ridges

The JST References in Study Guides by David J. Ridges

Note that some of the JST (The Joseph Smith Translation of the Bible) references I use in my study guides are not found in the King James English-speaking edition of the Bible, published by the Church, in the footnotes or in the Joseph Smith Translation section in the reference section in the back. The reason for this, as explained to me while writing curriculum materials for the Church, is simply that there is not enough room to include all of the JST additions and changes. As you can imagine, as was likewise explained to me, there were difficult decisions that had to be made by the Scriptures Committee of the Church as to which JST contributions were included and which were not.

The Joseph Smith Translation of the Bible in its entirety can generally be found in or ordered through bookstores or online. It was originally published under the auspices of the Reorganized Church of Jesus Christ of Latter Day Saints in Independence, Missouri. The version of the JST that I prefer to use is a parallel column version, *Joseph Smith's "New Translation" of the Bible*, published by Herald Publishing House, Independence, Missouri, in 1970. This parallel column version compares the King James Bible with the JST side by side and includes only the verses that have changes, additions, or deletions made by the Prophet Joseph Smith.

By the way, some members of the Church have wondered whether or not we can trust the JST since it was published by a breakaway faction from our Church. They worry that some changes from Joseph Smith's original manuscript might have been made to support doctrinal differences between us and the RLDS Church. This is not the case. Many years ago, Robert J. Matthews of the Brigham Young University Religion Department was given permission by leaders of the RLDS Church to go to their Independence, Missouri, headquarters and personally compare the original JST document word for word with their publication of the JST. Brother Matthews was thus able to verify that they had been meticulously true to the Prophet's original work.

Contents

Dedication

To my wife and eternal companion, Janette,
who has encouraged and supported me
every step of the way.

FOREWORD

In many years of teaching in the Church and for the Church Educational System, I have found that members of the Church encounter some common problems when it comes to understanding the scriptures. One problem is understanding the language of the scriptures themselves. Another is understanding symbolism. Another is how best to mark scriptures and perhaps make brief notes in them. Yet another concern is how to understand what the scriptures are actually teaching. In other words, what are the major messages being taught by the Lord through His prophets?

This study guide is designed to address each of the concerns mentioned above for Acts through James in the New Testament.

The format is intentionally simple, with some license taken with respect to capitalization and punctuation in order to minimize interruption of the flow. The format is designed to help readers to:

- Quickly gain a basic understanding of these scriptures through the use of brief explanatory notes in brackets within the verses as well as notes between some verses.
- Better understand the beautiful language of the scriptures. This is accomplished in this study guide with in-the-verse notes that define difficult scriptural terms.
- Mark their scriptures and put brief notes in the margins that will help them understand now and remember later what given passages of scripture teach.
- Better understand the symbolism of the parables of Jesus as well as many other passages where symbolism is used.
- Get a feel for the background and setting in which events and teachings take place. A basic understanding of Jewish culture in the days of the Savior is vital. Notes between verses help with these issues.

Over the years, one of the most common expressions of gratitude from my students has been, "Thanks for the notes you had us put in our scriptures." This book is dedicated to that purpose.

Sources for the notes given in this work are as follows:

- The standard works of The Church of Jesus Christ of Latter-day Saints.
- Footnotes in the Latter-day Saint version of the King James Bible.
- The Joseph Smith Translation of the Bible.
- The Bible Dictionary in the back of the Latter-day Saint version of the Bible.
- Various dictionaries.
- *Strong's Exhaustive Concordance of the Bible*, shown as [*Strong's* # or Strong's #].
- Various student manuals provided for our institutes of religion, including the New Testament student manual, Religion 211, *The Life and Teachings of Jesus and His Apostles.*
- James E. Talmage, *Jesus the Christ*, Deseret Book, 1982.
- Various translations of the Bible, including the Martin Luther edition of the German Bible, which Joseph Smith said was the most correct of any then available.
- *Doctrinal New Testament Commentary*, volumes 1, 2, and 3, by Apostle Bruce R. McConkie.
- *Teachings of the Prophet Joseph Smith*, 1976.
- *Understanding the Book of Revelation*, by Jay A. Parry and Donald W. Parry.
- *New International Version of the Bible*, Zondervan Publishing House, 1984.
- Other sources as noted in the text and in the "Sources" section.

I hope that this study guide will serve effectively as a "teacher in your hand" to members of the Church as they seek to increase their understanding of the writings and teachings of the Savior's Apostles. Above all, if this work serves to bring increased understanding and testimony of the Atonement of Christ, all the efforts to put it together will have been far more than worth it. A special thanks goes to my wife, Janette, and my children who have encouraged me every step of the way.

THE ACTS OF THE APOSTLES

It is helpful to know that Luke wrote both the Gospel of Luke and Acts (The Acts of the Apostles). As mentioned at the beginning of Luke in this study guide series, he was a physician, apparently a Greek convert to the gospel. Many believe that Luke addressed his writings to the Gentiles. See Bible Dictionary (at the back of our Bible), under "Luke." Both Luke and Acts were written to "Theophilus" (see Luke 1:3 and Acts 1:1). Theophilus is a Greek name meaning "friend of God" or "beloved of God." Some Bible scholars suggest that "Theophilus" could mean anyone who is a friend of God. However, most consider Theophilus to have been an actual person, probably a Greek official of high rank.

Acts deals mainly with the growth of the Church after the Savior had been resurrected and had ascended up to heaven. In it, Luke writes of the ministries of Peter and the other Apostles and especially gives us much detail about Paul's teaching and missionary journeys to the Gentiles.

We will include verses from the JST (the Joseph Smith Translation of the Bible) frequently for clarification. As we do so, you will be able to gain an even stronger testimony of the inspired work of the Prophet Joseph Smith.

ACTS 1

As this chapter begins, Luke explains that this account is a continuation of his former account (the Book of Luke) to Theophilus. After a very brief review of Luke, he proceeds to tell Theophilus what took place with the Church and spread of the gospel after the Savior's ascension into heaven. Among other things, you will see that Peter has now taken on his role as president of the Church, and you will see a new Apostle chosen to take the place of Judas Iscariot.

1 THE former treatise [*the former account, namely, the Gospel of Luke*] have I made, O Theophilus, of all that Jesus began both to do and teach,

2 Until the day in which he was taken up [*Acts 1:9–11*], after that he through the Holy Ghost had given commandments unto the apostles whom he had chosen:

In verse 3, next, you will see the word "passion." As used here it refers to the Savior's suffering for us, and includes His agony in the Garden of Gethsemane and on the cross. You will see that the Prophet Joseph Smith uses "sufferings" in place of "passion," as you read the JST [*Joseph Smith Translation of the Bible*], quoted after verse 3.

3 To whom also he shewed [*showed, pronounced "showed"*] himself alive after his passion by many infallible [*absolute*] proofs, being seen of them forty days, and speaking of the things pertaining to the kingdom of God:

JST Acts 1:3

3 To whom also he **showed** himself alive after his **sufferings** by many infallible proofs, being seen of them forty days, and speaking of the things pertaining to the kingdom of God;

In verse three, above, we learn that the Savior associated with His Apostles during the forty days following His resurrection. They saw Him and spent time with Him as He taught and instructed them in preparation for the time when they would lead the Church, after His departure.

4 And, being assembled together with them, commanded them that they should not depart from Jerusalem, but wait for the promise of the Father [*that they would receive the full power of the Gift of the Holy Ghost; see John 14:16–17, 26, etc.*], which, saith he, ye have heard of me [*which, Jesus reminded them, they had heard of from Him*].

JST Acts 1:4

3 And, being **with them when they were** assembled together, commanded them that they should not depart from Jerusalem, but wait for the promise of the Father, which, saith he, ye have heard of me.

5 For John truly baptized with water; but ye shall be baptized with the Holy Ghost not many days hence [*from now*]. [*This will happen on the day of Pentecost. See Acts 2:1–4.*]

We know from Luke 4:1, Matthew 3:13–17 and many other references that the Holy Ghost was actively functioning during the Savior's mortal ministry. Yet, in verse 5, above, the Apostles are told that, in a few days, they would be "baptized with the Holy Ghost." We understand that the full power of the Gift of the Holy Ghost was not given these men while the Savior was with them, and that it is what was given to them after the Savior departed. See Bible Dictionary under "Holy Ghost."

6 When they therefore were come together [*when they had met together, at the end of the forty days, to be instructed some more by the resurrected Savior*], they asked of him, saying, Lord, wilt thou at this time restore again the kingdom to Israel [*in other words, is the time for the Second Coming about here, when Israel will be restored and the gospel taught upon the whole earth*] ?

7 And he said unto them, It is not for you to know the times or the seasons [*the exact timing of these things*], which the Father hath put in his own power [*the Father is the one who will say when these things will happen; see Matthew 24:36, Mark 13:32, Revelation 15:15*].

8 But ye shall receive power, after

that the Holy Ghost is come upon you [*in full power; see note following verse 5, above*]: and ye shall be witnesses unto me both in Jerusalem, and in all Judea, and in Samaria, and unto the uttermost [*most distant*] part of the earth.

9 And when he had spoken these things, while they beheld [*watched*], he was taken up; and a cloud received him out of their sight.

10 And while they looked stedfastly [*in rapt attention*] toward heaven as he went up, behold, two men [*angels*] stood by them in white apparel [*clothing*];

11 Which also said, Ye men of Galilee, why stand ye gazing up into heaven? this same Jesus, which is taken up from you into heaven, shall so come in like manner as ye have seen him go into heaven. [The Savior will come in clouds of glory at the time of His Second Coming.]

It is interesting to note that the Second Coming is mentioned over 1500 times in the Old Testament and over 300 times in the New Testament.

12 Then returned they unto Jerusalem from the mount called Olivet [*the Mount of Olives, just outside Jerusalem*], which is from Jerusalem a sabbath day's journey [*about 3,000 feet; see Bible Dictionary under "Sabbath"*].

13 And when they were come in [*had come into the building*], they went up into an upper room, where abode [*lived*] both Peter, and James, and John, and Andrew, Philip, and Thomas, Bartholomew, and Matthew, James the son of Alphæus, and Simon Zelotes, and Judas the brother of James. [*All eleven remaining Apostles were apparently staying temporarily in Jerusalem, as commanded in verse 4, above.*]

14 These all continued with one accord [*in unity of purpose*] in prayer and supplication [*asking God for things they desired*], with the women, and Mary the mother of Jesus, and with his brethren [*Jesus' half brothers—He had at least four; see Mark 6:3*].

Next, beginning with verse 15, we see Peter take charge, indicating to us that he is now serving as the president of the Church. He will explain what happened to Judas Iscariot and the need to find a replacement for him to serve in the Quorum of the Twelve.

15 ¶ And in those days [*at a certain point during those days*] Peter stood up in the midst of the disciples, and said, (the number of names together [*the total number who were meeting together*] were about an hundred and twenty,)

16 Men and brethren, this scripture [*Psalm 41:9*] must needs have been fulfilled [*had to be fulfilled*], which the Holy Ghost by the mouth of [*through*] David spake before [*spoke in the past*] concerning Judas [*Iscariot*], which [*who*] was guide to them that took Jesus [*who*

guided the soldiers to arrest Jesus].

17 For he was numbered with us [*he was one of the Twelve*], and had obtained part of this ministry. [*Judas Iscariot worked with us as one of the twelve Apostles.*]

18 Now this man [*Judas*] purchased a field with the reward of iniquity [*money obtained through wickedness; the thirty pieces of silver Judas was paid for betraying Jesus was used to buy a field*]; and falling headlong, he burst asunder in the midst, and all his bowels gushed out.

Matthew 27:3–8 tells us that Judas hanged himself. From verse 18, above, we would conclude that the rope broke, or was cut later, and that Judas' body fell headfirst down a steep incline and burst open.

19 And it was known unto all the dwellers at Jerusalem [*everybody in Jerusalem knew about Judas Iscariot's awful death*]; insomuch as that field is called in their proper [*own*] tongue, Aceldama, that is to say, The field of blood.

20 For it is written in the book of Psalms [*69:25*], Let his habitation be desolate, and let no man dwell therein: and his bishoprick [*church calling; Psalm 109:8*] let another take.

21 Wherefore of these men which have companied with [*who have accompanied*] us all the time that the Lord Jesus went in and out [*came and went*] among us,

22 Beginning from the baptism of John [*beginning at the time John the Baptist baptized Jesus*], unto that same day that he [*Jesus*] was taken up from us, must one be ordained to be a witness with us of his resurrection. [*We need an Apostle to replace Judas Iscariot.*]

23 And they appointed two [*selected two men*], Joseph called Barsabas, who was surnamed [*whose family name was*] Justus, and Matthias.

24 And they prayed, and said, Thou, Lord, which knowest the hearts of all men, shew whether [*show which*] of these two thou hast chosen,

25 That he [*the new Apostle*] may take part of this ministry and apostleship, from which Judas by transgression fell, that he [*Judas*] might go to his own place [*reward*].

26 And they gave forth their lots; and the lot fell upon Matthias; and he was numbered with the eleven apostles. [*Matthias became a member of the twelve Apostles.*]

Praying, and then casting lots, sticks of wood, or whatever, with one being shorter than the other, such that the short stick would indicate Matthias, and the long stick Joseph Justus, might be the way the Lord indicated to the other Apostles that Matthias was to be the new Apostle. However, it may well be that "they gave forth their lots," verse 26, above, means that they gave their sustaining votes to Peter after he had selected the new Apostle, by inspiration. The Prophet today is the one who chooses new Apostles, and that choice is sustained by the members of the Quorum of the Twelve. See McConkie, *Doctrinal New Testament Commentary*, Vol. 2, p. 32.

ACTS 2

This chapter contains the rather well-known account of the marvelous out-pouring of the Holy Ghost on the Day of Pentecost. Peter will explain to the crowd that has gathered what has taken place and will preach a great sermon leading up to an invitation to be baptized and receive the gift of the Holy Ghost. You may well recognize verses 37–38 which are often used in our missionary work today.

1 AND when the day of Pentecost was fully come [*had arrived*], they [*the Apostles and other faithful Saints*] were all with one accord in one place [*were all gathered together in harmony and unity in one location*].

"Pentecost" means "fiftieth" in Greek. This feast of gratitude to God was held fifty days after Passover. Large numbers of faithful Jews gathered to Jerusalem to celebrate this special festival. See Bible Dictionary under "Feasts."

2 And suddenly there came a sound from heaven as of a rushing mighty wind, and it filled all the house where they were sitting.

3 And there appeared unto them cloven tongues like as of fire [*what appeared to be tongues of fire which separated*], and it sat upon each of them.

JST Acts 2:3

3 And there appeared unto them cloven tongues like as of fire, and it **rested** upon each of them.

4 And they were all filled with the Holy Ghost, and began to speak with other tongues [*in other languages*], as the Spirit gave them utterance [*the ability to speak*].

At the dedication of the Kirtland Temple, in Ohio, there was another "Day of Pentecost" type experience. During the dedicatory prayer, on March 27, 1836, the Prophet Joseph prayed for a special outpouring of the Holy Ghost. "Let it be fulfilled upon them as in the days of Pentecost," he prayed. "Let the gift of tongues be poured out upon thy people, even cloven tongues as of fire, and the interpretation thereof. And let thy house be filled, as with a rushing mighty wind, with thy glory." (D&C 109:35–37.)

This prayer was literally fulfilled, not once, but for several days following the initial dedicatory services. Joseph Smith reported that, on one occasion: "A noise was heard like the sound of a rushing mighty wind, which filled the Temple, and all the congregation simultaneously arose, being moved upon by an invisible power; many began to speak in tongues and prophesy; others saw glorious visions;

and I beheld the Temple was filled with angels, which fact I declared to the congregation. The people of the neighborhood came running together (hearing an unusual sound within, and seeing a bright light like a pillar of fire resting upon the Temple,) and were astonished at what was taking place. This continued until the meeting closed at eleven p.m." He reported the following as happening on March 30, 1836, as dedication services and worship continued: "I left the meeting in the charge of the Twelve, and retired about nine o'clock in the evening. The brethren continued exhorting, prophesying, and speaking in tongues until five o'clock in the morning. The Savior made His appearance to some, while angels ministered to others, and it was a Pentecost and an endowment indeed, long to be remembered, for the sound shall go forth from this place into all the world, and the occurrences of this day shall be handed down upon the pages of sacred history, to all generations; as the day of Pentecost, so shall this day be numbered and celebrated as a year of jubilee, and time of rejoicing to the Saints of the Most High God." See Joseph Smith, *History of The Church of Jesus Christ of Latter-day Saints*, Vol. 2, pp. 428 and 432–433.

5 And there were dwelling at Jerusalem [*staying in Jerusalem for the Pentecost worship and festivities*] Jews, devout men, out of every nation under heaven.

6 Now when this was noised abroad [*when the news about what happened (verses 2–4, above) was spread*], the multitude [*a crowd*] came together, and were confounded [*confused; astounded*], because that every man heard them speak in his own language.

7 And they [*people in the crowd*] were all amazed and marvelled, saying one to another, Behold, are not all these which speak Galilæans [*Aren't these men who are speaking all from Galilee*]?

8 And how hear we every man in our own tongue, wherein we were born [*then how is it that each of us is hearing them in our native language*]?

Next, in verses 9–11, Luke records some of the nationalities and foreign languages represented in the crowd.

9 Parthians, and Medes, and Elamites, and the dwellers in Mesopotamia, and in Judæa, and Cappadocia, in Pontus, and Asia,

10 Phrygia, and Pamphylia, in Egypt, and in the parts of Libya about Cyrene, and strangers of Rome, Jews and proselytes [*converts to Judaism*],

11 Cretes and Arabians, we do hear them speak in our tongues [*in our native language*] the wonderful works of God.

12 And they were all amazed, and were in doubt [*were confused*], saying one to another, What meaneth this?

13 Others mocking said, These men are full of new wine. [*Some ridiculed what was going on, saying that the Apostles were drunk, and that's how they could speak all those different languages.*]

14 ¶ But Peter, standing up with the eleven, lifted up [*raised*] his voice, and said unto them, Ye men of Judæa, and all ye that dwell at Jerusalem [*and all you from other countries who are visiting in Jerusalem*], be this known unto you, and hearken to [*listen and act upon*] my words:

15 For these are not drunken, as ye suppose, seeing it is but the third hour of the day [*it is only 9 AM*].

16 But this is that which was spoken by the prophet Joel;

In verses 17–21, next, Peter basically quotes Joel 2:28–32.

17 And it shall come to pass in the last days, saith God, I will pour out of my Spirit upon all flesh: and your sons and your daughters shall prophesy, and your young men shall see visions, and your old men shall dream dreams:

18 And on my servants and on my handmaidens I will pour out in those days of my Spirit; and they shall prophesy:

19 And I will shew wonders in heaven above, and signs in the earth beneath; blood, and fire, and vapour of smoke:

20 The sun shall be turned into darkness, and the moon into blood, before that great and notable day of the Lord come:

21 And it shall come to pass, that whosoever shall call on the name of the Lord shall be saved. [*End of quote from Joel. Peter now continues.*]

22 Ye men of Israel, hear these words; Jesus of Nazareth, a man approved of God among you by miracles and wonders and signs, which God did by him [*through Jesus*] in the midst of [*among*] you, as ye yourselves also know:

23 Him, being delivered by the determinate counsel [*according to the plan presented in the council in heaven where Christ was chosen to be our Redeemer*] and foreknowledge of God, ye have taken, and by wicked hands have crucified and slain:

24 Whom God hath raised up [*resurrected*], having loosed the pains of death [*having freed Jesus from the pains of death*]: because it was not possible that he [*Jesus*] should be holden of it [*it was not possible that Christ should be held captive by death and the grave*].

25 For David speaketh concerning him [*Psalm 16:8–11*], I foresaw the Lord always before my face, for he is on my right hand, that I should not be moved: [*"Right hand" is symbolic of making covenants. Being on the "right hand" of God is symbolic of being saved.*]

26 Therefore did my heart rejoice, and my tongue was glad; moreover also my flesh shall rest in hope:

27 Because thou wilt not leave my soul in hell, neither wilt thou suffer thine Holy One to see corruption.

JST Acts 2:27

27 Because thou wilt not leave my soul in prison, neither wilt thou suffer thine Holy One to see corruption.

28 Thou hast made known to me the ways of life; thou shalt make me full of joy with thy countenance. [*End of quote from Psalm.*]

29 Men and brethren, let me freely speak unto you of the patriarch [*of our ancestor*] David, that he is both dead and buried, and his sepulchre [*tomb, grave*] is with us unto this day. [*In other words, David is still dead and buried, meaning that he did not get resurrected with the righteous at the time of Christ's resurrection. See D&C 133:54–55 to see who was resurrected with the Savior.*]

30 Therefore being a prophet [*King David*], and knowing that God had sworn [*promised*] with an oath [*with a covenant*] to him, that of the fruit of his loins [*from his posterity*], according to the flesh [*here on earth*], he would raise up Christ to sit on his throne; [*David was promised that Christ would be one of his descendants and would be King.*]

31 He seeing this before [*David, having seen this before it happened*] spake [*spoke*] of the resurrection of Christ, that his soul was not left in hell, neither his flesh did see corruption.

The phrase "that his soul was not left in hell" in verse 31, above, seems to have a dual meaning, as is often the case in the scriptures. One meaning is that Satan and all the powers of hell would not succeed in overcoming Christ or preventing His resurrection. In this sense, the word "hell" in verse 31 would mean the spirit world. See Bible Dictionary under the topic "Hell," first four lines, where "hell," "Sheol," and "Hades" all refer to the world of departed spirits. In other words, Christ would not remain, as others had, in the world of departed spirits, but would be resurrected after a short three days.

A second meaning of the phrase "his soul was not left in hell" refers to King David. After having committed adultery with Uriah's wife, Bathsheba, and then being told that she was expecting his child, (2 Samuel 11:2–5), David arranged to have Uriah killed in battle and then quickly married Bathsheba, thus attempting to cover up his adultery with murder. This was a tragedy, and David pled with the Lord not to leave his soul in hell. Joseph Smith tells us that David got a promise that his soul would not be left in hell (*Teachings of the Prophet Joseph Smith*, p. 339). We understand the "hell" spoken of by David in reference to his own status to be perdition, meaning "outer darkness" as we commonly use the term. See McConkie, *Doctrinal New Testament Commentary*, Vol. 2, p. 39. According to D&C 42:18, murderers cannot be forgiven as far as gaining exaltation is concerned, but D&C 76:103 combined with Revelation 22:15 inform us that such murderers will go to telestial glory, and thus are out of Satan's grasp eternally. Tragically, David was a murderer, and will apparently go to telestial glory. D&C 132:39 confirms that David will not obtain exaltation. It also assures us that David's wives were not penalized eternally because of their husband's wickedness. They would be blessed to marry someone else and thus be exalted.

32 This Jesus hath God raised up [*resurrected*], whereof we all are witnesses.

33 Therefore being by the right hand [*covenant hand*] of God exalted [*Christ kept His covenants and the Father exalted him*], and having received of [*from*] the Father the promise of the Holy Ghost, he hath shed forth this, which ye now see and hear [*He sent the Holy Ghost, as promised, and this is why you witnessed the speaking in tongues which has amazed you so*].

34 For David is not ascended into the heavens [*David didn't make it to heaven; see footnote 34a in your Bible, which refers to D&C 132:39*]: but he saith himself [*but he prophesied; Psalm 110:1*], The LORD [*Heavenly Father*] said unto my Lord [*Christ*], Sit thou on my right hand [*sit down with Me in heaven*],

35 Until I make thy foes thy footstool [*until the Second Coming, and also, a thousand years later, at the end of the Millennium, after the final battle with Satan and his followers (the battle of Gog and Magog), when You will triumph over all enemies of righteousness*].

36 Therefore let all the house of Israel know assuredly, that God [*the Father*] hath made that same Jesus, whom ye have crucified, both Lord and Christ.

Above, in verse 36, Peter lays the blame for the Savior's crucifixion directly upon the Jews of that day, rather than upon the Romans. However, watch in verse 39, below, as repentance and forgiveness are extended to the Jews.

37 ¶ Now when they [*the people in the crowd who had heard the Apostles speak in tongues with the power of the Holy Ghost upon them*] heard this, they were pricked [*deeply touched*] in their heart, and said unto Peter and to the rest of the apostles, Men and brethren, what shall we do?

38 Then Peter said unto them, Repent, and be baptized every one of you in the name of Jesus Christ for the remission of sins [*to be forgiven of your sins*], and ye shall receive the gift of the Holy Ghost.

39 For the promise [*of forgiveness of sins*] is unto you [*is available to you*], and to your children, and to

all that are afar off [*to everyone*], even as many as the Lord our God shall call.

Verse 39, above, is most significant. In verse 36, Peter boldly told the Jews that they had crucified Christ. Yet, in this verse, mercy is still extended to them as they are invited to repent and be forgiven. This is a strong reminder of how patient and kind the Lord is and how anxious He is to forgive us and help us progress.

40 And with many other words did he [*Peter*] testify and exhort [*strongly counsel*], saying, Save yourselves from this untoward [*wicked and rebellious*] generation.

41 ¶ Then they that [*who*] gladly received his word were baptized: and the same day there were added unto them about three thousand souls. [*About 3,000 converts joined the Church that day.*]

42 And they [*the new converts*] continued stedfastly [*faithfully*] in the apostles' doctrine [*teachings*] and fellowship, and in breaking of bread [*the sacrament*], and in prayers.

43 And fear came upon every soul [*everyone was filled with awe and deep respect for God*]: and many wonders [*miracles and amazing things*] and signs were done by the apostles.

44 And all that believed were together [*were united and harmonious*], and had all things common [*they lived a united order*];

45 And sold their possessions and goods, and parted them to all men [*shared with everyone*], as every man had need [*according to each person's needs*].

46 And they, continuing daily with one accord [*in unity and peace*] in the temple, and breaking bread from house to house, did eat their meat [*food*] with gladness and singleness of heart,

Just a quick reminder. The word "meat" as used in verse 46, above, means "food." When the Bible refers to beef, chicken, lamb, etc., it uses the word "flesh."

47 Praising [*worshiping*] God, and having favour with all the people. And the Lord added to the church daily such as should be saved. [*With the help of the Lord, many people who wanted to be saved were baptized daily.*]

ACTS 3

Watch now as Peter and John fearlessly and faithfully go forth in their calling as Apostles of Jesus Christ. Imagine the excited talk among the people as these great servants of the Lord carry on the work of the Master. You will probably recognize verses 19–21, which prophesy of the restoration of the gospel in the latter-days.

1 NOW Peter and John went up together into the temple at the hour of prayer, being the ninth hour [*about 3 PM*].

JST Acts 3:1

1 Now Peter and John went up together into the temple at the **ninth hour, for prayer**.

2 And a certain man lame from his mother's womb [*who had been crippled since he was born*] was carried, whom they laid daily at the gate of the temple which is called Beautiful, to ask alms [*donations*] of them that entered into the temple;

There were several "gates" or doorways into the temple grounds. One of these was named "Beautiful," and it was here that friends left the cripple each day so he could beg for a living.

3 Who seeing Peter and John about to go into the temple [*into the inner courtyard of the temple complex*] asked an alms [*a donation*].

4 And Peter, fastening his eyes upon him with John, said, Look on us.

JST Acts 3:4

4 And Peter **and John**, fastening **their** eyes upon him, said, Look on us.

5 And he [*the crippled man*] gave heed unto them, expecting to receive something of them.

6 Then Peter said, Silver and gold have I none; but such as I have give I thee: In the name of Jesus Christ of Nazareth rise up and walk.

7 And he took him by the right hand, and lifted him up: and immediately his feet and ankle bones received strength.

8 And he [*the crippled man*] leaping up stood, and walked, and entered with them into the temple, walking, and leaping, and praising God.

9 And all the people saw him walking and praising God:

10 And they knew that it was he which [*who*] sat for alms at the Beautiful gate of the temple: and they were filled with wonder and amazement at that which had happened unto him.

11 And as the lame man which was healed held [*held onto*] Peter and John, all the people ran together unto them in the porch that is called Solomon's, greatly wondering [*astonished*].

12 ¶ And when Peter saw it, he answered unto [*responded to*] the people, Ye men of Israel, why marvel ye at this? or why look ye so earnestly on us [*so seriously at us*], as though by our own power or holiness we had made this man to walk?

JST Acts 3:12

12 And when Peter saw **this**, he answered **and said** unto the people, Ye men of Israel, why marvel ye at this? or why look ye so earnestly on us, as though by our own power or holiness we had made this man to walk?

13 The God of Abraham, and of Isaac, and of Jacob, the God

of our fathers, hath glorified his Son Jesus; whom ye delivered up [*whom you told Pilate to crucify*], and denied him [*you said "Crucify Him!"*] in the presence of Pilate, when he was determined to let him go.

14 But ye denied the Holy One [*Christ*] and the Just, and desired a murderer [*Barabbas; Luke 23:16–25*] to be granted [*released*] unto you;

Did you notice that the word "Just," in verse 14 above, is capitalized? When capitalized, it is another word for Christ.

15 And killed the Prince of life [*Jesus*], whom God hath raised from the dead; whereof we are witnesses. [*We are witnesses of the resurrected Christ whom you insisted be crucified.*]

The JST verse following Bible verse 16, next, will help you to better understand it.

16 And his name through faith in his [*Christ's*] name hath made this man strong, whom ye see and know: yea, the faith which is by him [*the faith which comes through Christ*] hath given him [*the crippled man*] this perfect soundness [*complete healing*] in the presence of you all.

JST Acts 3:16

16 And **this man**, through faith in his name, **hath been made strong**, whom ye see and know; yea, the faith which is **in** him hath given him this perfect soundness in the presence of you all.

17 And now, brethren, I wot that through ignorance ye did it [*insisted that Jesus be crucified*], as did also your rulers.

JST Acts 3:17

17 And now, brethren, I **know** that through ignorance ye **have done this**, **as also** your rulers.

18 But those things, which God before had shewed by the mouth of all his prophets, that Christ should suffer, he hath so fulfilled. [*Jesus fulfilled all the prophecies about the Messiah.*]

19 ¶ Repent ye therefore, and be converted, that your sins may be blotted out, when the times of refreshing shall come from the presence of the Lord;

20 And he [*the Father; see Mark 13:32*] shall send Jesus Christ [*the Second Coming; see footnote 19a in your Bible*], which [*who*] before [*in the Old Testament*] was preached unto you:

JST Acts 3:20

20 And he shall send Jesus Christ, which before was preached unto you, **whom ye have crucified**;

Just a note to emphasize that Peter has grown much in strength since the night he denied knowing Jesus three times before the rooster crowed. See Matthew 26:69–75. He now boldly preaches of Christ to the Jews in the face of certain arrest.

Verse 21, next, is often used by our missionaries to teach that the restoration of the gospel through Joseph Smith was clearly prophesied by Peter.

21 Whom the heaven must receive [*who will dwell in heaven*] until the times of restitution of all things [*the restoration of the gospel through the Prophet Joseph Smith and the fulfillment of all the signs of the times*], which God hath spoken by the mouth of all his holy prophets since the world began.

22 For Moses truly said [*Deuteronomy 18:15–19*] unto the fathers [*our ancestors in Old Testament times*], A prophet [*Jesus Christ*] shall the Lord your God raise up unto you of your brethren, like unto me; him shall ye hear in all things whatsoever he shall say unto you.

23 And it shall come to pass, that every soul, which will not hear that prophet [*Christ*], shall be destroyed from among the people.

24 Yea, and all the prophets from Samuel and those that follow after, as many as have spoken, have likewise foretold [*prophesied*] of these days.

Next, Peter will strongly teach these people to get on the covenant path, and that if they will repent and be converted, they will receive the blessings promised to Abraham and his descendants (see Abraham 2:9–11), meaning the blessings promised to covenant Israel; or, in other words, ultimately, exaltation. These blessings, especially the blessings of Abraham, Isaac, and Jacob, are often mentioned in patriarchal blessings.

25 Ye are the children of [*descendants of*] the prophets, and of the covenant which God made with our fathers, saying unto Abraham [*Genesis 12:3*], And in thy seed shall all the kindreds of the earth be blessed.

26 Unto you first [*the Jews received the gospel first from Jesus, then it went to the Gentiles*] God, having raised up his Son Jesus, sent him to bless you, in turning away every one of you from his iniquities [*in giving every one of you the opportunity to turn away from your sins*].

ACTS 4

Opposition will continue increasing as the Adversary seeks to stop the work of the Lord. Luke describes how Peter and John are arrested and threatened with serious consequences if they don't stop teaching about Jesus Christ. They don't stop.

1 AND as they [*Peter and John; see chapter three, verse one*] spake unto the people, the priests, and the captain of the temple, and the Sadducees, came upon them,

2 Being grieved [*disappointed, angry*] that they [*the Apostles*] taught the people, and preached through Jesus the resurrection from the dead.

The religious leaders of the Jews, mentioned in verse 1, above, were the main force behind getting the Savior crucified. They had hoped in their evil hearts to have stopped the religious movement started by Jesus. Now they find that the Apostles are continuing to teach about Jesus and His gospel, including the resurrection from the dead. The Sadducees did not believe in resurrection (see Bible Dictionary under "Sadducees"), therefore, such preaching is particularly irritating to them. Furthermore, a crippled man, whom many people knew, has been healed by Peter and John (Acts 3:6–7) and everybody is talking about it. These wicked religious rulers of the Jews are alarmed because they find that the people are excited about the Apostles' teachings and miracle, and many are joining the Church.

3 And they laid hands on them [*they arrested Peter and John*], and put them in hold [*in jail*] unto [*until*] the next day: for it was now eventide [*evening*].

4 Howbeit [*however*] many of them which heard the word [*the preaching*] believed; and the number of the men was about five thousand. [*5,000 more are ready to join the Church.*]

5 ¶ And it came to pass on the morrow, that their rulers [*the Jews' religious leaders*], and elders, and scribes,

6 And Annas the high priest, and Caiaphas [*who presided at the illegal trial of Christ during the night. See Matthew 26:57*], and John, and Alexander, and as many as were of the kindred [*relatives*] of the high priest, were gathered together [*had met in council*] at Jerusalem.

Israel was part of the Roman Empire at this time. However, the Romans allowed the Jews to pretty much have their own government and to govern their own affairs, with the exception that they were not allowed to execute anyone without Roman permission. The Jewish religious leaders mentioned in verses 5 and 6, above, represented the highest governing body of Jews. The fact that they quickly gathered together in council is evidence of how alarmed they were about Peter and John and their influence among the people. Watch now as they proceed to interrogate Peter and John.

7 And when they had set them [*Peter and John*] in the midst [*in the center of the court chambers*], they asked, By what power, or by what name, have ye done this [*by whose authority did you heal this lame man*]?

Watch now as Peter and John boldly answer. Notice also what the Holy Ghost can do for us when we are doing the Lord's work.

8 Then Peter, filled with the Holy Ghost, said unto them, Ye rulers of the people, and elders of Israel,

9 If we this day be examined of [*be placed on trial because of*] the good deed done to the impotent [*crippled*] man, by what means he

is made whole [*as to how he was healed*];

10 Be it known unto you all, and to all the people of Israel, that by the name of Jesus Christ of Nazareth, whom ye crucified, whom God raised from the dead, even by him doth this man stand here before you whole. [*In other words, we healed him in the name of Jesus Christ, whom you crucified and who is now resurrected. It is through Christ's power that the man is healed.*]

11 This [*Christ*] is the stone which was set at nought of [*which was rejected by*] you builders, which is become the head of the corner [*the capstone; the finishing of the whole building*].

Peter is quoting Psalm 118:22, where it was prophesied that builders would foolishly reject the very stone (Christ) or rock upon which God's work is built, in other words, upon which their salvation depends. The imagery is that wicked builders would foolishly refuse to use a solid foundation upon which to build, rather, would build their own kingdom, with no foundation, which guarantees that it will crumble. It reminds us of the "great and spacious building" in Lehi's dream (1 Nephi 8:26) which had no foundation at all! Peter tells these high rulers that they are the "builders" who have rejected the Stone, and have thus fulfilled the prophecy in Psalms!

Next, Peter bears testimony to those who have him on trial, that Jesus Christ is the only source of salvation.

12 Neither is there salvation in any other [*there is no other way to be saved, other than through Christ*]: for there is none other name under heaven given among men, whereby we must be saved.

The last phrase in verse 12, above, would be a good one for you to mark. It is powerful and very important doctrine.

13 ¶ Now when they saw the boldness of Peter and John, and perceived [*were aware*] that they were unlearned [*hadn't had the formal training which the Jewish religious leaders had had*] and ignorant men [*common, ordinary men*], they marvelled; and they took knowledge of them [*they took note*], that they had been with Jesus.

14 And beholding [*seeing*] the man which was healed standing with them, they could say nothing against it.

15 But when they had commanded them [*Peter and John*] to go aside out of the council [*to step outside the courtroom*], they conferred [*counseled*] among themselves,

16 Saying, What shall we do to these men? for that indeed a notable miracle hath been done by them is manifest to all them that dwell in Jerusalem [*everybody in Jerusalem knows that Peter and John have done a great miracle*]; and we cannot deny it [*we can't make it go away*].

17 But that it spread no further among the people, let us straitly [*strictly*] threaten them, that they speak henceforth [*from now on*] to no man in this name. [*Let's threaten them with most serious consequences if they do any more such things in the name of Jesus Christ.*]

It has been said that wickedness does not promote rational thought and behavior. Verse 18, next, is certainly an example of this.

18 And they called them [*back into the courtroom*], and commanded them not to speak at all nor teach in the name of Jesus.

19 But Peter and John answered and said unto them, Whether it be right in the sight of God to hearken unto you [*to obey you*] more than unto God, judge ye [*you decide*].

20 For we cannot but speak the things which we have seen and heard. [*In other words, we will obey God rather than you.*]

21 So when they had further threatened them, they let them go, finding nothing how they might punish them, because of the people: for all men glorified God for that which was done. [*They were afraid to do more than threaten Peter and John for fear of causing a riot among the people, because of their popularity.*]

JST Acts 4:21

21 So when they had further threatened them, they let them go, finding nothing how they might punish them, because of the people; for **many** glorified God for that which was done.

22 For the man was above [*over*] forty years old, on whom this miracle of healing was shewed [*showed*]. [*People had known of this crippled man for over forty years, so there were too many witnesses as to the miracle for the chief priests and elders to squelch it successfully.*]

23 ¶ And being let go, they [*Peter and John*] went to their own company [*to their group of Church members*], and reported all that the chief priests and elders had said unto them.

Watch next, in verses 24–30, as the members of the Church in this group pray powerfully for God to give Peter and John power to keep preaching. Some people get the idea from the Bible and elsewhere that certain rote or memorized prayers are best or more convenient to use. This prayer by these faithful Saints reminds us that spontaneous prayers that fit the occasion are very appropriate.

24 And when they [*the members*] heard that, they lifted up their voice to God with one accord [*in unity*], and said, Lord, thou art God, which hast made heaven, and earth, and the sea, and all that in them is:

25 Who by the mouth of thy servant David hast said [*Psalm 2:1–2*],

Why did the heathen rage, and the people imagine vain things?

26 The kings of the earth stood up, and the rulers were gathered together against the Lord, and against his Christ.

27 For of a truth [*just as was stated in David's prophecy,*] against thy holy child Jesus, whom thou hast anointed, both Herod, and Pontius Pilate, with the Gentiles, and the people of Israel, were gathered together, [*King Herod, Pontius Pilate, etc. have fulfilled the prophecy that they would gather together against Jesus.*]

28 For to do whatsoever thy hand and thy counsel determined before to be done. [*They did exactly as it was prophesied that they would do.*]

29 And now, Lord, behold [*consider*] their [*the rulers*] threatenings [*against Peter and John*]: and grant unto thy servants, that with all boldness they may speak thy word,

30 By stretching forth thine hand to heal; and that signs and wonders may be done by the name of thy holy child Jesus.

31 ¶ And when they had prayed, the place was shaken where they were assembled together; and they were all filled with the Holy Ghost, and they spake [*spoke*] the word of God with boldness.

32 And the multitude of them that believed were of one heart and of one soul: neither said any of them that ought of the things which he possessed was his own; but they had all things common. [*They lived in harmony, in a united order.*]

33 And with great power gave the apostles witness of [*the Apostles bore testimony with great power of*] the resurrection of the Lord Jesus: and great grace [*help from the Lord*] was upon them all.

In verses 34–37, next, we see these early Saints practicing the law of consecration.

34 Neither was there any among them that lacked: for as many as were possessors of lands or houses sold them, and brought the prices of the things that were sold,

35 And laid them down at the apostles' feet [*they gave the money they received from selling their possessions to the Apostles*]: and distribution was made unto every man according as he had need.

36 And Joses, who by the apostles was surnamed Barnabas, (which is, being interpreted, The son of consolation,) a Levite, and of the country of Cyprus,

37 Having land, sold it, and brought the money, and laid it at the apostles' feet.

ACTS 5

Luke begins this chapter by informing us that a certain man and his wife were intentionally dishonest with the Lord. They attempted to deceive the Apostles, claiming to be consecrating all they had to the Lord, but secretly holding back a portion for themselves.

1 BUT a certain man named Ananias, with Sapphira his wife, sold a possession [*some land; see verse 8*],

2 And kept back part of the price [*the money received*], his wife also being privy to it [*being fully aware of what he was doing*], and brought a certain part [*just part of the money*], and laid it at the apostles' feet [*donated it to the Apostles for the united order*].

3 But Peter said, Ananias, why hath Satan filled thine heart to lie to the Holy Ghost, and to keep back part of the price of the land? [*Why have you secretly kept back part of the money for yourself and pretended to donate all of it to the Church for the united order?*]

4 Whiles it remained, was it not thine own [*didn't it belong to you before you sold it*]? and after it was sold, was it not in thine own power [*wasn't all the money you got for it in your control*]? why hast thou conceived this thing [*hatched this plot*] in thine heart? thou hast not lied unto men, but unto God.

Those who intentionally lie to their bishop or stake president during an interview would do well to read and take to heart the last two phrases of verse 4, above.

5 And Ananias hearing these words fell down, and gave up the ghost [*died*]: and great fear came on all them that heard these things.

6 And the young men arose, wound him up [*wrapped him in strips of burial cloth*], and carried him out, and buried him.

7 And it was about the space of three hours after [*about three hours later*], when his wife, not knowing what was done [*not knowing what had happened to her husband*], came in.

Have you noticed that "answered unto" someone is quite often used in King James English (the language of our English version of the Bible) for "asked" or "responded to" a person? We see an example of this at the beginning of verse 8, next.

8 And Peter answered unto her [*asked her*], Tell me whether ye sold the land for so much [*is it true you sold the land for this much money*]? And she said, Yea, for so much [*yes, that's correct*].

9 Then Peter said unto her, How [*why*] is it that ye [*you and your husband*] have agreed [*plotted*] together to tempt [*test*] the Spirit of the Lord [*to find out whether or not we are inspired by the Holy Ghost*]? behold, the feet of them which have buried thy husband are at the door, and shall carry thee out.

10 Then fell she down straightway [*immediately*] at his feet, and

yielded up the ghost [*died*]: and the young men came in, and found her dead, and, carrying her forth, buried her by her husband.

11 And great fear came upon all the church, and upon as many as heard these things.

This is a rather strong reminder to us that it is a serious thing to lie to the Lord's servants. For most members who lie to their bishop or stake president, the penalty is not so final as with Ananias and Sapphira. However, it is equally as deadly and immediate in terms of spiritual damage to the liar.

By the way, have you noticed the backward "P" at the beginning of some verses in your English-speaking King James version of the Bible? An example is found at the beginning of verse 12, next. It generally means that a new topic is now being addressed.

12 ¶ And by the hands of the apostles were many signs and wonders wrought [*done*] among the people; and they were all with one accord [*gathered together in unity of purpose*] in Solomon's porch [*a part of the outer courtyard of the temple grounds in Jerusalem*].

13 And of the rest durst [*dared*] no man join himself to them: [*In other words, none of the religious rulers of the Jews dared join with them.*] but the people magnified them [*held the Apostles in very high regard*].

JST Acts 5:13

13 And **of the rulers** durst no man join himself to them; but the people magnified them.

14 And believers were the more added to the Lord [*many more converts joined the Church*], multitudes both of men and women."

15 Insomuch that [*as a result*] they brought forth the sick into the streets, and laid them on beds and couches, that at the least the shadow of Peter passing by might overshadow [*might touch*] some of them.

16 There came also a multitude [*large crowds of people*] out of the cities round about unto Jerusalem, bringing sick folks, and them which were vexed [*troubled*] with unclean [*evil*] spirits: and they were healed every one.

As you will see next, Satan is obviously successfully blinding these religious leaders of the Jews to what is going on right before their eyes, namely that Jesus truly was the Son of God and His Apostles truly do have power from Him to carry on the work. As you probably know, Satan uses anger and pride to blind people to spiritual things.

17 ¶ Then the high priest [*the chief religious leader of the Jews*] rose up, and all they that were with him [*along with his associates*], (which is the sect of the Sadducees,) and were filled with indignation [*anger*],

18 And laid their hands on [*arrested*] the apostles, and put them in the common prison [*the public jail*].

19 But the angel of the Lord by night [*during the night*] opened the prison doors, and brought them forth [*out*], and said,

20 Go, stand and speak in the temple to the people all the words of this life. [*Go back to the temple grounds and continue teaching the gospel.*]

21 And when they heard that [*the angel's instructions*], they [*the Apostles who had been freed from jail*] entered into the temple early in the morning, and taught. But the high priest came, and they that were with him [*the high priest and his associates came to their offices the next morning*], and called the council [*the Sanhedrin, the highest government body run by the Jews*] together, and all the senate [*senators*] of the children of Israel, and sent to the prison to have them brought [*to have the Apostles brought to appear before them*].

22 But when the officers came, and found them not in the prison, they returned, and told,

23 Saying, The prison truly found we shut with all safety [*the jail doors were all locked and secure*], and the keepers [*the men who guarded the jail*] standing without [*outside the jail*] before [*in front of*] the doors: but when we had opened [*the doors to the jail cells*], we found no man within [*inside*].

24 Now when the high priest and the captain of the temple and the chief priests heard these things, they doubted of them whereunto this would grow [*they were puzzled and worried as to what would happen when the people found about it and word of it spread*].

25 Then came one [*someone*] and told them, saying, Behold, the men whom ye put in prison are standing in the temple [*on the Jerusalem temple grounds*], and teaching the people.

26 Then went the captain [*of the police*] with the officers, and brought them without violence [*arrested the Apostles, handling them gently*]: for they feared the people, lest they should have been stoned. [*The police were worried that the people might throw rocks at them when they arrested the Apostles.*]

27 And when they [*the police*] had brought them [*the Apostles*], they set them before the council: and the high priest asked [*questioned*] them,

28 Saying, Did not we straitly [*strictly, strongly*] command you that ye should not teach in this name [*didn't we command you not to teach about Jesus*]? and, behold, ye have filled Jerusalem with your doctrine [*you have everyone in Jerusalem filled with excitement about Jesus*], and intend to bring this man's blood upon us [*you are trying to make us look guilty for crucifying Jesus*].

What Peter says next to these very worried and frustrated Jewish leaders is a wonderful understatement! (Last phrase of verse 29.)

29 ¶ Then Peter and the other apostles answered and said, We ought to obey God rather than men.

30 The God of our fathers [*ancestors*] raised up [*sent*] Jesus, whom ye slew [*killed*] and hanged on a tree [*crucified on a cross*].

31 Him [*Jesus*] hath God [*the Father*] exalted [*lifted up*] with his right hand [*to sit at his right hand; see Acts 5:31, footnote a*] to be a Prince and a Saviour, for to give repentance [*for the purpose of making repentance available*] to Israel, and forgiveness of sins.

Next, in verse 32, Peter reminds us all that the Holy Ghost bears witness to us of God and His work.

32 And we are his witnesses of these things; and so is also the Holy Ghost, whom God hath given to them that obey him.

33 ¶ When they [*the High Priest and his associates*] heard that, they were cut to the heart, and took counsel [*made plans*] to slay them [*to kill the Apostles*].

In verse 34, next, you will see that not all Pharisees were wicked and corrupt. Gamaliel was a Pharisee who had wisdom and integrity and was not afraid to stand up to peer pressure. Acts 22:3 informs us that Paul, in his younger days, was one of Gamaliel's students.

34 Then stood there up one in the council, a Pharisee, named Gamaliel, a doctor of the law, had in reputation [*highly respected*] among all the people, and commanded to put the apostles forth a little space [*ordered the Apostles to be taken out of the room for a few minutes*];

As mentioned in the note above, Gamaliel seems to have been a rare exception among the members of the Sanhedrin (the highest governing council of the Jews). Here, he has enough influence and confidence to successfully challenge the prevailing feeling in the Sanhedrin to execute the Apostles. The Bible Dictionary also tells us that the Apostle Paul was one of Gamaliel's students. See Bible Dictionary under "Gamaliel." Watch the logic Gamaliel uses to try to persuade his fellow council members to beware of what they do to these Apostles.

35 And [*Gamaliel*] said unto them [*the other members of the Sanhedrin*], Ye men [*rulers*] of Israel, take heed to yourselves [*stop and think about*] what ye intend to do as touching [*concerning*] these men [*Apostles*].

36 For before these days rose up Theudas [*remember back to the time when a fellow named Theudas came along*], boasting himself to be somebody [*claiming to be someone special*]; to whom a number of men, about four hundred, joined

themselves [*about four hundred men became his loyal followers*]: who was slain [*Theudas was killed*]; and all, as many as obeyed him, were scattered, and brought to nought [*his followers were scattered and his influence among the people died out*].

37 After this man rose up Judas of Galilee [*after Theudas was gone, a man named Judas, from Galilee, came along*] in the days of the taxing [*census*], and drew away much people after him [*Judas led a revolt at the time the Romans ordered that a census be taken among us for the purpose of taxation*]: he also perished [*he was also killed*]; and all, even as many as obeyed him, were dispersed [*all his followers scattered and nothing came of what he tried to start*].

38 And now I [*Gamaliel*] say unto you [*members of the Sanhedrin*], Refrain from these men, and let them alone [*don't do anything to these Apostles of Jesus*]: for if this counsel or this work be of men, it will come to nought [*if what Jesus started is man-made, it will eventually die out, like the movements started by Theudas and Judas*]:

39 But if it be of God [*if Jesus and His gospel are from God*], ye cannot overthrow it [*you can't stop it*]; lest haply [*perhaps*] ye be found even to fight against God.

JST Acts 5:39

39 But if it be of God, ye cannot overthrow it; **be careful, therefore,** lest ye be found even to fight against God.

As you will see in verse 40, next, these evil rulers of the Jews backed off some because of Gamaliel's counsel, but they still didn't get it. Also notice in verse 40 that these Apostles were beaten, a serious reminder that choosing the right does not always make our lives easier.

40 And to him they agreed: and when they had called the apostles, and beaten them, they commanded that they should not speak in the name of Jesus, and let them go.

41 ¶ And they [*the Apostles*] departed from the presence of the council, rejoicing that they were counted worthy to suffer shame [*to be persecuted*] for his name [*for Christ*].

42 And daily in the temple, and in every house, they ceased not [*did not stop*] to teach and preach Jesus Christ.

ACTS 6

As you will see in this chapter, the Church continues to experience rapid growth, and the Apostles can't keep up with everything. As a result, the Seventy were established and seven righteous men, including Stephen (who will be martyred in chapter 7) were called to serve. In a way, they experienced what we are experiencing in our day as the gospel expands into all the world and the quorums of General

Authority Seventies are being expanded to fill the needs.

1 AND in those days, when the number of the disciples was multiplied [*as the Church continued to grow*], there arose a murmuring [*a complaint*] of the Grecians [*the Greek members of the Church*] against the Hebrews [*the Jewish members*], because their widows were neglected in the daily ministration [*they felt that their widows were not being properly taken care of in the united order by the Church leaders*].

2 Then the twelve called the multitude of the disciples unto them [*the Twelve called a meeting of the members*], and said, It is not reason [*wise*] that we should leave the word of God [*stop preaching and handling administrative matters*], and serve tables [*spend all our time taking care of individual member needs*].

3 Wherefore [*therefore*], brethren, look ye out [*seek out*] among you seven men of honest report, full of the Holy Ghost and wisdom, whom we may appoint over this business [*managing the daily needs of the members, taking care of widows etc.*].

4 But we will give ourselves continually to prayer, and to the ministry of the word.

Next, we are given the names of the first General Authority Seventies in the early Church that were called and ordained by these early Apostles.

5 ¶ And the saying pleased the whole multitude: and they chose Stephen, a man full of faith and of the Holy Ghost, and Philip, and Prochorus, and Nicanor, and Timon, and Parmenas, and Nicolas a proselyte of Antioch [*a convert from Antioch*]:

6 Whom they set before the apostles: and when they had prayed, they laid their hands on them [*ordained them and set them apart for that work*].

7 And the word of God increased [*the gospel continued to spread*]; and the number of the disciples [*converts*] multiplied [*increased*] in Jerusalem greatly; and a great company [*a large group*] of the priests [*Jewish priests who were converted*] were obedient to the faith.

8 And Stephen, full of faith and power, did great wonders and miracles among the people.

9 ¶ Then there arose certain of the synagogue, which is called the synagogue of the Libertines [*Freed-men*], and, Cyrenians, and Alexandrians, and of them of Cilicia and of Asia, disputing [*debating, arguing against him*] with Stephen.

JST Acts 6:9

9 **And** there arose certain of the synagogue, **who are called Libertines,** and **also** Cyrenians, and Alexandrians, and of them of Cilicia, and of Asia, disputing with Stephen.

10 And they were not able to resist [*could not successfully contradict*] the wisdom and the spirit by which he spake.

11 Then they suborned men [*secretly bribed false witnesses*], which [*who*] said, We have heard him [*Stephen*] speak blasphemous words against Moses, and against God.

"Blasphemous words" or "blasphemy," meaning speaking mockingly or disrespectfully of God or prophets, was a sin which was punishable by death in the Jewish legal system.

12 And they [*the angry Jews mentioned in verse 9, above*] stirred up the people, and the elders, and the scribes, and came upon him, and caught him [*arrested Stephen*], and brought him to the council [*the Sanhedrin, the "supreme court" run by the Jews; see Bible Dictionary under "Sanhedrin"*],

13 And set up false witnesses, which said, This man ceaseth not to speak [*refuses to quit speaking*] blasphemous words against this holy place, and the law [*the law of Moses, as given in Genesis, Exodus, Leviticus, Numbers, and Deuteronomy*]:

14 For we have heard him say, that this Jesus of Nazareth shall destroy this place [*Jerusalem*], and shall change the customs which Moses delivered us.

Keep in mind that in the minds and general culture of the Jews at this time, the words of Moses (along with Abraham) were considered to be the supreme authority in matters of religion, and even in matters of daily living. That's one reason why these leaders were so upset, as stated in verse 14, above, that Jesus had been changing "the customs which Moses delivered us."

In verse 15, next, these leaders of the Jews are given a marvelous manifestation from God that Stephen is indeed His servant as this newly called Seventy is transfigured before them. (Be careful not to confuse "transfigured" with "translated." "Transfigured" means to glow or shine because of being filled with the Spirit. "Translated" means to be changed so as to keep on living, like the Three Nephites. See 3 Nephi chapter 28.)

15 And all that sat in the council, looking stedfastly on [*intently at*] him, saw his face as it had been the face of an angel. [*Stephen was transfigured in front of them so that his face shined with glory, and all the Sanhedrin and others there saw it happen.*]

ACTS 7

This chapter contains one of the finest reviews of the history of covenant Israel, beginning with Abraham, found anywhere in the scriptures. Included in it is a rather detailed history of Moses. The review is given by Stephen during his trial in answer to the Jewish high priest who asked if he was guilty of the accusations against him recorded in chapter 6, above.

1 THEN said the high priest [*the highest ruling official among the Jews*], Are these things so?

2 And he [*Stephen*] said, Men, brethren, and fathers [*leaders of the Jews*], hearken [*pay very close attention to what I say*]; The God of glory appeared unto our father [*ancestor*] Abraham, when he was in Mesopotamia [*the Persian Gulf area*], before he dwelt in Charran [*Haran; southern part of Turkey*],

3 And said unto him, Get thee out of thy country, and from thy kindred [*relatives*], and come into the land which I shall shew [*show*] thee.

4 Then came he [*Abraham*] out of the land of the Chaldaeans [*Babylon; Persian Gulf area*], and dwelt in Charran: and from thence [*from there*], when his father was dead, he removed him [*he traveled*] into this land [*the Holy Land*], wherein [*in which*] ye now dwell.

5 And he [*God*] gave him [*Abraham*] none [*no*] inheritance in it, no, not so much as to set his foot on: yet he promised that he would give it to him for a possession, and to his seed [*descendants*] after him, when as yet he had no child.

6 And God spake on this wise [*God said*], That his seed [*Abraham's posterity*] should sojourn [*would live temporarily*] in a strange [*foreign*] land; and that they [*the inhabitants of that foreign land; in other words, Egypt*] should [*would*] bring them into bondage [*slavery*], and entreat them evil [*treat them very badly*] four hundred years.

7 And the nation to whom they shall be in bondage will I judge [*punish*], said God: and after that [*after Abraham's posterity had spent four hundred years as slaves in Egypt*] shall they come forth [*leave Egypt*], and serve me [*God*] in this place [*in Israel*].

8 And he [*God*] gave him [*Abraham*] the covenant of circumcision [*see Bible Dictionary under "Circumcision."*]: and so Abraham begat [*fathered, sired*] Isaac, and circumcised him the eighth day [*eight days after Isaac was born*]; and Isaac begat Jacob; and Jacob begat [*was the father of*] the twelve patriarchs [*heads of the twelve tribes*]. [*Jacob had twelve sons, and that was the beginning of the twelve tribes of Israel.*]

9 And the patriarchs [*Joseph's older brothers*], moved with envy [*being jealous of him*], sold Joseph into Egypt [*Genesis, chapter 37*]: but God was with him,

10 And delivered him out of all his afflictions [*troubles*], and gave him favour and wisdom in the sight of Pharaoh king of Egypt; and he made him [*Joseph*] governor over Egypt and all his [*Pharaoh's*] house.

11 Now there came a dearth [*famine*] over all the land of Egypt and Chanaan [*where Joseph's father and eleven brothers were*

living; basically Israel or the Holy Land today], and great affliction: and our fathers [*Jacob and his eleven sons and their families*] found no sustenance [*were starving up in Israel*].

12 But when Jacob heard that there was corn [*grain*] in Egypt, he sent out our fathers [*ancestors; Joseph's older brothers*] first. [*Jacob sent his ten oldest sons to Egypt to see if they could buy food there and bring it back home to Israel.*]

13 And at the second time Joseph was made known to his brethren [*when Joseph's brothers came the second time to Egypt (Genesis 43–45,) Joseph told them who he was*]; and Joseph's kindred was [*relatives were*] made known unto Pharaoh [*were introduced to Pharaoh*].

14 Then sent Joseph, and called his father Jacob to him, and all his kindred, threescore and fifteen souls. [*Joseph brought his father, Jacob, and all seventy five of his father's family to Egypt to help them survive the famine.*]

15 So Jacob went down into Egypt, and died, he, and our fathers [*our ancestors*],

16 And were carried over into Sychem [*in southern Israel*], and laid in the sepulchre [*grave*] that Abraham bought for a sum of money of [*from*] the sons of Emmor the father of Sychem.

17 But when the time of the promise drew nigh [*when it came time for God to fulfill his promise to Abraham, namely that his posterity would someday be established in the Holy Land*], which God had sworn [*promised*] to Abraham, the people [*the children of Israel, slaves in Egypt*] grew and multiplied in Egypt,

18 Till another king arose, which knew not [*who had no respect for*] Joseph.

19 The same [*the new Pharaoh*] dealt subtilly [*treacherously*] with our kindred [*ancestors*], and evil entreated [*mistreated, abused*] our fathers [*ancestors*], so that they cast out their young children, to the end they might not live. [*The new Pharaoh, king of Egypt, commanded that every male child born to Israelite slaves be killed. See Exodus 1:15–16.*]

20 In which time Moses was born, and was exceeding fair, and nourished up in his father's house three months: [*Moses' parents successfully hid him for three months after he was born. See Exodus 2:1–2.*]

21 And when he was cast out [*when baby Moses was put in a tiny little waterproof basket and hidden in the bulrushes along side the river; Exodus 2:3–10*], Pharaoh's daughter took him up [*discovered baby Moses and kept him*], and nourished him for her own son.

22 And Moses was learned [*taught*] in all the wisdom of the Egyptians, and was mighty in words and in deeds.

23 And when he was full forty

years old, it came into his heart [*he had a desire*] to visit his brethren the children of Israel.

24 And seeing one of them [*the Israelite slaves*] suffer wrong [*he was being beaten by an Egyptian; Exodus 2:11*], he defended him, and avenged him that was oppressed [*made things fair for the slave being beaten*], and smote [*killed*] the Egyptian:

25 For he supposed his brethren would have understood how that God by his hand would deliver them: but they understood not.

> Verse 25, above, gives us a very significant insight regarding Moses. It informs us that he knew that he was to deliver the children of Israel out of slavery and bondage in Egypt. While we don't know for sure how Moses came to know this about himself, we would strongly believe that his mother taught him as she raised him in Pharaoh's household under the protection of Pharaoh's daughter (see Exodus 2:5–10). It is highly likely that his mother taught him about the prophecy made by Joseph who was sold into Egypt. Part of this prophecy is as follows: ". . . for a seer will I raise up to deliver my people out of the land of Egypt; and he shall be called Moses. And by this name he shall know that he is of thy house (he will know that he is an Israelite); for he shall be nursed by the king's daughter and shall be called her son." See JST Genesis 50:29, at the back of our Bible. See also 2 Nephi 3:9–10.

26 And the next day he shewed [*showed*] himself unto them [*some Israelite slaves*] as they strove [*as one hit the other; see Exodus 2:13*], and would have set them at one again [*tried to get them to make peace with each other*], saying, Sirs, ye are brethren; why do ye wrong one to another?

27 But he that did his neighbour wrong [*the Israelite slave who was hitting the other slave*] thrust him away [*pushed Moses away*], saying, Who made thee a ruler and a judge over us?

28 Wilt thou kill me, as thou diddest the Egyptian yesterday? [*Are you going to kill me like you did the Egyptian slave driver yesterday*?]

> This had to have been a terrible disappointment to Moses. It was also a reminder that during the centuries of slavery in Egypt, the Israelites had become a hardened, rough, people, who, for the most part, were spiritually lacking.

29 Then fled Moses at this saying [*Moses ended up having to flee for his life from Egypt because he defended a Hebrew slave and killed an Egyptian in the process*], and was a stranger in the land of Madian [*Midian, just east of Sinai*], where he begat [*had*] two sons.

30 And when forty years were expired [*at the end of another forty years, when Moses was 80 years old*], there appeared to him in the wilderness of mount Sina [*Sinai*] an angel of the Lord [*JST Exodus*

3:2 "The presence of the Lord"] in a flame of fire in a bush. [*The premortal Christ appeared to Moses in the burning bush.*]

31 When Moses saw it, he wondered at the sight: and as he drew near to behold it, the voice of the Lord [*Christ*] came unto him,

32 Saying, I am the God of thy fathers, the God of Abraham, and the God of Isaac, and the God of Jacob. [*In other words, Jesus Christ, as a spirit, was the God of the Old Testament, usually referred to as Jehovah.*] Then Moses trembled, and durst not behold [*didn't dare even look*].

33 Then said the Lord to him, Put off thy shoes from thy feet: for the place where thou standest is holy ground.

34 I [*Christ*] have seen, I have seen the affliction of my people [*the Israelite slaves*] which is in Egypt, and I have heard their groaning, and am come down to deliver them. And now come, I will send thee into Egypt.

Moses, in effect, led three lives, namely, forty years as a prince in Egypt, forty peaceful years as a shepherd in Midian, and forty years as a mighty prophet to the children of Israel. At age one hundred and twenty, he was translated and taken up without dying (see Bible Dictionary under "Moses"). He ministered to the Savior on the Mount of Transfiguration, about six months before the crucifixion (Matthew 17:1–3,) and was resurrected with the Savior (D&C 133:55).

35 This Moses whom they [*the Israelite slaves*] refused [*rejected*], saying, Who made thee a ruler and a judge? the same did God send to be a ruler and a deliverer by the hand of the angel [*the Lord, see JST Exodus 3:2*] which appeared to him in the bush.

36 He brought them out, after that he [*Moses*] had shewed wonders and signs [*including the ten plagues*] in the land of Egypt, and in the Red sea, and in the wilderness forty years.

Remember that Stephen is on trial before the Sanhedrin (Acts 6:12) and is still answering the high priest's question in verse one of this chapter. He is laying a foundation for bearing testimony to them of Christ. As stated earlier in a note for this chapter, Moses was probably the most important prophet in the eyes of the Jews at this time, and Stephen, with wonderful, inspired skill, has laid a strong foundation, leading up to the fact that Moses prophesied about Jesus, which Stephen says in verse 37, next.

37 ¶ This is that Moses, which [*who*] said unto the children of Israel, A prophet [*Christ*] shall the Lord your God raise up unto you of your brethren, like unto me; him [*Christ*] shall ye hear [*listen to and obey*].

38 This is he [*Moses*], that was in the church in the wilderness

with the angel which spake to him in the mount Sina, and with our fathers [*our ancestors, the children of Israel*]: who received the lively oracles [*revelations from the living God; see D&C 90:4, footnote a*] to give unto us:

39 To whom our fathers would not obey [*the children of Israel did not want to obey Moses*], but thrust him from them [*rejected him while he was up on Mount Sinai; see Exodus 32*], and in their hearts turned back again into Egypt,

JST Acts 7:39

39 **Whom** our fathers would not obey, but thrust him from them, and in their hearts turned back again into Egypt,

40 Saying unto Aaron [*Moses' brother*], Make us gods [*the gold calf*] to go before us [*to lead us*]: for as for this Moses, which brought us out of the land of Egypt, we wot not [*don't know*] what is become of him. [*Moses had been gone for many days on Mount Sinai, receiving commandments from the Lord, written on stone tablets. See Exodus 32:1–6.*]

JST Acts 7:40

40 Saying unto Aaron, Make us gods to go before us; for as for this Moses, which brought us out of the land of Egypt, we know not what is become of him.

41 And they made a calf [*the golden calf*] in those days, and offered sacrifice unto the idol, and rejoiced in the works of their own hands.

42 Then God turned, and gave them up to worship the host of heaven [*to worship idols*]; as it is written in the book of the prophets [*Amos 5:25–27*], O ye house of Israel, have ye offered to me slain beasts and sacrifices by the space of forty years in the wilderness?

43 Yea, ye took up the tabernacle of Moloch [*you worshiped the idol, Moloch (probably Molech "a fire god, worshiped by passing children through or burning them in fire; Deuteronomy 18:10") see Bible Dictionary under "Molech"*], and the star of your god Remphan, figures which ye made to worship them: and I will carry you away beyond Babylon [*the Babylonian captivity, about 600 B.C.*]

44 Our fathers [*ancestors*] had the tabernacle of witness in the wilderness, as he [*God*] had appointed [*instructed*], speaking unto Moses, that he should make it [*the Tabernacle*] according to the fashion that he had seen [*that the Lord had shown him in vision*].

JST Acts 7:44

44 Our fathers had the tabernacle of witness in the wilderness, as he had appointed, speaking unto Moses, that he should make it according to the **pattern** that he had seen.

The tabernacle, spoken of in verse 44, above, was a portable temple. See Bible Dictionary under "Tabernacle." It was about 45 feet long, 15 feet wide, and 15 feet tall, and was a very elaborate tent, which allowed it to be moved as needed. It was used for sacred worship by the children of Israel during their wanderings in the wilderness. It continued to be used until the building of Solomon's Temple.

Next, Stephen tells these Jewish religious leaders that, after Moses had been taken up, the children of Israel brought the Tabernacle into the Holy Land with them, under the direction of Joshua, who had taken Moses' place.

45 Which [*the Tabernacle*] also our fathers that came after [*after Moses was translated and taken up*] brought in with Jesus [*the Greek form of Joshua—see Bible Dictionary under "Jesus"*] into the possession of the Gentiles [*into the Holy Land, which was inhabited by Gentiles at that time*], whom God drave [*drove*] out before the face of our fathers [*ahead of the children of Israel, as they crossed over the Jordan River into the promised land*], unto the days of David [*until King David's time*];

46 Who found favour before God, and desired to find a tabernacle for the God of Jacob. [*King David wanted to build a permanent temple for the Lord, but was not allowed to. See 1 Kings 5:3–5. King Solomon, David's son, built the temple in Jerusalem. See 1 Kings, chapter 6.*]

47 But Solomon built him an house [*a temple*].

Next, in verse 48, Stephen will quote the prophet Isaiah, reminding them that even though they and their ancestors made a big fuss about building and maintaining a temple for God, He doesn't actually live in the temple. We know that God can and does come to His temples, and that they are built for our benefit. The point Stephen is making here is that these religious leaders and their ancestors, who built Solomon's Temple, claim to be righteous followers of God and take great pride in the temple, yet they live corrupt lives and persecute and kill the righteous. They are just like their wicked ancestors!

48 Howbeit [*however*] the most High [*God*] dwelleth not in temples made with hands; as saith the prophet [*Isaiah 66:1–2*],

49 Heaven is my throne, and earth is my footstool: what house will ye build me? saith the Lord: or what is the place of my rest?

50 Hath not my hand made all these things?

51 ¶ Ye stiffnecked [*proud*] and uncircumcised [*unrighteous, wicked*] in heart and ears, ye do always resist the Holy Ghost: as your fathers [*ancestors*] did, so do ye. [*You are just like your wicked ancestors.*]

52 Which of the prophets have not your fathers persecuted? and they have slain them which shewed [*prophesied*] before [*in times past*] of the coming of the Just One [*Christ*]; of whom ye have been

now the betrayers and murderers [*whom you murdered by crucifixion*]:

53 Who have received the law [*the law of Moses*] by the disposition [*ministering*] of angels, and have not kept it. [*In other words, you claim to follow Moses' laws and teachings exactly, yet, he prophesied of Christ, and you rejected Christ; therefore, you have rejected Moses.*]

54 ¶ When they heard these things, they were cut to the heart [*the truth cut them deeply and made them furious*], and they gnashed on him with their teeth [*they bit Stephen*].

55 But he, being full of the Holy Ghost, looked up stedfastly [*steadily*] into heaven, and saw the glory of God, and Jesus standing on the right hand of God,

56 And said, Behold, I see the heavens opened, and the Son of man [*Jesus*] standing on the right hand of God.

Verses 55–56, above, are wonderful scriptures to use to teach that the Godhead consists of three distinct, separate beings. Jesus is standing to the right of the Father, and the Holy Ghost is upon Stephen.

57 Then they cried out with a loud voice [*they shouted*], and stopped their ears [*plugged their ears because they didn't want to hear his testimony*], and ran upon him with one accord [*rushed upon him with the same objective in mind*],

58 And cast him out of the city, and stoned him [*killed him with rocks*]: and the witnesses [*the men who killed Stephen*] laid down their clothes [*so they wouldn't get dirty while they killed Stephen*] at a young [*under 40 years of age*] man's feet, whose name was Saul. [*Saul will be converted and his name will be changed to Paul. He will become the Apostle Paul.*]

59 And they stoned Stephen, calling upon God, and saying, Lord Jesus, receive my spirit.

JST Acts 7:59

59 And they stoned Stephen; **and he**, calling upon God, **said**, Lord Jesus, receive my spirit.

60 And he kneeled down, and cried with a loud voice, Lord, lay not this sin to their charge [*allow these men, who are killing me, to repent*]. And when he had said this, he fell asleep [*he died*].

ACTS 8

In verse one of this chapter, Luke will introduce us to Saul, a devout Pharisee who felt that the followers of Jesus Christ were a real threat to established Jewish religion. In fact, Saul was authorized by the highest Jewish religious authorities to persecute the Christians, including rounding them up and putting them in prison. After his conversion, Saul's name will be changed to Paul, and he will eventually become the Apostle Paul. We will read of his conversion in chapter 9.

In the meantime, in chapter 8, we see the spread of the gospel to other areas. Luke tells us about Philip, one of the original Seventy, and his successful missionary work in Samaria. You will see Peter and John come to Samaria from Jerusalem and, upon discovering that Philip's converts had been baptized but had not received the gift of the Holy Ghost yet, proceeded to bestow the gift of the Holy Ghost (see verses 16–17). One of the better-known converts in this chapter is Simon the Sorcerer, who will try to buy the priesthood (verses 13, 18–24.) The JST makes no changes to this chapter.

1 AND Saul was consenting unto his death [*Saul felt that it was right to stone Stephen*]. And at that time [*at the time Stephen was killed*] there was a great persecution against the church which was at Jerusalem; and they [*the members of the Church*] were all scattered abroad throughout the regions of Judæa and Samaria, except the apostles.

2 And devout men [*faithful members*] carried Stephen to his burial, and made great lamentation over him [*mourned his death*].

3 As for Saul, he made havock of the church [*caused terrible trouble for the Church*], entering into every house, and haling [*arresting*] men and women committed them to prison.

4 Therefore they [*the members*] that were scattered abroad went every where preaching the word.

> This terrible persecution of members, which scattered them everywhere, actually resulted in the gospel being spread and much missionary work being done.

5 Then Philip [*one of the seven chosen, along with Stephen, to assist the Apostles in ministering to the temporal (physical) needs of the Saints; Acts 6:5*] went down to the city of Samaria, and preached Christ unto them. [*As instructed in Acts 1:8, they were to take the gospel to Samaria and to all the world.*]

6 And the people with one accord [*unitedly*] gave heed [*paid close attention*] unto those things which Philip spake, hearing and seeing the miracles which he did.

7 For unclean spirits [*evil spirits*], crying with loud voice, came out of many that were possessed with them: and many taken with [*sick with*] palsies, and that were lame [*crippled*], were healed.

8 And there was great joy in that city.

9 But there was a certain man, called Simon, which beforetime [*in the past*] in the same city used sorcery [*used Satan's power along with superstition*], and bewitched [*deceived*] the people of Samaria, giving out that himself was some great one [*building himself up in the eyes of the people*]:

10 To whom they all gave heed, from the least to the greatest, saying, This man is the great power

of God. [*Simon had great influence among the people, who believed that his power came from God.*]

11 And to him they had regard [*fear and respect*], because that of long time he had bewitched them with sorceries [*because, for a long time, he had exercised unrighteous influence over them with his evil powers and pretending*].

12 But when they believed Philip preaching the things concerning the kingdom of God, and the name of Jesus Christ, they were baptized, both men and women.

13 Then Simon [*the Sorcerer*] himself believed also: and when he was baptized, he continued [*traveled*] with Philip, and wondered [*was amazed*], beholding [*seeing*] the miracles and signs which were done.

14 Now when the apostles which were at Jerusalem heard that Samaria [*many people in Samaria*] had received the word of God [*had been baptized*], they sent unto them Peter and John:

15 Who, when they were come down, prayed for them, that they might receive the Holy Ghost:

16 (For as yet he was fallen upon none of them: only they were baptized in the name of the Lord Jesus.) [*None of those baptized had yet been confirmed and given the Gift of the Holy Ghost.*]

17 Then laid they [*the Apostles Peter and John*] their hands on them, and they received the Holy Ghost.

18 And when Simon saw that through laying on of the apostles' hands the Holy Ghost was given, he offered them money [*offered to buy the Melchizedek Priesthood from them*],

19 Saying, Give me also this power, that on whomsoever I lay hands, he may receive the Holy Ghost.

20 But Peter said unto him, Thy money perish with thee, because thou hast thought that the gift of God may be purchased with money. [*The priesthood is not for sale.*]

21 Thou hast neither part nor lot in this matter: for thy heart is not right in the sight of God. [*You can't participate in the priesthood because you have wrong motives for wanting it.*]

22 Repent therefore of this thy wickedness, and pray God, if perhaps the thought of thine heart may be forgiven thee.

23 For I perceive [*know*] that thou art in the gall of bitterness [*you are a bitter man*], and in the bond of iniquity [*caught up in wickedness*].

24 Then answered [*responded*] Simon, and said, Pray ye to the Lord for me, that none of these things which ye have spoken come upon me.

25 And they [*Peter and John*], when they had testified and preached the word of the Lord, returned to Jerusalem, and preached the gospel in

many villages of the Samaritans.

26 And the angel of the Lord spake [*spoke*] unto Philip, saying, Arise, and go toward the south unto the way that goeth down from Jerusalem unto Gaza, which is desert [*go down to the Gaza Strip*].

27 And he arose and went: and, behold, a man of [*from*] Ethiopia [*a nation in eastern Africa, south of Egypt*], an eunuch [*a man, who had been surgically rendered incapable of fathering children; see Bible Dictionary under "Eunuch"*] of great authority under Candace queen of the Ethiopians, who had the charge of all her treasure, and had come to Jerusalem for to worship,

> Next, you will be introduced to a man who had trouble understanding the writings of Isaiah. Many members today can sympathize with him. Philip will help us a bit.

28 Was returning [*the eunuch was returning home to Ethiopia from Jerusalem*], and sitting in his chariot read Esaias [*Isaiah*] the prophet.

29 Then the Spirit said unto Philip, Go near, and join thyself to this chariot [*go over to the chariot where the man is reading the scriptures*].

30 And Philip ran thither [*there*] to him, and heard him read the prophet Esaias [*Isaiah*], and said, Understandest thou what thou readest?

31 And he said, How can I, except some man should guide me? [*How can I understand Isaiah, unless someone helps me*?] And he desired Philip that he would come up and sit with him.

32 The place of the scripture which he read [*the verse of Isaiah he was reading*] was this [*Isaiah 53:7–8*], He was led as a sheep to the slaughter; and like a lamb dumb before his shearer, so opened he not his mouth:

33 In his humiliation his judgment was taken away: and who shall declare his generation? for his life is taken from the earth.

34 And the eunuch answered [*asked*] Philip, and said, I pray thee, of whom speaketh the prophet this? of himself, or of some other man? [*Please tell me. Was Isaiah speaking of himself or of some other man?*]

35 Then Philip opened his mouth [*started talking*], and began at the same scripture, and preached unto him Jesus. [*Philip used the Isaiah verses to teach the eunuch about Jesus.*]

> We will take a moment and give a few brief explanations of the verses from Isaiah about the Savior, which the eunuch was trying to understand (in verses 32–33, above):
>
> 32 He was led as a sheep to the slaughter [*the Savior went peacefully to His trial and crucifixion*]; and like a lamb dumb [*does not make noise*] before his shearer, so opened he not his mouth [*Christ refused to answer*

most of the questions put to Him during His illegal trial]:

33 In his humiliation, his judgment was taken away [*He was subject to humiliation, ridicule, and mocking and did not get a fair or legal trial*]: and who shall declare his generation [*who will even care about Him or what happens to Him*]? for his life is taken from the earth [*He is killed and His mortal mission is over*].

36 And as they went on their way, they came unto a certain water [*a body of water*]: and the eunuch said, See, here is water; what doth hinder me to be baptized [*is there any reason why I shouldn't be baptized*]?

37 And Philip said, If thou believest with all thine heart, thou mayest. And he answered and said, I believe that Jesus Christ is the Son of God.

38 And he commanded the chariot to stand still [*the eunuch commanded the chariot driver to stop*]: and they went down both into the water, both Philip and the eunuch; and he baptized him.

Here is another reminder (verse 38, above) that baptism was done by immersion in the Bible.

39 And when they were come up out of the water, the Spirit of the Lord caught away Philip, that the eunuch saw him no more: and he went on his way rejoicing. [*The eunuch went home to Ethiopia rejoicing that he was now baptized.*]

40 But Philip was found at Azotus [*about 20 miles north of Gaza*]: and passing through he preached in all the cities, till he came to Cæsarea [*about 80 miles north of Gaza, on the coast of the Mediterranean Sea*].

ACTS 9

As mentioned in the note at the beginning of Acts, chapter 8, in this study guide, Saul approved of the stoning of Stephen and was a major leader in persecuting the Church (see Acts 7:58 and 8:1–3). In chapter 9, we will see the conversion of this misguided man of integrity and watch as he enters the path to becoming one of the most influential Apostles ever. His name will be changed to Paul, and he will become the Apostle Paul, who became "the Apostle to the Gentiles" and who wrote fourteen of the books of the New Testament (Romans through Hebrews).

Just a note about the JST (Joseph Smith Translation of the Bible) quotes provided in this chapter as well as elsewhere in this study guide. As you will notice, some of the JST changes are not major doctrinal or information changes. We included them to demonstrate that the Prophet Joseph Smith, under the direction of the Lord, paid attention to "smaller matters" as well as "weightier matters."

1 AND Saul [*whose name will be changed to Paul, when he is converted*], yet breathing out threatenings and slaughter against the

disciples of the Lord [*against the members of the early Church*], went unto the high priest [*the chief religious leader among the Jews*],

2 And desired of him letters [*letters of permission to empower him to arrest Christians*] to Damascus [*a major city in Syria, north and a bit east of Israel*] to the synagogues, that if he found any of this way [*any members of the Church*], whether they were men or women, he might bring them bound unto Jerusalem. [*Saul got permission to arrest any Christians he found as he traveled to Damascus, and to put them in chains and bring them back to Jerusalem.*]

Next, Luke will tell us about Saul's marvelous conversion.

3 And as he journeyed, he came near Damascus: and suddenly there shined round about him a light from heaven:

4 And he fell to the earth, and heard a voice saying unto him, Saul, Saul, why persecutest thou me? [*Why are you fighting against Me by persecuting My Saints?*]

5 And he said, Who art thou, Lord? And the Lord said, I am Jesus whom thou persecutest: it is hard for thee to kick against the pricks.

A prick was a goad, a sharp stick or pointed instrument of any type which could be used to poke animals when herding them along or keeping them moving when pulling a cart, etc. The tendency of many animals, when poked with the goad, was to stubbornly kick back against it, thus driving it deeper into their hide. The imagery here seems to be that Saul's conscience has begun to bother him, as he rounds up Christians, breaks up families, etc. He has been kicking against the pricks of his conscience and perhaps has been feeling more and more miserable about what he is doing to members of the Church.

In verse 6, next, Luke helps us see that Saul is actually a man of high integrity but is completely misguided about Jesus and His disciples at this point. He is an honest man and sincerely humble.

6 And he trembling and astonished said, Lord, what wilt thou have me to do? And the Lord said unto him, Arise, and go into the city, and it shall be told thee what thou must do.

7 And the men which journeyed with him stood speechless, hearing a voice, but seeing no man.

As you will see, the JST version of verse 7, above, makes a significant change. Inspired changes such as this can significantly strengthen our testimonies of the Prophet Joseph Smith.

JST Acts 9:7

7 And **they who were journeying** with him **saw indeed the light, and were afraid; but they heard not the voice of him who spake to him**.

8 And Saul arose from the earth; and when his eyes were opened, he saw no man [*he was blind*]: but they led him by the hand, and brought him into Damascus.

9 And he was three days without sight, and neither did eat nor drink.

10 ¶ And there was a certain disciple [*faithful member of the Church*] at Damascus, named Ananias; and to him said the Lord in a vision, Ananias. And he said, Behold, I am here, Lord [*tell me what you need me to do, Lord*].

11 And the Lord said unto him, Arise, and go into the street which is called Straight, and enquire [*ask*] in the house of Judas for one called Saul, of Tarsus: for, behold, he prayeth,

12 And hath seen in a vision a man named Ananias coming in, and putting his hand on him, that he might receive his sight.

This had to have been a startling request from the Savior to Ananias. He knew how dangerous Saul was to the members of the Church, and how much damage had already been caused by him. It would seem to be a blessing that Saul had been struck blind and perhaps would not persecute the Saints any more. Watch, beginning in verse 13, next, as Ananias expresses concern about using the priesthood to restore Saul's sight.

13 Then Ananias answered, Lord, I have heard by many of this man [*Saul*], how much evil he hath done to thy Saints at Jerusalem:

14 And here [*in Damascus*] he hath authority from the chief priests to bind [*arrest*] all that call on thy name [*all who are members of the Church*].

15 But the Lord said unto him, Go thy way [*go ahead and do what I have asked*]: for he is a chosen vessel [*servant*] unto me, to bear [*carry*] my name before the [*to the*] Gentiles, and kings, and the children of Israel:

16 For I will shew [*show*] him how great things [*how many things*] he must suffer for my name's sake [*as he serves Me*].

17 And Ananias went his way, and entered into the house; and putting his hands on him [*Saul*] said, Brother Saul, the Lord, even Jesus, that appeared unto thee in the way [*on the road*] as thou camest, hath sent me, that thou mightest receive thy sight, and be filled with the Holy Ghost.

18 And immediately there fell from his [*Saul's*] eyes as it had been scales: and he received sight forthwith [*immediately*], and arose, and was baptized.

19 And when he had received meat [*food*], he was strengthened. Then was Saul certain days with the disciples [*Saul stayed with members of the Church for a few days*] which were at Damascus.

20 And straightway [*immediately*] he preached Christ in the

synagogues, that he is the Son of God. [*After the few days with members, Saul went to the Jewish church buildings and began to teach about Christ.*]

A Description of Paul

Saul, whose name will be changed to Paul (Acts 13:9,) was a very loyal, energetic, humble man who did things thoroughly. When he felt that the Christians were a threat to the church Moses had set up, he did everything he could to destroy the Christian movement. But as soon as he found out he was wrong, and that Jesus was indeed the promised Messiah, he immediately began using his full energy to preach the gospel of Christ. The Prophet Joseph Smith gave a physical description of Paul as follows: "He is about five feet high; very dark hair; dark complexion; dark skin; large Roman nose; sharp face; small black eyes, penetrating as eternity; round shoulders; a whining voice, except when elevated, and then it almost resembled the roaring of a lion. He was a good orator, active and diligent, always employing himself in doing good to his fellow man." (*Teachings of the Prophet Joseph Smith*, p. 180.)

21 But all that heard him [*Saul*] were amazed, and said; Is not this he that destroyed them [*members of the Church*] which called on this name [*who were loyal followers of Jesus*] in Jerusalem, and came hither [*here to Damascus*] for that intent [*purpose*], that he might bring them bound [*arrest them and bring them in chains*] unto the chief priests?

22 But Saul increased the more in strength [*continued growing in the gospel*], and confounded the Jews which dwelt at Damascus, proving that this is very Christ. [*Paul successfully debated the Jews in Damascus, showing them that Jesus was indeed the Christ, the promised Messiah.*]

23 ¶ And after that many days were fulfilled [*after many days*], the Jews took counsel to kill him [*the Jews plotted to kill Saul*]:

24 But their laying await was known of Saul [*Saul was aware of their plans to ambush him*]. And they watched the gates [*the city gates*] day and night to kill him.

JST Acts 9:24

24 But their **lying in wait** was known of Saul. And they watched the gates day and night to kill him.

25 Then the disciples took him by night, and let him down by the wall in a basket.

26 And when Saul was come to Jerusalem, he assayed [*attempted*] to join himself to the disciples: but they were all afraid of him, and believed not that he was a disciple [*a follower of Christ*].

27 But Barnabas took him, and brought him to the apostles, and declared [*explained*] unto them

how he [*Saul*] had seen the Lord in the way [*on the way to Damascus*], and that he [*the Lord*] had spoken to him, and how he [*Saul*] had preached boldly at Damascus in the name of Jesus.

28 And he was with them coming in and going out at Jerusalem. [*And so, Saul was permitted to associate with the members of the Church in Jerusalem.*]

29 And he spake boldly in the name of the Lord Jesus, and disputed against [*debated with*] the Grecians [*the Grecian Jews*]: but they went about to slay him.

30 Which when the brethren knew [*found out*], they brought him down to Cæsarea [*about 60 miles north of Jerusalem, on the coast of the Mediterranean Sea*], and sent him forth to Tarsus [*Saul's home town, in what is known as southern Turkey today*].

JST Acts 9:30

30 **When the brethren knew this**, they brought him down to Caesarea, and sent him forth to Tarsus.

31 Then had the churches [*wards and branches*] rest [*because Saul wasn't persecuting them any more*] throughout all Judæa and Galilee and Samaria, and were edified [*strengthened and built up*]; and walking in the fear [*respect and knowledge*] of the Lord, and in the comfort of the Holy Ghost, were multiplied [*continued growing*].

Next, you will see Peter as the chief Apostle, or, in effect, the "President of the Church," traveling throughout the Church. He will heal a bedridden man in verses 33–34.

32 ¶ And it came to pass, as Peter passed throughout all quarters [*as Peter traveled throughout the Church*], he came down also to the saints which dwelt at Lydda [*about 20 miles northwest of Jerusalem*].

JST Acts 9:32

32 And it came to pass, as Peter passed throughout all **these regions**, he came down also to the saints which dwelt at Lydda.

33 And there he found a certain man named Æneas, which had kept his bed eight years [*who had been bedridden for eight years*], and was sick of the palsy.

34 And Peter said unto him, Æneas, Jesus Christ maketh thee whole: arise, and make thy bed. And he arose immediately.

35 And all that dwelt at Lydda and Saron saw him [*the man who had been healed*], and turned to the Lord.

In verses 36–41, we will watch Peter use the power of God to bring Tabitha, sometimes called Dorcas, a faithful member of the Church, back to life.

36 ¶ Now there was at Joppa [*about 12 miles northwest of Lydda and 35 miles northwest of Jerusalem*] a certain disciple named Tabitha,

which by interpretation is called Dorcas: this woman was full of good works and almsdeeds [*helping the poor*] which she did.

37 And it came to pass in those days, that she was sick, and died: whom when they had washed [*prepared her body for burial*], they laid her in an upper chamber [*an upstairs room*].

38 And forasmuch as [*since*] Lydda was nigh [*near*] to Joppa, and the disciples [*the members in Joppa*] had heard that Peter was there, they sent unto him two men, desiring him that he would not delay to come to them.

JST Acts 9:38

38 And forasmuch as Lydda was nigh to Joppa, and the disciples had heard that Peter was there, they sent unto him two men, **desiring that** he would not delay to come to them.

39 Then Peter arose and went with them. When he was come [*when he arrived in Joppa*], they brought him into the upper chamber: and all the widows stood by him weeping, and shewing the coats and garments [*clothing*] which Dorcas made, while she was with them [*while she was alive*].

40 But Peter put them all forth [*had them all leave the room*], and kneeled down, and prayed; and turning him to the body [*turning toward Tabitha's body*] said, Tabitha, arise. And she opened her eyes: and when she saw Peter, she sat up.

JST Acts 9:40

40 But Peter put them all forth, and kneeled down, and prayed; and **turning to the body** said, Tabitha, arise. And she opened her eyes; and when she saw Peter, she sat up.

41 And he gave her his hand, and lifted her up, and when he had called the saints and widows, presented her alive.

JST Acts 9:41

41 And he gave her his hand, and lifted her up; and when he had called the saints and widows; **he** presented her alive.

42 And it was known throughout all Joppa; and many believed in the Lord.

43 And it came to pass, that he [*Peter*] tarried [*stayed*], many days in Joppa with one Simon a tanner [*a man who made his living by making leather goods*].

ACTS 10

One of the major messages which the Savior gave to His Apostles after He was resurrected was that the gospel was now to be taken to all the world—see Mark 16:15. For the Jewish members of the Church, this was a major change and went against their cultural traditions and upbringing. In this chapter, we will see the rather well-known account of a Roman soldier, a Gentile named Cornelius, who is ministered to by an angel in preparation for his conversion to the gospel of

Jesus Christ. The angel tells Cornelius to send for the Apostle Peter. In the meantime, Peter is prepared by a vision to preach the gospel to the Gentiles, and specifically to Cornelius and his household. Watch now as the work of the Lord is extended to the Gentiles.

1 THERE was a certain man in Cæsarea [*about 30 miles north of Joppa and 70 miles northwest of Jerusalem, on the coast of the Mediterraenean Sea*] called Cornelius, a centurion [*a Roman soldier in charge of one hundred soldiers*] of the band called the Italian band,

2 A devout man, and one that feared [*respected, worshipped*] God with all his house [*along with all the people in his household*], which gave much alms [*financial assistance*] to the people, and prayed to God alway.

3 He saw in a vision evidently about the ninth hour of the day [*about 3:00 PM*] an angel of God coming in to him, and saying unto him, Cornelius.

4 And when he looked on him, he was afraid, and said, What is it, Lord? And he said unto him, Thy prayers and thine alms are come up for a memorial before God. [*God has heard your prayers and knows of your contributions to the poor.*]

5 And now send men to Joppa, and call for one Simon, whose surname is Peter:

6 He lodgeth with [*is living with*] one Simon a tanner, whose house is by the sea side: he shall tell thee what thou oughtest to do.

7 And when the angel which spake unto Cornelius was departed [*had left*], he called two of his household servants, and a devout soldier of them that waited on [*served*] him continually;

8 And when he had declared all these things unto them, he sent them to Joppa.

9 ¶ On the morrow [*the next day*], as they went on their journey, and drew nigh [*near*] unto the city, Peter went up upon the housetop [*remember that the houses in the Holy Land had flat roofs and were commonly used for living quarters when weather permitted*] to pray about the sixth hour [*about noon*]:

10 And he became very hungry, and would have eaten: but while they made ready [*while lunch was being prepared*], he fell into a trance [*the Spirit came upon him and his physical surroundings faded out of his mind as a vision opened to him*],

11 And saw heaven opened, and a certain vessel descending [*coming down*] unto him, as it had been [*like*] a great sheet knit [*held*] at the four corners, and let down to the earth:

12 Wherein [*on the sheet*] were all manner of [*all kinds of*] four-footed beasts of the earth, and wild beasts, and creeping things, and fowls of the air.

The Jews had a very detailed "word of wisdom," telling them

what they should and should not eat, as faithful followers of the law of Moses. For instance, they were allowed to eat any animals which had cloven hoofs and chewed the cud, such as sheep, goats, and cows. However, they were not allowed to eat blood, camels, rabbits, pigs, eagles, vultures, ravens, owls, storks, bats, mice, tortoises, ferrets, lizards, snails, moles, etc. All of these were considered "unclean" under the law of Moses. They were permitted to eat locusts, bald locusts, beetles, and grasshoppers, but no other bugs. For more details, see Leviticus, chapter 11. This "word of wisdom" for them was a great blessing because it prevented them from getting many diseases carried by such creatures. With this as background, the sheet in Peter's vision contained many "unclean" creatures, eating of which was against Peter's religious background, training, and commitments. Peter is startled when told by the voice to eat these "unclean" things.

13 And there came a voice to him, Rise, Peter; kill, and eat.

14 But Peter said, Not so, Lord; for I have never eaten any thing that is common or unclean.

15 And the voice spake unto him again the second time, What God hath cleansed, that call not thou common. [*Do not say that what the Lord has made clean is still unclean.*]

16 This was done thrice [*three times*]: and the vessel was received up again into heaven.

By the way, in the Jewish culture of the day, three times ("thrice," in verse 16 above) was the superlative, the best, and the most important. So, when the vision was presented to Peter three times, he knew that whatever the message was, it was of the highest importance.

17 Now while Peter doubted in himself what this vision which he had seen should mean [*as Peter was wondering what the meaning of this vision was*], behold, the men which were sent from Cornelius [*the Roman centurion, who was a Gentile, not a Jew*] had made enquiry for Simon's house [*had asked directions for and finally found Simon's house*], and stood before the gate,

18 And called, and asked whether Simon, which was surnamed Peter, were lodged there [*asked whether or not Simon Peter was staying there*].

19 ¶ While Peter thought on the vision [*while Peter was still trying to figure out the meaning of the vision*], the Spirit said unto him, Behold, three men seek thee.

20 Arise therefore, and get thee down [*go downstairs*], and go with them, doubting nothing [*don't question My instructions*]: for I have sent them.

21 Then Peter went down to the men which were sent unto him from Cornelius; and said, Behold, I am he whom ye seek: what is the

cause wherefore ye are come [*why have you come to see me*]?

22 And they said, Cornelius the centurion, a just man [*a righteous man; one who lives his beliefs with exactness*], and one that feareth God, and of good report [*good reputation*] among all the nation of the Jews, was warned from God by an holy angel to send for thee into his house [*was told by an angel to ask you to come to his house*], and to hear words of thee.

23 Then called he them in, and lodged them [*then Peter invited them in and had them stay overnight*]. And on the morrow Peter went away with them, and certain brethren from Joppa accompanied him.

24 And the morrow after [*the day after*] they entered into Cæsarea. And Cornelius waited for them, and had called together his kinsmen [*relatives*] and near friends.

Although Roman Centurians were powerful men of authority, notice how humble Cornelius is in verse 25, next.

25 And as Peter was coming in, Cornelius met him, and fell down at his feet, and worshipped him.

26 But Peter took him up, saying, Stand up; I myself also am a man. [*In other words, don't worship me; I am just a man.*]

27 And as he talked with him, he went in [*into Cornelius' house*], and found many that were come together [*and met many who had gathered there*].

Peter now understands the meaning of the dream or vision of the sheet with unclean animals, birds, etc., which he was commanded to eat. Jewish law made it illegal to closely associate with Gentiles (non-Jews), or go into their homes. The message of the vision was that he was no longer to follow this law. The time had now come to take the gospel to all people and to associate with them freely.

28 And he said unto them, Ye know how that it is an unlawful thing for a man that is a Jew to keep company [*associate with*], or come unto one of another nation; but God hath shewed [*showed*] me that I should not call any man common or unclean.

29 Therefore [*for this reason*] came I unto you without gainsaying [*without opposing what God told me*], as soon as I was sent for: I ask therefore for what intent ye have sent for me?

30 And Cornelius said, Four days ago I was fasting until this hour; and at the ninth hour [*about 3:00 PM*] I prayed in my house, and, behold, a man [*angel*] stood before me in bright clothing,

31 And said, Cornelius, thy prayer is heard, and thine alms [*contributions to the poor*] are had in remembrance in the sight of God.

32 Send therefore to Joppa, and call hither [*invite to come to your home*]

Simon, whose surname is Peter; he is lodged in the house of one Simon a tanner by the sea side: who, when he cometh, shall speak unto thee.

33 Immediately therefore I sent to thee; and thou hast well done that thou art come [*it was good of you to come*]. Now therefore are we all here present before God [*now this is why we are all here*], to hear all things that are commanded thee of God.

Verse 34, next, has a rather well-known and oft-quoted doctrine. It is "God is no respecter of persons."

34 ¶ Then Peter opened his mouth, and said, Of a truth I perceive that God is no respecter of persons: [*In other words, I understand for sure that God will treat all people equally.*]

Remember that the resurrected Savior clearly instructed His disciples to take the gospel to all the world, even though He had limited His mortal mission to the Jews. (See Mark 16:15.) Now Peter, in his role as the Prophet and head of the Church, is having this new doctrine strongly emphasized in a very personal interaction with Cornelius, a Gentile, and his household. He will thus be strongly motivated to implement this change in doctrine; namely, to now take the gospel to all people.

35 But in every nation he that feareth him [*he who has respect and reverence for God*], and worketh righteousness, is accepted with him.

36 The word which God sent unto the children of Israel, preaching peace by Jesus Christ: (he is Lord of all:)

37 That word, I say, ye know [*you are familiar with*], which was published throughout all Judæa, and began from Galilee, after the baptism which John [*the Baptist*] preached;

38 How God [*the Father*] anointed [*prepared*] Jesus of Nazareth with the Holy Ghost and with power: who went about doing good, and healing all that were oppressed of the devil; for God was with him.

39 And we are witnesses of all things which he [*Jesus*] did both in the land of the Jews, and in Jerusalem; whom they slew [*killed*] and hanged on a tree [*crucified*]:

40 Him God raised up [*resurrected*] the third day, and shewed him openly [*had the resurrected Jesus appear to many*];

41 Not to all the people, but unto witnesses chosen before of God [*Jesus didn't appear to everyone, but to many who serve as witnesses*], even to us, who did eat and drink with him after he rose from the dead [*as recorded in Luke 24:36–43 and elsewhere*].

42 And he commanded us to preach unto the people, and to testify that it is he which was ordained of God to be the Judge of quick [*the living*] and dead.

43 To him give all the prophets witness [*all the Old Testament prophets bore witness of Christ*], that through his name whosoever believeth in him shall receive remission [*forgiveness*] of sins.

44 ¶ While Peter yet spake these words, the Holy Ghost fell on all them which heard the word [*all the people who were listening to Peter in Cornelius' house*].

45 And they of the circumcision which believed [*the Jewish members of the Church who had accompanied Peter from Joppa to Cornelius' house in Caesarea*] were astonished, as many as came with Peter, because that on the Gentiles also was poured out the gift of the Holy Ghost. [*They were shocked that the Holy Ghost actually came upon non-Jews.*]

46 For they heard them speak with tongues, and magnify God. Then answered Peter [*Peter responded by saying*],

47 Can any man forbid water, that these should not be baptized [*would any of you dare to forbid baptism for these Gentiles*], which have received the Holy Ghost as well as we [*who have received the Holy Ghost just like we have*]?

48 And he commanded them to be baptized in the name of the Lord. Then prayed they him to tarry certain days. [*Then these new converts asked Peter to stay with them for a few days.*]

ACTS 11

As you will see in this chapter, the fact that the gospel, including baptism, had actually been taken to Gentiles, stirred up strong feelings among Jewish members of the Church. They had grown up in a culture and tradition that Israelites were superior in the eyes of God and that Gentiles, no matter how righteous, would always be second class people as far as the kingdom of God is concerned.

Even though the Savior instructed that the gospel be taken to all the world (Mark 16:15 and elsewhere), it has not sunk in yet in the heads and hearts of Jewish members that the ordinances and rituals of the law of Moses, including circumcision, are no longer required in the Church Jesus Christ established. Thus, you will see a rather heated debate when Peter and his fellow travelers return to Jerusalem. The debate is about the fact that Peter has actually associated with Gentiles and baptized Cornelius and his household.

As mentioned earlier, there are always growing pains as the Church and gospel are taken to other cultures and nations. We see a considerable amount of this today, so it ought to be relatively easy for us to be patient with these folks as they go through some rather painful growth toward becoming Zion people.

1 AND the apostles and brethren that were in Judæa heard that the Gentiles [*people who were not Jews*] had also received the word

of God [*been baptized into the Church*].

2 And when Peter was come up to [*had arrived in*] Jerusalem, they that were of the circumcision contended with him [*Jewish members of the Church, who believed strongly that male converts should be circumcised according to the law of Moses in order to join the Church (see "Circumcision" in the Bible Dictionary), argued the point with Peter*],

3 Saying, Thou wentest in to men uncircumcised, and didst eat with them [*you not only went into the homes of uncircumcised men (or in other words, Gentiles) but you actually ate with them, which was forbidden by the laws of the Jewish Elders*].

4 But Peter rehearsed the matter [*explained everything*] from the beginning, and expounded it by order unto them [*explained the events, in order, which led up to his actions*], saying,

5 I was in the city of Joppa praying: and in a trance I saw a vision [*see Acts 10:10–16*], A certain vessel descend, as it had been [*as if it were*] a great [*large*] sheet, let down from heaven by four corners; and it came even to me [*it came right down to me*]:

6 Upon the which when I had fastened mine eyes, I considered, and saw [*when I looked closely, I saw*] fourfooted beasts of the earth, and wild beasts, and creeping things, and fowls of the air.

7 And I heard a voice saying unto me, Arise, Peter; slay and eat.

8 But I said, Not so, Lord: for nothing common or unclean hath at any time entered into my mouth. [*I can't do it, Lord. I have never broken the law of Moses by eating unclean things.*]

9 But the voice answered [*said to*] me again from heaven, What God hath cleansed, that call not thou common.

10 And this was done [*repeated*] three times: and all were drawn up again into heaven [*all the things in the vision were taken back up into heaven*].

11 And, behold, immediately there were three men already come unto [*already arrived at*] the house where I was, sent from Cæsarea unto me.

12 And the Spirit bade me go [*told me to go*] with them, nothing doubting [*without questioning the instructions*]. Moreover these six brethren [*six Jewish members of the Church*] accompanied me, and we entered into the man's [*Cornelius'*] house:

13 And he shewed [*told*] us how he had seen an angel in his house, which stood and said unto him, Send men to Joppa, and call for Simon, whose surname is Peter;

14 Who shall tell thee words [*who will preach the gospel to you*], whereby thou [*through which you*] and all thy house shall be saved.

15 And as I [*Peter*] began to speak, the Holy Ghost fell on them [*the Gentiles in Cornelius' house*], as on us at the beginning [*just like it did upon us when we first heard of the gospel*].

16 Then remembered I the word of the Lord, how that he said, John [*the Baptist*] indeed baptized with water; but ye shall be baptized with the Holy Ghost.

17 Forasmuch then as [*therefore, since*] God gave them [*Cornelius and his family and friends*] the like gift [*the same manifestation of the Holy Ghost*] as he did unto us, who believed on the Lord Jesus Christ; what was I, that I could withstand God [*do you really think I should have told God He made a mistake*]?

18 When they heard these things, they held their peace [*they quit criticizing Peter and arguing with him*], and glorified [*praised*] God, saying, Then hath God also to the Gentiles granted repentance unto life. [*So, the fact is, God allows Gentiles to repent and attain eternal life (exaltation) also.*]

19 ¶ Now they which were scattered abroad upon the persecution that arose about Stephen [*members of the Church, who had been scattered far and wide by persecutions which started with the stoning of Stephen,*] travelled as far as Phenice, and Cyprus, and Antioch, preaching the word to none but unto the Jews only [*taught the gospel only to Jews*].

20 And some of them were men of Cyprus and Cyrene, which, when they were come to Antioch, spake unto the Grecians, preaching the Lord Jesus. [*Now, they taught the gospel to some citizens of Greece, who were Gentiles.*]

21 And the hand of the Lord was with them: and a great number believed, and turned unto the Lord [*many Greeks were converted to Christ*].

22 ¶ Then tidings [*news*] of these things came unto the ears of the church which was [*to members of the Church who were*] in Jerusalem: and they sent forth Barnabas [*who will later become one of Paul's missionary companions*], that he should go as far as Antioch.

23 Who, when he came, and had seen the grace of God [*had seen the work of conversion among Gentiles there*], was glad, and exhorted [*counseled*] them all, that with purpose of heart [*with deep determination*] they would cleave unto [*stay true to*] the Lord.

24 For he [*Barnabas*] was a good man, and full of the Holy Ghost and of faith: and much people was added unto the Lord [*many converts were added to the Church*].

25 Then departed Barnabas to Tarsus, for to seek Saul [*Barnabas then left Antioch to go to Tarsus to try to find Saul*]:

26 And when he had found him, he brought him unto Antioch. And it came to pass, that a whole year they assembled themselves

with the church, and taught much people. [*Barnabas and Saul stayed for a whole year with the Saints and did much teaching.*] And the disciples were called Christians first in Antioch. [*Antioch was the first place where people began referring to members of the Church as "Christians."*]

27 ¶ And in these days came prophets from Jerusalem unto Antioch.

28 And there stood up one of them [*one of the prophets*] named Agabus, and signified by the Spirit [*and prophesied by the power of the Holy Ghost*] that there should be great dearth [*that there would be a wide-spread famine*] throughout all the world: which came to pass [*happened*] in the days of Claudius Cæsar [*Emperor of Rome from A.D. 41–51*].

29 Then the disciples [*members in Antioch*], every man according to his ability, determined to send relief unto the brethren which dwelt in Judæa [*the Jerusalem area*]:

30 Which also they did, and sent it to the elders by the hands of Barnabas and Saul. [*Members in Antioch sent relief to the leaders of the Church in Jerusalem for them to distribute to needy members during the famine.*]

ACTS 12

In this chapter, Luke will tell us about the persecution of the Church by King Herod. James, the brother of John, will be martyred. Peter will be placed in prison but will be set free by an angel. Just like in our day, the Church will continue to grow in spite of opposition.

1 NOW about that time Herod the king stretched forth his hands to vex certain of the church [*King Herod started persecuting members of the Church*].

2 And he killed James the brother of John with the sword. [*James was one of the original Apostles.*]

3 And because he saw it pleased the Jews, he proceeded further to take [*arrest*] Peter also. (Then were the days of unleavened bread.) [*This was during the Passover season, and would be around our Easter season. See Bible Dictionary under "Feasts".*]

4 And when he had apprehended him [*had arrested Peter*], he put him in prison, and delivered him to four quaternions of soldiers [*four teams of four soldiers each*] to keep him; intending after Easter [*Passover*] to bring him forth to the people [*intending to have a public trial for Peter*].

5 Peter therefore [*for that reason*] was kept in prison: but prayer was made without ceasing of the church unto God for him. [*Members of the Church prayed constantly for Peter.*]

6 And when Herod would have brought him forth [*the night before King Herod was to have Peter brought to him from the prison*],

the same night [*that night*] Peter was sleeping between two soldiers, bound with two chains: and the keepers before [*in front of*] the door kept the prison.

As we continue our study, you will notice that we refer occasionally to word definitions given by *Strong's Exhaustive Concordance of the Bible.* This highly respected reference work lists Biblical words by number and gives helpful alternate definitions for many words used in the Bible. It is much-used among Bible scholars, including Bible scholars in our Church. You will see an example in verse 7, next.

7 And, behold, the angel of the Lord came upon him, and a light shined in the prison: and he smote [*tapped;* Strong's *#3960*] Peter on the side, and raised him up, saying, Arise up quickly. And his chains fell off from his hands.

JST Acts 12:7

7 And, behold, the angel of the Lord came **unto him**, and a light shined in the prison; and he smote Peter on the side, and raised him up, saying, Arise up quickly. And his chains fell off from his hands.

8 And the angel said unto him, Gird thyself [*get dressed*], and bind on thy sandals [*put on your sandals*]. And so he did. And he [*the angel*] saith unto him, Cast thy garment about thee [*put on your robe*], and follow me.

9 And he went out, and followed him; and wist [*knew*] not that it was true which was done by the angel; but thought he saw a vision. [*Peter didn't realize this was actually happening to him, rather, thought he was seeing it in a vision.*]

10 When they were past the first and the second ward [*when they had passed the first and second sets of guards in their assigned stations*], they came unto the iron gate [*the main gate to the prison*] that leadeth unto the city; which opened to them of his own accord [*which opened by itself*]: and they went out, and passed on through one street; and forthwith [*at that point*] the angel departed from him.

11 And when Peter was come to himself [*when Peter realized he wasn't dreaming or seeing a vision*], he said, Now I know of a surety [*for sure*], that the Lord hath sent his angel, and hath delivered me out of the hand of Herod, and from all the expectation of the people of the Jews. [*Peter now knew for sure that this was actually happening and that the Lord had sent an angel to free him from Herod and from the public trial expected by the Jews the next day.*]

12 And when he had considered the thing [*had decided what to do*], he came to the house of Mary the mother of John, whose surname was Mark; where many were gathered together praying.

The member of the Church named Mark, referred to in verse 12 above, was the Mark to whom the writing of the Gospel of Mark is attributed. Peter came to Mark's mother's house directly from the prison and had a bit of difficulty getting in, as seen in the next verses.

13 And as Peter knocked at the door of the gate, a damsel [*a young lady*] came to hearken [*came to where she could hear the person at the gate*], named Rhoda.

14 And when she knew [*recognized*] Peter's voice, she opened not the gate for gladness [*she was so happy she forgot to open the gate*], but ran in, and told how Peter stood before the gate [*she ran to the others who had gathered at Mary's house to pray for Peter, and told them Peter was standing outside*].

15 And they said unto her, Thou art mad [*You are crazy!*]. But she constantly affirmed that it was even so [*she insisted that it was true*]. Then said they, It is his angel. [*In other words, Peter is dead, and it must be his spirit standing out there.*]

16 But Peter continued knocking: and when they had opened the door, and saw him, they were astonished.

17 But he, beckoning unto them with the hand to hold their peace [*Peter signaled for them to quiet down*], declared [*explained*] unto them how the Lord had brought him out of the prison. And he said, Go shew [*show*] these things unto James [*perhaps James, the Savior's half-brother (see Mark 6:3) or James, son of Alpheus (see Luke 6:15) who was also an Apostle*], and to the brethren. And he departed, and went into another place.

18 Now as soon as it was day, there was no small stir among the soldiers, what was become of Peter [*the soldiers who had been guarding Peter in prison were very worried because he was gone*].

19 And when Herod had sought [*sent*] for him, and found him not, he examined the keepers [*questioned the prison guards*], and commanded that they should be put to death. And he [*Peter*] went down from Judæa to Cæsarea, and there abode [*and stayed there*].

At the beginning of verse 20, below, if you are using the King James Version of the Bible (the one English-speaking members of the Church use, as authorized by the Church), you will notice a "¶" which looks like a fancy backward P. As mentioned previously, It is a symbol which means that this verse starts a new topic. There are many ¶'s in our Bible, and each one signals the beginning of a different topic.

20 ¶ And Herod was highly displeased [*very angry*] with them of Tyre and Sidon: but they came with one accord [*united in purpose*] to him, and, having made Blastus the king's chamberlain [*personal servant*] their friend, desired peace; because their country was nourished by [*was receiving aid from*] the king's country.

21 And upon a set day Herod, arrayed in royal apparel [*dressed in fine royal robe, etc.*], sat upon his

throne, and made an oration [*gave a speech*] unto them.

22 And the people gave a shout, saying, It is the voice of a god, and not of a man.

23 And immediately the angel of the Lord smote him, because he gave not God the glory: and he was eaten of worms, and gave up the ghost [*he died*].

> We don't know quite what to do with verses 21–23 above, except to perhaps learn the lesson that sometimes the wicked are punished immediately, whereas, most of the time, they are punished later, even in the next life.

24 ¶ But the word of God grew and multiplied [*the gospel continued to spread*].

25 And Barnabas and Saul returned from Jerusalem, when they had fulfilled their ministry [*when they had finished their assignment*], and took with them John, whose surname was Mark. [*Mark will later write the Gospel of Mark.*]

ACTS 13

In this chapter, Paul (called "Saul" until verse 9 where Luke—the writer of Acts—starts referring to him as "Paul," which is the Latin name for "Saul") is sent on a mission with Barnabus. It will be the first of three major missionary journeys for Paul. As you will see, Paul is a master teacher. Watch as he gives a history of God's dealings with Israel in Old Testament times, setting the stage for teaching these people about the coming of Jesus Christ in fulfillment of the law of Moses.

1 NOW there were in the church that was at Antioch [*a city in Syria, about 300 miles north of Jerusalem*] certain prophets and teachers; as [*including*] Barnabas, and Simeon that was called Niger, and Lucius of Cyrene, and Manaen, which had been brought up with Herod the tetrarch, and Saul.

2 As they ministered to the Lord, and fasted, the Holy Ghost said [*in other words, Christ told them through the Holy Ghost*], Separate me [*set apart*] Barnabas and Saul for the work whereunto I have called them [*send Saul and Barnabas on a mission*].

> This mission, started probably in the spring of AD 48, will be the first of three major missionary journeys for Paul over the next several years. This first mission will take him from Antioch (in Syria) to the Island of Cyprus, and then to what is known today as southern Turkey, where the Galatians lived. Paul will become known as the missionary to the Gentiles. This first missionary journey is reported in Acts 13:1 through Acts 14:26. See Bible Dictionary under "Paul."

3 And when they had fasted and prayed, and laid their hands on them [*set them apart by the laying on of hands*], they sent them away.

4 ¶ So they, being sent forth by the Holy Ghost [*by the Savior,*

through inspiration of the Holy Ghost], departed unto Seleucia [*near Antioch*]; and from thence they sailed to Cyprus.

5 And when they were at Salamis [*on the east coast of Cyprus*], they preached the word of God in the synagogues [*church buildings*] of the Jews: and they had also John to their minister [*someone named John was their assistant*].

6 And when they had gone through the isle [*island*] unto Paphos [*on the southwest coast of Cyprus*], they found a certain sorcerer, a false prophet, a Jew, whose name was Bar-jesus [*also called Elymas; see verse 8, below*]:

7 Which was with [*who associated with*] the deputy of the country [*a powerful Roman official*], Sergius Paulus, a prudent [*wise*] man; who called for Barnabas and Saul, and desired to hear the word of God.

8 But Elymas the sorcerer (for so is his name by interpretation) withstood them [*tried to stop them*], seeking to turn away the deputy [*Sergius Paulus*] from the faith [*the gospel*].

In verse 9, below, we note (as stated above) that Luke now starts referring to Saul as "Paul," which is his Latin name. He will be called Paul during the rest of Acts. Later, he will be called to be an Apostle.

9 Then Saul, (who also is called Paul,) filled with the Holy Ghost, set his eyes on him [*looked straight at Elymas*],

10 And said, O full of all subtilty [*deception*] and all mischief [*dishonesty*], thou child of the devil [*you follower of Satan*], thou enemy of all righteousness, wilt thou not cease to pervert [*plot against*] the right ways of the Lord?

11 And now, behold, the hand of [*the power of*] the Lord is upon thee, and thou shalt be blind, not seeing the sun for a season. And immediately there fell on him a mist and a darkness; and he went about seeking some to lead him by the hand.

12 Then the deputy [*the Roman official, Sergius Paulus*], when he saw what was done, believed, being astonished at the doctrine of the Lord.

13 Now when Paul and his company [*group*] loosed [*departed*] from Paphos, they came to Perga in Pamphylia [*in southern Turkey, northwest of Cyprus*]: and John [*Mark*] departing from them returned to Jerusalem.

John Mark (or Mark) sailed with Paul, Barnabas, and the others to Pamphylia [*see Acts 15:38*], in what today is southern Turkey. Then, for whatever reason, Mark left them and returned to Jerusalem. This irritated Paul and he refused to take Mark with him on his second missionary journey. See Acts 15:36–41.

14 ¶ But when they departed from Perga, they came to Antioch in Pisidia [*this Antioch is in southern Turkey, and is not the Antioch from*

which Paul started on this journey in Acts 13:1–3], and went into the synagogue on the sabbath day, and sat down.

15 And after the reading of the law and the prophets [*the reading of some Old Testament scriptures*] the rulers of the synagogue sent unto them [*sent word to Paul and Barnabas*], saying, Ye men and brethren, if ye have any word of exhortation [*instruction, encouragement*] for the people, say on [*go ahead and talk to us*].

16 Then Paul stood up, and beckoning [*motioning*] with his hand said, Men of Israel, and ye that fear God, give audience.

Pay close attention now (in verses 16–41) as Paul gives a brief and concentrated review of the history of the children of Israel from the time Moses led them out of Egyptian bondage. He recounts 40 years of wandering in the wilderness, the settling of the Holy Land, four hundred and fifty years of having judges and no prophets until Samuel, the reign of Kings Saul, David, and Solomon, the preaching of John the Baptist, and the ministry, crucifixion, and resurrection of Christ. He is giving them a short review of their heritage as descendants of Abraham, or, in other words, as covenant Israel, and inviting them to fully embrace the full gospel brought by Jesus Christ. His major purpose is to show them that they cannot be saved by adhering to the law of Moses. Rather, by carefully studying the words of Moses, they will see that he was pointing them toward Jesus Christ, whose gospel can save them.

17 The God of this people of Israel chose our fathers [*ancestors*], and exalted [*blessed and strengthened*] the people when they dwelt as strangers in the land of Egypt, and with an high arm [*with power*] brought he [*God*] them [*the children of Israel*] out of it [*Egyptian bondage*].

18 And about the time of forty years suffered he their manners in the wilderness [*Israel wandered in the wilderness for about forty years because of their wickedness*].

JST Acts 13:18

18 And about the time **for** forty years suffered he their manners in the wilderness.

19 And when he [*God*] had destroyed seven nations in the land of Chanaan [*in what is now Palestine*], he divided their land to them by lot [*He divided up the land of Canaan among the twelve tribes of Israel in a fair manner*].

20 And after that he gave unto them judges about the space of four hundred and fifty years, until Samuel the prophet. [*Israel had a loose system of judges to rule over them for about 450 years, after Joshua and up until Samuel.*]

21 And afterward they desired a king: and God gave unto them Saul the son of Cis, a man of the tribe

of Benjamin, by the space of forty years. [*King Saul ruled Israel for 40 years.*]

22 And when he [*God*] had removed him [*Saul*], he raised up unto them David to be their king; to whom also he gave testimony [*God said that David was a righteous man at the time, and He made him king*], and said, I have found David the son of Jesse, a man after mine own heart, which shall fulfil all my will.

23 Of this man's seed [*from King David's descendants*] hath God according to his promise raised unto Israel a Saviour, Jesus: [*Jesus, as prophesied, was a descendant of David.*]

24 When John [*the Baptist*] had first preached before his [*Christ's*] coming the baptism of repentance to all the people of Israel.

25 And as John fulfilled his course [*as John the Baptist fulfilled his mission*], he said, Whom think ye that I am? I am not he [*I am not Christ*]. But, behold, there cometh one after me, whose shoes of his feet I am not worthy to loose [*whose sandals I am not worthy to take off His feet*].

26 Men and brethren, children of the stock of Abraham [*you descendants of Abraham*], and whosoever among you feareth God, to you is the word of this salvation sent [*this message of salvation through Jesus is directed at you*].

27 For they that dwell at Jerusalem [*the inhabitants of Jerusalem*], and their rulers, because they knew him not [*refused to accept Jesus for who He was*], nor yet the voices of the prophets which are read every sabbath day [*they refused to acknowledge the prophecies about Jesus, which they read every Sabbath in their meetings*], they have fulfilled them in condemning him [*they fulfilled the prophecies that they would condemn Jesus to death*].

28 And though they found no cause of death in him [*they could not come up with a valid reason to kill Jesus*], yet desired they Pilate [*the Roman governor*] that he [*Jesus*] should be slain.

29 And when they had fulfilled all that was written of him [*when they had fulfilled all the prophecies about Christ's crucifixion*], they took him down from the tree [*the cross*], and laid him in a sepulchre [*tomb*].

30 But God raised him from the dead:

31 And he [*Jesus*] was seen many days of them which came up with him from Galilee to Jerusalem, who are his witnesses unto the people. [*His disciples saw Jesus many times after His resurrection, and are now teaching others about Him.*]

Paul is now going to refer to scriptures, which the Jews in this meeting in the synagogue know well, to explain to them that Jesus fulfilled those prophecies and thus was truly the promised Messiah.

32 And we declare unto you glad tidings [*good news*], how that the promise which was made unto the fathers,

33 God hath fulfilled the same unto us their children [*the promise which God made to our ancestors has been fulfilled among us in our day*], in that he hath raised up Jesus again; as it is also written in the second psalm [*Psalm 2:7*], Thou art my Son, this day have I begotten thee [*Jesus is God's only begotten Son*].

34 And as concerning that he [*the Father*] raised him [*Jesus*] up from the dead [*resurrected Him*], now no more to return to corruption [*Jesus will never die again*], he said on this wise [*in these words*], I will give you the sure mercies [*blessings*] of David.

35 Wherefore he saith also in another psalm [*Psalm 16:10*], Thou shalt not suffer thine Holy One to see corruption. [*Christ's body will not die again.*]

36 For David, after he had served his own generation by the will of God, fell on sleep [*died*], and was laid unto his fathers [*was buried with his ancestors*], and saw corruption [*his body rotted in the grave*]:

37 But he [*Christ*], whom God raised again [*resurrected*], saw no corruption [*did not decompose in the tomb*].

38 ¶ Be it known unto you therefore, men and brethren, that through this man [*through Jesus*] is preached unto you the forgiveness of sins [*through Christ's Atonement, you can be forgiven of sins*]:

39 And by him [*through Christ*] all that believe are justified [*saved*] from all things, from which ye could not be justified [*redeemed*] by the law of Moses.

Did you catch the vital message that Paul led into in verse 39, above, concerning the law of Moses? These people to whom Paul is speaking have been taught the false doctrine all their lives that salvation comes through the law of Moses. This is not so. The law of Moses in its pure form was designed to lead people to Jesus Christ, through whom salvation comes. Watch now to see where Paul goes from here with his inspired message.

40 Beware therefore, lest that come upon you, which is spoken of in the prophets [*watch out that what the prophet Habakkuk said doesn't happen to you, quoting Habakkuk 1:5*];

41 Behold, ye despisers [*watch out, you skeptics and mockers*], and wonder, and perish [*marvel at Christ's life and teachings but still reject Him and die spiritually*]: for I [*God*] work a work in your days, a work which ye shall in no wise believe, though a man declare it unto you. [*I will do something so marvelous in your day that, even if someone explains it to you, you still won't believe it, referring to*

Christ's gospel and His Atonement.]

Watch now as the Gentiles in the group wait until the Jews have departed and then request that Paul and Barnabas teach them more the following week.

42 And when the Jews were gone out of [*had left*] the synagogue, the Gentiles [*non-Jews*] besought [*requested*] that these words [*this same message from Paul*] might be preached to them the next sabbath.

43 Now when the congregation was broken up [*was dismissed to go home*], many of the Jews and religious proselytes [*devout converts to Jewish religion*] followed Paul and Barnabas: who, speaking to them, persuaded [*encouraged*] them to continue in the grace of God [*continue to be faithful to God*].

By the next week, word has spread, and large crowds come to listen to Paul and Barnabas. But the jealous Jews, who do not believe these missionaries, confront them and speak strongly against what they are teaching—that Christ is the fulfillment of the law of Moses.

44 ¶ And the next sabbath day came almost the whole city together to hear the word of God.

45 But when the Jews saw the multitudes [*the large crowds coming to hear Paul and Barnabas*], they were filled with envy, and spake [*spoke*] against those things which were spoken by Paul, contradicting and blaspheming [*speaking abusively against what he was preaching*].

46 Then Paul and Barnabas waxed [*grew*] bold, and said, It was necessary that the word of God should first have been spoken to you [*the Jews who are now criticizing them*]: but seeing ye put it from you [*since you are rejecting it*], and judge yourselves unworthy of everlasting life, lo, we turn to the Gentiles.

47 For so hath the Lord commanded us, saying, I have set thee to be a light of the Gentiles, that thou shouldest be for salvation unto the ends of the earth [*to all the world*].

The JST makes an important change to verse 48, next.

48 And when the Gentiles heard this, they were glad, and glorified [*praised*] the word of the Lord: and as many as were ordained to eternal life believed.

<u>JST Acts 13:48</u>

48 And when the Gentiles heard this, they were glad, and glorified the word of the Lord; and as many as **believed** were ordained unto eternal life.

Did you catch it? Joseph Smith changed things to the proper order; namely, first you believe, then you live the gospel, which will lead you ultimately to eternal life, which is exaltation in the highest degree of glory in the celestial kingdom.

49 And the word of the Lord was

published [*preached*] throughout all the region.

50 But the Jews stirred up the devout [*loyal*] and honourable [*leading*] women, and the chief men of the city, and raised persecution against Paul and Barnabas, and expelled them out of their coasts [*region*].

51 But they [*Paul and Barnabas*] shook off the dust of their feet against them [*as a testimony that they had tried to teach them the gospel; see D&C 60:15*], and came unto Iconium [*about 70 miles to the east*].

52 And the disciples were filled with joy, and with the Holy Ghost.

ACTS 14

This is an action-packed chapter in which you feel the energy and determination of Paul, as he and Barnabus preach despite mounting opposition. They will be declared gods by the people in one place, and Paul will be stoned and left for dead in another.

1 AND it came to pass in Iconium, that they [*Paul and Barnabas*] went both together into the synagogue [*church building*] of the Jews, and so spake, that a great multitude both of the Jews and also of the Greeks believed.

2 But the unbelieving Jews stirred up the Gentiles [*people who were not Jews*], and made their minds evil affected [*prejudiced*] against the brethren [*Paul and Barnabas*].

3 Long time therefore abode they speaking boldly in the Lord [*Paul and Barnabas spent quite a long time preaching boldly under the direction of the Spirit*], which gave testimony unto the word of his grace [*which bore witness of the gospel of Christ*], and granted signs and wonders to be done by their hands [*the Spirit blessed them such that they did a number of miracles*].

4 But the multitude of the city was divided: and part held [*took sides*] with the Jews, and part with the apostles.

5 And when there was an assault [*an attack against Paul and Barnabas*] made both of [*by*] the Gentiles, and also of the Jews with their rulers, to use them despitefully [*to abuse them*], and to stone them [*kill them by stoning*],

6 They were ware of it [*they became aware of it*], and fled unto Lystra [*south of Iconium, about 20 miles*] and Derbe [*about 20 miles southeast of Lystra*], cities of Lycaonia, and unto the region that lieth round about:

7 And there they preached the gospel.

8 ¶ And there sat a certain man at Lystra, impotent [*crippled*] in his feet, being a cripple from his mother's womb [*from birth*], who never had walked:

9 The same heard Paul speak: who stedfastly beholding him [*Paul*

looked straight at the crippled man for several moments], and perceiving [*knowing*] that he had faith to be healed,

10 Said with a loud voice, Stand upright on thy feet. And he [*the crippled man*] leaped [*jumped up*] and walked.

11 And when the people saw what Paul had done, they lifted up their voices, saying in the speech [*language*] of Lycaonia, The gods are [*have*] come down to us in the likeness [*form*] of men.

12 And they called Barnabas, Jupiter [*the chief of the Roman gods; see Bible Dictionary under "Jupiter"*]; and Paul, Mercurius [*Mercury, the speaker for the Roman gods; see Bible Dictionary under "Mercurius"*], because he was the chief speaker [*Paul did most of the speaking as Paul and Barnabas preached*].

13 Then the priest of Jupiter, which was before their city [*the priest of the temple of Jupiter, which was just outside the city walls*], brought oxen and garlands unto the gates, and would have done sacrifice with the people [*and wanted to offer sacrifices to Barnabas and Paul, with the crowds*].

14 Which when the apostles, Barnabas and Paul, heard of, they rent [*tore*] their clothes, and ran in among the people, crying out,

JST Acts 14:14

14 **When the apostles, Barnabas and Paul, heard this**, they rent their clothes, and ran in among the people, crying out,

In the culture of these people, tearing one's clothing was a sign of deep distress and extreme emotion.

15 And saying, Sirs, why do ye these things? We also are men of like passions with you [*we are not gods, rather, just ordinary mortals like you*], and preach unto you that ye should turn from these vanities unto the living God, which made heaven, and earth, and the sea, and all things that are therein [*our message is that you should turn away from such worthless worship of Jupiter, Mercury, etc., and worship the living God instead*]:

16 Who in times past suffered [*allowed*] all nations to walk in their own ways [*in other words, gave all of us our agency*].

17 Nevertheless he left not himself without witness [*evidence*], in that he did good, and gave us rain from heaven, and fruitful seasons, filling our hearts with food and gladness. [*Even though people left the true God and worshiped as they pleased, there is much evidence of His existence and kindness in giving rain and crops to all. (See Moses 6:63.)*]

18 And with these sayings scarce restrained they the people, that they had not done sacrifice unto them. [*It was all Paul and Barnabas could do, even with such strong words, to stop the priest and the people from worshiping them.*]

19 ¶ And there came thither [*to Lystra*] certain Jews from Antioch and Iconium [*who had already tried to kill Paul and Barnabas*], who persuaded the people [*who talked the people in Lystra into stoning Paul*], and, having stoned Paul, drew [*dragged*] him out of the city, supposing he had been dead [*thinking he was dead*].

20 Howbeit [*however*], as the disciples [*members of the church*] stood round about him, he rose up, and came into the city: and the next day he departed with Barnabas to Derbe.

We gain additional insights into Paul's personality as he continues on this first missionary journey. Once he has made up his mind to do something, he is unstoppable! He seems to have no fear, and, in defiance of the Jews who stoned him and left him for dead, goes right back through their cities and ministers to new converts there, as you will see beginning with verse 21, next.

21 And when they had preached the gospel to that city, and had taught many, they returned again to Lystra, and to Iconium, and Antioch,

22 Confirming [*strengthening*] the souls of the disciples, and exhorting [*urging*] them to continue in the faith, and that we must through much tribulation enter into the kingdom of God. [*We can only get to celestial glory by staying faithful in spite of trials and troubles which stand in our way.*]

23 And when they had ordained them elders in every church [*ward or branch*], and had prayed with fasting, they commended them to the Lord, on whom they believed. [*After Paul and Barnabas had organized priesthood leadership in each ward and branch, they turned the new converts over to the Lord and continued their missionary journey.*]

24 And after they had passed throughout Pisidia, they came to Pamphylia [*both are regions in what is now east-central Turkey, near the coast of the Mediterranean Sea*].

25 And when they had preached the word in Perga, they went down into Attalia [*on the coast*]:

26 And thence [*from there*] sailed to Antioch, from whence they had been recommended to the grace of God for the work which they fulfilled [*from which they had been sent on this mission*].

27 And when they were come [*when they arrived*], and had gathered the church together, they rehearsed [*told*] all that God had done with them, and how he had opened the door of faith unto the Gentiles [*how the gospel was taking hold among the Gentiles*].

28 And there they abode long time with the disciples [*they stayed in Antioch for a long time with the members of the church*].

ACTS 15

Remember that when Stephen was stoned to death (Acts 7:55–60,) it signaled the beginning of intense persecution against the Church. Consequently, many faithful Jewish members fled from Jerusalem and settled far away in foreign cities. Thus, the stage was set for many Gentiles to hear the gospel and join the Church. Antioch (in northern Syria, over 300 miles north of Jerusalem and near eastern Turkey today) was one of these cities. Paul and Barnabas have just returned to Antioch from a very important mission, in which the gospel was successfully taken to the Island of Cyprus, plus many cities in what is now south central Turkey. Along with a number of Jews, many Gentiles have also been converted and have joined the Church. Antioch has become a significant gathering place for members and new converts, including a large number of Gentile converts (see Acts 11:20–21).

As we begin our study of chapter 15, we find that some Jewish members, men from Church headquarters in Jerusalem, have come to Antioch and are disturbed that the male Gentile converts have been allowed to join the Church without being required to be circumcised according to the requirements of the law of Moses (see Bible Dictionary under "Circumcision"). Paul and Barnabas are angry with these Jerusalem brethren for imposing cultural Judaism upon Gentile converts as a requirement for church membership. Lest we be too critical of these Jerusalem brethren, who are still learning, we might note that members of the Church today should be careful not to mix "cultural Mormonism" in with actual doctrines and ordinances required for exaltation.

1 AND certain men which came down from Judea [*from Church headquarters*] taught the brethren, and said, Except ye be circumcised after the manner of Moses [*unless you are circumcised, as taught by Moses*], ye cannot be saved.

2 When therefore Paul and Barnabas had no small dissension and disputation with them [*after Paul and Barnabas had argued strongly that these Jerusalem brethren were wrong*], they determined that Paul and Barnabas, and certain other of them, should go up to Jerusalem unto the apostles and elders about this question [*it was decided that Paul and Barnabas, with some other members, should go to Church headquarters in Jerusalem and check with the leaders of the Church on this matter*].

3 And being brought on their way by the church [*as they headed toward Jerusalem on this official business of the Church*], they passed through Phenice and Samaria, declaring [*telling about*] the conversion of the Gentiles: and they caused great joy unto all the brethren.

4 And when they were come to Jerusalem, they were received of the church, and of [*by*] the apos-

tles and elders, and they declared [*explained*] all things that God had done with them.

5 But there rose up certain of the sect of the Pharisees which believed [*some Pharisees who had joined the Church, stood up*], saying, That it was needful to circumcise them, and to command them to keep the law of Moses.

The Pharisees (see Bible Dictionary under "Pharisees," for more about these men) had been very influential in getting Jesus crucified. They were powerful political and religious leaders among the Jews, and constantly accused Christ of violating the law of Moses. Now, apparently, some of them had been converted and baptized and joined the Church. They want Peter and the brethren to command that the law of Moses be kept by the Church, even though Jesus had taught that He came to fulfill the law of Moses, and such things were no longer required.

6 ¶ And the apostles and elders came together [*met together*] for to consider of this matter.

7 And when there had been much disputing [*after much debate*], Peter rose up [*note that Peter is now presiding as the President of the Church*], and said unto them, Men and brethren, ye know how that a good while ago God made choice among us, that the Gentiles by my mouth should hear the word of the gospel, and believe [*You know that some time ago (see Acts, chapter 10), God told us that we should now take the gospel to the Gentiles. (See also Mark 16:15.)*].

8 And God, which knoweth the hearts, bare them witness, giving them the Holy Ghost, even as he did unto us [*God has born witness to the Gentiles and given them the Holy Ghost, just like us*];

9 And put no difference between us and them [*God has shown us that there is no difference between them and us*], purifying their hearts by faith.

10 Now therefore why tempt ye God [*why do you want to try God's patience with you*], to put a yoke [*burden*] upon the neck of the disciples [*Gentile converts*], which neither our fathers nor we were able to bear [*which neither our ancestors nor we Jews could fully live ourselves? In other words, circumcision is not necessary for exaltation.*]

11 But we believe that through the grace [*help*] of the Lord Jesus Christ we shall be saved, even as they.

12 ¶ Then all the multitude kept silence, and gave audience [*turned their attention*] to Barnabas and Paul, declaring [*who began explaining*] what miracles and wonders God had wrought [*performed*] among the Gentiles by them [*on their missionary journey*].

13 ¶ And after they had held their peace [*after Paul and Barnabas were through talking*], James answered [*responded*], saying,

Men and brethren, hearken [*listen*] unto me:

We understand that James, in verse 13, above, is the brother of Jesus, and is one of Mary and Joseph's own children. See Bible Dictionary under "James." Paul informs us that James became an Apostle. See Galatians 1:19.

14 Simeon [*Peter*] hath declared [*explained*] how God at the first did visit the Gentiles, to take out of them a people for his name. [*Peter has explained to you that the "chosen people" originally came from the Gentiles.*]

Abraham was the beginning of the "chosen people" referred to in verse 14, above. He and his posterity were chosen to carry the wonderful and often heavy burden of carrying the gospel and the priesthood ordinances to all people of the earth. See Abraham 2:9–11.

15 And to this agree the words of the prophets [*the words of the prophets in the Old Testament agree with what Peter has told you about this*]; as it is written [*in Amos 9:11–12*],

Verses 16 and 17, next, are New Testament quotes of Amos 9:11–12. You will see that the wording varies a bit. You will also see that the word "heathen" in Amos means "Gentiles," or, in other words, non-Jews.

16 After this I will return, and will build again the tabernacle of David, which is fallen down; and I will build again the ruins thereof, and I will set it up: [*The Lord will gather Israel back and restore the gospel to them.*]

17 That the residue of men [*the people who remain*] might seek after the Lord, and all the Gentiles, upon whom my name is called [*that the Gentiles also may join the Church and take My name upon them*], saith the Lord, who doeth all these things.

18 Known unto God are all his works from the beginning of the world. [*The Lord knows what He is doing.*]

19 Wherefore my sentence [*recommendation*] is, that we trouble not them, which from among the Gentiles are turned to God: [*I recommend that we do not require Gentile converts to live the law of Moses, including circumcision, in order to join the Church.*]

20 But that we write unto them, that they abstain from pollutions of idols, and from fornication, and from things strangled, and from blood. [*I recommend that we put our decision in writing and also tell them to avoid idol worship, sexual immorality, and other things associated with idol worship.*]

21 For Moses of old time hath in every city them that preach him, being read in the synagogues every sabbath day. [*It is likely that James is referring here back to what he said in verse 19, and warning that there is still a lot of pressure for all Jews to live the law of

Moses, which was done away with by Christ.]

22 Then pleased it the apostles and elders, with the whole church [*the unanimous decision was then made*], to send chosen men of their own company [*from the Church leadership in Jerusalem*] to Antioch with Paul and Barnabas; namely, Judas surnamed [*whose family name was*] Barsabas, and Silas, chief men [*men who had much influence and authority*] among the brethren:

23 And they wrote letters by them after this manner [*this is what they wrote in their letters of instruction to Gentile converts*]; The apostles and elders and brethren send greeting unto the brethren which are of the Gentiles [*to the brothers who are Gentile converts*] in Antioch and Syria and Cilicia:

24 Forasmuch [*inasmuch*] as we have heard, that certain which went out from us [*that some members who came from here*] have troubled you with words [*have given you instructions which worried you*], subverting your souls [*damaging your testimonies*], saying, Ye must be circumcised, and keep the law: to whom we gave no such commandment [*we did not authorize them to give you such instructions*]:

JST Acts 15:24

24 Forasmuch as we have heard, that certain **men** which went out from us have troubled you with words, subverting your souls, saying, Ye must be circumcised, and keep the law; to whom we gave no such commandment;

25 It seemed good unto us, being assembled with one accord [*having met and come to unity on this matter*], to send chosen men unto you with our beloved Barnabas and Paul,

26 Men that have hazarded their lives [*men who have put their lives in danger*] for the name of our Lord Jesus Christ.

27 We have sent therefore Judas [*Not Judas Iscariot—the one who betrayed Jesus—rather, an influential member of the Church in Jerusalem. (See Bible Dictionary under "Judas.")*] and Silas, who shall also tell you the same things by mouth [*verbally*].

28 For it seemed good to the Holy Ghost, and to us [*the Holy Ghost approves of this*], to lay upon you no greater burden than these necessary things;

29 That ye abstain from meats offered to idols, and from blood, and from things strangled, and from fornication [*see explanation in verse 20, above*]: from which if ye keep yourselves, ye shall do well. Fare ye well.

30 So when they were dismissed, they came to Antioch: and when they had gathered the multitude together, they delivered the epistle [*the letter from Peter and the Brethren*]:

31 Which when they [*the Gentile converts in Antioch and the*

surrounding areas] had read, they rejoiced for the consolation [*because it was very comforting*].

32 And Judas and Silas, being prophets also themselves, exhorted [*taught and explained things to*] the brethren [*the Gentile converts*] with many words, and confirmed them [*and verbally confirmed what had been written in the letter*].

33 And after they [*Judas, Silas, and others who had accompanied them from Church headquarters*] had tarried there a space [*had stayed for a while in Antioch*], they were let go in peace from the brethren unto the apostles [*they left, in peace, and returned to Church headquarters in Jerusalem*].

34 Notwithstanding it pleased Silas to abide there still [*however, Silas chose to remain in Antioch*].

35 Paul also and Barnabas continued [*stayed*] in Antioch, teaching and preaching the word of the Lord, with many others also.

Beginning with verse 36, next, Paul will make preparations and leave on what is known as his second missionary journey. It is reported in Acts 15:36 through Acts 18:22. See Bible Dictionary under "Paul."

36 ¶ And some days after Paul said unto Barnabas, Let us go again and visit our brethren in every city where we have preached the word of the Lord [*let's visit the converts in every city we went to on our first missionary journey*], and see how they do.

37 And Barnabas determined to take with them John, whose surname was Mark [*Barnabas wanted to take Mark with them*].

38 But Paul thought not good to take him with them, who departed from them from Pamphylia, and went not with them to the work. [*But Paul didn't want to take Mark with them because he considered Mark to be a quitter, because he left them and went home from Pamphylia (see Acts 13:13) while they were on their first missionary journey*].

39 And the contention was so sharp between them, that they departed asunder one from the other [*Paul and Barnabas disagreed with each other so sharply that they parted company over the issue*]: and so Barnabas took Mark, and sailed unto Cyprus [*the first destination on the first missionary journey of Paul and Barnabas*];

40 And Paul chose Silas, and departed, being recommended by the brethren unto the grace of God. [*The Brethren wisely sent Paul and Silas in a different direction than Barnabas and Mark.*]

The above contention between Paul and Barnabas is a reminder that these great men were still human, and still had some growing to do. Fortunately for us all, God is patient and allows us to grow also.

41 And he [*Paul*] went through Syria and Cilicia, confirming [*strengthening*] the churches.

As mentioned previously, this is the beginning of what is known as Paul's second missionary journey. He and Silas will head north from Antioch, through the northern part of Syria, then west through what is known as Turkey today, then west to what is modern-day Greece, preaching to many, including the Philippians, the Thessalonians, the Corinthians and the Ephesians, and finally ending up in Jerusalem, after traveling thousands of miles.

ACTS 16

Paul continues his energetic missionary work as he boldly returns to the sites of previous persecution. Timothy will join him as a missionary companion and will no doubt be taught much to prepare him for his ministry.

1 THEN came he [*Paul*] to Derbe and Lystra [*remember that Paul was stoned and left for dead in Lystra during his first missionary journey; see Acts 14:8–20*]: and, behold, a certain disciple [*member of the Church*] was there, named Timotheus [*Timothy*], the son of a certain woman, which was a Jewess, and believed [*was a member of the Church*]; but his father was a Greek [*a Gentile and apparently not a member of the Church*]:

Timothy will join Paul and Silas on their missionary journey as they leave Lystra. Timothy will become a very important assistant to Paul. First and Second Timothy are letters written to Timothy by Paul. For more about him, see Bible Dictionary under "Timothy."

2 Which was well reported of by the brethren that were at Lystra and Iconium. [*The local leaders of the Church at Lystra and Iconium told Paul that Timothy was a very faithful young man*].

There is a bit of a side issue presented in verse 3, next. It is a matter of wisdom rather than doctrine. As you read, you will see that Paul circumcised Timothy in preparation for him to join him on his next missionary journey. As you know, from the discussions in chapter 15, above, the decision had been made by Church leaders that circumcision was no longer required for membership in the Church. However, many Jewish converts to the Church, who were still very human and set in their ways, felt strongly that the law of Moses, which required circumcision, should still be required. So, as a matter of wisdom, to keep the peace, and to help Timothy be a more effective missionary among the Jews, he was circumcised.

Perhaps you can think of similar situations that might be encountered in the Church today. One example might be the following: A Jewish family has been converted in your ward boundaries. You have decided to invite them to dinner. Because you are aware that, as a matter of religion and culture, they formerly avoided eating pork or pork products, you would not serve them pork in the meal you fixed. While doctrinally there is no problem with eating pork, it would not be wise or nice to put them in a potentially embarrassing situation.

3 Him would Paul have to go forth with him [*Paul wanted him to accompany him on this mission*]; and took and circumcised him because of the Jews [*so that he could work more effectively with Jewish members of the Church*] which were in those quarters [*in that region*]: for they knew all that his father was a Greek [*a Gentile*].

4 And as they went through the cities, they delivered them the decrees for to keep, that were ordained of the apostles and elders which were at Jerusalem [*they delivered instructions from the Brethren at Church headquarters in Jerusalem*].

5 And so were the churches [*wards and branches*] established [*strengthened*] in the faith, and increased in number daily [*received new converts daily*].

6 Now when they had gone throughout Phrygia [*west-central Turkey today*] and the region of Galatia [*north-central Turkey today*], and were forbidden of the Holy Ghost to preach the word in Asia [*the Spirit prompted them not to preach in Asia, which would be in western Turkey today*],

7 After they were come to Mysia [*far northwestern Turkey today*], they assayed to go [*discussed the possibilities of going*] into Bithynia [*extreme north-central Turkey today*]: but the Spirit suffered them not [*did not permit it*].

8 And they passing by Mysia came down to Troas [*on the extreme northwestern tip of Turkey today*].

9 And a vision appeared to Paul in the night; There stood a man of Macedonia [*northern Greece today*], and prayed [*urgently asked*] him, saying, Come over into Macedonia, and help us.

10 And after he had seen the vision, immediately we [*Luke has now joined them*] endeavoured [*made plans*] to go into Macedonia, assuredly gathering [*knowing for sure*] that the Lord had called us for to preach the gospel unto them.

The use of "we" and "us" in verse 10, above, is interesting. As mentioned in the note at the beginning of Acts, Luke is the author of Acts. Up to Acts 16:10, Luke has used the pronoun "they" in describing what is happening. Now, he uses the pronoun "we"—thus informing us that he has joined Paul, Silas, and Timothy at this point of Paul's second missionary journey. The verses of Acts that follow verse 9 are sometimes called the "we" passages.

11 Therefore loosing [*sailing*] from Troas, we came with a straight course to Samothracia [*an island in the northern part of the Aegean Sea*], and the next day to Neapolis [*in extreme north-eastern Greece today*];

12 And from thence [*there*] to Philippi [*in northeastern Greece today*], which is the chief [*main*] city of that part of Macedonia, and a colony [*a colony planted by the Roman Empire under Octavius*]: and we were in that city abiding certain days [*staying for several days*].

13 And on the sabbath we went out of the city by a river side, where prayer was wont to be made [*where it was customary for citizens of the city to come to pray*]; and we sat down, and spake unto the women which resorted thither [*who came there*].

JST Acts 16:13

13 And on the Sabbath we went out of the city by a river side, where **the people resorted for prayer to be made**; and we sat down, and spake unto the women which resorted thither.

14 ¶ And a certain woman named Lydia, a seller of purple [*a merchant who sold purple cloth*], of [*from*] the city of Thyatira [*in modern-day western Turkey*], which worshipped God [*who believed in God*], heard us: whose heart the Lord opened [*the Spirit touched her heart*], that she attended [*paid close attention*] unto the things which were spoken of Paul.

15 And when she was baptized, and her household [*along with members of her household*], she besought [*asked*] us, saying, If ye have judged me to be faithful to the Lord [*if you consider me worthy*], come into my house, and abide there [*come stay at my home*]. And she constrained us [*convinced us to stay with her*].

Next, you will see Paul ruin a local business by casting an evil spirit out of a young slave woman who was telling fortunes and making considerable money for her owners.

16 ¶ And it came to pass, as we went to prayer, a certain damsel [*young woman slave*] possessed with a spirit of divination [*possessed by an evil spirit which helped her tell fortunes and predict the future*] met us, which brought her masters much gain by soothsaying: [*Her fortune-telling earned her owners much money.*]

17 The same [*the young slave girl*] followed Paul and us, and cried [*shouted*], saying, These men are the servants of the most high God, which shew [*who will show*] unto us the way of salvation.

18 And this did she many days. But Paul, being grieved [*saddened by this*], turned and said to the spirit [*the evil spirit who possessed her*], I command thee in the name of Jesus Christ to come out of her. And he came out the same hour [*NIV, "at that moment"*].

19 ¶ And when her masters [*owners*] saw that the hope of their gains [*that their source of income*] was gone, they caught Paul and Silas, and drew [*dragged*] them into the marketplace unto the rulers,

20 And brought them to the magistrates [*city judges*], saying, These men, being Jews, do exceedingly trouble our city,

21 And teach customs, which are not lawful [*legal*] for us to receive [*to accept*], neither to observe [*to practice*], being Romans [*since we are Roman citizens*].

22 And the multitude rose up together against them [*joined in attacking Paul and Silas*]: and the magistrates rent off their clothes, and commanded to beat them. [*The judges tore off Paul and Silas' clothes and ordered that they be beaten.*]

23 And when they had laid many stripes upon them [*when they had beaten them with several lashes of the whip*], they cast them into prison, charging [*commanding*] the jailor to keep them safely [*to make sure they didn't get away*]:

24 Who, having received such a charge, thrust them into the inner prison, and made their feet fast in the stocks. [*The jailor, having received such strict orders, put Paul and Silas in the inner dungeon and locked their feet in the stocks, so that there was no chance they would escape.*]

25 ¶ And at midnight Paul and Silas prayed, and sang praises unto God: and the prisoners heard them.

26 And suddenly there was a great earthquake, so that the foundations of the prison were shaken: and immediately all the doors were opened, and every one's bands were loosed [*every prisoner's shackles were unlocked so they could escape*].

27 And the keeper of the prison awaking out of his sleep, and seeing the prison doors open, he drew out his sword, and would have killed himself, supposing that the prisoners had been fled [*assuming that all the prisoners had escaped*].

28 But Paul cried with a loud voice, saying, Do thyself no harm [*don't hurt yourself*]: for we are all here.

29 Then he [*the jailor*] called for a light, and sprang in [*ran into the dungeon*], and came trembling, and fell [*bowed*] down before Paul and Silas,

30 And brought them out, and said, Sirs, what must I do to be saved?

31 And they said, Believe on the Lord Jesus Christ, and thou shalt be saved, and thy house [*and your family too*].

32 And they spake unto him the word of the Lord, and to all that were in his house [*they taught him and his family the gospel*].

33 And he took them [*Paul and Silas*] the same hour of the night [*immediately*], and washed their stripes [*washed their wounds from*

their whipping]; and was baptized, he and all his [*family*], straightway [*immediately*].

34 And when he had brought them [*Paul and Silas*] into his house, he set meat [*food*] before them, and rejoiced, believing in God with all his house.

35 And when it was day [*in the morning*], the magistrates [*judges, city officials*] sent the serjeants [*sergeants to the jailor*], saying, Let those men go [*release Paul and Silas from jail*].

36 And the keeper of the prison [*the jailor*] told this saying to Paul [*gave Paul the following message*:], The magistrates have sent to let you go: now therefore depart, and go in peace.

Next, we gain more insights into Paul's personality. He's feisty!

37 But Paul said unto them, They have beaten us openly [*in pub*lic] uncondemned [*without a proper trial according to Roman law*], being Romans [*and we are Roman citizens*], and have cast us into prison; and now do they thrust us out privily [*very quietly*]? nay verily [*absolutely not*!]; but let them come themselves and fetch us out [*let them come personally and release us*!].

38 And the serjeants told these words unto the magistrates: and they feared [*were very worried because they themselves could get into serious trouble for abusing Roman citizens without due process of law*], when they heard that they were Romans.

39 And they came and besought them [*begged their forgiveness*], and brought them out [*personally escorted them out of the prison*], and desired them [*asked them*] to depart out of the city.

40 And they went out of the prison, and entered into the house of Lydia and when they had seen the brethren [*probably local leaders and members of the Church*], they comforted them, and departed [*left town*].

ACTS 17

This chapter contains Paul's masterful sermon about the "Unknown God" (see verse 23). It was given in Athens and is an excellent example of Paul's skill as a speaker. You will also see one of the best references in the Bible teaching clearly that we are literally spirit children of God (verses 28–29).

1 NOW when they had passed through Amphipolis and Apollonia [*both cities were in what is known as northeastern Greece today*], they came to Thessalonica [*in northeastern Greece, on the coast of the Aegean Sea*], where was a synagogue [*church building*] of the Jews:

2 And Paul, as his manner [*custom*] was, went in unto them, and three sabbath days reasoned with them out of the scriptures [*taught and discussed the scriptures with them*

each Sabbath day for three weeks],

3 Opening and alleging [*presenting to them*], that Christ must needs have suffered [*that it was necessary for Christ to suffer for our sins*], and risen again from the dead [*and be resurrected*]; and that this Jesus, whom I preach unto you, is Christ [*that Jesus, about whom I am teaching you, is the Messiah (Christ) as promised in the scriptures*].

4 And some of them [*Jews who belonged to this synagogue*] believed, and consorted [*joined*] with Paul and Silas; and of the devout Greeks [*Gentiles*] a great multitude [*a large number joined*], and of the chief women not a few [*many prominent, influential women joined the Church also*].

Often, the word "Greeks," as used in verse 4, above, refers to Gentiles rather than just Greeks. In *Strong's Concordance*, under word #1671, it says the following regarding the word "Greek": "In a wider sense the name embraces all nations not Jews that made the language, customs, and learning of the Greeks their own . . ."

5 ¶ But the Jews which believed not [*who did not believe Paul and refused to join the Church*], moved with [*motivated by*] envy, took unto them [*gathered up*] certain lewd [*evil, wicked*] fellows of the baser sort [*who were vulgar idlers, hanging around the market place*] and gathered a company [*a mob*], and set all the city on an uproar [*caused a riot*], and assaulted [*attacked*] the house of Jason [*Romans 16:21 informs us that Jason was one of Paul's relatives*], and sought to bring them [*Paul and Silas*] out to the people [*to turn them over to the mob*].

It appears that Jason was a Thessalonican citizen who had joined the Church and that Paul and his associates visited in Jason's home. This incident took place about AD 48.

6 And when they found them not, they drew [*dragged*] Jason and certain brethren unto the rulers of the city, crying [*shouting*], These that have turned the world upside down are come hither also [*Paul, Silas and their group, who have stirred things up everywhere they have been, have come to our city too*];

7 Whom Jason hath received [*Jason accepted them and their teachings*]: and these all do contrary to the decrees of Cæsar, saying that there is another king, one Jesus [*Paul and his people are undermining Caesar and the Roman government by saying that there is another king, namely Jesus*].

8 And they troubled [*stirred up*] the people and the rulers of the city, when they heard these things.

9 And when they had taken security of Jason, and of the other, they let them go. [*When they had made Jason and other members pay bail, they released them.*]

10 ¶ And the brethren immediately sent away Paul and Silas by night unto Berea [*about 40 miles west of Thessalonica*]: who coming thither [*having arrived there*] went into the synagogue of the Jews.

11 These were more noble than those in Thessalonica, in that they received the word with all readiness of mind, and searched the scriptures daily, whether those things were so. [*The Jews in Berea were more receptive to the gospel than those in Thessalonica, and sincerely searched the scriptures to see if what Paul and Silas said was true.*]

12 Therefore many of them believed; also of honourable women which were Greeks, and of men, not a few [*many Gentile men and women were converted also*].

13 But when the Jews of Thessalonica had knowledge [*became aware*] that the word of God was preached of [*by*] Paul at Berea, they came thither [*there*] also, and stirred up the people.

14 And then immediately the brethren sent away Paul to go as it were to the sea [*to catch a ship and get away*]: but Silas and Timotheus abode there still [*stayed in Berea*].

15 And they that conducted [*the sailors who escorted*] Paul brought him unto Athens [*in southeastern Greece*]: and receiving a commandment unto Silas and Timotheus for to come to him with all speed [*receiving instructions from Paul to tell Silas and Timothy to join him in Athens as soon as possible*], they departed [*the sailors left for Berea*].

16 ¶ Now while Paul waited for them [*Silas and Timothy*] at Athens, his spirit was stirred in him, when he saw the city wholly given to idolatry [*completely involved in idol worship*].

17 Therefore disputed he [*he debated*] in the synagogue with the Jews, and with the devout [*religious*] persons, and in the market daily with them that met with him.

18 Then certain philosophers of the Epicureans, and of the Stoicks [*Stoics*], encountered [*met with Paul*] him. And some said, What will this babbler say? other some [*others said*], He seemeth to be a setter forth of strange gods [*he is preaching about some strange gods*]: because he preached unto them Jesus, and the resurrection.

Epicureans and Stoics, as mentioned in verse 18, above, taught Greek philosophies that were opposite each other. The Epicureans basically believed in pleasure and materialism as the source of true happiness in life. The Stoics, on the other hand, taught their followers to completely ignore pleasure, pain, and all external good or evil. They taught that the desired goal was complete independence from all external, physical influences.

19 And they took him [*Paul*], and brought him unto Areopagus [*a rocky hill in Athens, known as*

Mars Hill], saying, May we know what this new doctrine, whereof thou speakest, is?

JST Acts 17:19

19 And they took him and brought him unto the Areopagus, saying, May we know what this new doctrine **is, whereof thou speakest?**

20 For thou bringest certain strange things to our ears: we would know therefore [*we would like to know*] what these things mean.

21 (For all the Athenians [*citizens of Athens*] and strangers [*foreigners*] which were there spent their time in nothing else, but either to tell, or to hear some new thing.)

Paul's sermon at Mars Hill, beginning with verse 22, next, is one of the more famous of his addresses. You can get a good feel for his inspired skill as a teacher as he sets the stage for preaching about the true God.

22 ¶ Then Paul stood in the midst of Mars' hill, and said, Ye men of Athens, I perceive that in all things ye are too superstitious [*you are very religious; see Acts 17:22, footnote a*].

23 For as I passed by, and beheld [*saw*] your devotions [*your sacred statues, etc.*], I found an altar with this inscription, TO THE UNKNOWN GOD. Whom therefore ye ignorantly [*without understanding*] worship, him declare I unto you. [*I am going to explain to you who the UNKNOWN GOD is.*]

24 [*He is the*] God that made the world and all things therein [*in it*], seeing that he is Lord of heaven and earth, dwelleth not in temples made with hands [*He does not actually live in temples built by people*];

25 Neither is worshipped with men's hands, as though he needed any thing [*you don't have to fix or repair Him like you would a damaged statue (see* Strong's *#2324, definition 2) because He doesn't need such things*], seeing he giveth to all life, and breath, and all things [*The true God gives life to everything; D&C 88:41*];

26 And hath made of one blood [*from Adam and Eve*] all nations of men [*we are all brothers and sisters*] for to dwell on all the face of the earth, and hath determined the times before appointed [*"God sends his spirit children to earth on a regular, organized schedule. There is nothing haphazard or accidental about the peopling of the earth . . ." McConkie,* Doctrinal New Testament Commentary, *Vol. 2, p. 159*], and the bounds of their habitation [*God has planned that certain races would inhabit certain lands*];

27 That they should seek the Lord [*God planned all this so that He would be available to help us as we seek Him*], if haply [*if perhaps*] they might feel after him [*seek Him*], and find him, though he be not far from every one of us [*it doesn't take much looking because He is close by and anxious to help us*]:

JST Acts 17:27

27 That they should seek the Lord, **if they are willing to find him, for he is not far from every one of us;**

28 For in him we live, and move, and have our being [*God is everything to us*]; as certain also of your own poets have said, For we are also his offspring.

Verse 28, above, and verse 29, below, contain simple, clear doctrine, namely, that we are the offspring of God. In most verses in scripture, we are referred to as "creations" of God, which, of course, we are. But the word "offspring" is even more specific. It means that we were born as spirit sons and daughters of our Heavenly Parents. See Proclamation on the Family, paragraph two. It means that we are not "creations" in the sense that trees, mountains, cows, horses, sheep, birds, etc., are. Rather, we are literally children of God, and thus, through righteousness, can become like Him and become gods. (See D&C 132:19–20.) To have this correct doctrine right in the Bible can be helpful to us as we teach our nonmember friends who they really are.

29 Forasmuch then as we are the offspring of God, we ought not to think that the Godhead is like unto gold, or silver, or stone, graven by art and man's device. [*Since we are God's literal children, and we are not made of gold, silver, or stone, carved or sculpted by some artist, then it follows that the Godhead is composed of real people like us, not of statues made by man.*]

30 And the times of this ignorance God winked at [*God has been patient up to now with such foolish notions about who He is*]; but now commandeth all men every where to repent [*but now you know the truth about Him and who you are, and it is time to repent and begin worshiping the true God*]:

31 Because he [*the Father*] hath appointed a day [*Judgment Day*], in the which he will judge the world in righteousness by that man [*by Jesus who is the Christ*] whom he hath ordained [*sent*]; whereof he hath given assurance unto all men, in that he hath raised him from the dead [*the fact that the Father raised Jesus from the dead is proof that Jesus is indeed the promised Messiah*].

JST Acts 17:31

31 Because he hath appointed a day, in the which he will judge the world in righteousness **by him whom** he hath ordained; **and he** hath given assurance **of this** unto all men, in that he hath raised him from the dead.

32 ¶ And when they heard of the resurrection of the dead, some mocked [*made fun of it*]: and others said, We will hear thee again of this matter [*we would like to hear more about this from you*].

33 So Paul departed from among them.

34 Howbeit [*however*] certain men clave unto him [*joined Paul*], and believed [*and were converted*]: among the which was Dionysius the Areopagite [*a member of the Supreme Court of Athens; see* Strong's *#0697*], and a woman named Damaris, and others with them.

ACTS 18

In this chapter, Paul will visit Corinth, a city widely known for its wealth and wicked lifestyle. He will meet a faithful couple named Aquila and Priscilla and they will form a life-long friendship.

1 AFTER these things Paul departed from Athens, and came to Corinth [*a wealthy, worldly, wild seaport city in Paul's day, in southern Greece*];

2 And found a certain Jew named Aquila, born in Pontus, lately [*recently*] come from Italy, with his wife Priscilla; (because that Claudius had commanded all Jews to depart from Rome:) and came unto them.

3 And because he was of the same craft [*Aquila and Paul were both skilled in making fabric for tentmaking*], he abode [*stayed*] with them, and wrought [*worked*]: for by their occupation they were tentmakers.

After a year and a half, Paul will leave Corinth, and Aquila and Priscilla will leave with him.

4 And he reasoned [*taught and discussed the gospel*] in the synagogue every sabbath, and persuaded [*taught*] the Jews and the Greeks [*Gentiles*].

5 And when Silas and Timotheus [*Timothy*] were come [*finally arrived; see Acts 17:10–15*] from Macedonia, Paul was pressed in the spirit [*strongly felt the urgency to teach of Christ*], and testified to the Jews that Jesus was Christ.

6 And when they [*the Jews*] opposed themselves [*angrily resisted*], and blasphemed [*reviled and insulted Paul*], he shook his raiment [*he took his robe off and shook it in front of them, a sign of extreme disgust, grief, etc., in Jewish culture*], and said unto them, Your blood be upon your own heads; I am clean [*I have tried, therefore I am no longer responsible for you*]: from henceforth [*from now on*] I will go unto the Gentiles. [*I've had it with you Jews! From now on, I will preach to the Gentiles.*]

Paul's feisty personality shows strongly here. He apparently felt that all the Jews in that synagogue had rejected him, but as it turns out, the leader of the synagogue and all his family believed and were converted, as shown in the next verses, below. This is a good reminder to all of us that we sometimes don't know when someone has been helped by our efforts to bring them to Christ, even though it appears hopeless at the time.

7 ¶ And he departed thence [*from those Jews*], and entered into a certain man's house, named Justus, one that worshipped God [*one who believed in God*], whose house joined hard [*was right next door*] to the synagogue [*the building where the Jews worshiped*].

8 And Crispus, the chief ruler of the synagogue, believed on the Lord [*Christ*] with all his house [*along with his whole family*]; and many of the Corinthians hearing [*that Crispus had joined the Church*] believed, and were baptized.

9 Then spake the Lord [*the Savior*] to Paul in the night by a vision, Be not afraid, but speak, and hold not thy peace [*don't hold back, go ahead and preach to these people*]:

10 For I am with thee, and no man shall set on thee to hurt thee [*I will protect you here in Corinth*]: for I have much people in this city [*I have many people here in Corinth who will join the Church*].

11 And he continued there a year and six months, teaching the word of God among them.

12 ¶ And when Gallio was the deputy [*the Roman governor*] of Achaia [*southern Greece*], the Jews made insurrection with one accord [*joined together*] against Paul, and brought him to the judgment seat [*brought him to Gallio*],

13 Saying, This fellow persuadeth men to worship God contrary to the law [*which is against our law*].

14 And when Paul was now about to open his mouth [*was about to start speaking in his defense*], Gallio said unto the Jews, If it were a matter of wrong or wicked lewdness [*crime against our laws*], O ye Jews, reason would [*logic would dictate*] that I should bear with you [*that I would hear this case*]:

15 But if it be a question of words and names, and of your law [*but if it is a matter of your wanting me to enforce your religious laws for you*], look ye to it [*you take care of it*]; for I will be no judge of such matters [*I want nothing to do with such matters*].

16 And he drave them [*had them driven out*] from the judgment seat [*from his court room*].

17 Then all the Greeks took Sosthenes, the chief ruler of the synagogue, and beat him before [*within sight of*] the judgment seat [*Gallio's courtroom*]. And Gallio cared for none of those things [*payed no attention to it*].

18 ¶ And Paul after this tarried [*stayed*] there yet a good while, and then took his leave of the brethren [*said goodbye to the members in Corinth*], and sailed thence into Syria, and with him Priscilla and Aquila [*members of the Church; see Acts 18:2–3*]; having shorn his head [*cut his hair off*] in Cenchrea [*just a few miles south of Corinth*]: for he had a vow.

We do not know what Paul's vow or promise was. The cutting off of his hair was a sign in his culture and reminder to him that he had made a promise that he was determined to keep.

19 And he came to Ephesus [*near the coast of the Aegean Sea in southwestern Turkey*], and left them [*Aquila, and Priscilla, Aquila's wife*] there: but he himself entered into the synagogue, and reasoned [*discussed the gospel*] with the Jews.

20 When they desired him to tarry longer time [*to stay longer*] with them, he consented not [*he did not agree to*];

21 But bade them farewell [*said "Goodbye"*], saying, I must by all means keep this feast that cometh in Jerusalem [*I must at all costs, keep my vow to attend the feast that is coming up in Jerusalem*]: but I will return again unto you, if God will. And he sailed from Ephesus.

Acts 20:16 tells us that it was the Feast of Pentacost, held in Jerusalem, that Paul was so anxious to attend. He was absolutely determined not to arrive late to it.

22 And when he had landed at Cæsarea [*on the coast of the Mediterranean Sea, about 50 miles northwest of Jerusalem*], and gone up [*to Jerusalem*], and saluted the church [*greeted the members of the Church there*], he went down to Antioch [*about 350 miles north of Jerusalem, in northern Syria*].

Starting in verse 23, next, Paul will begin what is known as his third missionary journey. His travels on this journey are reported in Acts 18:23 through Acts 21:15. See Bible Dictionary under "Paul." This missionary journey will be his last (about four years), and he will travel farther on this journey than he did on either of his first two.

23 And after he had spent some time there, he departed, and went over all the country of Galatia and Phrygia in order [*he traveled back to visit his converts in what would be central Turkey today*], strengthening all the disciples [*members*].

24 ¶ And a certain Jew named Apollos, born at Alexandria [*probably about a hundred miles north of Antioch in northern Syria*], an eloquent man [*an excellent speaker*], and mighty in the scriptures [*who knew the scriptures very well*], came to Ephesus.

25 This man was instructed in the way of the Lord; and being fervent in the spirit, he spake and taught diligently the things of the Lord, knowing only the baptism of John. [*Apollos had considerable gospel knowledge and was a spiritual man, but was only acquainted with the teachings of John the Baptist, not of Jesus.*]

26 And he began to speak boldly in the synagogue: whom when Aquila and Priscilla [*faithful members from Corinth, who had followed Paul to Ephesus, and stayed there while he went to Jerusalem*] had heard, they took him unto them, and expounded [*explained*] unto him the way of God more perfectly

[*taught him about Christ and his teachings*].

27 And when he [*Apollos*] was disposed to pass into [*decided to go to*] Achaia [*the region of southern Greece, where Athens and Corinth were*], the brethren wrote, exhorting [*urging*] the disciples [*the members in southern Greece*] to receive [*accept*] him: who, when he was come, helped them much which had believed through grace: [*When Appolos arrived among the Saints in southern Greece, he taught them much and strengthened their knowledge of the gospel.*]

28 For he mightily convinced the Jews, and that publickly [*he was very successful in public debates with the non-believing Jews*], shewing by the scriptures that Jesus was Christ [*proving from their scriptures that Jesus was indeed the Messiah promised by Old Testament prophets*].

ACTS 19

One of the more well-known incidents recorded by Luke in this chapter is the account of the seven sons of Sceva who try without priesthood authority to cast out an evil spirit (verses 13–16).

1 AND it came to pass [*it so happened*], that, while Apollos was at Corinth, Paul having passed through the upper coasts [*having passed through the upper regions of what is today Turkey*] came to Ephesus: and finding certain disciples.

Did you notice Corinth and Ephesus in verse 1, above? They probably sound familiar to you. Paul wrote letters to the Saints living in these and other cities (such as Galatia in Acts 18:23) where he had taught and baptized. These letters or epistles became the New Testament books of 1 Corinthians, 2 Corinthians, Galatians, and so forth.

2 He said unto them, Have ye received the Holy Ghost since ye believed [*since you were converted*]? And they said unto him, We have not so much as heard whether there be any Holy Ghost [*we haven't even heard of the Holy Ghost*].

3 And he said unto them, Unto what then were ye baptized? And they said, Unto John's [*John the Baptist's*] baptism.

4 Then said Paul, John verily [*indeed*] baptized with the baptism of repentance, saying unto the people, that they should believe on him [*Christ*] which should come after him [*John the Baptist*], that is, on Christ Jesus.

5 When they [*the disciples at the end of verse 1*] heard this, they were baptized in the name of the Lord Jesus.

Verse 6, next, along with verse 5, above, is helpful in teaching investigators that the gift of the Holy Ghost is bestowed after baptism by the laying on of hands.

6 And when Paul had laid his

hands upon [*confirmed*] them, the Holy Ghost came on them; and they spake [*spoke*] with tongues, and prophesied.

7 And all the men were about twelve [*there were about twelve who were baptized and confirmed*].

8 And he went into the synagogue, and spake boldly for the space of three months, disputing [*reasoning with them*] and persuading [*teaching*] the things concerning the kingdom of God.

9 But when divers [*various Jews there*] were hardened [*hard-hearted*], and believed not, but spake evil of that way [*severely criticized Paul's teachings about God's kingdom*] before the multitude [*in front of the crowds*], he departed from them [*he left that synagogue*], and separated [*set apart*] the disciples, disputing [*reasoning and debating*] daily in the school of one Tyrannus.

Scholars presume that Tyrannus (a name which means "sovereign") was a Greek philosopher who taught philosophy in a public school setting in Ephesus. He obviously allowed Paul to meet with his students.

10 And this continued by the space of [*for*] two years; so that all they which dwelt in Asia heard the word of the Lord Jesus, both Jews and Greeks [*Gentiles*].

11 And God wrought [*performed*] special miracles by the hands of Paul:

12 So that from his body were brought unto the sick handkerchiefs or aprons, and the diseases departed from them, and the evil spirits went out of them. [*The power of God was upon Paul so much that people were able to take handkerchiefs or aprons, which had touched Paul, to sick people, including those possessed by evil spirits, and they were healed.*]

13 ¶ Then certain of the vagabond Jews, exorcists [*wandering Jews who went around trying to cast out evil spirits*], took upon them [*took upon themselves*] to call over them which had evil spirits the name of the Lord Jesus [*decided to try using the name of Jesus Christ in their attempts to cast evil spirits out of people*], saying [*to the evil spirits*], We adjure [*command*] you by Jesus whom Paul preacheth.

14 And there were seven sons of one Sceva [*a name meaning "mind reader"*], a Jew, and chief of the priests, which did so. [*A Jew who was high in authority had seven sons who tried to cast an evil spirit out of a man in the name of Jesus Christ.*]

15 And the evil spirit answered and said, Jesus I know, and Paul I know; but who are ye?

Did you notice the doctrine we get about evil spirits from verse 15 above? It is that the spirits who followed Satan in the war in heaven (Revelation 12:9), who are now here on earth as evil spirits, do not have the veil over their memory of the premortal life like we do. Thus, they remember and recognize Jesus.

16 And the man in whom the evil spirit was [*the man whom the evil spirit controlled*] leaped on them [*attacked them*], and overcame them, and prevailed against them [*beat them up*], so that they fled out of that house naked and wounded.

17 And this was known [*word of this spread rapidly*] to all the Jews and Greeks [*Gentiles*] also dwelling at Ephesus; and fear fell on them all, and the name of the Lord Jesus was magnified [*became much more famous and honored*].

18 And many that believed [*who were converted*] came [*to Paul and his brethren*], and confessed, and shewed their deeds [*and openly confessed their sins and evil deeds*].

19 Many of them also which used curious arts [*magic, sorcery, witchcraft, etc.*] brought their books together [*gathered together their books about sorcery, etc.*], and burned them before all men [*burned them in public*]: and they counted the price of them, and found it fifty thousand pieces of silver [*they figured the cost of the books they burned to be about 50,000 pieces of silver*].

20 So mightily grew the word of God and prevailed [*had much success*].

21 ¶ After these things were ended, Paul purposed in the spirit [*felt prompted by the Spirit*], when [*after*] he had passed through Macedonia and Achaia [*modern Greece today*], to go to Jerusalem, saying, After I have been there, I must also see Rome.

22 So he sent into Macedonia [*northern Greece*] two of them that ministered unto him, Timotheus [*Timothy*] and Erastus; but he himself stayed in Asia [*the Ephesus region in what is western Turkey today*] for a season.

23 And the same time there arose no small stir [*in the region around Ephesus*] about that way [*the way of living taught by the gospel*].

24 For a certain man named Demetrius, a silversmith, which made silver shrines for Diana, brought no small gain [*profit*] unto the craftsmen;

Diana, also known as Artemis, was a Greek goddess and was worshiped by many people in that region. See Bible Dictionary under "Diana." A temple to honor her had been built at Ephesus, and silversmiths in the area made an excellent living making statues of Diana, models of the temple, etc., to sell to worshipers of this false god. Watch next as these businessmen meet together to plot a strategy to stop Paul's teaching in the area that is threatening to ruin their business.

25 Whom he called together with the workmen of like occupation [*Demetrius called an emergency meeting of the silversmiths*], and said, Sirs, ye know that by this craft [*making things to sell to worshipers of Diana*] we have our wealth.

26 Moreover [*furthermore*] ye see and hear, that not alone at Ephesus [*not only at Ephesus*], but almost throughout all Asia, this Paul hath persuaded and turned away much [*many*] people, saying that they be no gods, which are made with hands: [*In other words, Paul is ruining our business by convincing people everywhere that the idols we make are not real gods.*]

27 So that not only this our craft [*our occupation*] is in danger to be set at nought [*to be ruined*]; but also that the temple of the great goddess Diana should be despised, and her magnificence should be destroyed, whom all Asia and the world worshippeth. [*Not only is Paul ruining our very profitable business, but he is convincing people not to respect and worship Diana nor her temple.*]

28 And when they heard these sayings, they were full of wrath [*anger*], and cried out, saying, Great is Diana of the Ephesians.

29 And the whole city was filled with confusion [*a riot started*]: and having caught Gaius and Aristarchus, men of Macedonia, Paul's companions in travel [*missionary companions of Paul*], they [*the mob*] rushed with one accord [*together*] into the theatre [*a place where large events, games, etc., were held. This theater was capable of holding 25,000 to 30,000 spectators and was the largest built by the Greeks, according to information given in conjunction with* Strong's *#2181.*]

30 And when Paul would have entered in unto the people, the disciples suffered him not [*Paul wanted to go in and speak to the mob, but the members of the Church would not let him*].

31 And certain of the chief of Asia [*leading government officials*], which were his friends, sent unto him [*sent a message to him*], desiring him that he would not adventure himself into the theatre [*telling him not to go in where the mob was*].

32 Some [*members of the mob*] therefore cried one thing, and some another: for the assembly was confused; and the more part knew not wherefore they were come together.

This seems to be typical mob mentality. Many of them have joined in the uproar but don't even know what it is all about, as stated at the end of verse 32, above.

33 And they drew Alexander [*most likely one of Paul's followers*] out of the multitude, the Jews putting him forward [*the Jews pushed him out where he could be heard*]. And Alexander beckoned [*motioned for quiet*] with the hand, and would have made his defence unto the people.

34 But when they [*the mob*] knew [*discovered*] that he was a Jew, all with one voice about the space of two hours cried out, Great is Diana of the Ephesians [*they shouted for about two solid hours, "Great is Diana of the Ephesians"*] and wouldn't listen to Alexander.

35 And when the townclerk [*a public official*] had appeased the people [*had settled the mob down sufficiently*], he said, Ye men of Ephesus, what man is there that knoweth not how that the city of the Ephesians is a worshipper of [*is the host city for*] the great goddess Diana, and of the image which fell down from Jupiter [*doesn't everybody know that Diana came from Zeus, in other words, directly from heaven*]?

36 Seeing then that these things cannot be spoken against, ye ought to be quiet, and to do nothing rashly. [*There is nothing to worry about. No one can successfully speak against Diana. So, you ought to settle down and not do anything rash.*]

37 For ye have brought hither [*here to the theater*] these men [*disciples of Paul*], which are neither robbers of churches, nor yet blasphemers of your goddess [*these men have not committed any crimes*].

38 Wherefore if Demetrius, and the craftsmen which are with him, have a matter against any man, the law is open [*our courts are available to them*], and there are deputies [*judges*]: let them implead one another [*let Demetrius and the silversmiths bring formal charges against these men if they so desire, in proper manner in our public courts*].

39 But if ye enquire any thing concerning other matters, it shall be determined in a lawful assembly. [*If you have any other matters to bring up, do it legally.*]

40 For we are in danger to be called in question for this day's uproar [*we could get in big trouble with the Romans because of the riot you caused today*], there being no cause whereby we may give an account of this concourse [*we would not have a good excuse to the Romans for what happened*].

41 And when he had thus spoken, he dismissed the assembly [*he sent the crowd home*].

ACTS 20

Sometimes we are challenged as to why Sunday is our holy day and Sabbath rather than Saturday, which was the Sabbath in Old Testament times. This chapter explains why. After the crucifixion and resurrection of the Savior, the members of the Church began meeting on the first day of the week, which was Sunday, rather than Saturday. (See verse 7.)

1 AND after the uproar was ceased [*after the riot had been settled down*], Paul called unto him the disciples [*the members of the Church in Ephesus*], and embraced them, and departed for to go into Macedonia [*northern Greece today*].

2 And when he had gone over those parts [*when he had visited the members in those regions*], and had given them much exhortation [*counsel and teachings*], he came into Greece [*southern Greece today*],

3 And there abode [*stayed*] three months. And when the Jews laid

wait for him, as he was about to sail into Syria [*when he discovered that the Jews had plans to attack him as he set sail for Syria*], he purposed to [*decided instead to*] return through Macedonia.

4 And there accompanied him into Asia [*Turkey today*] Sopater of Berea [*Sopater was apparently a member of the Church from the city of Berea, in the northeastern region of central Greece*]; and of the Thessalonians [*from among the members in Thessalonica–northeastern Greece*], Aristarchus and Secundus; and Gaius of Derbe [*in southern Turkey today*], and Timotheus [*Timothy*]; and of [*from*] Asia, Tychicus and Trophimus.

5 These going before tarried [*waited*] for us [*Luke, Paul, and whoever else was with Paul—remember, Luke is the one writing Acts*] at Troas.

6 [*The seven men mentioned in verse 4, above, who were members of the Church from the various cities mentioned, went ahead and waited for Paul, Luke, and their companions at Troas, a coastal city in what is northwestern Turkey today.*] And we sailed away from Philippi [*northeastern Greece today*] after the days of unleavened bread [*after Passover; see Bible Dictionary under "Feasts"*], and came unto them to [*met them in*] Troas in five days; where we abode [*stayed*] seven days.

As mentioned in the note at the beginning of this chapter, in verse 7, next, we see that the members of the Church were now meeting on Sunday, the first day of the week, for their sacrament meetings, etc. After the Savior's resurrection, Sunday became the Sabbath, the holy day of the week for the Saints. Before that, Saturday (the seventh day of the week) was the Sabbath, the holy day.

7 And upon the first day of the week [*on Sunday*], when the disciples [*members*] came together to break bread [*to partake of the sacrament*], Paul preached unto them, ready to depart on the morrow; and continued his speech until midnight. [*Paul kept speaking until midnight because he knew he was leaving in the morning.*]

Next, Luke tells us about a wonderful miracle. As mentioned above, Paul spoke to a large crowd until midnight. The following verses report that a young man in attendance, who was sitting on a windowsill by an open window on the third floor of the building, dozed off and went into a deep sleep, which resulted in him falling to his death three stories down. He is brought back to life, a clear and marvelous miracle!

8 And there were many lights in the upper chamber, where they were gathered together.

9 And there sat in a window a certain young man named Eutychus, being fallen into a deep sleep [*who fell sound asleep*]: and as Paul was long preaching, he sunk down with sleep, and fell down from the third

loft, and was taken up dead. [*As Paul continued talking, Eutychus sunk into even deeper sleep and fell from the third story window and was killed. See heading to Acts, chapter 20 in our Bible.*]

10 And Paul went down, and fell on him [*bent down to him*], and embracing him said, Trouble not yourselves; for his life is in him. [*Paul brought him back to life and told the people not to worry because he was alive again.*]

11 When he [*Paul*] therefore was come up again, and had broken bread, and eaten, and talked a long while, even till break of day, so he departed. [*After bringing Eutychus back to life, Paul went back upstairs, had something to eat and then talked until dawn. Then he left and continued his journey.*]

12 And they brought the young man alive, and were not a little comforted. [*The people were very comforted because Eutychus had been brought back to life.*]

13 ¶ And we [*Luke and some of the others*] went before to ship [*went ahead of Paul to the ship*], and sailed unto Assos [*on the seacoast, about 25 miles south of Troas*], there intending to take in Paul: for so had he appointed, minding himself to go afoot. [*We planned to pick Paul up there in Assos, according to his instructions. He, himself, wanted to travel to Assos on foot.*]

14 And when he met with us at Assos, we took him in [*aboard the ship*], and came [*sailed*] to Mitylene [*about 30 miles south of Assos*].

15 And we sailed thence [*from there*], and came the next day over against Chios [*the next day we sailed along close to the shores of the island of Chios—about 60 miles south of Mitylene*]; and the next day we arrived at Samos [*an island off the western coast of Turkey, about 40 miles southeast of Chios*], and tarried [*stayed*] at Trogyllium; and the next day we came to Miletus [*a distance of about 50 or 60 miles, to the southwestern coast of what is Turkey today*].

16 For Paul had determined to sail by [*past*] Ephesus, because he would not [*didn't want to*] spend the time in Asia [*what we know as western Turkey today*]: for he hasted [*was in a hurry*], if it were possible for him, to be at Jerusalem the day of Pentecost.

Luke seems to be anxious to explain why Paul didn't stop to visit the Saints at Ephesus, which would have been a logical stop en route from Chios to Miletus. Earlier, during Paul's third missionary journey, which is close to over at this point in Acts, he had spent about three years in Ephesus, ministering, teaching, and writing letters to the Saints in Corinth (First and Second Corinthians) and to the Saints in Rome (Romans) and Galatia (Galatians). Luke explains that Paul didn't have time to do justice to a visit in the Ephesus region. Paul was very anxious to get to Jerusalem for the Feast of Pentecost (see Bible Dictionary under "Feasts"), which was held 50 days after the Feast of Passover. Remember, in verse 6, above, that Paul had spent Passover ("the days of unleavened bread") in northeastern Greece. Thus, he only had about 50 days to make the journey from Philippi (in northeastern Greece today) to Jerusalem.

17 ¶ And from Miletus he sent [*a message*] to Ephesus, and called the elders of the church [*asked church leaders in Ephesus to meet him in Miletus*].

18 And when they were come to him [*when they arrived in Miletus*], he said unto them, Ye know, from the first day that I came into Asia, after what manner I have been with you at all seasons [*as you know, I have spent a lot of time with you previously*],

19 Serving the Lord with all humility of mind, and with many tears, and temptations [*trials, troubles*], which befell me by the lying in wait of the Jews [*which came upon me because of the plots of the Jews to ambush me*]:

20 And how I kept back nothing that was profitable unto you [*I spared no effort in bringing you the gospel*], but have shewed [*showed*] you, and have taught you publickly, and from house to house,

21 Testifying both to the Jews, and also to the Greeks [*Gentiles*], repentance toward God, and faith toward our Lord Jesus Christ.

JST Acts 20:21

21 Testifying both to the Jews, and also to the Greeks, repentance toward God, and faith **on the name of** our Lord Jesus Christ.

22 And now, behold, I go bound in the spirit unto Jerusalem [*I am required by the Spirit to go to Jerusalem*], not knowing the things that shall befall [*happen to*] me there:

23 Save [*except*] that the Holy Ghost witnesseth in every city, saying that bonds and afflictions abide me [*the Holy Ghost tells me everywhere I go that prison and persecutions await me*].

24 But none of these things move me [*none of these things make me want to change my mind about going to Jerusalem*], neither count I my life dear unto myself, so that I might finish my course with joy, and the ministry, which I have received of the Lord Jesus, to testify the gospel of the grace of God. [*If I lose my life as a result of finishing the work to which the Lord called me, so be it.*]

25 And now, behold, I know that ye all, among whom I have gone preaching the kingdom of God, shall see my face no more [*I know that none of you will see me again*].

26 Wherefore [*therefore*] I take you to record this day [*you are my witnesses*], that I am pure from the blood of all men [*since I have done

my best, I am free from accountability for the sins of all people].

27 For I have not shunned [*hesitated*] to declare unto you all the counsel of God [*I have not held back anything as I taught you the gospel*].

28 ¶ Take heed [*pay close attention to your responsibilities*] therefore unto yourselves, and to all the flock [*members*], over the which the Holy Ghost [*the Savior directs the work through the Holy Ghost*] hath made you overseers [*leaders*], to feed [*take care of*] the church of God, which he hath purchased with his own blood [*Christ "purchased" us from the law of justice, in other words, "redeemed" us from our sins, with His Atonement*].

Verses 29–30, next, are much-used in our missionary work. Paul is clearly prophesying that the Great Apostasy will take place. In other words, the true Church, established by the Savior during His mortal ministry, will die out, setting the stage for the necessary restoration through the Prophet Joseph Smith.

29 For I know this, that after my departing [*after I leave*] shall grievous [*vicious*] wolves [*people who will tear the Church apart*] enter in among you, not sparing the flock.

30 Also of [*from*] your own selves shall men arise [*some among you will step forward*], speaking perverse things [*teaching false doctrines; twisting the truths of the gospel*], to draw away disciples [*followers*] after them.

31 Therefore watch, and remember, that by the space of three years I ceased not to warn every one night and day with tears. [*Stick firmly to what I have unceasingly taught you with deep emotion and conviction over these past three years.*]

32 And now, brethren, I commend you to God [*I turn you over to God*], and to the word of his grace [*and to the gospel and Atonement of Christ*], which is able to build you up, and to give you an inheritance among all them which are sanctified [*which can give you exaltation among those who are made holy and clean and fit to be in the presence of God*].

33 I have coveted no man's silver, or gold, or apparel [*I have not desired other peoples' wealth or support for me*].

34 Yea, ye yourselves know, that these hands have ministered unto my necessities, and to them that were with me. [*You know that I have worked with my own hands to support myself and others traveling with me.*]

35 I have shewed you all things [*I have been an example to you*], how that so labouring [*working*] ye ought to support the weak, and to remember the words of the Lord Jesus, how he said, It is more blessed to give than to receive.

36 ¶ And when he had thus spoken, he kneeled down, and prayed with them all.

37 And they all wept sore [*much*], and fell on Paul's neck [*hugged him*], and kissed him,

38 Sorrowing most of all for the words which he spake, that they should see his face no more [*saddened most by his telling them that they would not see him again*]. And they accompanied him unto the ship.

ACTS 21

We know from the use of "we" in verse 1, that Luke is again traveling with Paul. These "we passages" continue through Acts 28:16, indicating that Luke is with him all this time.

As you will see, Paul continues taking a direct course for Jerusalem. When he arrives, he will be persecuted and arrested. You will probably smile a bit in admiration of Paul at the end of this chapter when, after a mob has beaten him and he is rescued in the nick of time by Roman soldiers, he stands in chains on the stairs and requests permission to preach to the mob, while under the protection of the soldiers. His sermon will be recorded in chapter 22.

1 AND it came to pass, that after we were gotten from them, and had launched [*after Paul, Luke, and the other traveling companions of Paul had sailed from Miletus (see Acts 20:15)*], we came with a straight course unto Coos [*we sailed straight to the island of Coos (about 50 miles south of Miletus)*], and the day following unto Rhodes [*an island about 60 miles east of Coos*], and from thence unto Patara [*about 70 miles east of Rhodes (this would be the coast of southern Turkey today)*]:

2 And finding a ship sailing over unto Phenicia [*east to Phoenicia, which would be on the eastern coast of the Mediterranean Sea today*], we went aboard, and set forth.

3 Now when we had discovered [*sighted*] Cyprus, we left it on the left hand [*we sailed south of the Island of Cyprus*], and sailed into Syria, and landed at Tyre [*about 100 miles north of Jerusalem*]: for there the ship was to unlade [*unload*] her burden.

4 And finding disciples [*Church members*], we tarried [*stayed*] there seven days: who said to Paul through the Spirit, that he should not go up to Jerusalem [*members at Tyre told Paul that they felt inspired to tell him not to go to Jerusalem*].

5 And when we had accomplished those days [*after the seven days*], we departed and went our way; and they all brought us on our way [*they all accompanied us*], with wives and children, till we were out of the city: and we kneeled down on the shore, and prayed.

6 And when we had taken our leave one of another [*said goodbye to each other*], we took ship [*boarded a ship*]; and they returned home again.

7 And when we had finished our course from Tyre, we came to Ptolemais [*about 25 miles south of Tyre*], and saluted [*greeted*] the brethren, and abode [*stayed*] with them one day.

8 And the next day we that were of Paul's company [*we who were traveling with Paul*] departed, and came unto Cæsarea [*about 30 miles south of Ptolemais and about 72 miles northwest of Jerusalem*]: and we entered into the house of Philip the evangelist, which was one of the seven [*one of the seven in Acts 6:5 who were chosen to assist the Apostles in ministering to the members as the Church grew*]; and abode [*stayed*] with him.

The word "evangelist" used in verse 8, would likely mean "patriarch." See Ephesians, 4:11, footnote d. Also see McConkie, *Doctrinal New Testament Commentary*, Vol. 2, p. 181. Philip, along with Stephen who was killed by stoning (Acts 7:57–60), was chosen to assist the apostles (Acts 6:1–7). It would appear that by the time Paul and his traveling companions arrive at Caesarea, Philip has been given the added responsibility of being ordained a patriarch.

9 And the same man [*Philip*] had four daughters, virgins [*who were not married*], which did prophesy [*who had the gift of prophesying, as mentioned in D&C 46:22 and elsewhere in the scriptures*].

10 And as we [*Luke, who wrote Acts, and Paul's other missionary companions*] tarried [*stayed*] there many days, there came down from Judæa [*from the Jerusalem area*] a certain prophet, named Agabus.

We don't know who Agabus was except that he prophesied that there would be a severe famine (see Acts 11:28) and that he prophesied in verse 11, next, that Paul would be imprisoned in Jerusalem. See Bible Dictionary under "Agabus."

11 And when he was come unto us [*when Agabus came to where we were staying*], he took Paul's girdle [*belt*], and bound [*tied up*] his own hands and feet, and said, Thus saith the Holy Ghost, So shall the Jews at Jerusalem bind [*tie up; put in chains; arrest*] the man that owneth this girdle, and shall deliver him into the hands of the Gentiles. [*The Jews at Jerusalem will arrest Paul and turn him over to the Gentiles.*]

12 And when we heard these things, both we, and they of that place [*the local members in Caesarea*], besought him [*begged him*] not to go up to Jerusalem.

13 Then Paul answered, What mean ye to weep and to break mine heart [*do you think you can stop me by breaking my heart*]? for I am ready not to be bound only, but also to die at Jerusalem for the name of the Lord Jesus.

14 And when he would not be persuaded [*when we saw that we could not persuade him to stay away from Jerusalem*], we ceased [*stopped trying*], saying, The will of the Lord be done.

15 And after those days we took up our carriages [*we packed our bags*], and went up to Jerusalem.

16 There went with us also certain of the disciples of [*members of the Church from*] Cæsarea, and brought with them one Mnason of Cyprus [*originally from Cyprus*], an old disciple [*member*], with whom we should lodge.

17 And when we were come to [*when we arrived at*] Jerusalem, the brethren [*leaders of the Church there*] received us gladly.

Next, Paul reports his missionary journey to the leaders of the Church in Jerusalem.

18 And the day following Paul went in with us unto James [*one of the Apostles*]; and all the elders were present.

19 And when he [*Paul*] had saluted [*greeted*] them [*the Brethren*], he declared [*reported*] particularly what things God had wrought [*done*] among the Gentiles by his ministry [*as a result of his missionary efforts*].

20 And when they heard it, they glorified [*praised*] the Lord, and said unto him [*Paul*], Thou seest, brother, how many thousands of Jews there are which believe [*you have obviously noticed that thousands of Jews have joined the Church*]; and they are all zealous of the law [*and they still keep the law of Moses*]:

21 And they are informed of thee [*they know about you*], that thou teachest all the Jews which are among the Gentiles to forsake Moses, saying that they ought not to circumcise their children, neither to walk after the customs. [*They know that you teach Jewish converts in Gentile nations that they don't have to keep the law of Moses, including circumcision, and that you teach them that they don't have to live according to our Jewish customs.*]

22 What is it therefore [*what shall we do now*]? the multitude must needs come together: for they will hear that thou art come [*no doubt many of our Jewish members here will assemble together to discuss this when they find out that you are in town*].

23 Do therefore this that we say to thee [*therefore, do what we say in order to try to resolve this problem*]: We have four men which have a vow [*covenant*] on them [*we have four men who have made a vow according to Jewish custom in keeping with the law of Moses*];

24 Them take [*take them to the temple*], and purify thyself with them [*participate in the law of Moses purification ritual along with them*], and be at charges with them [*pay their expenses*], that they may shave their heads [*according to Moses' instructions*

in Leviticus 14:8–9]: and all may know that those things, whereof they were informed concerning thee, are nothing [*so that those local Jewish members who have heard troubling things about you will stop worrying*]; but that thou thyself also walkest orderly, and keepest the law [*rather, they will understand that you are keeping the law of Moses yourself*].

25 As touching the Gentiles [*non-Jews*] which believe [*as far as the Gentile converts are concerned*], we have written and concluded that they observe no such thing [*we have written to them and instructed them that they do not need to keep these laws of Moses or customs of the Jews*], save only that they keep themselves from [*except that they must avoid*] things offered to idols [*food left over from idol worship*], and from blood [*eating blood*], and from strangled [*eating birds or animals which were strangled so that their blood is still in the meat*], and from fornication [*from sexual immorality*].

The situation described in verses 24 and 25 above can seem rather strange at first. Obviously, Paul has stirred up some bad feelings among the Jewish converts in the Jerusalem area, who still have not caught the vision that the law of Moses has been fulfilled by the Savior, and it is no longer necessary to keep the law of circumcision, nor does one have to keep the customs and traditions of the Jews in order to be a good member of the Church. The Church leaders in Jerusalem are anxious to keep the peace and to not have things stirred up unnecessarily. Realizing that change comes slowly (see Jacob 5:65–66) and the Jewish members in Jerusalem are no exception, they ask Paul to soothe feelings of local members by participating in a law of Moses cleansing ritual, which he does as seen in verse 26, next. Knowing Paul's feisty personality as we do, we see it as a credit to him that he did follow the counsel of the leaders of the Church.

26 Then Paul took the men, and the next day purifying himself with them entered into the temple, to signify the accomplishment of the days of purification, until that an offering should be offered for every one of them. [*Paul followed counsel and participated in the law of Moses cleansing ritual.*]

27 And when the seven days were almost ended, the Jews which were of Asia [*anti-Christian Jews from what is Turkey today, who fought against Paul in Asia*], when they saw him in the temple, stirred up all the people, and laid hands on him [*grabbed him*],

28 Crying out [*shouting*], Men of Israel, help: This [*Paul*] is the man, that teacheth all men every where against the people, and the law, and this place [*this is the man who is teaching everybody, everywhere, not to believe in our Jewish customs nor in the law of Moses, nor in what we have been doing in this temple under Moses' law*]: and further

brought Greeks [*Gentiles*] also into the temple, and hath polluted this holy place [*furthermore, Paul has taken Gentiles into our temple and has thus polluted it*].

29 (For they had seen before with him in the city Trophimus an Ephesian, whom they supposed that Paul had brought into the temple.)

30 And all the city was moved [*a mob formed*], and the people [*the mob*] ran together: and they took Paul, and drew [*dragged*] him out of the temple: and forthwith the doors were shut [*and immediately shut the gates of the temple grounds*].

31 And as they went about to kill him [*as they dragged him off to kill him*], tidings [*news of the riot*] came unto the chief captain of the band [*the leader of the Roman soldiers*], that all Jerusalem was in an uproar.

32 Who [*the Roman military leader*] immediately took soldiers and centurions [*Roman leaders of 100 Roman soldiers each*], and ran down unto them [*the Jews who were beating Paul to kill him*]: and when they saw the chief captain and the soldiers, they left beating of Paul [*they quit beating Paul*].

33 Then the chief captain came near, and took him [*Paul*], and commanded him to be bound with two chains; and demanded who he was, and what he had done.

34 And some cried [*shouted*] one thing, some another, among the multitude [*mob; crowd*]: and when he could not know the certainty for the tumult [*when the commander of the Roman soldiers could not get a clear answer from the mob*], he commanded him [*Paul*] to be carried into the castle [*the castle of Antonia in Jerusalem, where the Roman soldiers had their barracks*].

35 And when he came upon the stairs [*when he got to the stairs of the castle*], so it was, that he was borne of the soldiers for the violence of the people [*he had to be carried by the soldiers and protected from the violence of the mob*].

36 For [*because*] the multitude [*mob*] of the people followed after, crying [*shouting*], Away with him.

37 And as Paul was to be led into the castle [*at the top of the stairs*], he said unto the chief captain [*the Roman commander*], May I speak unto thee? Who said, Canst thou speak Greek? [*The Roman commander was surprised that Paul could speak Greek.*]

Next we see that this Roman commander mistakenly thought Paul was someone else.

38 Art not thou that Egyptian, which before these days madest an uproar, and leddest out into the wilderness four thousand men that were murderers? [*I thought you were the Egyptian who recently caused trouble by leading 4,000 assassins and cutthroats out into the wilderness.*]

39 But Paul said, I am a man

which am a Jew of [*from*] Tarsus, a city in Cilicia [*southeastern Turkey today*], a citizen of no mean city [*by no means a small city*]: and, I beseech [*ask*] thee, suffer [*allow*] me to speak unto the people [*to the mob*].

40 And when he [*the Roman commander*] had given him licence [*permission*], Paul stood on the stairs, and beckoned with the hand [*motioned for silence*] unto the people. And when there was made a great silence, he spake [*spoke*] unto them in the Hebrew tongue, saying,

ACTS 22

As Paul defends himself to the mob, he will recount the story of his conversion, which includes seeing the resurrected Christ in vision.

You will gain additional insight into Paul's personality after his sermon, when the Roman officer commands that he be whipped. At exactly the right moment for dramatic effect, Paul will casually mention that he is a Roman citizen (see verse 25) which makes what the Roman soldiers were going to do to him illegal.

1 MEN, brethren, and fathers [*honored men*], hear ye my defence which I make now unto you [*listen carefully while I defend my actions to you*].

Among other talents, Paul also speaks several languages. The fact that he speaks Hebrew (the language of the Old Testament and the main native language spoken by most of the citizens of Jerusalem) surprises and impresses the mob, and they settle down to listen to him, as mentioned in verse 2, next.

2 (And when they heard that he spake in the Hebrew tongue to them, they kept the more silence: and he saith,)

3 I am verily a man which am a Jew [*I am actually a Jew*], born in Tarsus [*a coastal town in what is southeast Turkey today*], a city in Cilicia, yet brought up in this city at the feet of Gamaliel [*I was taught here in Jerusalem by Gamaliel (a prominent Pharisee and respected Jewish teacher of the day); see Bible Dictionary under "Gamaliel"*], and taught according to the perfect manner of the law of the fathers [*I was taught and trained in the law of Moses, and am a Pharisee; see Acts 23:6*], and was zealous [*faithful*] toward God, as ye all are this day.

The Pharisees were powerful religious leaders among the Jews, and played a strong role in getting Jesus crucified. See Bible Dictionary under "Pharisee."

4 And I persecuted this way [*this way of living, in other words, the Christians*] unto the death, binding [*arresting them*] and delivering into prisons both men and women.

5 As also the high priest [*the chief religious leader of the Jews*] doth

bear me witness, and all the estate of the elders [*your religious leaders here know me and will tell you I am telling you the truth*]: from whom also I received letters unto the brethren [*I obtained letters from your leaders here to the Jewish religious leaders in Damascus, giving me permission to arrest Christians there*], and went to Damascus [*a major city in southern Syria today*], to bring them [*the Christians*] which were there bound [*who had been arrested in Damascus*] unto Jerusalem, for to be punished.

6 And it came to pass, that, as I made my journey, and was come nigh [*had come near*] unto Damascus about noon, suddenly there shone [*shined*] from heaven a great light round about me.

7 And I fell unto the ground, and heard a voice saying unto me, Saul, Saul, why persecutest thou me?

8 And I answered, Who art thou, Lord? And he said unto me, I am Jesus of Nazareth, whom thou persecutest.

9 And they that were with me [*the people traveling with me*] saw indeed the light, and were afraid; but they heard not the voice of him that spake to me.

> This is one of those places in the Bible where one verse conflicts with a verse in another place. Verse 9, above, says that Paul's traveling companions saw the light but did not hear the voice of Jesus. However, in the Bible, in Acts 9:7, it says that Paul's companions heard the voice. The Joseph Smith Translation of the Bible (the JST) straightens this out by correcting Acts 9:7 to read "And they who were journeying with him saw indeed the light, and were afraid; but they heard not the voice of him who spake to him." This is another testimony of the calling of the Prophet Joseph Smith, and a reminder that the Bible is not always translated correctly as indicated in our eighth article of faith.

10 And I said, What shall I do, Lord? And the Lord said unto me, Arise, and go into Damascus; and there it shall be told thee of all things which are appointed for thee to do.

11 And when I could not see for the glory of that light [*I had become blind because of the brightness of the light*], being led by the hand of them that were with me, I came into Damascus.

12 And one Ananias [*a faithful convert and priesthood holder in the Church in Damascus*], a devout man according to the law, having a good report [*a good reputation*] of all the Jews which dwelt there,

13 Came unto me, and stood, and said unto me, Brother Saul, receive thy sight. And the same hour I looked up upon him [*immediately my blindness was healed and I could see Ananias*].

14 And he said, The God of our fathers [*our ancestors, including*

Abraham, Isaac, and Jacob] hath chosen thee, that thou shouldest know his will, and see that Just One [*Christ*], and shouldest hear the voice of his mouth.

15 For thou shalt be his witness unto all men of what thou hast seen and heard.

16 And now why tarriest thou [*what are you waiting for*]? arise, and be baptized, and wash away thy sins, calling on the name of the Lord.

17 And it came to pass, that, when I was come again to Jerusalem, even while I prayed in the temple, I was in a trance [*I had a vision*];

18 And saw him [*Jesus*] saying unto me, Make haste [*hurry*], and get thee quickly out of Jerusalem: for they will not receive [*accept*] thy testimony concerning me.

19 And I said, Lord, they know that I imprisoned and beat in every synagogue them that believed on thee [*these people in Jerusalem know that I rounded up Christians from every synagogue and had them beaten and put in prison*]:

20 And when the blood of thy martyr Stephen was shed [*when Stephen was killed; Acts 7:55–60*], I also was standing by, and consenting unto his death [*I agreed that he should be killed; Acts 8:1*], and kept the raiment of them that slew him [*I kept watch over the robes, clothing that the men who killed Stephen had taken off while they stoned him to death*].

21 And he [*Jesus*] said unto me, Depart: for I will send thee far hence unto the Gentiles [*I will send you far away from here to the Gentiles*].

22 And they [*the Jerusalem mob to whom Paul was speaking while standing at the top of the stairs leading into the Roman barracks; see Acts 21:40*] gave him audience unto this word [*listened to him while he spoke*], and then lifted up their voices [*shouted out*], and said, Away with such a fellow from the earth: for it is not fit that he should live [*in other words, they ignored what he had just told them and shouted "Kill him!"*].

23 And as they cried out [*screamed and yelled*], and cast off their clothes, and threw dust into the air [*a sign of deep emotion in Jewish culture of the day*],

24 The chief captain [*the Roman commander*] commanded him to be brought into the castle, and bade [*requested*] that he should be examined by scourging; that he might know wherefore they cried so against him. [*The commander of the Roman soldiers commanded that Paul be whipped to get the truth out of him as to why the Jewish mob was so angry with him.*]

As mentioned previously, Paul is indeed an interesting character and a master of strategy! In the middle of all this uproar and life-threatening situation, he has not yet mentioned to the Roman soldiers that he himself is a Roman citizen. As we see in the next verses, he waits until the timing is perfect to mention this fact.

25 And as they bound [*tied*] him with thongs, Paul said unto the centurion [*the Roman soldier*] that stood by, Is it lawful [*legal*] for you to scourge [*whip*] a man that is a Roman, and uncondemned [*a man who is a Roman citizen and who has not had a proper trial*]?

26 When the centurion heard that, he went and told the chief captain [*the Roman commanding officer*], saying, Take heed what thou doest [*be careful what you do*]: for this man is a Roman [*a Roman citizen*].

27 Then the chief captain came, and said unto him [*Paul*], Tell me, art thou a Roman? He said, Yea [*Yes, I am*].

28 And the chief captain answered, With a great sum obtained I this freedom [*I had to buy my Roman citizenship with a large sum of money (implying "So, how did somebody like you obtain Roman citizenship?")*]. And Paul said, But I was free born [*I was born a Roman citizen*].

29 Then straightway [*immediately*] they departed from him which should have examined him [*the Roman soldiers who planned to ask him questions while whipping him left in a big hurry*]: and the chief captain also was afraid, after he knew that he was a Roman, and because he had bound him [*the Roman commander was also very worried because he had violated Paul's legal rights as a Roman citizen*].

30 On the morrow [*in the morning*], because he [*the Roman commander*] would have known the certainty wherefore he was accused of the Jews [*wanted to know exactly what the Jews had against Paul*], he loosed [*untied*] him [*Paul*] from his bands, and commanded the chief priests and all their council to appear [*he commanded the Jewish religious leaders to appear in court*], and brought Paul down, and set him before them.

Verses 29–30, above, are a bit confusing. The Roman commander was very concerned about having had Paul tied up illegally [*probably put in chains*], since Paul was a Roman citizen. Yet, he waited to set him free until the next morning (verse 30). The JST shows us what really happened as follows:

JST Acts 22:29–30

29 Then straightway they departed from him which should have examined him, and the chief captain also was afraid after he knew that he was a Roman, **because** he had bound him, **and he loosed him** [*set him free*] **from his bands**.

30 On the morrow, because he would have known the certainty wherefore he was accused of the Jews, **he commanded** the chief priests and all their council to appear, and brought Paul down, and set him before them.

Thus, the JST informs us that indeed the commander untied him immediately, then arranged for Paul to appear in court the next day, in front of the Jewish high priest and other leaders, assuring Paul of a fair trial according to Roman law.

ACTS 23

The highest governing council, controlled by the Jews, was the Sanhedrin. The high priest presided over it. (See Bible Dictionary under "Sanhedrin.") The Roman commander instructed that the high priest and the Sanhedrin face Paul in a legal court setting. We will now watch as Paul defends himself and his actions in front of this council.

1 AND Paul, earnestly beholding [*looking directly at*] the council, said, Men and brethren, I have lived in all good conscience before God until this day [*I have done my best to live strictly according to God's commandments right up to this day*].

2 And the high priest Ananias commanded them that stood by him [*Paul*] to smite [*hit*] him on the mouth.

Ananias, the high priest, was an evil man who was later murdered during an uprising at Jerusalem. See Bible Dictionary under Ananias.

3 Then said Paul unto him, God shall smite thee, thou whited [*white-washed*] wall [*in other words, you hypocrite; see Matthew 23:27*]: for sittest thou to judge me after the law, and commandest me to be smitten contrary to the law [*how can you claim to judge me according to the law and still command me to be hit which is against the law*]?

4 And they that stood by said, Revilest thou God's high priest [*how dare you speak to God's high priest like that*]?

5 Then said Paul, I wist not, brethren, that he was the high priest: for it is written, Thou shalt not speak evil of the ruler of thy people [*Exodus 22:28*].

JST Acts 23:5

5 Then said Paul, I **did not know**, brethren, that he was the high priest; for it is written, Thou shalt not speak evil of the ruler of thy people.

6 But when Paul perceived [*noticed*] that the one part [*part of the group of Jewish leaders there in court*] were Sadducees, and the other Pharisees, he cried out in the council, Men and brethren, I am a Pharisee, the son of a Pharisee: of the hope and resurrection of the dead I am called in question [*the real reason I have been arrested and brought here is because I believe in resurrection*].

Again, in these verses we see Paul's skill in using strategy. He is now going to pit the Pharisees against the Saddducees and get them arguing among themselves. The Pharisees believed in resurrection, but the Sadducees did not, and the topic of resurrection was a long-standing point of heated contention between them.

7 And when he had so said, there arose a dissension [*argument*] between the Pharisees and the Sadducees: and the multitude [*crowd in the courtroom*] was divided [*took sides on the issue*].

8 For the Sadducees say [*teach*] that there is no resurrection, neither angel [*messengers from God*], nor spirit [*in other words, there is no such thing as a spirit, which leaves the body when it dies*]: but the Pharisees confess both [*believe in resurrection and in spirits*].

9 And there arose a great cry: and the scribes [*who interpret the scriptures for the people*] that were of the Pharisees' part [*who belonged to the Pharisees*] arose, and strove [*argued*], saying, We find no evil in this man [*we do not find anything wrong with what Paul has taught*]: but if a spirit or an angel hath spoken to him, let us not fight against God.

10 And when there arose a great dissension [*a huge uproar*], the chief captain [*the commander of the Roman soldiers*], fearing lest Paul should have been pulled in pieces of them [*afraid that they would tear Paul apart physically*], commanded the soldiers to go down, and to take him by force from among them, and to bring him into the castle [*where the Roman soldiers had their barracks*].

Next, the Savior appeared to Paul.

11 And the night following the Lord stood by him [*the Savior appeared to him*], and said, Be of good cheer [*cheer up*], Paul: for as thou hast testified of me in Jerusalem, so must thou bear witness also at Rome [*I need you to testify of Me in Rome, like you have done here in Jerusalem*].

12 And when it was day [*in the morning*], certain of the Jews banded together, and bound themselves under a curse [*made a vow, made an oath*], saying that they would neither eat nor drink till they had killed Paul.

In the Jewish culture of the day, to make a vow was the most serious commitment possible. Here, more than forty men promise each other that they will not eat or drink until they have killed Paul. It is a foolish vow and a strong reminder that wickedness does not promote rational thought. If they try to keep it and are unsuccessful, they will die of thirst and hunger.

13 And they were more than forty which had made this conspiracy [*plot*].

14 And they came to the chief priests and elders [*the main religious leaders of the Jews*], and said, We have bound ourselves under a great curse [*we have made a solemn vow*], that we will eat nothing until we have slain [*killed*] Paul.

15 Now therefore ye with the council [*you members of the council*] signify to [*make a request to*] the chief captain [*the chief Roman commander*] that he bring him [*Paul*] down unto you to morrow, as though ye would enquire something more perfectly concerning him [*ask the Roman commander to bring Paul to you again tomorrow and pretend that you want to get additional clarification from him on some matters*]: and we, or ever [*before*] he come near, are ready to kill him [*we will kill him before he arrives at the courtroom*].

JST Acts 23:15

15 Now therefore ye with the council signify to the chief captain that he bring him down unto you **tomorrow**, as though **you** would inquire something more perfectly concerning him; **and we, before he come near**, are ready to kill him.

16 And when Paul's sister's son heard of their lying in wait [*their plot to ambush him*], he went and entered into the castle [*the Antonia Fortress or castle, where the Roman soldiers in Jerusalem were headquarted*], and told Paul.

17 Then Paul called one of the centurions [*a Roman soldier in charge of 100 soldiers*] unto him, and said, Bring this young man unto the chief captain [*take my nephew to the chief Roman captain*]: for he hath a certain thing to tell him.

18 So he took him, and brought him to the chief captain, and said, Paul the prisoner called me unto him, and prayed [*asked*] me to bring this young man unto thee, who hath something to say unto thee.

19 Then the chief captain took him by the hand, and went with him aside privately, and asked him, What is that thou hast to tell me?

20 And he said, The Jews have agreed [*plotted*] to desire thee [*to send a request to you*] that thou wouldest bring down Paul to morrow into the council, as though they would enquire somewhat of him more perfectly [*pretending that they want to ask him additional questions*].

21 But do not thou yield unto them [*don't let them do it*]: for there lie in wait for him of them more than forty men [*over forty men will be waiting in ambush for Paul*], which have [*who have*] bound themselves with an oath [*a vow*], that they will neither eat nor drink till they have killed him: and now are they ready, looking for a promise from thee.

22 So the chief captain then let the young man depart, and charged [*commanded*] him, See thou tell no man that thou hast shewed these things to me [*don't tell anyone that you have informed me about this*].

23 And he called unto him two centurions [*Roman soldiers in charge of one hundred soldiers each*], saying, Make ready two hundred soldiers to go to Cæsarea [*about 72 miles northwest of Jerusalem*], and horsemen threescore and ten [*70 horsemen*], and spearmen two

hundred [*200 foot soldiers carrying spears*], at the third hour of the night [*at 9 PM tonight*];

24 And provide them beasts, that they may set Paul on [*make sure they have mounts for Paul to ride*], and bring him safe unto Felix the governor [*the chief Roman official in Caesarea*].

25 And he [*the Roman commander (Claudius Lysias) in Jerusalem*] wrote a letter after this manner [*which read as follows*]:

26 Claudius Lysias unto the most excellent governor Felix sendeth greeting [*greetings from Claudius Lysias to his excellency, Governor Felix*].

27 This man [*Paul*] was taken of [*grabbed by*] the Jews, and should have [*would have*] been killed of [*by*] them: then came I with an army, and rescued him, having understood that he was a Roman.

JST Acts 23:27

27 This man was taken of the Jews, and **would** have been killed of them; then came I with an army, and rescued him, having understood that he was a Roman.

28 And when I would have known the cause wherefore they accused him [*because I wanted to know what they had against him*], I brought him forth into their council [*I took him to appear before the Sanhedrin*]:

29 Whom I perceived to be accused of questions of their law, but to have nothing laid to his charge worthy of death or of bonds. [*As I watched them question him, it became clear that it had to do with their religious laws, but there was nothing he had done that was worthy of death or imprisonment.*]

30 And when it was told me how that the Jews laid wait for [*were waiting to ambush*] the man, I sent straightway [*immediately*] to thee, and gave commandment to his accusers also [*and commanded the Jews who brought charges against him*] to say before thee what they had against him [*to appear in your court to bring charges against him*]. Farewell.

31 Then the soldiers, as it was commanded them, took Paul, and brought him by night to Antipatris [*a city near Caesarea, named after Herod the Great's father, Antipater*].

32 On the morrow [*in the morning*] they left the horsemen to go with him [*Paul*], and returned to the castle [*returned to Jerusalem*]:

33 Who [*the Roman soldiers who accompanied Paul on to Caesarea*], when they came to Cæsarea, and delivered the epistle [*the letter from Claudius Lysias; see verse 26, above*] to the governor [*Felix*], presented Paul also before him.

34 And when the governor had read the letter, he asked of what province he was [*he asked Paul which province he was from originally*]. And when he understood that he was of Cilicia [*would be in southeastern Turkey today*];

35 I will hear thee, said he, when thine accusers are also come [*I will convene the court and hear your case when the Jews who accuse you of criminal behavior arrive from Jerusalem*]. And he commanded him to be kept in Herod's judgment hall. [*He commanded that Paul be kept at Governor Felix's headquarters; see Acts 23:35, footnote a.*]

ACTS 24

In this chapter, Paul's trial continues and he skillfully teaches the gospel as he provides his own defense.

1 AND after five days Ananias the high priest descended [*arrived from Jerusalem*] with the elders, and with a certain orator [*lawyer*] named Tertullus, who informed the governor against Paul [*who presented the case against Paul to Governor Felix*].

Watch now, as Tertullus attempts to flatter Felix with compliments and pretended loyalty of the Jewish religious leaders. In actuality, the Jews despised their Roman rulers.

2 And when he was called forth [*invited to speak*], Tertullus began to accuse him [*Paul*], saying, Seeing that by thee [*through you, Felix*] we enjoy great quietness [*we enjoy wonderful peace*], and that very worthy deeds are done unto this nation by thy providence [*you have done very noble things for our nation through your kindness and generosity*],

3 We accept it always, and in all places, most noble Felix, with all thankfulness [*we accept your kindness and generosity always and everywhere with deep gratitude*].

4 Notwithstanding [*however*], that I be not further tedious unto thee [*let me get right to the point, so that I don't waste your valuable time*], I pray thee that thou wouldest hear us of thy clemency a few words [*I humbly ask that you be so kind as to hear a few words from us*].

5 For we have found this man [*Paul*] a pestilent fellow [*to be a troublemaker*], and a mover of sedition [*who undermines leadership*] among all the Jews throughout the world, and a ringleader of the sect of the Nazarenes [*the followers of Jesus; see* Strong's *#3478*]:

6 Who also hath gone about to profane [*defile, to make unclean*] the temple: whom we took, and would have judged according to our law [*we arrested Paul and wanted to handle this matter ourselves. Remember that the way these Jews wanted to deal with Paul was to kill him on the spot after they dragged him out of the temple. See Acts 21:30–31.*]

7 But the chief captain Lysias came upon us, and with great violence took him away out of our hands [*but Lysias, commander of the Roman soldiers in Jerusalem, using unnecessary force, took Paul from us*],

The implication in Tertullus' words to Felix is that if

the Roman commander hadn't intervened in the Jews' private business, using inappropriate violence, then Felix wouldn't even have to be bothered with this whole thing.

8 Commanding his accusers to come unto thee [*Lysias commanded us to come to you to present our case against Paul*]: by examining of whom thyself mayest take knowledge of all these things, whereof we accuse him [*if you will now cross-examine Paul, you will see why we are so upset with him*].

9 And the Jews also assented, saying that these things were so [*the Jewish religious leaders confirmed that what Tertullus had told Felix was true*].

Watch now as Paul begins his own defense.

10 Then Paul, after that the governor had beckoned unto him [*had motioned for him*] to speak, answered [*responded*], Forasmuch as I know [*since I am aware*] that thou hast been of many years [*for many years*] a judge unto this nation, I do the more cheerfully answer for myself [*I am happy to defend myself because I know that you have had many years of experience judging cases brought before you by the Jews*]:

Paul will now tell Felix that he is not the cause of trouble and rioting, rather the religious leaders of the Jews themselves, who are in the courtroom now, are the ones who destroyed the peace and caused riots.

11 Because that thou mayest understand, that there are yet but twelve days since I went up to Jerusalem for to worship [*I want you to understand that I arrived in Jerusalem just twelve days ago*].

12 And they neither found me in the temple disputing with any man [*I was reverent in the temple, not arguing with anyone*], neither raising up the people [*I didn't stir the people up*], neither in the synagogues, nor in the city:

13 Neither can they prove the things whereof they now accuse me [*they can't prove any of the things they are accusing me of*].

14 But this I confess unto thee [*but I will admit this to you*], that after the way which they call heresy [*in opposition to what they believe about me*], so worship I the God of my fathers, believing all things which are written in the law and in the prophets [*I do indeed worship in the way they are accusing me of, namely, I worship the God of Abraham, Isaac and Jacob and believe very exactly all the things written by Moses and the other prophets in our scriptures*]:

15 And have hope toward God, which they themselves also allow [*I have the same hope and faith that my accusers claim to have in God*], that there shall be a resurrection of the dead, both of the just and unjust [*namely, that everyone, whether righteous or wicked, will be resurrected*].

You may wish to mark the important doctrine about the resurrection taught in verse 15, above, in your own scriptures. Many Christians believe that only the righteous will be resurrected. Here, Paul teaches clearly that both the righteous and the wicked will be resurrected. (He teaches the same doctrine in 1 Corinthians 15:22.)

16 And herein do I exercise myself [*I follow these religious beliefs very carefully*], to have always [*in order to always have*] a conscience void of offence toward God, and toward men.

17 Now after many years I came to bring alms to my nation, and offerings [*now, after many years I came to Jerusalem to bring money we collected for the poor*].

18 Whereupon certain Jews from Asia found me purified in the temple, neither with multitude, nor with tumult. [*While I was purifying myself, according to the law of Moses, in the temple, some Jews from Asia (Turkey today; see Acts 14, and who tried to stone Paul) found me, and I did not have a crowd around me nor was I causing a disturbance.*]

19 Who ought to have been here before thee, and object, if they had ought against me [*they are the ones who ought to be here bearing witness against me, if they have anything to say in your court.*].

20 Or else let these same here say, if they have found any evil doing in me, while I stood before the council [*since the Jews from Asia, who dragged me from the temple in Jerusalem are not here today, perhaps you could have these Jews who are here testify before you as to what evil they found in me when I stood before their council; see Acts 22:30 through Acts 23:1–9*],

21 Except it be for this one voice, that I cried standing among them [*there was one thing I said that apparently has bothered them*], Touching the resurrection of the dead [*I told them that I believe in the resurrection*] I am called in question by you this day. [*The only reason I am standing before you this day is because I told them I believe in the resurrection of the dead.*]

22 And when Felix heard these things, having more perfect knowledge of that way [*having a good understanding now of the situation*], he deferred them [*he postponed the rest of the trial*], and said, When Lysias the chief captain [*the Roman commander in Jerusalem*] shall come down [*arrives from Jerusalem*], I will know the uttermost of your matter [*I will get the details I need to make a decision about your case*].

23 And he commanded a centurion to keep Paul [*to keep Paul under guard*], and to let him have liberty, and that he should forbid none of his acquaintance to minister or come unto him [*allow Paul's friends to come and go, visiting Paul whenever they wanted to*].

24 And after certain days [*a few days later*], when Felix came with his wife Drusilla, which [*who*] was a Jewess [*she was a Jew*], he sent for Paul, and heard him concerning the faith in Christ [*Felix asked Paul to teach them about Christ*].

25 And as he reasoned of [*as Paul taught them about*] righteousness, temperance [*self-control*], and judgment to come [*being judged by God for our actions here on earth*], Felix trembled, and answered [*responded*], Go thy way for this time [*leave for the time being because I can't handle any more*]; when I have a convenient season, I will call for thee [*when it is convenient for me, I will have you come and tell us more*].

26 He hoped also that money should have been given him of Paul, that he might loose him [*Felix was hoping that Paul would offer to bribe him to let him go free*]: wherefore he sent for him the oftener, and communed with him [*and so Felix sent for Paul quite often and talked with him*].

This went on for two years, after which Felix was replaced by Porcuis Festus. Festus was sent by Nero to take Felix's place, probably in the autumn of AD 60.

27 But after two years Porcius Festus came into Felix' room [*to take Felix's place*]: and Felix, willing to shew the Jews a pleasure, left Paul bound [*and, in order to please the Jews who hated Paul, he left Paul under guard rather than releasing him when he left office*].

ACTS 25

In this chapter, in order to prevent being turned over to the Jews who would kill him, Paul, as a Roman citizen, exercises his right to appear before Caesar to be tried.

1 NOW when Festus was come into the province, after three days he ascended from Cæsarea to Jerusalem [*three days after Governor Festus arrived in Caesarea, to take Felix's place, he traveled up to Jerusalem*].

2 Then the high priest [*the highest Jewish religious leader*] and the chief of the Jews [*and other Jewish religious leaders*] informed him [*informed him of their charges*] against Paul, and besought him [*and urgently asked him*],

3 And desired favour against him [*Paul*], that he would send for him [*Paul*] to Jerusalem, laying wait in the way to kill him. [*In other words, the Jewish rulers tried to bias Festus against Paul and asked him to command that Paul be brought to Jerusalem so they could ambush and murder Paul as he came along the road.*]

4 But Festus answered, that Paul should be kept at Cæsarea, and that he himself would depart shortly thither [*but Festus turned down their request and told them that he himself would soon be leaving for Caesarea*].

5 Let them therefore, said he, which among you are able, go down with me, and accuse this man, if there be any wickedness in him. [*He*

invited the Jewish leaders, whoever could come with him, to come and present their case against Paul in Caesarea.]

6 And when he had tarried [*stayed*] among them more than ten days, he went down unto Cæsarea; and the next day sitting on the judgment seat commanded Paul to be brought.

7 And when he was come [*when Paul arrived in the court room*], the Jews which came down from Jerusalem stood round about, and laid [*presented*] many and grievous [*serious*] complaints against Paul, which they could not prove.

8 While he answered for himself [*when Paul answered the charges, he said*], Neither against the law of the Jews, neither against the temple, nor yet against Cæsar, have I offended any thing at all [*I have done nothing at all against the law of the Jews, nor the temple, nor against Caesar*].

9 But Festus, willing to do the Jews a pleasure [*a favor*], answered Paul, and said, Wilt thou go up to Jerusalem, and there be judged of these things before me [*would you like me to take you to Jerusalem and hold court there on these charges against you*]?

As a Roman citizen by birth, Paul will now exercise his legal right to trial in a Roman court, in person, in Rome, by appealing to Caesar. In this way, he will escape being turned back over to the Jews.

10 Then said Paul, I stand at Cæsar's judgment seat, where I ought to be judged [*I am where I belong, in a Roman courtroom*]: to the Jews have I done no wrong, as thou very well knowest [*you know very well that I have done no wrong to the Jews*].

11 For if I be an offender [*a lawbreaker*], or have committed any thing worthy of death, I refuse not to die [*if I have done anything worthy of death, I am willing to die for it*]: but if there be none of these things whereof these accuse me [*if the accusations against me are false*], no man may deliver me unto them [*the Jews*]. I appeal unto Cæsar.

12 Then Festus, when he had conferred with the council [*with his legal counselors*], answered, Hast thou appealed unto Cæsar? unto Cæsar shalt thou go [*since you have appealed to Caesar, to Caesar you will go*].

13 And after certain days [*after a few days*] king Agrippa and Bernice came unto Cæsarea to salute [*to pay their respects to*] Festus.

King Agrippa was the son of Herod Agrippa I, who is mentioned in Acts 12:1–23. Bernice was his sister. Drusilla, Felix's wife (Acts 24:24), was also his sister. See chart in Bible Dictionary under "Herod." We are dealing with members of the royal family, the ruling royal family in the Palestine area at the time, all of which was under Roman rule.

14 And when they had been there many days, Festus declared [*explained*] Paul's cause unto the king, saying, There is a certain man left in bonds by Felix: [*Felix left a prisoner here when he turned things over to me.*]

15 About whom, when I was at Jerusalem, the chief priests and the elders of the Jews informed me [*told me of several charges they had against him*], desiring to have judgment against him [*wanting me to turn Paul over to them*].

16 To whom I answered, It is not the manner of the Romans to deliver any man to die [*it is not legal, according to Roman law, to give any man to anyone to be executed*], before that he which is accused have the accusers face to face [*until they have faced the accused in our courts*], and have licence to answer for himself concerning the crime laid against him [*so that the accused has a chance to defend himself against the charges*].

JST Acts 25:16

16 To whom I answered, It is not the **matter** of the Romans to deliver any man to die, before that he which is accused have the accusers face to face, and have license to answer for himself concerning the crime laid against him.

17 Therefore, when they [*the Jews*] were come hither [*arrived here in Caesarea*], without any delay on the morrow [*the next day*] I sat on the judgment seat [*I convened court*], and commanded the man [*Paul*] to be brought forth [*in*].

JST Acts 25:17

17 Therefore, when they were come hither, without any delay **on the day following** I sat on the judgment seat, and commanded the man to be brought forth.

18 Against whom when the accusers stood up, they brought none accusation of such things as I supposed [*they didn't accuse Paul of any of the things I expected they would*]:

19 But had certain questions [*presented charges*] against him of their own superstition [*which came out of their own religious beliefs*], and of one Jesus, which was dead, whom Paul affirmed [*claimed*] to be alive.

20 And because I doubted of such manner of questions [*because I didn't feel qualified to deal with such questions, knowing nothing about such things*], I asked him whether he would go to Jerusalem, and there be judged of these matters [*I asked Paul if he would prefer to go to Jerusalem and appear in the Jews' court system where they would be more knowledgeable about such things*].

21 But when Paul had appealed to be reserved unto the hearing of Augustus [*when Paul demanded his right to be tried by Caesar Augustus (the Roman emperor)*], I commanded him to be kept [*in prison*] till I might send him to Cæsar.

22 Then Agrippa said unto Festus, I would also hear the man myself [*I would like to listen to Paul myself*]. To morrow, said he [*Festus*], thou shalt hear him.

23 And on the morrow [*the next day*], when Agrippa was come, and Bernice, with great pomp, and was entered into the place of hearing [*after King Agrippa and Bernice had arrived with much pomp and ceremony*], with the chief captains, and principal men of the city, at Festus' commandment Paul was brought forth [*into the court room*].

24 And Festus said, King Agrippa, and all men which are here present with us, ye see this man [*now all of you can see this man, Paul, with your own eyes*], about whom all the multitude of the Jews have dealt with me, both at Jerusalem, and also here, crying that he ought not to live any longer [*about whom large numbers of Jews from Jerusalem as well as here have complained to me long and loud, saying he should be executed*].

25 But when I found that he had committed nothing worthy of death, and that he himself hath appealed to Augustus [*Caesar*], I have determined to send him [*to Caesar*].

26 Of whom I have no certain thing to write unto my lord [*I haven't been able to come up with anything definite to write to Caesar about him*]. Wherefore [*therefore*] I have brought him forth before you [*all the people gathered in the courtroom*], and specially before thee, O king Agrippa, that, after examination had [*so that, after today's court proceedings are over*], I might have somewhat to write [*I will have specific charges against Paul which I can include in a letter to Caesar*].

27 For it seemeth to me unreasonable to send a prisoner, and not withal [*along with him*] to signify [*to explain*] the crimes laid against him. [*In other words, it would be quite awkward to send a prisoner to Caesar without including specific charges against him.*]

ACTS 26

As Paul defends himself before King Agrippa, he will again tell the story of his conversion. Paul is a great teacher and a skilled speaker and before this session is over, Agrippa will exclaim that Paul has almost persuaded him to become a Christian. Watch Paul's skill and inspiration now as he draws his listeners into his defense, which will focus on resurrection and on Christ.

1 THEN Agrippa said unto Paul, Thou art permitted to speak for thyself [*you are permitted to defend yourself now*]. Then Paul stretched forth the hand, and answered for [*defended*] himself:

2 I think myself happy, king Agrippa, because I shall answer for myself this day before thee touching all the things whereof I am accused of the Jews [*I consider myself fortunate to defend myself*

to you regarding each accusation which the Jews have brought against me]:

3 Especially because I know thee to be expert in all customs and questions which are among the Jews: wherefore I beseech [*ask*] thee to hear me patiently.

4 My manner of life from my youth, which was at the first among mine own nation at Jerusalem, know all the Jews; [*The Jews know me and that I grew up in Jerusalem from the time of my youth.*]

5 Which knew me from the beginning, if they would testify, that after the most straitest sect of our religion I lived a Pharisee. [*Those who actually knew me from my youth, if they would tell you the truth about me, would testify that I was a Pharisee, the strictest religious group among the Jews.*]

6 And now I stand and am judged for the hope of the promise made of God unto our fathers: [*I am on trial here today because I believe in the promise God made to our ancestors.*]

7 Unto which promise our twelve tribes [*the descendants of Jacob*], instantly [*earnestly*] serving God day and night, hope to come. [*It is the same promise which all our people, the twelve tribes of Israel, hope to gain through faithfully serving God day and night.*] For which hope's sake, king Agrippa, I am accused of the Jews [*it is my belief in this promise and my hope for its fulfillment for which the Jews have brought me to trial*].

8 Why should it be thought a thing incredible with you, that God should raise the dead [*why should it be so difficult to believe that God can resurrect us*]?

9 I verily [*truly*] thought with myself, that I ought to do many things contrary to the name of Jesus of Nazareth [*In my earlier years, I was convinced that I ought to do everything possible to oppose Jesus and his followers*].

10 Which thing I also did in Jerusalem: and many of the saints [*the followers of Jesus*] did I shut up in prison, having received authority from the chief priests [*Jewish religious leaders*]; and when they [*Christians*] were put to death, I gave my voice against them [*I testified against them*].

11 And I punished them oft [*often*] in every synagogue [*congregation*], and compelled them to blaspheme [*say things which would justify their death*]; and being exceedingly [*very*] mad against them, I persecuted them even unto strange [*foreign*] cities [*I even went to foreign cities to round up and arrest Christians*].

12 Whereupon as I went [*in pursuit of this cause, I was traveling*] to Damascus [*about 140 miles north of Jerusalem, in Syria*] with authority and commission [*letters of authorization*] from the chief priests [*to arrest more Christians*],

13 At midday [*noon*], O king,

I saw in the way [*while traveling along the road*] a light from heaven, above the brightness of the sun, shining round about me and them which journeyed with me.

14 And when we were [*when we had*] all fallen to the earth, I heard a voice speaking unto me, and saying in the Hebrew tongue [*language*], Saul, Saul, why persecutest thou me? it is hard for thee to kick against the pricks [*it is hard for you to keep going against your conscience*].

15 And I said, Who art thou, Lord? And he said, I am Jesus whom thou persecutest.

In verse 16, next, the Savior calls Paul to full-time service in the Church and tells him that he is to bear witness of this appearance of Jesus to him and also that more will be revealed to him in future appearances and revelations from Christ.

16 But rise, and stand upon thy feet: for I have appeared unto thee for this purpose, to make thee a minister and a witness both of these things which thou hast seen, and of those things in the which I will appear unto thee;

17 Delivering thee from the people, and from the Gentiles [*I will rescue you from the Jews and from the Gentiles*], unto whom now I send thee,

18 To open their eyes [*spiritually*], and to turn them from darkness [*spiritual darkness*] to light, and from the power of Satan unto God, that they may receive forgiveness of sins, and inheritance among them which are sanctified [*who obtain celestial glory; "sanctified" means being made clean, pure, holy, and fit to be in the presence of God*] by faith that is in me.

19 Whereupon, O king Agrippa, I was not disobedient unto the heavenly vision [*from that point on, I have been obedient to instructions given me in that vision*]:

20 But shewed first unto them of Damascus, and at Jerusalem, and throughout all the coasts [*borders*] of Judæa, and then to the Gentiles, that they should repent and turn to God, and do works meet for repentance. [*I taught the people, beginning in Damascus, then at Jerusalem, and the Jews throughout the region of Judea, and then the Gentiles that they must repent and turn to God and demonstrate their sincere repentance by righteous living.*]

21 For these causes the Jews caught me in the temple, and went about to kill me [*these are the reasons the Jews grabbed me in the temple and tried to kill me*].

22 Having therefore obtained help of God [*because of God's help and protection*], I continue unto this day, witnessing both to small and great [*testifying to everyone I meet, both the little known and the famous*], saying none other things than those which the prophets and Moses did say should come [*saying*

nothing but what the prophets and Moses prophesied would happen, namely]:

23 That Christ should suffer [*would suffer for our sins and be crucified*], and that he should be the first that should rise from the dead [*and that He would be the first to be resurrected*], and should shew light [*and would bring the light of the gospel*] unto the people [*the Jews*], and to the Gentiles [*everyone who is not a Jew or member of the Twelve Tribes*].

24 And as he [*Paul*] thus spake for himself [*spoke in his own defense*], Festus [*the Roman ruler over Judea, the Jerusalem area, whom King Agrippa was visiting*] said [*interrupted*] with a loud voice, Paul, thou art beside thyself; much learning doth make thee mad [*Paul, you are out of your mind! Too much education has made you crazy!*].

25 But he said, I am not mad, most noble Festus; but speak forth the words of truth and soberness.

26 For the king [*Agrippa*] knoweth of these things, before whom also I speak freely [*King Agrippa knows what I am talking about; that's why I have spoken so openly in front of him*]: for I am persuaded [*convinced*] that none of these things are hidden from him; for this thing was not done in a corner. [*I am convinced that he is very aware of the things about which I have spoken because all of this was done in public, not secretly.*]

27 King Agrippa, believest thou the prophets [*do you believe the words of the Old Testament prophets*]? I know that thou believest.

King Agrippa's statement to Paul, next, is quite well known.

28 Then Agrippa said unto Paul, Almost thou persuadest me to be a Christian [*you have almost convinced me to become a Christian*].

29 And Paul said, I would to God [*I wish with all my heart*], that not only thou [*you*], but also all that hear me this day [*everyone in this room*], were both almost, and altogether such as I am [*were almost, in fact, exactly like me*], except these bonds [*except for being a prisoner*].

30 And when he had thus spoken, the king [*Agrippa*] rose up, and the governor [*Festus*], and Bernice [*Agrippa's sister*], and they that sat with them [*and other officials who were in their group*]:

31 And when they were gone aside [*had gone where they could talk privately*], they talked between themselves, saying, This man doeth nothing worthy of death or of bonds [*Paul has done nothing that justifies his being executed or even being held prisoner*].

32 Then said Agrippa unto Festus, This man might have been set at liberty, if he had not appealed unto Cæsar [*we could set Paul free right now if he had not made a formal request for a trial before Caesar; see Acts 25:11*].

ACTS 27

Just a reminder (as previously noted) that when you see the word "we" in verse 1, next, it tells you that Luke (who wrote the Gospel of Luke as well as Acts) is with Paul and his companions at this time. In fact, it appears that Luke has been traveling with Paul since Acts 16:10. Paul's journey to Rome takes place in AD 55. As you will see, in this chapter, Paul's journey to Rome to be tried there before Caesar was just as eventful as most of his other travels, for him and his companions. Among other things, he will be shipwrecked.

1 AND when it was determined that we should sail into Italy [*to Rome*], they delivered Paul and certain other prisoners unto one named Julius, a centurion of Augustus' band.

The "Augustus band" mentioned in verse 1, above, would probably be one of the elite detachments of Roman soldiers, who had been honored for valor and effective in fighting for the Roman Empire. See *Strong's* #4575. A "band" of soldiers has various definitions, but would quite likely be 600 Roman soldiers which would be one tenth of a Roman legion. Julius (verse 1, above), as a centurion, would be in charge of 100 Roman soldiers.

2 And entering into a ship of [*from*] Adramyttium [*a seaport in what would be far northwestern Turkey today*], we launched, meaning [*planning*] to sail by the coasts of Asia [*along the southern coasts of Turkey today*]; one Aristarchus, a Macedonian of Thessalonica [*a faithful member of the Church from Thessalonica, who will stay with Paul during his Roman imprisonment; see Colossians 4:10*], being with us.

3 And the next day we touched at Sidon [*a seacoast city about 130 miles north of Jerusalem on the Mediterranean Sea*]. And Julius [*the Roman centurion in charge of Paul and other prisoners on the ship*] courteously entreated Paul [*treated Paul very courteously*], and gave him liberty [*permission and freedom*] to go unto his friends [*to go ashore and visit friends*] and to refresh himself.

4 And when we had launched from thence [*set sail from there*], we sailed under Cyprus [*along the leeward side, or eastern side, of the Island of Cyprus; "leeward" means the side of the island which offers some protection from the wind*], because the winds were contrary [*not blowing in the right direction for us*].

5 And when we had sailed over the sea of Cilicia and Pamphylia [*along the coast of what would be southern Turkey today*], we came to Myra, a city of Lycia [*on the coast of southwestern Turkey today*].

6 And there the centurion found a ship of [*from*] Alexandria sailing into Italy; and he put us therein.

7 And when we had sailed slowly

many days, and scarce were [*just barely had*] come over against Cnidus [*had only come about 150 miles and were approaching Cnidus, on the southwestern coast of southern Turkey today*], the wind not suffering us [*still not blowing in our favor*], we sailed under Crete [*for protection from the wind to the leeward side of Crete*], over against [*close to*] Salmone [*on the eastern end of Crete*];

8 And, hardly [*with much difficulty*] passing it, came unto a place which is called The fair havens [*on the southern coast of central Crete*]; nigh [*near*] whereunto was the city of Lasea.

9 Now when much time was spent [*we had already lost a lot of time*], and when sailing was now dangerous [*it was the dangerous time of year for sailing in this region because of frequent storms*], because the fast was now already past, Paul admonished [*warned*] them,

> The "fast" referred to in verse 9, above, which was already past, identifies the time of year when this dangerous sailing is taking place as autumn. This public fast was required by the law of Moses. It was to be held on the tenth of the month of Tisri which is equivalent to mid-September to mid-October on our modern calendar. This "fast" in autumn, was held in conjunction with the Day of Atonement or Yom Kippur, as it is better known today on our calendars.

10 And said unto them, Sirs, I perceive [*I am inspired to tell you*] that this voyage will be with hurt and much damage [*that if we continue this journey now, it will result in disaster*], not only of [*for*] the lading [*cargo*] and ship, but also of [*for*] our lives.

11 Nevertheless the centurion [*the Roman commander*] believed the master [*captain*] and the owner of the ship, more than those things which were spoken by Paul.

12 And because the haven [*harbor where they were located at that time*] was not commodious [*suitable*] to winter in [*to stay in for the winter*], the more part [*the majority of the people on board*] advised to depart thence also [*counseled them to set sail from there*], if by any means they might attain to Phenice [*and try to sail to Phenice, on the southwestern end of Crete*], and there to winter [*and stay there for the winter*]; which is an haven of Crete, and lieth toward the south west and north west [*a harbor in western Crete which faced both southwest and northwest*].

13 And when the south wind blew softly [*and so, when a gentle south wind began to blow*], supposing that they had obtained their purpose [*thinking that luck was with them*], loosing thence [*taking up their anchor from there*], they sailed close by Crete [*they sailed along, keeping close to the shores of Crete*].

14 But not long after there arose against it [*their ship*] a tempestuous

[*hurricane-like*] wind, called Euroclydon [*the "Northeaster" in other words, a severe north east wind which occurred often enough to be given a name; see* Strong's *#2148*].

15 And when the ship was caught, and could not bear up [*sail*] into the wind, we let her drive [*we let the ship be driven with the wind*].

16 And running under [*using the island as a windbreak, in other words, on the lee side of*] a certain island which is called Clauda [*about 30 miles due south of Phenice, verse 12*], we had much work to come by the boat [*it was all we could do to get the lifeboat ready*]:

17 Which when they had taken up, they used helps, undergirding the ship [*the crew ran ropes under the ship and tied them together in an attempt to keep the ship from breaking apart*]; and, fearing lest they should fall into the quicksands [*afraid that they would be blown into the sandbars off the coast of northern Africa*], strake sail [*lowered the ships sails*], and so were driven [*and drifted with the wind*].

18 And we being exceedingly tossed with a tempest, the next day they lightened the ship [*because we were being so badly tossed about in the storm, the next day the crew began throwing cargo overboard to lighten the ship*];

19 And the third day we cast out [*threw overboard*] with our own hands the tackling [*equipment, furniture, and so forth*] of the ship.

20 And when neither sun nor stars in many days appeared [*we saw neither sun nor stars for many days*], and no small tempest lay on us [*and the storm kept beating on us*], all hope that we should be saved was then taken away [*we lost all hope of surviving*].

21 But after long abstinence [NIV, *after the men had gone a long time without food*] Paul stood forth [*stood up*] in the midst [*middle*] of them, and said, Sirs, ye should have hearkened unto me [*you should have listened to me*], and not have loosed from Crete [*and not have left Crete*], and to have gained this harm and loss [*and then you would not have suffered this damage and loss of your cargo*].

22 And now I exhort you to be of good cheer [*however, cheer up*]: for there shall be no loss of any man's life among you, but of the ship [*none of you will lose your lives; all we will lose is the ship*].

23 For there stood by me this night the angel of God [*an angel of the Lord appeared to me last night*], whose I am, and whom I serve,

24 Saying, Fear not, Paul; thou must be brought before Cæsar [*you must appear before Caesar*]: and, lo, God hath given thee all them that sail with thee [*none who are sailing with you will die*].

25 Wherefore, sirs, be of good cheer [*cheer up*]: for I believe God, that it shall be even as it was told me [*I know that what God had the angel tell me will happen*].

26 Howbeit [*however*] we must be cast [*we will be shipwrecked*] upon a certain island.

27 But when the fourteenth night was come [*on the fourteenth night of the storm*], as we were driven up and down in Adria [*as we were driven back and forth on the Adriatic Sea, east of Italy*], about midnight the shipmen [*sailors*] deemed [*felt*] that they drew near to [*were approaching*] some country [*land*];

28 And sounded [*lowered a weighted rope to determine how deep the water was*], and found it twenty fathoms [*120 feet deep*]: and when they had gone a little further, they sounded again, and found it fifteen fathoms [*90 feet deep*].

29 Then fearing lest we should have fallen upon rocks [*afraid that the ship would hit rocks and be broken up*], they cast four anchors out of the stern [*the back of the ship*], and wished for the day [*wished that daylight would come*].

30 And as the shipmen were about to flee out of the ship [*making plans to escape overboard*], when [*after*] they had let down the boat [*the lifeboat*] into the sea, under colour [*pretending*] as though they would have cast anchors out of the foreship [*pretending that they were going to do something with the forward anchors*],

31 Paul said to the centurion [*the Roman commander of the soldiers*] and to the soldiers, Except these abide in the ship, ye cannot be saved [*unless these sailors remain in the ship, none of you will survive*].

32 Then the soldiers cut off the ropes of the boat, and let her fall off [*so the soldiers cut the ropes that were holding the lifeboat and let it drift away so the sailors could not use it to escape the ship*].

33 And while the day was coming on [*at about dawn*], Paul besought [*encouraged*] them all to take meat [*to eat food, thus breaking their fast*], saying, This day is the fourteenth day that ye have tarried and continued fasting, having taken nothing [*this is the fourteenth day you have fasted to be saved from the storm*].

34 Wherefore I pray you [*I urge you*] to take some meat [*to eat some food*]: for this is for your health [*you must do this in order to survive*]: for there shall not an hair fall from the head of any of you [*if you follow my instructions, each of you will be saved without injury*].

Next, in verse 35, Luke describes for us the incredible courage and fortitude of Paul in seemingly unsurmountable odds.

35 And when he had thus spoken, he took bread, and gave thanks to God in presence of them all: and when he had broken it, he began to eat.

36 Then were they all of good cheer, and they also took some meat [*then they cheered up and ate also*].

37 And we were in all in the ship

two hundred threescore and sixteen souls [*there were 276 of us on board the ship*].

38 And when they had eaten enough, they lightened the ship, and cast out the wheat into the sea [*they threw more things overboard, including the wheat they were carrying*].

39 And when it was day [*when daylight came*], they knew not the land [*didn't recognize where they were*]: but they discovered a certain creek [*a bay where a river entered the sea*] with a shore [*beach*], into the which they were minded, if it were possible, to thrust in the ship [*they decided to try to get the wind to push the ship into the bay, if possible*].

40 And when they had taken up the anchors, they committed themselves unto the sea [*turned themselves over to the sea*], and loosed the rudder bands [*untied the ropes from the rudders*], and hoised [*hoisted, lifted*] up the mainsail to the wind, and made [*headed*] toward shore.

41 And falling into a place where two seas met, they ran the ship aground [*but the ship hit a sandbar before getting to the beach*]; and the forepart stuck fast, and remained unmoveable [*and the bow, the front of the ship was stuck and would not move*], but the hinder part was broken with the violence of the waves [*but the back of the ship was broken off by the pounding of the waves*].

42 And the soldiers' counsel [*plan*] was to kill the prisoners, lest any of them should swim out, and escape.

43 But the centurion [*the Roman commander of the soldiers*], willing [*wanting*] to save Paul, kept them from their purpose [*commanded the soldiers not to kill anyone*]; and commanded that they which could swim should cast themselves first into the sea, and get to land [*the centurion told all who were able to dive in and swim to shore*]:

44 And the rest, some on boards, and some on broken pieces of the ship [*the centurion told the rest, who were not good enough swimmers, to grab hold of boards and broken pieces of the ship and make their way to shore*]. And so it came to pass, that they escaped all safe to land [*thus, all of them arrived safely on the beach*].

ACTS 28

As you have already seen, Paul is always a missionary. He will be bitten by a poisonous snake as he helps gather wood for the fire and it will turn into an excellent opportunity for spreading the gospel.

1 AND when they were escaped, then they knew [*found out*] that the island was called Melita [*Malta, south of Sicily in southern Italy; they had been blown about 600 miles by the storm*].

2 And the barbarous people [*native people of the island*] shewed us no little kindness [*were very kind to us*]: for they kindled a fire, and

received [*welcomed*] us every one, because of the present [*continuing*] rain, and because of the cold.

In the following verses, the local people on the island will get quite an introduction to the Apostle Paul, and much good will be done by this great missionary.

3 And when [*after*] Paul had gathered a bundle of sticks, and laid them on the fire, there came a viper [*a very poisonous snake*] out of the heat, and fastened on his hand [*and bit him on the hand and then continued to hang on to Paul's hand*].

4 And when the barbarians [*the inhabitants of the island*] saw the venomous [*poisonous*] beast [*snake*] hang on his hand, they said among themselves, No doubt this man is a murderer, whom, though he hath escaped the sea, yet vengeance suffereth not to live. [*They thought Paul must be a murderer and that although he escaped successfully from the ship, the gods were not going to let him get away; rather, they caused the snake to bite him so he would die.*]

Paul has an advantage over these people who believe that he will now die. Remember that Paul had been told by an angel (Acts 27:23–24) that he would be brought safely to Rome to appear in court before Caesar. One can almost imagine a bit of a twinkle in Paul's determined and energetic eyes as the people watch in rapt attention for him to die after the snake has been shaken off into the fire. He no doubt knew what they were waiting for, but simply went innocently about his activities on the beach.

5 And he shook off the beast [*snake*] into the fire, and felt no harm [*felt no negative effects from the bite*].

6 Howbeit [*in the meantime*] they looked when he should have swollen, or fallen down dead suddenly [*the people watched to see Paul's hand swell up or for him to drop dead*]: but after they had looked [*watched*] a great while, and saw no harm come to him, they changed their minds, and said that he was a god.

7 In the same quarters [*in that same area of the island*] were possessions of [*was an estate which belonged to*] the chief man [*probably the governor*] of the island, whose name was Publius; who received [*welcomed*] us, and lodged us [*had us stay at his place*] three days courteously.

8 And it came to pass, that the father of Publius lay sick of a fever and of a bloody flux [*bloody diarrhea, dysentery; see* Strong's *#1420*]: to whom Paul entered in [*Paul entered his room*], and prayed, and laid his hands on him [*administered to him*], and healed him.

9 So when [*after*] this was done, others also, which had diseases in the island, came, and were healed:

10 Who also honoured us with many honours; and when we departed, they laded us with such

things as were necessary [*they provided us with necessities for our journey*].

11 And after three months we departed in a ship of [*from*] Alexandria, which had wintered in the isle [*which had spent the winter on Malta*], whose sign was Castor and Pollux [*the ship had figureheads of the gods Castor and Pollux*].

Castor and Pollux, in verse 11, above, were mythological gods, the twin sons of Jupiter and Leda, and were regarded as the gods who protected ships and sailors.

12 And landing at Syracuse [*in southeastern Sicily*], we tarried there three days.

13 And from thence we fetched a compass [*took a roundabout course*], and came to Rhegium [*on the southwestern tip of Italy, across the bay from the northeast tip of Sicily*]: and after one day the south wind blew, and we came the next day to Puteoli [*they covered about 230 miles and came to Puteoli, on the western coast of Italy, about 100 miles south of Rome*]:

14 Where we found brethren [*members of the Church*], and were desired to tarry with them seven days [*and stayed with them, according to their request, for seven days*]: and so we went toward Rome.

15 And from thence [*from Rome*], when the brethren heard of us, they came to meet us as far as Appii forum, and The three taverns [*when the brethren at Rome heard we were coming, they came as far as Appii Forum and The Three Taverns, about 25 to 30 miles to meet us*]: whom when Paul saw, he thanked God, and took courage [*which was very encouraging to Paul*].

16 And when we came to Rome, the centurion [*Roman commander*] delivered the prisoners to the captain of the guard: but Paul was suffered [*allowed*] to dwell by himself with a soldier that kept [*guarded*] him. [*In other words, Paul was allowed to live in a place of his own, under house arrest, with a soldier assigned to watch him, rather than being put in prison.*]

Three days after his arrival in Rome, Paul will call the local leaders of the Jews together and explain how he ended up in Rome. He will explain that, even though he was innocent of any wrongdoing, he had to request a trial before Caesar in order to avoid being murdered by the Jews at home in Jerusalem.

17 And it came to pass, that after three days Paul called the chief of the Jews [*the leaders of the Jews*] together: and when they were come together [*when they had assembled*], he said unto them, Men and brethren, though I have committed nothing against the people [*even though I am innocent of any crime*], or customs of our fathers [*ancestors*], yet was I delivered prisoner from Jerusalem [*I was arrested in Jerusalem*] into the

hands of the Romans [*and turned over to the Romans*].

18 Who, when they had examined me [*had finished with my trial*], would have let me go, because there was no cause of death in me [*I had done nothing worthy of being executed*].

19 But when the Jews spake against it [*but when the Jews violently objected to the decision of the court*], I was constrained to [*I had to*] appeal unto Cæsar; not that I had ought to accuse my nation of [*not that I wanted to accuse my own nation of anything*].

20 For this cause therefore have I called for you [*this is why I've asked you to come here to me*], to see you, and to speak with you: because that for the hope of Israel I am bound with this chain [*the reason I am a prisoner, bound in chains, is that I believe in the God of Israel*].

21 And they said unto him, We neither received letters out of Judea concerning thee [*the Jewish religious leaders in the Jerusalem area have written nothing to us about you*], neither any of the brethren that came shewed or spake any harm of thee [*and none of our leaders who have visited us has said anything negative concerning you*].

Next, the leaders of the Jews living in the area around Rome agree to set a time during which they will listen to Paul present his story since they have heard nothing but bad things about Christians from the leaders of the Jews everywhere.

22 But we desire to hear of thee what thou thinkest [*we would like to have you talk to us about your beliefs*]: for as concerning this sect [*the Christians*], we know that every where it is spoken against [*we have heard nothing but bad about the Christians*].

23 And when they had appointed him a day, there came many to him into his lodging [*on a day which they had decided upon, many Jews living in Rome came to Paul's quarters*]; to whom he expounded and testified the kingdom of God [*and he taught them and testified of the kingdom of God*], persuading [*teaching*] them concerning Jesus, both out of the law of Moses, and out of the prophets [*using the teachings of Moses and the other Old Testament prophets*], from morning till evening.

In verses 24–25, next, Luke tells us the outcome of these local leaders of the Jews having listened to Paul. It is disappointing.

24 And some believed the things which were spoken, and some believed not.

25 And when they agreed not among themselves, they departed, after that Paul had spoken one word [*After discussing Paul's teachings among themselves, they couldn't agree about them, so they started to leave, after Paul had said this last thing, quoting Isaiah 6:9–10*], Well spake the Holy Ghost by

Esaias [*through Isaiah*] the prophet unto our fathers [*ancestors*],

In other words, Isaiah was certainly inspired by the Holy Ghost when he described such people as these as follows:

26 Saying, Go unto this people, and say, Hearing ye shall hear, and shall not understand [*you are spiritually deaf*]; and seeing ye shall see, and not perceive [*you are spiritually blind*]:

27 For the heart of this people is waxed gross [*the people are hard-hearted, spiritually insensitive*], and their ears are dull of hearing [*they are spiritually deaf*], and their eyes have they closed [*they don't want to understand spiritual things*]; lest they should see with their eyes, and hear with their ears, and understand with their heart, and should be converted, and I should heal them.

28 Be it known therefore unto you [*the Jews here in Rome*], that the salvation of God [*the gospel*] is sent unto the Gentiles [*is being taken to non-Jews*], and that they will hear it [*they will accept it*].

29 And when he had said these words, the Jews departed, and had great reasoning among themselves [*and had many arguments among themselves about Paul's teachings*].

30 And Paul dwelt two whole years in his own hired [*rented*] house, and received [*welcomed*] all that came in unto him [*who came to visit him*],

31 Preaching the kingdom of God, and teaching those things which concern the Lord Jesus Christ, with all confidence, no man forbidding him [*no one ordered him to stop teaching*].

As indicated by Luke in verse 30, above, Paul will spend two years as a prisoner in Rome. He will be under house arrest, living in his own rented quarters, at his own expense. Even though he is a prisoner, he will be given many freedoms and privileges, including the freedom to have people visit him whenever they want to and to teach anything he wants to. During this first Roman imprisonment, Paul will write at least four of his letters (called "epistles") to his converts in various locations along the routes of his missionary journeys. These four letters appear as books in our New Testament. They are: Philippians, Colossians, Ephesians, and Philemon. After two years, he will be released from prison and will visit members of the Church in many locations, traveling perhaps as far as Spain. After four years, he will again be taken prisoner to Rome and will be executed by Nero, the emperor or "Caesar" of the Roman Empire, about AD 65. See Bible Dictionary under "Paul."

A General Note about Paul's Writings

Our Bible contains 14 epistles (letters) written by the Apostle Paul to members of the Church in various locations. Of the 14 letters, 13 of them, Romans through Philemon, are placed in the Bible generally according to length, the longest being Romans and the shortest being Philemon. The reason Hebrews is placed last is because some scholars question whether or not Paul is the author of Hebrews. See Bible Dictionary under "Pauline Epistles." We know that Paul did write Hebrews because the Prophet Joseph Smith said he did. In *Teachings of the Prophet Joseph Smith*, p. 59, he simply said, "It is said by Paul in his letter to the Hebrew brethren…"

THE EPISTLE OF PAUL THE APOSTLE TO THE ROMANS

The epistle (letter) from the Apostle Paul to the Romans was written from Corinth (in southern Greece), probably in the winter of AD 57 to AD 58, near the end of Paul's third missionary journey. Major themes of Romans include a strong condemnation of every form of wickedness and Paul's teachings about the relationship between our own works and the grace of God. With respect to grace and works, or faith and works, many Christians use quotes from Romans to prove that one needs only grace in order to be saved. We will give some examples here:

Example: Romans 3:27–28

27 Where is boasting then? It is excluded. By what law? of works? Nay: but by the law of faith.

28 Therefore we conclude that a man is justified by faith without the deeds of the law.

Others quote Romans to show that works are also necessary in order to be saved.

Example: Romans 2:13

13 For not the hearers of the law are just before God, but the doers of the law shall be justified.

What is going on here? The answer is simple. We must keep Paul's writings in their context, in their setting in the scriptures. For instance, in our example, above, of Romans 3:27–28, Paul is speaking to Jewish members of the Church who, because of their past tradition and culture before their baptism, are going through the motions of religion, who do the rituals and sacrifices and works, etc., but don't have faith and are not living the true gospel. Therefore, Paul emphasizes faith to them, and downplays empty works, which won't save them. Also, the "law" in verse 28 refers to the law of Moses, which was fulfilled by the Savior.

On the other hand, in Romans 2:13, quoted above, Paul's audience is Gentile members of the Church who are not as concerned as they should be about works, rather are thinking that since they have been baptized and are members, they don't need much else. Therefore, Paul's emphasis to them is that they must pay much closer attention to righteous works and deeds, and avoid sin and unrighteous behaviors.

ROMANS 1

In Romans, chapter 1, Paul's emphasis is mainly on works, and on avoiding the evils of that day. You will notice that many in our world today are caught up in the same sins.

The Joseph Smith Translation of the Bible (JST) is very significant in helping us understand this chapter. The Prophet Joseph Smith made many changes, additions, and clarifications. We will include all of the changes he made for this chapter.

Also, you will see that I have made considerable use of *Strong's Exhaustive Concordance of the Bible*, which is much-used among Bible scholars as a highly respected reference work on definitions of Bible vocabulary.

1 PAUL, a servant of Jesus Christ, called to be an apostle, separated [*set apart*] unto the gospel of God,

JST Romans 1:1

1 Paul, **an apostle,** a servant of **God, called of Jesus Christ, and separated to preach the gospel**,

2 (Which he had promised afore [*which gospel He promised in times past*] by [*through*] his prophets in the holy scriptures,)

JST Romans 1:2

2 (Which he had promised **before** by his prophets in the holy scriptures,)

3 Concerning his Son Jesus Christ our Lord, which was made of the seed of David [*was a descendant of* David] according to the flesh [*who was a descendant of King David, in terms of his mortal birth*];

4 And declared to be the Son of God with power, according to the spirit of holiness, by the resurrection from the dead: [*God testifies, with great power, through the Holy Ghost, that Christ is the Son of God, as witnessed by His resurrection from the dead.*]

JST Romans 1:4

4 And **declared the Son of God** with power, **by the Spirit according to the truth through the resurrection from the dead**;

5 By whom we have received grace and apostleship, for obedience to the faith among all nations, for his name:

JST Romans 1:5

5 By whom we have received grace and apostleship, **through obedience, and faith in his name, to preach the gospel among all nations**;

6 Among whom are ye also the called of Jesus Christ: [*You also are among those who have been called by Jesus Christ to bear witness of Him and help spread the gospel everywhere.*]

JST Romans 1:6

6 **Among whom ye also are called** of Jesus Christ;

7 To all [*the members of the Church*] that be in Rome, beloved of God, called to be saints: Grace to you and peace from God our Father, and the Lord Jesus Christ.

JST Romans 1:7

7 **Wherefore I write to all who are** in Rome, beloved of God, **called saints**; Grace to you, and peace, from God our Father, and the Lord Jesus Christ.

Verse 7, above, is one of many verses which are helpful in showing that the Father and Jesus are separate individuals.

8 First, I thank my God [*Heavenly Father*] through [*in the name of*] Jesus Christ for you all, that your faith is spoken of throughout the whole world [*the whole region of the Mediterranean Sea; the Roman "world"*].

JST Romans 1:8

8 First, I thank my God through Jesus Christ, **that you all are steadfast, and** your faith is spoken of throughout the whole world.

9 For God is my witness [*God knows that what I'm telling you is true*], whom I serve with my spirit in the gospel of his Son, that without ceasing I make mention of you always in my prayers [*that I pray for you continually*];

JST Romans 1:9

9 For God is my witness, whom I serve, that without ceasing I make mention of you always in my prayers, **that you may be kept through the Spirit, in the gospel of his Son**,

10 Making request, if by any means now at length [*in due time*] I might have a prosperous journey by the will of God to come unto you.

JST Romans 1:10

10 Making request **of you, to remember me in your prayers, I now write unto you, that you will ask him in faith, that** if by any means, at length, **I may serve you with my labors, and may** have a prosperous journey by the will of God, to come unto you.

11 For I long to see you, that I may impart unto you some spiritual gift, to the end ye may be established [*I would like to visit you so that I can strengthen you spiritually for the rest of your lives*];

JST Romans 1:11

11 For I long to see you, that I may impart unto you some spiritual gift, **that it may be established in you to the end**;

12 That is, that I may be comforted together with you by the mutual faith both of you and me [*that we might strengthen and comfort each other; see* Strong's *#4837*].

JST Romans 1:12

12 That I may be comforted together with you by the mutual faith both of you and me.

13 Now I would not have you ignorant [*I want you to be aware*], brethren, that oftentimes I purposed [*planned*] to come unto you, (but was let hitherto) [*every time*], that I might have some fruit [*success*] among you also, even as among other Gentiles.

JST Romans 1:13

13 Now I would not have you ignorant, brethren, that oftentimes I purposed to come unto you, (but was **hindered** hitherto,) that I might have some fruit among you also, even as among other Gentiles.

14 I am debtor [*obligated*] both to the Greeks, and to the Barbarians [*people of other nations; this does not have a negative connotation–see* Strong's *#0915*]; both to the wise, and to the unwise. [*In other words, I owe all people my best efforts to teach them of Christ.*]

15 So, as much as in me is [*with my best efforts*], I am ready to preach the gospel to you that are at Rome also.

JST Romans 1:15

15 **And**, as much as in me is, I am ready to preach the gospel to you that are at Rome also.

The first 24 words of verse 16, next, are one of the best-known quotes from the Apostle Paul.

16 For I am not ashamed of the gospel of Christ: for it is the power of God unto salvation to every one that believeth; to the Jew first, and also to the Greek [*to the Gentiles*]. [*The gospel was given to the Jews first, then, after the Savior's resurrection, was taken to the Gentiles as well as the Jews.*]

17 For therein [*in the gospel of Jesus Christ*] is the righteousness [*the standard for personal righteousness*] of God revealed [*made known*] from faith to faith: as it is written, The just [*the righteous*] shall live by faith.

JST Romans 1:17

17 For therein is the righteousness of God revealed **through** faith on his name; as it is written, The just shall live by faith.

18 For the wrath [*anger*] of God is revealed from heaven against all ungodliness and unrighteousness of men, who hold the truth in unrighteousness [*who do not repent once they know the truth*];

JST Romans 1:18

18 For the wrath of God is revealed from heaven against all ungodliness and unrighteousness of men; who **love not the truth, but remain in unrighteousness**,

19 Because that which may be known of God is manifest in them; for God hath shewed it unto them. [*In other words, after they have been taught the gospel*]

JST Romans 1:19

19 **After that which may be known of God is manifest to them**.

20 For the invisible things of him from the creation of the world are clearly seen [*evidence of the existence of God is everywhere to be seen*], being understood by the things that are made [*the earth and all creation bear witness of God*], even his eternal power and Godhead; so that they are without excuse: [*In other words, all creation clearly bears witness of God, therefore, the people described in verses 18–19 have no excuse for not believing in God and living His gospel.*]

JST Romans 1:20

20 **For God hath revealed unto them the invisible things of him, from the creation of the world, which are clearly seen; things which are not seen being understood by the things that are made, through his eternal power and Godhead**; so that they are without excuse;

21 Because that, when they knew God [*after they had been taught about God*], they glorified him not as God [*they did not worship Him as they should*], neither were thankful [*neither did they express gratitude; see D&C 59:21*]; but became vain in their imaginations [*they became corrupt in their thinking and desires*], and their foolish heart was darkened [*they became spiritually darkened*].

JST Romans 1:21

21 Because that, when they knew God, they glorified him not as God, neither were **they** thankful, but became vain in their imaginations, and their foolish **hearts were** darkened.

22 Professing [*claiming*] themselves to be wise, they became fools,

23 And changed [*reduced*] the glory of the uncorruptible [*immortal, eternal*] God into an image made like to corruptible man [*they brought God down to the level of man, as with Greek gods*], and to birds, and fourfooted beasts, and creeping things [*including making idols to worship*].

By way of warning from God, Paul will now describe some of the worst sins being committed by people in Rome at the time, including sexual immorality in many different forms such as masturbation, lesbianism, and homosexuality. See the heading to chapter 1 in our Bible, where it confirms that Paul is referring to practicing homosexuality. See also Topical Guide, under "Homosexuality" for additional references to the sin of homosexual behavior.

24 Wherefore God also gave them up [*allowed them to use their agency and thus turned them over*] to uncleanness [*immorality*] through the lusts [*evil, immoral desires*] of their own hearts, to dishonour their own bodies between themselves [*by themselves; see* Strong's *#1722*; in other words, *masturbation*]:

25 Who changed the truth of God into a lie [*they changed the righteous use of the power of*

procreation into perversion], and worshipped and served the creature [*lusts of the flesh*] more than the Creator, who is blessed [*is to be praised*] for ever. Amen.

26 For this cause [*because they desired wickedness*] God gave them up unto [*because of agency, God allowed them to become involved in*] vile [*unrighteous*] affections [*depraved passion; see* Strong's *#3806*]: for even their women did change the natural use [*of the powers of procreation*] into that which is against nature [*perversion; see* Strong's *#5449*]: [*In other words, women got involved in lesbianism, homosexuality, and so forth. See McConkie,* Doctrinal New Testament Commentary, *Vol. 2, p. 220.*]

27 And likewise also the men [*the men did similar things*], leaving the natural use of the woman [*departing from normal, proper sexual relations with their wives*], burned in their lust one toward another [*became inflamed with sexual attraction toward other men*]; men with men [*homosexuality; see Romans 1:27, footnote a*] working that which is unseemly [*shameful; involving nakedness; see* Strong's *#0808*], and receiving in themselves that recompence of their error which was meet [*required by God's laws; in other words, setting themselves up for the punishment of God for their perversion*].

28 And even as they did not like [*choose*] to retain God in their knowledge [*to acknowledge God's laws*], God gave them over to a reprobate [*depraved*] mind [*allowed them to exercise their agency leading toward acting out on the thoughts and desires of their evil minds*], to do those things which are not convenient [*which they ought not to be doing*];

JST Romans 1:28

28 And even as they did not like to retain God **according to some knowledge**, God gave them over to a reprobate mind, to do those things which are not convenient;

29 Being filled with all unrighteousness [*with all kinds of sins*], fornication [*sexual immorality*], wickedness [*depravity; see* Strong's *#4189*], covetousness, maliciousness [*meanness*]; full of envy, murder, debate [*strife, arguing*], deceit [*dishonesty*], malignity [*plotting evil against others*]; whisperers [*gossipers*],

30 Backbiters [*slanderers; people who ruin other peoples' reputations*], haters of God, despiteful [*violent, overbearing*], proud, boasters, inventors of evil things [*thinking up more ways to be wicked*], disobedient to parents,

31 Without understanding [*foolish, stupid; see* Strong's *#0801*], covenantbreakers, without natural affection [*heartless*], implacable [*refuse to make covenants; see* Strong's *#0786*], unmerciful:

32 Who knowing the judgment of God [*they are sinning against knowledge*], that they which

commit such things are worthy of death [*They know God's commandments and that people who commit such sins will die spiritually and will eventually be cut off from God*], not only do the same [*they not only commit such sins*], but have pleasure in them that do them [*they approve of and encourage others to commit such sins*]. [*In other words, members of the Church who have been taught the gospel and understand it, and still commit such sins, are very accountable. The effects on their spirituality are tragic. A major problem is that they not only commit such sins themselves, but they also encourage others to do the same.*]

JST Romans 1:32

32 **And some** who, knowing the judgment of God, that they which commit such things are worthy of death, **are inexcusable**, not only do the same, but have pleasure in them that do them.

ROMANS 2

In verses 1–16, Paul will talk mainly to Gentiles who have joined the Church, counseling them to avoid hypocrisy and emphasizing good works. He then talks to Jewish converts in verses 17–29, counseling them to avoid merely going through the motions of true religion, while lacking faith and internal commitment to personal righteousness.

1 THEREFORE thou art inexcusable [*there is no excuse for the following behavior*], O man, whosoever thou art that judgest [*this warning applies to anyone who judges others unrighteously*]: for wherein thou judgest another, thou condemnest thyself [*when you criticize and judge others unrighteously you condemn yourself*]; for thou that judgest doest the same things [*because you do the same things you criticize them for*].

JST Romans 2:1

1 Therefore thou art inexcusable, O man, whosoever thou art that **thus** judgest; for wherein thou judgest another, thou condemnest thyself; for thou that judgest doest the same things.

Paul is teaching strongly against hypocrisy, which is defined as criticizing others for wrong things they do when we ourselves are secretly committing the same sins.

2 But we are sure that the judgment of God is according to truth against them which commit such things [*God's judgment against people who do such things is fair*].

3 And thinkest thou this, O man, that judgest them which do such things, and doest the same, that thou shalt escape the judgment of God [*do you really think that you can be hypocrites and avoid the punishments of God*]?

4 Or despisest thou the riches of his goodness and forbearance and longsuffering; not knowing that the goodness of God leadeth thee to repentance [*do you take*

God's goodness and tolerance and patience so lightly that you miss the chance to repent]? [*In other words, do you misinterpret the fact that God hasn't smitten you yet to be a signal that the sins you are committing are not that bad?*]

5 But after thy hardness and impenitent heart treasurest up unto thyself wrath against the day of wrath and revelation of the righteous judgment of God [*but instead, you follow your hard and unrepentant heart and continue storing up reasons for God's righteous anger to eventually condemn you*];

6 Who will render to every man according to his deeds [*God will judge every man according to his deeds*]:

7 To them who by patient continuance in well doing seek for glory and honour and immortality, eternal life [*to those who patiently and constantly persevere in doing righteous deeds, faithfully seeking to develop the attributes of God, He will give eternal life, exaltation*]:

8 But unto them that are contentious [*those who like to cause contention*], and do not obey the truth, but obey unrighteousness [*and commit other sins also*], indignation and wrath [*will call the righteous anger of God upon themselves*],

9 Tribulation [*trouble*] and anguish [*sorrow*], upon [*will come upon*] every soul of man that doeth evil, of the Jew first, and also of the Gentile [*the Jews were first to hear the gospel, and now the Gentiles have the same accountability*];

10 But glory, honour, and peace, to every man that worketh good, to the Jew first, and also to the Gentile [*the rewards for righteous living will come to everyone who performs good works; this was taught first to the Jews and then to the Gentiles*]:

Verse 11, next, is often quoted in gospel sermons and discussions.

11 For there is no respect of persons with God [*because all people are of equal worth to God*].

12 For as many as have sinned without law [*without knowing the gospel*] shall also perish without law: and as many as have sinned in the law [*who continue sinning even though they know the gospel*] shall be judged by the law [*will be held accountable for what they know*];

Just so you know, the parenthesis in your Bible, at the beginning of verse 13, next, is closed at the end of verse 15.

13 (For not the hearers of the law are just before God [*it is not those who have heard the commandments of God whom God considers to be righteous*], but the doers of the law shall be justified [*but rather it is those who live the gospel who will be saved in celestial glory; "justified" means being exalted in celestial glory—see 1 Nephi 16:2, wherein "lifted up" means exalted*].

In verses 14–15, next, Paul calls

attention to an interesting and important truth, namely that all people are born with the Spirit of Christ, which includes a conscience. And when people follow the promptings of conscience, they naturally tend to live in harmony with the principles and commandments of the gospel, or, as Paul puts it, the "law." Also, remember that the use of the word "Gentile" in Paul's writings, means everyone who is not a Jew.

14 For when the Gentiles, which have not the law [*who do not have the gospel of Christ*], do by nature the things contained in the law [*naturally live in harmony with the laws of the gospel*], these, having not the law, are a law unto themselves [*are doing what they consider to be right*]:

15 Which shew the work of the law written in their hearts [*as they live in harmony with the things their hearts tell them, their lives demonstrate the purpose and desired outcomes of the laws and commandments of the gospel*], their conscience also bearing witness [*being guided by their conscience*], and their thoughts the mean while accusing or else excusing one another;) [*in other words, being guided by their own conscience, they either approve or disapprove of each other's actions*]

It is easy to get confused as we go from verse 15 to verse 16. Verse 16 refers back to the judgment mentioned at the end of verse 12 and expands a bit on that subject. As mentioned previously, verses 13 through 15 were enclosed in parentheses and contained a separate topic about the effects of following one's conscience on the part of people who have not heard of the gospel.

16 In the day when God shall judge the secrets of men by Jesus Christ [*on Judgment Day, when the Father has Jesus judge the secret acts of people (see John 5:22)*] according to my gospel. [*In other words, going back to the end of verse 12 and then back to verse 16, those who know the gospel will be held accountable for their knowledge and actions on the final Judgment Day by the Savior, who serves as our final judge, under the direction of the Father.*]

JST Romans 2:16

16 In the day when God shall judge the secrets of men by Jesus Christ according to **the** gospel.

Did you notice that Joseph Smith changed only one word in verse 16, above? It is a little word that makes a big difference. He changed "**my** gospel" to "**the** gospel," making it the gospel of Jesus Christ rather than Paul's gospel.

Paul, who has been mainly addressing Gentile converts in this chapter so far, now specifically addresses the Jewish converts and warns them against inappropriate ethnic pride and the hypocrisy of telling everyone else exactly how to live the gospel but not practicing what they preach.

17 Behold, thou art called a Jew [*you are proud of your Jewish heritage*], and restest in the law [*you still rely on the law of Moses*], and makest thy boast of God [*and boast of your fine relationship with God*],

18 And knowest his will [*you claim to know God's will*], and approvest the things that are more excellent, being instructed out of the law [*and you carefully compare all things against the standards of the law of Moses in order to choose the best in your lives*] ;

19 And art confident that thou thyself art [*you thus have confidence in your ability to serve as*] a guide of the blind [*the spiritually blind*], a light of them which are in darkness [*who are in spiritual darkness*],

20 An instructor of the foolish, a teacher of babes [*those who know very little about the gospel*], which hast the form of knowledge and of the truth in the law [*you appear to have great gospel knowledge because of your knowledge of details of the law of Moses*].

21 Thou therefore which teachest another [*you, who take it upon yourself to teach others*], teachest thou not thyself [*do you live the gospel yourself or are you a hypocrite (see Romans 2:21, footnote a)*]? thou that preachest a man should not steal, dost thou steal [*do you steal*]?

22 Thou that sayest a man should not commit adultery, dost thou commit adultery? thou that abhorrest idols [*you who claim to be terribly offended by idol worship and claim to stay far away from idols and their associated shrines, so you don't get "contaminated" by them*], dost thou commit sacrilege [*are you among those who enter into those shrines and rob and plunder them; see Romans 2:22, footnote b; also see* Strong's *#2416*]?

23 Thou that makest thy boast of the law, through breaking the law dishonourest thou God [*you who boast that you keep the law of God, do you dishonor God by breaking His laws*]?

24 For the name of God is blasphemed among the Gentiles through you, as it is written [*God's name is ridiculed by Gentiles because of your poor example, just like it said in Isaiah 52:5 and Ezekiel 36:22*].

In verses 25–29, next, Paul brings up the topic of circumcision, which, in his day, is still held by many Jewish converts to be very important, even though Christ did away with that part of the law of Moses and even though the Church leaders ruled that circumcision was not required of Gentile converts. See Acts 15:1–31. Also see Bible Dictionary under "Circumcision." Paul is a diplomat and a wise servant of God, so, instead of taking the Jews to task for still being adamant about circumcision, he simply teaches them to avoid the hypocrisy of making covenants and keeping them outwardly, but not keeping them with the heart.

25 For circumcision verily profiteth, if thou keep the law [*circumcision can have value, if you keep the covenant associated with it to be loyal and true to God*]: but if thou be a breaker of the law, thy circumcision is made uncircumcision [*but if you don't keep God's commandments, you might just as well not have been circumcised*].

26 Therefore if the uncircumcision [*if an uncircumcised convert*] keep the righteousness of the law [*keeps God's commandments as taught by Christ*], shall not his uncircumcision be counted for circumcision [*isn't it as if he were circumcised*]?

27 And shall not uncircumcision which is by nature, if it fulfil the law, judge thee, who by the letter and circumcision dost transgress the law? [*Won't you be condemned, who live the letter of the law of Moses but don't live the gospel, by converts who naturally are not circumcised but do live the gospel?*]

> Paul now drives home the point that outward appearance alone does not make a person a true member of God's covenant people.

28 For he is not a Jew [*he is not truly one of God's covenant people*], which is one outwardly [*who outwardly appears to be, but who merely goes through the outward motions of being righteous*]; neither is that circumcision, which is outward in the flesh [*neither is the outward surgery of being circumcised, true commitment to God; it does not automatically make one "circumcised of heart" or truly committed to God, inwardly righteous*]:

29 But he is a Jew [*he is truly a member of God's covenant people*], which is one inwardly [*who is one deep inside*]; and circumcision [*symbolic of true loyalty to God*] is that of the heart, in the spirit [*is a matter of heart and soul*], and not in the letter [*and not in outward appearance, conforming to the letter of the law*]; whose praise is not of men, but of God [*for those who look to God rather than men for approval*].

ROMANS 3

As stated in the introduction to Romans in this study guide, chapter three can be taken out of context and used to show that works are not necessary and that faith and grace are all that count. In context, this chapter is addressed to Jews who have joined the Church in Rome. Many of them at the time of Paul's writing are still caught up in their previous culture and traditions before baptism. They still believe that strict adherence to the outward details and requirements of the law of Moses will assure them salvation. Thus, Paul will emphasize the role of faith in Christ and the role of grace rather than works. He will emphasize that personal righteousness, not external appearance alone, enables the Savior's grace and mercy to cleanse us and save us. Examples of this emphasis are found, among others, in verses 24, 27 and 28. The first verses of chapter three are a continuation of the theme of the last verses of chapter two, namely that personal righteousness and covenant keeping, not outward appearance and empty ritual, are the things that lead to salvation in celestial glory.

The issue in verses 1 and 2 is whether or not a Jewish member of the Church, who strictly keeps the law of Moses but is not a true follower of Christ in his heart, has any advantage over a Gentile member who is truly converted to Christ? Answer: Of course not!

The JST (Joseph Smith Translation of the Bible) is very important to our understanding of these two verses.

1 WHAT advantage then hath the Jew? or what profit is there of circumcision?

JST Romans 3:1

1 What advantage then hath the Jew **over the Gentile**? or **what profit of circumcision, who is not a Jew from the heart?**

2 Much every way: chiefly, because that unto them were committed the oracles of God.

JST Romans 3:2

2 **But he who is a Jew from the heart, I say hath** much every way; chiefly because that unto them were committed the oracles of God.

The word "Jew," as used here, can represent the covenant people of the Lord. In other words, anyone who is truly converted and makes and keeps covenants with God, and gets on and stays on the covenant path, has the advantage in every way because they have been given the "oracles" or true words of God. The phrase "oracles of God" can also mean "the prophets of God;" see D&C 90:5, footnote 5a. See also Topical Guide, under "Oracle."

3 For what if some did not believe? shall their unbelief make the faith of God without effect? [*In other words, when have the wicked ever nullified God or made faith in Him of no value? Answer: Never!*]

4 God forbid [*that will never happen*]: yea, let God be true, but every man a liar [*even if everyone refused to obey God, it still would not change the fact that God is true*]; as it is written [*in Psalm 51:4*], That thou [*God*] mightest be justified [*will be proven right*] in thy sayings [*in everything You say*], and mightest overcome [*will triumph*] when thou art judged [*when people judge Your revelations to be of no value*].

In the next two verses, Paul says, in effect, that God's righteousness is constant, and that when people are wicked, God's righteousness shows up even more, by comparison and contrast with the wicked. He also points out that wicked people want God to "water down" His commandments so that they don't look so wicked. Paul asks the question, "How could God judge the world righteously if He yielded to the desires of the wicked to do away with His commandments?"

5 But if our unrighteousness commend [*serves to point out*] the righteousness of God, what shall we say [*are we justified in asking*]? Is God unrighteous who taketh vengeance? (I speak as a man) [*In other words, if we say, "Isn't it unfair for God to punish the wicked who, in a helpful way, are serving to point out His righteousness?"*]

JST Romans 3:5

5 But if **we remain in our unrighteousness and** commend the righteousness of God [*thus demonstrate by contrast the righteousness of God*], **how dare we say, God is unrighteous** who taketh vengeance? (I speak as a man **who fears God**,) [*In other words, if we, through our unrighteousness, emphasize God's righteousness even more, because of the contrast between Him and us, how could we possibly criticize Him for judging us and punishing us?*]

6 God forbid [*never!*]: for then how shall God judge the world? [*How would God be able to judge the world properly if He gave in to peoples' criticism of Him?*]

Judging by what Paul is saying here, he has apparently heard that some members of the Church in Rome are excusing their sinful behavior by saying, in effect, there has to be opposition so we are just helping God's work by being the opposition.

Watch, next, as Paul continues to tackle this issue head on. He will, in effect, ask his readers, "If our unrighteousness serves to emphasize God's righteousness, is it fair for Him to punish us? Aren't we actually doing good?" In other words, the wicked are apt to say that somebody has to be wicked so that others can see God's righteousness. Therefore, is it fair for Him to punish the wicked?

7 For if the truth of God hath more abounded through my lie unto his glory; why yet am I also judged as a sinner?

JST Romans 3:7

7 For if the truth of God hath more abounded through my lie, **(as it is called of the Jews,)** unto his glory; why yet am I also judged as a sinner? **and not received? Because we are slanderously reported**;

8 And not rather, (as we be slanderously reported, and as some affirm that we say,) Let us do evil, that good may come? whose damnation is just.

JST Romans 3:8

8 And **some affirm** [*claim*] **that we say, (whose damnation is**

just), Let us do evil that good may come. But **this is false**.

Apparently, as we learn in the JST above, Paul and the brethren have been falsely accused of teaching that it is okay to do evil because good comes from it. As you saw in the middle of JST verse 8, Paul said those false accusers deserved to be damned. And at the end of JST verse 8, Paul says this accusation is absolutely false.

In the next verses, Paul will teach clearly that no one is perfect, including Jews, Gentiles, Apostles, and members of the Church. Thus, all need the Atonement of Christ.

9 What then? are we better than they? No, in no wise [*no, not at all*]: for we have before proved both Jews and Gentiles [*all people*], that they are all under sin [*everyone has committed sin, no one is perfect*];

JST Romans 3:9

9 **If not so**; what then are we better than they? No, in no wise; for we have **proved before, that Jews and Gentiles are all under sin**.

Paul, as a master teacher, and as one who knows the Old Testament very thoroughly, will now quote scripture to powerfully prove to his listeners that everyone is caught up in sin and thus all need the gospel of Christ and His Atonement.

In an even tighter context, Paul is describing many of the self-righteous Jews of his day who engineered the crucifixion of Christ. They meticulously keep the details of the law of Moses, and outwardly appear religious and righteous, when in reality their hearts are full of filth, corruption, and evil and they spew poison from their mouths (see verses 13–14, below) as they teach others to be like them.

10 As it is written [*in Psalm 14:1–3*], There is none righteous, no, not one [*nobody is completely righteous; everyone needs to repent*]:

11 There is none that understandeth, there is none that seeketh after God.

12 They are all gone out of the way, they are together become unprofitable; there is none that doeth good, no, not one [*absolutely no one is perfect*].

13 [*Next, quoting Psalm 5:9.*] Their throat is an open sepulchre [*their throat is like an open grave, accepting rot and corruption, sin and filth*]; with their tongues they have used deceit [*they lie with their tongues*]; the poison of asps [*poisonous snakes*] is under their lips [*poisonous things which kill spirituality spew forth from their lips*]:

14 [*Next, quoting Psalm 10:7.*] Whose mouth is full of cursing and bitterness:

15 [*Next, quoting Isaiah 59:7–8.*] Their feet are swift to shed blood [*they move quickly to execute prophets and other righteous people*]:

16 Destruction and misery are in their ways [*theirs is a lifestyle of destroying good and causing misery*]:

17 And the way of peace have they not known [*they don't even know what peace is*]:

18 [*Next, quoting Psalm 36*:1.] There is no fear of God before their eyes [*they don't even have enough sense to be afraid of God because of their wickedness*].

Having quoted several Old Testament scriptures, blasting the hypocrisy of Jewish religious leaders, and reminding all of us that we too have sins and shortcomings and all need Christ's grace, help, mercy and Atonement, he now goes on to teach that the preaching of the gospel makes everyone accountable.

19 Now we know that what things soever the law saith, it saith to them who are under the law [*those who have been taught the gospel*]: that every mouth may be stopped [*silenced*], and all the world may become guilty [*accountable*] before God.

20 Therefore by the deeds of the law [*the law of Moses*] there shall no flesh [*person*] be justified [*be made worthy to enter into celestial glory*] in his sight: for by the law is the knowledge of sin [*knowledge of God's laws makes people accountable*]

JST Romans 3:20

20 **For by the law is the knowledge of sin**; therefore by the deeds of the law shall no flesh be justified in his sight.

Paul has emphasized, over and over in these verses, that one cannot be saved by complying with the law of Moses, but rather must come unto Christ and comply with His laws and commandments in order to enter celestial glory. Remember, the law of Moses was given as a "schoolmaster law" (Galatians 3:24) to elevate the people to a level where they would be capable of living the higher laws given by the Savior which lead to exaltation. The problem which Paul faces is the same as that faced by the Savior among the Jews. They have become so caught up in the tiny details of the law of Moses that they have departed from the intent of that law, namely to point their minds toward the Messiah who was to come. They have strayed far away from the wonderful outcomes built into the law of Moses such as those in Exodus 23: 1–13, Leviticus 19:18 [*"Thou shalt love thy neighbour as thyself:"*], Deuteronomy, chapter 8, and Deuteronomy 11:18–19.

21 But now the righteousness of God [*the standards required by God*] without [*outside of*] the law [*the law of Moses; in other words, separate and apart from the law of Moses*] is manifested [*has been revealed by Christ*], being witnessed by the law and the prophets

[*the "law"—that is, the writings of Moses in Genesis, Exodus, Leviticus, Numbers, and Deuteronomy*—along *with other Old Testament prophets, all testified that Christ would come and restore the higher laws and ordinances necessary for exaltation*];

22 Even the righteousness of God [*God's standards and gospel*] which is by faith of Jesus Christ unto all and upon all them that believe [*which is available to all people who believe Christ*]: for there is no difference [*there is no difference between Jew and Gentile, they all need Christ*]:

Verse 23, next, is rather well-known among students of the Bible as a brief, concise statement that we all need to repent.

23 For all have sinned, and come short of the glory of God [*everyone has sinned and fallen short of God's requirements for salvation*];

24 Being justified [*in this context, "justified" means to be lined up in harmony with God's laws, thus worthy to be ratified on judgment day and approved for exaltation*] freely by his grace [*the help of Christ, ". . . after all we can do." (2 Nephi 25:23)*] through the redemption that is in Christ Jesus: [*In other words, the only way we can be made clean, free from sin, and fit to be in the presence of God again, is through Christ.*]

JST Romans 3:24

24 **Therefore** being justified **only** by his grace through the redemption that is in Christ Jesus;

25 Whom [*referring to Christ*] God hath set forth [*appointed*] to be a propitiation [*an atonement; a sacrifice for our sins*] through faith in his blood [*through our faith in His atoning sacrifice*], to declare [*announce; proclaim*] his righteousness [*Christ's Atonement*] for the remission of sins that are past [*so that we can be cleansed of past sins*], through the forbearance [*patience*] of God [*in other words, through the patience which God has with us, which gives us sufficient time to repent, do good and be cleansed from sin*];

26 To declare [*present to us*], I say, at this time his righteousness [*Christ and His Atonement*]: that he [*the sinner*] might be just [*might be made clean*], and the justifier [*and to present unto us Christ, the Atoner*] of him [*the sinner*] which [*who*] believeth in Jesus [*Christ's Atonement works for those who believe him*].

Paul will now summarize by reminding his audience that boasting of outwardly going through the motions of religion is of no value. In other words, going through the outward ritual and detail of the law of Moses while the inward soul remains evil and corrupt, is worthless.

27 Where is boasting then [*what good does boasting and outward religious appearance do*]? It is excluded [*it is of no value*]. By what law? of works [*will empty,*

insincere, hypocritical outward show of complying with the law of Moses save a person]? Nay: but by the law of faith [*we are saved by faith in Christ, which requires sincere, deep, personal righteousness*].

28 Therefore we conclude that a man is justified by faith without [*outside of*] the deeds of the law [*in summary, we must conclude that a person is prepared to return to God by faith, which requires true personal righteousness, rather than merely going through the outward appearance of keeping the law of Moses*].

JST Romans 3:28

28 Therefore we conclude that a man is justified by faith **alone** without the deeds of the law [*the performances, rites, and rituals of the law of Moses*].

29 Is he the God of the Jews only? is he not also of the Gentiles? Yes, of the Gentiles also [*in other words, God is everybody's God*]:

30 Seeing it is one God [*since there is just one God for everyone*], which shall justify the circumcision [*the Jews*] by faith, and uncircumcision [*the Gentiles*] through faith [*everyone who is willing to follow Christ will be saved, justified, because of their faith in Him and keeping his commandments*].

JST Romans 3:30

30 Seeing that **God will** justify the circumcision by faith, and uncircumcision through faith.

31 Do we then make void [*destroy*] the law [*the law of Moses*] through faith? God forbid: yea, we stablish [*fulfill the purposes of*] the law. [*The whole purpose of the law of Moses was to point our minds toward Christ. Therefore, when we demonstrate true faith in Jesus, which involves action and covenants, we are indeed fulfilling the major purpose of the law of Moses, rather than destroying it.*]

ROMANS 4

The word "faith" is used often in this chapter. One of the common mistakes that many people make in interpreting Paul's writings is that they assume that "faith" is passive, meaning simply believing in Christ, requiring no action on the part of the believer. To believe this about faith is not only false, but also terribly unfortunate. Faith is much more than mere belief. Joseph Smith said that faith is a "principal of action"—see *Lectures on Faith*, lecture number one. Thus, when Paul speaks of belief and faith, he is speaking of all the actions, ordinances, good works, repenting, and changing done by one who truly has faith in Jesus Christ and who desires to be cleansed by the Atonement. Generally speaking, in this chapter, when Paul refers to the "law" and to "works," he is referring to the detailed external behaviors and requirements of the law of Moses, which the Jews had come to falsely believe would be sufficient to lead them to salvation.

Remember also that in this chapter Paul is speaking to Jewish converts to the Church, who still tend to be caught up in the details of the law of Moses rather than seeing the need for faith in Christ and His grace (the help He offers us constantly) which lead to personal, internalized, genuine righteousness.

1 WHAT shall we say then that Abraham our father, as pertaining to the flesh [*our mortal ancestor*], hath found? [*In other words, if Abraham, our common ancestor were here, what would he tell us about faith and works?*]

2 For if Abraham were justified by [*shown to be faithful by his*] works, he hath whereof to glory [*he has something to boast about*]; but not before God [*but it is not sufficient to save him as far as God is concerned*]

JST Romans 4:2

2 For if Abraham were justified by **the law of works, he hath to glory in himself; but not of God**.

3 For what saith the scripture [*what does it say in the scriptures about Abraham*]? [*Answer*] Abraham believed God, and it was counted unto him for righteousness. [*He was given credit for being righteous because he believed God*].

4 Now to him that worketh is the reward not reckoned [*calculated*] of grace, but of debt. [*In other words, no matter how many "works" a person has, he is still in debt to God and cannot be saved without the grace of Christ. See Mosiah 2:24.*]

JST Romans 4:4

4 Now to him **who is justified by the law of works, is the reward reckoned, not of grace**, but of debt.

As you have perhaps noticed already in your own Bible, verse 5, next, came through the various translations quite garbled and confusing. As it stands, it sounds like the "ungodly" are "justified" or saved. Without the help of the JST corrections, we would be quite lost when it comes to understanding it. Remember that "justified," in this context, means to be made worthy of exaltation through the Atonement of Christ.

5 But to him that worketh not, but believeth on him that justifieth the ungodly, his faith is counted for righteousness.

JST Romans 4:5

5 But to him that **seeketh not to be justified by the law of works,** but believeth on him **who** justifieth **not** the ungodly, his faith is counted for righteousness. [*In other words, to him who understands correctly and does not attempt to gain salvation through living the law of Moses, but rather exercises faith in Jesus Christ, Who will not justify or save the unrighteous, his faith is accepted by God.*]

Paul is a master at quoting people from the Old Testament

whom the Jewish converts highly respect, in order to prove his point about faith and works. He now quotes David from Psalm 32:1–2.

6 Even as David also describeth the blessedness of the man, unto whom God imputeth righteousness without works, [*In other words, David described the blessings which come to the righteous who do not live the law of Moses.*]

JST Romans 4:6

6 Even as David also describeth the blessedness of the man, unto whom God imputeth righteousness without **the law of** works,

7 Saying, [*quoting Psalm 32:1*] Blessed are they whose iniquities are forgiven, and whose sins are covered [*JST, Psalm 32:1 "Blessed are they whose transgressions are forgiven, and who have no sins to be covered."*].

JST Romans 4:7

7 Saying, Blessed are they **through faith** whose iniquities are forgiven, and whose sins are covered.

8 [*Quoting Psalm 32:2.*] Blessed is the man to whom the Lord will not impute sin [*hold accountable for sins, because he has repented and has thus been forgiven*].

The phrase "the circumcision" is often used by Paul to refer to Jewish converts to the Church who have come from a background of living the law of Moses. He uses the phrase "the uncircumcision" to refer to Gentile converts to the Church, who have not come from a background of living the law of Moses. Knowing this helps understand verse 9, next.

9 Cometh this blessedness then upon the circumcision only [*do these blessings of being forgiven of sin come only upon Jewish converts*], or upon the uncircumcision also [*or are they available to Gentile converts also*]? for we say [*we have established, in this presentation to you*] that faith was reckoned to Abraham for righteousness [*God considered Abraham to be righteous because of his faith*].

10 How was it then reckoned [*under what circumstances was Abraham credited with being righteous by God*]? when he was in circumcision, or in uncircumcision [*before or after he was circumcised*]? Not in circumcision, but in uncircumcision [*Answer: before he was circumcised*].

Having established that Abraham was considered to be righteous by the Lord, before he was circumcised, Paul will now emphasize that point again in verse 11, next. Remember that what Paul is trying to get across to these Jewish converts to the Church in Rome is that it is indeed possible to be righteous without adhering to the law of Moses, including circumcision, which the Jews considered to be extremely important in terms of loyalty to God. Paul points out that Abraham received great promises and blessings, the blessings of exaltation with eternal posterity [*Genesis 17:1–8*], before he was actually circumcised [*Genesis 17:9–14*], thus emphasizing that it is possible to be very righteous and worthy of exaltation, without circumcision. His use of Abraham as an example of one who was considered by God to be righteous, without circumcision, in other words, without the law of Moses, is designed to have real clout with these Jewish converts.

11 And he [*Abraham*] received the sign of circumcision [*great blessings promised to him by the Lord; see Genesis 17:1–8*], a seal of the righteousness of the faith which he had yet being uncircumcised [*a confirmation from God that he was righteous, before he was circumcised (in Genesis 17:9–11)*]: that he might be the father of all them that believe [*so that all worthy believers, whether Jew or Gentile, could also receive the blessings promised to Abraham*], though they be not circumcised [*even if they were not living according to the law of Moses*]; that righteousness might be imputed unto them also [*that they might be considered righteous in the eyes of the Lord also*]:

In verse 12, next, Paul will refer to Abraham as "the father of circumcision"—in other words, "the father (ancestor) of the covenant people." As mentioned in a note in verse 11, above, God chose Abraham to be the "father" of the covenant people, in other words, Abraham was called of God to make covenants of exaltation (see Genesis 17:1–8) and to carry the gospel and priesthood to all nations through his posterity. (See also Abraham 2:9–11.) His posterity became the "covenant" people. We, as members of the Church, are part of this covenant people. As stated in our patriarchal blessings, one way or another, we are entitled to the blessings of Abraham, Isaac, and Jacob, which are the blessings of exaltation, through our worthiness.

12 And the father of circumcision [*Abraham is the "father" or "ancestor" of all covenant people*] to them who are not of the circumcision only, but who also walk in the steps of that faith of our father Abraham, which he had being yet uncircumcised. [*In other words, Abraham is the one through whom the blessings of exaltation come, not only to his direct descendants, the Israelites, who lived the law of Moses, but also to those who are not his direct descendants and did not keep the law of Moses, but who faithfully live as Abraham did before he was circumcised.*]

13 For the promise, that he should be the heir of the world, was not to Abraham, or to his seed, through the law [*the law of Moses*], but through the righteousness of faith. [*Abraham and his posterity did not receive the great promises of the Lord (Genesis 17:1–8) because of works alone, rather, also because of faith.*]

14 For if they which are of the law be heirs, faith is made void, and the promise made of none effect: [*If people were to automatically inherit the highest blessings of God merely because they are descendants of Abraham who live the law of Moses, then faith would not be necessary and the promises of God to Abraham and his posterity would not effect or cause personal righteousness in people.*]

15 Because the law worketh wrath [*the law of Moses brings accountability and punishment for those who know the law and violate it*]: for where no law is, there is no transgression [*people are not held accountable if they don't know the law*].

The JST is of great importance in helping us understand verse 16, next. The JST puts the word "works" back into the verse. As it stands in our Bible, the word "works" has been left out, and thus the powerful relationship between faith, works, and grace has been removed (faith, as a principle of action leads to good works and to personal righteousness which enable the grace of Christ's Atonement to cleanse us).

16 Therefore it is of faith, that it might be by grace; to the end the promise might be sure to all the seed; not to that only which is of the law, but to that also which is of the faith of Abraham; who is the father of us all [*the ancestor of us all, whether literal or by "adoption," through whom all of us, Jew or Gentile, receive the blessings of exaltation, if worthy*],

JST Romans 4:16

16 **Therefore ye are justified of** [*saved by*] **faith and works, through grace**, to the end the promise might be sure to all the seed [*to all people*]; not to **them** only **who are** of the law [*not only to the Jews*], but to **them** also **who are** of the faith of Abraham [*but also to the Gentiles who have the faith that Abraham had*]; who is the father of us all [*the one through whom all of us can inherit the blessings of exaltation; see Abraham 2:9–11*],

17 (As it is written [*in Genesis 17:4*], I have made thee [*Abraham*] a father [*an ancestor*] of many nations,) before him [*in the presence of God*] whom he [*Abraham*] believed, even God, who quickeneth [*resurrects*] the dead, and calleth those things which be not as though they were [*and tells of things which have not yet happened as if they had already taken place*].

In verse 18, next, Paul continues emphasizing the role of faith and hope. He uses Abraham as an example of one who had great faith and hoped against all odds, who had faith in the promises of God against all obvious evidence to the contrary. Remember that Abraham and Sarah had been promised by the Lord that they would have posterity. See Genesis 17:19. Abraham was 62 years old and Sarah was 52 years old at the time the promise of posterity was given. (See Abraham 2:9 and 14.) Abraham was 100 and Sarah was 90 when Isaac was born. Sarah had already passed the time of life when she could be expected to bear a child. (See Genesis 18:11.) Thus, a "miracle child" was born to them, as promised by God.

18 [*Abraham*] Who against hope believed in hope, that he might become the father [*ancestor*] of many nations, according to that which was spoken [*according to the promise of numerous posterity spoken by the Lord; see Genesis 17:16*], So shall thy seed [*posterity*] be.

19 And being not weak in faith, he [*Abraham*] considered not his own body now dead [*didn't let the fact that his body was so old that it was nearly dead, shut down his faith that God's promise of posterity to him and Sarah would be fulfilled*], when he was about an hundred years old, neither yet the deadness of Sara's womb [*the physiological fact that Sarah was way past the age of childbearing*]:

20 He [*Abraham*] staggered not at the promise of God through unbelief [*he did not doubt the promise of God*]; but was strong in faith, giving glory [*praise and honor*] to God;

21 And being fully persuaded that, what he [*the Lord*] had promised, he [*the Lord*] was able also to perform.

22 And therefore it [*Abraham's faith*] was imputed to him for [*credited to him by the Lord as*] righteousness.

As you have already noticed, when Paul is trying to make an important point, he repeats it over and over. In this chapter, you have seen him do that with the topic of faith, using Abraham as the example. Remember that he is trying to convince Jewish converts to the Church that faith in Jesus Christ is an essential ingredient for salvation. As mentioned already, many of these converts still tended to think that strict adherence to the outward performances required by the traditions of the Jews would save them.

23 Now it was not written for his [*Abraham's*] sake alone, that it [*faith*] was imputed to him [*that he was given credit by the Lord for his great faith*];

24 But for us also, to whom it shall be imputed [*we also must demonstrate great faith in order to have it credited to us*], if we believe on him [*Heavenly Father*] that raised up Jesus our Lord from the dead;

25 Who was delivered [*who was turned over to suffer in Gethsemane and to be crucified*] for our offences [*because of our sins*], and was raised again [*resurrected*] for our justification [*was resurrected in order to complete the Atonement so that we can be "justified," that is, cleansed and made worthy to be exalted and to live again with God*].

ROMANS 5

As you have perhaps noticed, Paul uses the word "justified" often in his teaching. Generally speaking, "justified" means "saved," "ratified," "approved." Therefore, in the context of Paul's writings, it can be considered to mean, in effect, "lined up in harmony with God's commandments" and thus being made worthy of exaltation. The word is used in a similar way in computer word processing. When typing a document on a computer, people usually "justify" the left margin and sometimes "justify" both margins. In other words, they do the key stroke sequence or the mouse click necessary to make the margins of the document line up perfectly. So it is with our lives. When we are "justified," it means that we have been faithful, have followed the promptings of the Holy Ghost who leads us to live righteously and participate in the saving ordinances and covenants of the gospel. Thus we become worthy to be cleansed by the Atonement and therefore are lined up in harmony with God such that we are worthy to live with Him forever in exaltation. See Moses 6:59–60. Also in this chapter, Paul will teach us the highly important role that hope plays in our lives as we strive to go forward on the covenant path.

1 THEREFORE being justified by faith, we have peace with God [*the Father*] through our Lord Jesus Christ [*through Christ's Atonement*]:

2 By whom [*through Christ*] also we have access by faith into this grace [*"grace" can be considered to be the help and mercy of Christ*] wherein we stand [*which we are now enjoying*], and rejoice in hope of the glory of God [*and rejoice in anticipating exaltation, which is the glory in which God lives; see McConkie,* Doctrinal New Testament Commentary, *Vol. 2, p. 239*].

3 And not only so, but we glory in tribulations also [*we rejoice that we have problems here in mortality*]: knowing that tribulation [*trouble*] worketh patience [*develops patience, perseverance, and so forth in us*];

JST Romans 5:3

3 And not only **this**, but we glory in tribulations also; knowing that tribulation worketh patience;

4 And patience, [*develops*] experience; and experience, [*develops*] hope:

5 And hope maketh not ashamed [*keeps us from quitting in our efforts to live the gospel*]; because the love of God is shed abroad in our hearts by the Holy Ghost which is given unto us [*the Holy Ghost bears witness to us of God's love and encourages us to continue striving to live righteously*].

6 For when we were yet without strength [*before Christ's Atonement, we were helpless to save ourselves; see 2 Nephi 9:7–9*], in due time [*at the appropriate time*

in God's plan] Christ died for the ungodly [*for all of us sinners*].

Paul will now point out how, on occasions among us mortals, some person gives his or her life for another, and that when this does take place, it is usually for someone who is righteous or at least good. The point is that it is truly amazing that someone (namely Christ) would give His life for all people, including the wicked.

7 For scarcely for a righteous man will one die: yet peradventure [*perhaps*] for a good man some would even dare [*be willing*] to die.

8 But God commendeth [*shows*] his love toward us, in that, while we were yet sinners, Christ died for us.

9 Much more then [*and there is much more to what the Savior did for us*], being now justified [*cleansed, saved*] by his blood, we shall be saved from wrath [*from the punishments required by the Law of Justice*] through him.

10 For if, when we were enemies [*in opposition to God because of our sins*], we were reconciled to God [*the Atonement was put in place whereby we could be redeemed and placed in harmony with him*] by the death of his Son, much more, being reconciled, we shall be saved by his life [*we will be saved also by His resurrection, and, if we are willing to live such that His Atonement saves us from our sins (reconciles us with God), we can continue toward eternal life, which is exaltation*].

11 And not only so [*And not only that*], but we also joy in God through our Lord Jesus Christ, by whom we have now received the atonement. [*In other words, the Atonement brings great joy into our lives and lets us enjoy a wonderful relationship with the Father.*]

Paul's teaching in verse 11, above, that we can have joy in our relationship with God, is more significant than many of us might realize. Typically, most Jews, by the time Paul came along, had been taught to fear God. They had been taught in their culture that God was a God of anger and vengeance. His mercy, kindness, patience, gentleness, etc., as taught in Deuteronomy 4:31, 2 Chronicles 30:9, Isaiah 54:7, Micah 7:18, and so forth, had been either downplayed or eliminated in the culture of the Jews.

12 Wherefore, as by one man [*Adam*] sin entered into the world, and death by sin [*see 1 Corinthians 15:21–22*]; and so death passed upon all men, for that all have sinned [*because everyone has sinned*]:

The parenthesis which you see at the beginning of verse 13, next in your Bible, is closed at the end of verse 17, in your Bible.

13 (For until the law sin was in the world: but sin is not imputed when there is no law [*people are not held accountable when they don't know the law and commandments*].

<u>**JST Romans 5:13**</u>

13 (For, before the law, sin was in the world; **yet** sin is not imputed **to those who have no law**.

14 Nevertheless death reigned [*ruled*] from Adam to Moses, even over them that had not sinned after the similitude of Adam's transgression, who [*referring to Adam*] is the figure of him [*is symbolic of Christ*] that was to come [*who would come sometime in the future*].

<u>**JST Romans 5:14**</u>

14 Nevertheless, death reigned from Adam to Moses, even over them that had not sinned after the similitude of Adam's transgression, who is the figure of him that was to come. **For I say, that through the offense, death reigned over all**.

Verse 14, above, is a bit complex. First of all, Paul's logic is that since people were living and dying for about 2500 years from Adam to Moses, and since the law of Moses wasn't given until Moses came on the scene, there had to be a way for those people to be saved without knowing the law of Moses, and the way is through Christ and His Atonement. Next, Paul says that Adam is "the figure of" or symbolic of Christ. We get some help with Paul's vocabulary by reading 1 Corinthians 15:45 where Paul refers to two "Adams," namely, "the first man Adam," who was Eve's husband, and "the last Adam" (Christ), who is a "quickening spirit" or one who makes people come alive again. What Paul is teaching is that everyone will eventually die and thus, all of us need Christ's resurrection to free us from death. He also teaches that Adam was a "type" of Christ or symbolic of Christ, in the sense that Adam (and Eve) got things going for us to be born into mortality, and thus is a type of "savior" for us. In summary, Adam (and Eve) brought transgression, physical death, and the potential for spiritual death into the world. Christ brought forgiveness, immortality, and the potential for exaltation into the world.

15 But not as the offence, so also is the free gift. For if through the offence of one many be dead, much more the grace of God, and the gift by grace, which is by one man, Jesus Christ, hath abounded unto many.

<u>**JST Romans 5:15**</u>

15 But **the offense is not as the free gift, for the gift aboundeth**. For, if through the offense of one, many be dead; much more the grace of God, and the gift by grace, **hath abounded by one man, Jesus Christ, unto many.**

The "offense" spoken of above is the fall of Adam—see end of JST verse 14, above. The free gift is the Atonement of Christ. The gift includes the grace of Christ made available to us through His Atonement, which "aboundeth," in other words, continues to bless our lives abundantly forever. Among other things, Paul is saying, in effect, that the fall of Adam and the Atonement of Christ are not equal to each other. The Atonement is more powerful. The fall of Adam brought death into the world, but the Atonement overcomes physical death for everyone—see 1 Corinthians 15:22—and continues to give immeasurably to all the righteous as it enables them to attain eternal life.

16 And not as it was by one that sinned, so is the gift: for the judgment [*the condemnation which followed Adam's fall*] was by one to condemnation, but the free gift is of many offences unto justification. [*Again, the Atonement of Christ is far more powerful than Adam's transgression*];

JST Romans 5:16

16 And **not as, by one that sinned, is the gift**; for the judgment **is** by one to condemnation [*the fall of Adam was caused by one transgression*], but the free gift is of many offenses [*the Atonement is effective for innumerable sins*] unto justification [*and leads the righteous to exaltation*].

Through repetition, Paul is still emphasizing the fact that Christ's Atonement, which provides resurrection for all and represents the grace of God to all who will live worthily, overcomes the fall of Adam. The main point is still that the Jewish converts to the Church must make the transition from their religious and cultural upbringing as followers of the law of Moses to faithfully accepting Jesus of Nazareth as the promised Messiah. They will all be resurrected because of the Atonement, but must fully accept and follow the Savior's teachings in order to overcome spiritual death and to be redeemed by the grace of God, after all they can do (2 Nephi 25:23).

Paul's repetition of this topic continues in the next verses.

17 For if by one man's offence [*Adam's transgression*] death reigned by one [*death was caused by one man (Adam)*]; much more they which receive abundance of grace and of the gift of righteousness [*those who accept the gift of being made clean through the Atonement*] shall reign in life [*shall rule as Gods in eternal life*] by one, Jesus Christ [*because of one man, namely Jesus Christ*].)

By the way, as mentioned above, the parenthesis which ends verse 17 in your Bible, began with the parenthesis at the beginning of verse 13.

Remember also, as stated previously, that Paul uses repetition to drive home his point. You will see this again in the next verses.

18 Therefore as by the offence of one [*Adam*] judgment came upon all men to condemnation [*therefore, because of Adam's transgression, all people became subject to sin*]; even so by the righteousness of one [*Christ*] the free gift came upon all men unto justification of life [*the Atonement made eternal life available to all upon condition*

that they live worthy of being "justified," meaning to be cleansed from sin and "approved" to dwell in the presence of God forever.]

19 For as by one man's disobedience many were made sinners [*because of Adam's transgression, many became involved in sin*], so by the obedience of one [*because of Christ's obedience to the Father*] shall many be made righteous [*many can become righteous through being cleansed from their sins*].

20 Moreover the law entered, that the offence might abound [*when the law of Moses was given, it made people more accountable*]. But where sin abounded [*where there were abundant sins*], grace did much more abound [*the Atonement is more powerful than sins and can overcome them*]:

21 That as sin hath reigned unto death [*whereas sin leads toward spiritual death*], even so might grace reign through righteousness unto eternal life by Jesus Christ our Lord [*the grace of God, demonstrated by the Atonement, enables us to attain eternal life through personal righteousness*].

ROMANS 6

Having taught that the Atonement of Jesus Christ overcomes the Fall of Adam, Paul will now turn his attention to the opportunity for these people to repent and be baptized, in order to benefit from the full gospel of Jesus Christ, who fulfilled the law of Moses and brought the higher law that enables us to attain exaltation.

1 WHAT shall we say then? Shall we continue in sin, that grace may abound [*should we go right on committing more and more sins so that there is more and more opportunity for the Atonement to work for us*]?

2 God forbid [*absolutely not*]. How shall we, that are dead to sin, live any longer therein [*how could we who are trying to stop sinning possibly be content to continue in our sins*]?

Paul will now give a beautiful explanation of why we are baptized, including the symbolism involved in baptism by immersion. Pay close attention to his careful use of highly descriptive vocabulary words as he teaches that when we are baptized, we, in effect, bury our old sinful selves with Christ in the grave. Then, we come forth with Christ as new people, "born again," starting a new life of dedication to the gospel and personal righteousness. Compare with Mosiah 27:26.

3 Know ye not, that so many of us as were baptized into Jesus Christ were baptized into his death [*are you aware that those of us who have been baptized were baptized so that Christ's death, resurrection, and so forth could cleanse us*]?

4 Therefore we are buried with him by baptism into death [*being*

buried in the waters of baptism is symbolic of accepting Christ's invitation to join Him in burying our old sinful selves and thus letting our sinful ways die]: that like as Christ was raised up from the dead by the glory of the Father, even so we also should walk in newness of life [*so that, just as Christ came forth from the grave in glory, we can come forth from the waters of baptism into a new life filled with the glory and influence of the Father*].

5 For if we have been planted [*buried*] together in the likeness of his death [*if we have buried our old sinful lives, through His Atonement*], we shall be also in the likeness of his resurrection [*we will have a glorious new life in the gospel*]:

In verse 6, next, Paul uses a very strong word to describe the effort sometimes needed on our part to repent of sins. He uses the word "crucify." This implies that some sins require much pain and godly sorrow to be rid of. Indeed, changing friends, being cut off from family, going through withdrawals from chemical dependency, confessing serious sin to the bishop and facing possible consequences, refraining from Sabbath-breaking activities, cutting back on expenses in order to pay an honest tithe, and so forth, can be painful, but walking in "newness of life" (verse 4) makes it far more than worthwhile to "crucify" our sins.

6 Knowing this, that our old man [*our old lifestyle*] is crucified with him [*Christ*], that the body of sin [*our past sins*] might be destroyed, that henceforth [*from now on*] we should not serve sin.

The JST makes a very significant doctrinal change to verse 7, next.

7 For he that is dead is freed from sin.

JST Romans 6:7

7 For he that is dead **to sin** is freed from sin.

8 Now if we be dead with Christ [*if we follow Christ such that our sins die through His Atoning sacrifice*], we believe that we shall also live with him [*we will come alive in the sweetness of the gospel life here on earth and will live with Him eternally*]:

9 Knowing that Christ being raised from the dead dieth no more [*will never die again*]; death hath no more dominion [*power*] over him.

10 For in that he died, he died unto sin once [*in dying, the Savior suffered once for all sins; see 2 Nephi 9:21–22*]: but in that he liveth, he liveth unto God [*in being resurrected, He now joins the Father in eternal life*].

11 Likewise reckon ye also yourselves to be dead indeed unto sin [*consider your sins to be dead and buried*], but alive unto God through Jesus Christ our Lord [*and now you are alive spiritually and*

enjoy the blessings the Father has for you because of the Atonement of Jesus Christ].

12 Let not sin therefore reign in your mortal body, that ye should obey it in the lusts thereof [*do not let sin rule over you here in mortality*].

In verse 13, next, Paul uses "members," meaning body parts such as head, arms, legs, eyes, ears, etc., to represent the possibility that some parts of your life and personality may be vulnerable to certain temptations.

13 Neither yield ye your members as instruments of unrighteousness unto sin [*don't allow yourself to give in to specific sins for which you may have particular weakness*]: but yield yourselves unto God [*give in to God's commandments rather than giving in to sin*], as those that are alive from the dead [*like those Saints have done who repented from sinful lifestyles and are now "alive" in Christ*], and your members as instruments of righteousness unto God [*exercise self-control such that your "members," in other words, all aspects of your life and personality, are in harmony with God*].

14 For sin shall not have dominion over you [*sin will not rule over you*]: for ye are not under the law [*because you are not living under the law of Moses*], but under grace [*rather, you are living under the grace of God which allows the Atonement to cleanse you from sin*].

JST Romans 6:14

14 **For in so doing** sin shall not have dominion over you; for ye are not under the law, but under grace.

15 What then? shall we sin, because we are not under the law [*the law of Moses*], but under grace [*the higher law brought by Christ; in other words, do we have license to sin and not worry about "works" anymore because of "grace"*]? God forbid [*absolutely not*].

16 Know ye not, that to whom ye yield yourselves servants to obey, his servants ye are to whom ye obey; whether of sin unto death [*spiritual death*], or of obedience unto righteousness [*don't you realize that if you yield to sin, you are sin's servants, and if you yield to God, you are God's servants*]? [*In other words, whose servants would you rather be?*]

17 But God be thanked, that ye were the servants of sin, but ye have obeyed from the heart that form of doctrine which was delivered you [*thanks be to God that you, who once had sin as your master, have now repented deep in your hearts and obeyed the true doctrine of Christ which was preached to you*].

JST Romans 6:17

17 But God be thanked, that ye **are not** the servants of sin, **for** ye have obeyed from the heart that form of doctrine which was delivered you.

18 Being then made free from

sin [*having repented and been cleansed from sin*], ye became the servants of righteousness.

19 I speak after the manner of men because of the infirmity of your flesh [*I have to put what I am saying in simple terms, using examples from your daily lives because you are still weak in the gospel of Christ*]: for as ye have yielded your members servants to uncleanness [*since you have yielded to various sins in the past and thus been servants of sin*] and to iniquity unto iniquity [*and your own wickedness then invited you to commit additional sins*]; even so now yield your members servants to righteousness unto holiness [*now exercise self-control and become servants of righteousness and holiness*].

JST Romans 6:19

19 I speak after the manner of men because of the infirmity of your flesh; for as ye have **in times past yielded** your members servants to uncleanness and to iniquity unto iniquity; even so now yield your members servants to righteousness unto holiness.

20 For when ye were the servants of sin, ye were free from righteousness [*when you were ruled by your sins, you were free from the blessings of righteousness*].

21 What fruit [*results in your lives*] had ye then in those things whereof ye are now ashamed [*what good did your sins, of which you are now ashamed, do for you*]? for the end of those things [*the end result of sin and wickedness*] is death [*spiritual death*].

22 But now being made free from sin, and become servants to God, ye have your fruit unto holiness, and the end everlasting life. [*Having been cleansed from sin through faith, repentance, baptism, and so forth, and having become worthy servants of God, you have become holy, and your goal is now exaltation.*]

By the way, "everlasting life," in verse 22, above, means "exaltation." "Eternal life" is another term for exaltation. As you know, everyone will be resurrected, no matter what their lifestyle is. So, everybody will live forever. This is referred to in the scriptures as "immortality" (see Moses 1:39). "Everlasting life, "exaltation," and "eternal life" all mean the kind of life that God has.

Verse 23, next, is rather well-known and oft-quoted.

23 For the wages of sin is death [*the ultimate pay for unrepentant sin is spiritual death and being cut off from the presence of God forever*]; but the gift of God is eternal life [*exaltation*] through Jesus Christ our Lord.

ROMANS 7

Paul will now emphasize again that the law of Moses is no longer in force, that it was fulfilled by Christ and that obedience to Christ's gospel is designed to develop and strengthen inward righteousness. He will use the imagery of marriage between a husband and wife, in Jewish culture, to represent the temporary nature and purpose of the law of Moses. He will, in effect, teach that just as when her husband dies, the wife is no longer bound to him, so also with the law of Moses. During the time it was in effect, from Moses to the beginning of Christ's mission, the people were bound to it. But with the coming of Christ, the law "died," having fulfilled its purpose, and thus, people are no longer bound to it.

1 KNOW ye not, brethren, (for I speak to them that know the law,) [*the law of Moses*] how that the law hath dominion over a man as long as he liveth?

JST Romans 7:1

1 Know ye not, brethren, (for I speak to them that know the law,) how that the law hath dominion over a man **only** as long as he liveth?

2 For the woman which hath an husband is bound by the law to her husband so long as he liveth; but if the husband be dead, she is loosed from the law of her husband [*she is no longer bound to her marriage vows made to her husband*].

JST Romans 7:2

2 For the woman which hath **a** husband is bound by the law to her husband **only as** long as he liveth; **for** if the husband be dead, she is loosed from the law of her husband.

3 So then if, while her husband liveth, she be married to another man [*if she were to marry another man while her husband is still alive*], she shall be called an adulteress [*she would be an adulteress*]: but if her husband be dead [*has died*], she is free from that law; so that she is no adulteress, though [*even though*] she be married [*gets married*] to another man.

4 Wherefore [*therefore*], my brethren, ye also are become dead to the law [*you are set free from the law of Moses because it has died, in effect*] by the body of Christ [*by the gospel brought by Jesus Christ*]; that ye should be married to another [*it is time for you to "marry" another gospel*], even to him [*Christ*] who is raised [*who has been resurrected*] from the dead, that we should bring forth fruit [*worthy lives*] unto God [*so that we can live lives worthy of living with God*].

We will need a lot of help from the JST [*Joseph Smith Translation of the Bible*] to understand verses 5 through 25. Remember, also, that Paul will continue to use much repetition to drive home the point that the Jews are no longer bound to the law of Moses, which was a schoolmaster law to help prepare them for the full gospel taught by the Savior. Because he uses so much repetition, some readers begin to look for other meanings to what Paul is saying, thinking to themselves, "Surely he wouldn't keep saying the same thing over and over so many times, so there must be some additional meaning I am missing." Such is usually not the case. He is repeating because it is a tremendous transition for the Jews to change from an entire culture and upbringing, where the law of Moses was everything to most people, to the gospel of Christ where inward, deep personal righteousness is the emphasis, along with the ordinances of salvation and exaltation.

5 For when we were in the flesh [*carnally minded, living sinfully, not yet redeemed by Christ*], the motions of sins, which were by the law, did work in our members to bring forth fruit [*unworthy lives*] unto death [*which would ultimately lead to spiritual death*].

The JST makes a major change to verse 5, above.

JST Romans 7:5

5 For when we were in the flesh, the motions of sin, which were **not according to** the law, did work in our members to bring forth fruit unto death.

6 But now we are delivered from the law [*In other words, we are now set free from the law of Moses, to which we were previously bound, by the gospel of Christ.*], that being dead wherein we were held [*In other words, we are no longer bound to the law of Moses*]; that we should serve in newness of spirit [*so that we can be "new people" serving Christ*], and not in the oldness of the letter [*and not be caught up in the old "letter of the law" which did not have power to save us*].

JST Romans 7:6

6 But now we are delivered from the law **wherein we were held, being dead to the law**, that we should serve in newness of spirit, and not in the oldness of the letter.

7 What shall we say then? Is the law sin [*was it a sin to live the law of Moses*]? God forbid [*absolutely not*]. Nay, I had not known sin, but by the law [*I would not have known what sin was without the teachings of the law of Moses*]: for I had not known lust [*unrighteous desire for something*], except the law had said, Thou shalt not covet [*without the law of Moses, I would not have known that it is a sin to covet*].

8 But sin, taking occasion by the commandment, wrought [*caused*] in me all manner [*kinds*] of concupiscence [*strong desires for that which God forbids*]. [*In other words, once the law of Moses pointed out to us what things were sinful and thus forbidden by God, it seems that those sins became all the more tempting.*] For without the law sin was dead [*when people don't know the law, they are not held accountable*].

9 For I was alive without the law once: but when the commandment came, sin revived, and I died. [*In other words, at one time in my life, I (Paul) lived the law of Moses very strictly and felt spiritually alive. I was not accountable for Christ's*

gospel because I was not familiar with it. However, when I became aware of the commandments of Christ, I became accountable and thus was a sinner, and found myself to be spiritually dead.]

JST Romans 7:9

9 For **once I was alive without transgression of the law**, but when the commandment **of Christ** came, sin revived, and I died.

10 And the commandment, which was ordained to life, I found to be unto death. [*When I heard the gospel and commandments of Christ, which lead to eternal life, but didn't yet believe, it made me accountable and thus condemned me to spiritual death and being separated from God forever.*]

JST Romans 7:10

10 **And when I believed not the commandment of Christ which came, which was ordained to life, I found it condemned me unto death.**

11 For sin, taking occasion by the commandment, deceived me, and by it slew me.

JST Romans 7:11

11 For sin, taking occasion, **denied the commandment, and deceived me; and by it I was slain** [*spiritually*].

12 Wherefore the law is holy, and the commandment holy, and just, and good. [*In spite of the wrong way I was heading, I found out that Christ's gospel is holy, correct, and good.*]

JST Romans 7:12

12 **Nevertheless, I found the law to be holy, and the commandment to be** holy, and just, and good.

13 Was then that which is good [*Christ's gospel*] made death unto me [*did Christ's gospel ultimately cause spiritual death in me*]? God forbid [*absolutely not*]. But sin, that it might appear sin, working death in me by that which is good; that sin by the commandment might become exceeding sinful.

JST Romans 7:13

13 Was then that which is good made death unto me? God forbid. But sin, that it might appear sin **by that which is good working death in me** [*sin clearly shows up as sin in the light of the gospel of Christ, and thus we see how dangerous it is*]; that sin, by the commandment, might become exceeding sinful [*as we compare sin against the gospel of Christ, we see all the better how dangerous sin is*]."

14 For we know that the law is spiritual: but I am carnal, sold under sin.

JST Romans 7:14

14 For we know that the **commandment** [*the gospel of Christ*] is spiritual [*leads to worthiness for eternal life*] but **when I was under law** [*when I was living the law of Moses*], **I was yet carnal**

[*I was not redeemed, not living the higher law required for exaltation*], sold under sin [*still living under the burden of sin.*]

Verse 15, next, seems to have been completely scrambled somewhere in the process of being put in our King James Bible. It provides a wonderful opportunity for us to witness the inspiration and power of God coming to us through the Prophet Joseph Smith. Through the Prophet's inspired translation, we see that Paul is telling the Roman Saints that he has gained great spiritual strength from the gospel of Christ.

15 For that which I do I allow not: for what I would, that do I not; but what I hate, that do I.

JST Romans 7:15–16

15 **But now I am spiritual; for that which I am commanded to do, I do; and that which I am commanded not to allow, I allow not.**

16 **For what I know is not right, I would not do; for that which is sin, I hate.**

16 If then I do that which I would not, I consent unto the law that it is good. [*I acknowledge by my actions that the gospel of Christ is good*]; and I am not condemned [*and thus I am not stopped in my progression toward eternal life with God*].

JST Romans 7:17

17 If then I do not that which I would not **allow**, I consent unto the law, that it is good; and I am not condemned.

Remember that the JST verse numbers are sometimes not the same as the verse numbers in the Bible.

17 Now then it is no more I that do it, but sin that dwelleth in me. [*Now I am truly trying to live Christ's gospel and overcome and repent of my sins.*]

JST Romans 7:18

18 Now then, it is no more I that **do sin**; but **I seek to subdue that sin which dwelleth in me.**

18 For I know that in me (*that is, in my flesh,*) dwelleth no good thing: for to will [*to want to do right*] is present with me; but how to perform that which is good I find not.

JST Romans 7:19

19 For I know that in me, that is, in my flesh [*my mortal weaknesses*], dwelleth no good thing; for to will is present with me, **but to perform** that which is good I find not, **only in Christ**.[*In other words, the flesh is weak; there is no good in yielding to my sins, imperfections, weaknesses, etc. I want to do good and be righteous. The only way to become righteous is through Christ and His Atonement.*]

19 For the good that I would I do not: but the evil which I would not, that I do.

The JST uses two verses to deal with Bible verse 19, above.

JST Romans 7:20–21

20 For the good that I would **have done when under the law, I find not to be good; therefore, I do it not**. [*In other words, I have learned that all the good I wanted to do in harmony with the law of Moses still couldn't save me and therefore was not good for me in the ultimate sense of gaining eternal life. Therefore, I no longer build my life around the law of Moses.*]

21 But the evil which I would not do **under the law, I find to be good; that, I do.** [*But the law of Moses pointed out many sins which we should avoid. This is good, and I avoid those sins.*]

Remember that the Savior was constantly criticized by the Jewish religious leaders for violating the law of Moses and their nit-picky interpretations of it. For example, they criticized Him for healing the sick on the Sabbath. They criticized Him for associating with sinners, for eating with them, for teaching that it is inward righteousness rather than outward appearance that saves us. They criticized Him and His disciples for not washing their hands ritually before eating, as prescribed by the law of Moses and embellished by the traditions of the Jews. They criticized Him for teaching that the law of Moses could not save them and that they must repent and be baptized and receive the Gift of the Holy Ghost and follow its promptings in order to have eternal life. This cultural and religious background and setting is helpful in understanding Joseph Smith's corrections of what Paul says next in verse 20.

20 Now if I do that I would not, it is no more I that do it, but sin that dwelleth in me.

JST Romans 7:22

22 Now if I do that, **through the assistance of Christ, I would not do under the law, I am not under the law; and it is no more that I seek to do wrong, but to subdue** sin that dwelleth in me. [*In other words, If, with the help of Christ and His gospel, I now do things that I would not have done under the law of Moses, because I am no longer bound to the law of Moses, it is because my focus has changed from constantly studying what sins to avoid according to the law, to simply wanting to be good deep down inside myself.*]

21 I find then a law, that, when I would do good, evil is present with me.

22 For I delight in the law of God after the inward man: [*note that JST verse 23, next, covers both Bible verses 21 and 22 here.*]

JST Romans 7:23

23 I find then **that under the law, that** when I would do good evil **was** present with me; for I delight in the law of God after the inward man. [*I find that when*

I was living strictly according to the law of Moses, focusing so intently on outward appearances, it still allowed me to be evil while appearing good. Now, I find delight in living the gospel of Christ which focuses on cleansing the inner man.]

Remember that the word "members" as used next in verse 23, are members of the body such as eyes, ears, tongue, hands, feet, etc. which can get us into temptation and trouble.

23 But I see another law in my members, warring against the law of my mind, and bringing me into captivity to the law of sin which is in my members. [*In other words, the gospel of Christ is now firmly imprinted in my mind. I want to live true to it, but my weaknesses, imperfections, sins, etc. still make war against the righteous intent of my mind.*]

JST Romans 7:24–25

24 **And now** I see another law, **even the commandment of Christ, and it is imprinted in my mind**.

25 **But my members are** warring against the law of my mind, and bringing me into captivity to the law of sin which is in my members.

24 O wretched man that I am! who shall deliver me from the body of this death?

JST Romans 7:26

26 **And if I subdue not the sin which is in me** [*if I do not control my tendencies to commit sin*], **but with the flesh serve the law of sin** [*but give in to my mortal weaknesses and thus commit sins*]; O wretched man that I am! who shall deliver me from the body of this death [*from the sins and temptations of mortality which could lead me to spiritual death*]?

25 I thank God through Jesus Christ our Lord. So then with the mind I myself serve the law of God; but with the flesh the law of sin.

JST Romans 7:27

27 I thank God through Jesus Christ our Lord, **then, that so** with the mind I myself serve the law of God [*I rejoice in thanksgiving to the Father, that because of Christ and his Atonement, the desire of my mind to be righteous can be fulfilled as I serve and follow Christ's gospel*].

Did you notice that the JST verse above leaves out the last phrase of verse 25 in the Bible?

ROMANS 8

Remember that Paul is addressing members of the Church, Jewish converts in Rome, who still tend to be very caught up in trying to keep the law of Moses according to their culture and upbringing before joining the Church. Many of them struggle with the transition from the law of Moses, with its exacting rites and daily spelled-out performances to the much less structured gospel brought by Christ which emphasizes genuine personal righteousness. They still believe that any convert who does not keep the law of Moses, even though they have been baptized and have received the Gift of the Holy Ghost, will be condemned. Paul, with great teaching skill and inspiration, continues in this chapter to remind these Saints that salvation and eternal life come through Christ and His gospel, not through the law of Moses. As mentioned previously, Paul is using much repetition in these chapters to drive home his main teaching points.

1 THERE is therefore now no condemnation [*being stopped in progression toward eternal life*] to them which are in Christ Jesus [*to those who follow Christ*], who walk not after the flesh [*who do not yield to the temptations of mortality nor follow the details of the law of Moses*], but after the Spirit [*but yield to the guidance of the Holy Ghost*].

2 For the law of the Spirit of life in Christ Jesus [*Following the law of the Spirit which leads to eternal life through Christ's gospel*] hath made me free from the law of sin and death [*has set me free from the lasting effects of sin and spiritual death*].

3 For what the law [*the law of Moses*] could not do, in that it was weak through the flesh [*it was given to people who were very weak and caught up in sins of the flesh, to strengthen them to the point, eventually, that they could accept Christ's gospel*], God [*the Father*] sending his own Son [*Jesus Christ*] in the likeness of sinful flesh [*in a mortal body*], and for sin [*to atone for our sins*], condemned sin in the flesh [*condemned all forms of wickedness*]:

4 That the righteousness of the law might be fulfilled in us [*so that the goal of the law of Moses might find fulfillment in us, having helped us become righteous enough to accept Jesus and His higher laws*], who walk not after the flesh [*who have turned from sin*], but after the Spirit [*and are following the promptings of the Holy Ghost*].

5 For they that are after the flesh [*those who focus on desires of the mortal body*] do mind the things of the flesh [*yield to the temptations of the flesh*]; but they that are after the Spirit [*but those who are spiritual*] the things of the Spirit [*yield to the promptings of the Holy Ghost*].

Verse 6, next, is often quoted in gospel lessons and discussions.

6 For to be carnally minded is death [*to focus on bodily appetites and to give in to them leads us to spiritual death*]; but to be spiritually minded is life and peace [*but to focus on spiritual things brings peace now and eternal life in the world to come*].

7 Because the carnal mind is enmity against God [*to be focused*

on worldly sins pits us against God]: for it is not subject to the law of God, neither indeed can be [*the carnal mind does not allow itself to be ruled by God's laws, therefore it is very dangerous to us and our potential for exaltation*].

8 So then they that are in the flesh cannot please God. [*In other words, those who yield to the temptations of the flesh cannot be pleasing to God.*]

JST Romans 8:8

> 8 So then they that are **after** the flesh cannot please God.

9 But ye [*you Jewish converts to the Church in Rome*] are not in the flesh, but in the Spirit, if so be that the Spirit of God dwell in you. [*In other words, you Saints in Rome are no longer following the desires of the flesh but are following the Spirit toward salvation.*] Now if any man have not the Spirit of Christ, he is none of his [*if anyone does not have and follow the Spirit of Christ, he does not yet belong to Christ*].

JST Romans 8:9

> 9 But ye are not **after** the flesh, but **after** the Spirit, if so be that the Spirit of God dwell in you. Now if any man have not the Spirit of Christ, he is none of his.

10 And if Christ be in you, the body is dead because of sin; but the Spirit is life because of righteousness.

JST Romans 8:10

> 10 And if Christ be in you, **though the body shall die because of sin, yet the Spirit is life**, because of righteousness [*If you allow Christ to rule your life, even though your body dies because of Adam's transgression, your personal righteousness will yet lead to eternal life*].

11 But if the Spirit of him [*Heavenly Father*] that raised up [*resurrected*] Jesus from the dead dwell in you, he [*Heavenly Father who*] that raised up Christ from the dead shall also quicken your mortal bodies [*will make you spiritually alive, born again, during your life on earth*] by his Spirit that dwelleth in you.

JST Romans 8:11

> 11 **And** if the Spirit of him that raised up Jesus from the dead, dwell in you, he that raised up Christ from the dead shall also quicken your mortal bodies by his Spirit that dwelleth in you.

12 Therefore, brethren, we are debtors, not to the flesh, to live after the flesh [*in other words, we have an obligation to avoid yielding to the temptations of the mortal body*].

13 For if ye live after the flesh, ye shall die [*if you submit to sin and live wickedly, you will die spiritually*]: but if ye through the Spirit [*with the help of the Spirit*] do mortify [*kill, do away with*] the deeds of the body [*the sins of the flesh*], ye shall live. [*In other words, if*

you follow the promptings of the Holy Ghost and thus keep repenting successfully, you will do away with evil in your lives and will be spiritually alive and will come unto Christ.]

JST Romans 8:13

13 For if ye live after the flesh, **unto sin**, ye shall die; but if ye through the Spirit do mortify the deeds of the body, ye shall live **unto Christ.**

The phrase "sons of God" in verse 14, next, is a term meaning exaltation. See Mosiah 5:7 and D&C 76:24.

14 For as many as are led by the Spirit of God, they are the sons of God [*ultimately end up in exaltation, meaning the highest degree of glory in the celestial kingdom*].

15 For ye have not received the spirit of bondage again to fear [*with the gospel of Christ, you have not been given something which focuses on fear and bondage, as did the law of Moses*]; but ye have received the Spirit of adoption [*through Christ's gospel, you receive the Spirit of being included in God's family, which is intimate, loving, and close*], whereby we cry [*which enables us to exclaim*], Abba, Father [*Abba is an intimate, familiar name for our Father in Heaven, see Bible Dictionary under "Abba."*]

The end of verse 15, above, is most beautiful indeed. Paul tells these converts that, through following the Savior's gospel, they will return to their rightful status of being true sons and daughters of God, belonging to Him and being privileged to call him "Daddy." This is a pleasant reminder that the family unit exists in exaltation.

In verses 16–17, next, Paul uses vocabulary which specifically reminds the Roman Saints, and us, that we are literally the children of God and can literally become like Him. These are two of the most important doctrinal verses in Paul's writings.

16 The Spirit itself beareth witness with our spirit, that we are the children of God [*the Holy Ghost tells our spirit that we are indeed Heavenly Father's children; see Acts 17:28–29, Hebrews 12:9*]:

17 And if children [*since we are the Father's children*], then heirs; heirs of God [*then we stand to inherit all he has; see D&C 84:36–38*], and joint-heirs with Christ [*we inherit all things, jointly with Christ*]; if so be that we suffer with him [*if we sacrifice whatever in necessary to follow the Savior*], that we may be also glorified together [*that we may be received into celestial glory and exaltation with Him*].

18 For I reckon that the sufferings of this present time are not worthy to be compared with the glory which shall be revealed in us. [*There is no comparison between the small price we pay to attain exaltation and the actual glory of it.*]

JST Romans 8:18

18 For I reckon that the sufferings of this present time are not worthy to be **named** with the glory which shall be revealed in us.

19 For the earnest expectation of the creature [*creation, material universe; see Romans 8:19, footnote b*] waiteth for the manifestation of the sons of God. [*All creation is waiting anxiously for the righteous to become "sons of God." In other words, the whole purpose of the creation was to enable us to become sons and daughters of God who are lifted up or exalted to become like He is.*]

20 For the creature [*mankind*] was made subject to vanity, not willingly, but by reason of him [*Christ*] who hath subjected the same in hope, [*In other words, we, mankind, were given the trials and tribulations of mortality and were given hope of overcoming them through Christ who was subjected to all tribulations and overcame them, thus giving us the bright hope (2 Nephi 31:20) of overcoming them also with His help.*]

JST Romans 8:20

20 For the creature was made subject to **tribulation** not willingly, but by reason of him who hath subjected **it** in hope;

Next, in verse 21, Paul explains why we can have such an encouraging "hope."

21 Because the creature itself [*people who follow Christ*] also shall be delivered from the bondage of corruption [*the captivity of sin*] into the glorious liberty of the children of God [*to the freedom which comes to the followers of God; see John 8:32 where we are taught that "the truth shall make you free"*].

22 For we know that the whole creation [*all people*] groaneth and travaileth in pain together until now. [*All people groan and suffer in sin until they accept the redemption which is now being made available to you through Christ and His gospel.*]

23 And not only they, but ourselves also, which have the firstfruits of the Spirit [*even those of us who are among the first to have been baptized and received the Gift of the Holy Ghost*], even we ourselves groan within ourselves, waiting for the adoption [*struggling against sin as we await adoption as joint heirs with Christ, i.e., redemption and exaltation*], to wit [*namely*], the redemption of our body [*possibly referring to the future when our mortal body, which is subject to all kinds of temptations now, has been resurrected and we are in celestial glory where such temptations no longer abound*].

24 For we are saved by hope: but hope that is seen is not hope: for what a man seeth, why doth he yet hope for? [*In other words, if we could see the end result of our hope, we wouldn't have to have hope.*]

25 But if we hope for that we see not [*if we have hope to see God and live with Him eventually*], then do we with patience wait for it. [*Hope gives us the patience to wait for and live worthy of eternal life.*]

JST Romans 8:25

25 But if we hope for that we see not, then **with patience we do** wait for it.

26 Likewise the Spirit also helpeth our infirmities [*the Holy Ghost helps us overcome our sins, weaknesses, imperfections, etc.*]: for we know not what we should pray for as we ought [*even our prayers fall short of being what they should be*]: but the Spirit itself maketh intercession for us with groanings which cannot be uttered [*the Holy Ghost is very interested in helping us come unto Christ*].

27 And he [*Christ*] that searcheth the hearts [*who knows what is in our hearts, even though we fall short in expressing our feelings in prayer*] knoweth what is the mind of the Spirit, because he [*Christ*] maketh intercession [*performed the Atonement*] for the saints according to the will of God [*the Father*].

Next, in verses 28–31, Paul refers to the doctrine of foreordination and God's foreknowledge of us because we lived with Him in premortal life. We understand that each person who comes to earth "is a beloved spirit son or daughter of heavenly parents" (Proclamation on the Family, September 23, 1995) and that as such, each is "called" or "foreordained" to come to earth and to successfully return to live with God forever. Unfortunately, the King James Bible translators chose to use the word "predestinate" instead of the word "foreordain," which reflects the meaning of the original Greek from which they translated. "Predestination" indicates loss of agency. "Foreordination" indicates being called and capable but preserves agency as to whether or not we live true to our potential. Because of this unfortunate use of "predestination" in these and other verses, many are burdened and shackled with the false belief that some have been chosen or "predestinated" by God to succeed, whereas others are predestinated by God to fail.

28 And we know that all things work together for good to them that love God, to them who are the called [*who are foreordained; see verses 29–30, next*] according to his purpose.

29 For whom he did foreknow [*which includes the noble and great in premortality, as mentioned in Abraham 3:22*], he also did predestinate [*foreordain, see footnote 29c in your Bible*] to be conformed to the image of his Son [*to successfully follow the Savior and become "joint heirs" (Romans 8:17) with Him, and thus become like the Father*], that he might be the firstborn among many brethren [*that such might be exalted*].

JST Romans 8:29

29 For him whom he did foreknow, he also did predestinate to be conformed to **his own image**, that he might be the firstborn among many brethren.

30 Moreover whom he did predestinate [*foreordain*], them he also called: and whom he called, them he also justified: and whom he justified, them he also glorified.

JST Romans 8:30

30 Moreover, **him whom** he did predestinate, **him** he also called; and **him** whom he called, **him** he also **sanctified** [*meaning to be made pure and holy, fit to be in the presence of God, because of their worthiness to have the Atonement cleanse them*]; and **him** whom he **sanctified**, **him** he also glorified.

31 What shall we then say to these things [*how should we respond to these wonderful doctrines*]? [*Answer: with great hope and confidence in our potential for exaltation!*] If God be for us, who can be against us?

JST Romans 8:31

31 What shall we then say to these things? If God be for us, who can **prevail** against us?

Did you notice the important change in the JST verse above? Joseph Smith changed "who can **be** against us" to "who can **prevail** against us?" Anyone can be against us and try to keep us from salvation, but if we strive faithfully to get on and stay on the covenant path, with God on our side, no one can "prevail," meaning win against us or keep us from succeeding!

32 He [*the Father*] that spared not his own Son [*Christ*], but delivered him up [*allowed Jesus to go through the suffering and humiliation of the Atonement*] for us all, how shall he not with him also freely give us all things? [*If the Father went through so much to give us the Atonement through His own Son, why wouldn't He also give us all things (meaning exaltation), which is the whole purpose of everything we have been talking about?*]

33 Who shall lay any thing to the charge of God's elect [*who could possibly hold the Saints of God back from exaltation*]? It is God that justifieth [*it is Christ who is the final judge; see John 5:22*].

34 Who is he that condemneth [*who is in charge of determining who does and who does not make it to exaltation*]? It is Christ that died, yea rather, that is risen again, who is even at the right hand of God, who also maketh intercession for us. [*In other words, in effect, we have great cause to hope for exaltation, in fact, to plan on it if we repent and follow the Savior, because Christ, who suffered and died and was resurrected for us is in a position of power at the right hand of the Father and wants us to succeed! In fact, He*

is our advocate with the Father, interceding between us and our sins as we repent.]

35 Who shall separate us from the love of Christ [*who shall keep the Savior from helping us*]? shall tribulation, or distress, or persecution, or famine, or nakedness, or peril, or sword? [*The answer is given in verse 37.*]

36 As it is written [*in Psalm 44:22*], For thy sake we are killed all the day long; we are accounted as sheep for the slaughter [*we are all mortal and will die one way or another, so, in the eternal perspective, the tribulation, distress, persecution, etc., mentioned in verse 35 are not really important compared to whether or not we live righteously*].

37 Nay, in all these things we are more than conquerors through him that loved us [*we overcome all these things because of the Father's love as demonstrated in offering His Son for our sins*].

38 For I am persuaded, that neither death, nor life, nor angels, nor principalities, nor powers, nor things present, nor things to come,

39 Nor height, nor depth, nor any other creature, shall be able to separate us from the love of God, which is in Christ Jesus our Lord. [*If we are willing and faithful, nothing at all can prevent us from attaining exaltation through Jesus Christ.*]

ROMANS 9

The heading for this chapter, in the Joseph Smith Translation of the Bible (JST) tells us that Paul has tender feelings for these new converts in Rome and in the opening verses of this chapter, he tells them he wishes that he could carry more of their burdens, sorrows, and troubles himself.

Paul will explain how the law of "election" (foreordination) works and will use Israel as an example.

1 I SAY the truth in Christ, I lie not, my conscience also bearing me witness in the Holy Ghost [*I am telling you the absolute truth when I tell you what I'm going to say to you next*],

2 That I have great heaviness and continual sorrow in my heart [*your sorrows and troubles weight heavily in my heart*].

3 For I could wish that myself were accursed from Christ for my brethren, my kinsmen according to the flesh [*in other words, for my fellow Israelites*]:

JST Romans 9:3

3 **(For once I could have wished that myself were accursed from Christ,)** for my brethren, my kinsmen according to the flesh; [*In other words, because of my tender feelings for you, I have felt at times that if you don't make it, I don't want to make it either. See Romans 9:3, footnote b, which refers you to*

Exodus 32:32 where Moses had similar feelings about his people, the children of Israel.]

Paul uses the word "adoption" in verse 4, next. "Adoption" is another word for "election" or being "elected" by God to gain exaltation, because of personal worthiness. See Romans 9:4, footnote 4a. In the sense that Paul uses it, the word "adoption" means to become part of the family of God, by joining the Church, becoming faithful Saints and to thus be "adopted" into the family of God and Christ in exaltation forever. Whereas we are all literal spirit children of God, and thus belonged to His family from the time of our spirit birth in premortality, we now must use our agency wisely, as mortals, to determine whether or not we are "adopted" back into His celestial family to live with Him forever.

4 Who are Israelites; to whom pertaineth the adoption, and the glory, and the covenants, and the giving of the law, and the service of God, and the promises;

JST Romans 9:4

4 Who are Israelites; **of whom are the adoption**, and the glory, and the covenants, and the giving of the law, and the service of God [*In other words, those who are "adopted," are adopted into God's Church and family through making and keeping covenants and receiving all the blessings of the gospel*],

5 Whose are the fathers, and of whom as concerning the flesh Christ came, who is over all, God blessed for ever. Amen.

JST Romans 9:5

5 **And the promises which are made unto the fathers;** and of whom, as concerning the flesh, Christ **was, who is God over all**, blessed **forever**. [*In other words, the promises of exaltation made to our ancestors, particularly Abraham (see Abraham 2:9–11), Isaac, and Jacob, came from God. Christ was from God and came into mortality as the Son of God and has charge of all things on earth, under the Father's direction*]. Amen.

Some Jews held the belief that, because they were direct descendants of Abraham, to whom the blessings of exaltation were promised (Abraham 2:9–11; Genesis 12:1–3; 17:1–8), they were guaranteed entrance to heaven. Furthermore, they believed that all other people, because they were not direct descendants of Abraham, Isaac, and Jacob, would forever be second-class citizens in God's kingdom. Paul deals with that false belief, beginning in verse 6, next.

6 Not as though the word of God hath taken none effect. For they are not all Israel, which are of Israel: [*All people who are bloodline Israelites are not necessarily true, covenant-keeping Israel, or God's people. In other words, it is not as if God's promises are not valid, in the fact that some*

of Abraham's descendants won't make it to heaven. It is simply that some of His descendants are not worthy of receiving God's promises of exaltation.]

Paul uses repetition much, as a teaching tool, and will repeat the message of verse 6 again in verses 7 and 8.

7 Neither, because they are the seed of Abraham, are they all children [*in other words, just because they are all the descendants of Abraham doesn't necessarily mean they are all "children of God" or righteous Saints*]: but, In Isaac shall thy seed be called [*Isaac had the same blessings promised to him and his posterity*].

JST Romans 9:7

7 Neither, because they are **all children of Abraham, are they the seed** [*the Lord's people*]; but, In Isaac shall thy seed be called.

8 That is, They which are the children of the flesh [*those who are literal descendants of Abraham and Isaac*], these are not the children of God [*do not automatically get exaltation*]: but the children of the promise [*those who live righteously*] are counted for the seed [*are ultimately the Lord's people and the ones to whom the blessings promised to Abraham's seed or descendants will come*].

9 For this is the word of promise [*Here is what the Lord promised Abraham; see Genesis 17:16*], At this time will I come, and Sara [*Abraham's* wife] shall have a son.

10 And not only this; but when Rebecca [*Isaac's wife*] also had conceived by one, even by our father Isaac [*see Genesis 25:20–23*];

JST Romans 9:10

10 And not only **Sarah**; but when Rebecca also had conceived by one, **our father Isaac**,

11 (For the children being not yet born, neither having done any good or evil [*even though Rebecca and Isaac's twins had not been born yet, God told Rebecca about them*], that the purpose of God according to election [*foreordination*] might stand [*might take place*], not of works, but of him [*not merely because of genealogy, etc., but because of the will of God*] that calleth;)

12 It was said unto her [*Rebecca, the mother of twins, Esau and Jacob*], The elder [*the older twin*] shall serve the younger [*Esau will serve Jacob*].

13 As it is written [*Malachi 1:2–3*], Jacob have I loved, but Esau have I hated [*in effect, I was able to bless Jacob but had to withhold blessings from Esau*].

The word "hated" in verse 13, above, can cause problems. Obviously, God loves everyone. See John 3:16. Therefore, the word "hated" in this context has to mean people whom God can't bless as He would like to because of their personal wickedness.

14 What shall we say then? Is there unrighteousness with God [*Is God unrighteous? Is He prejudiced*]? God forbid [*Absolutely not!*].

15 For he saith to Moses, I will have mercy on whom I will have mercy, and I will have compassion on whom I will have compassion. [*In other words, I am the Judge and know how to strike the proper balance between justice and mercy.*]

16 So then it is not of him that willeth, nor of him that runneth, but of God that sheweth mercy. [*We do not dictate to God as to how He should run things, rather, He determines when mercy is appropriate and beneficial.*]

17 For the scripture [*Exodus 9:13–21*] saith unto Pharaoh, Even for this same purpose have I raised thee up, that I might shew my power in thee, and that my name might be declared throughout all the earth. [*God used Pharaoh to show His power. Because of Pharaoh's arrogance and refusal to humble himself before God, God's power was dramatically displayed to the children of Israel.*]

18 Therefore hath he [*God*] mercy on whom he will have mercy, and whom he will he hardeneth [*leaves to his own stubbornness, hardheartedness; see Romans 9:18, footnote b*].

19 Thou wilt say then unto me [*in spite of what I have been teaching you so far, some of you Roman converts will still ask me*], Why doth he [*God*] yet find fault [*why does God still bless some people more than others*]? For who hath resisted his will [*who would go against God once they know His will*]?

20 Nay [*you know better than that*] but, O man, who art thou that repliest against God [*who do you think you are, criticizing God*]? Shall the thing formed say to him that formed it, Why hast thou made me thus [*is it proper for the thing that is made to say to the person who made it, "Why did you make me this way?"*] ?

21 Hath not the potter [*one who makes clay pots*] power over the clay, of [*with*] the same lump to make one vessel [*pot*] unto honour, and another unto dishonour?

Unless you think in terms of premortal life and our agency to choose there, and of mortal life and our agency to choose here, between right and wrong, you might end up believing in predestination because of what Paul says here. The potter in verse 21, above, symbolizes God, and the clay pots symbolize people. Taken out of the context of all the scriptures, this verse makes it sound like God makes some people good and some people evil in order to work out His plan for us here on earth. Such is definitely not the case. Jesus Christ is the righteous judge of all people (see John 5:22), and on final Judgment Day, He will, by virtue of His role as our final judge, "make" or designate some as righteous or "honorable" (end of verse 21) and some as unrighteous or "dishonorable" (verse 21), depending on how each used agency.

22 What if God, willing [*able*] to shew his wrath, and to make his power known, endured with much longsuffering [*patience*] the vessels of wrath [*the wicked*] fitted to destruction [*who are worthy of destruction*]: [*In other words, what if God showed great patience toward the wicked rather than destroying them when they seem to deserve it?*]

3 And that he might make known the riches of his glory on the vessels of mercy [*people to whom He shows mercy*], which he had afore prepared [*whom he had foreordained, not predestined*] unto glory,

24 Even us [*like each of us*], whom he hath called, not of the Jews only, but also of the Gentiles [*not just those of us who are Abraham's descendants, but all others too*]?

25 As he saith also in Osee [*Hosea 2:23; Zechariah 13:9*], I will call them my people, which were not my people; and her beloved, which was not beloved.

Paul's message here is that none of us is perfect, and all deserve punishment, but God is very patient and merciful and encouraging. He wants us each to return worthily to live with Him forever. Therefore, the Savior "stretches forth His hands unto [*us*] all the day long" (Jacob 6:4), encouraging us to repent, be faithful, and return to the Father through Him.

26 And it shall come to pass, that in the place where it was said unto them, Ye are not my people; there shall they be called the children of the living God. [*The Savior's Atonement will have much success, and many who once were not worthy of returning to the Father, therefore were "not My people" at the time, will repent, be forgiven, and become "children of the living God," or, as Paul would put it, will be "adopted" into the family of God and live with Him in exaltation forever.*]

Paul is emphasizing the mercy of God now. He is reminding his readers that even though God could wipe out all of the wicked right now, He doesn't want to nor will He. Through His mercy and patience, He will yet save a large remnant of Israel.

27 Esaias [*Isaiah*] also crieth [*speaks out*] concerning Israel [*in Isaiah 10:22*], Though the number of the children of Israel be as the sand of the sea, a remnant shall be saved:

28 For he will finish the work [*of saving souls*], and cut it short in righteousness [*and bring it to an end with much power*]: because a short work will the Lord make upon the earth.

29 And as Esaias [*Isaiah*] said before [*in Isaiah 1:9*], Except the Lord of Sabaoth [*the Lord of Hosts, Jehovah, Christ; see Bible*

Dictionary under "Sabaoth"] had left us a seed, we had been as Sodoma [*Sodom*], and been made like unto Gomorrha [*Gomorrah*]. [*In other words, if God had not intervened with mercy, Israel would have been destroyed as completely as Sodom and Gomorrah.*]

30 What shall we say then [*what conclusion should we draw from all this*]? [*Answer:*] That the Gentiles, which followed not after righteousness [*who did not live the law of Moses*], have attained to righteousness [*can attain salvation*], even the righteousness which is of faith [*even the salvation which comes through faith in Jesus Christ*].

31 But Israel [*the "chosen" people, the descendants of Abraham, Isaac, and Jacob*], which followed after the law of righteousness [*who lived according to the law of Moses*], hath not attained to the law of righteousness [*cannot attain salvation through it*]. [*In other words, one cannot be saved by the law of Moses, but we must accept Christ and follow His gospel in order to be saved.*]

32 Wherefore [*why*]? Because they sought it [*salvation*] not by faith [*in Christ*], but as it were by the works of the law [*the law of Moses*]. For they stumbled at that stumblingstone; [*In other words, the law of Moses, which was designed to help them prepare for Christ's gospel, became a stumbling stone to them because they stubbornly remained loyal to it and rejected Christ.*]

JST Romans 9:32

32 Wherefore **they stumbled at that stumbling stone**, not by faith, but as it were by the works of the law;

33 As it is written [*in Isaiah 8:14; 28:16*], Behold, I lay in Sion [*Zion*] a stumblingstone [*Christ*] and rock of offence [*Christ; in other words, many Israelites will be offended by Jesus and His gospel*]: and whosoever believeth on him shall not be ashamed [*will not be stopped in their progression toward eternal life*].

ROMANS 10

Paul continues his letter to these members of the Church in Rome by emphasizing that salvation comes through living righteously and having faith in Jesus Christ. He will emphasize that the purpose of the law of Moses was to prepare and lead people to accept Christ and His gospel (see verse 4). We will point out that verses 9–11, when taken out of the context of the whole Bible, lead some Christians to believe that all they have to do to be saved is to verbally accept Christ as the Savior.

1 BRETHREN, my heart's desire and prayer to God for Israel is, that they might be saved.

2 For I bear them [*Israel*] record that they have a zeal of God [*they are attempting to worship God properly*], but not according to knowledge [*but they don't have*

correct knowledge about Him and what He requires for salvation].

3 For they being ignorant of God's righteousness [*they do not have correct knowledge of God and how he wants to go about saving them; see* Strong's *#1342*], and going about to establish their own righteousness [*they are going around making their own rules about how to be saved by God*], have not submitted themselves unto the righteousness of God [*therefore, they are not living the correct gospel*].

4 For Christ is the end of the law [*Christ is the whole purpose and end goal of the law of Moses*] for righteousness to every one that believeth [*Christ's gospel leads to true righteousness for every one who believes in Him*].

5 For Moses describeth the righteousness which is of the law [*Moses gave us the law of Moses to lead to a certain degree of righteousness*], That the man which doeth those things shall live by them [*and instructed his people to live according to the law of Moses*].

In Deuteronomy 30:10–14, Moses told his people, the children of Israel, that they didn't have to hunt all over the place for the laws of God by which they should live. They didn't have to send someone to heaven to find God's laws, neither did they have to send beyond the sea for information. Rather, the laws and commandments were to be found in what Moses had written and they should be "in thy mouth" (verse 14) and "in thy heart" (verse 14). In other words, he told his people that God's laws and commandments should be in their conversations, their hearts, and their behavior always.

Next, in Romans 10:6–8, as he continues to instruct the Saints living in Rome, Paul uses their knowledge of Deuteronomy 30:10–14 to remind them that they have the true gospel of Christ right in front of them and that they don't have to look far and wide for it.

6 But the righteousness which is of faith [*but the higher personal righteousness which comes through faith in Christ*] speaketh on this wise, Say not in thine heart, Who shall ascend into heaven? (that is, to bring Christ down *from above:*) *in other words, you don't have to send someone to heaven to find out about Christ and then come back and report to you. Christ has already been here and given us His gospel.*]

7 Or, Who shall descend into the deep? (that is, to bring up Christ again from the dead.) [*in other words, you don't have to send someone to the world of the departed dead to access Christ's word for you, as Moses said in Deuteronomy 30:13*].

8 But what saith it [*what did Moses say, in Deuteronomy 30:14*]? The word [*God's instruction to you*] is nigh thee [*near you; in fact, right here!*], even in thy mouth, and in

thy heart: that is, the word of faith [*of faith in Jesus Christ*], which we preach;

As mentioned in the notes at the beginning of this chapter, verses 9–11, next, are often badly misused by taking them out of the bigger context of all Paul's writings as well as the rest of the scriptures. Some people use verses 9–11 to teach that all that is necessary to be "saved" is to believe in Jesus and to confess that he is the Christ with one's mouth. They forget that what Moses taught in Deuteronomy 30:10–14 and what Paul is teaching here is that, in order to be saved, in addition to ordinances, covenants, and so forth, we must have personal righteousness to the point that Jesus is constantly in our conversation and in our hearts.

9 That if thou shalt confess with thy mouth the Lord Jesus, and shalt believe in thine heart that God hath raised him from the dead, thou shalt be saved.

10 For with the heart man believeth unto righteousness [*when you truly believe in Christ, it leads to personal righteousness*]; and with the mouth confession is made unto salvation.

11 For the scripture saith, Whosoever believeth on him shall not be ashamed [*will not be stopped in progressing to eventual exaltation*].

12 For there is no difference between the Jew and the Greek [*Gentile*]: for the same Lord over all is rich unto all that call upon him. [*The Lord gives all people the same rich blessings of exaltation, if they come unto Christ and live His gospel.*]

13 For whosoever shall call upon the name of the Lord shall be saved [*anyone who calls upon the name of Christ, meaning anyone who learns the gospel and lives it, earnestly striving to stay on the covenant path, will be saved*].

Next, Paul will say, in effect, that in order to properly worship Christ and keep His commandments, people have to be taught by authorized servants of God.

14 How then shall they call on him [*the true God*] in whom they have not believed? and how shall they believe in him of whom they have not heard? and how shall they hear without a preacher?

15 And how shall they preach, except they be sent [*who can teach the true gospel unless sent from God*]? as it is written [*in Isaiah 52:7*], How beautiful are the feet of them that preach the gospel of peace, and bring glad tidings of good things!

16 But they have not all obeyed the gospel [*every Israelite has not necessarily listened to God's messengers and obeyed*]. For Esaias [*Isaiah*] saith [*in Isaiah 53:1*], Lord, who hath believed our report [*in effect, who listens to us prophets, anyway*]?

17 So then faith cometh by hearing and hearing by the word of God, [*the only way we can exercise true faith is by hearing the true gospel*].

18 But I say, Have they not heard [*haven't the Israelites had a chance to hear the word of God*]? Yes verily [*absolutely yes*], their sound went into all the earth, and their words unto the ends of the world [*they have had prophets and more prophets who have taught them throughout the whole world*].

19 But I say [*I ask the question again*], Did not Israel know [*Israel (the Israelites) heard, but did they understand with their hearts*]? First Moses saith, I will provoke you to jealousy by them that are no people [*non-Israelites*], and by a foolish nation I will anger you. [*The answer to the question is "No." They did not understand with their hearts. They refused to. Therefore, Moses told them that the Lord would "provoke" them, or punish them by Gentiles to the point that they would return to Him.*]

JST Romans 10:19

19 But I say, Did not Israel know? **Now** Moses saith, I will provoke you to jealousy by them that are no people, and by a foolish nation I will anger you.

20 But Esaias [*Isaiah*] is very bold, and saith [*in Isaiah 65:1*], I was found of them that sought me not; I was made manifest unto them that asked not after me. [*JST Isaiah 65:1 "I am found of them* ***who seek after me, I give unto all them that ask of me; I am not found of them that sought me not, or that inquireth*** *not after me."*]

21 But to Israel he saith [*in Isaiah 65:2*], All day long I have stretched forth my hands unto a disobedient and gainsaying people [*a people who oppose and deny Me*]. [*In other words, "all day long" I continue to invite them to repent, even though they are wicked and oppose Me in everything I try to do for them. Compare with Jacob 6:4–5.*]

ROMANS 11

One of the interesting pieces of information in this chapter is that Paul is from the tribe of Benjamin (verse 1), which, historically, was the smallest and least prestigious of all the tribes of Israel. Some members of the Church today feel a bit disappointed if their lineage is designated to be a tribe other than Ephraim, or Manasseh, or Judah or whatever they expected, when they receive their patriarchal blessing. Here we see that Paul, one of the greatest Apostles ever to have lived on earth, is from the tribe of Benjamin. Sometimes we forget that all of the tribes of Israel are given the charge to spread the gospel and blessings of the priesthood to all the world, as descendants of Abraham, Isaac, and Jacob (see Abraham 2:9–11). And the blessings of exaltation are promised to all of Israel if they are righteous, whether as direct descendants or as those who join Israel by making gospel covenants, starting with baptism.

Paul continues his message to the Saints in Rome by discussing the foreordination of Israel and pointing out how Gentiles can become members of Israel in the kingdom of God. This is very important doctrine.

1 I SAY then [*I ask the question*], Hath God cast away his people [*has God deserted His people*]? God forbid [*absolutely not*!]. For I also am an Israelite, of the seed of Abraham, of the tribe of Benjamin [*I am a descendant of Abraham, coming through the tribe of Benjamin*].

2 God hath not cast away his people which he foreknew [*foreordained*]. Wot ye not what the scripture saith of Elias [*about Elijah*]? how he maketh intercession to God against Israel, saying [*in 1 Kings 19:10 and 14*],

JST Romans 11:2

2 God hath not cast away his people which he foreknew. **Know** ye not what the scripture saith of Elias? how he maketh **complaint** to God against Israel, saying,

3 Lord, they have killed thy prophets, and digged down thine altars; and I am left alone, and they seek my life.

4 But what saith the answer of God unto him [*what did God say when he answered Elijah's complaint*]? I have reserved to myself seven thousand men, who have not bowed the knee to the image of Baal [*there are still 7,000 righteous men in Israel, so you are not alone; see 1 Kings 19:18*].

5 Even so then at this present time [*the time of Paul*] also there is a remnant according to the election of grace [*even so there are many righteous Israelites now who are dedicated to God through the grace of Christ*].

6 And if by grace, then is it no more of works [*since they are being saved by the grace or help of Christ, then it is obvious that they are not being saved by the works of the law of Moses*]: otherwise grace is no more grace [*otherwise, grace would not really be grace*]. But if it be of works, then is it no more grace [*if they were to be saved by compliance with the law of Moses, there would be no need for the grace of Christ*]: otherwise work is no more work [*if they are being saved by grace, the works of the law of Moses are not effective in saving them*].

7 What then [*so what is this all leading to*]? Israel hath not obtained that which he seeketh for; [*In other words, every one in Israel is not going to gain salvation.*] but the election hath obtained it [*those of Israel who honor their foreordination by living righteously have attained God's grace, through Christ, and are on their way to exaltation*], and the rest [*of Israel*] were blinded [*spiritually*]

JST Romans 11:7

7 What then? Israel hath not obtained that which **they seek** for; but the election hath obtained it, and the rest were blinded.

8 (According as it is written [*in Isaiah 29:10*], God hath given them the spirit of slumber, eyes that they should not see, and ears that they should not hear;) unto this day. [*In other words, God allows agency choice, and when used to choose wickedness, people end up being spiritually blind and deaf.*]

9 And David saith [*Psalm 69:22–23*], Let their table be made a snare, and a trap, and a stumbling block, and a recompence [*reward*] unto them: [*Let the wicked be rewarded appropriately for their wicked choices.*]

10 Let their eyes be darkened, that they may not see [*let them become spiritually blind*], and bow down their back alway [*and let the burdens of their wickedness bend them over always*].

11 I say then [*the next question is:*], Have they [*Israel*] stumbled that they should fall [*has Israel lost their chance for salvation forever*]? God forbid [*absolutely not!*]: but rather through their fall salvation is come unto the Gentiles [*because of their failure to keep the commandments and lead out in spreading the gospel, the gospel will be given to the Gentiles*], for to provoke them [*Israel*] to jealousy [*eventually Israel will be humbled, repent, and be gathered*].

12 Now if the fall of them [*Israel*] be the riches of the world [*if the failure of the Jews and Israelites in the Holy Land and elsewhere to be worthy of being the chosen people leads to the gospel being given to the rest of the world instead*], and the diminishing of them the riches of the Gentiles [*and leads to the taking of the gospel from them and giving it to the Gentiles (especially through Joseph Smith and the restoration)*]; how much more their fulness [*how much more will Israel appreciate the fulness of the gospel when they are gathered to the fold in the last days gathering of Israel*]?

13 For I speak to you Gentiles [*Gentile converts to the Church*], inasmuch as [*since*] I am the apostle of the Gentiles, I magnify mine office [*I am carrying out my special calling to take the gospel to the Gentiles*]:

Next, in verse 14, it helps to know that "emulation" means to follow someone else's example.

14 If by any means I may provoke to emulation them which are my flesh [*my fellow Israelites*], and might save some of them [*perhaps I can provoke some of my fellow Israelites to follow the good example of you Gentile converts and thus save some of them*].

15 For if the casting away of them [*if the casting off of Israel, because of their wickedness*] be the reconciling of the world [*leads to the teaching of the gospel of Christ to the whole world, so that they can*

be "reconciled"—be "joined to God" through the Atonement of Christ], what shall the receiving of them be, but life from the dead [*when Israel is finally restored and gathered in the last days, won't it be like bringing someone back from the dead*]?

JST Romans 11:15

15 For if the casting away of them is the reconciling of the world, what shall the **restoring** of them be, but life from the dead?

In order to understand what Paul says next in verses 16–26, one needs to understand the parable or "allegory of the tame and wild olive trees" given in Jacob, chapter 5, in the Book of Mormon. The olive tree represents Israel, God's covenant people. Tame branches represent righteous people. Wild branches represent apostate, wicked people and can also represent Gentiles. Roots can represent gospel covenants. Branches, basically, represent various groups of people. You may wish to read Jacob 5 before continuing with Paul's sermon here.

16 For if the firstfruit [*the first lump of dough or loaf of bread made from the first grain harvested; see Numbers 15:17–21*] be holy, the lump is also holy [*the rest of the harvest has the potential to be holy also*]: and if the root be holy, so are the branches. [*In other words, since Israel was once holy, a remnant of Israel can become holy again (and will in the last days after the restoration by Joseph Smith).*]

17 And if some of the branches be broken off [*if some of Israel goes into apostasy (falls away from God)*], and thou [*Gentiles*] being a wild olive tree, wert graffed [*grafted, joined*] in among them [*the people of God*], and with them partakest of the root and fatness of the olive tree [*and with them enjoy the blessings of being righteous, covenant people, in other words, Israel*];

Next, in verses 18–20, Paul warns these Gentile converts to the Church not to think they are better than Jews who have neither accepted the gospel of Christ nor joined the Church.

18 Boast not against the branches. But if thou boast, thou bearest not the root, but the root thee. [*Don't become prideful and think you are better than the Jews who refuse to join the Church. Remember that God is giving you strength through covenants, rather than you giving God strength by keeping covenants.*]

JST Romans 11:18

18 Boast not against the branches, **for** thou bearest not the root, but the root thee.

19 Thou [*Gentiles*] wilt say then, The branches were broken off, that I might be graffed in. [*Don't get caught up in boasting that some Jews have been cut off to make room for you to be brought into the Church.*]

JST Romans 11:19

19 **For if thou boast,** thou wilt say, The branches were broken off, that **we** might be grafted in.

20 Well; because of unbelief they were broken off [*it is true that they, the wicked of Israel, were "cut off the olive tree" because of unbelief and resulting wickedness*], and thou standest by faith [*and you Gentile members are in good standing before God because of your faith*]. Be not highminded [*don't get cocky or prideful*], but fear:

21 For if God spared not the natural branches, take heed lest he also spare not thee [*if God cut off the natural branches (covenant Israel) from the olive tree, because of their wickedness, don't think for a moment that you can't get cut off too if you turn to wickedness*].

22 Behold therefore [*make sure you understand*] the goodness and severity of God: on them which fell, severity [*He has had to deal severely with those who fell away from the gospel*]; but toward thee, goodness, if thou continue in his goodness [*but you will receive of His goodness and blessings, if you continue faithful*]: otherwise thou also shalt be cut off.

23 And they [*those who fell away*] also, if they abide not still in unbelief [*if they repent*], shall be graffed [*grafted*] in [*brought back into the Lord's covenant people*]: for God is able to graff [*graft*] them in again.

The invitation in verse 23, above, is the same invitation given often today by our Church leaders; namely, if you have fallen off the covenant path, get back on. God welcomes you to return! Paul's statement that "God is able to graff them in again" is a big understatement!

24 For if thou [*you Gentiles*] wert [*were*] cut out of the olive tree which is wild by nature [*were taken from a Gentile culture which promotes lifestyles which are contrary to Christ's gospel*], and wert graffed contrary to nature into a good olive tree [*and were converted, seemingly against all odds, and brought into Christ's true Church*]: how much more shall these, which be the natural branches, be graffed into their own olive tree [*what do you think the chances are that wicked Israel will be brought back, gathered to Christ in the last days*]?

25 For I would not, brethren, that ye should be ignorant of this mystery [*I don't want you to remain ignorant about this matter*], lest ye should be wise in your own conceits [*for fear that you would become prideful about it*]; that blindness in part is happened to Israel, until the fulness of the Gentiles be come in [*namely, that through wickedness, Israel (particularly the Jews) have become spiritually blind and will remain that way until the last days after the times of the Gentiles—see Joseph Smith History 1:41—are fulfilled, or, in other words, until the gospel has been preached to the Gentiles*].

The "fulness of the Gentiles"

referred to in verse 25, above, is one of the signs of the times which is to be fulfilled before the Second Coming. Basically, it goes like this: In the days of the Savior's mortal mission, the Jews were "first" and the Gentiles "last," meaning that the gospel was taken first to the Jews, and then, after the Savior's crucifixion and resurrection, the Apostles took the gospel to the Gentiles. In the last days, the Gentiles will be "first" and the Jews "last," meaning that the gospel will go first to all the rest of the world, and then it will go to the Jews.

26 And so all Israel [*who repent; see Isaiah 59, heading*] shall be saved: as it is written [*in Isaiah 59:20–21; 27:9; Jeremiah 31:33–34*], There shall come out of Sion [*Zion*] the Deliverer [*the Redeemer*], and shall turn away ungodliness from Jacob [*and Jacob (Israel) will repent of wickedness*]:

<u>JST Romans 11:26</u>

26 And **then** all Israel shall be saved; as it is written, There shall come out of Sion the Deliverer, and shall turn away ungodliness from Jacob;

27 For this is my covenant unto them, when I shall take away their sins.

28 As concerning the gospel, they are enemies for your sakes [*the fact that the Jews reject the gospel actually works to your advantage because the prophecy gets fulfilled that the gospel is then taken to you, the Gentiles*]: but as touching the election [*but, speaking of Israel, who were foreordained to accept the gospel and take it to all the world*], they are beloved for the fathers' sakes [*the promises made to Abraham, Isaac, and Jacob by God concerning their posterity will yet be fulfilled, and they will be successfully gathered into Christ's Church in the last days*].

29 For the gifts and calling of God are without repentance. [*In other words, God blesses sinners and calls them, through the preaching of the gospel, before they even start to repent. He does not wait until they have repented before He starts calling them to return to Him.*]

30 For as ye in times past have not believed God, yet have now obtained mercy through their unbelief [*it is just like with you: in times past you didn't believe in God either, but He reached out to you and now you have joined the Church and obtained mercy and forgiveness because the Jews rejected it first and then it was preached to you*]:

31 Even so have these [*the Jews*] also now not believed, that through your mercy [*through the mercy of God to the Gentiles, they will get the gospel first in the last days*] they [*the Jews in the last days*] also may obtain mercy [*also will get the gospel, after the "fulness of the Gentiles" (verse 25) has taken place, before the Second Coming*].

32 For God hath concluded [*gathered, as fish are gathered in a net;*

see Strong's *#4788*] them all [*will do everything possible to gather them all*] in unbelief [*despite their unbelief*], that he might have mercy upon all.

33 O the depth of the riches both of the wisdom and knowledge of God! how unsearchable are his judgments, and his ways past finding out! [*God's kindness, mercy, wisdom, knowledge, etc., are far beyond man's capability to comprehend!*]

34 For who hath known the mind of the Lord? or who hath been his counsellor? [*Who can understand the mind of the Lord, or who can tell Him how to improve His reaching out to us?*]

35 Or who [*what person*] hath first given to him [*God*], and it shall be recompensed [*paid back*] unto him again? [*In other words, who has ever put God in his debt, or done things for God such that God owes him? Answer: No one! See Mosiah 2:24*]

36 For of him, and through him, and to him, are all things [*we are forever indebted to Him*]: to whom be glory for ever. Amen.

ROMANS 12

Since Satan has much success in luring people to follow him by giving in to the temptations to which the mortal body is subject, Paul now invites the members of the Church to exercise extra self-control over their physical bodies, "sacrificing" sins of the flesh such as impatience, temper, sexual immorality, jealousy, etc., and thus presenting their bodies as a living sacrifice to God. There is a bit of a play on words here. All animals used for sacrifices under the law of Moses, of course, ended up as dead bodies, symbolic of giving their "all" to God. Since the law of animal sacrifice has now, at this point when Paul is preaching, been done away with by the Savior's Atonement, Paul invites the Saints to offer their bodies to God, in other words, to give their "all" to God, but their bodies stay alive, symbolic of the newness of life brought by the gospel of Christ.

In this chapter, Paul mentions a number of the gifts of the Spirit, including a number that members of the Church may not normally think of as being specific spiritual gifts. You may wish to mark these (verses 6–13) in your scriptures by way of emphasizing that there are many gifts of the Spirit in addition to the most commonly discussed ones.

Also, in this chapter, Paul gives us straightforward and simple advice on how to be good Christians.

1 I BESEECH you therefore, brethren, by the mercies of God [*I urgently counsel you, through your using the mercies of God made available to you through the Atonement*], that ye present your bodies a living sacrifice [*that you offer yourselves as a living sacrifice*, holy, acceptable unto God, which

is your reasonable service [*this sacrifice shows up in your serving God*].

2 And be not conformed to this world [*don't live by the world's standards*]: but be ye transformed [*but let yourselves be changed*] by the renewing of your mind [*by the energizing and renewing of your minds which comes through the gospel of Christ*], that ye may prove [*recognize, discern*] what is that good, and acceptable, and perfect, will of God.

JST Romans 12:2

2 And be not conformed to this world; but be ye transformed by the renewing of your mind, that ye may prove **what that good**, and acceptable, and perfect will of God is.

3 For I say, through the grace given unto me [*through the help Christ has given me to understand these things*], to every man that is among you, not to think of himself more highly than he ought to think [*in other words, be humble*]; but to think soberly [*be serious minded about the gospel*], according as God hath dealt [*given out*] to every man the measure of faith.

4 For as we have many members in one body [*just as our physical bodies have many "members"—eyes, ears, head, feet, arms, hands, etc.*], and all members have not the same office [*and each of our body parts doesn't do the same thing for us, in other words, each has a different function*]:

5 So we [*members of the Church*], being many [*even though there are many of us and each is an individual*], are one body in Christ [*all work together in Christ's church*], and every one members one of another [*and each of us belongs to all the other members*]. [*In other words, it is very important that we work together with each other in unity for the good of the Church and each other.*]

Paul will now mention that there are different gifts of the Spirit, and one member has one and another has a different one. Working together in unity and harmony, all members of the Church benefit from each others' spiritual gifts. For a list of several gifts of the Spirit, see D&C 46:8–26; Moroni 10:8–19; 1 Corinthians 12:1–12.

As we continue, we will use **bold** to point out several of the spiritual gifts mentioned by Paul in verses 6–13.

Gifts of the Spirit

6 Having then gifts differing according to the grace that is given to us, whether **prophecy** [*if we have the gift of prophecy*], let us prophesy according to the proportion of faith [*according to how much faith we have*];

7 Or **ministry** [*if we have the gift of serving others*], let us wait on [*attend to*] our ministering [*let us serve others*]: or he that **teacheth** [*he who has the gift of teaching*], on teaching [*let him teach*];

8 Or he that **exhorteth** [*he who has the gift of speaking and encouraging others to do right*], on exhortation: he that **giveth** [*he who has the gift of generosity*], let him do it with simplicity [*without drawing much attention to himself*]; he that **ruleth** [*has the gift of leadership*], with diligence [*let him be diligent in leading and fulfilling his duties*]; he that **sheweth mercy** [*he who has the gift of mercy*], with **cheerfulness** [*some are given the gift of having a cheerful disposition*].

9 Let **love** be without dissimulation [*let the gift of love be used sincerely, without hypocrisy*]. **Abhor that which is evil** [*the gift of shunning evil*]; **cleave to that which is good** [*the gift of deeply desiring to be involved with good*].

<u>**JST Romans 12:9**</u>

9 Let love be without dissimulation. Abhor that which is evil **and** cleave to that which is good.

10 Be **kindly affectioned** [*the gift of being kind to others*] one to another with **brotherly love** [*the gift of showing extra concern and kindness toward others*]; in honour **preferring one another** [*the gift of leading by good example and honor*];

The word "preferring" in verse 10, above, is an example of Old English vocabulary which has changed in our day. "Pre" is used in association with going in advance. "Prefer" means "go before or show the way." See *Strong's* #4285. If we think of "prefer" in our modern English, we think of preferring one person over another and thus miss Paul's point completely. Another example of how words have changed drastically in meaning from Old English to modern American English is found in Matthew 17:25, where Jesus "prevented" Peter. It sounds like Jesus stopped Peter from doing something. Not so. Old English "prevented" means Christ spoke first, before Peter even had a chance to ask him about paying the temple tax. See Matthew 17:25, footnote a.

11 **Not slothful in business** [*the gift of being skilled in business*]; **fervent in spirit** [*the gift of spirituality*]; **serving the Lord** [*the gift of happily serving in Church callings; also the gift of serving others—see Mosiah 2:17*];

12 Rejoicing in **hope** [*the hope and confidence which comes through living Christ's gospel*]; **patient** in tribulation [*the gift of being patient during times of trials and troubles*]; **continuing instant in prayer** [*the gift of being in constant communication with God*];

13 **Distributing** [*the gift of sharing*] to the necessity of saints [*sharing according to the needs of the Saints*]; given to **hospitality** [*the gift of being a gracious hostess or host*].

14 Bless them which persecute you: bless, and curse not.

15 Rejoice with them that do rejoice, and weep with them that weep.

16 Be of the same mind one toward another [*be united, live in harmony*]. Mind not high things [*don't be arrogant, conceited*], but condescend to men of low estate [*be willing to associate with people of low social status*]. Be not wise in your own conceits [*avoid pride*].

17 Recompense to no man evil for evil [*don't try to get revenge*]. Provide things honest in the sight of all men [*be honest in your dealings with all people*].

18 If it be possible, as much as lieth in you [*as much as you possibly can*], live peaceably with all men.

19 Dearly beloved, avenge not yourselves [*please avoid getting revenge*], but rather give place unto wrath [*step aside and let God be the judge and take care of it; see D&C 64:11*]: for it is written [*in Deuteronomy 32:35*], Vengeance is mine; I will repay, saith the Lord.

20 Therefore if thine enemy hunger, feed him; if he thirst, give him drink: for in so doing thou shalt heap coals of fire on his head. [*In other words, in being kind to your enemies, in doing good to people who treat you badly, you save your own soul from bitterness and hatred and you shift the full burden of accountability for his or her behavior to your enemy.*]

21 Be not overcome of evil [*don't let evil overcome you*], but overcome evil with good.

ROMANS 13

Paul now reminds the members in Rome how important it is for them to sustain and support the leaders of the Church. This same counsel applies to us today. If we sustain the leaders God has called to preside over us, we will not go astray and become subject to the punishments of God.

It is interesting to note that Joseph Smith made changes to seven out of the fourteen verses in this chapter in the JST.

1 LET every soul be subject unto the higher powers [*the leaders of the Church*]. For there is no power but of God: the powers that be [*the Church leaders*] are ordained of God.

JST Romans 13:1

1 Let every soul be subject unto the higher powers. For there is no power **in the church but of God;** the powers that be are ordained of God.

2 Whosoever therefore resisteth the power, resisteth the ordinance of God: and they that resist shall receive to themselves damnation. [*In other words, if you don't sustain and support the leaders of the Church, you are stopping your own progress toward exaltation and will receive God's punishment instead.*]

JST Romans 13:2

2 Whosoever therefore resisteth the power, resisteth the ordinance of God; and they that resist shall receive to themselves **punishment**.

3 For rulers are not a terror to good works [*the leaders of the Church are not feared by those who are faithful*], but to the evil [*but the wicked often fear them*]. Wilt thou then not be afraid of the power [*do you desire not to be afraid of Church leaders*]? do that which is good [*then live righteously*], and thou shalt have praise of the same [*and you will have their praise and appreciation*]:

4 For he is the minister of God to thee for good [*the Church leaders are called by God for your benefit*]. But if thou do that which is evil [*if you choose to break God's commandments*], be afraid [*you should fear the leaders of the Church*]; for he beareth not the sword in vain [*for there are good reasons God has given leaders power and authority over you*]: for he [*each Church leader*] is the minister of God, a revenger [*judge*] to execute wrath upon him that doeth evil [*authorized leaders of the Church are judges and sometimes have to be strict with members involved in serious sin, even to the point of disfellowshipping or excommunicating them*].

JST Romans 13:4

4 For he is the minister of God to thee for good. But if thou do that which is evil be afraid; for he beareth not the **rod** [*"rod" in the scriptures is often symbolic of authority*] in vain; for he is the minister of God, a revenger to execute wrath upon him that doeth evil.

5 Wherefore ye must needs be subject, not only for wrath, but also for conscience sake [*therefore you need to be subject to Church leaders, not only to avoid Church discipline, but also simply because your conscience tells you to*].

In verses 6–7, next, Paul reminds the Saints that many of the leaders of the Church are required by their callings to serve full time, much the same as our current First Presidency, Twelve, and Seventies do. Since they can't work for a living, they and their families are often supported out of funds donated to the Church by members.

6 For for this cause pay ye tribute [*tithes and offerings*] also; for they are God's ministers, attending continually upon this very thing [*many of our leaders serve full time*].

JST Romans 13:6

6 For, for this cause pay ye **your consecrations also unto them**; for they are God's ministers, attending continually upon this very thing.

Next, Paul counsels these members to pay their obligations, whether to the government, to other men, to the Church, or to anyone they owe.

7 Render therefore to all their dues

[*give to everyone that which is properly due them*]: tribute [*tax*] to whom tribute [*tax*] is due; custom [*income*] to whom custom [*income is due*]; fear [*respect*] to whom fear [*respect is due*]; honour to whom honour.

JST Romans 13:7

7 **But first, render** to all their dues, **according to custom**, tribute to whom tribute, custom to whom custom, **that your consecrations may be done in fear of him to whom fear belongs, and in honor of him to whom honor belongs.**

8 Owe no man any thing [*don't let any debts remain outstanding or unpaid*], but to love one another [*except for the ongoing debt of loving one another*]: for he that loveth another hath fulfilled the law [*the whole purpose of the laws and commandments is to teach us to love one another*].

JST Romans 13:8

8 **Therefore** owe no man **anything**, but to love one another; for he that loveth another hath fulfilled the law.

9 For this [*the purpose of all the commandments, including*], Thou shalt not commit adultery, Thou shalt not kill, Thou shalt not steal, Thou shalt not bear false witness, Thou shalt not covet; and if there be any other commandment, it [*its purpose*] is briefly comprehended [*can be briefly summarized*] in this saying, namely, Thou shalt love thy neighbour as thyself.

10 Love worketh no ill to his neighbour [*if you truly love other people, you will do them no harm*]: therefore [*this is why*] love is the fulfilling of the law [*this is why you are fulfilling the laws of the gospel when you show love toward others*].

11 And that, knowing the time, that now it is high time to awake out of sleep [*it is time to wake up to the urgency of keeping the commandments*]: for now is our salvation nearer than when we believed [*we have more accountability now than when we first joined the Church*].

12 The night is far spent, the day is at hand: let us therefore cast off the works of darkness [*let us repent of our sins*], and let us put on the armour of light [*and put on the protection of the gospel light*].

13 Let us walk honestly [*let us behave decently; see Romans 13:13, footnote a*], as in the day; not in rioting [*wild parties in the night*] and drunkenness, not in chambering [*sleeping around, bed-hopping, as in sexual immorality*] and wantonness [*whoredoms, lustfulness*], not in strife [*contention, arguing*] and envying [*jealousy*].

14 But put ye on the Lord Jesus Christ [*put on the full armor or protection of Christ and His gospel*], and make not provision for the flesh [*don't keep thinking of ways to satisfy your desires for sin and the lustful tendencies of your physical bodies*], to fulfil the lusts thereof.

JST Romans 13:14

14 But put ye on the Lord Jesus Christ, and make not provision for the flesh, to **gratify** the lusts thereof.

ROMANS 14

There is a great lesson for us in Paul's teaching about "doubtful disputations" in the next verses. "Doubtful disputations" are arguing, debating, criticizing, judging one another, and so forth, over trivial things and personal preferences. Often, members become critical of each other in such less significant or "doubtful" matters. For example, one member likes whole wheat bread, another prefers white bread, one prefers honey as a sweetener, another enjoys white sugar. One member finds great value in herbs and prefers mainly a vegetarian diet while another seems to enjoy and devour about anything that gets in the path of his knife and fork, including meat. Paul counsels members not to get caught up in the sin of being critical of each other in matters of individual preference, especially in reference to new members of the Church, whose preferences and tastes, over time, may well grow to reflect the finer details of scriptural counsel. Ultimately, this is a chapter counseling us not to judge one another unrighteously (compare with JST Matthew 7:1–2).

1 HIM that is weak in the faith receive ye, but not to doubtful disputations [*don't be critical of likes and preferences, etc., that are not specific gospel commandments*].

2 For one believeth that he may eat all things: another, who is weak, eateth herbs.

3 Let not him that eateth [*let not the member who likes to eat about anything and everything*] despise him that eateth not [*be critical of a member who is very choosy and particular about what he or she eats*]; and let not him which eateth not judge him that eateth [*on the other hand, the picky eater should avoid criticizing the member who eats everything*]: for God hath received him [*God accepts both types in His Church*].

4 Who art thou that judgest another man's servant? [*In other words, who are you to judge the Lord's servants who answer to Him, not you?*] to his own master he standeth or falleth [*it is the Master's job to judge His servants, not your job*]. Yea, he shall be holden up [*each of us is helped and supported by God, despite our weaknesses*]: for God is able to make him stand [*God is capable of helping each of us to come unto Him*].

5 One man esteemeth one day above another [*one convert considers special days under the law of Moses to still be special*]: another esteemeth every day alike [*another convert considers each day to be a day dedicated to God's work*]. Let every man be fully persuaded in his own mind [*allow each person*

to act according to the convictions in his own mind].

6 He that regardeth the day, regardeth it unto the Lord [*the person who considers a particular day to have religious significance, has his mind on the Lord that day*]; and he that regardeth not the day, to the Lord he doth not regard it [*but the member who no longer considers it to be a religious holiday (because it pertained to the law of Moses), no longer celebrates it as a special holy day*]. He that eateth [*he who eats everything (verses 2 and 3*), eateth to the Lord, for he giveth God thanks [*remembers the Lord and gives Him thanks as he eats*]; and he that eateth not [*he who doesn't eat everything, rather eats herbs* [*verses 2 and 3*], to the Lord he eateth not, and giveth God thanks [*even though there are many things he won't eat, he still gives thanks to the Lord for what he does eat*].

7 For none of us liveth to himself, and no man dieth to himself. [*We are not alone. We all need and receive God's help.*]

8 For whether [*if*] we live, we live unto the Lord; and whether [*if*] we die, we die unto the Lord: whether we live therefore, or die, we are the Lord's. [*Whether we live or die, we all belong to the Lord.*]

9 For to this end [*for this purpose*] Christ both died, and rose, and revived [*came back to life; was resurrected*], that he might be Lord both of the dead and living. [*Christ performed the Atonement in order to have all people be accountable to Him so He can help everyone and be everyone's judge.*]

10 But why dost thou judge thy brother [*So, why would any of you take it upon yourselves to judge of one another*]? or why dost thou set at nought thy brother [*or why do you criticize each other and put each other down*]? for we shall all stand before the judgment seat of Christ.

11 For it is written [*in Isaiah 45:23*], As I live, saith the Lord, every knee shall bow to me, and every tongue shall confess to God. [*In other words, Christ is the final judge (see John 5:22) and everyone will ultimately acknowledge that Jesus is the Christ, whether or not they accept His gospel. See D&C 76:110.*]

JST Romans 14:11

11 **For I live, saith the Lord, as it is written. And** every knee shall bow to me, and every tongue shall **swear** to God [*confess to God that He is indeed God—see D&C 76:110*].

12 So then every one of us shall give account of himself to God [*all of us will ultimately give an accounting of our lives to God. He, Christ will be our judge (John 5:22)*].

13 Let us not therefore judge one another any more: but judge this rather [*but judge ourselves on the following very important matter, namely*], that no man put a stum-

blingblock or an occasion to fall in his brother's way [*that we do not do things that would cause others to be less faithful to God or cause them harm or trouble of any kind*].

14 I know, and am persuaded by the Lord Jesus, that there is nothing unclean of itself: but to him that esteemeth any thing to be unclean, to him it is unclean. [*In other words, I realize that food, in and of itself, is neither clean nor unclean. But if a member considers certain foods to be unclean, then to him it is unclean. It is just that simple.*]

Paul gives some very wise counsel in verses 15–23, next. We would all do well to avoid offending new members or weak members or nonmembers by eating or drinking things which they believe "Mormons" don't use, even though they are a matter of personal choice rather than right or wrong. For instance, many members do not drink cola drinks, but many do. A faithful member can still get a temple recommend in spite of drinking cola drinks because the recommend questions do not prohibit cola drinks. However, a new convert or a nonmember might be offended or confused or bothered that a long-time member drinks such drinks because he or she has always heard that faithful members of the Church don't drink such things. Another example might be that if you are eating at a restaurant with a Jewish friend, it would be insensitive for you to order pork and eat it in his presence. Paul counsels us to be sensitive and to do our best not to offend or damage someone else's view of the Church by indulging in things which might offend. See especially verse 21.

15 But if thy brother be grieved with thy meat [*if an acquaintance is bothered from a religious standpoint by your choice of food*], now walkest thou not charitably [*you are not being charitable if you eat it in front of him*]. Destroy not him with thy meat [*don't destroy his respect for the Church and perhaps his potential testimony by your insensitive choice of food in his presence*], for whom Christ died. [*In other words, don't undo Christ's work to save him or her by your insensitive choice of foods around them.*]

<u>JST Romans 14:15</u>

15 But if thy brother be grieved with thy meat, **thou walkest not charitably if thou eatest**. Therefore destroy not him with thy meat, for whom Christ died.

16 Let not then your good be evil spoken of: [*Don't undo the good you can do by being unwise or insensitive in such matters.*]

17 For the kingdom of God is not meat and drink; but righteousness, and peace, and joy in the Holy Ghost. [*The ultimate focus of the kingdom of God is not on food or drink, but on personal righteousness, peace and joy from following the promptings of the Holy Ghost.*]

18 For he that in these things serveth Christ is acceptable to God, and approved of men. [*If you follow my counsel in these matters, you will be serving Christ, you will be acceptable to God and won't be offending others unnecessarily.*]

19 Let us therefore follow after the things which make for peace [*lets do everything we can to promote peace*], and things wherewith one may edify another [*and do things which build and strengthen one another*].

Just a reminder that the word "meat," as used by Paul in these verses, means "food." The word "flesh" is used in the Bible when referring to what we call meat, such as chicken, beef, lamb, etc.

20 For [*because of*] meat [*your choices of food*] destroy not the work of God [*don't destroy God's work with people by being insensitive about your choice of foods around them*]. All things indeed are pure [*all food is clean, since that part of the law of Moses, Leviticus 11, is no longer in effect*] ; but it is evil for that man who eateth with offence [*but it is evil to offend people with insensitive choices of food in their presence*].

21 It is good [*better*] neither to eat flesh [*meat*], nor to drink wine, nor any thing whereby thy brother stumbleth, or is offended, or is made weak. [*It is better not to eat or drink anything, in the presence of others, which might weaken their testimony or commitment to God. In other words, don't offend others needlessly!*]

22 Hast thou faith? have it to thyself before God. [*If you have faith in the gospel of Christ, such that the dietary restrictions in the law of Moses are no longer part of your life, keep it to yourself and between you and God, rather than offending others for whom it might be offensive.*] Happy is he that condemneth not himself in that thing which he alloweth. [*You will be happier if you don't condemn yourself by offending others unnecessarily.*]

23 And he that doubteth is damned if he eat, because he eateth not of faith: for whatsoever is not of faith is sin. [*In other words, if a new member were to eat something forbidden by the law of Moses, and doesn't yet have enough faith in the gospel of Christ to be convinced that the dietary laws of old are done away with, it could weaken his determination to follow God and thus stop his progress.*]

JST Romans 14:23

23 And he that doubteth is **condemned** if he eat, **because it is not of faith**; for whatsoever is not of faith is sin.

ROMANS 15

As Paul begins to bring his letter to the Saints in Rome to a close (written from Corinth—see Bible Dictionary under "Pauline Epistles," "Epistle to the Romans"), he reminds them that the strong ought to support and help the weak in the Church. Among other things, he acknowledges that he has written very boldly to them (verse 15), and once again reminds them that the Gentile converts to the Church are entitled to every blessing of the gospel, through their faithfulness to the promptings of the Holy Ghost (verse 16). He tells them that he will now head for Jerusalem (verse 25) which will bring to a close his third missionary journey which has taken about three and a half years.

Once again, in this chapter, we see that Paul knew the Old Testament very well and was a master at using specific verses, with which the Jews would be familiar because of their upbringing in the tradition of the law of Moses, to teach them the gospel of Jesus Christ. Here, he will especially use Old Testament prophesy to drive home the point to these Jewish converts that the Gentiles are to have the full gospel too.

1 WE then that are strong [*in the gospel*] ought to bear [*be patient with*] the infirmities [*shortcomings, weaknesses*] of the weak, and not to please ourselves [*not only be interested in our own needs*].

2 Let every one of us please [*be sensitive to the needs of*] his neighbour for his good to edification [*to build him up in the gospel*].

3 For even Christ pleased not himself [*did not give in to His own needs*]; but, as it is written [*in Psalm 69:9*], The reproaches of them that reproached thee fell on me [*the insults and caustic criticisms aimed at you came upon Me*].

4 For whatsoever things were written aforetime were written for our learning, that we through patience and comfort of the scriptures might have hope. [*Since ancient times, the scriptures have encouraged us to learn patience with others so that we might have hope of salvation ourselves.*]

5 Now the God of patience and consolation [*comfort*] grant you to be likeminded [*patient*] one toward another according to Christ Jesus [*like Jesus was with us*]:

JST Romans 15:5

5 Now the God of patience and consolation grant you to be likeminded one toward another according **as was** Christ Jesus;

6 That ye may with one mind and one mouth [*with unity*] glorify God, even the Father of our Lord Jesus Christ.

7 Wherefore receive ye one another [*accept one another with patience*], as Christ [*with great patience*] also received us to the glory of God.

As previously mentioned, the phrase "the circumcision" in Paul's writings means "the Jewish converts to the Church." We see this phrase in verse 8, next.

8 Now I say that Jesus Christ was a minister of the circumcision [*Jesus Christ was sent by the Father as a minister to the Jews*] for the truth of God, to confirm [*fulfill*] the promises made unto the fathers [*their ancestors*]:

9 And that the Gentiles [*the non-Jews*] might glorify [*be able to praise*] God for his mercy; as it is written [*in Psalm 18:49*], For this cause I will confess to thee among the Gentiles, and sing unto thy name. [*In other words, it was prophesied in the Old Testament that the gospel would be taken to the Gentiles too.*]

10 And again he saith [*in Deuteronomy 32:43*], Rejoice, ye Gentiles, with his people. [*The faithful Gentiles will join with the faithful covenant people and all will be the Lord's covenant people.*]

11 And again [*in Psalm 117:1*], Praise the Lord, all ye Gentiles; and laud him, all ye people.

12 And again, Esaias saith [*Isaiah prophesied, recorded in Isaiah 11:10*], There shall be a root of Jesse [*a descendant of Jesse (David's father), in other words, Christ; see Romans 15:12, footnote b*], and he that shall rise to reign over the Gentiles; in him shall the Gentiles trust [*the Gentiles will be brought into Christ's gospel*].

13 Now the God of hope fill you with all joy and peace in believing, that ye may abound in hope [*that you may have abundant hope*], through the power of the Holy Ghost.

Next, in verse 14, Paul uses a very effective teaching method; namely, complimenting people for the good that is already in them.

14 And I myself also am persuaded of you, my brethren, that ye also are full of goodness, filled with all knowledge, able also to admonish one another. [*I am convinced by what I hear of you that you are wonderful Saints and are helping and strengthening each other.*]

15 Nevertheless, brethren, I have written the more boldly unto you in some sort, as putting you in mind, because of the grace that is given to me of God, [*Nevertheless, I have been quite blunt in what I have written you in this letter because of the responsibility God has given me.*]

16 That I should be the minister of Jesus Christ to the Gentiles [*namely, that I have been called to take the gospel to the Gentiles*], ministering the gospel of God, that the offering up of the Gentiles might be acceptable [*in order that the Gentiles might know the gospel too, and be able to live it*], being sanctified by the Holy Ghost [*"sanctified" means being made holy and fit to be in the presence of God by being led by the Gift of the Holy Ghost as members of the Church*].

17 I have therefore whereof I may glory through Jesus Christ in those things which pertain to God. [*I have great joy in the Savior and His teachings which point us to the Father.*]

18 For I will not dare to speak of any of those things which Christ hath not wrought by me [*I will not venture to speak of anything at*

this time except what Christ has accomplished, using me as His instrument], to make the Gentiles obedient, by word and deed [*to bring the gospel to the Gentiles, so that they might be obedient to God in word as well as in their actions*],

19 Through mighty signs and wonders, by the power of the Spirit of God [*the Spirit of God has prepared the way and performed many miracles during my missionary journeys*]; so that from Jerusalem, and round about unto Illyricum [*all the way from Jerusalem through the eastern coast of the Adriatic Sea*], I have fully preached the gospel of Christ.

20 Yea, so have I strived to preach the gospel, not where Christ was named [*it has been my desire to preach the gospel in places where people hadn't even heard of Christ*], lest I should build upon another man's foundation [*because I didn't want to build upon what others had already started*]:

21 But as it is written [*you are familiar with what Isaiah said, in Isaiah 52:15, where he prophesied*], To whom he [*Christ*] was not spoken of, they shall see [*the gospel will be taken to people to whom Christ did not go*]: and they that have not heard shall understand [*and they who have never heard of Christ shall someday understand His gospel*].

22 For which cause also I have been much hindered from coming to you [*because of my involvement in taking the gospel to the Gentiles, I have experienced many delays in coming to visit you in Rome*].

23 But now having no more place in these parts [*but now that I am no longer traveling and preaching in all those areas*], and having a great desire these many years to come unto you [*and having desired to visit you for many years*];

24 Whensoever I take my journey into Spain, I will come to you [*when I finally get on my way to Spain, I will stop by and visit you*]: for I trust to see you in my journey, and to be brought on my way thitherward [*toward Spain*] by you, if first I be somewhat filled with your company.

JST Romans 15:24

24 **When** I take my journey into Spain, I will come to you; for I trust to see you in my journey, and to be brought on my way thitherward by you, if first I be somewhat filled **through your prayers**.

25 But now I go unto Jerusalem to minister unto the Saints.

26 For it hath pleased them of Macedonia and Achaia to make a certain contribution for the poor Saints which are at Jerusalem. [*The members in northern and southern Greece have gathered a donation for the poverty-stricken Saints in Jerusalem.*]

27 It hath pleased them verily [*they were very pleased to gather up this donation*]; and their debtors they are [*and indeed they owe it to the*

Saints in Jerusalem]. For if the Gentiles have been made partakers of their spiritual things, their duty is also to minister unto them in carnal things. [*Since the gospel came to the Gentiles through the Jews and Christ's ministry among them, the Gentiles certainly have a responsibility to help the Jewish Saints in their physical or temporal needs.*]

28 When therefore I have performed this, and have sealed to them this fruit [*after I have personally delivered the donation to the Saints in Jerusalem*], I will come by you into Spain [*I will come to you, and then go on to Spain from Rome*].

29 And I am sure that, when I come unto you, I shall come in the fulness of the blessing of the gospel of Christ.

30 Now I beseech you [*I have an urgent request*], brethren, for the Lord Jesus Christ's sake, and for the love of the Spirit, that ye strive together [*join together*] with me in your prayers to God for me;

31 That I may be delivered from them that do not believe in Judea [*that I be protected from those unbelievers in Judea and Jerusalem who want to arrest me*]; and that my service [*so that the contributions from the Saints in Greece*] which I have for Jerusalem may be accepted of the Saints [*might get into the hands of the Saints in Jerusalem*];

32 That I may come unto you with joy by the will of God, and may with you be refreshed.

33 Now the God of peace be with you all. Amen.

ROMANS 16

As Paul finishes his letter to the members of the Church in Rome, he sends greetings to a number of individuals and leaves some final counsel about avoiding people who cause contention.

1 I COMMEND [*introduce and recommend*] unto you Phebe our sister, which is a servant [*a faithful member*] of the church which is at Cenchrea [*a city in the eastern harbor of Corinth*]: [*Paul is writing this letter to the Roman Saints from Corinth (in what today is in southern Greece) and Phebe is the one who carries it in person to the members in Rome. See note in your King James Bible at the end of Romans 16.*]

2 That ye receive her in the Lord, as becometh saints [*please accept her among you as proper Saints would do*], and that ye assist her in whatsoever business she hath need of you [*and help her in whatever her needs are*]: for she hath been a succourer of many, and of myself also [*she has assisted many here in Corinth, including me*].

The word "succor," a form of which is used in verse 2, above, means "to hurry to help another."

3 Greet Priscilla and Aquila [*Priscilla is Aquila's wife*] my helpers in Christ Jesus:

4 Who have for my life laid down their own necks [*who risked their necks for me and many other members*]: unto whom not only I give thanks, but also all the churches [*wards and branches*] of the Gentiles.

5 Likewise greet the church [*the members*] that is in their house [*who meet in their home*]. Salute [*give my greetings to*] my wellbeloved Epænetus, who is the firstfruits of Achaia unto Christ [*who was the first convert to the Church in southern Greece*].

6 Greet Mary, who bestowed much labour on us.

7 Salute [*greet*] Andronicus and Junia, my kinsmen [*my relatives*], and my fellowprisoners [*who spent some time in prison with me*], who are of note among the apostles [*who are well known by the Apostles*], who also were in Christ before me [*who were converted to Christ before I was*].

8 Greet Amplias my beloved in the Lord.

9 Salute Urbane, our helper in Christ, and Stachys my beloved [*my dear friend*].

10 Salute Apelles approved in Christ [*who has proven faithful*]. Salute them which are of Aristobulus' household.

JST Romans 16:10

10 Salute Apelles approved in Christ. Salute them which are of Aristobulus' **church** [*ward or branch*].

11 Salute Herodion my kinsman [*relative*]. Greet them that be of the household of Narcissus, which are in the Lord [*who are members of the Church*].

JST Romans 16:11

11 Salute Herodian my kinsman. Greet them that be of the **church** of Narcissus, which are in the Lord.

12 Salute Tryphena and Tryphosa [*faithful women*], who labour in the Lord. Salute the beloved Persis [*another faithful sister*], which laboured much in the Lord.

13 Salute [*greet*] Rufus chosen in the Lord, and his mother and mine [*and his mother who is like a mother to me too*].

14 Salute Asyncritus, Phlegon, Hermas, Patrobas, Hermes, and the brethren which are with them.

15 Salute Philologus, and Julia, Nereus, and his sister, and Olympas, and all the saints which are with them.

16 Salute [*greet*] one another with an holy kiss. The churches of Christ salute you [*the members in other wards and branches of the Church send their greetings to you*].

JST Romans 16:16

16 Salute one another with a holy **salutation**. The churches of Christ salute you.

Next, Paul urges the members of the Church to avoid those who cause contention. Contention can be very damaging and can drive the Spirit away. Christ warned strongly against contention in His first words to the Nephites as He visited them. (See 3 Nephi 11:22, 28–30.)

17 Now I beseech [*urge*] you, brethren, mark them which [*take note of those who*] cause divisions and offences contrary to the doctrine which ye have learned; and avoid them.

18 For they that are such [*those who cause contention*] serve not our Lord Jesus Christ, but their own belly [*their own appetites and selfish interests*]; and by good words [*smooth talk*] and fair speeches [*flattery*] deceive the hearts of the simple [*the naive, easy to deceive*].

19 For your obedience is come abroad unto all men [*your reputation for being obedient is known far and wide*]. I am glad therefore on your behalf [*I have had much reason to be happy because of you*]: but yet I would have you wise unto that which is good, and simple concerning evil [*I still want to remind you to always be on guard to do good and avoid evil*].

20 And the God of peace shall bruise Satan under your feet shortly [*God will ultimately give you power over Satan and his influence*]. The grace of our Lord Jesus Christ be with you. Amen.

21 Timotheus [*Timothy, the one to whom Paul will later write two letters, known today as 1 and 2 Timothy*] my workfellow [*my companion*], and Lucius, and Jason, and Sosipater, my kinsmen [*my relatives*], salute you.

22 I Tertius [*Paul's scribe*], who wrote this epistle [*who wrote down this letter as Paul dictated it*], salute [*greet*] you in the Lord.

23 Gaius mine host, and of the whole church [*who has hosted us and the whole church here in Corinth*], saluteth [*greets*] you. Erastus the chamberlain of the city [*the city manager*] saluteth you, and Quartus a brother.

24 The grace [*help, mercy, and kindness*] of our Lord Jesus Christ be with you all. Amen.

Verses 25–27 can be confusing. If you look closely, you will see that they are one long sentence, with all kinds of clauses and phrases. If you were to take all the modifying clauses and phrases out, you would have, basically, "Now to him (the Father)," at the beginning of verse 25. . ." be glory through Christ and his gospel," at the end of verse 27.

By the way, as you compare verse 25 in the Bible to the JST verse 25, you will see that Joseph Smith changed the wording from "my gospel" in the Bible, to "the gospel" in the JST, because it is not Paul's gospel.

25 Now to him [*God*] that is of power to stablish you [*who has power to save you and establish you in His kingdom*] according to my gospel, and the preaching of Jesus Christ [*according to the gospel which Christ preached*], according to the revelation of the mystery [*Christ himself was a revelation from God, which to many remains a mystery*], which was kept secret since the world began [*which, unfortunately, many have remained unaware of since the beginning of history*],

JST Romans 16:25

25 Now to him that is of power to stablish you according to **the** gospel, and the preaching of Jesus Christ, according to the revelation of the mystery, which was kept secret since the world began,

26 But now is made manifest [*but now Jesus has come*], and by the scriptures of the prophets [*just as prophesied by ancient prophets*], according to the commandment of the everlasting God, made known to all nations [*being preached to all nations, Jew and Gentile*] for the obedience of faith [*to make obedience available to everyone who has faith in Jesus Christ*]:

27 To God only wise, be glory through Jesus Christ for ever. Amen.

THE FIRST EPISTLE OF PAUL THE APOSTLE TO THE CORINTHIANS

This letter from the Apostle Paul to the members of the Church in Corinth [*in southern Greece today*], was probably written from Philippi [*in northeastern Greece*], probably in March or April of AD 57. Corinth was a wealthy commercial center, with ideas, philosophies, and religions from both East and West. Idol worship dominated the area, with 12 different temples in the city of Corinth alone. Sexual immorality was rampant everywhere. The people engaged in prostitution as part of their worship ceremonies in the temple of Aphrodite. In fact, leaders encouraged sexual immorality and other immoral behavior. Paul wrote three letters to the Corinthian Saints. We don't have the first one, referred to in

1 Corinthians 5:9. Thus, First Corinthians is actually the second letter Paul wrote to them. In it he responds to several issues and questions they asked him in the letter they sent to him in reply to his first (see 1 Corinthians 7:1).

Paul established the Church in Corinth during his second missionary journey, about AD 50. He had lived in Corinth himself for about a year and a half (see Acts 18:8–11).

FIRST CORINTHIANS 1

Paul begins his letter by greeting the Saints at Corinth and greets them for members all over the Church. He will then teach these members to avoid contention and seek to be unified in the gospel. From his letter, we see that some apostasy had already made its way into the Church at Corinth.

1 PAUL, called to be an apostle of Jesus Christ through the will of God, and Sosthenes our brother [*Sosthenes, who was a member of the Church and had been publically beaten because of his association with Paul; see Acts 18:17*],

JST 1 Corinthians 1:1

1 Paul, **an apostle, called of Jesus Christ** through the will of God; and Sosthenes our brother,

2 Unto the church of God which is at Corinth, to them that are sanctified in [Strong's *#0037; who have dedicated themselves to*] Christ Jesus, called to be saints [*holy ones*], with all that in every place [*along with all other Saints who*] call upon the name of Jesus Christ our Lord, both theirs and ours [*their Lord and our Lord*]:

3 Grace be unto you, and peace, from God our Father, and from the Lord Jesus Christ.

Verse 3, above, is another good reminder that the Father and Son are separate individuals.

4 I thank my God always on your behalf, for the grace of God which is given you by Jesus Christ [*I give thanks constantly for the gospel and the Atonement, which the Father has given you through Jesus Christ*];

The only change made by Joseph Smith in both verses 4 and 5 was to change "by" to "of." We included these JST verses as a testimony that the Prophet paid much inspired attention to detail.

JST 1 Corinthians 1:4

4 I thank my God always on your behalf, for the grace of God which is given you **of** Jesus Christ;

5 That in every thing ye are enriched by him, in all utterance, and in all knowledge [*which enriches and blesses every aspect of your lives*];

JST 1 Corinthians 1:5

5 That in everything ye are enriched **of** him, in all utterance, and in all knowledge;

6 Even as the testimony of Christ was confirmed [*strengthened*] in you:

7 So that ye come behind in no gift [*so that you do not lack any spiritual gifts*]; waiting for the coming of our Lord Jesus Christ:

8 Who shall also confirm you [*strengthen you, make you strong and stable*] unto the end, that ye may be blameless in the day of our Lord Jesus Christ. [*Verses 7 and 8 are basically saying that you have all that is necessary so that you can prepare to appear before Christ and have a pleasant judgment day.*]

9 God is faithful [*you can rely on God*], by whom ye were called unto the fellowship of his Son Jesus Christ our Lord [*who called you to join with His son Jesus Christ and be saved*].

10 Now I beseech you, brethren, by the name of our Lord Jesus Christ, that ye all speak the same thing [*stay true to the gospel*], and that there be no divisions among you [*that you don't start falling away from the Church*]; but that ye be perfectly joined together in the same mind and in the same judgment [*that you stick absolutely with the gospel that we taught you*].

JST 1 Corinthians 1:10

10 Now I beseech you, brethren, **in** the name of our Lord Jesus Christ, that ye all speak the same thing, and that there be no divisions among you; but that ye be perfectly joined together in the same mind and in the same judgment.

11 For it hath been declared unto me of you, my brethren, by them which are of the house of Chloe, that there are contentions among you [*I have been told by members of Chloe's household that there are arguments among you as to Church doctrines*].

All of the men mentioned along with the Savior in verse 12, next, were faithful members of the Church. Paul is warning the Saints against becoming part of splinter groups who break off from the true Church, using as their excuse that they prefer one leader or another in the Church.

12 Now this I say, that every one of you saith [*I understand that some among you are saying*], I am of Paul [*I follow Paul*]; and I of Apollos [*I follow Apollos (a learned member of the Church; see Acts 18:24–19:5)*]; and I of Cephas [*I follow Peter*]; and I of Christ [*I follow Jesus*].

JST 1 Corinthians 1:12

12 Now this I say, that **many** of you saith, I am of Paul; and I of Apollos; and I of Cephas; and I of Christ.

What Paul says next is strong evidence for the fact that there is one true church. Different churches with different doctrines cannot all lead to celestial glory and exaltation.

13 Is Christ divided [*What's going on here? Did Christ preach several*

conflicting doctrines]? was Paul crucified for you? or were ye baptized in the name of Paul? [*In other words, whose church is this?*]

14 I thank God that I baptized none of you, but Crispus and Gaius;

15 Lest any should say that I had baptized in mine own name. [*This is strong language. Paul sounds disgusted that these members are so caught up in divisive arguing and doctrinal bickering that they are in danger of falling away from the Church.*]

16 And I baptized also the household of Stephanas: besides, I know not whether I baptized any other. [*I can't remember whether or not I personally baptized any others there in Corinth.*]

17 For Christ sent me not to baptize [*Christ didn't send me to baptize people in my own name to get converts for my church*], but to preach the gospel: not with wisdom of words [*not with the wisdom of man*], lest the cross of Christ should be made of none effect [*which would make the sacrifices required by Christ's gospel ineffective*].

18 For the preaching of the cross is to them that perish foolishness [*the gospel of Christ appears foolish to unbelievers*]; but unto us which are saved [*the Greek language gives this phrase as "to us who are being saved"*] it is the power of God.

"We believe the Bible to be the word of God as far as it is translated correctly" (Article of Faith number 8). The phrase "unto us which are saved," in verse 18, above, appears to be one of those places where the Bible wording was deliberately changed to reflect the idea of predestination. It includes the idea that one can confess believing in Christ and thus be saved, with no other thoughts or concerns about salvation. In the original Greek, from which our New Testament was translated, this phrase clearly said "being saved," indicating an ongoing process of effort and learning, rather than "are saved," which could indicate no further concern about being saved in heaven.

19 For it is written [*in Isaiah 29:14*], I will destroy the wisdom of the wise, and will bring to nothing the understanding of the prudent. [*In other words, the pure gospel of Jesus Christ will expose false teachings, false philosophies, etc., and destroy them in the minds of faithful Saints so they are not led astray by such things.*]

20 Where is the wise? where is the scribe [*scribes were the religious scholars among the Jews who interpreted the scriptures and came up with all kinds of false doctrines*]? where is the disputer [*debater, scholar*] of this world? hath not God made foolish the wisdom of this world? [*In other words, hasn't the true gospel exposed the foolishness of man-made doctrines and philosophies*]?

21 For after that in the wisdom of

God the world by wisdom knew not God [*since God has allowed people agency to follow man-made wisdom and make up their own false teachings to the point that they do not even believe in him*], it pleased God by the foolishness of preaching to save them that believe [*it pleased God to use what many worldly-wise people call "foolish preaching" of Christ to save those who will believe*] .

22 For the Jews require a sign [*the Jews always seem to say "show me a sign" to prove the gospel of Christ*], and the Greeks seek after wisdom [*and the Gentiles seem to always want to compare the gospel to their man-made philosophies to see if they should believe in Christ*]:

Just a reminder, as stated previously, the word "Greek" is generally used here as a generic term for "Gentiles" no matter where the Gentiles mentioned live.

23 But we preach Christ crucified, unto the Jews a stumblingblock [*we preach the simple truth about the Savior's Atonement, and the Jews stumble all over it because Jesus didn't keep the law of Moses*], and unto the Greeks foolishness [*and the Gentiles think our gospel teaching is foolish because it doesn't fit into their man-made false philosophies*];

24 But unto them which are called, both Jews and Greeks [*Gentiles*], Christ the power of God, and the wisdom of God [*Christ represents the power and wisdom of the Father*].

JST 1 Corinthians 1:24

24 But unto them **who believe** [*in other words, to those who are converted to Christ*], both Jews and Greeks, Christ the power of God, and the wisdom of God.

25 Because the foolishness of God is wiser than men [*the most foolish-looking aspect of God's teaching is wiser than the most impressive wisdom men can come up with*]; and the weakness of God is stronger than men. [*In other words, the wisdom of men can't even begin to compare with the wisdom of God.*]

26 For ye see your calling, brethren, how that not many wise men after the flesh, not many mighty, not many noble, are called: [*You see, with the perspective you have as members of the Church, that very few men who are wise, powerful, and high in society, in the eyes of the world, accept the gospel of Christ.*]

JST 1 Corinthians 1:26

26 For ye see your calling, brethren, how that not many wise men after the flesh, not many mighty, not many noble, are **chosen** [*to preach the gospel (see verse 27) and ultimately to receive the blessings of the gospel because they choose not to accept it*];

27 But God hath chosen the foolish things of the world [*the humble Saints, whose beliefs look foolish and whose intellect appears weak to the so-called "wise" of the world*] to confound [*to successfully*

stand up to] the wise; and God hath chosen the weak things of the world to confound the things [*the people*] which are mighty;

JST 1 Corinthians 1:27

27 **For** God hath chosen the foolish things of the world to confound the wise; and God hath chosen the weak things of the world to confound the things which are mighty;

28 And base things of the world [*the lowly, simple, humble people, whom scholars, intellectuals, philosophers, etc., consider to be naive, unintelligent, so simple they can be easily led around without thinking*], and things which [*people who*] are despised, hath God chosen [*to be in His Church and to lead His Church*], yea [*indeed*], and things [*people*] which are not [*people whom the worldly wise consider to be nothing are chosen by God*], to bring to nought [*to destroy*] things that are: [*In other words, the humble Saints, upon whom the people of the world look down, will continue to carry the true gospel of Christ forth until it fills the whole earth (Daniel 2:35, 44–45) and until all the false, proud, arrogant teachings of the worldly-wise are put down in the light of truth.*]

JST 1 Corinthians 1:28

28 And base things of the world, and things which are despised, hath God chosen, yea, and things which are not, to bring to naught things that are **mighty**;

29 That no flesh should glory in his presence [*so that no people who are arrogant and wise in their own opinion will be able to boast of themselves in the presence of God*].

30 But of him [*from the Father; in other words, because of the kindness of the Father*] are ye in Christ Jesus [*you have been brought to Christ*], who of God [*who was sent from God*] is made unto us [*who becomes our source of*] wisdom, and righteousness, and sanctification [*salvation*], and redemption [*being saved from our sins and the false philosophies of the world*]:

31 That, according as it is written [*in Jeremiah 9:24*], He that glorieth, let him glory in the Lord. [*In other words, because we have the true gospel, we can take pleasure and satisfaction in glorious truths from the Lord, rather than getting caught up in man-made philosophies and false worldly doctrines*]

FIRST CORINTHIANS 2

Paul begins here by humbly confessing that he was very concerned by his lack of speaking and teaching ability when he first came to Corinth as a missionary on his second major missionary journey. He goes on to write a powerful sermon to these members of the Church in Corinth, teaching that the Holy Ghost is the real teacher when the gospel is preached. You may well recognize some verses here which are often quoted in sermons and lessons today. They include verses 9, 11, and 14.

1 AND I, brethren, when I came to you [*in Corinth*], came not with excellency of speech [*as a skilled speaker*] or of wisdom [*or with a lot of worldly wisdom*], declaring unto you the testimony of God [*as I taught you the gospel of Jesus Christ*].

2 For I determined not to know any thing among you, save Jesus Christ, and him crucified. [*Indeed, I kept my message very simple, focusing only on teaching you about Jesus and His Atonement.*]

3 And I was with you in weakness [*my weaknesses and imperfections were obvious to you and to me*], and in fear, and in much trembling.

4 And my speech and my preaching was not with enticing words of man's wisdom [*I did not use cunning, flattering words to teach you man's wisdom*], but in demonstration of the Spirit and of power [*rather, I came with the Holy Ghost and power of God*]:

5 That your faith should not stand in the wisdom of men [*so that your faith in Christ would not be based on the wisdom of men, intellectual, academic, etc.*], but in the power of God.

6 Howbeit [*however*] we speak wisdom among them that are perfect [*however, the spiritually mature among you will recognize the great wisdom contained in the gospel*]: yet not the wisdom of this world, nor of the princes [*leaders*] of this world, that come to nought: [*The wisdom contained in the gospel is not the wisdom of the world, which will ultimately come to nothing.*]

7 But we speak the wisdom of God in a mystery [*the wisdom of God and His teachings remain a mystery to unbelievers*], even the hidden wisdom [*the wisdom, the gospel, which is hidden from the worldly by their own unbelief*], which God ordained before the world unto our glory [*which the Father prepared for us clear back before the world was created to bring us back to Him in glory*]:

8 Which none of the princes [*the unbelieving leaders*] of this world knew [*accepted*]: for had they known [*accepted*] it, they would not have crucified the Lord of glory [*Jesus*].

9 But as it is written [*in Isaiah 64:4*], Eye hath not seen, nor ear heard, neither have entered into the heart of man, the things which God hath prepared for them that love him [*it is impossible to imagine the wonderful blessings the Father has in store for those who love Him enough to keep His commandments and thus return to live with Him someday*].

Next, Paul gives us important insights as to the great value of having the Holy Ghost as a constant companion.

10 But God hath revealed them unto us by his Spirit [*God does reveal these things to us by the power of the Holy Ghost*]: for the Spirit searcheth [*helps us explore,*

investigate] all things, yea, the deep things of God.

11 For what man knoweth the things of a man, save the spirit of man which is in him? even so the things of God knoweth no man, but the Spirit of God. [*In effect, we understand other people because we are human, but we can only understand the things of God and gain a testimony of Him through the Holy Ghost.*]

JST 1 Corinthians 2:11

> 11 For what man knoweth the things of a man, save the spirit of man which is in him? even so the things of God knoweth no man, **except he has the Spirit of God**.

12 Now we [*as members of the Church*] have received, not the spirit of the world [*not the understanding which comes through worldly wisdom*], but the spirit which is of God [*rather, the understanding which comes from the Holy Ghost*]; that we might know [*understand and have testimonies of*] the things that are freely given to us of God.

13 Which things also we speak [*preach, teach*], not in the words which man's wisdom teacheth [*we don't use worldly vocabulary and wisdom to teach the gospel*], but which the Holy Ghost teacheth [*rather, we use special gospel vocabulary and wisdom, accompanied by the Holy Ghost*]; comparing spiritual things with spiritual.

14 But the natural man [*unbelievers who won't listen to the Holy Ghost*] receiveth not [*won't accept*] the things of the Spirit of God: for they are foolishness unto him [*they consider the gospel of Christ to be foolishness*]: neither can he know them [*understand them through intellectual and academic methods*], because they are spiritually discerned [*they can only be examined and understood with the help of the Holy Ghost*].

15 But he that is spiritual judgeth all things [*people who are spiritual are able to see all things in the light of the gospel and with the help of the Holy Ghost*], yet he himself is judged of no man [*the only judge he has to worry about is Christ*].

16 [*Paul now quotes Isaiah 40:13*] For who hath known the mind of the Lord, that he may instruct him [*who is wise enough to teach the Lord anything*]? [*Answer: No one, so don't let the wisdom and teachings of men take priority over the teachings of God in your lives.*] But we have the mind of Christ [*we know the mind of Christ, in other words, He has taught us His mind and will, and thus we don't have to get caught up in the confusion and falseness of much of the teaching and wisdom of men*].

FIRST CORINTHIANS 3

Paul is straightforward (some would even say he is blunt), but it is because of his love for these new members in Corinth as he encourages them to separate themselves from the worldly philosophies and lifestyles in Corinth. He tells them that he must speak to them as he would to children who are yet immature in the Church and urges them to build their lives upon the principles of the gospel, making their lives and bodies fit for the Spirit of the Lord to dwell in.

One of the better-known quotes in this chapter, among Latter-day Saints, is that found in verses 16–17, where Paul teaches us that our bodies are temples of God.

1 AND I, brethren, could not speak unto you as unto spiritual [*I can't yet speak to you as I would to spiritually mature members*], but as unto carnal [*rather, as to converts who are yet caught up much in worldly thinking and behaving*], even as unto babes in Christ [*in fact, I must speak to you as brand new in the gospel of Christ*].

2 I have fed you with milk [*I have given you the very basics of the gospel*], and not with meat [*not with advanced doctrines*]: for hitherto ye were not able to bear it, neither yet now are ye able [*because you have not been able to handle it up to now and, in fact, you are still not able to handle it*].

JST 1 Corinthians 3:2

2 I have fed you with milk, and not with meat; for hitherto ye were not able to **receive** it, neither yet now are ye able.

3 For ye are yet carnal [*you are still too worldly*]: for whereas [*let me tell you what I mean*] there is among you envying [*jealousy*], and strife [*contention, arguing, bickering*], and divisions [*apostasy*], are ye not carnal, and walk as men [*isn't that sufficient evidence that you are still worldly, and acting like everyone else in Corinth*]?

4 For while [*as long as*] one saith, I am of Paul; and another, I am of Apollos; [*as long as you remain separated into factions—as mentioned in 1 Corinthians 1:11–13—rather than being united, following Christ*] are ye not carnal [*are you not proving that you have not yet been spiritually reborn*]?

5 Who then is Paul [*the Apostle*], and who is Apollos [*a faithful member and excellent teacher; see Acts 18:24–28*], but ministers by whom ye believed [*aren't we (Apollos and I) just servants of the Lord who brought you the gospel*], even as the Lord gave to every man [*simply following the Lord's instructions to teach you the gospel*]?

It may seem strange to us that these converts in Corinth would be dividing up into groups, some claiming to follow Paul, some claiming to be loyal to Apollos, or Peter (chapter 1, verse 12) or whomever. But if we remember that many different idols were worshiped in Corinth and that it was common in Corinthian culture for people to choose among several available "gods" for their family or neighborhood, school or business, etc., then it becomes more understandable as to what was going on among the members and why Paul had to repeat himself so many times in trying to get them to understand the principle of one God only, and His Son, Jesus Christ.

6 I have planted [*I came along first and preached the gospel to you, planting the seeds in your minds and hearts; compare with Alma 32*], Apollos watered [*then Apollos came among you and nourished the gospel seeds in you by his excellent teaching*]; but God gave the increase [*but God is the one who made them grow*].

7 So then neither is he that planteth any thing, neither he that watereth [*the servants of the Lord who plant the gospel seeds in your hearts and nourish them by teaching you are nothing compared to God*]; but God that giveth the increase [*God is everything and must be the focus of your loyalty as He causes the seeds to grow within you*].

8 Now he that planteth and he that watereth are one [*have just one purpose, that is, to bring the gospel to others*]: and every man shall receive his own reward according to his own labour [*the Lord's servants, missionaries, teachers, and so forth are rewarded by the Lord for their labors*].

9 For we are labourers together with God [*we work in unity with God*]: ye are God's husbandry [*you are His garden*], ye are God's building [*He is growing His gospel in you*].

10 According to the grace [*kindness and help*] of God which is given unto me, as a wise masterbuilder [*God is like a wise master builder*], I have laid the foundation, and another buildeth thereon [*other servants of the Lord come along after me and build upon the foundation which I have laid, under God's direction*]. But let every man take heed how he buildeth thereupon [*each of you must be very careful how you build upon the foundation of the gospel which has been laid for you*].

11 For other foundation can no man lay than that is laid, which is Jesus Christ. [*If you choose to build your lives upon any foundation other than Christ, you will fail.*]

12 Now if any man build upon this foundation gold, silver, precious stones, wood, hay, stubble [*if you choose to try to build upon the foundation of wealth or any material priority*];

13 Every man's work shall be made manifest [*your work will eventually be exposed for what it is*]: for the day shall declare it [*the test of time will reveal it*], because it shall be revealed by fire [*the "trial by fire" eventually reveals whether or not we have built our lives on a firm foundation or not*]; and the fire shall try [*test*] every man's work of what sort it is [*and show what it is really made of*].

14 If any man's work abide [*stands through the trial by fire, in other words, if our lives stand up to trials, troubles, persecutions, etc., and we remain loyal to our cov-*

enants and commitments to Christ] which he hath built thereupon, he shall receive a reward [*we will be well rewarded for building upon the foundation of Jesus Christ*].

Verse 15, next, is an example of the importance of the Joseph Smith Translation of the Bible (JST). The Prophet changed just one word in this verse, but it changes the meaning dramatically. Joseph Smith changed the word "shall" to "may." This is very important because it changes the meaning of the verse from saying that people who foolishly build their lives upon material things "shall be saved" to saying that they "may be saved," if they use their agency to repent when they discover that they have built upon a foundation other than Christ.

15 If any man's work shall be burned [*if the things a person has built his life around are not in harmony with the gospel and thus don't survive the trials by fire*], he shall suffer loss: but he himself shall be saved; yet so as by fire [*if he will let the Holy Ghost "burn" the sins and imperfections out of his life by inspiring him to repent and use the Atonement*].

JST 1 Corinthians 3:15

15 If any man's work shall be burned, he shall suffer loss; but he himself **may** be saved; yet so as by fire.

16 Know ye not that ye are the temple of God, and that the Spirit of God dwelleth in you [*don't you realize that you are the temple of God and should take care of your mind and body in such a way that the Holy Ghost can dwell in you and direct you constantly*]?

Remember, as mentioned in notes at the beginning of First Corinthians in this study guide, that temples were a part of everyday life in Corinth. In fact, there were twelve temples set up in that area to worship various idols. Paul is very skillfully using this background and cultural setting to remind these relatively new members of the Church that each of them can be a "temple" in which the Holy Ghost will dwell, if they will build themselves upon the foundation of Jesus Christ, thus keeping their "temples" clean.

17 If any man defile the temple of God [*makes his temple unclean through sin, evil, personal corruption, crudeness, and so forth*], him shall God destroy [*if he doesn't repent*]; for the temple of God is holy, which temple ye are.

18 Let no man deceive himself [*don't fool yourselves*]. If any man among you seemeth to be wise in this world, let him become a fool [*let him humble himself*], that he may be wise [*that he may be taught by God and thus become truly wise*].

19 For the wisdom of this world is foolishness with God [*man's worldly wisdom becomes foolishness in the light of the gospel*]. For it is written [*in Job 5:13*], He taketh

the wise in their own craftiness. [*In other words, those who think they are "crafty" or cunning enough to work around God's laws will ultimately be "taken" or caught, trapped by the law of justice.*]

20 And again, The Lord knoweth the thoughts of the wise [*worldly wise*] are vain [*lead to no good*].

21 Therefore let no man glory in men [*don't get caught up in and trust the thinking of worldly people*]. For all things are yours [*exaltation is available to you, if you will just follow Christ*];

22 Whether Paul, or Apollos, or Cephas [*Peter*], or the world, or life, or death, or things present, or things to come; all are yours;

23 And ye are Christ's; and Christ is God's. [*See also Romans 8:17 where Paul teaches that we can become "joint heirs with Christ." In other words, through your faithfulness, you will belong to Christ (Mosiah 5:7), and He will belong to the Father (Revelation 3:21), thus you will belong to the Father and have exaltation.*]

FIRST CORINTHIANS 4

The word "mysteries" as used next in verse 1, is commonly used in the scriptures to mean the simple basics of the gospel, such as the Ten Commandments, repentance, baptism, the Gift of the Holy Ghost, three degrees of glory, exaltation, eternal family units, life after death, the spirit world, and so forth, which remain a "mystery" to people who have never heard of the gospel or who do not believe it. Joseph Fielding Smith said "Until it is understood, however, a simple truth may be a great mystery." *Doctrines of Salvation*, Vol. 1, p. 296. In Mosiah 1:5, King Benjamin taught his sons that without the scriptures, they would not be able to understand the "mysteries." He said "I say unto you, my sons, were it not for these things, which have been kept and preserved by the hand of God, that we might read and understand of his mysteries, and have his commandments always before our eyes, that even our fathers would have dwindled in unbelief, and we should have been like unto our brethren, the Lamanites, who know nothing concerning these things, or even do not believe them when they are taught them, because of the traditions of their fathers, which are not correct."

1 LET a man so account of us, as of the ministers of Christ, and stewards of the mysteries of God. [*Please consider us to be ministers of Christ who bring you the simple basics of the gospel, which remain mysteries to unbelievers and those who have not heard the gospel.*]

2 Moreover it is required in stewards, that a man be found faithful. [*All ministers of Christ must be worthy.*]

JST 1 Corinthians 4:2

2 Moreover it is required of stewards, that a man be found faithful.

3 But with me it is a very small thing that I should be judged of you, or of man's judgment [*I really don't worry much about what you think of me or what others think of me*]: yea, I judge not mine own self [*I don't even judge myself*].

4 For I know nothing by myself; yet am I not hereby justified [*that doesn't mean that I can sit back and relax with respect to striving to be righteous*]: but he that judgeth me is the Lord [*what really counts is what the Lord thinks of me*].

JST 1 Corinthians 4:4

4 **For though I know nothing against myself** [*In other words, even though I have a clear conscience*]; yet I am not hereby justified; but he who judgeth me is the Lord.

5 Therefore judge nothing before the time, [*I am careful not to judge anything or anyone prematurely*] until the Lord come [*but will wait for the Lord to Judge people*], who both will bring to light the hidden things of darkness [*who will expose all the hidden wickedness of people*], and will make manifest the counsels [*thoughts, plans, desires*] of the hearts: and then shall every man have praise of God. [*All who deserve it will then have the praise of God, when Christ Himself judges us.*]

JST 1 Corinthians 4:5

5 Therefore **I** judge nothing before the time, until the Lord come, who both will bring to light the hidden things of darkness, and will make manifest the counsels of the hearts; and then shall every man have praise of God.

6 And these things, brethren, I have in a figure transferred to myself and to Apollos [*I have, for example, applied these things to myself and to Apollos (a convert who was a great teacher among the Corinthian Saints)*] for your sakes [*for your benefit*]; that ye might learn in us [*by our example*] not to think of men above [*beyond*] that which is written [*that we should not judge one another unrighteously*], that no one of you be puffed up [*become proud, arrogant, and judgmental*] for one against another.

7 For who maketh thee to differ from another [*who makes one of you different from another; who makes one of you superior to another*]? and what hast thou that thou didst not receive [*What do you have that you did not receive from God? In other words, why should you think yourself superior to another, as if you truly earned what you have received from God*]? now if thou didst receive it [*since you receive everything you have from God*], why dost thou glory [*why should you think you are anything special above anyone else*], as if thou hadst not received it [*as if you had earned it completely yourself rather than receiving it from God*]? [*This is very similar to the message King*

Benjamin gave his people in Mosiah 4:19, namely, that we are all beggars and are completely dependant on God for everything we have.]

8 Now ye are full [*you are very well off*], now ye are rich [*you are wealthy as to worldly goods there in Corinth*], ye have reigned as kings without us [*you are living like kings*]: and I would to God ye did reign, that we also might reign with you [*I wish that you really were kings of righteousness and that we could be there in Corinth with you*].

9 For I think that God hath set forth us the apostles last [*it sometimes seems to me that God has placed us Apostles last when it comes to money, wealth, homes, and so forth*], as it were appointed to death [*as if we were supposed to plan on trials, persecutions, even death as a result of our calling and service to others*]: for we are made a spectacle unto the world, and to angels, and to men [*we are often ridiculed in public for all to see, including angels as well as people*].

10 We are fools for Christ's sake [*we look like fools to many because of our commitment to Christ*], but ye are wise in Christ [*you will be made wise if you remain loyal to Christ*]; we are weak [*we have been weakened physically by persecutions and hard times*], but ye are strong [*you still have it good*]; ye are honourable [*many people still respect you*], but we are despised [*many unbelievers know and despise us*].

11 Even unto this present hour [*even now*] we both hunger, and thirst, and are naked, and are buffeted, and have no certain dwellingplace [*we suffer from hunger, thirst, inadequate clothing, and don't know for sure from day to day where we will be staying*];

12 And labour, working with our own hands [*we earn our own way*]: being reviled, we bless [*we return good for evil*]; being persecuted, we suffer it [*we put up with a lot of persecution*]:

13 Being defamed [*slandered*], we intreat [*answer with kindness*]: we are made as the filth of the world [*we are treated as trash*], and are the offscouring of all things [*are treated as the scum of the earth*] unto this day.

14 I write not these things to shame you [*to make you feel ashamed that you have it so good*], but as my beloved sons [*as my own much-loved children*] I warn you.

15 For though ye have ten thousand instructors in Christ [*even though you have many gospel teachers now*], yet have ye not many fathers [*I am like a father to you, because I first brought you life in the gospel of Christ*]: for in Christ Jesus I have begotten you through the gospel. [*You have become like family to me because of the gospel. I introduced it to you, and, in that sense, I am your father.*]

16 Wherefore I beseech [*urge*] you, be ye followers of me [*follow my example*].

17 For this cause have I sent unto you Timotheus [*Timothy, who became a missionary companion to Paul; see Acts 16:1*], who is my beloved son [*who has become like a son to me*], and faithful in the Lord, who shall bring you into remembrance of my ways which be in Christ, as I teach every where in every church. [*When Timothy arrives in Corinth, he will remind you about the things I taught you, which are the same things I teach in wards and branches everywhere.*]

18 Now some are puffed up [*have become arrogant and are preaching false doctrines, apostate doctrines*], as though I would not come to you [*as if they think I will not come to you in Corinth and straighten them out*].

19 But I will come to you shortly, if the Lord will, and will know, not the speech of them which are puffed up, but the power [*and will see first hand what actual influence and power these teachers of apostasy have among you*].

20 For the kingdom of God is not in word, but in power [*the true Church of God on earth is not sustained by the confusing and contentious words of men but by the power of God*].

21 What will ye? shall I come unto you with a rod, or in love, and in the spirit of meekness? [*What do you prefer, that I come to you, crashing down severely upon the false teachers and their followers among you, or would you prefer that I come in gentleness and love*?]

FIRST CORINTHIANS 5

Remember that sexual immorality was very common in Corinthian society and culture and was considered normal behavior. Many members of the Church had the same attitudes about sexual involvements outside of marriage as their nonmember fellow citizens. Thus, in this chapter, Paul attacks this serious sinful behavior head on.

Just a note about the JST references given in this study guide. Not all of the JST changes are provided in our Latter-day Saint edition of the Bible. Decisions had to be made as to what to include and what not to include because of space limitations. Therefore, you will not find some of the JST references we give in this study guide, in our Bible. But, you can find them in the full version of the Joseph Smith Translation of the Bible, which is available in some Latter-day Saint oriented bookstores or online.

1 IT is reported commonly that there is fornication among you [*I understand that there is much sexual immorality among you*], and such fornication as is not so much as named among the Gentiles [*and even one type of sinful sexual intercourse that is not even known among Gentile nonmembers*], that one should have his father's

wife [*namely, incest, wherein one has sexual relations with his mother, his father's wife*].

2 And ye are puffed up [*are you so arrogant and prideful that you find this acceptable!*], and have not rather mourned, that he that hath done this deed might be taken away from among you [*whereas you should have been so shocked and saddened about such behavior that you would have excommunicated such sinners and no longer associated with them*].

3 For I verily, as absent in body, but present in spirit, have judged already, as though I were present, concerning him that hath so done this deed [*Even though I am physically away from you, I am there among you in spirit and have already passed judgment on those who are involved in this type of behavior*],

JST 1 Corinthians 5:3

3 For verily, as absent in body but present in spirit, **I have judged already him who hath so done this deed, as though I were present**.

4 In the name of our Lord Jesus Christ, when ye are gathered together, and my spirit, with the power of our Lord Jesus Christ,

JST 1 Corinthians 5:4

4 In the name of our Lord Jesus Christ, when ye are gathered together, **and have the Spirit, with the power of our Lord Jesus Christ**,

5 To deliver such an one unto Satan [*to excommunicate such members and turn them over to the buffetings of Satan*] for the destruction of the flesh [*which will cause them much anguish during the next part of their mortal lives*], that the spirit may be saved in the day of the Lord Jesus [*in order that they might repent and ultimately be saved on Judgment Day*].

JST 1 Corinthians 5:5

5 To deliver such **a** one unto Satan for the destruction of the flesh, that the spirit may be saved in the day of the Lord Jesus.

6 Your glorying is not good [*your boasting that "anything goes" among you is not good*]. Know ye not that a little leaven [*yeast*] leaveneth the whole lump [*of dough*]? [*If you do not deal properly with this terrible problem, it will continue to spread among you until everyone in the Church is affected by it, just as a little bit of yeast works through the whole lump of dough and affects it all.*]

7 Purge out therefore the old leaven [*get rid of the old sinful behaviors and attitudes which permeate the culture of Corinth, even to the extent of excommunicating some members if needed*], that ye may be a new lump [*so that you may be a new, pure and clean "lump of dough"*], as ye are unleavened [*and remain free of the old sins and corruption of your environment*]. For even Christ our passover is sacrificed for us [*Christ is our "unleavened bread"*

and was sacrificed for us that we may be freed from our enemies, including sin]:

> The reference in verse 7, above, to Passover, refers to the commandment Moses gave to the children of Israel (see Exodus 12:3–8) to prepare to be redeemed from their slavery in Egypt by putting lamb's blood (representing Christ's redeeming blood) on their door posts and eating unleavened bread (representing not being corrupted by the "leaven" or yeast of the society around them).

8 Therefore let us keep the feast [*of Passover*], not with old leaven [*not with old or past sins and wickedness*], neither with the leaven of malice [*evil intentions*] and wickedness; but with the unleavened bread [*the new influence of the gospel which is free from the corruption of the world*] of sincerity and truth.

9 I wrote unto you in an epistle not to company with fornicators [*I told you in a previous letter not to associate with people involved in sexual immorality*]:

10 Yet not altogether with the fornicators [*sexually immoral*] of this world, or with the covetous [*greedy*], or extortioners [*swindlers, cheaters*], or with idolaters [*but what I meant was not to allow them to have the privileges of Church membership, unless they repent*]; for then must ye needs go out of the world [*because if you never associated at all with such people, it would require that you leave this world, and that is not very practical*].

11 But now I have written unto you [*but now I am counseling you*] not to keep company [*not to associate with people*], if any man that is called a brother [*a member*] be a fornicator, or covetous, or an idolater, or a railer [*one who yells and screams at others or is always criticizing others*], or a drunkard, or an extortioner; with such an one no not to eat [*don't even eat with him or her*].

> The message in the above verses about choosing friends and associates wisely is very important. Peer pressure causes many to commit sin.

12 For what have I to do to judge them also that are without [*outside of the Church*]? do not ye judge them that are within?

<u>JST 1 Corinthians 5:12</u>

> 12 For what have I to do to judge them also that are without? do not **they** judge them that are within [*aren't nonmembers critical of church members who won't join them in sinning*]?

13 But them that are without [*who are outside the Church, in other words, not members*] God judgeth. Therefore put away from among yourselves that wicked person [*you must do what is necessary to cleanse the Church from wickedness, even if it means excommunication; compare with D&C 42:24–26*].

FIRST CORINTHIANS 6

Paul continues in this chapter by counseling the members of the Church in Corinth to avoid living like the world does. He counsels them to avoid the common practice in Corinth of taking each other to court to settle disputes, instead of working things out peaceably among themselves. In fact, he scolds them for using courts of law when they should be acting more like Saints and settling things with each other. He reminds them that they have the potential to someday be gods and thus are behaving far beneath their potential by being petty with each other.

1 DARE any of you, having a matter [*a dispute or disagreement*] against another, go to law [*take him or her to court*] before the unjust [*going before judges who often turn out to be corrupt*], and not before the saints [*rather than going to local leaders of the Church for help in settling things*]?

2 Do ye not know that the saints shall judge the world? [*This phrase has at least two meanings. First, the world will ultimately be judged by the standards of the gospel, which true Saints keep. Second, during the Millennium, the true Saints will rule and reign on earth with the Savior. See Revelation 20:4*] and if the world shall be judged by you, are ye unworthy to judge the smallest matters [*if you are someday going to judge the world, shouldn't you be able to take care of these relatively small or trivial matters among yourselves*]?

> In the first phrase of verse 3, next, Paul clearly teaches that worthy Saints will someday have power over angels, in other words, they will someday become gods. Compare with D&C 132:20.

3 Know ye not that we shall judge angels [*don't you know you will someday be gods*]? how much more things that pertain to this life [*shouldn't you be very capable then of handling disputes, etc., that come among you in this mortal life*]?

4 If then ye have judgments of things pertaining to this life, set them to judge who are least esteemed in the church. [*It would be better for you to take your disputes before the least respected judge who is a member of the Church than to go before worldly judges.*]

5 I speak to your shame [*shame on you for being so petty with each other!*]. Is it so, that there is not a wise man among you [*are there no wise men among you members there in Corinth*]? no, not one that shall be able to judge between his brethren [*not even one to whom you could go to get help in working out disagreements*]?

6 But brother goeth to law with brother, and that before the unbelievers [*one member takes another to court, and to make things worse,*

they do it in the court system of unbelievers].

7 Now therefore there is utterly a fault among you, because ye go to law one with another [*you are way out of line in participating in this type of behavior*]. Why do ye not rather take wrong [*why don't you follow the Savior's council to turn the other cheek, to endure wrong; Matthew 5:38–48*]? why do ye not rather suffer yourselves to be defrauded [*why don't you allow yourselves to be cheated rather than getting all tied up with contention among yourselves*]?

8 Nay, ye do wrong [*you are the ones who are in the wrong, by not following the Savior's counsel*], and defraud [*you are the real cheaters!*], and that your brethren [*and the sad thing is that you are doing it to other members of the Church*].

In verses 9 and 10, next, Paul gives quite a list of sins which would qualify people for telestial glory, if not repented of.

9 Know ye not that the unrighteous shall not inherit the kingdom of God [*don't you realize that your contentious behavior puts you in the same category as the unrighteous and you will not get celestial glory if you continue*]? Be not deceived [*don't be fooled*]: neither fornicators [*those who break the law of chastity*], nor idolaters [*idol worshipers*], nor adulterers [*those who commit adultery*], nor effeminate [*men who use boys in homosexual acts; see* Strong's *#3120*], nor abusers of themselves with mankind [*practicing male homosexuals*],

10 Nor thieves, nor covetous, nor drunkards, nor revilers [*people who are mean-tempered; who constantly criticize others; who mock and make fun of that which is good*], nor extortioners [*people who rob others through fear and intimidation*], shall inherit the kingdom of God.

In verse 11, next, we are reminded of the wonderful power of the Atonement to cleanse and heal. After naming several very serious and abominable sins, in the above verses, which were common behavior in Corinth, and which some members there have committed, Paul reminds them that they can be completely forgiven upon deep repentance.

11 And such were some of you [*some of you were involved in these kinds of sins*]: but ye are washed [*you have been baptized, cleansed*], but ye are sanctified [*you have been made holy and fit to be in the presence of God*], but ye are justified [*you have followed the promptings of the Holy Ghost and thus been lined up in harmony with God's commandments so that you are ratified and approved to be in the presence of God*] in the name of the Lord Jesus [*this has happened to you because of the Savior*], and by the Spirit of our God [*and because you have followed the promptings of the Holy Ghost*].

The Joseph Smith Translation of the Bible makes very significant changes in verse 12, next.

12 All things are lawful unto me, but all things are not expedient: all things are lawful for me, but I will not be brought under the power of any.

JST 1 Corinthians 6:12

12 All **these** things are **not** lawful unto me [*the commandments teach against all of these sins*], **and** all **these** things are not expedient [*there is no reason for any of us to commit such sins*]. All things are **not** lawful for me, **therefore** I will not be brought under the power of any [*therefore I will not allow any such sins to have power over me*].

13 Meats [*foods*] for the belly [*satisfy the stomach's hunger*], and the belly for meats: [*The Corinthians had a saying that just as it is permissible to eat food to satisfy the stomach's hunger, so also it is proper to satisfy one's sexual appetites by fornication, adultery, homosexuality, child sexual partners, etc. See also McConkie,* Doctrinal New Testament Commentary, *Vol. 2, p. 340.*] but God shall destroy both it and them. [*All such sinners who don't repent will be destroyed spiritually and eventually will be punished by God.*] Now the body is not for fornication, but for the Lord [*remember, the body is the temple of the Spirit of God (1 Corinthians 3:16) and should not be defiled by sexual immorality*]; and the Lord for the body [*the Spirit of the Lord would like to dwell in your bodies*].

14 And God [*the Father*] hath both raised up the Lord [*has exalted Christ*], and will also raise up us by his own power [*and will exalt us if we keep the commandments*].

15 Know ye not that your bodies are the members of Christ [*don't you realize that, as baptized members of the Church, you have joined yourselves to Christ, and, in a sense, have become part of His body*]? shall I then take the members of Christ, and make them the members of an harlot [*would it be proper to take part of Christ and have it involved with a prostitute*]? God forbid [*absolutely not!*].

16 What? know ye not that he which is joined to an harlot is one body [*don't you realize that when you join yourself to another in sexual immorality, you both become part of a body of sin*]? for two, saith he [*God, in Genesis 2:24*], shall be one flesh [*just as God said that a husband and wife become one flesh, in other words, one family unit and have children, so also those who get involved with each other in acts of sexual immorality become one unit of sin*].

17 But he that is joined unto the Lord is one spirit [*those who join with the Lord in purity and righteousness become united with Him and will be saved*].

Again, we must have the Prophet Joseph Smith's help to understand a verse. The JST makes significant changes to verse 18, next.

18 Flee fornication [*avoid sexual immorality at all costs!*]. Every sin that a man doeth is without the body; but he that committeth fornication sinneth against his own body. [*when you commit sexual sin, you are committing serious sin against yourself*].

JST 1 Corinthians 6:18

18 Flee fornication. Every sin that a man **committeth** is **against** the body **of Christ**, **and** he **who** committeth fornication sinneth against his own body.

19 What? know ye not that your body is the temple of the Holy Ghost which is in you, which ye have of God, and ye are not your own [*don't you realize that you can be a "temple" in which the Holy Ghost dwells, which gift you get from God, and that you have given yourselves to God? In other words, how would you dare defile and pollute a part of God, which you are, having given yourselves to him by covenant at baptism?*]

20 For ye are bought with a price [*Christ paid a heavy price to redeem you from your sins*]: therefore glorify God in your body [*worship God by treating your body as a temple, keeping it clean and pure*], and in your spirit [*and keep your mind clean and pure too*], which are God's [*both of which you have dedicated to God through the covenants you have made with Him*].

FIRST CORINTHIANS 7

The JST makes changes in seventeen verses in this chapter. As you will see, without the Prophet's inspired changes, this chapter could lead to a number of damaging false doctrines. Indeed, many Christians have been confused or stumbled because of this chapter as it stands in the Bible.

Paul will deal with some issues which the Corinthian Saints brought up in the letter they wrote back to him in response to his first letter to them (which we don't have). See note about Paul's first letter to the Corinthians at the beginning of First Corinthians in this study guide.

Verse 1 contains what the Corinthian Saints said to Paul in their reply to him. They are wrong and have obviously misunderstood some basics of the gospel with respect to honorable relations between men and women, including marriage. Unfortunately, many in the world consider the powers of procreation to be inherently unclean and evil. This is not so. They are beautiful and wonderful and are key in happy marriages. They only become ugly, evil and destructive when misused. In fact, in the next life, after Judgment Day, when people have been placed in the three degrees of glory or outer darkness, the only ones who will have the powers of procreation and the privilege of using them will be those who become gods and bring forth spirit children to send to their own worlds. See Smith, *Doctrines of Salvation*, Vol. 2, pp. 286–288. Thus, the powers of procreation are pure, clean, holy, sacred, and wonderful when properly used in marriage between a man and a woman (see Proclamation on the Family, September 23, 1995, paragraph number 4). Just so you don't miss it, make sure you notice in verse 2 that Paul tells the members in Corinth that it is good to get married.

As we begin our study of this chapter, note that verse 1, as it stands, says that Paul says that it is good for a man not even to touch a woman. JST verse 1, however, changes the meaning completely. It informs us that it was the Corinthian Saints who said in their letter to Paul that "it is good for a man not to touch a woman." Paul will straighten out this false idea.

1 NOW concerning the things whereof ye wrote unto me: It is good for a man not to touch a woman.

JST 1 Corinthians 7:1

Now concerning the things whereof ye wrote unto me, **saying**, It is good for a man not to touch a woman.

2 Nevertheless, to avoid fornication, let every man have his own wife, and let every woman have her own husband. [*In other words, in your letter back to me, you said that it would actually be best if men and women had nothing to do with each other. However, I say that marriage is fine and helps people avoid sexual immorality.*]

JST 1 Corinthians 7:2

2 Nevertheless, **I say**, to avoid fornication, let every man have his own wife, and let every woman have her own husband.

Paul now responds, teaching that marriage is not just something which is second best to never marrying, or something to get involved in by those who are so weak that they can't control sexual urges. Rather, marriage is honorable, and husbands and wives should treat each other with love and kindness and as equals.

3 Let the husband render unto the wife due benevolence [*proper kindness and respect*]: and likewise also the wife unto the husband.

4 The wife hath not power of her own body, but the husband: and likewise also the husband hath not power of his own body, but the wife. [*They have given themselves to each other and are equal partners. Sexual relations will be desired by each and it is proper for them to give themselves to each other in physical intimacy.*]

5 Defraud ye not one the other, except it be with consent for a time, that ye may give yourselves to fasting and prayer [*do not be apart from each other except by mutual agreement for brief periods of time*

when you want to dedicate some time to fasting and prayer]; and come together again [*then resume sexual relations again; see* Strong's *#4905 "conjugal cohabitation"*], that Satan tempt you not for your incontinency [*so that you don't give Satan extra power to tempt you to become unfaithful to your spouse because of lack of self-control or because you are not finding physical satisfaction in your marriage*].

JST 1 Corinthians 7:5

5 **Depart ye not one from the other**, except it be with consent for a time, that ye may give yourselves to fasting and prayer; and come together again, that Satan tempt you not for your incontinency.

6 But I speak this by permission, and not of commandment [*I give this as my opinion and not by way of commandment from the Lord*].

JST 1 Corinthians 7:6

6 **And now what I speak is** by permission, and not by commandment.

Some people teach that Paul chose to remain single and use verses 7 and 8, next, to claim that he taught that it is better not to be married. Some groups use these verses to teach celibacy (deliberately remaining single as a form of devotion to God). Elder Spencer W. Kimball said that this is not so and explained it as follows: "Taking such statements in conjunction with others [*Paul*] made, it is clear that he is not talking about celibacy, but is urging the normal and controlled sex living in marriage and total continence [*refraining from sexual relations*] outside marriage. [*There is no real evidence that Paul was never married, as some students claim, and there are in fact indications to the contrary.*]" *Miracle of Forgiveness*, p. 64.

7 For I would that all men were even as I myself. [*Apostle Bruce R. McConkie explained that Paul was, in effect, saying: "I would that all men understood the law of marriage, that all had self-mastery over their appetites, and that all obeyed the laws of God in these respects." McConkie, Doctrinal New Testament Commentary, Vol. 2, p. 344.*] But every man hath his proper gift of God, one after this manner, and another after that [*each of us has gifts and strengths, one this and another that*].

JST 1 Corinthians 7:7

7 For I would that all men were even **as myself**. But every man hath his proper gift of God, one after this manner, and another after that.

8 I say therefore to the unmarried and widows, It is good for them if they abide even as I. [*Perhaps Paul is a widower and knows what it means to be single again and is counseling single members to be extra strong in controlling sexual desires. Perhaps he is saying something else, namely, that being single allows him to devote full attention*

to his missionary labors.]

9 But if they cannot contain, let them marry: for it is better to marry than to burn.

JST 1 Corinthians 7:9

9 But if they cannot **abide**, let them marry; for it is better to marry than **that any should commit sin**.

No matter how we explain or interpret verses 7–9, above, one thing is certain. Paul taught that celestial marriage is necessary. He said "Nevertheless neither is the man without the woman, neither the woman without the man, in the Lord." (1 Corinthians 11:11.) Also, there is no question as to whether or not Paul himself was or had been married (perhaps his wife had passed away). As a strict Pharisee (Acts 26:5), which he was before his conversion, he would have been required to be married, according to Jewish culture.

In verses 10 and 11, next, Paul counsels against divorce.

10 And unto the married I command, yet not I, but the Lord [*this is not my opinion, rather, it is what the Lord says*], Let not the wife depart from [*divorce*] her husband:

11 But and if she depart [*if she divorces him*], let her remain unmarried, or be reconciled to [*or work things out again with*] her husband: and let not the husband put away [*divorce*] his wife.

JST 1 Corinthians 7:11

11 **But if she depart**, let her remain unmarried, or be reconciled to her husband; **but** let not the husband put away his wife.

12 But to the rest speak I, not the Lord [*what I say next is my opinion, not a commandment from the Lord*]: If any brother [*member*] hath a wife that believeth not [*has a nonmember wife*], and she be pleased to dwell with him [*and she desires to stay with him, even though he joined the Church*], let him not put her away [*don't divorce her*].

13 And the woman [*member*] which hath an husband that believeth not [*who has a nonmember husband*], and if he be pleased to dwell with her [*and if he would like to stay married to her, even though she joined the Church*], let her not leave him [*don't divorce him*].

14 [*Be sure to look at the note after this verse.*] For the unbelieving [*nonmember*] husband is sanctified [*saved*] by the wife [*who is a faithful member*], and the unbelieving [*nonmember*] wife is sanctified [*saved*] by the husband [*who is a faithful member*]: else [*otherwise*] were your children unclean [*your children would not be saved*]; but now are they holy.

Having explained the wording in verse 14, above, we are now left to ask "Is that true doctrine?" Answer: "No." We would do well to suspect that something vital was left out in the translation. Article of Faith number eight reminds us that "We believe the Bible to be the word of God as far as it is translated correctly;" It is very likely that verse 14 is a quote from the letter the Corinthian Saints wrote Paul, expressing their beliefs on certain matters, as indicated in verse one of this chapter where Paul wrote "Now concerning the things whereof ye wrote unto me..." At any rate, the beliefs represented in verse 14 are not correct. This verse caused the Prophet Joseph Smith enough concern, when he was working on the Joseph Smith Translation of the Bible (JST), that he received D&C 74 by way of background for verse 14. You may wish to read section 74 now. You will find that nonmembers who were married to members in Corinth wanted their male children circumcised as required by the law of Moses, which had been fulfilled by Christ. This was causing much contention in the Church. The net result was that when a member married a nonmember, and the nonmember's religion was practiced in the home, the children generally grew up as non-believers in Christ. Thus, they were not "holy," in other words, they were not being saved. There was also a tradition among the Jews that little children were unholy, which is completely false doctrine and was apparently being perpetuated in these part-member homes. See D&C 137:10 where we are taught that all children who die before the years of accountability "are saved in the celestial kingdom of heaven." Perhaps, in the last two phrases of verse 14, Paul was responding and saying, in effect, "If things were indeed as is being taught in many of your part-member homes, little children would be unclean and thus lost. But, with the true gospel of Jesus Christ, we know that little children are holy, and thus, are saved."

15 But if the unbelieving depart [*if the nonmember spouse decides to divorce the spouse who is a member*], let him depart [*let him get a divorce*]. A brother or a sister is not under bondage [*is not guilty of sin*] in such cases: but God hath called us to peace [*to do our best to try to work things out and keep the peace*].

16 For what knowest thou, O wife, whether thou shalt save thy husband [*who knows but what your good example might someday cause your husband to be converted*]? or how knowest thou, O man, whether thou shalt save thy wife?

17 But as God hath distributed to every man [*but each case is different*], as the Lord hath called every one, so let him walk [*each member should follow the inspiration of the Lord in each individual situation*]. And so ordain I in all churches [*this is my advice to all the wards and branches of the Church who have to deal with these things*].

18 Is any man called being circumcised? let him not become uncircumcised. [*If a male convert was circumcised, according to the law*

of Moses, don't worry about it.] Is any called in uncircumcision? let him not be circumcised. [*If a man is converted to the Church, but was not circumcised, don't give in to the pressure from some members who still believe in the law of Moses and circumcision.*]

19 Circumcision is nothing, and uncircumcision is nothing, but the keeping of the commandments of God. [*Circumcision and uncircumcision are not issues anymore. The issue is to keep the commandments given by the Savior.*]

Verses 20–24 deal with the legal status of slaves, or indentured servants or free people, etc., who join the Church. Paul counsels them that joining the Church doesn't necessarily change their legal status. This could obviously become a problem for some, because the gospel of Christ teaches of the equality and worth of all souls.

20 Let every man abide in the same calling wherein he was called [*remain in the same legal status as you were in at the time you joined the Church*].

21 Art thou called being a servant [*did you join the Church while a servant who belongs to someone*]? care not for it [*don't be overly concerned about it*]: but if thou mayest be made free, use it rather [*but if you can obtain your freedom, do it*].

22 For he that is called in the Lord, being a servant, is the Lord's freeman [*even if you are still a slave or a servant who still owes your owner a few more years of work before you are free, remember that if you live the gospel, you are free in the eternal sense that matters*]: likewise also he that is called, being free, is Christ's servant [*those who were free citizens when baptized, are now "servants" to Christ. In other words, living the gospel makes all of us free and living the gospel makes all of us servants*].

23 Ye are bought with a price; be not ye the servants of men [*Christ paid an enormous price to purchase you from your sins, therefore, look upon yourselves as His servants, rather that being the servants of men*].

24 Brethren, let every man, wherein he is called, therein abide with God [*regardless of your social or legal status, be faithful to God*].

Paul now switches topics and deals with special issues concerning those involved in missionary service or other service which can require longer periods of time away from home. For instance, should engaged persons marry first, then go, or remain single? Also, would it be best for married members to get divorced, so that they can focus more effectively on their missionary service or whatever the calling may be? Paul is obviously answering questions raised by these members in their letter to him, as indicated in verse 1.

25 Now concerning virgins [*single sisters*] I have no commandment of the Lord [*I don't have any specific direction from the Lord*]: yet I give my judgment [*I will give my opinion*], as one that hath obtained mercy of the Lord to be faithful [*as one who has been helped much by the Lord and who is trustworthy*].

26 I suppose therefore that this is good for the present distress [*the current missionary work*], I say, that it is good for a man so to be.

JST 1 Corinthians 7:26

26 I suppose therefore that this is good for the present distress, **for a man so to remain that he may do greater good** [*In other words, I suppose that it is best for a man to remain single while he is involved fully in missionary work, so that he can be more effective*].

27 Art thou bound unto a wife? seek not to be loosed [*If you are married, don't seek a divorce so you can serve a full-time mission*]. Art thou loosed from a wife? seek not a wife. [*If you are already a widower or divorced, don't get married for the time being so you can focus on the missionary service to which you are called.*]

28 But and if thou marry, thou hast not sinned [*however, if you choose to marry, it is not a sin*]; and if a virgin marry [*and if a single sister gets married, rather than going into full-time missionary service*], she hath not sinned. Nevertheless such shall have trouble in the flesh: but I spare you.

JST 1 Corinthians 7:28

28 **But if** thou marry, thou hast not sinned; and if a virgin marry, she hath not sinned. Nevertheless, such shall have trouble in the flesh. **For I spare you not** [*No matter what you choose to do, you will not be spared the trials and tribulations that come with mortal life*].

29 But this I say, brethren, the time is short: it remaineth, that both they that have wives be as though they had none; [*In other words, for a short while yet, those of you who are married will have to be away from home so much that it will almost seem to you as if you were not married.*]

JST 1 Corinthians 7:29

29 But I **speak unto you who are called unto the ministry. For** this I say, brethren, **the time that remaineth is but short, that ye shall be sent forth unto the ministry. Even they who have wives, shall be as though they had none; for ye are called and chosen to do the Lord's work**.

30 And they that weep, as though they wept not; and they that rejoice, as though they rejoiced not; and they that buy, as though they possessed not; [*The intensity of the work and the fast pace of it will hardly give you time to weep for missionary efforts that failed, or to rejoice for very long*

because of successes, or to even enjoy material things.]

JST 1 Corinthians 7:30

30 **And it shall be with them who weep, as though they wept not; and them who** rejoice, as though they rejoiced not**, and them** who buy, as though they possessed not;

31 And they that use this world, as not abusing it: for the fashion of this world passeth away.

JST 1 Corinthians 7:31

31 And **them who** use this world, as not **using** it; for the fashion of this world passeth away [*Because of the fast pace of the work, worldly concerns, likes and interests in material things will fade to the point that you don't hardly even feel like a part of the world*].

32 But I would have you without carefulness. He that is unmarried careth for the things that belong to the Lord, how he may please the Lord:

JST 1 Corinthians 7:32

32 But I would, **brethren, that ye magnify your calling**. I would have you without carefulness [*I would like you to be free from worldly cares during the time of your missionary service*]. **For** he **who** is unmarried, careth for the things that belong to the Lord [*a single person can focus more effectively on the things of missionary work*], how he may please the Lord; **therefore he prevaileth** [*has success*].

33 But he that is married careth for the things that are of the world, how he may please his wife. [*Single missionaries can focus more on the work, therefore, there is a difference between them and married members, because married members have more distractions and can't be as effective.*]

JST 1 Corinthians 7:33

33 But he **who** is married, careth for the things that are of the world, how he may please his wife; **therefore there is a difference, for he is hindered**.

34 There is difference also between a wife and a virgin. [*The same thing holds true for married women as opposed to single sisters, as holds for married men as opposed to single brethren.*] The unmarried woman careth for [*is better able to focus full-time on*] the things of the Lord, that she may be holy [*may be set apart and be spiritually focused*] both in body and in spirit: but she that is married careth for the things of the world [*has to devote time and energy to daily responsibilities of homemaking*], how she may please her husband.

JST 1 Corinthians 7:34

34 There is a difference also, between a wife and a virgin. The unmarried woman careth for the things of the Lord, that she may be holy both in body and in spirit; but she that is married careth for the things of the world, how she may please her husband.

By the way, the only difference between verse 34, above, and the JST is that the Prophet put a semicolon after "spirit" in place of the colon in verse 34. This is another example of Joseph Smith's inspired attention to detail.

35 And this I speak for your own profit [*I am giving you this counsel for your own good*]; not that I may cast a snare upon you [*not trying to cause trouble for you*], but for that which is comely [*honorable and appropriate*], and that ye may attend upon the Lord without distraction [*so that you can focus on temporary full-time service of the Lord without being distracted*].

36 But if any man think that he behaveth himself uncomely [*unkindly*] toward his virgin [*his fiancée*], if she pass the flower of her age [*the best years for her to bear children*], and need so require, let him do what he will, he sinneth not: let them marry. [*If a single man is engaged and thinks that going into full-time service of the Lord will cause his fiancée to be past the best years for child bearing when he returns, keep your promise to her. Stay home and marry her. It is not a sin to do so.*]

JST 1 Corinthians 7:36

36 But if any man think that he behaveth himself uncomely toward his virgin **whom he hath espoused**, if she pass the flower of age, and need so require, let him do what he **hath promised**, he sinneth not; let them marry.

37 Nevertheless, he that standeth stedfast in his heart [*who really wants to serve a mission*], having no necessity [*and his fiancee will not be too far along in years when he returns*], but hath power over his own will [*and has good self control*], and hath so decreed in his heart that he will keep his virgin and decides to remain espoused [*engaged*], doeth well.

The JST completely changes the meaning of the first phrase of verse 38.

38 So then he that giveth her in marriage doeth well; but he that giveth her not in marriage doeth better. [*So, to summarize, if a man desires to go ahead and marry his fiancée, that is fine. But, if he could go on a mission first, that would be even better.*]

JST 1 Corinthians 7:38

38 **So then he that giveth himself in marriage** doeth well; **but he that giveth himself not in marriage** doeth better.

39 The wife is bound by the law [*the obligations that go along with marriage*] as long as her husband liveth [*so don't divorce your husbands so you can go on full-time missions*]; but if her husband be dead, she is at liberty to be married to whom she will; only in the Lord [*and in the case of a woman whose husband is a nonmember, if he dies, she of course can remarry, but she ought to marry a man who is a member of the Church*].

40 But she is happier if she so abide, after my judgment [*but, she will be happier if she remains faithful and marries a member of the Church, in my opinion*]: and I think also that I have the Spirit of God [*and I think that I have the Spirit of the Lord with me*].

FIRST CORINTHIANS 8

It appears that one of the questions the Saints in Corinth asked Paul in their letter to him (see note at the beginning of chapter 7 in this study guide) had to do with whether or not it was okay for members to eat things left over from sacrifices offered by pagans to their idols. There were twelve temples to various idols in Corinth, consequently, there were many sacrifices. As a result, there was a significant market for leftover meat and whatever remained from these offerings. These Saints are apparently asking Paul if it is permissible for them to purchase such stuff in the open market and eat it.

1 NOW as touching [*concerning*] things offered unto idols, we know that we all have knowledge. Knowledge puffeth up [*knowledge can make us prideful*], but charity edifieth [*but the Christlike virtue of charity builds us up and strengthens us*].

2 And if any man think that he knoweth any thing, he knoweth nothing yet as he ought to know [*none of us knows near what we ought to know yet*].

3 But if any man love God, the same is known of him [*but God knows His faithful followers*].

4 As concerning therefore the eating of those things that are offered in sacrifice unto idols [*now, back to your question about eating things left over from pagan sacrifices*], we know that an idol is nothing in the world [*we know that idols are not really gods*], and that there is none other God but one [*and that there is only one true God*].

JST 1 Corinthians 8:4

4 As concerning therefore the eating of those things which are **in the world** offered in sacrifice unto idols, we know that an idol is nothing, and that there is none other God but one.

Before Paul continues to answer their questions about eating meat left over from pagan idol worship, he takes a minute to review the true doctrine of plurality of gods with them. We know from D&C 132:19–20, that all who are worthy will become gods over their own worlds, and will send their own spirit offspring to those worlds to go through the same plan of salvation as we are going through here. Therefore, because of the success of the Father's plan, there are many gods in the universe. But there is only one Heavenly Father for us. Thus, Paul reminds these Corinthian Saints that there actually are many gods out there.

5 For though there be that are called gods, whether in heaven or in earth, (as there be gods many, and lords many,)

> The Prophet Joseph Smith tells us that the parentheses in verse 5, above, teach a marvelous doctrine; namely that there, indeed, are many gods. This reminds us that we can all become gods. (By the way, Abraham, Isaac, and Jacob from our world have already become gods. See D&C 132:27. This would include their wives. See D&C 132, 19–20.) He taught that the word "gods" in verse 5 does not refer to idols or, in other words, heathen gods. He said: "Some say I do not interpret the Scripture the same as they do. They say it means the heathen's gods. Paul says there are Gods many and Lords many; and that makes a plurality of Gods, in spite of the whims of all men. . . You know and I testify that Paul had no allusion to the heathen gods. I have it from God, and get over it if you can. I have a witness of the Holy Ghost, and a testimony that Paul had no allusion to the heathen gods in the text." (Joseph Smith, *Teachings of the Prophet Joseph Smith*, selected and arranged by Joseph Fielding Smith, Salt Lake City: Deseret Book, 1976, p. 371.)

6 But to us [*but for us*] there is but one God, the Father, of whom are all things [*from whom all our blessings come*], and we in him [*and we belong to Him*]; and one Lord Jesus Christ [*and there is but one Savior*], by whom are all things [*through whom the Father makes all His blessings of exaltation available to us*], and we by him [*we come to the Father only through Jesus Christ*].

> Having said, in verse 4, that idols are not actual gods, implying that there is nothing wrong with buying meat left over from pagan idol worship to help feed the family, Paul now cautions members that newer or weaker members of the Church might be shocked and offended to see members buying and eating such stuff, thinking that they are secretly or openly involved in idol worship themselves.

7 Howbeit [*however*] there is not in every man that knowledge [*everyone doesn't realize that idols are absurd and are nothing, in and of themselves*]: for some with conscience of the idol unto this hour eat it as a thing offered unto an idol [*many idol worshipers, even now, eat such things as part of worshiping the idol*]; and their conscience being weak is defiled [*and they are thus defiled by it*].

8 But meat commendeth us not to God: for neither, if we eat, are we the better; neither, if we eat not, are we the worse. [*Food by itself doesn't save us or condemn us with God.*]

9 But take heed lest by any means this liberty of yours become a stumblingblock to them that are weak. [*But be careful, for fear that the liberty which this knowledge*

gives you (namely that in and of themselves, various foods used in idol worship are neither good nor evil, so you can eat it if you want to) could cause your behavior to become a stumbling block for weaker members, who don't understand these things as you do.]

10 For if any man see thee which hast knowledge sit at meat in the idol's temple [*if some weaker members see you (who understand this) sit down at a buffet in an idol worship temple for lunch*], shall not the conscience of him which is weak be emboldened to eat those things which are offered to idols [*isn't it possible that your example would make them think that they can be a member of our Church and still worship idols also*?];

11 And through thy knowledge shall the weak brother perish [*and thus, even though you know that the food itself is neither good nor evil, your example could cause a weaker member to lose salvation*], for whom Christ died [*thus undoing the work of the Savior which He did for them*]?

12 But when ye sin so against the brethren, and wound their weak conscience, ye sin against Christ [*if you go against the counsel of the Brethren and thus wound a member whose conscience and understanding is yet weak, it is a sin against the Savior*].

13 Wherefore, if meat make my brother to offend, I will eat no flesh while the world standeth, lest I make my brother to offend. [*Therefore, I will avoid things which I know are neither good or evil, but which might destroy another member's testimony.*]

FIRST CORINTHIANS 9

Later in this chapter, Paul will continue with the theme in the last verses of chapter eight, namely that when we are in the presence of others, we need to be sensitive to their perceptions and feelings, so as to avoid offending them unnecessarily. But first, he will give a rather detailed treatment of the fact that Apostles and other full-time leaders in the Church need the support of the members for the physical needs of them and their families.

1 AM I not an apostle? am I not free? have I not seen Jesus Christ our Lord? are not ye my work in the Lord [*aren't you members of the Church because of the help the Lord gave me as a missionary to you*]?

2 If I be not an apostle unto others, yet doubtless I am to you [*even if others don't consider me to be an Apostle, at least you do*]: for the seal of mine apostleship are ye in the Lord [*you are the proof of my apostleship*].

3 Mine answer to them that do examine me is this [*my answer to those who challenge me about the counsel I just gave you is this*],

4 Have we [*the Apostles*] not power [*agency*] to eat and to drink?

5 Have we not power to lead about a sister, a wife [*don't we have the right to be married too*?], as well as other apostles [*just like other Apostles*], and as the brethren of the Lord, and Cephas [*including Peter, the president of the Church*]?

6 Or I only and Barnabas, have not we power to forbear working [*or are Barnabas and I the only ones who could quit working for the Lord if we chose to*]?

7 Who goeth a warfare any time at his own charges [*who else can you think of who serves as a soldier at his own expense*]? who planteth a vineyard, and eateth not of the fruit thereof [*who plants but never gets to be there to harvest*]? or who feedeth a flock, and eateth not of the milk of the flock [*who nourishes a ward or branch but doesn't get to be with them to enjoy the blessings with them in person*]?

8 Say I these things as a man [*am I just giving an opinion*]? or saith not the law the same also [*or is this what the law of Moses said*]?

9 For it is written in the law of Moses, Thou shalt not muzzle the mouth of the ox that treadeth out the corn [*you are not allowed to leave a muzzle on an ox which is working on the threshing floor*]. Doth God take care for oxen [*is God only concerned for oxen*]?

10 Or saith he it altogether for our sakes [*or is he telling us this for our sakes*]? For our sakes, no doubt, this is written: that he that ploweth should plow in hope; and that he that thresheth in hope should be partaker of his hope [*God expects us to plow and plant with the hope of a good harvest, and those who actually harvest the crops get to participate in the satisfaction of all involved in the whole process*].

11 If we have sown unto you spiritual things [*since we have planted spiritual seed, namely the seeds of the gospel of Christ among you*], is it a great thing if we shall reap your carnal things [*is it too much for us to expect your support in our physical needs as missionaries and full-time servants of God*]?

12 If others be partakers of this power over you, are not we rather [*if you support others among you, who need temporal and physical help from you, aren't we even more entitled to such help*]? Nevertheless we have not used this power [*we haven't used our authority to request such help*]; but suffer all things [*but often do without*], lest we should hinder the gospel of Christ [*for fear of offending some and thus hindering the work*].

13 Do ye not know that they which minister about holy things live of the things of the temple [*are you not aware that those who serve full-time in the temple are fed and taken care of by the donations to the temple*]? and they which wait [*those who serve*] at the alter [*in the temple*] are partakers with the alter [*take part of the flesh*

from the animal sacrifices to feed themselves and their families]?

14 Even so hath the Lord ordained that they which preach the gospel should live of the gospel [*the Lord has commanded that his full-time servants should be supported by the members*].

15 But I have used none of these things [*but I have worked for my own living, rather than be supported by members*]: neither have I written these things, that it should be so done unto me [*and I am not writing these things to you for my own benefit, but so that you will be aware of God's will on this matter and will be more willing to support the physical needs of other leaders*] : for it were better for me to die [*I would rather die*], than that any man should make my glorying void [*than have my independence in earning my own way taken from me; see Acts 20:34*].

16 For though I preach the gospel, I have nothing to glory [*boast*] of: for necessity is laid upon me [*I am obligated to do it*]; yea, woe is unto me, if I preach not the gospel [*after all the blessings I have received from the Lord, I would be in deep trouble if I didn't preach the gospel*]!

17 For if I do this thing willingly, I have a reward [*I have the reward of extra joy and satisfaction*]: but if against my will [*if not willingly*], a dispensation of the gospel is committed unto me [*I still have an obligation to preach*].

18 What is my reward then? Verily that, when I preach the gospel, I may make the gospel of Christ without charge [*I preach without thought of monetary support*], that I abuse not my power in the gospel.

19 For though I be free [*am independent*] from all men, yet have I made myself servant unto all, that I might gain the more.

Paul now tells these members that he has always done his best to fit in with people, no matter who they were, so that he could avoid offending them and thus could gain their confidence in order to be effective in teaching the gospel. However, he assures his readers that he has never compromised the standards and commandments of the Savior in so doing.

20 And unto the Jews I became as a Jew, that I might gain the Jews [*while preaching to the Jews, I lived as much as possible like them so that they would be more willing to listen to me*]; to them that are under the law [*the law of Moses*], as under the law, that I might gain them that are under the law;

21 To them [*Gentiles*] that are without law [*who do not live the law of Moses*], as without law, (being not without law to God, but under the law to Christ,) [*I assure you I still kept the standards and commandments of the gospel as taught by Christ*] that I might gain them that are without law [*those who do not live the law of Moses*].

22 To the weak became I as weak, that I might gain the weak: I am made all things to all men [*I try to fit in as well as possible with all people*], that I might by all means save some.

This "fitting in" as well as possible wherever he went would have been particularly hard for Paul because of his upbringing as a strict Pharisee, perhaps the strictest of all religious sects among the Jews. Most Pharisees were very judgmental of others who did not believe as they did and strictly avoided even associating with them. One must admire Paul for his willingness to quickly learn the Christ-like attribute of considering all people to be of equal worth.

23 And this I do for the gospel's sake, that I might be partaker thereof with you [*so that I might enjoy associating with you in the gospel*].

24 Know ye not that they which run in a race run all, but one receiveth the prize [*you know that lots of people run in a race, but only one is the winner*]? So run, that ye may obtain [*live the gospel so that you may get the prize, namely exaltation*].

JST 1 Corinthians 9:24

24 Know ye not that they which run in a race **all run**, but **only** one receiveth the prize? So run, that ye may obtain.

25 And every man that striveth for the mastery [*every participant in local athletic events*] is temperate [*goes through strict training*] in all things. Now they do it to obtain a corruptible crown [*they go through a lot to get a worldly honor*]; but we an incorruptible [*but we are training for an eternal crown*].

26 I therefore so run, not as uncertainly [*since the gospel crown is available to all who will live worthy, I do not run aimlessly*]; so fight I, not as one that beateth the air [*I do not fight for the prize like one who merely beats the air and puts on a show*]:

27 But I keep under my body, and bring it into subjection [*I control and discipline my body rigorously*]: lest that by any means [*for fear that through some temptation or another*], when I have preached to others, I myself should be a castaway [*my own soul should be lost*].

FIRST CORINTHIANS 10

Paul will turn his attention to explaining that Jesus Christ was the God who let ancient Israel out of Egypt and into the promised land. This is crucial doctrine for those converts who are trying to understand why they should leave the law of Moses rites and rituals and follow Christ as Paul has been teaching them to do. He will warn them not to fall into the same sins as the children of Israel did, which led many to destruction.

Verse 13 is one of the most often-quoted verses in the New Testament in our church meetings and lessons.

1 MOREOVER [*in addition*], brethren, I would not that ye should be ignorant [*I wouldn't want you to miss the fact*], how that all our fathers [*ancestors*] were under the cloud [*were guided by the Lord by a "pillar of a cloud"; Exodus 13:21*], and all passed through the sea [*all passed to safety, escaping from Egypt through the Red Sea*];

Paul uses much symbolism in verses 2–4.

2 And were all baptized [*immersed*] unto Moses in the cloud and in the sea; [*Symbolically, they were "immersed" in God's leadership through Moses and "came up out of the waters of redemption," symbolic of being baptized in order to be freed from our enemies of sin and evil and led into the "promised land" (symbolic of heaven)*].

3 And did all eat the same spiritual meat [*they partook of the same manna, symbolic of being nourished by the gospel, sent down to them from heaven*];

4 And did all drink the same spiritual drink [*they were refreshed and saved by water which came out from the rock (Exodus 17:6), symbolic of the "living water" (John 4:10 and 14) which comes to us from Christ (the "Rock")*]: for they drank of that spiritual Rock [*the solid and sure foundation upon which we can safely build our lives*] that followed them: and that Rock was Christ.

5 But with many of them [*the children of Israel*] God was not well pleased: for they were overthrown [*destroyed*] in the wilderness.

6 Now these things were our examples, to the intent [*for the purpose of teaching us that*] we should not lust after evil things, as they also lusted.

7 Neither be ye idolaters [*don't be idol worshipers*], as were some of them; as it is written [*in Exodus 32:1–6*], The people sat down to eat and drink, and rose up to play [*to engage in pagan idol worship, including sexual immorality as part of the idol worship of the golden calf*].

8 Neither let us commit fornication [*let us avoid sexual immorality*], as some of them [*children of Israel*] committed, and fell in one day three and twenty thousand [*which caused 23,000 of them to get destroyed in one day*].

9 Neither let us tempt [*test or ignore*] Christ, as some of them also tempted [*did*], and were destroyed of serpents [*which led to their being destroyed by poisonous snakes*].

10 Neither murmur ye [*don't complain and mumble against the Lord and His leaders*], as some of them also murmured, and were destroyed of the destroyer [*were destroyed by the plague as recorded in Numbers 14:37*].

11 Now all these things happened unto them for ensamples [*all these things happened to them to try to teach them a lesson*]: and they

are written for our admonition [*to warn us also*], upon whom the ends of the world are come.

JST 1 Corinthians 10:11

11 Now, all these things happened unto them for ensamples; and they **were** written for our admonition also, and for an admonition **for those upon whom the end of the world shall come** [*in other words, these things should serve as a warning to all those who will be destroyed if they don't repent, including those who live shortly before the Second Coming*].

12 Wherefore let him that thinketh he standeth take heed lest he fall. [*Let those who don't think these warnings apply to them think again and repent so they won't be destroyed.*]

13 There hath no temptation taken you but such as is common to man [*all of us are subject to temptation*]: but God is faithful, who will not suffer you to be tempted above that ye are able [*God will not allow you to be tempted beyond what you can resist*]; but will with the temptation also make a way to escape [*will help you overcome it*], that ye may be able to bear it [*so that you can handle it*].

Elder Joseph B. Worthlin, of the Quorum of the Twelve, explained verse 13, above, in a talk given in the October 1989 General Conference. He said, "I suppose some of you, at one time or another, feel that you are 'hitting the wall', feeling an almost compelling urge to quit, give up, or give in to temptation. You will meet challenges, adversities, and temptations that seem to be more than you can bear. In times of sickness, death, financial need, and other hardships, you many wonder whether you have the strength, courage, or ability to continue . . . be sure you understand that God will not allow you to be tempted beyond your ability to resist (see 1 Corinthians 10:13). He does not give you challenges that you cannot surmount. He will not ask more than you can do but may ask right up to your limits so you can prove yourselves."

14 Wherefore, my dearly beloved, flee from idolatry [*avoid idol worship at all costs*].

15 I speak as to wise men [*I consider you to be wise men*]; judge ye what I say [*you be the judge of what I am teaching you*].

Paul will now compare the true sacrament with false "sacraments" partaken of by idol worshipers.

16 The cup of blessing [*the sacrament*] which we bless, is it not the communion [*sacrament*] of the blood of Christ? The bread which we break [*as we partake of the sacrament*], is it not the communion of the [*does it not represent*] body of Christ?

17 For we being many are one bread, and one body [*we are all united by Christ's sacrificing His body for us*]: for we are all

partakers of that one bread [*we all partake of the gospel, represented by the sacrament bread*].

18 Behold Israel after the flesh [*think about the Israelites who have become so worldly*]: are not they which eat of the sacrifices partakers of the altar [*don't those apostate Israelites who eat the food used for the sacrifices to idols in effect participate in offering the sacrifice at the altar*]?

19 What say I then [*what am I saying*]? that the idol is any thing [*other than a piece of wood or stone*], or that which is offered in sacrifice to idols is any thing [*or that there is anything special about the food that is offered to it*]?

20 But I say, that the things which the Gentiles sacrifice, they sacrifice to devils [*the sacrifices the Gentiles offer to their idols are in effect sacrifices offered to false gods or devils*], and not to God: and I would not that ye should have fellowship with devils [*and I don't want you associating with devils*].

21 Ye cannot drink the cup of the Lord, and the cup of devils [*you can't worship the Lord and worship devils at the same time*]: ye cannot be partakers of the Lord's table, and of the table of devils [*you can't be nourished by the Lord and by devils at the same time*].

22 Do we provoke the Lord to jealousy [*is the Lord just another idol or god*]? are we stronger than he [*do we run His life like idol worshipers run the lives of their idols*]?

We would be lost and very confused by verse 23 without the JST.

23 All things are lawful for me, but all things are not expedient: all things are lawful for me, but all things edify not.

JST 1 Corinthians 10:23

23 All things are not lawful for me, for all things are not expedient; all things are not lawful, for all things edify not.

24 Let no man seek his own, but every man another's wealth.

JST 1 Corinthians 10:24

24 Let no man seek **therefore** his own, but every man another's **good**.

The word "shambles" in verse 25, next, refers to the meat markets in Corinth where left over meat from idol worship was sold.

25 Whatsoever is sold in the shambles, that eat, asking no question for conscience sake [*don't worry about buying and eating meat that is left over from pagan idol worship*]:

26 For the earth is the Lord's, and the fulness thereof.

27 If any of them that believe not bid you to a feast, and ye be disposed to go; whatsoever is set before you, eat, asking no question for conscience sake [*if any*

nonmembers invite you to dinner, and you would like to accept their invitation, go ahead and eat whatever they serve].

JST 1 Corinthians 10:27

27 If any of them that believe not bid you to a feast, and ye be disposed to **eat**; whatsoever is set before you, eat, asking no **questions** for conscience' sake.

28 But if any man say unto you, This is offered in sacrifice unto idols, eat not for his sake that shewed it, and for conscience sake [*but if the host or any others attending the feast tell you that eating this meat is part of their idol worship ceremonies, don't eat it as a matter of respect for him and his beliefs, and also as a matter of not participating in idol worship*]: for the earth is the Lord's, and the fulness thereof:

29 Conscience, I say [*let me explain a bit more of what I mean by conscience*], not thine own, but of the other [*I'm not referring to yours but rather to your host's or that of other dinner guests*]: for why is my liberty judged of another man's conscience [*why should my freedom to do as I please be limited by another man's beliefs*]?

30 For if I by grace be a partaker [*if through the kindness of God I am blessed with a good meal*], why am I evil spoken of for that for which I give thanks [*why do I get criticized for something I personally am thankful for*]?

31 Whether therefore ye eat, or drink, or whatsoever ye do, do all to the glory of God [*therefore, no matter what you do, make sure it furthers the work of God among your fellow beings*].

32 Give none offence, neither to the Jews, nor to the Gentiles, nor to the church of God [*do your best not to offend anyone*]:

33 Even as I please all men in all things [*just like I try not to offend anyone in anything*], not seeking mine own profits [*often not doing what I would prefer to do*], but the profit of many [*rather trying to do what will be best for many others*], that they may be saved [*so that they are encouraged to come to Christ and be saved*].

JST 1 Corinthians 10:33

33 Even as I please all men in all things, not seeking mine own **profit**, **but of the many**, that they may be saved.

FIRST CORINTHIANS 11

In this chapter, the Apostle Paul will deal with a number of issues among the Corinthian Saints, including local customs of hair and grooming, marriage, and husband and wife roles, some of which he approves and some of which he disapproves. His counsel regarding some of these matters, if taken out of context, can become a problem. He will also give a beautiful written sermon regarding the sacrament.

1 BE ye followers of me, even as I also am of Christ [*follow me as I follow Christ*].

2 Now I praise [*compliment*] you, brethren, that ye remember [*for remembering*] me in all things, and keep the ordinances, as I delivered them to you [*and that you are keeping the ordinances and teachings of the gospel just as I taught you to*].

In verse 3, next, Paul teaches the organization and relationship of husband and wife, which he compares to the organization and relationship of Christ and the Father, implying that the husband and wife should work together in love, unity, and harmony just as the Father and Son do.

Be sure to read the note provided after verse 9.

3 But I would have you know, that the head of every man is Christ; and the head of the woman is the man; and the head of Christ is God [*the Father*].

In verses 4–7, Paul deals with local customs used to show respect for God while worshiping. In Corinth, men took their hats or caps off as a way of showing respect for God while worshiping, whereas, local custom required women to wear head coverings while worshiping.

4 Every man praying or prophesying [*worshiping*], having his head covered, dishonoureth his head [*is showing disrespect*].

5 But every woman that prayeth or prophesieth [*worships*] with her head uncovered dishonoureth her head [*is showing disrespect*]: for that is even all one as if she were shaven [*it is just as if she had shaved her head bald, which, in Corinthian culture, was the sign of a woman who was an adulteress*].

JST 1 Corinthians 11:5

5 But every woman that prayeth or prophesieth with her head uncovered dishonoreth her head; for that is even all one as if she were shaven.

Notice, again, that the only change made by the JST is changing a colon to a semicolon in JST verses 5 and 6.

6 For if the woman be not covered [*if she is not willing to cover her head while worshiping*], let her also be shorn [*let her head be shaved*]: but if it be a shame for a woman to be shorn or shaven, let her be covered. [*In other words, even though this is just a local custom, there is wisdom in going along with it in order not to cause unnecessary distraction or criticism during worship.*]

JST 1 Corinthians 11:6

6 For if the woman be not covered, let her also be shorn; but if it be a shame for a woman to be shorn or shaven, let her be covered.

7 For a man indeed ought not to cover his head [*during worship*], forasmuch as he is the image and

glory of God: but the woman is the glory of the man. [*The woman should bring glory and honor to her husband just as the husband should bring glory and honor to God.*]

8 For the man is not of the woman; but the woman of the man. [*Adam did not come from Eve, rather Eve came from Adam.*]

9 Neither was the man created for the woman; but the woman for the man.

Verses 8 and 9, above, can be misinterpreted to mean that men are superior to women in God's eyes. This is not true. James E. Faust said, "Nowhere does the doctrine of this Church declare that men are superior to women." (Conference Report, April 1988, p. 43.) We should study the word of the Lord through our modern First Presidency and Quorum of the Twelve given in "The Family, a Proclamation to the World," September 23, 1995, wherein they said "fathers and mothers are obligated to help one another as equal partners." You may wish to read the notes in this study guide that go along with Ephesians 5:21–33, which help with this topic.

D&C 132:19–20 also teaches us correct doctrine, namely, that worthy husbands and wives, sealed together for eternity, are gods and serve together and are "above all, because all things are subject unto them. . . and the angels are subject to them." Elder Bruce R. McConkie explained D&C 132:20 as follows: "Exaltation grows out of the eternal union of a man and his wife. Of those whose marriage endures in eternity, the Lord says, 'Then shall they be gods' (D&C 132:20); that is each of them, the man and the woman, will be a god. As such they will rule over their dominions forever." See *Mormon Doctrine*, p. 613.

10 For this cause ought the woman to have power on her head because of the angels. [*Out of respect for heaven.*]

JST 1 Corinthians 11:10

10 For this cause ought the woman to have **a covering** on her head because of the angels.

Next, in verse 11, Paul teaches eternal marriage, explaining that a man and a woman can remain married when they live with the Lord in His kingdom in heaven. Compare with D&C 132:19–20. Also, see Matthew 19:6.

11 Nevertheless neither is the man without the woman, neither the woman without the man, in the Lord.

12 For as the woman is of the man, even so is the man also by the woman [*Eve came from Adam, but all men come from women through birth*]; but all things of God [*and all things come from God*]. [*In other words, men and women should respect each other and sustain and build each other up, because they all come from God, and thus have great worth.*]

13 Judge in yourselves [*you be the judge*]: is it comely [*appropriate, fitting*] that a woman pray unto God uncovered [*with her head uncovered*]? [*In other words, in your local Corinthian culture, would it be appropriate for a righteous woman to pray with her head uncovered, since it would make everyone think she is an adulteress?*]

14 Doth not even nature itself teach you, that, if a man have long hair, it is a shame unto him?

Apparently, in the local Corinthian culture and society, there was something about men having long hair which was offensive and signaled that they were involved in evil or inappropriate behaviors. Thus, Paul counsels local Saints, in verse 14, above, to be sensitive to their culture and not wear hairstyles which directly associate them with wicked lifestyles. Certainly there was not anything inherently wrong with long hair on men. The Savior had long hair, signaling in His local culture that He was dedicated to God.

15 But if a woman have long hair, it is a glory to her [*it accentuates her beauty*]: for her hair is given her for a covering.

16 But if any man seem to be contentious [*if anyone gets upset about what I have just said*], we have no such custom, neither the churches of God [*remind them that we are dealing here with local customs, not a universal policy throughout the Church*].

17 Now in this that I declare unto you I praise you not [*now, in the next matter I am going to bring up, I can't compliment you*], that ye come together not for the better, but for the worse [*that when you meet together, you are causing more problems than you are solving.*].

18 For first of all, when ye come together in the church, I hear that there be divisions among you [*I hear that you are breaking up the Church into apostate groups and factions*]; and I partly believe it [*and I am inclined to believe that it is happening among you to some degree*].

19 For there must be also heresies among you, that they which are approved [*those who remain faithful to what I have taught you, and are thus approved by God*] may be made manifest [*may show up as steadfast Saints*] among you. [*In other words, as stated in 2 Nephi 2:11, "It must needs be that there is an opposition in all things" in order to test us.*]

<u>**JST 1 Corinthians 11:19**</u>

19 For there must be also **divisions** among you, that they which are approved may be made manifest among you.

20 When ye come together therefore into one place, this is not to eat the Lord's supper [*the sacrament*].

<u>**JST 1 Corinthians 11:20**</u>

20 When ye come **together into** one place, **is it not to eat the Lord's supper?**

In verses 21–22, next, Paul is apparently dealing with a specific problem which has developed among the Corinthian members. It appears that their meetings have degenerated into thoughtless and quarrelsome times of contention, where some selfishly eat while others go hungry, some get drunk, etc., all of which is contrary to the peaceful coming together of kind and faithful Saints to reverence the Savior through partaking of the sacrament.

21 For in eating every one taketh before other his own supper: and one is hungry, and another is drunken.

JST 1 Corinthians 11:21

21 **But** in eating everyone taketh **before his** own supper; and one is hungry, and another is drunken.

22 What? have ye not houses to eat and to drink in [*can't you eat and drink at home, instead of during sacred meetings*]? or despise ye the church of God, and shame them that have not [*are you so disrespectful of the Church of God that you bring expensive foods and then embarrass members who can't afford such lavish food by not sharing with them*]? What shall I say to you? shall I praise you in this? I praise you not.

Paul will now teach these members the background of the sacrament and thus illustrate to them why it is so sacred.

23 For I have received of the Lord [*I have been taught by the Lord*] that which also I delivered unto you [*that which I taught you*], That the Lord Jesus the same night in which he was betrayed took bread:

24 And when he had given thanks, he brake [*broke*] it, and said, Take, eat: this is my body, which is broken for you: this do in remembrance of me.

25 After the same manner [*in the same way*] also he took the cup, when he had supped [*after supper*], saying, This cup is the new testament [*the new covenant*] in my blood: this do ye, as oft as ye drink it, in remembrance of me.

26 For as often as ye eat this bread, and drink this cup, ye do shew the Lord's death [*you are remembering that Christ gave His life for you*] till he come. [*In other words, whenever you take the sacrament, you are bearing witness of Christ, and so it will continue until the Second Coming when He Himself will bear witness to everyone.*]

27 Wherefore whosoever shall eat this bread, and drink this cup of the Lord, unworthily [*whoever partakes of the sacrament unworthily*], shall be guilty of the body and blood of the Lord [*is guilty of being disrespectful or mocking the Savior's sacrifice of His body and blood for us*].

28 But let a man examine himself [*you judge yourselves carefully as to whether or not you are worthy to partake of the sacrament*], and

so [*if he feels worthy*] let him eat of that bread, and drink of that cup.

29 For he that eateth and drinketh unworthily, eateth and drinketh damnation to himself, not discerning the Lord's body [*not being aware of how important the sacrament is and what it represents*].

JST 1 Corinthians 11:29

29 For he that eateth and drinketh unworthily, eateth and drinketh **condemnation** to himself, not discerning the Lord's body.

30 For this cause many are weak [*spiritually*] and sickly [*spiritually*] among you, and many sleep [*many have died spiritually*].

Based on what Paul counsels about the sacrament in the above verses, it would be easy for members to go too far and be afraid to ever take it. This is not the purpose of the sacrament. Bruce R. McConkie said, "This penalty [*referring to what Paul said in verse 27*] applies only to those who partake of the sacrament in total and complete unworthiness and rebellion." *Doctrinal New Testament Commentary*, Vol. 2, p. 365.

31 For if we would judge ourselves, we should not be judged [*if we were more careful not to take the sacrament unworthily, we wouldn't be in danger of being judged severely by God*].

32 But when we are judged, we are chastened of the Lord, that we should not be condemned with the world [*the Lord scolds us as needed so we can repent so we will not be condemned with the rest of the world*].

33 Wherefore, my brethren, when ye come together to eat, tarry [*wait*] one for another.

34 And if any man hunger, let him eat at home; that ye come not together unto condemnation [*so that you don't get condemned because of your contention and irreverence in your meetings*]. And the rest will I set in order when I come [*I will straighten out some other things when I get there*].

FIRST CORINTHIANS 12

This chapter is well-known for mentioning several spiritual gifts. Each person who has received the gift of the Holy Ghost is given one or more gifts of the Spirit. Elder Orson Pratt described this privilege as follows: "Whenever the Holy Ghost takes up its residence in a person, it not only cleanses, sanctifies, and purifies him, in proportion as he yields himself to its influence, but also imparts to him some gift, intended for the benefit of himself and others . . . all Saints who constitute the Church of Christ, are baptized into the same Spirit; and each one, without any exception, is made a partaker of some spiritual gift. . . Each member does not receive all these gifts; [*they*] are distributed among the members of the Church, according to their faithfulness, circumstances, natural abilities, duties, and callings; that the whole may be properly instructed, confirmed, perfected, and saved." (*Masterful Discourses*, pp. 539–41. Institute of Religion *Doctrine and Covenants Student Manual*, p. 100.) Two other major references in the scriptures which also list a number of these gifts are Moroni 10:8–18 and D&C, 46:8–27. Romans 12:6–13 lists several additional gifts. These are gifts which are given by the Holy Ghost. See D&C 46:13. Many of the definitions of spiritual gifts, used in the notes for the following verses, derive from the Institute of Religion *Doctrine and Covenants Student Manual*, Religion 324–325, pp. 100–101.

We will use **bold** to point out specific gifts of the Spirit.

1 NOW concerning spiritual gifts, brethren, I would not have you ignorant [*not knowing about them*].

JST 1 Corinthians 12:1

1 Now concerning spiritual **things**, brethren, I would not have you ignorant.

2 Ye know that ye were Gentiles [*nonmembers*], carried away unto these dumb idols [*worshiping idols which can't talk*], even as ye were led [*having been led to do so by false religions and philosophies*].

3 Wherefore I give you to understand, that no man speaking by the Spirit of God calleth Jesus accursed [*no person who has the Holy Ghost opposes Jesus*]: and that **no man can say that Jesus is the Lord, but by the Holy Ghost** [*you cannot have a full testimony of the Savior unless it is given you by the Holy Ghost*].

In reference to the last phrase in verse 3, above, Joseph Smith said that it should be translated as "No man can know that Jesus is the Lord, but by the Holy Ghost." See *Teachings of the Prophet Joseph Smith*, p. 223.

4 Now there are diversities of gifts [*there are various spiritual gifts*], but the same Spirit [*but they all come from the Holy Ghost; see D&C 46:11 and 13*].

5 And there are [*one of these gifts is*] **differences of administrations** [*being able to use the organizations within the Church effectively, the gift of leadership in the Church*], but the same Lord [*each gift comes from the same God*].

The last phrase in verse 5, above, may appear a bit unnecessary to those of us who have always believed in one Lord, but to the Corinthian Saints, who lived in an environment of many false gods, it is an important clarification. Otherwise, members might be tempted to believe that one spiritual gift came from one idol, and another from another god, etc.

6 And there are [*another gift is*] **diversities of operations** [*the ability to distinguish between truth and false philosophies and ideas*], but it is the same God which

worketh all in all [*each of these gifts comes from God*].

7 But the manifestation of the Spirit is given to every man to profit withal. [*These gifts of the Spirit are given to individuals so that everyone can benefit.*]

8 For to one [*faithful member*] is given by the Spirit [*the Holy Ghost*] the word of **wisdom** [*the gift of wisdom*]; to another the word of **knowledge** [*the gift of acquiring and retaining knowledge, especially of the gospel*] by the same Spirit;

9 To another **faith** [*another member is given the gift of faith*] by the same Spirit; to another the **gifts of healing** by the same Spirit;

> With respect to the gift of healing, in verse 9, above, Joseph Smith taught that both men and women can have this gift. "These signs, such as healing the sick, casting out devils, etc., should follow all that believe, whether male or female." *Teachings of the Prophet Joseph Smith*, p. 224.

10 To another the **working of miracles**; to another **prophecy** [*the gift of knowing the future (which must be used properly within one's own stewardship)*]; to another **discerning of spirits** [*the gift of detecting evil which others don't see; also, the gift of seeing the good in others*]; to another divers [*various*] kinds of **tongues** [*the gift of tongues, which includes the ability to rather quickly learn a foreign language as a missionary*]; to another the **interpretation of tongues**:

> Joseph Smith warned that speaking in tongues is often used by Satan to deceive people. He said "Be not so curious about tongues, do not speak in tongues except there be an interpreter present; the ultimate design of tongues is to speak to foreigners, and if persons are very anxious to display their intelligence, let them speak to such in their own tongues. The gifts of God are all useful in their place, but when they are applied to that which God does not intend, they prove an injury, a snare, and a curse instead of a blessing." *History of the Church*, Vol. 5, pp. 31–32.

11 But all these worketh that one and the selfsame Spirit [*all these gifts come from the same Spirit, namely the Holy Ghost*], dividing [*giving*] to every man severally [*his own*] as he will.

12 For as the body is one [*is one unit*], and hath many members [*such as arms, legs, hands, eyes, and so forth*], and all the members of that one body, being many, are one body: so also is Christ. [*Just as the body consists of many individual body parts, all belonging to the same body, so also is it with these gifts of the Spirit. Even though there are many different ones, given to various members of the Church, they all work together to bring us to unity in Christ's gospel.*]

13 For by one Spirit are we all baptized into one body, whether we be Jews or Gentiles, whether we be bond [*a slave or servant*] or free; and have been all made to drink into one Spirit. [*Regardless of our background, culture, etc., the same Spirit unites us in the gospel. In other words, the purpose of the gifts of the Spirit is to help us work in harmony as a team, each benefiting from the other's gifts. See D&C 46:11–12.*]

14 For the body is not one member, but many [*the body is not composed of just one part, but many parts*].

15 If the foot shall say, Because I am not the hand, I am not of the body; is it therefore not of the body? [*For instance, if a member who has the gift of faith but not the gift of knowledge were to say, "Since I don't have the gift of knowledge, I am left out," does that mean that he or she is not a valid member of the Church?*]

16 And if the ear shall say, Because I am not the eye, I am not of the body; is it therefore not of the body?

17 If the whole body were an eye, where were the hearing [*how would we hear*]? If the whole were hearing, where were the smelling [*how would we be able to smell things*]? [*The point is that we as a "body" of Saints need each member and the gifts which each member has been given.*]

18 But now hath God set the members every one of them in the body [*the Church*], as it hath pleased him [*God has given each member one or more gifts of the Spirit according to His will, and placed them in the Church*].

19 And if they were all one member, where were the body [*and if each of them were the same body part (such as a foot), what kind of a body would that be*]?

20 But now are they many members, yet but one body. [*God has given many different gifts of the Spirit, thus creating a well-balanced "body" of the Church.*]

By now you are probably quite used to the fact that Paul often uses much repetition to drive home his point when he is teaching.

21 And the eye cannot say unto the hand [*a member with one spiritual gift can't say to another*], I have no need of thee: nor again the head to the feet, I have no need of you.

22 Nay, much more [*on the contrary*] those members of the body, which seem to be more feeble [*weak; see 1 Corinthians 12:22, footnote a, in your Bible*], are necessary [*the weaker members of the Church are very necessary*]:

23 And those members of the body [*those members of the Church*], which we think to be less honourable [*not as capable; not as valuable to the Church—see* Teachings of the Prophet Joseph Smith, *pp. 223–224*], upon these we bestow more abundant honour [*we treat as*

more valuable]; and our uncomely parts have more abundant comeliness [*and our members who are less influential and capable in the Church become more capable and thus more influential*].

The word "comely" has various meanings in the scriptures, depending on context. *Strong's Concordance* (definition #2158) defines it various ways, including "of elegant figure, shapely, graceful, bearing one's self becomingly in speech or behavior, of good standing, honourable, influential, respectable." In verse 23, above, "uncomely" seems to have the connotation of being less influential or less experienced in the Church. In verse 24, next, "comely" seems to include the concept of "experienced," "influential," "bringing honor to the Church," and "being stable and solid in the Church." In speaking of these verses in 1 Corinthians, chapter 12, Joseph Smith warned members against being jealous of those called to leadership. In *Teachings of the Prophet Joseph Smith*, pp. 223–224, it tells us what the Prophet said about this. "He spoke of the disposition of many men to consider the lower offices in the Church dishonorable, and to look with jealous eyes upon the standing of others who are called to preside over them."

24 For our comely parts [*our stronger members*] have no need [*are already aware of their worth and value to God*]: but God hath tempered [*mixed*] the body [*members of the Church*] together, having given more abundant honour [*value, worth;* Strong's *#5092*] to that part [*weaker members; see verse 22*] which lacked: [*In other words, a major purpose of the Lord's mixing weaker members with stronger members is to increase the weaker members' self-esteem and sense of worth in God's eyes, as well as training them for future leadership callings.*]

25 That there should be no schism [*divisions*] in the body [*the Church*]; but that the members should have the same care one for another.

26 And whether one member suffer [*if one member is suffering*], all the members suffer with it; or one member be honoured, all the members rejoice with it. [*This is similar to Mosiah 18:8–9, which includes "willing to bear one another's burdens, that they may be light; . . . and are willing to mourn with those that mourn; and comfort those that stand in need of comfort, . . ."*]

27 Now ye are the body of Christ [*you all belong to Christ's Church*], and members in particular [*and each of you has individual skills, spiritual gifts, abilities, etc.*].

Next, Paul will summarize this chapter by emphasizing the importance of Church organization and the role each member has in strengthening the Church with his or her own unique gifts and abilities. He will also emphasize the importance of those who teach in the Church, placing them next in influence to Apostles and prophets.

28 And God hath set some in the church [*and God has organized the Church with*], first apostles, secondarily prophets, thirdly teachers, after that miracles, then gifts of healings, helps, governments, diversities of tongues [*the gift of tongues*].

29 Are all apostles? are all prophets? are all teachers? are all workers of miracles? [*Answer: No.*]

30 Have all the gifts of healing? do all speak with tongues? do all interpret? [*Answer: No.*]

31 But covet [*seek*] earnestly the best gifts [*D&C 46:8 ". . . seek ye earnestly the best gifts,"*]: and yet shew I unto you a more excellent way.

JST 1 Corinthians 12:31

31 **I say unto you, Nay; for I have shown unto you a more excellent way, therefore covet earnestly the best gifts.**

The "more excellent way" spoken of by Paul in verse 31, would seem to include the concept that spiritual gifts given to individual members open up the opportunity for unity, harmony, strengthening each other and all working together for the good of each other. Indeed, this "more excellent way" is the way to celestial glory and exaltation.

FIRST CORINTHIANS 13

Having taught the Corinthian Saints about the role of spiritual gifts in strengthening the Church and its individual members, in chapter 12, Paul now focuses on the very essence of Christ like living for each of us, namely, having charity toward each other. He will teach us, in effect, that no matter how qualified we are in other areas, if we lack charity we are nothing.

The word "charity" in the original New Testament Greek is defined as "brotherly love, good will, love, benevolence." In Moroni 7:47, it is defined as "the pure love of Christ." This is one of the best known and beautiful of Paul's teachings. The Prophet Joseph Smith made no JST changes to this chapter.

1 THOUGH I speak with the tongues of men and of angels [*even though I speak many different languages and even speak like an angel*], and have not charity, I am become as sounding brass, or a tinkling cymbal [*I am nothing but a loud brass gong or a clanging cymbal*].

2 And though I have the gift of prophecy, and understand all mysteries, and all knowledge; and though I have all faith, so that I could remove mountains, and have not charity, I am nothing.

3 And though I bestow [*give*] all my goods [*material possessions*] to

feed the poor, and though I give my body to be burned [*if I were to give my life for the gospel*], and have not charity, it profiteth me nothing.

4 Charity suffereth long [*is patient*], and is kind; charity envieth not [*does not resent others for what they have*]; charity vaunteth not itself [*does not brag*], is not puffed up [*is not prideful*],

5 Doth not behave itself unseemly [*indecently (see 1 Corinthians 13:5, footnote a), inappropriately, rudely*], seeketh not her own [*is not selfish*], is not easily provoked [*is not irritable; doesn't lose its temper*], thinketh no evil [*the word "thinketh" as used here, means "keeps a list of; keeps an account of";* Strong's *#3049; see also the Institute of Religion's New Testament student manual,* The Life and Teachings of Jesus and His Apostles, *p. 296. In other words, doesn't hold grudges, doesn't keep a list of wrongs done to him or her by others*];

6 Rejoiceth not in iniquity [*does not delight in or take pleasure in wickedness*], but rejoiceth in the truth;

7 Beareth all things [*keeps quiet about the errors and faults of others; see* Strong's *#4722; does not give in to resentment (see Institute New Testament student manual, p. 296)*], believeth all things [*is completely trusting of and committed to God and Christ;* Strong's *#4100*], hopeth all things [*in the Book of Mormon, the word "hope" implies "courage," "assurance," and "determination" (see Alma 58:11–12) and optimistically planning on success in following God, a "perfect brightness of hope" (see 2 Nephi 31:20)*], endureth all things [*never gives up in following Christ*].

The phrase "Charity never faileth" in verse 8, next, has many possible interpretations and lessons for us. For instance, it can mean that exercising charity never fails to make us a better person. It never fails to make the world a better place. Another lesson for us could be found in *Strong's Concordance* #1601, which defines "faileth" as being ineffective, in other words, "charity" is never ineffective. Even in the case where Christ like love and patience is rejected by others, charity still brings the one who has it back to God. Yet another use of the word "fail" is found in the phrase "Men's hearts failing them for fear," as used in Luke 21:26. Here, the word "failing" means "to run out of," as in running out of hope, courage, optimism, etc. Thus, "Charity never faileth" could mean that a truly Christ like person never runs out of charity toward others. Still another help for understanding the word "faileth" is found in the Institute of Religion's New Testament student manual, p. 296, where "faileth" is used in conjunction with a leaf falling off a tree or a flower. The message is that "charity" will never be removed from its place as a central focus of celestial, Christ like behavior.

8 Charity never faileth [*see note above*]: but whether there be prophecies [*in the case of prophecies*], they shall fail [*they eventually finish up by being fulfilled*]; whether there be tongues [*in the case of speaking various languages*], they shall cease [*it will no longer be necessary when we all learn the same language; it will no longer be necessary after the Second Coming because we will all speak the same language; see Zephaniah 3:9*]; whether there be knowledge [*in the case of knowledge*], it shall vanish away [*partial knowledge, false assumptions, philosophies, and opinions will vanish away in the light of truth*].

9 For we know in part, and we prophesy in part. [*In other words, we don't know all things, and the prophesying we do does not reveal all truth yet.*]

10 But when that [*Christ*] which is perfect is come, then that which is in part shall be done away. [*In other words, when Christ comes, He will "reveal all things." See D&C 101:32–34.*]

11 When I was a child, I spake [*spoke*] as a child, I understood as a child, I thought as a child: but when I became a man, I put away childish things. [*One of the messages in this verse is that as we develop Christ like charity, we put away "childish" or spiritually-immature behaviors, such as self-centeredness, selfishness, losing our temper, being impatient with others, gossiping, taking pleasure in wickedness, etc., as mentioned in the earlier verses in this chapter.*]

In order to better understand Paul's imagery about seeing "through a glass darkly" in the next verse, we need a bit of information about Paul's day. Page 296 of the Institute of Religion's New Testament student manual, *The Life and Teachings of Jesus and His Apostles*, has the following explanation: "The word translated glass is actually mirror. To those of us accustomed to the high quality mirrors of today, Paul's imagery is not clear. 'The thought of imperfect seeing is emphasized by the character of the ancient mirror, which was of polished metal, and required constant polishing, so that a sponge with pounded pumice-stone was generally attached to it.' (Vincent Word Studies, 2:795–96.") In other words, even with our best efforts, with our current limitations, we have a hard time seeing clearly who we are and what we can become as we develop charity and follow Christ. It is like looking at ourselves in a hazy, distorted mirror and saying, "That's the real me."

12 For now [*with our mortal limitations*] we see through a glass, darkly; but then face to face [*when we are face to face with God, and have become gods, we will see who we really are, that we are "like him"; see 1 John 3:2, where we are told "we shall be like him; for we shall see him as he is"; see also D&C 130:1*]: now I know in part [*now, I do not know*

all things]; but then shall I know even as also I am known [*by God, in celestial exaltation; see D&C 76:94. In other words, via true doctrine, you must "see" your potential, and that you and I have the potential of becoming gods, and of knowing all things, just as our God, our Father knows us.*]

13 And now abideth faith, hope, charity, these three [*now, these three things are our main focus, faith, hope, and charity*]; but the greatest of these [*the character trait we need most, and to which faith in Christ and hope lead*] is charity.

In verse 13, above, faith, hope, and charity are a dynamic combination of cause and effect, and might be summarized as follows: Faith in Jesus Christ leads to personal change and improvement, thus, to hope for ourselves as far as exaltation is concerned. Both faith and hope lead us to the essence of Christ like living, which is charity toward all others. Apostle Bruce R. McConkie explained verse 13, above, as follows: "But some things shall 'abide' forever. Among them: Faith, which is the very power of God himself; hope, which is the assurance of eternal life and everlasting progression; and charity, which is the pure love of Christ." *Doctrinal New Testament Commentary*, Vol. 2, p. 380.

FIRST CORINTHIANS 14

Chapter 14 is a continuation of Paul's teachings dealing with gifts of the Spirit (chapter 12) and charity (chapter 13). By way of background, it would seem that many of the Corinthian members of the Church have gone overboard with speaking in tongues. It has become a matter of prestige among them and has become a type of false spirituality, leaving them subject to Satan's deceptions. Joseph Smith cautioned the members of the Church on several occasions about the dangers of deception when it comes to speaking in tongues and other so-called "manifestations of the Spirit." In *History of the Church*, Vol. 4, p. 572, he taught: "One great evil is, that men are ignorant of the nature of spirits; their power, laws, government, intelligence, &c., and imagine that when there is anything like power, revelation, or vision manifested, that it must be of God. Hence the Methodists, Presbyterians, and others frequently possess a spirit that will cause them to lie down, and during its operation, animation is frequently entirely suspended; they consider it to be the power of God, and a glorious manifestation from God—a manifestation of what? Is there any intelligence communicated? Are the curtains of heaven withdrawn, or the purposes of God developed? Have they seen and conversed with an angel—or have the glories of futurity burst upon their view? No! but their body has been inanimate, the operation of their spirit suspended, and all the intelligence that can be obtained from them when they arise, is a shout of 'glory,' or 'hallelujah,' or some incoherent expression; but they have had 'the power.' The Shaker will whirl around on his heel, impelled by a supernatural agency or spirit, and think that he is governed by the Spirit of God; and the Jumper will jump and enter into all kinds of extravagances. A Primitive Methodist will shout under the influence of that spirit, until he will rend the heavens with his cries; while the Quakers (or Friends) moved as they think, by the Spirit of God, will sit still and say nothing. Is God the author of all this? If not of all of it, which does He recognize? Surely, such a heterogeneous mass of confusion never can enter into the kingdom of heaven."

We will include other such cautions from the Prophet as we study this chapter.

1 FOLLOW [*eagerly pursue; seek*] after charity, and desire [*seek; see D&C 46:8*] spiritual gifts, but rather that ye may prophesy.

The word "prophesy" in verse 1, above, has more than one meaning in scripture. It usually means to foretell the future, especially predicting future events which pertain to the gospel. It can also mean to have the influence of the Holy Ghost upon you such that you know the gospel is true. Thus, for instance, you can "prophesy" that everyone will some day know that God exists. We are taught this in the Bible Dictionary, p. 754, where it says "In a general sense a prophet is anyone who has a testimony of Jesus Christ by the Holy Ghost, as in Numbers 11:25–29; Revelation 19:10."

"Prophesying" can also mean "bearing one's testimony," for instance, in a church meeting. Yet another definition of "prophesy" is found in *Strong's Concordance* #4395, where it is defined as "to teach, refute, reprove, admonish, comfort others." This last definition may fit Paul's intent in verse 1 so that it basically says for us to seek to develop charity and to seek spiritual gifts so that we can more effectively teach and minister to one another by word and example. This seems to fit the context of verses 3 and 4.

2 For he that speaketh in an unknown tongue [*language*] speaketh not unto men, but unto God: for no man understandeth him [*perhaps meaning that it doesn't do anyone any good, because only God can understand him*]; howbeit [*however*] in the spirit he speaketh mysteries [*perhaps meaning that what he says while under the influence of such a spirit remains a mystery to others*].

JST 1 Corinthians 14:2

2 For he that speaketh in **another** tongue speaketh not unto men, but unto God; for no man understandeth him; howbeit

in the spirit he speaketh mysteries.

It may be that the Prophet Joseph Smith's counsel about speaking in tongues fits in with this verse. He said:

"Not every spirit, or vision, or singing, is of God. The devil is an orator; he is powerful. . . Speak not in the gift of tongues without understanding it, or without interpretation. The devil can speak in tongues . . . he can tempt all classes; can speak in English or Dutch. Let no one speak in tongues unless he interpret, except by the consent of the one who is placed to preside; then he may discern or interpret, or another may." (*Teachings of the Prophet Joseph Smith*, p. 162.)

3 But he that prophesieth speaketh unto men to edification [*builds them up, strengthens them spiritually*], and exhortation [*encouragement*], and comfort.

4 He that speaketh in an unknown tongue edifieth himself [*builds himself up*]; but he that prophesieth [*teaches correct doctrine and ministers to others with the pure love of Christ; see note for verse 1*] edifieth [*builds and strengthens*] the church.

JST 1 Corinthians 14:4

4 He that speaketh in **another** tongue edifieth himself; but he that prophesieth edifieth the church.

As mentioned in the note at the beginning of this chapter, there seems to have been a problem among the Corinthian Saints with speaking in tongues. Paul appears to be trying to convince them to downplay speaking in tongues into its proper place as a gift of the Spirit as opposed to using it to build themselves up in the eyes of others. In verse 5, next, he is rather gentle and diplomatic with them.

5 I would that ye all spake with tongues [*it would be nice if you could all speak in different languages*], but rather that ye prophesied [*but I would rather have you teach and strengthen each other rather than yourselves*]: for greater is he that prophesieth than he that speaketh with tongues [*the member who humbly teaches others is actually greater than the member who speaks in tongues*], except he interpret [*unless the gift of interpretation of tongues is also present*], that the church may receive edifying [*may be strengthened*].

Joseph Smith addressed this issue as he explained Paul's teachings about gifts of the Spirit in 1 Corinthians, chapter 12. He said "There are several gifts mentioned here, yet which of them all could be known by an observer at the imposition of hands? The word of wisdom, and the word of knowledge, are as much gifts as any other, yet if a person possessed both of these gifts, or received them by the imposition of hands [*laying on of hands*], who would know it? Another might receive the gift of faith, and they would be as ignorant of it. Or suppose a man had the gift of healing or power to work miracles, that would not then be known; it would require time and circumstances to call these gifts into operation. Suppose a man had the discerning of spirits, who would be the wiser of it? Or if he had the interpretation of tongues, unless someone spoke in an unknown tongue, he of course would have to be silent; there are only two gifts that could be made visible—the gift of tongues and the gift of prophecy. These are the things that are the most talked about, and yet if a person spoke in an unknown tongue, according to Paul's testimony, he would be a barbarian to those present. They would say that it was gibberish; and if he prophesied they would call it nonsense. The gift of tongues is the smallest gift perhaps of the whole, and yet it is one that is the most sought after. (*Teachings of the Prophet Joseph Smith*, p. 246.) The Prophet went on to say, "Be not so curious about tongues, do not speak in tongues except there be an interpreter present; the ultimate design of tongues is to speak to foreigners, and if persons are very anxious to display their intelligence, let them speak to such in their own tongues. The gifts of God are all useful in their place, but when they are applied to that which God does not intend, they prove an injury, a snare and a curse instead of a blessing. (*Teachings of the Prophet Joseph Smith*, p. 247.)

6 Now, brethren, if I come unto you speaking with tongues, what shall I profit you [*what good will it do*], except [*unless*] I shall speak to you either by revelation, or by knowledge, or by prophesying, or by doctrine?

7 And even things without life giving sound, whether pipe or harp [*even in the case of lifeless things such as a flute or a harp which give out specific sounds*], except [*unless*] they give a distinction in the sounds [*if they all sounded the same, if notes were played indiscriminately, like when you speak in tongues and* no *one understands*], how shall it be known what is piped or harped [*how would a listener know what is being played*]?

8 For if the trumpet give an uncertain sound [*like when you are speaking in tongues and no one understands*], who shall prepare himself to the battle [*who would understand the message*]?

9 So likewise ye [*such is the case with you*], except ye utter by the tongue words easy to be understood [*unless you speak in words easy for others to understand*], how shall it be known what is spoken [*how would anyone understand the message*]? for ye shall speak into the air [*you are just talking into the wind*].

10 There are, it may be, so many kinds of voices [*languages; see* Strong's *#5456*] in the world, and none of them is without signification [*and each language has meaning*].

11 Therefore if I know not the meaning of the voice, I shall be unto him that speaketh a barbarian [*a foreigner*], and he that speaketh shall be a barbarian [*a foreigner*] unto me. [*In other words, it doesn't do us any good if we can't understand each other.*]

12 Even so ye [*it should be the case with you*], forasmuch as ye are zealous of spiritual gifts [*since you are anxious to obtain spiritual gifts*], seek that ye may excel to the edifying of the church [*seek gifts of the Spirit that will allow you to build up the Church and its members, rather than gifts such as the gift of tongues which build you up in their eyes*].

13 Wherefore let him that speaketh in an unknown tongue pray that he may interpret.

JST 1 Corinthians 14:13

13 Wherefore let him that speaketh in **another** tongue pray that he may interpret.

14 For if I pray in an unknown tongue, my spirit prayeth, but my understanding is unfruitful [*doesn't help anyone else*].

JST 1 Corinthians 14:14

14 For if I pray in **another** tongue, my spirit prayeth, but my understanding is unfruitful.

15 What is it then [*so what should I do*]? I will pray with the spirit, and I will pray with the understanding [*with my mind*] also: I will sing with the spirit, and I will sing with the understanding also.

16 Else [*otherwise*] when thou shalt bless with the spirit [*if you pray in tongues*], how shall he that occupieth the room of the unlearned say Amen at thy giving of thanks, seeing he understandeth not what thou sayest [*how would someone in the room with you, who does not understand that language, know whether or not to say "Amen," at the end of the prayer (which means "I agree.")*]?

17 For thou verily givest thanks well [*you did a right good job of praying in tongues*], but the other is not edified [*but it didn't do the person who couldn't understand any good*].

18 I thank my God, I speak with tongues more than ye all [*I am grateful that I can speak more languages than any of you*]:

19 Yet in the church I had rather speak five words with my understanding, that by my voice I might teach others also [*Yet, I would rather speak five words which members in the congregation can understand, and thus teach them something*], than ten thousand words in an unknown tongue.

JST 1 Corinthians 14:19

19 Yet in the church I had rather speak five words with my understanding, that by my voice I might teach others also, than ten thousand words in **another** tongue.

20 Brethren, be not children in understanding [*don't think like children; in other words, don't be*

so spiritually immature that you want to build yourselves up in the eyes of others by speaking in tongues]: howbeit [*however*] in malice [*wickedness, depravity; see 1 Corinthians 14:20, footnote c*] be ye children [*be like little children who are pure, not wicked*], but in understanding be men [*think like men*].

21 In the law it is written [*in Isaiah 28:11–12*], With men of other tongues [*foreign languages*] and other lips [*other languages, including the inspiration of the Holy Ghost*] will I speak unto this people; and yet for all that will they not hear [*pay attention to*] me, saith the Lord.

22 Wherefore tongues are [*the gift of tongues is*] for a sign, not to them that believe [*not to members of the Church*], but to them that believe not [*but for nonmembers, such as on the Day of Pentecost (Acts 21:1–11) when people from many nations heard the preaching of Peter and the Apostles in their own language*] but prophesying serveth not for them that believe not, but for them which believe.

Joseph Smith spoke of the use of the gift of tongues in missionary work to enable missionaries to speak to people in their own mother tongue. He said, "I read the 13th chapter of First Corinthians, also a part of the 14th chapter, and remarked that the gift of tongues was necessary in the Church. . .the gift of tongues by the power of the Holy Ghost in the Church, is for the benefit of the servants of God to preach to unbelievers, as on the day of Pentecost. When devout men from every nation shall assemble to hear the things of God, let the Elders preach to them in their own mother tongue, whether it is German, French, Spanish or Irish, or any other, and let those interpret who understand the language spoken, in their own mother tongue, and this is what the Apostle meant in First Corinthians 14:27." (*Teachings of the Prophet Joseph Smith*, p. 195.)

23 If therefore the whole church be come together into one place, and all speak with tongues, and there come in those that are unlearned, or unbelievers, will they not say that ye are mad [*if you are meeting together and all speaking in different languages, won't it make newer members or nonmembers who visit your meetings think you are all crazy*]?

24 But if all prophesy [*if all teach the gospel simply in the language of the members, and minister with Christlike love*], and there come in one that believeth not [*if a nonmember visits your meetings*], or one unlearned [*or if one who doesn't understand the gospel very well visits your meetings*], he is convinced [*convicted, shamed;* Strong's *#1651*] of all [*in other words, when he sees your righteousness and hears you preach the gospel, he is ashamed of his lifestyle and convicted in his mind that he should change and join the Church*], he is judged of all [*he is "judged" by your righteous*

behaviors and clear teachings, and thus is motivated to change his lifestyle]:

25 And thus are the secrets of his heart made manifest [*his unrighteousness and need for repentance become clear in his mind*]; and so falling down on his face [*in humility*] he will worship God, and report that God is in you of a truth [*that you members have the true gospel for sure*].

26 How is it then, brethren? when ye come together, every one of you hath a psalm [*a hymn*], hath a doctrine, hath a tongue, hath a revelation, hath an interpretation. Let all things be done unto edifying. [*In other words, each member has something good to contribute in your meetings. Things must be done in an orderly fashion so that all will be strengthened and built up in the gospel.*]

Obviously, Paul is very concerned about the wild, confusing, circus-like atmosphere that speaking in tongues has created in some of the meetings of the Corinthian Saints and he has said much about it so far in this chapter. Next, however, he assures these members that there is a place in the Church, on rare occasions, for speaking in tongues. When it comes from God, rather than from Satan, the gift of tongues will be done in an orderly fashion.

27 If any man speak in an unknown tongue, let it be by two, or at the most by three [*just two or at the most, three of you*], and that by course [*one at a time*]; and let one interpret.

JST 1 Corinthians 14:27

27 If any man speak in **another** tongue, let it be by two, or at the most by three, and that by course; and let one interpret.

28 But if there be no interpreter, let him keep silence in the church; and let him speak to himself, and to God.

29 Let the prophets speak two or three, and let the other judge [*listen attentively and weigh what is being said against the revealed word of God*].

The word "prophets" as used in verse 29, above, means members of the Church who have strong personal testimonies of the gospel. Referring to 1 Corinthians 14:29, Bruce R. McConkie explained this as follows: "Let those speak who have the testimony of Jesus, who know of spiritual things by revelation, who have tasted the good word of God; let those speak to whom the heavens have been opened, who can testify from personal knowledge, who have gained "words of wisdom. . . even by study and also by faith." (D&C 88:118.) Let those speak who can tell what God has revealed to them about his glorious gospel, 'for one truth revealed from heaven is worth all the sectarian notions in existence.' (*Teachings of the Prophet Joseph Smith*, p. 338.)" *Doctrinal New Testament Commentary*, Vol. 2, p. 386.

30 If any thing be revealed to another that sitteth by [*if the Spirit reveals something to you and you want to share it with others in the meeting*], let the first hold his peace [*be courteous and let the one who is speaking finish what he has to say before you stand and bear your testimony*].

31 For ye [*members of the Church*] may all prophesy [*bear testimony; Revelation 19:10 says "... the testimony of Jesus is the spirit of prophecy."*] one by one, that all may learn, and all may be comforted.

32 And the spirits of the prophets [*the members of the Church*] are subject to the prophets [*are under the direction of the presiding priesthood authorities; see McConkie,* Doctrinal New Testament Commentary, *Vol. 2, p. 387*].

33 For God is not the author of confusion, but of peace, as in all churches [*wards, branches*] of the saints. [*In other words, God's true Church is run under the direction of presiding priesthood authorities in each ward, branch, stake, etc., which provides an atmosphere of confidence and peace rather than the confusion and wrangling for position which is often found in other organizations.*]

The next two verses can cause much trouble and misunderstanding unless kept very strictly in the context in which Paul gives them. What is the context? Answer: Verses 32 and 33, wherein Paul teaches the Corinthian Saints that God places presiding authorities in each congregation. Who are the presiding authorities in the true Church? Answer: The priesthood brethren, such as the First Presidency, Quorum of the Twelve, Seventies, Area Seventies, mission presidents, stake presidents, district presidents, bishops, and branch presidents, who preside over members, male and female, in Church units. What is Paul telling the Corinthian Saints in verses 34 and 35? As you will see, the JST changes give us the answer. Joseph Smith changed the word "speak" to "rule." President Spencer W. Kimball used the word "preside" in place of "rule" as he explained Genesis 3:16 "and he shall rule over thee." See *Ensign*, March 1976, p. 71. With these things in mind, Paul is telling the Corinthian Saints that women may not preside over Church units. Rather, it is the responsibility of the priesthood to do so.

34 Let your women keep silence in the churches [*wards, branches*]: for it is not permitted unto them to speak; but they are commanded to be under obedience, as also saith the law.

JST 1 Corinthians 14:34

34 Let your women keep silence in the churches; for it is not permitted unto them to **rule**; but to be under obedience, as also saith the law.

35 And if they will learn any thing, let them ask their husbands at home: for it is a shame [*not proper*] for women to speak in the church.

JST 1 Corinthians 14:35

35 And if they will learn any thing, let them ask their husbands at home; for it is a shame for women to **rule** in the church.

When confusion arises through such verses as 34 and 35 above, as they stand in the Bible, we would do well to remember that the Bible is not always complete nor is it always translated correctly. There is a simple and very important principle which can help members avoid hurt and confusion because of such incompleteness or incorrectness in the Bible. It is this: Simply ask, "What do the Brethren do or say on this matter?" There is always safety in following the Brethren. And in this matter, do the Brethren allow women to speak, teach, serve as auxiliary presidents, bear testimony, etc., in church meetings? Answer: Yes! So, can women speak in the true Church, contrary to what the Bible says in these two verses? Answer: Yes.

36 What? came the word of God out from you [*did the word of God originate with you*]? or came it unto you only [*are you the only people it comes to*]?

37 If any man think himself to be a prophet, or spiritual [*if any of you has a true testimony*], let him acknowledge [*recognize*] that the things that I write unto you are the commandments of the Lord.

38 But if any man be ignorant, let him be ignorant [*wrong, mistaken; see* Strong's *#0050*]. [*In other words, if any members disagree with the counsel I have given, which comes from the Lord, realize that they are mistaken about it.*]

39 Wherefore, brethren, covet [*earnestly seek*] to prophesy [*emphasize orderly bearing of testimony, teaching and ministering in your meetings, under the inspiration of the Holy Ghost*], and forbid not to speak with tongues [*when it is appropriate*].

40 Let all things be done decently [*appropriately*] and in order.

FIRST CORINTHIANS 15

This chapter is one of the better known ones as far as doctrine is concerned. We quote from it often in our missionary work and teaching in the Church. Among other things, Paul wrote of resurrection for everyone, baptism for the dead, and the three degrees of glory to the Corinthian Saints. It is interesting and significant to realize that these Saints in the early Church had the same true doctrines as we have. They are all a part of the great plan of happiness, the Father's plan of salvation for us.

Paul begins his review of what he has taught the Corinthians by bearing witness of the resurrected Christ.

1 MOREOVER [*in addition*], brethren, I declare unto you the gospel which I preached unto you [*when I was there in Corinth among you*], which also ye have received [*which you accepted*], and wherein ye stand [*as members of the Church*];

2 By which also ye are saved, if ye keep in memory what I preached unto you [*if you remember what I taught*], unless ye have believed in vain [*unless you are not living what you believe*].

Paul will now emphasize that Jesus fulfilled the scriptural prophecies about the promised Messiah.

3 For I delivered unto you first of all that which I also received, how that Christ died for our sins according to the scriptures [*according to Old Testament prophecies*];

4 And that he was buried, and that he rose again the third day according to the scriptures:

Just a quick comment about "rose again" in verse 4, above. Once in a while, a student will see the word "again" and start wondering if it means that Jesus had been resurrected previously on other earths and thus, was being resurrected "again" here on our earth, after performing an atonement for us. Furthermore, some start wondering if Jesus gets born, crucified, and resurrected over and over on each of Father's worlds. This is not true. The word "again" simply means that Jesus became alive "again" through the process of resurrection. We know from D&C 76:24, that the Atonement, which Jesus performed on our earth, works for all other worlds he has created or will create for the Father. He will never die again. Neither will we, once we have been resurrected—see Hebrews 9:27.

5 And that he [*the resurrected Christ*] was seen of [*by*] Cephas [*Peter*], then of the twelve:

6 After that, he was seen of above [*more than*] five hundred brethren at once; of whom the greater part remain unto this present [*are still alive today*], but some are fallen asleep [*some have died*].

7 After that, he was seen of [*by*] James; then of all the apostles.

8 And last of all he was seen of me also [*as recorded in Acts 9:1–6*], as of one born out of due time [*as one born too late to see Him during His mortal ministry*].

9 For I am the least of the apostles, that am not meet to be called an apostle [*I am a very inadequate Apostle*], because I persecuted the church of God [*Acts 8:1–3*].

10 But by the grace of God [*because of the mercy, forgiveness, and help of God*] I am what I am [*I am a member of the Church and an Apostle*]: and his grace which was bestowed upon me was not in vain [*was not unproductive*]; but I laboured more abundantly than

they all [*I had to work harder than any other convert to get my life in order and to take the gospel to others*]: yet not I, but the grace of God which was with me [*I do not take the credit, rather, I give all credit to God*].

JST 1 Corinthians 15:10

10 But by the grace of God I am what I am; and his grace which was bestowed upon me was not in vain; **for** I labored more abundantly than they all; yet not I, but the grace of God which was with me.

11 Therefore whether it were I or they, so we preach, and so ye believed [*it makes no difference whether I or others brought the gospel to you; the important thing is that you believed and joined the Church*].

There were apparently a number of members in Corinth who still did not believe in the resurrection of Christ or anyone else, because of their past traditions before joining the Church. You might remember that the Sadducees were an influential religious group among the Jews who did not believe in resurrection. See Bible Dictionary under "Sadducees." Paul will now address this issue.

12 Now if Christ be preached that he rose from the dead, how say some among you that there is no resurrection of the dead? [*In other words, you have been taught that Christ was resurrected from the dead, so why is it that some of you don't believe in resurrection?*]

13 But if there be no resurrection of the dead, then is Christ not risen [*if there were no resurrection from the dead, then Christ couldn't have resurrected*]:

14 And if Christ be not risen [*was not resurrected*], then is our preaching vain [*our preaching is worthless*], and your faith is also vain [*of no value*].

15 Yea, and we are found false witnesses of God [*and if that were the case, then we would be false witnesses of God because what we said about His resurrecting Christ (Acts 4:33) would have been false*]; because we have testified of God [*about the Father*] that he raised up Christ: whom he raised not up, if so be that the dead rise not [*are not resurrected*].

16 For if the dead rise not [*if there is no such thing as resurrection*], then is not Christ raised [*then Christ would not have been resurrected*]:

17 And if Christ be not raised, your faith is vain; ye are yet in your sins [*if Christ was not resurrected, then your faith in Him is worth nothing, and you have not been forgiven of your sins*].

18 Then they also which are fallen asleep in Christ [*furthermore, those who joined the Church and remained faithful until death*] are perished [*will not be resurrected nor saved in heaven because the*

Atonement they relied on would not be in effect].

19 If in this life only we have hope in Christ [*if our belief in Christ only serves to give us hope during mortality, but is not based on eternal reality*], we are of all men most miserable [*we are to be pitied more than any other people because we have been so badly fooled*].

20 But now is Christ risen from the dead [*but, the truth of the matter is that Christ was indeed resurrected*], and become the firstfruits of them that slept [*and He was the first person from this earth to be resurrected, of all who had died up to the time of His resurrection*].

The reason we emphasize that Christ was the first person from this earth to be resurrected, in our note in verse 20, above, is that, obviously, Heavenly Father was resurrected long ago, before this earth was even created. And He had already had "worlds without number" created by the Son before our earth was created, which have already passed away. See Moses 1:32–35. Thus, there were already countless resurrections in the universe before our earth was even created.

Now let's come back down to earth and listen to more of Paul's teaching.

21 For since by [*because of*] man [*Adam*] came death, by man [*Christ; the "mortal" Messiah*] came also the resurrection of the dead. [*In other words, since physical death was introduced into the world through Adam and Eve, by the Fall, so also was the resurrection from the dead brought about by a mortal, namely the Savior.*]

Verse 22, next, is a rather famous and often-quoted verse in the New Testament by members of the Church. It teaches the wonderful true doctrine that everyone who has been or ever will be born will be resurrected. We will all get our bodies back and live forever. In fact, there is nothing anyone could do, no sin anyone could commit, including becoming a son of perdition during mortal life, which could prevent one from being resurrected. See D&C 88:97–102.

22 For as in Adam all die, even so in Christ [*because of Christ*] shall all be made alive [*all will be resurrected*].

23 But every man in his own order [*there is an order to the resurrection*]: Christ the firstfruits [*Christ is the first*]; afterward they that are Christ's at his coming [*then those who will go to the celestial kingdom*].

The Order of the Resurrection

As Latter-day Saints, we are privileged to have considerable detail about the "order" of the resurrection, as referred to by Paul in verse 23, above. We know of five major groups and the order in which they have been or will be resurrected:

1. The first group resurrected on this earth consisted of the righteous, from Adam and Eve down to the time of Christ's resurrection. These are spoken of in D&C 133:54–55. This group, led by the Savior, included John the Baptist and involved only those worthy of celestial glory. Qualifications for celestial glory are given in D&C 76:50–53 and elsewhere.

2. Next comes the large group who will be resurrected first at the Second Coming of the Savior. This resurrection is spoken of in D&C 88:97–98. In our day, this group is often spoken of as "the morning of the first resurrection," "the resurrection of the just," "the resurrection of the righteous," and so on. It includes only those worthy of celestial glory who died after Christ's resurrection or who will have died up to the time of His Second Coming.

3. Next come those who are found worthy to enter terrestrial glory. Qualifications for terrestrial glory are given in D&C 76:71–80. They will be resurrected near the beginning of the Millennium, but after the celestials spoken of in #2, above, have been resurrected. This resurrection is spoken of in D&C 88:99. This group consists of all those who will go to terrestrial glory who lived from the time of Adam and Eve up to the Second Coming. This will be the first time any terrestrials will have been resurrected. This group is sometimes referred to as "the afternoon of the first resurrection."

4. The next major group to be resurrected "in order" consists of those who will go to telestial glory. They are spoken of in D&C 88:100–101. They must wait for their resurrection until after the Millennium is over. No telestials have been resurrected yet. Qualifications for attaining telestial glory are given in D&C 76:81–85, 103–106; Revelation 22:15 and other places.

5. Last of all, those who were born on earth but who then became sons of perdition will be resurrected. This resurrection is referred to in D&C 88:102. Qualifications for becoming sons of perdition are detailed in D&C 76:31–35.

24 Then cometh the end [*of the mortal world*], when he [*Christ*] shall have delivered up the kingdom to God, even the Father [*see D&C 76:107–108*]; when he [*Christ*] shall have put down all rule [*brought to an end all earthly governments*] and all authority and power [*when Christ will have triumphed over all things; see D&C 76:106*].

JST 1 Corinthians 15:24

24 **Afterward** cometh the end, when he shall have delivered up the kingdom to God, even the Father; when he shall have put down all rule, and all authority and power.

25 For he [*Christ*] must reign, till he hath put all enemies under his feet.

26 The last enemy that shall be destroyed is death.

JST 1 Corinthians 15:26

26 **The last enemy, death, shall be destroyed**.

27 For he [*Christ*] hath put all things under his feet [*has attained power over all things*]. But when he saith all things are put under him, it is manifest [*it is clear*] that he [*the Father; see verse 28*] is excepted, which did put all things under him. [*In other words, when we say that Christ will triumph over all things, we do not mean he will triumph over the Father, who gave Jesus power to overcome all things so that we can be exalted, if we so choose.*]

JST 1 Corinthians 15:27

27 **For he saith, When it is manifest that he hath put all things under his feet, and that all things are put under, he is excepted of the Father who did put all things under him**.

28 And when all things shall be subdued unto him [*Christ*], then shall the Son also himself be subject unto him [*the Father*] that put all things under him, that God [*the Father*] may be all in all [*may be over all things; see Ephesians 4:6*].

Verse 29, next, is another often-quoted verse of scripture. We use it to teach people that baptism for the dead was practiced in Bible times as well as in the latter days. It is interesting to note that the main point of these next verses is not baptism for the dead. Rather, Paul is emphasizing the point that people will be resurrected. Otherwise, Paul asks, what good does it do to get baptized for the dead if the dead are not resurrected? From this we gather that baptism for the dead was such a common practice that Paul used it as a backdrop to strengthen his teaching about resurrection.

29 Else what shall they do which are baptized for the dead, if the dead rise not at all [*are not resurrected*]? why are they then baptized for the dead?

30 And why stand we in jeopardy [*in danger*] every hour?

31 I protest [*promise you, confirm with an oath;* Strong's *#3513*] by your rejoicing which I have in Christ Jesus our Lord, I die daily.

JST 1 Corinthians 15:31

31 **I protest** [*testify*] **unto you the resurrection of the dead; and this is my rejoicing** which I have in Christ Jesus our Lord **daily, though I die.**

Paul's reference to fighting with wild beasts in the city of Ephesus, verse 32, next, may well imply that this was one of the things he suffered because of his loyalty to the Savior, and survived. There was a large stadium in Ephesus, which was the Roman capital in that part of Asia, which was 685 feet by 200 feet, and in which spectators gathered to watch as people were forced to fight ferocious beasts; see information in conjunction with *Strong's* #2181.

32 If after the manner of men I have fought with beasts at Ephesus [*as mentioned in the note above, Paul may be saying "When I was thrown to the wild beasts in Ephesus, because of my loyalty to Christ"*], what advantageth it me, if the dead rise not [*what good was it for me to be loyal to Christ if we don't get resurrected*]? let us eat and drink; for to morrow we die [*if there is no resurrection, then Christ was a fraud and we might just as well live it up in mortality because we won't exist after we die*].

33 Be not deceived [*don't be fooled into thinking that there is no life after death, and thus feeling free to live riotously, eating, drinking, and being merry*]: evil communications [*wicked associations and conversations;* Strong's *#3657*] corrupt good manners [*morals, character;* Strong's *#2239*].

34 Awake to righteousness, and sin not; for some [*of your members*] have not the knowledge of God: I speak this to your shame.

Paul will now be very direct with any members who challenge or do not believe in the doctrine of resurrection.

35 But some man will say, How are the dead raised up? and with what body do they come [*what kind of a body will they have when they are resurrected*]?

36 Thou fool, that which thou sowest [*the seed that you plant in the ground*] is not quickened [*does not grow and become a new plant*] except it die [*unless you bury it in the ground, just as our bodies are buried when we die*]: [*In other words, you are being foolish to challenge the doctrine of resurrection because there are examples of "death" and "resurrection" all around you in the daily world of agriculture.*]

37 And that which thou sowest [*and when you plant a seed*], thou sowest not that body that shall be [*you are not planting the plant which the seed will become*], but bare grain [*a mere seed, not the plant itself;* Strong's *#1131*], it may chance of wheat, or of some other grain [*whether it is wheat or any other type of grain*]:

<u>JST 1 Corinthians 15:37</u>

37 And that which thou sowest, thou sowest not that body which shall be, **but grain, it may be of wheat, or some other**;

38 But God giveth it a body as it hath pleased him, and to every seed his own body [*every seed that is planted and grows has a body unique to it, according to God's plan*].

Now Paul is focusing in on the question in verse 35, above, which asked what kind of a body people will have when they are resurrected. Paul's answer provides us with some very specific doctrine about types of bodies people will have in the resurrection. It tells us that there will be differences between the bodies of celestials and terrestrials and telestials. Let's see what he says.

39 All flesh is not the same flesh: but there is one kind of flesh of men, another flesh of beasts, another of fishes, and another of birds.

40 There are also celestial bodies [*the bodies of those who are resurrected and go to celestial glory*], and bodies terrestrial [*bodies for those in the terrestrial kingdom*]: but the glory of the celestial is one, and the glory of the terrestrial is another [*there is a difference between the bodies of celestials and the bodies of terrestrials*].

JST 1 Corinthians 15:40

40 **Also** celestial bodies, and bodies terrestrial, **and bodies telestial**; but the glory of the celestial, one; **and the terrestrial, another; and the telestial, another.**

Did you notice that the JST for verse 40, above, adds telestial bodies? In other words, it adds the telestial kingdom. This is a most important doctrinal addition.

41 There is one glory of the sun, and another glory of the moon, and another glory of the stars: for one star differeth from another star in glory [*one of the differences between resurrected bodies is that there will be a difference in the glory radiating from the bodies of celestials, terrestrials, and telestials*].

The fact that there will be differences in resurrected bodies, depending on which kingdom of glory people go to, is taught in D&C 88:28–32. Apostle Joseph Fielding Smith explained these things as follows:

"KINDS OF RESURRECTED BODIES. In the resurrection there will be different kinds of bodies; they will not all be alike. The body a man receives will determine his place hereafter. There will be celestial bodies, terrestrial bodies, and telestial bodies . . . Elder Orson Pratt many years ago in writing of the resurrection and the kind of bodies which would be raised in these kingdoms said: '. . . There will be several classes of resurrected bodies; some celestial, some terrestrial, some telestial, and some sons of perdition. Each of these classes will differ from the others by prominent and marked distinctions;'

Continuing, Joseph Fielding Smith pointed out that procreation will be limited to those who gain exaltation. He said "Some will gain celestial bodies with all the powers of exaltation and eternal increase. These bodies will shine like the sun as our Savior's does, as described by John (in Revelation 1:16). Those who enter the terrestrial kingdom will have terrestrial bodies, and they will not shine like the sun, but they will be more glorious than the bodies of those who receive the telestial glory. In both of these kingdoms (terrestrial and telestial) there will be changes in the bodies and limitations. They will not have the power of increase, neither the power or nature to live as husbands and wives, for this will be denied them and they cannot increase. Those who receive the exaltation in the celestial kingdom will have the 'continuation of the seeds forever' (D&C 132:19.) They will live in the family relationship. In the terrestrial and in the telestial kingdoms there will be no marriage. Those who enter there will remain 'separately and singly' forever (D&C 132:17). Some of the functions in the celestial body will not appear in the terrestrial body, neither in the telestial body, and the power of procreation will be removed." (*Doctrines of Salvation*, Vol. 2, p. 286.)

The resurrection is, in fact, a partial judgment. We will know which degree of glory we will go to by what kind of a body we get in the resurrection.

42 So also is the resurrection of the dead [*this is how it will be in the resurrection of the dead*]. It is sown in corruption [*our mortal bodies will be buried and will decompose*]; it is raised in incorruption [*when we are resurrected, our resurrected bodies will never be subject to deterioration again*]:

43 It [*our mortal body*] is sown [*buried*] in dishonour [*having failed to sustain our life any longer*]; it is raised [*resurrected*] in glory: it is sown [*buried*] in weakness [*demonstrating mortal frailty*]; it is raised [*resurrected*] in power:

44 It is sown [*buried*] a natural [*mortal*] body; it is raised a spiritual body. [*Not a "spirit" body, rather, a "spiritual" body, meaning an immortal body of flesh, bone, and spirit.*] There is a natural body, and there is a spiritual body.

Apostle Howard W. Hunter, who later became the president of the Church, explained the meaning of the phrase "spiritual body" as used in verse 44, above. He taught "There is a separation of the spirit and the body at the time of death. The resurrection will again unite the spirit with the body, and the body becomes a spiritual body, one of flesh and bones but quickened [*made alive*] by the spirit instead of blood. Thus, our bodies after the resurrection, quickened by the spirit, shall become immortal and never die. This is the meaning of the statements of Paul that 'there is a natural body, and there is a spiritual body' and 'that flesh and blood cannot inherit the kingdom of God.' The natural body is flesh and blood, but quickened by the spirit instead of blood, it can and will enter the kingdom." [*General Conference, April 1969.*]

45 And so it is written, The first man Adam was made a living soul; the last Adam was made a quickening spirit.

We need some help with Paul's vocabulary in verse 45, above. Paul refers to two "Adams," namely, "the first man Adam," who was Eve's husband, and "the last Adam" (*Christ*), who is a "quickening spirit" or one who makes people come alive again, i.e., enables us to be resurrected. What Paul is teaching is that Adam's spirit was given a mortal body, and thus became a "living soul." The definition of "soul" is given in D&C 88:15 where it says "And the spirit and the body are the soul of man." Everyone will eventually die and thus, all of us need Christ's resurrection to free us from death.

46 Howbeit [*however*] that was not first which is spiritual, but that which is natural; and afterward that which is spiritual. [*In other words, first we get our mortal bodies. Next, we get our immortal, resurrected bodies.*]

JST 1 Corinthians 15:46

46 Howbeit, **that which is natural first, and not that which is spiritual**; **but** afterwards, that which is spiritual;

47 The first man [*Adam*] is of the earth, earthy [*Adam got a mortal body, first, made of earthly elements*]: the second man [*Christ*] is the Lord from heaven.

48 As is the earthy [*just like Adam*], such are they also that are earthy [*all of us mortals get a mortal body, subject to death*]: and as is the heavenly [*just as Christ received a resurrected celestial body*], such are they also that are heavenly [*so also will all the righteous get a celestial resurrected body*].

49 And as we have borne the image of the earthy [*we are just like Adam in the sense that our mortal bodies will die*], we shall also bear the image of the heavenly [*we will also be resurrected, like Christ was*].

50 Now this I say, brethren, that flesh and blood cannot inherit the kingdom of God [*physical, mortal bodies cannot go to heaven to be with God without being resurrected first, because mortal bodies could not survive in the fiery glory surrounding God. See* Teachings of the Prophet Joseph Smith, *pp. 367, 326, and 199–200.*]; neither doth corruption inherit incorruption [*mortal bodies, which are subject to decay upon burial, cannot inherit the presence of God*].

51 Behold, I shew you a mystery [*let me share an interesting exception to the general rule that all of us will be buried when we die, to await our resurrection*]; We shall not all sleep [*not everyone will be buried in the ground*], but we shall all be changed,

52 In a moment, in the twinkling of an eye [*those who live during the Millennium will not be buried when they die, rather, they will die and then be resurrected instantly; see D&C 101:31 as referred to in 1 Corinthians 15:52, footnote c*], at the last trump: for the trumpet shall sound, and the dead shall be raised incorruptible [*with immortal*

bodies of flesh and bone], and we shall be changed.

JST 1 Corinthians 15:52

52 In a moment, in the twinkling of an eye, at the **sound of** the last trump; for the trumpet shall sound, and the dead shall be raised incorruptible, and we shall be changed.

53 For this corruptible [*this mortal body*] must put on incorruption [*must be resurrected*], and this mortal must put on immortality.

54 So when this corruptible shall have put on incorruption [*so, when we are all resurrected*], and this mortal shall have put on immortality, then shall be brought to pass the saying that is written [*in Isaiah 25:8*], Death is swallowed up in victory.

55 O death, where is thy sting? O grave, where is thy victory?

56 The sting of death is sin [*the thing that really hurts us is unrepented of sin*]; and the strength of sin [*the power that sin has over us*] is the law [*of justice*].

57 But thanks be to God, which giveth us the victory through our Lord Jesus Christ [*we can triumph over sin through the Atonement of Christ*].

58 Therefore, my beloved brethren, be ye stedfast, unmoveable [*remain faithful*], always abounding in the work of the Lord [*remain active in the Church*], forasmuch as ye know that your labour is not in vain in the Lord.

FIRST CORINTHIANS 16

Several of the members of the Church in the Jerusalem area had come upon hard times and needed welfare assistance from members elsewhere. Paul has been very active in taking up collections to be taken to these needy Saints. In the first few verses of this chapter, he gives instructions to the Corinthian Saints regarding collecting money for this cause.

1 NOW concerning the collection for the saints [*the donations being collected to be taken to the members of the Church who are in need of welfare help in the Jerusalem area*], as I have given order to the churches of Galatia, even so do ye [*please set things up for collecting donations from your wards and branches the same way I set things up among the Galatian Saints*].

2 Upon the first day of the week [*Sunday; see Acts 20:7; see also Bible Dictionary under "Sabbath"*] let every one of you lay by him in store, as God hath prospered him [*on each Sunday, gather up donations to the cause according to members' ability to give*], that there be no gatherings when I come [*so that I don't have to take time to gather up donations when I come*].

3 And when I come, whomsoever ye shall approve by your letters [*letters of recommendation*], them will I send to bring your liberality [*generosities; in other words, your donations*] unto Jerusalem.

4 And if it be meet [*and if it is necessary*] that I go also, they shall go with me.

5 Now I will come unto you, when I shall pass through Macedonia [*northern Greece, today*]: for I do pass through Macedonia.

6 And it may be that I will abide, yea, and winter with you [*it may be that I will spend the winter there with you*], that ye may bring me on my journey whithersoever [*wherever*] I go.

Paul is writing this letter to the Corinthians from Philippi, which is in the far northeastern part of Greece.

7 For I will not see you now by the way [*I don't want to visit you now, because I wouldn't have time to stay*]; but I trust to tarry [*stay*] a while with you, if the Lord permit.

8 But I will tarry at Ephesus [*in western Turkey, today*] until Pentecost [*a major religious celebration in Jerusalem, held fifty days after Passover; see Bible Dictionary under "Feasts"*].

9 For a great door and effectual is opened unto me [*I have many wonderful opportunities to serve that opened up for me*], and there are many adversaries [*and I have many enemies trying to stop me*].

10 Now if Timotheus [*Timothy*] come [*comes to Corinth*], see that he may be with you without fear: for he worketh the work of the Lord [*he is serving the Lord*], as I also do.

11 Let no man therefore despise him [*not take him seriously because he is so young; see 1 Timothy 4:12*]: but conduct him forth in peace [*help him get on his way without undue difficulties*], that he may come unto me: for I look for him with the brethren.

12 As touching our brother Apollos [*a faithful convert to the Church, who is with Paul as he writes this letter to the Corinthian members; see information given with* Strong's *#0625*], I greatly desired him to come unto you with the brethren: but his will was not at all to come at this time; but he will come when he shall have convenient time.

Just a reminder, that when we refer to "*Strong's #*" we mean the definition of a particular word as given in *Strong's Exhaustive Concordance of the Bible*.

13 Watch ye [*be alert*], stand fast [*firm*] in the faith, quit you [*behave*] like men, be strong.

14 Let all your things be done with charity.

15 I beseech [*urge*] you, brethren, (ye know the house [*the household*] of Stephanas [*the first people I baptized in Corinth, when I came through on my missionary journey*], that it is the firstfruits of Achaia [*the general area of southern Greece*], and that they have addicted [*devoted*] themselves to the ministry of the saints,)

16 That ye submit yourselves unto such [*listen to their advice and*

counsel; Strong's *#5293*], and to every one that helpeth with us, and laboureth.

17 I am glad of the coming [*I am happy about the arrival here*] of Stephanas [*one of the first converts in Corinth, referred to in verse 15, above*] and Fortunatus [*apparently a convert from Corinth;* Strong's *#5415*] and Achaicus [*a convert from Corinth; see* Strong's *#0883*]: for that which was lacking on your part they have supplied [*they have supplied me with information I was lacking about you*].

18 For they have refreshed my spirit and yours: therefore acknowledge ye them that are such [*such men deserve recognition by you*].

19 The churches of Asia salute you [*send their greetings to you*]. Aquila and Priscilla salute you much in the Lord, with the church that is in their house [*along with the members of the Church who meet in their home*].

20 All the brethren greet you [*send their greetings to you*]. Greet ye one another with an holy kiss.

JST 1 Corinthians 16:20

20 All the brethren greet you. Greet ye one another with **a holy salutation**.

21 The salutation of [*greeting from*] me Paul with mine own hand [*which I have written with my own hand, rather than having it written by one of my scribes*].

22 If any man love not the Lord Jesus Christ, let him be Anathema Maranatha.

The two words, "Anathema" and "Maranatha", used in verse 22, above, are a bit puzzling to us. Some possible interpretations are given in the Institute of Religion's New Testament student manual, *The Life and Teachings of Jesus and His Apostles*, p. 298, as follows:

"This strange inclusion of two Aramaic words together in Paul's closing words of the epistle [*letter*] has raised many questions. The meaning of both words is known, but the strange combination is what puzzles most scholars. Anathema means literally 'something set apart or consecrated,' and came to carry the meaning of 'cursed' or 'accursed.' This is the word Paul uses in Galatians 1:8 when he says that anyone preaching another gospel than the true one should be accursed. Maranatha has been variously translated as 'the Lord comes,' 'the Lord will come,' 'the Lord is at hand,' and so on. It seems to have been a common Christian greeting or watchword. As far as the combination of the two are concerned, two basic interpretations are made. Some versions assume that there should be a period between the two. Thus it reads: 'If anyone has no love for the Lord, let him be accursed. Our Lord, come!' Most scholars seem to prefer this separation. But one has suggested that Paul combines them deliberately, using an old Syriac exclamation,

'Let him be accursed, the Lord is at hand,' suggesting that at the Lord's coming, punishment will be meted out. (See Fallows, The Popular and Critical Bible Encyclopedia and Scriptural Dictionary, 1:104.)

23 The grace [*mercy, help, forgiveness, etc.*] of our Lord Jesus Christ be with you.

24 My love be with you all in Christ Jesus. Amen.

THE SECOND EPISTLE OF PAUL THE APOSTLE TO THE CORINTHIANS

This is Paul's follow-up letter to First Corinthians. Most Bible scholars believe that it was written about AD 57 from Macedonia, which would be the northern area of modern-day Greece. The first nine chapters are comparatively conciliatory and kind. The last four chapters are somewhat strong and blunt like much of First Corinthians was.

SECOND CORINTHIANS 1

In this opening chapter of his follow-up letter to what we know as 1 Corinthians, you will see that Paul is quite personal and down-to-earth with these members of the Church in Corinth. He will emphasize that these Saints are a valued comfort and support to him and his missionary companions, just as he hopes he and those with him have been a strength and comfort to them.

1 PAUL, an apostle of Jesus Christ by the will of God, and Timothy our brother, unto the church of God which is at Corinth, with all the saints which are in all Achaia [*southern Greece*]:

2 Grace be to you and peace from God our Father, and from the Lord Jesus Christ. [*Another reminder that the Father and the Son are separate personages.*]

3 Blessed be [*praised be*] God, even the Father of our Lord Jesus Christ, the Father of mercies, and the God of all comfort;

An important message for us all is found in verse 4, next. It is that since we are blessed with comfort from above, we should also be willing to comfort and help others.

4 Who comforteth us in all our tribulation [*trials and troubles*], that we may be able to comfort

them [*others*] which are in any trouble, by the [*because of the*] comfort wherewith [*with which*] we ourselves are comforted of [*by*] God.

5 For as the sufferings of Christ abound in us [*we are persecuted because we believe in Christ*], so our consolation also aboundeth by Christ [*we receive much comfort from Christ as we go through persecutions*].

6 And whether [*if*] we [*Paul and his direct associates*] be afflicted [*are persecuted*], it is for your consolation and salvation, which is effectual in the enduring of the same sufferings which we also suffer [*our suffering helps you endure similar suffering because of your faithfulness to Christ*]: or whether [*if*] we be [*are*] comforted, it is for your consolation and salvation [*it helps to comfort you and strengthen your testimonies, leading to salvation*].

7 And our hope of you is stedfast [*we have full confidence in you*], knowing, that as ye are partakers of the sufferings, so shall ye be also of the consolation [*knowing that just as you suffer because of your loyalty to Christ, so also you will be comforted and strengthened by Him*].

8 For we would not, brethren, have you ignorant of our trouble which came to us in Asia [*and, speaking of suffering, may we remind you of the troubles we went through in Asia (western Turkey today)*], that we were pressed out of measure, above strength [*how we had troubles, seemingly far beyond our ability to survive*], insomuch that we despaired even of life [*to the point that we expected to die*]:

9 But we had the sentence of death in ourselves [*we felt in our hearts that we were facing certain death*], that we should not trust in ourselves, but in God which raiseth the dead [*we knew that we could not rely on our own abilities, rather that we must trust in God who can raise the dead*]:

10 Who delivered us from so great a death [*who saved us from the life-threatening dangers we faced in Asia*], and doth deliver [*and continues to deliver us from such perils*]: in whom we trust that he will yet deliver us [*and we trust that he will yet deliver us from additional dangers*];

11 Ye also helping together by prayer for us [*your prayers for us are a great help*], that for the gift bestowed upon us by the means of many persons thanks may be given by many on our behalf.

12 For our rejoicing is this [*consists of this*], the testimony of our conscience [*in good conscience*], that in simplicity [*with no other motive*] and godly sincerity, not with fleshly wisdom [*not with the wisdom of man*], but by the grace of God, we have had our conversation [*our associations*] in the world, and more abundantly to you-ward [*and our rejoicing is because of our association with you*].

13 For we write none other things unto you, than what ye read or acknowledge [*we write nothing to you but what you can easily understand*]; and I trust ye shall acknowledge [*understand*] even to the end;

14 As also ye have acknowledged [*understood*] us in part [*to some degree*], that we are your rejoicing [*that we are the source of your rejoicing because we brought you the gospel*], even as ye also are ours [*even as you are the source of great rejoicing in our hearts*] in the day of the Lord Jesus [*as we all look forward to returning to be with Jesus*].

15 And in this confidence [*assurance that you are glad that we brought you the gospel*] I was minded [*I intended*] to come unto you before [*earlier*], that ye might have a second [*additional*] benefit [*that I might help you understand even more of the gospel*];

16 And to pass by you into Macedonia [*and to stop by and visit you on my way to Macedonia—northern Greece*], and to come again out of Macedonia unto you, and of you to be brought [*and to have your help in getting*] on my way toward Judea [*the Jerusalem area*].

17 When I therefore was thus minded [*when my intention was to come visit you*], did I use lightness [*do you think I was being overly light-minded, optimistic, or unrealistic*]? or the things that I purpose, do I purpose according to the flesh [*or do you think that I am being a bit selfish, desiring the personal pleasure which it would bring me to be among you again*], that with me there should be yea yea, and nay nay [*do you think I am too indecisive*]?

18 But as God is true [*just as surely as God is trustworthy*], our word toward you was not yea and nay [*there was nothing indecisive in our message to you about Christ*].

19 For the Son of God, Jesus Christ, who was preached among you by us, even by me and Silvanus and Timotheus [*Timothy*], was not yea and nay [*Christ, whom we preached to you, was not indecisive*], but in him was yea [*in Christ was definitely the one road to salvation*].

20 For all the promises of God [*the Father*] in him [*through Christ*] are yea [*positive*], and in him Amen [*Christ; Christ is often referred to as "the Amen"; see Bible Dictionary under "Amen"*], unto the glory of God by us [*our salvation through Christ adds to the glory of God*].

21 Now he which establisheth us with you in Christ [*who establishes us with you in his kingdom via Christ*], and hath anointed us [*and who has given us the Gift of the Holy Ghost, with its accompanying gifts; see* Strong's *#5548*], is God [*is the Father*];

22 Who hath also sealed us [*who has put His seal of ownership upon*

us], and given the earnest of the Spirit in our hearts [*and has put "earnest money," so to speak, on us in the form of the Gift of the Holy Ghost, which, if followed, assures that we will someday belong to the Father in exaltation forever*].

As indicated in the note in verse 22, above, the word "earnest" as used in verse 22, above, is the same as the phrase "earnest money" as used today. It means to pay earnest money to secure the right to purchase a car, or house or whatever at a later date. Symbolically, the Gift of the Holy Ghost is given to members of the Church to secure the right for Christ's Atonement to purchase us for the Father, later, on Judgment Day, to live with Him forever in exaltation, if we will hearken to the promptings of the Holy Ghost.

23 Moreover [*furthermore*] I call God for a record upon my soul [*I call upon God as my witness that I am telling you the truth*], that to spare you I came not as yet unto Corinth. [*In other words, the reason I haven't yet come to Corinth is to spare you further preaching from me which might cause you more pain (see 2 Corinthians 2:1–5). In other words, Paul realizes that what he wrote them in 1 Corinthians was very direct and no doubt caused many of them considerable pain. Paul is obviously a very sensitive, though energetic, Apostle, and doesn't like to hurt people's feelings, even though it is sometimes necessary in order to open their eyes and hearts to the need for change.*]

24 Not for that we have dominion over your faith [*not that we want to dominate you*], but are helpers of your joy [*rather, we want to help your faith and joy grow*]: for by faith ye stand [*faith in Christ is the key to your remaining faithful in the Church and being in good standing with God*].

SECOND CORINTHIANS 2

As previously mentioned, it was hard on Paul to be as direct and blunt with these members of the Church as he sometimes had to be, as seen in 1 Corinthians. Now his deep tenderness and gentleness emerges as he shows forth "an increase of love toward [*those*] whom [*he has*] reproved" (Compare with D&C 121:43.)

1 BUT I determined this with myself, that I would not come again to you in heaviness [*scolding you and causing you grief and worry*].

2 For if I make you sorry, who is he then that maketh me glad, but the same which is made sorry by me? [*In other words, if I make you unhappy, who is left to make me happy? Answer: only you whom I have made sad, and that doesn't seem to work.*]

3 And I wrote this same unto you, lest, when I came, I should have sorrow from them of whom I ought to rejoice [*the reason I wrote rather harsh things to you in my last letter is that I was worried for fear you*

would continue going in wrong directions, thus causing me sorrow instead of joy because of you]; having confidence in you all, that my joy is the joy of you all [*having confidence that the joy which obedience to Christ brings me is the same joy which such obedience will bring you*].

4 For out of much affliction and anguish of heart I wrote unto you with many tears [*I was deeply worried about you*]; not that ye should be grieved [*I didn't want to cause you grief*], but that ye might know the love which I have more abundantly unto you [*I just wanted you to know how much I love you and care about your salvation*].

5 But if any have caused grief [*if some among you have caused trouble in the Church there in Corinth*], he hath not grieved me, but in part [*they haven't caused me as much grief as they have you*]: that I may not overcharge you all [*I need to be careful not to blame all of you for the misdeeds and apostasy of some among you*].

6 Sufficient to such a man is this punishment, which was inflicted of many [*the punishment inflicted upon such by the majority of you, who are faithful, should be sufficient*].

We don't know what the "punishment" in verse 6, above, was. Perhaps it was something as simple as disapproval or as strong as withdrawing from associating with them. Whatever it was, Paul considers it sufficient and now counsels these Saints to forgive one another and show increased love for those members who had caused trouble.

7 So that contrariwise [*instead*] ye ought rather to forgive him, and comfort him, lest perhaps [*for fear that*] such a one should be swallowed up with overmuch [*too much*] sorrow. [*Compare this with D&C 121:43.*]

8 Wherefore [*therefore*] I beseech [*urge*] you that ye would confirm [*demonstrate*] your love toward him.

9 For to this end also did I write [*another reason I wrote to you is*], that I might know the proof of you [*that I might receive evidence from you*], whether ye be obedient in all things.

10 To whom ye forgive any thing, I forgive also [*whomever you forgive, I will forgive*]: for if I forgave any thing [*in any cases where I needed to forgive anything*], to whom I forgave it, for your sakes forgave I it in the person of Christ [*I forgave them under the direction of Christ*];

11 Lest Satan should get an advantage of us: for we are not ignorant of his devices. [*In other words, we know how Satan works, and it is essential that we forgive one another so that he doesn't get the advantage over us.*]

12 Furthermore [*let me mention another thing now*], when I came to Troas [*on the western tip of*

northern Turkey] to preach Christ's gospel, and a door was opened unto me of the Lord [*and the Lord opened up many opportunities for successful preaching there*],

13 I had no rest in my spirit [*I couldn't relax*], because I found not Titus my brother [*because I couldn't locate Titus*]: [*Titus was one of Paul's favorite and most faithful associates in the Church. He was a Greek convert and was very familiar with the Saints in Corinth; see information associated with* Strong's *#5103*] but taking my leave of them, I went from thence into Macedonia [*so I left Troas and went to northern Greece*].

14 Now thanks be unto God [*the Father*], which always causeth us to triumph in Christ [*because of Christ and his Atonement*], and maketh manifest the savour of his knowledge by us in every place.

Paul will use the word "savour" several times as this chapter comes to a close. It is translated from the Greek and means "smell," "odor" or "fragrance." The smell of sacrifices in Old Testament times would remind God's people of Him and their loyalty to Him. Incense was also used in worshiping God and was symbolic of the prayers of the Saints. See Bible Dictionary under "Incense," and also Revelation 5:8. Thus, when the Saints would smell the fragrance of incense, it would remind them of the Lord. Paul refers to the members of the Church, symbolically, as "savour" or fragrance.

15 For we are unto God [*the Father*] a sweet savour of Christ, in them that are saved [*in Greek, it says "are being saved"*], [*In other words, righteous Saints are like a sweet "fragrance," i.e., a pleasant result of Christ's mission to save us*], and in them that perish [*standing out among those who will not come to Christ*]: [*Another way to say this might be "Our righteous lives, based on Christ, are a prayer of gratitude rising up like incense to the Father," in contrast to those who will not return to Him through Christ.*]

16 To the one we are the savour of death unto death [*to those who reject our example as followers of Christ, we become the smell of spiritual death and damnation, because our example will help condemn them on Judgment Day*]; and to the other the savour of life [*of being "born again"*] unto life [*eternal life*]. And who is sufficient for these things [*how many of us are up to the task, equal to the opportunities before us to spread the pleasant fragrance of the gospel to others*]?

17 For we are not as [*like*] many, which corrupt the word of God [*peddle for personal gain and financial profit; see* Strong's *#2585*]: [*Paul seems to be referring to "priestcraft," as defined in Alma 1:16.*] but as of sincerity [*but we teach the word of God sincerely, without thought of personal gain or profit*], but as of God [*as servants sent from God*], in the sight of God speak we in Christ [*God is our*

witness that we speak the truth about Christ].

SECOND CORINTHIANS 3

Paul will now reemphasize that the gospel, as brought by Christ, takes the place of the law of Moses. He will begin by asking if he and the brethren who are with him need additional identification as authorized servants of the Lord. He uses this as the background for complimenting them and telling them that their lives as members of the Church are all the recommendation others need to see that the gospel brought to them by Paul is true.

1 DO we begin again to commend ourselves [*are our names sufficient recommendation for you*]? or need we, as some others, epistles of commendation to you [*or do we need, as some others do, letters of recommendation*], or letters of commendation [*of recommendation*] from you?

2 Ye are our epistle written in our hearts, known and read of all men: [*In other words, the answer is "No." Your righteous lives are all the "letter of recommendation" necessary, witnessing that the gospel we brought to you, as authorized servants of God, is true. Your lives are the "letter of recommendation" which others read to find out about God.*]

3 Forasmuch as [*since*] ye are manifestly [*obviously*] declared to be the epistle of Christ [*you are the "letter" from Christ to be "read" by others*] ministered by us, written not with ink, but with the Spirit of the living God [*not literally a letter written with ink, but rather you are a "letter" which radiates the Spirit of the living God for others to "read"*]; not in tables of stone, [*not written in stone tablets like the Ten Commandments were*], but in fleshy tables of the heart [*but written deep in your hearts*].

4 And such trust have we through Christ to God-ward:

<u>JST 2 Corinthians 3:4</u>

4 And such trust have we through Christ **toward God**.

5 Not that we are sufficient of ourselves to think any thing as of ourselves; but our sufficiency is of God; [*Not that we are capable of doing the work of God because of any great talents or abilities we ourselves have, rather we are instruments in God's hand, and He makes us adequate to do His work.*]

You may wish to mark "the letter killeth, but the spirit giveth life," found in verse 6, next, in your own scriptures. It is a very important part of the gospel of Jesus Christ.

6 Who also [*God*] hath made us able ministers of the new testament [*the new covenant, brought by Christ, which replaces the law of Moses*]; not of the letter [*the detailed performances required by the law of Moses*], but of the spirit [*the "spirit" or "intent" of all*

God's commandments is to make us Christ like]: for the letter killeth, but the spirit giveth life. [*Those who pay attention only to the "letter of the law" eventually die spiritually; whereas, those who strive to grow spiritually, understanding the intent of all God's laws for us, grow spiritually toward eternal life.*]

7 But if the ministration of death [*if the law of Moses, followed exclusively, would still lead to spiritual death*], written and engraven in stones, was glorious [*yet was a relatively high law*], so that the children of Israel could not stedfastly behold [*look directly at*] the face of Moses [*it still didn't enable the children of Israel to look directly at Moses' face when it shined*] for [*because of*] the glory of his countenance [*because his face shined with glory after he had been in the presence of the Lord for 40 days in the mountain; see Exodus 34:29–35*]; which glory was to be done away [*which glory was not the full glory which God has*]:

Verse 7, above, is saying, in effect, that if we were to follow only the law of Moses, which included the Ten Commandments engraved in stone, and which was glorious indeed compared to the depraved lifestyles the children of Israel learned in Egypt, we would not be able to return to the presence of God in celestial glory and would thus suffer spiritual death (meaning being cut off from the direct presence of God forever); see Bible Dictionary under "Death" for the definition of spiritual death. The law of Moses didn't even get the children of Israel to the point where they could stand to be in the presence of Moses after he had been in the presence of the Lord. And the light radiating from Moses' face was nothing compared to the light you would have to be able to stand if you go to celestial glory.]

8 How shall not the ministration of the spirit be rather glorious [*don't you think the Spirit which attends Christ's gospel will be even more glorious*]?

9 For if the ministration of condemnation be glory [*if the law of Moses had much glory along with it*], much more doth the ministration of righteousness exceed in glory [*the personal righteousness which comes through following Christ will lead to much more glory*].

10 For even that which was made glorious had no glory in this respect, by reason of the glory that excelleth [*when you compare the glory brought by following the law of Moses to the glory which will come through following Christ, it is as if there were not glory at all accompanying the law of Moses*].

11 For if that which is done away was glorious [*if the law of Moses, which has been done away with now, was glorious, which it was*], much more that which remaineth is glorious [*the glory attained by following Christ far exceeds it*].

In 2 Corinthians 4:17, Paul will emphasize again the tremendous difference in glory between those who attain celestial glory and all others, when he says they will obtain "a far more exceeding and eternal weight of glory."

12 Seeing then that we have such hope [*because we know what God has in store for us*], we use great plainness of speech [*we speak plainly with boldness; see 2 Corinthians 3:12, footnote a*]:

13 And not as Moses [*who had to hold back*], which put a vail over his face [*symbolically, we are not hiding the glory of God from you, like Moses had to because of their unbelief*], that the children of Israel could not stedfastly look to the end [*see the purpose*] of that which is abolished [*of the law of Moses*]:

14 But their minds were blinded [*they were spiritually blind and could not see the purpose of the law of Moses*]: for until this day remaineth the same vail untaken away in the reading of the old testament [*it is as if, even today, the same veil were still in place, hiding the glory of God from spiritually blind Israel who are still stuck in Old Testament times*]; which vail is done away in Christ [*even though that "veil" has been removed by the gospel which Christ brought*].

15 But even unto this day, when Moses is read [*when they read the Old Testament*], the vail is upon their heart [*Israelites today are still spiritually blind and hard-hearted*].

16 Nevertheless when it [*Israel*] shall turn to the Lord, the vail shall be taken away. [*When Israelites repent and turn to Christ, the veil of spiritual darkness and hard-heartedness will be taken from them.*]

JST 2 Corinthians 3:16

16 Nevertheless, when **their heart** shall turn to the Lord, the **veil** shall be taken away.

17 Now the Lord is that Spirit: and where the Spirit of the Lord is, there is liberty [*there is freedom from spiritual darkness and bondage*].

In verse 18, next, Paul says, in effect, that we are just beginning to catch a glimpse of the glory which will be ours as we progress toward becoming "joint heirs" with Christ (Romans 8:17), in other words, exalted beings, through the help of the Holy Ghost.

Paul uses a clever play on words here as he refers to our faces which are beginning to shine just a bit.

18 But we all, with open face beholding as in a glass the glory of the Lord [*seeing, as if in an imperfect mirror*], are changed [*Greek: "are being transformed"*] into the same image [*to look like Christ*] from glory to glory [*with continually increasing glory and light*], even as by the Spirit of the Lord [*by the power of the gift of the Holy Ghost*].

SECOND CORINTHIANS 4

After reminding the Corinthian Saints that he and his companions are authorized servants of God, Paul will continue, warning them against such things as dishonesty, and reminding them that troubles for the righteous in mortality are nothing compared to the blessings of eternity with God.

1 THEREFORE seeing we have this ministry, as we have received mercy [*the fact that we have been called of God to do this work, along with the fact that we, ourselves, have been blessed by the Atonement, gives us strength and courage so that*], we faint not [*we do not give up*];

2 But have renounced the hidden things of dishonesty [*we have turned away from the hidden evils which come from dishonesty*], not walking in craftiness [*not deceiving others*], nor handling the word of God deceitfully [*nor corrupting (*Strong's *#1389) God's word to make it more acceptable to people*]; but by manifestation of the truth [*we teach the true gospel plainly*] commending ourselves to every man's conscience in the sight of God [*presenting ourselves and our message to all people so that they can follow their conscience and come to God.*]

3 But if our gospel be hid, it is hid to them that are lost [*if it seems to some that our message is hard to understand, be aware that it only seems so to those who are spiritually lost*]:

4 In whom the god of this world [*the devil, Satan*] hath blinded the minds of them which believe not [*it is because the "god of this world," the devil (see 2 Corinthians 4:4, footnote a), has blinded their minds because of their unbelief*], lest [*for fear that*] the light of the glorious gospel of Christ, who is the image of God [*who literally looks like the Father (Hebrews 1:3) and also represents the Father*], should shine unto them [*those who are under Satan's influence*].

5 For we preach not ourselves [*about ourselves and our own ideas*], but Christ Jesus the Lord [*the Messiah;* Strong's *#2962*]; and ourselves your servants [*as your servants*] for Jesus' sake [*sent by Christ*].

6 For God, who commanded the light to shine out of darkness [*Genesis 1:3–5*], hath shined in our hearts [*has shined the gospel light into our hearts*], to give the light of the knowledge of the glory of God in the face of Jesus Christ [*and has let us see His glory as it shined from Him to us through the face of Christ*].

7 But we have this treasure [*the gospel light*] in earthen vessels [*in our mortal lives*], that the excellency of the power may be of God, and not of us [*the source of this powerful gospel light is God, not us*].

8 We are troubled on every side [*every way we turn, we run into trouble as we fulfill our missions*], yet not distressed [*yet we are not detoured, stopped*]; we are perplexed, but not in despair;

9 Persecuted, but not forsaken [*not abandoned by the Lord*]; cast down, but not destroyed;

10 Always bearing about in the body the dying of the Lord Jesus [*always remembering that Jesus went through trials in His mortal life also*], that the life also of Jesus might be made manifest in our body [*that, through our faithfulness, we might be resurrected to eternal life with Christ; see McConkie,* Doctrinal New Testament Commentary, *Vol. 2, p. 419*].

11 For we which live are alway [*always*] delivered unto death for Jesus' sake [*are always repenting because of Christ*], that the life also of Jesus [*that the newness of life from Jesus, being "born again" constantly*] might be made manifest in our mortal flesh [*might happen to us during our mortal lives*].

> Verse 11, above, seems to tie in with Romans 6:4–6, where we continue going through the process of dying or repenting, "burying" our old sinful ways, and "crucifying" our sins in order to "walk in newness of life" through the Atonement. It also ties in with Alma 5:14, where, through repentance, we "receive his image in [*our*] countenances." All of this is an ongoing process during our mortal lives.

12 So then death worketh in us, but life in you. [*Perhaps Paul is saying in effect, based on the context of previous verses, "So, then, the gospel inspires us to put our own sins and worldly ways to death, so that we can more effectively bring the gospel of Christ to you, which brings new life to you."*]

JST 2 Corinthians 4:12

12 So then **it worketh death unto us, but life unto you**.

13 We having the same spirit of faith, according as it is written [*like it says in Psalm 116:10*], I believed, and therefore have I spoken; we also believe [*in Christ*], and therefore speak [*of Christ*];

14 Knowing that he [*the Father*] which raised up [*resurrected*] the Lord Jesus shall raise up us also by Jesus [*will resurrect us also, through Jesus*], and shall present us with you [*and we will meet together at the judgment bar of God (compare with 2 Nephi 33:15)*].

15 For all things are for your sakes, that the abundant grace might through the thanksgiving [*gratitude*] of many redound [*overflow; see* Strong's *#4052*] to the glory of God. [*In other words, we put up with whatever we have to in order to help you understand the gospel so that there will be many who are grateful for the Atonement to the point that their gratitude overflows in praising God and bringing glory to Him.*]

JST 2 Corinthians 4:15

15 For **we bear all things** for your sakes, that the abundant grace might, through the thanksgiving of many, redound to the glory of God.

It might be hard to notice, but can you see that the JST adds two commas to the verse above? Just another reminder that Joseph Smith paid very close attention to detail as he worked on the JST.

16 For which cause we faint not [*we never give up in this cause*]; but though our outward man perish [*even though our physical bodies get exhausted*], yet the inward man is renewed day by day [*our minds and spirits are constantly being strengthened and refreshed*].

17 For our light affliction [*the little suffering we are called to endure*], which is but for a moment, worketh for us [*prepares for us*] a far more exceeding and eternal weight of glory [*exaltation in the kingdom of God; see D&C 132:16*];

18 While we look not at the things which are seen, but at the things which are not seen [*we prioritize on spiritual things rather than on the things of the world*]: for the things which are seen are temporal [*temporary;* Strong's *#4340*]; but the things which are not seen [*the things of God*] are eternal.

SECOND CORINTHIANS 5

In this chapter, Paul starts out by teaching the doctrine of the resurrection of our mortal bodies. He emphasizes how wonderful it will be to eventually get a resurrected body. He will go on to teach the doctrine that we will all appear before the Lord on Judgment Day, and then teach the Atonement of Jesus Christ.

1 FOR we know that if our earthly house [*our mortal body*] of this tabernacle [*mortal body*] were dissolved [*decomposed when we die*], we have a building [*we will have a resurrected body*] of [*from*] God, an house [*a body*] not made with hands [*not mortal*], eternal in the heavens [*which will last forever; see McConkie,* Doctrinal New Testament Commentary, *Vol. 2, p. 420*].

2 For in this we groan, earnestly desiring to be clothed upon with our house which is from heaven [*we sigh in anticipation, looking forward to our resurrected bodies*]:

3 If so be that being clothed [*with a resurrected body*] we shall not be found naked.

4 For we that are in this tabernacle [*this mortal body*] do groan [*sigh*], being burdened [*burdened with the pains, sicknesses, weariness, etc., to which our mortal bodies are subject*]: not for that we would be unclothed [*not that we want to die*

right now], but clothed upon [*but look forward to the resurrection*], that mortality might be swallowed up of life [*when our mortal bodies will become resurrected bodies which live for ever*].

5 Now he that hath wrought us for the selfsame thing [*He who made it possible for us to be resurrected*] is God [*the Father; see notes with 2 Corinthians 1:21–22 in this study guide*], who also hath given unto us the earnest of the Spirit [*who, in effect, put "earnest money" on us in the form of the Holy Ghost to ensure that we return to Him*].

6 Therefore we are always confident [*cheerful; see 2 Corinthians 5:6, footnote a*], knowing that, whilst we are at home in the body [*while we live in our mortal bodies*], we are absent from the Lord [*we are merely absent for a while longer from living with the Lord in heaven*]:

7 (For we walk by faith, not by sight)

8 We are confident [*cheerful, of good courage;* Strong's *#2292*], I say, and willing [*looking forward*] rather to be absent from the body [*to leave the mortal body*], and to be present with the Lord [*to live with the Lord*].

9 Wherefore we labour, that, whether present or absent, we may be accepted of him [*we strive to be worthy to be acceptable to the Lord, whether alive or dead*].

10 For we must all appear before the judgment seat of Christ; that every one may receive the things done in his body, according to that he hath done [*may be rewarded or punished, according to what we did in mortality*], whether it be good or bad.

JST 2 Corinthians 5:10

10 For we must all appear before the judgment seat of Christ, that **everyone** may **receive a reward of the deeds done in the body; things according to what he hath done,** whether good or bad.

11 Knowing therefore the terror of the Lord [*since we know what fear the wicked will have when they face the Lord*], we persuade men [*we try to persuade them to follow Christ*]; but we are made manifest unto God [*God knows that we are trying*]; and I trust also are made manifest in your consciences [*and I trust that we have had a positive impact on you*].

12 For we commend not ourselves again unto you [*we are not going to talk ourselves up or brag to you*], but give you occasion to glory on our behalf [*but you can judge us by our works and praise us if you so choose*], that ye may have somewhat to answer them which glory in appearance [*people who want to look righteous*], and not in heart [*but don't want to be righteous in their hearts*].

13 For whether [*if*] we be beside ourselves [*out of our minds;*

Strong's *#1839*], it is to God: or whether we be sober, it is for your cause.

JST 2 Corinthians 5:13

13 For **we bear record that we are not beside ourselves** [*we assure you that we are not out of our minds*]; **for whether we glory, it is to God, or whether we be sober** [*sober-minded, serious*], it is for your **sakes**.

14 For the love of Christ constraineth us [*keeps us from coming apart, giving up;* Strong's *#4912*]; because we thus judge, that if one died for all [*if Christ had to die for everyone*], then were all dead [*then everyone must have needed His Atonement, otherwise they would all remain spiritually dead*]:

15 And that he [*Christ*] died for all, that they which live [*all people*] should not henceforth live unto themselves [*should not live according to their own knowledge and rules*], but unto him [*Christ*] which died for them, and rose again.

JST 2 Corinthians 5:15

15 **And he died for all**, that they which live should not henceforth live unto themselves, but unto him which died for them, and rose again.

16 Wherefore henceforth know we no man after the flesh: yea, though we have known Christ after the flesh, yet now henceforth know we him no more.

JST 2 Corinthians 5:16

Wherefore, henceforth **live we no more after the flesh** [*from now on, we no longer live according to worldly standards*]; yea, though **we once lived after the flesh** [*though we were once worldly*], **yet since we have known Christ** [*since we are now converted to Christ*], **now henceforth live we no more after the flesh** [*we no longer live according to the ways of the world*].

17 Therefore if any man be in Christ [*if anyone has been converted and come unto Christ*], he is a new creature [*he becomes a new person, born again*]: old things are passed away [*old lifestyles are gone*]; behold, all things are become new [*he has a new life*].

JST 2 Corinthians 5:17

17 Therefore if any man **live in Christ**, he is a new creature; old things are passed away; behold, all things are become new,

18 And all things are of God [*all these things come from the Father*], who hath reconciled us to himself by Jesus Christ [*who brings us back to his presence through Jesus Christ*], and hath given to us the ministry of reconciliation [*and has given us the Atonement*];

JST 2 Corinthians 5:18

18 **And receiveth all the things of God** [*". . . all that my Father hath shall be given unto him."; D&C 84:38; in other words,*

exaltation], who hath reconciled us to himself by Jesus Christ, and hath given to us the ministry of reconciliation;

19 To wit [*namely; in other words, the "ministry of reconciliation" spoken of in verse 18, above, is*], that God [*the Father*] was in Christ [*was made known to us by Christ*], reconciling the world unto himself [*in order to bring us back to His presence*], not imputing their trespasses unto them [*not holding us accountable for sins we repent of*]; and hath committed unto us the word [*the gospel*] of reconciliation [*of the Atonement*].

20 Now then we are ambassadors [*messengers*] for Christ, as though God did beseech you by us [*what we say to you is the same as if God were speaking to you; compare with "whether by mine own voice or by the voice of my servants, it is the same." D&C 1:38*]: we pray you in Christ's stead [*we urge you, standing in for Christ*], be ye reconciled to God [*be brought into harmony with the Father through the Atonement of Christ*].

Next, in verse 21, Paul tells us, in effect, that Christ, the Sinless One, was made to bear all our sins as if He, personally, had committed them all.

21 For he [*the Father*] hath made him [*Christ*] to be sin for us [*the Father has given us the Savior to pay for our sins*], who knew no sin [*Christ was perfect*]; that we might be made the righteousness of God in him. [*that we might be sanctified, made clean, pure, holy, righteous, through Christ*].

SECOND CORINTHIANS 6

Paul reminds these Corinthian members of the Church that now is the time for them to accept the gospel, since the opportunity is now being given to them. He reminds them to be good examples so that they don't hurt the work of spreading the gospel. He recounts the many things he and his missionary companions have gone through in order to bring the gospel to many.

1 WE then, as workers together with him, beseech you [*urge you*] also that ye receive not the grace of God in vain [*that you not fail to take full advantage of the Father's grace in giving us the Atonement of Christ*].

JST 2 Corinthians 6:1

1 We then, as workers together with **Christ**, beseech you also that ye receive not the grace of God in vain.

2 (For he saith [*in Isaiah 49:8*], I have heard thee in a time accepted, and in the day of salvation have I succoured thee [*rushed to your aid; in other words, the Lord will gather people in to the gospel as described in Isaiah 49:6*]: behold, now is the accepted time; behold, now is the day of salvation.) [*Paul is telling these members of the*

Church in Corinth that this time is their opportunity to accept the gospel; don't waste the opportunity.]

3 Giving no offence in any thing, that the ministry be not blamed [*be good examples so you don't hurt the work of the Lord*]:

4 But in all things approving ourselves [*we (Paul and his companions) have always tried to be good examples*] as the ministers of God, in much patience, in afflictions [*troubles*], in necessities [*in times of need*], in distresses,

5 In stripes [*we have been beaten*], in imprisonments [*we have been in prisons*], in tumults [*we have been attacked by mobs during riots*], in labours [*hard work*], in watchings [*in sleepless nights;* Strong's *#0070*], in fastings;

6 By pureness, by knowledge, by longsuffering [*not seeking revenge;* Strong's *#3115*], by kindness, by the Holy Ghost, by love unfeigned [*love which is genuine, not pretended*],

7 By the word of truth, by the power of God, by the armour of righteousness on the right hand and on the left,

8 By [*through*] honour and dishonour [*slander*], by evil report [*lies told about us*] and good report: as deceivers [*being thought of by many as deceivers*], and yet true [*yet as true servants of God*];

9 As unknown [*not known by most*], and yet well known [*by some*]; as dying [*going through times when it looked like we would not survive*], and, behold, we live [*and, as you see, we are still alive*]; as chastened [*beaten;* Strong's *#3811*], and not killed;

10 As sorrowful [*sad and mourning at times*], yet alway rejoicing [*because of Christ*]; as poor [*often having to ask for alms, financial help, etc.*], yet making many rich [*by bringing them the gospel*]; as having nothing [*in terms of worldly possessions and riches*], and yet possessing all things [*the gospel and potential exaltation*].

11 O ye Corinthians, our mouth is open unto you [*we have spoken clearly and straightforward to you*], our heart is enlarged [*swells with love and compassion for you*].

In the next verse, Paul uses the word "bowels." This word is used differently in modern English than in Old English. *Strong's Exhaustive Concordance of the Bible* defines this word as used by Paul here, as "inward affection, tender mercy, kindness, benevolence, compassion."

12 Ye are not straitened in us [*there is much room in our hearts for you*], but ye are straitened in your own bowels [*but there is not as much love and compassion in your hearts as there needs to be*].

13 Now for a recompence in the same [*now, in order to correct this*], (I speak as unto my children [*I'm speaking to you as I would to my children*],) be ye also enlarged

[*make more room in your hearts for Christlike love of others*].

Next, Paul will warn the Corinthian Saints and all of us about the dangers of trying to merge our LDS lifestyles in with the lifestyles of the world around us, through commitments and relationships which could lead us away from Christ.

14 Be ye not unequally yoked together with unbelievers [*don't get yourselves tied up in dealings and commitments with nonmembers which would lead you to be unfaithful to Christ; this could even include marrying out of the Church*]: for what fellowship hath righteousness with unrighteousness [*what business would righteousness have in trying to make unholy alliances with sin*]? and what communion [*association*] hath light with darkness [*are light and darkness compatible*]?

15 And what concord [*harmony, agreement;* Strong's *#4857*] hath Christ with Belial [*Satan;* Strong's *#0955*]? or what part hath he that believeth with an infidel [*a faithless unbeliever;* Strong's *#0571*]?

16 And what agreement hath the temple of God with idols [*in what way could true temples of God be compatible with idols and their temples*]? for ye are the temple of the living God; as God hath said [*in Leviticus 26:12*], I will dwell in them, and walk in them; and I will be their God, and they shall be my people.

17 Wherefore come out from among them [*leave associations which take you away from Christ*], and be ye separate, saith the Lord, and touch not the unclean thing; and I will receive you,

JST 2 Corinthians 6:17

17 Wherefore come out from among them, and be ye **the** separate, saith the Lord, and touch not the unclean thing; and I will receive you,

18 And will be a Father unto you, and ye shall be my sons and daughters, saith the Lord Almighty. [*This is a beautiful reminder to us that if we will leave the ways of the world, whatever the cost, we will become "family" with God, becoming His "sons and daughters," which is a scriptural phrase which means exaltation. See D&C 76:24 and Mosiah 5:7.*]

SECOND CORINTHIANS 7

This chapter is one of the more famous and oft-quoted of Paul's writings, because it defines "godly sorrow" (being truly sorry for sins committed, rather than merely being sorry you got caught) in verses 9–11. Godly sorrow is an essential part of true repentance and coming unto Christ.

The JST makes no corrections in this chapter.

1 HAVING therefore these promises [*including the promises in verse 18 of chapter 6, above*], dearly beloved, let us cleanse ourselves [*let us repent*] from all filthiness of the flesh and spirit [*of body and mind*], perfecting holiness in the fear of God [*working toward perfection with a realization that we are accountable to God*].

2 Receive us [*please accept our efforts in your behalf*]; we have wronged no man, we have corrupted no man, we have defrauded [*deceived for personal gain*] no man.

3 I speak not this to condemn you [*I am not comparing you to us to make you feel inferior*]: for I have said before, that ye are in our hearts to die and live with you.

4 Great is my boldness of speech toward you [*I have spoken very plainly to you*], great is my glorying of you [*I have great confidence in you*]: I am filled with comfort [*I am greatly encouraged by your progress*], I am exceeding joyful in all our tribulation [*I have much joy in spite of persecutions*].

5 For, when we were come [*when we came*] into Macedonia [*northern Greece*], our flesh had no rest [*we were physically exhausted*], but we were troubled on every side [*we were persecuted on every side*]; without were fightings [*externally, we were fighting for survival*], within [*inside of us*] were fears.

6 Nevertheless God, that comforteth those that are cast down [*discouraged*], comforted us by the coming of Titus; [*When Titus (one of Paul's favorite missionary companions) came, it cheered us up.*]

7 And not by his coming only, but by the consolation wherewith he was comforted in you, when he told us your earnest desire, your mourning, your fervent mind toward me; so that I rejoiced the more. [*Not only were we cheered up by Titus' coming, but I was cheered up even more when he told us about your concerns and worries for my well-being.*]

8 For though I made you sorry with a letter [*even though I caused you sorrow when I scolded you in my last letter to you (First Corinthians)*], I do not repent [*I don't take back what I said because you needed it*], though I did repent [*though I did regret hurting your feelings*]: for I perceive that the same epistle [*that letter*] hath made you sorry, though it were but for a season [*even though you got over it after while*].

9 Now I rejoice, not that ye were made sorry [*I'm not happy because I caused you pain*], but that ye sorrowed to repentance [*but because you actually repented because of what I said to you*]: for ye were made sorry after a godly manner [*my letter caused you to have "godly sorrow" so that you truly repented*], that ye might receive damage by us in nothing [*so that, as it ultimately turned out, we did not hurt you in any way*].

Paul now defines "godly sorrow,"

which is a vital part of truly repenting.

10 For godly sorrow worketh repentance [*causes us to repent*] to salvation [*and thus obtain exaltation*] not to be repented of [*and leaves us with no regrets*]: but the sorrow of the world [*being sorry you got caught, or sorry because you are embarrassed, or sorry that your opportunity to continue committing that sin has been taken away, etc.*] worketh death [*leads to spiritual death*].

Now, Paul describes some components of "godly sorrow," which make it so effective in cleansing us from sin and leading us to truly change and become more righteous.

11 For behold this selfsame thing [*this godly sorrow, the very thing I'm teaching you about, namely*], that ye sorrowed [*were sorry for sins*] after a godly sort [*in the way God wants you to be*], what carefulness [*sincerity, anxiety*] it wrought [*caused*] in you, yea, what clearing of yourselves [*eagerness to become clear of the sin*], yea, what indignation [*irritation, anger at yourself for committing the sin*], yea, what fear [*alarm*], yea, what vehement desire [*strong desire to change*], yea, what zeal [*enthusiasm to change*], yea, what revenge [*punishment; suffering whatever is necessary to make permanent change*]! In all things ye have approved yourselves to be clear in this matter [*in everything you have done, you have demonstrated that you understand godly sorrow*].

12 Wherefore, though I wrote unto you [*even though I wrote to all of you*], I did it not for his cause that had done the wrong [*I did not write it only to the members guilty of sinning*] , nor for his cause that suffered wrong [*nor did I write only to support the victims of others' sins*], but that our care for you in the sight of God might appear unto you [*but so that all of you would know that we care about you, with God as our witness*].

13 Therefore we were comforted in your comfort [*we were comforted by your concern for our comfort and well-being*]: yea, and exceedingly the more joyed we for the joy of Titus, because his spirit was refreshed by you all [*and we had all the more joy because of your kindnesses to Titus when he was among you*].

14 For if I have boasted any thing to him of you, I am not ashamed [*I told him what great Saints you are, and what he found when he visited you proved me right*]; but as we spake all things to you in truth, even so our boasting, which I made before Titus, is found a truth. [*In other words, when Titus arrived among us (see verse 6), and we talked about you and his visit among you, he verified that all the good things we said about you were true.*]

15 And his [*Titus'*] inward affection is more abundant toward you [*his affection for you swells up in his heart*], whilst he remembereth the obedience of you all [*as he talks*

to us about you and your obedience to the gospel], how with fear and trembling ye received him [*and how you humbly and respectfully welcomed him in your midst*].

16 I rejoice therefore that I have confidence in you in all things [*it brings me great joy that I can have such confidence in you in all these things*].

SECOND CORINTHIANS 8

Paul has been raising funds from members of the Church everywhere to take back to the impoverished Saints in the Jerusalem area. He now mentions to the members in Corinth the contributions made by members in northern Greece.

1 MOREOVER, brethren, we do you to wit of the grace of God bestowed on the churches [*wards and branches*] of Macedonia [*the area known as northern Greece today*];

JST 2 Corinthians 8:1

1 Moreover, brethren, we **would have you to know** of the grace of God bestowed on the churches of Macedonia;

2 How that in a great trial of affliction [*even though they have many afflictions themselves*] the abundance of their joy and their deep poverty abounded unto the riches of their liberality [*they were still very liberal and generous in joyfully giving money, despite their own poverty, to the fund for the Saints in Jerusalem*].

3 For to their power, I bear record, yea, and beyond their power they were willing of themselves [*they went far beyond their ability to contribute*];

4 Praying us with much intreaty [*asking us, indeed pleading with us*] that we would receive the gift [*accept their donations to the fund*], and take upon us the fellowship of the ministering to the saints [*and thus allow them to join in ministering to their fellow Saints*].

5 And this they did, not as we hoped, [*In other words, they did not do it because we required it of them.*] but first gave their own selves to the Lord [*rather, they did it because they had dedicated themselves to the Lord*], and unto us by the will of God [*and thus, they recognized the will of God and gave generously to us for the fund*].

JST 2 Corinthians 8:5

5 And this they did, not as we **required**, but first gave their own selves to the Lord, and unto us by the will of God.

6 Insomuch that we desired Titus, that as he had begun, so he would also finish in you the same grace also [*so we asked Titus, who had helped raise money for this fund elsewhere, to work with you to raise money for this fund*].

7 Therefore, as ye abound [*since you excel*] in every thing, in faith,

and utterance [*in doctrine; see* Strong's *#3056*], and knowledge, and in all diligence, and in your love to us, see that ye abound in this grace also [*see that you excel in contributing to this fund also*].

8 I speak not by commandment [*I am not commanding you to do this*], but by occasion of the forwardness of others [*but since others elsewhere have been so generous*], and to prove the sincerity of your love [*I think this is a test of your sincerity and love to see if you will contribute as generously as they have*].

9 For ye know the grace of our Lord Jesus Christ, that, though he was rich [*in heaven*], yet for your sakes [*in order to help you*] he became poor [*He came to earth*], that ye through his poverty [*through His sacrifices*] might be rich [*gain eternal life*]. [*In other words, you know that the Savior gave His all in order to make you rich in eternity, indeed, to give you the Atonement.*]

10 And herein I give my advice [*here is my advice to you about raising money for this fund*]: for this is expedient [*this advice is necessary*] for you, who have begun before [*who were the first to start contributing to this fund*], not only to do, but also to be forward [*desirous;* Strong's *#2309*] a year ago. [*In other words, you were the first to express a desire to contribute, and to actually start contributing to this fund a year ago.*]

11 Now therefore perform the doing of it [*now I counsel you to finish the job*]; that as there was a readiness to will [*since you were so willing to begin with*], so there may be a performance also out of that which ye have [*let's have your performance match your expressed commitment, according to your ability to pay*].

12 For if there be first a willing mind [*if the desire to contribute is in your hearts in the first place*], it is accepted according to that a man hath, and not according to that he hath not [*the actual amount you contribute must be according to what you have, not according to what you don't have*]. [*This reminds us of King Benjamin's counsel about giving to the poor in Mosiah 4:24.*]

13 For I mean not that other men be eased, and ye burdened [*I do not mean to imply that you should be overburdened in contributing in order to ease the needs of the Saints in Jerusalem and the surrounding area*]:

14 But by an equality [*I just think there should be a type of equality produced between you and them by your generosity*], that now at this time your abundance may be a supply for their want [*you help them now*], that their abundance also may be a supply for your want [*perhaps they will be the ones to help you another day*]: that there may be equality:

The principle of helping each other, as given in verse 14, above, is one of the guiding principles for our welfare system today within the Church.

15 As it is written [*in Exodus 16:18*], He that had gathered much had nothing over [*left over*]; and he that had gathered little had no lack [*had plenty*].

16 But thanks be to God, which put the same earnest care into the heart of Titus for you [*I am thankful that Titus cares for you as much as I do*].

17 For indeed he accepted the exhortation [*he accepted the challenge we gave him to collect these funds*]; but being more forward [*but being very enthusiastic about it himself*], of his own accord [*on his own initiative*] he went unto you [*he is coming to you*].

18 And we have sent with him the brother [*Bible scholars don't know who this brother is, but he has a good reputation*], whose praise is in the gospel throughout all the churches [*who is very well thought of by all the members here*];

19 And not that only, but who was also chosen of the churches [*wards and branches*] to travel with us with this grace [*with the money that has been raised so far*], which is administered by us to the glory of the same Lord [*which we are raising to honor the principles taught us by the Savior*], and declaration of your ready mind [*and because we understand that you are ready to finish the fundraising project among yourselves*]:

20 Avoiding this, that no man should blame us in this abundance [*money which has been raised*] which is administered by us [*we don't want to do anything in this matter of raising money for the impoverished Saints in Jerusalem and in taking it to them that would set us up for valid criticism*]:

21 Providing for honest things, not only in the sight of the Lord, but also in the sight of men [*we want to be considered honest by God and also by our fellow men*].

22 And we have sent with them our brother [*we have also sent another brother with Titus and his companion (verse 18)*], whom we have oftentimes proved diligent [*enthusiastic;* Strong's *#4707*] in many things [*who has proven his enthusiasm to us already in many things*], but now much more diligent [*even more enthusiastic*], upon [*because of*] the great confidence which I have in you.

23 Whether any do enquire of Titus, he is my partner and fellowhelper concerning you: or our brethren be enquired of, they are the messengers of the churches, and the glory of Christ.

The JST combines portions of verses 22 and 23 as follows:

JST 2 Corinthians 8:23

23 **Therefore we send him unto you, in consequence of the great confidence which we have in you, that you will receive the things concerning you, to the glory of Christ;**

whether we send by the hand of Titus, my partner and fellow laborer, or our brethren, the messengers of the churches.

24 Wherefore shew ye to them [*Titus and those traveling with him, plus any others Paul might send to them*], and before the churches [*wards and branches*], the proof of your love, and of our boasting on your behalf. [*In other words, we've bragged a lot about you, so please don't let us down.*]

SECOND CORINTHIANS 9

In this chapter, Paul will continue the theme he started in chapter 8 He will tell the members of the Church in Corinth who are being asked to continue donating to the fund for helping poverty-stricken Saints in Jerusalem, that the Lord loves people who give willingly and cheerfully (verse 7).

1 FOR as touching [*regarding*] the ministering to the saints [*this fundraising for the needy Saints in Jerusalem*], it is superfluous [*unnecessary*] for me to write to you:

2 For I know the forwardness of your mind [*I know how eager you are to participate in it*], for which I boast of you to them of Macedonia [*for which I have already bragged about you to the members in northern Greece*], that Achaia [*the area known as southern Greece today, including Corinth*] was ready [*to start contributing*] a year ago; and your zeal [*enthusiasm*] hath provoked very many [*inspired many to action already*].

3 Yet have I sent the brethren [*however, I have sent Titus (2 Corinthians 8:6) and his companions to follow up with you in this collection*], lest our boasting of you should be in vain in this behalf [*just in case you are not coming through with the needed contributions*]; that, as I said, ye may be ready [*so that you can have the job done when he gets there*]:

4 Lest haply [*for fear*] if they [*any members*] of Macedonia [*northern Greece today*] come with me, and find you unprepared, we (that we say not, ye) [*let alone you*] should be ashamed [*embarrassed, disappointed*] in this same confident boasting [*because of how we talked you up to others*].

5 Therefore I thought it necessary to exhort [*urge*] the brethren [*Titus and his companions*], that they would go before [*ahead of me and my companions*] unto you, and make up beforehand your bounty [*and make sure the welfare collection for the needy members in the Jerusalem area*], whereof ye had notice before [*about which we previously talked*], that the same might be ready [*might be in place*], as a matter of bounty [*as a generous gift, given over a longer period of time*], and not as of covetousness [*rather than a gift given grudgingly because of too short a time to collect it*].

6 But this I say, He which soweth sparingly shall reap also sparingly; and he which soweth bountifully shall reap also bountifully. [*But let me remind you that those who donate little will harvest fewer blessings from God and those who donate generously will have a bounteous harvest of blessings from God.*]

7 Every man according as he purposeth in his heart [*it is up to each person to decide how much he will give to this cause*], so let him give; not grudgingly, or of necessity [*or because he feels forced*]: for God loveth a cheerful giver.

8 And God is able to make all grace abound toward you [*God can bless you abundantly*]; that ye, always having all sufficiency in all things, may abound to every good work [*so that you can give abundantly to help others*]:

9 (As it is written [*in Psalm 112:9*], He hath dispersed abroad; he hath given to the poor: his righteousness remaineth for ever.

10 Now he [*God*] that ministereth [*provides*] seed to the sower [*planter, farmer*] both minister [*supplies*] bread for your food, and multiply your seed sown [*multiplies your harvest*], and increase the fruits of your righteousness [*and multiplies the rewards given to you because of your righteousness*];)

11 Being enriched in every thing to all bountifulness [*you will be blessed in every way by God so that you can be generous in giving to this fund*], which causeth through us thanksgiving to God [*which, when we bring it to the destitute members in Jerusalem, will cause them to give thanksgiving to God*].

12 For the administration of this service [*your giving of this money*] not only supplieth [*takes care of*] the want of the saints [*in the Jerusalem area*], but is abundant also by many thanksgivings unto God [*but will be the cause of much gratitude to God*];

13 Whiles by the experiment of this ministration [*meanwhile, the result of your ministry to them is that*] they glorify God for [*because of*] your professed subjection [*observable loyalty*] unto the gospel of Christ, and for your liberal distribution [*contribution*] unto them, and unto all men;

14 And by their prayer for you [*and in their prayers for you*], which long after you [*which reach out to you*] for [*because of*] the exceeding grace of God in you [*the great blessings of God which came to them through you*].

15 Thanks be unto God for his unspeakable [*indescribable*] gift.

SECOND CORINTHIANS 10

Paul is apparently concerned about criticism aimed at him by some who say his letters strike terror in people (see verse 9), but that he is less than impressive in person (see verse 10) and, furthermore, listening to him talk is of no value at all (see verse 10). It might be interesting here to read the Prophet Joseph Smith's description of Paul so that we can better understand why some unthinking people might be critical of him. The Prophet said, "He is about five feet high; very dark hair; dark complexion; dark skin; large Roman nose; sharp face; small black eyes, penetrating as eternity; round shoulders; a whining voice, except when elevated, and then it almost resembled the roaring of a lion. He was a good orator, active and diligent, always employing himself in doing good to his fellow man."

(*Teachings of the Prophet Joseph Smith*, p. 180.)

1 NOW I Paul myself beseech [*urge*] you by the meekness and gentleness of Christ [*in meekness and gentleness as taught by Christ*], who in presence [*when I am in your presence*] am base [*I am humble;* Strong's *#5011*] among you, but being absent am bold toward you [*but since I am away from you now, I have written rather boldly about issues and concerns to you*]:

2 But I beseech you [*I urge you to follow the counsel I have given you*], that I may not be bold when I am present [*so that I don't have to be too bold with you when I come to you*] with that confidence, wherewith I think to be bold against some, which think of us as if we walked according to the flesh [*like I think I will have to be with some who think of us as living according to the ways of the world*].

Paul will now use the imagery of war and weapons to describe the "war" against evil in which the members of the Church are involved.

3 For though we walk in the flesh [*though we live in the world*], we do not war after the flesh [*the war we fight is not like that of the world*]:

4 (For the weapons of our warfare are not carnal [*worldly*], but mighty through God [*but mighty because of God's power*] to the pulling down of strong holds [*and able to destroy the strongholds of the devil*];)

5 Casting down imaginations [*false doctrines and philosophies*], and every high [*prideful*] thing that exalteth itself [*rises up to fight*] against the knowledge of God, and bringing into captivity every thought to the obedience of Christ [*and overcoming every inappropriate thought or idea and making it subject to Christ*];

6 And having in a readiness to revenge [*punish*] all disobedience [*we are prepared to punish any disobedience on the part of others*], when your obedience is fulfilled [*once you yourselves have obeyed the counsel we have given you*].

7 Do ye look on things after the outward appearance [*do you really think that outward appearance is all that important*]? If any man trust to himself that he is Christ's,

let him of himself think this again [*if anyone who is being critical of us thinks that he belongs to Christ, he should rethink it*], that, as he is Christ's, even so are we Christ's [*that we have just as much right to belong to Christ as he does*].

8 For though I should boast somewhat more of our authority, which the Lord hath given us for edification, and not for your destruction, I should not be ashamed: [*It wouldn't embarrass me to remind you that the Lord has given us authority over you, but He didn't give us this authority with the intent that we should tear you down, rather that we should use it to build you up.*]

9 That I may not seem as if I would terrify you by letters. [*I don't want it to seem as if I am trying to frighten you with my letters.*]

10 For his letters, say they [*some people say Paul's letters*], are weighty [*severe;* Strong's *#0926*] and powerful [*too forceful;* Strong's *#2478*]; but his bodily presence is weak, and his speech contemptible. [*Some say that my letters are too severe and forceful, and they say that, in person, I am less than impressive, and my voice and speech are to be despised.*]

11 Let such an one [*let those who criticize*] think this, that, such as we are in word by letters when we are absent, such will we be also in deed when we are present [*we will be just as bold when we are among you as we are in letter writing*].

12 For we dare not make ourselves of the number [*we would not want to be numbered among those*], or compare ourselves with some that commend themselves [*who think too highly of themselves*]: but they measuring themselves by themselves [*they measure themselves against others of their own group*], and comparing themselves among themselves, are not wise.

13 But we will not boast of things without [*outside of*] our measure, but according to the measure of the rule which God hath distributed to us, a measure to reach even unto you. [*We do not measure ourselves against other people; rather, we measure ourselves according to the rules God has given us, which included instructions to bring the gospel as far as your city.*]

14 For we stretch not ourselves beyond our measure, as though we reached not unto you [*we have not overstated things in our letter or overreacted in what we wrote to you, as if we don't really know you or hadn't ever lived among you*]: for we are come [*did come*] as far as to you also in preaching the gospel of Christ:

15 Not boasting [*glorying*] of things without our measure [*outside of our stewardship*], that is, of other men's labours [*we are not trying to take glory for what others have accomplished*]; but having hope, when your faith is increased [*when your faith becomes stronger*], that we shall be enlarged by you [*we hope that we will have more work among you*] according to our rule

[*according to the responsibilities given us by God; see verse 13, above*] abundantly,

16 To preach the gospel in the regions beyond you [*beyond Corinth*], and not to boast in another man's line of things made ready to our hand [*and we do not want to take any credit for work already done by others*].

In verse 16, above, Paul must have been responding to something not recorded in what we have, such as someone criticizing him for allegedly taking credit for work which others had done.

17 But he that glorieth, let him glory in the Lord. [*See Alma 26:11–16 for similar counsel.*]

18 For not he that commendeth [*praises*] himself is approved [*by the Lord*], but whom the Lord commendeth [*praises*].

SECOND CORINTHIANS 11

One of the important messages from Paul, in this chapter, is his teaching about "the simplicity that is in Christ." From that we can conclude that the gospel of Jesus Christ promotes simplicity, and conversely, Satan promotes complexity.

Among other things, Paul will briefly review some of the trials and tribulations he has gone through in order to be faithful to his commitment to God (verses 23–28).

He begins by asking the Saints to be patient with him and his imperfections.

1 WOULD to God ye [*I wish that you*] could bear with me a little in my folly [*shortcomings and imperfections*]: and indeed bear with me [*be patient with me*].

Next, Paul uses marriage and covenant symbolism, common in the scriptures. In symbolism, we, as members, are the "bride." Christ is the "bridegroom" or "groom." We "marry" ourselves to Him, by making and keeping gospel covenants, and thus ensure that we will be with Him in celestial exaltation forever.

2 For I am jealous [*protective*] over you with godly jealousy [*concern*]: for I have espoused you [*joined you via covenants you made*] to one husband [*Christ*], that I may present you as a chaste virgin [*as clean and pure*] to Christ.

3 But I fear, lest by any means, as the serpent [*Lucifer*] beguiled Eve through his subtilty [*cunning*], so your minds should be corrupted [*taken away*] from the simplicity that is in Christ. [*In other words, the gospel we preached to you when you were converted is very simple, and I worry that Satan will tempt you to make it more complex, and thus corrupt your simple and pure understanding of Christ.*]

4 For if he that cometh preacheth [*if any messengers come to you and preach*] another Jesus [*a different kind of Jesus, with different*

commandments, etc.], whom we have not preached, or if ye receive [*accept*] another spirit, which ye have not received [*from us*], or another gospel, which ye have not accepted [*which does not go along in harmony with the one we preached to you*], ye might well bear with him. [*In other words, if anyone comes along and preaches something different than what I taught you about Christ, you would do well to stick with me.*]

JST 2 Corinthians 11:4

4 For if he that cometh preacheth another Jesus, whom we have not preached, or if ye receive another spirit, which ye have not received, or another gospel, which ye have not accepted, ye might well bear with **me**.

In verse 4, above, the JST change from "him" to "me" makes a huge difference in the meaning of the verse.

5 For I suppose I was not a whit [*not one bit*] behind the very chiefest apostles. [*I dare say that in my preaching the gospel to you, I did not "water it down" one bit from what the chief Apostles (Peter, James, John, etc.) would have taught if they had been the ones teaching you.*]

6 But though I be rude in speech [*blunt when I preach; can also mean less qualified in public speaking than the chiefest apostles; see* Strong's #2399], yet not in knowledge [*I have as good a knowledge of the gospel as they have*]; but we have been throughly made manifest among you in all things [*we have made this thoroughly clear in everything we have done among you*].

7 Have I committed an offence in abasing myself that ye might be exalted, because I have preached to you the gospel of God freely [*without your having to support me financially*]? [*In other words, was it offensive to you that I earned my own living as a common tentmaker in order to elevate you in the gospel without having you support me financially, as is often the case in other religions?*]

8 I robbed other churches, taking wages of them, to do you service [*there were times when I accepted contributions from Church members elsewhere so that I could spend more time serving you*].

9 And when I was present with you, and wanted, I was chargeable to no man [*when I was among you, and had need of financial help, I didn't ask you for anything*]: for that which was lacking to me the brethren which came from Macedonia supplied [*because the brethren who came from northern Greece gave me what I needed*]: and in all things I have kept myself from being burdensome unto you, and so will I keep myself [*and when I come to you again, I will likewise make sure that I am not a financial burden to you*].

10 As the truth of Christ is in me [*as God is my witness*], no man shall stop me of this boasting in

the regions of Achaia [*no one in the whole region of southern Greece will stop me from rejoicing*].

11 Wherefore [*Why*]? because I love you not? God knoweth [*God knows I do love you*].

Paul now directs his readers to the dangers of Satan-sponsored false prophets, false apostles, and other deceitful workers who apparently have worked themselves into positions of influence among some members in Corinth.

12 But what I do, that I will do [*what I have been doing I will continue to do. In other words, I have been speaking boldly against things which pose a spiritual danger to you, and I will continue to do so*], that I may cut off occasion [*the opportunity to deceive you*] from them which desire occasion [*from those who seek such opportunity among you*]; that wherein they glory, they may be found even as we [*in order to take away their advantage among you*].

13 For such are false apostles, deceitful workers, transforming themselves into the apostles of Christ [*trying to make you think they are true Apostles of Jesus Christ*].

14 And no marvel [*and it is no wonder that they are trying to do this*]; for Satan himself is transformed into [*appears as*] an angel of light.

Paul's statement that Satan can transform himself into an angel of light in order to deceive people is a very important matter for us to understand. D&C 129:8 was given by Joseph Smith to inform members of this danger. Furthermore, Joseph Smith said, "One great evil is, that men are ignorant of the nature of spirits; their power, laws, government, intelligence, etc., and imagine that when there is anything like power, revelation, or vision manifested, that it must be of God." (*Teachings of the Prophet Joseph Smith*, p. 203.)

The Prophet further warned that "nothing is a greater injury to the children of men than to be under the influence of a false spirit when they think they have the Spirit of God." He continued in the same sermon to say, "There have also been ministering angels in the Church which were of Satan appearing as an angel of light. A sister. . . saw a glorious personage descending, arrayed in white, with sandy colored hair;" (*Teachings of the Prophet Joseph Smith*, p. 205 and 214.)

Now, one last comment about avoiding such cunning and, in some cases, spectacular deception: How can we tell the difference between Satan and his evil spirits appearing as angels of light and angels from God? Answer: We have the Gift of the Holy Ghost. Furthermore, we have the gifts of the Spirit, which are given to enable us to avoid deception as explained in D&C 46:8.

15 Therefore it is no great thing [*therefore, it is not surprising*] if his [*Satan's*] ministers also be transformed as [*also try to make us think that they are*] the ministers of righteousness; whose end [*punishment*] shall be according to their works.

Next, Paul will use a little play on words to emphasize a point. He will use variations of the word "fool" and, in effect, say that some consider those who believe in Christ to be fools, yet, these so-called fools are wiser than those who don't believe, and thus allow themselves to become real fools, deceived by Satan.

16 I say again, Let no man think me a fool [*let no one consider me to be a fool*]; if otherwise [*but if they can't bring themselves to not consider me a fool*], yet as a fool receive me [*if it is foolish to believe in Christ, then accept me as a fool*], that I may boast myself a little [*that I may show how smart a "fool" can be*].

17 That which I speak [*what I am now going to say*], I speak it not after the Lord [*I do not speak in the manner the Lord would normally have me speak*], but as it were foolishly, in this confidence of boasting [*rather in a way that may sound foolish and a bit boastful*].

18 Seeing that many glory after the flesh, I will glory also [*since many boast of some of their own accomplishments, I will do a little boasting also, about some of the things I have survived—see verses 23–28*].

19 For ye suffer [*listen to*] fools gladly, seeing ye yourselves are wise.

20 For ye suffer [*put up with it*], if a man bring you into bondage [*enslaves you*], if a man devour [*destroys*] you, if a man take of you [*takes advantage of you*], if a man exalt himself [*lords it over you*], if a man smite [*slaps*] you on the face.

21 I speak as concerning reproach, as though we had been weak [*we are not strong enough to put up with some of the things you put up with*]. Howbeit [*however*] whereinsoever any is bold [*when it comes to things in which others are bold*], (I speak foolishly) [*I speak as a fool*], I am bold also [*I will be bold also*].

In order to accomplish what he did, Paul had to have a very strong personality. He was very humble and obedient to the Lord. He was sweet and gentle and tender. He was brilliant, energetic, powerful, and virtually unstoppable when he made up his mind to do something. He was also feisty, and we see this side of his personality in the next verses.

22 Are they Hebrews? so am I. Are they Israelites? so am I. Are they the seed [*descendants*] of Abraham? so am I.

23 Are they ministers of Christ? (I speak as a fool) [*you will think I have lost my mind when I say what I say next*] I am more; in

labours more abundant [*I have worked harder than they have*], in stripes above measure [*I can't even count how many times I have been whipped*], in prisons more frequent [*I have spent more time in prison than they have*], in deaths oft [*I have been nearly killed time and time again*].

JST 2 Corinthians 11:23

23 Are they ministers of Christ? (I speak as a fool.) **so am I**; in **labors** more abundant, in stripes above measure, in prisons more frequent, in deaths oft.

24 Of the Jews five times received I forty stripes [*lashes of a whip*] save one [*five times, the Jews flogged me with 39 lashes of the whip*].

Under Jewish law, it was illegal to flog a person with a whip more than 40 times (see Deuteronomy 25:3), therefore, they never struck a person more than 39 times with a whip in order to avoid breaking the law if they slipped up and miscounted. A description of this whipping is as follows: "Both of (the victim's) hands were tied to . . . a stake a cubit and a half high (about 27 inches high). The public officer then tore down his robe until his breast was laid bare. The executioner stood on a stone behind the criminal. The scourge consisted of two thongs, one of which was composed of four strands of calfskin, and one of two strands of ass's-skin, which passed through a hole in a handle. . . . The prisoner bent to receive the blows, which were inflicted with one hand, but with all the force of the striker, thirteen on the breast, thirteen on the right, and thirteen on the left shoulder. While the punishment was going on, the chief judge read aloud (Deuteronomy 28:58, 59; 24:9; and Psalm 78:38, 39 which dealt with God's commandments, the punishment for their nonobservance, and the Lord's compassion on the sinner) . . . If the punishment was not over by the time that these three passages were read, they were again repeated, and so timed as to end exactly with the punishment itself. Meanwhile a second judge numbered the blows, and a third before each blow exclaimed 'Hakkehu' (strike him)." (Farrar, *The Life and Works of St. Paul*, pp. 715–16. Quoted in the Institute of Religion's New Testament student manual, *The Life and Teachings of Jesus and His Apostles*, p. 303.)

25 Thrice [*three times*] was I beaten with rods, once was I stoned [*see Acts 14:19 where Jews stoned Paul and left him for dead*], thrice I suffered shipwreck [*I was shipwrecked three times*], a night and a day I have been in the deep [*I spent a night and a day in the sea*];

26 In journeyings often [*I have been constantly on the go*], in perils of [*in dangers from*] waters, in perils of robbers, in perils by mine own countrymen [*in dangers from the Jews*], in perils by the heathen [*in dangers from the Gentiles*], in perils in the city, in perils in the wilderness [*the country*], in perils

in the sea, in perils among false brethren [*in dangers because of members who betrayed me*];

27 In weariness [*I have gone through much toil and trouble*] and painfulness [*and pain*], in watchings often [*I have often gone without sleep*], in hunger and thirst [*I have been hungry and thirsty*], in fastings often [*I have often fasted; can also mean he had gone without food*], in cold and nakedness [*I have endured cold and nakedness (perhaps when he was in prison)*].

28 Beside those things that are without [*in addition to these things which are matters of physical suffering*], that which cometh upon me daily, the care of all the churches [*I have had the daily worries and concerns of caring for all the wards and branches of the Church under my stewardship*].

29 Who is weak, and I am not weak [*when a member shows weakness, does it not require energy from me*]? who is offended, and I burn not? [*In other words, the daily needs of members take a lot out of me.*]

JST 2 Corinthians 11:29

29 Who is weak, and I am not weak? who is offended, and I **anger** not?

30 If I must needs glory [*if I am going to rejoice;* Strong's *#2744*], I will glory of the things which concern mine infirmities [*I will rejoice in the fact that God has given me weaknesses; compare to Ether 12:27; see also 2 Corinthians 12:10, where Paul says "I take pleasure in infirmitie. . . for when I am weak, then am I strong."*]

31 The God and Father of our Lord Jesus Christ, which is blessed [*praised*] for evermore, knoweth that I lie not.

32 In Damascus the governor under Aretas the king kept the city of the Damascenes with a garrison, desirous to apprehend me: [*In other words, let me mention one more hardship I have been through, namely, that some years ago, I was hiding from soldiers in Damascus who were under orders to arrest me.*]

33 And through a window in a basket was I let down by the wall, and escaped his hands [*and I had to be let down the outside wall of the city from a window, in a basket, to escape*].

SECOND CORINTHIANS 12

This chapter is very important doctrinally, because it mentions the "third heaven" in verse 2, in other words, the celestial kingdom. Paul shares some sacred experiences with us that strengthen our testimonies.

1 IT is not expedient [*not necessary*] for me doubtless to glory [*to keep talking about these things*]. I will come to visions and revelations of the Lord [*I will mention more*

important things, namely visions and revelations from the Lord].

Joseph Smith confirms that the "man in Christ" referred to next, in verse 2, is Paul himself. See *Teachings of the Prophet Joseph Smith*, pp. 301, 304–305. Paul is being modest and doesn't give his name, initially, as he tells of the experience. But when he uses the word "I" in verses 2 and 3, it becomes obvious that he is the man.

2 I knew a man in Christ above fourteen years ago [*over fourteen years ago*], (whether in the body, I cannot tell; or whether out of the body, I cannot tell [*I couldn't tell whether or not I was in my body when this happened*]: God knoweth;) such an one caught up to the third heaven [*one who was taken up to the celestial glory*].

3 And I knew such a man, (whether in the body, or out of the body, I cannot tell: God knoweth;)

4 How that he was caught up into paradise [*the third heaven*], and heard unspeakable words, which it is not lawful for a man to utter [*talk about*].

Joseph Smith explained a bit of what Paul saw during this experience as follows: "Paul ascended into the third heavens, and he could understand the three principal rounds of Jacob's ladder—the telestial, the terrestrial, and the celestial glories or kingdoms, where Paul saw and heard things which were not lawful for him to utter." (*Teachings of the Prophet Joseph Smith*, p. 304.)

5 Of such an one will I glory [*I can rejoice about such a person*]: yet of myself I will not glory, but in mine infirmities [*I don't want to boast about myself, rather, I will limit myself to rejoicing in my shortcomings and weaknesses which allow God to teach and strengthen me; see verses 7 and 9, next*].

6 For though I would desire to glory [*even if I wanted to boast a bit*], I shall not be a fool; for I will say the truth [*I would be telling the truth*]: but now I forbear [*I will hold back*], lest any man should think of me above that which he seeth me to be, or that he heareth of me [*for fear that people would hold me up higher than I am*].

JST 2 Corinthians 12:6

6 For though I would desire to glory, I shall not be a fool; for I will say the truth; but now I forbear, lest any man should think of me above that which he seeth **of me**, or that he heareth of me.

7 And lest I should be exalted above measure through the abundance of the revelations [*and just in case I were to become prideful because of the many revelations I have been given*], there was given to me a thorn in the flesh, the messenger of Satan to buffet me [*strike me down, hit me;* Strong's *#2852; this "thorn in the flesh" serves to pound me down and keep me humble*], lest I should be exalted above measure [*for fear that I should become prideful*].

We do not know what Paul's "thorn in the flesh" was. Whether it was some physical problem or spiritual difficulty or persistent difficulty with someone close to him or whatever, it served to keep him humble as he explains in verses 9 and 10.

There is comfort for us in what Paul tells us next. Many humble members pray with great faith for God to heal them or a loved one, or to remove a problem from their lives, etc., but it doesn't happen. It is comforting to know that someone with as much faith as Paul had didn't get what he asked for either. The Lord's will is done in such matters, and that is important for us to understand so that we do not get bitter or angry with God.

8 For this thing [*my "thorn in the flesh"*] I besought the Lord thrice, that it might depart from me [*I pleaded with the Lord on three different occasions to remove this from me*].

9 And he said unto me, My grace [*My will, My mercy, My understanding*] is sufficient for thee: [*In other words, My will for you in this matter will be better for you than My granting your desire*] for my strength is made perfect in weakness [*my weaknesses keep me humble and allow God to strengthen me as I grow toward perfection*]. Most gladly therefore will I rather glory [*rejoice*] in my infirmities [*problems and weaknesses*], that the power of Christ may rest upon me.

The message in verse 9, above, is very similar to what Moroni said in Ether 12:27 when he quoted the Lord who said, "And if men come unto me I will show unto them their weakness. I give unto men weakness that they may be humble; and my grace is sufficient for all men that humble themselves before me; for if they humble themselves before me, and have faith in me, then will I make weak things become strong unto them."

10 Therefore I take pleasure in infirmities, in reproaches [*insults*], in necessities [*hardships*], in persecutions, in distresses [*difficulties*] for Christ's sake [*because of my commitment to Christ*]: for when I am weak, then am I strong [*then I become strong; Compare with Ether 12:27*].

11 I am become a fool in glorying [*I have overdone it in telling you all this*]; ye have compelled me [*but you encouraged me to do it*]: for I ought to have been commended of you [*it is proper for me to be well-thought of by you*]: for in nothing am I behind the very chiefest apostles [*because I have taught you and dealt with you exactly like the senior Apostles would have if they had been here in my place*], though I be nothing [*even though I am nothing compared to them*].

12 Truly the signs of an apostle were wrought [*done*] among you in all patience, in signs, and wonders, and mighty deeds [*truly, I have ministered among you as a true Apostle*].

13 For what is it wherein ye were inferior to other churches, except it be that I myself was not burdensome to you [*can you think of any way in which you are inferior to other members elsewhere, except in that you had to put up with me*]? forgive me this wrong.

14 Behold, the third time I am ready to come to you [*when I come to you again, it will be for the third time*]; and I will not be burdensome to you [*and I will not be a burden to you*]: for I seek not yours, but you [*I do not seek material support from you, rather to help you*]: for the children ought not to lay up for the parents, but the parents for the children [*the children are not supposed to have to take care of the parents, rather, the parents take care of the children; in other words, you (my "children") should not have to take care of me (your "parent" in the gospel)*].

15 And I will very gladly spend and be spent [*be worn out*] for you; though the more abundantly I love you, the less I be loved.

16 But be it so, I did not burden you: nevertheless, being crafty, I caught you with guile.

17 Did I make a gain [*take advantage*] of you by any of them whom I sent unto you?

18 I desired Titus, and with him I sent a brother. Did Titus make a gain of you [*take advantage of you in any way*]? walked we not in the same spirit? walked we not in the same steps [*isn't it true that Titus and I treat you the same*]?

19 Again, think ye that we excuse ourselves unto you [*do you think we owe you an apology for being too hard on you*]? we speak before God in Christ [*God is our witness that we teach you what Christ wants us to*]: but we do all things, dearly beloved, for your edifying [*but everything we do is designed to build you up and strengthen you*].

20 For I fear, lest, when I come, I shall not find you such as I would [*I worry that when I come to you, I will not find everything in order*], and that I shall be found unto you such as ye would not [*and that I will not be as pleasant to you as you would like*]: lest there be [*I worry that you still have among you*] debates [*quarreling*], envyings [*jealousy*], wraths [*uncontrolled tempers; outbursts of anger;* Strong's *#2372*], strifes [*dividing into factions*], backbitings [*slander*], whisperings [*gossiping*], swellings [*pride*], tumults [*disorder*]:

21 And lest [*I worry for fear that*], when I come again, my God will humble me among you, and that I shall bewail [*be saddened because of*] many which have sinned already, and have not repented of the uncleanness and fornication and lasciviousness [*sexual immorality in thought and deed*] which they have committed.

SECOND CORINTHIANS 13

Paul now concludes this letter to the members of the Church living in Corinth. He begins by reminding them about the law of witnesses.

1 THIS is the third time I am coming to you [*this will be the third time I have visited you*]. In the mouth of two or three witnesses shall every word be established [*Deuteronomy 19:15*].

2 I told you before, and foretell you, as if I were present, the second time [*I warned you when I was visiting you for the second time, and I repeat the warning now*]; and being absent now [*in my absence*] I write to them which heretofore [*in the past*] have sinned, and to all other, that, if I come again, I will not spare: [*In other words, I am warning you that when I come for this next visit, I will once again speak out boldly against sin among you as I have in times past.*]

3 Since ye seek a proof of Christ speaking in me [*since some of you are still seeking proof that Christ is speaking to you through me*], which to you-ward is not weak, but is mighty in you [*Christ does not demonstrate weakness toward you as He deals with you; rather, He shows His mighty power among you*].

4 For though he was crucified through weakness [*because He was mortal*], yet he liveth [*has been resurrected*] by the power of God [*the Father*]. For we also are weak in him [*we are weak compared to Him*], but we shall [*be resurrected and*] live with him by the power of God toward you [*because of the power which the Father has demonstrated to you*].

5 Examine yourselves, whether ye be in the faith [*look at yourselves to see whether or not you are being faithful to Christ*]; prove your own selves. Know ye not your own selves, how that Jesus Christ is in you, except ye be reprobates [*don't you realize that Christ can help you unless you are unfit, unless you fail the test;* Strong's *#0096*]?

6 But I trust that ye shall know that we are not reprobates [*unfit for the kingdom of God*].

7 Now I pray to God that ye do no evil; not that we should appear approved [*not so that people praise us for bringing you the gospel*], but that ye should do that which is honest, though we be as reprobates [*you should do right whether or not we do right*].

8 For we can do nothing against the truth, but for the truth [*everything we do is in harmony with the truth*].

9 For we are glad, when we are weak, and ye are strong [*we are happy when you live the gospel even better than we do*]: and this also we wish, even your perfection [*because we want you to progress toward perfection*].

10 Therefore I write these things being absent, lest being present I should use sharpness, according to the power which the Lord hath given me to edification, and not to destruction. [*In effect, I'm writing these things in advance, before my third visit to you, so that you can work on any problems before I arrive so that I won't have to be sharp with you. That way, I can build you up and strengthen you, rather than having to tear you down to try to get you to repent.*]

11 Finally, brethren, farewell. Be perfect [*keep working toward perfection*], be of good comfort, be of one mind [*be united*], live in peace; and the God of love and peace shall be with you.

12 Greet one another with an holy kiss.

JST 2 Corinthians 13:12

12 Greet one another with a holy **salutation** [*greeting*].

13 All the saints salute [*greet*] you.

14 The grace of the Lord Jesus Christ, and the love of God, and the communion [*companionship*] of the Holy Ghost, be with you all. Amen.

The Epistle of Paul the Apostle to the Galatians

Galatia was in what is now central Turkey. Paul had many converts in Galatia during his first missionary journey and wrote this letter to them somewhere around AD 57, which would be about 23 years after the crucifixion of the Savior. We do not know for sure where he was when he wrote this epistle (letter). Some scholars believe it was Rome, others believe he wrote it to the Galatian Saints while in Corinth.

The main theme of this letter is that the Gospel of Jesus Christ is the only source of true freedom. A major problem which Paul addresses in this letter is the "Judaizers." These were Jewish converts to the Church who insisted on keeping the law of Moses in spite of the fact that they had joined the Church and had been taught that the law of Moses had been fulfilled by Christ. Thus, the higher laws taught by Christ and the accompanying freedom from letter-of-the-law daily ritual were being undermined by the Judaizers. We encounter similar problems today when some members attempt to emphasize the words of dead prophets over the words of the current living prophets.

GALATIANS 1

In this chapter we learn that the prophesied apostasy is already under way. Paul warns these members that those among them who are attempting to change the true gospel are already in apostasy. No one is authorized to change the true gospel. Among other things, Paul will review his conversion for these Galatian members of the Church.

1 PAUL, an apostle, (not of men, neither by man, but by Jesus Christ, and God the Father, who raised him from the dead;) [*In other words, Paul, an Apostle who was called of God.*]

2 And all the brethren which are with me, unto the churches [*wards and branches*] of Galatia:

> Verse 3, below, is another scriptural verification that the Father and the Son are separate beings.

3 Grace be to you and peace from God the Father, and from our Lord Jesus Christ,

4 Who gave himself for our sins [*who gave us the Atonement*], that he might deliver us from this present evil world, according to the will of God and our Father [*who is our Father*]:

5 To whom be glory for ever and ever. Amen.

6 I marvel that ye are so soon removed from him that called you into the grace of Christ unto another gospel [*I am amazed that you are going into apostasy (falling away from the Church) so soon*]:

7 Which is not another [*actually, there is no such thing as "another gospel"*]; but there be [*are*] some that trouble you, and would pervert [*corrupt, change*] the gospel of Christ.

8 But though [*even if*] we, or an angel from heaven, preach [*were to preach*] any other gospel unto you than that which we have preached unto you, let him be accursed [*let him be doomed to destruction;* Strong's *#0331*].

9 As we said before, so say I now again, If any man preach any other gospel unto you than that ye have received, let him be accursed [*damned for eternity*].

10 For do I now persuade men, or God [*do you think I am trying to win the approval of men, or of God*]? or do I seek to please men [*the approval of men*]? for if I yet pleased men [*if my goal were to gain the approval of men*], I should not [*could not*] be the servant of Christ.

JST Galatians 1:10

> 10 For do I now **please** men, or God? or do I seek to please men? for if I yet pleased men, I should not be the servant of Christ.

11 But I certify [*assure*] you, brethren, that the gospel which was preached of me is not after man [*does not come from the philosophies of men*].

12 For I neither received it of man, neither was I taught it, but by [*through*] the revelation of Jesus Christ.

13 For ye have heard of my conversation [*behavior, lifestyle;* Strong's *#0391*] in time past in the Jews' religion [*as a Pharisee who strictly kept the law of Moses and saw the new "Christian" church as a threat to the established Jewish religion*], how that beyond measure [*without limits*] I persecuted the church of God, and wasted it [*destroyed it wherever I could*]:

14 And profited [*I was a success*] in the Jews' religion above many my equals [*over and above my peers*] in mine own nation, being more exceedingly zealous of the traditions of my fathers [*I was stricter than most Jews in keeping the law of Moses and the religious traditions of my ancestors*].

Paul will now briefly tell of his conversion.

15 But when it pleased God [*when it was God's will*], who separated me from my mother's womb [*who gave me life*], and called me by his grace [*and showed mercy and kindness to me*],

16 To reveal his Son in me [*to use me as an instrument to reveal His Son to others*], that I might preach him [*Christ*] among the heathen [*Gentiles*]; immediately I conferred not with flesh and blood [*I did not consult with men*]:

17 Neither went I up [*neither did I go*] to Jerusalem to them which were apostles before me [*to those who were called to be Apostles before I was*]; but I went into Arabia, and returned again unto Damascus [*in Syria*].

It is worth noting that it usually takes time for real change to take place. Paul needed a period of at least three years to let the gospel sink deeply into his soul and lifestyle, then he went to the Apostles for instructions, as indicated in verse 18, next.

18 Then after three years I went up to Jerusalem to see Peter [*who was the president of the Church*], and abode [*stayed*] with him fifteen days.

19 But other of the apostles saw I none, save James the Lord's brother [*the only other Apostle I saw was Jesus' half-brother James*].

Jesus' brother, James, mentioned in verse 19, above, is generally considered to be the author of the Book of James in the New Testament. See Bible Dictionary under "James."

20 Now the things which I write unto you, behold, before God [*as God is my witness*], I lie not.

21 Afterwards [*after that*] I came into the regions of Syria and Cilicia [*southeastern Turkey today*];

22 And was unknown by face unto the churches of Judæa which were in Christ [*so none of the members there even knew what I looked like*]:

23 But they had heard only, That he which persecuted us in times past now preacheth the faith which once he destroyed. [*All they knew was that the man who once tried to destroy the Church was now preaching to convert others to Christ.*]

24 And they glorified [*praised*] God in me [*because of me*].

JST Galatians 1:24

24 And they glorified God **on account of me**.

GALATIANS 2

Paul continues reviewing his ministry, talking about two of his missionary companions named Barnabas and Titus.

1 THEN fourteen years after [*later*] I went up again to Jerusalem with Barnabas, and took Titus with me also.

Barnabas was a faithful Jewish convert who served as a missionary companion to Paul. See Bible Dictionary under "Barnabas" for more information about him. Titus was a Gentile convert, possibly from the area of south central Turkey, today, who likewise was a missionary companion of Paul. See Bible Dictionary under "Titus."

2 And I went up by revelation [*as directed in a revelation I received*], and communicated unto them that gospel which I preach among the Gentiles [*and explained to the members in Jerusalem what I was preaching among the Gentiles*], but privately to them which were of reputation [*to the leaders of the Church*], lest by any means I should run, or had run, in vain [*in order to have their approval of what I was teaching and doing among the Gentiles*].

In Paul's writings, the word "Greek" is a general reference to all Gentiles.

3 But neither Titus [*not even Titus*], who was with me, being a Greek [*a Gentile;* Strong's *#1672*], was compelled to be circumcised: [*In other words, the Brethren did not require Titus to be circumcised, which validated what I had been teaching about that issue.*]

The Judaizers, as mentioned in the opening note for Galatians, were Jewish converts who insisted that Jewish Christians should still keep the law of Moses, especially the law of circumcision. This demand from them caused much controversy in the early Church, as mentioned in Bible Dictionary under "Circumcision." These members caused much trouble for Paul, who taught that Gentile male converts did not have to be circumcised in order to join the Church. Much of the rest of this chapter deals with Paul's battle against converts who believed that the law of Moses should still be lived.

4 And that because of false brethren unawares brought in, who came in privily to spy out our liberty which we have in Christ Jesus, that they might bring us into bondage:

JST Galatians 2:4

4 **Notwithstanding** [*even though the Brethren said Titus didn't have to be circumcised*], **there were some brought in by false brethren** [*apostates*] unawares, who came in privily [*who infiltrated among us*] to spy out our liberty [*to verify that we were not living the law of Moses and to destroy the freedom*] which we have in Christ Jesus, that they might bring us into bondage [*in an attempt to put us under the requirements of the law of Moses again*];

5 To whom we gave place by subjection, no, not for an hour [*and we did not give in to them for even a moment*]; that the truth of the gospel might continue with you [*so that they could not destroy the gospel we taught to you*].

6 But of these [*apostates*] who seemed to be somewhat [*who seemed to think they were pretty important*], (whatsoever they were, it maketh no matter to me: God accepteth no man's person [*does not show favoritism*]:) for they who seemed to be somewhat in conference added nothing to me [*didn't persuade me at all*]:

7 But contrariwise [*on the contrary*], when they saw that the gospel of the uncircumcision [*the gospel which did not require keeping the law of Moses*] was committed unto me [*when they saw that I was to be the Apostle to the Gentiles*], as the gospel of the circumcision was unto Peter [*just as Peter was the apostle to the Jews*];

8 (For he [*Christ*] that wrought effectually in Peter to the apostleship of the circumcision [*who worked effectively through Peter with the Jews*], the same [*Christ*] was mighty in me toward the Gentiles [*worked effectively through me with the Gentiles*])

9 And when James, Cephas [*Peter*], and John, who seemed to be pillars [*who were obviously pillars in the Church*], perceived the grace that was given unto me [*saw that I was working under Christ's direction*], they gave to me and Barnabas the right hands of fellowship [*their full approval*]; that we should go unto the heathen [*that we should preach the gospel among the Gentiles*], and they unto the circumcision [*and they would continue teaching the gospel among the Jews*].

The phrase "the right hand of fellowship" used in verse 9, above, is a saying in both Greek and Hebrew, which means full partnership, agreement and unity. See p. 309 of the Institute of Religion's New Testament student manual. It is interesting to note that this is the phrase the Prophet Joseph Smith used in a letter welcoming William W. Phelps (who wrote several hymns including *Praise to the Man*, *The Spirit of God*, *Now Let Us Rejoice*, and *If You Could Hie to Kolob*) back into the Church. See *History of the Church*, Vol 4, p. 162.

10 Only they would that we should remember the poor; the same which I also was forward to do. [*All they asked was that we remember to collect money for the impoverished Saints in the Jerusalem area (see the note at the beginning of 2 Corinthians 8 in this study guide) which I was already eager to do.*]

11 But when Peter was come [*came*] to Antioch [*a Gentile city in what is central Turkey today, where Paul and his companions had baptized many Gentile converts*], I withstood him to the face [*I stood up to him*], because he was to be blamed [*because he was wrong*].

Apostle Bruce R. McConkie explained the situation in verse 11, above, as follows: "Peter and Paul—both of whom were apostles, both of whom received revelations, saw angels, and were approved of the Lord, and both of whom shall inherit the fulness of the Father's kingdom—these same righteous and mighty preachers disagreed on a basic matter of church policy. Peter was the President of the Church; Paul, an apostle and Peter's junior in the church hierarchy, was subject to the direction of the chief apostle. But Paul was right, and Peter was wrong. Paul stood firm, determined that they should walk "uprightly according to the truth of the gospel"; Peter temporized (rationalized) for fear of offending Jewish semi-converts who still kept the law of Moses. The issue was not whether the Gentiles should receive the gospel. Peter himself had received the revelation that God was no respecter of persons, and that those of all lineages were now to be heirs of salvation along with the Jews. (Acts 10:21–35.) Further, the heads of the Church, in council assembled, with the Holy Ghost guiding their minds and directing their decisions, had determined that the Gentiles who received the gospel should not be subject to the law of Moses. (Acts 15:1–35.) The Jewish members of the Church, however, had not been able to accept this decision without reservation. They themselves continued to conform to Mosaic performances, and they expected Gentile converts to do likewise. Peter sided with them; Paul publicly withstood the chief apostle and won the debate, as could not otherwise have been the case. Without question, if we had the full account, we would find Peter reversing himself and doing all in his power to get the Jewish Saints to believe that the law of Moses was fulfilled in Christ and no longer applied to anyone, Jew or Gentile. (*Doctrinal New Testament Commentary*, Vol. 2: pp. 463–464.)

Beginning with verse 12, next, Paul explains what caused him to challenge Peter.

12 For before that certain came from James [*before some Jewish converts (Judaizers; see note after verse 3 of Galatians, chapter 2 in this study guide) came to Antioch*], he [*Peter*] did eat with the Gentiles [*associated freely with our Gentile converts, including eating with them*]: but when they [*the Jewish converts who felt strongly that all Gentile converts should live the law of Moses*] were come [*arrived on the scene*], he [*Peter*] withdrew and separated himself [*and wouldn't eat with Gentile converts*], fearing them which were of the circumcision [*fearing what the Jewish converts thought*].

13 And the other Jews dissembled likewise with him [*followed Peter's example*]; insomuch that Barnabas [*a Jewish convert and one of Paul's missionary companions*] also was carried away with their dissimulation [*hypocrisy;* Strong's *#5272*].

14 But when I saw that they walked not uprightly according to the truth of the gospel [*when I saw that they were not living according to Christ's teachings*], I said unto Peter before them all [*in front of all of them*], If thou, being a Jew, livest after the manner of [*live like the*] Gentiles, and not as do the Jews [*and not like a Jew*], why compellest thou [*why do you require*] the Gentiles to live as do the Jews [*according to Jewish customs*]?

JST Galatians 2:14

14 But when I saw that they walked not uprightly according to the truth of the gospel, I said unto Peter before them all, If thou, being a Jew, livest after the manner of **the** Gentiles, and not as do the Jews, why compellest thou the Gentiles to live as do the Jews?

15 We who are Jews by nature [*by birth*], and not sinners of the Gentiles [*and not sinners who come from the Gentiles*], [*In other words, every one of us is a sinner, and even we Jews know that we will not get to heaven by the law of Moses. This explanation includes the first part of verse 16, next.*]

16 Knowing that a man is not justified by the works of the law [*the law of Moses*], but by the faith of Jesus Christ, even we [*Jews*] have believed in Jesus Christ, that we might be justified [*brought into full harmony with God*] by the faith of Christ, and not by the works of the law [*the law of Moses*]: for by the works of the law shall no flesh be justified [*the law of Moses won't get anyone to heaven*].

17 But if, while we seek to be justified by Christ, we ourselves also are found sinners [*if, while we are striving for salvation through Christ, we are still found to be sinners*], is therefore Christ the minister of sin [*does that mean that Christ supports sin*]? God forbid.

18 For if I build again the things which I destroyed, I make myself a transgressor [*if I go back to my old ways, after having repented and having started following Christ, I make myself a sinner*]. [*In other words, Paul is, in effect, saying*

"Peter, if you, who know better, decide to side with the Jews and not eat with Gentile converts, because of peer pressure, in spite of what Christ showed you in your vision about taking the gospel to the Gentiles (Acts, chapter 10), you are making yourself a sinner.]

19 For I through the law [*of Christ*] am dead to the law [*have quit living the law of Moses*], that I might live unto God [*in order that I might progress to exaltation with God*].

20 I am crucified with Christ [*I crucified my old self, with my sins, through Christ's Atonement; see Romans 6:4–6*]: nevertheless I live [*but I am not literally dead*]; yet not I, but Christ liveth in me [*Christ is alive in me*]: and the life which I now live in the flesh [*in mortality*] I live by the faith of the Son of God, who loved me, and gave himself for me [*because of Christ's confidence in me, so much in fact that He died for me*].

21 I do not frustrate [*set aside;* Strong's *#0114*] the grace of God: for if righteousness come by the law [*because if we can be saved from our sins by the law of Moses*], then Christ is dead in vain [*then Christ died for nothing*].

GALATIANS 3

Paul will now give a masterful discourse explaining the role of the law of Moses as a "schoolmaster law," given to bring the children of Israel up to the point where they can accept the higher laws of Christ's full gospel which will lead them to exaltation.

1 O FOOLISH Galatians, who hath bewitched [*deceived*] you, that ye should not obey the truth, before whose eyes Jesus Christ hath been evidently set forth, crucified among you [*before whose very eyes Christ and His crucifixion was obviously and clearly taught*]?

2 This only would I learn of you [*just answer one question for me*], Received ye the Spirit by the works of the law, or by the hearing of faith [*did you get the Holy Ghost through the law of Moses or through the gospel of faith in Christ*]?

3 Are ye so foolish [*how could you be so foolish*]? having begun in the Spirit [*having begun a new life in the gospel of Christ and started to feel the effects of the Holy Ghost*], are ye now made perfect by the flesh [*how can you revert back to the law of Moses*]?

4 Have ye suffered so many things in vain [*have you gone through the persecutions heaped upon you as Christians in vain*]? if it be yet in vain [*if indeed it is in vain*].

5 He [*God*] therefore that ministereth to you the Spirit [*who gives you the Holy Ghost*], and worketh miracles among you, doeth he it by the works of the law [*does He give you these things through the law of Moses*], or by the hearing of faith [*or because of your faith in Christ*]?

Next, Paul will use the logic that Abraham (one of the most respected prophets among the Jews) did not have the law of Moses, and yet God considered him to be righteous.

6 Even as Abraham [*who did not have the law of Moses*] believed God, and it was accounted to him for righteousness [*and God considered him to be righteous*].

7 Know ye therefore [*you must realize*] that they which are of faith [*who have faith in Christ*], the same are the children of Abraham [*will have the same reward as Abraham*].

The phrase "children of" as used in verse 7, above, is a scriptural phrase which means "followers of" and, in context, usually means "they will receive the same reward as." Paul uses it in this sense in Romans 8:16–17, where he says "children of God" will be "heirs of God" and "joint heirs with Christ."

8 And the scripture, foreseeing [*prophesying*] that God would justify [*save*] the heathen [*the Gentiles*] through faith [*in Christ*], preached before [*back then*] the gospel unto Abraham, saying [*in Genesis 12:3*], In thee shall all nations be blessed.

9 So then they which be of faith are blessed with faithful Abraham [*therefore, those who believe in Christ will be blessed like Abraham was*].

10 For as many as are of the works of the law are under the curse [*those who try to gain salvation through the law of Moses, will be stopped in progression*]: for it is written [*in Deuteronomy 27:26*], Cursed is every one that continueth not in all things which are written in the book of the law to do them.

11 But that no man is justified by the law [*no one is saved by the law of Moses*] in the sight of God, it is evident [*is obvious*]: for, The just [*the righteous*] shall live by faith [*Habakkuk 2:4*].

12 And the law is not of faith [*the law of Moses does not emphasize faith*]: but, The man that doeth them shall live in them [*quoting Leviticus 18:5*].

As evidenced above and elsewhere, Paul has a remarkably detailed knowledge of the Old Testament and is thus able to quote from the very sources that the Judaizers hang on to in order to justify their continuing to live the law of Moses.

13 Christ hath redeemed us from the curse of the law [*Christ has freed us from the bondage of the law of Moses*], being made a curse for us: for it is written [*in Deuteronomy 21:22–23*], Cursed is every one that hangeth on a tree: [*In other words, Christ subjected Himself to the curse of being hung on a tree (the cross).*]

14 That [*so that*] the blessing of Abraham [*the blessings of exaltation; see Abraham 2:9–11*] might come on the Gentiles through Jesus Christ; that we might receive the promise of the Spirit through faith.

JST Galatians 3:14

14 That the blessing of Abraham might come on the Gentiles through Jesus Christ; that **they** might receive the promise of the Spirit through faith.

15 Brethren, I speak after the manner of men [*I'm going to use an example from everyday life so you can understand me*]; Though it be but a man's covenant, yet if it be confirmed, no man disannulleth, or addeth thereto [*when two men make a legal contract or covenant, no one can change or nullify it*].

JST Galatians 3:15

15 Brethren, I speak after the manner of men; Though it be but a man's covenant, yet **when** it be confirmed, no man disannulleth, or addeth thereto.

16 Now to Abraham and his seed were the promises made. He saith not [*God didn't say*], And to seeds, as of many [*meaning many people*]; but as of one, And to thy seed [*but just one*], which is Christ [*meaning Christ*].

17 And this I say, that the covenant [*the covenant with Abraham*], that was confirmed before [*before Moses came along*] of God in Christ, the law, which was four hundred and thirty years after [*the law of Moses which was given 430 years after God's covenant with Abraham*], cannot disannul [*nullify God's covenant with Abraham*], that it should make the promise [*God's promise to Abraham*] of none effect. [*In other words, it wouldn't be fair for God to tell Abraham, "Sorry, I've changed My mind. The covenant I made with you is void. The only way for people to be saved is through the law of Moses."*]

18 For if the inheritance be of the law [*if the only way we can get to heaven is through the law of Moses*], it is no more of promise [*the promise God gave to Abraham is broken*]: but God gave it to Abraham by promise [*but God did promise Abraham*]. [*In other words, God doesn't break promises.*]

JST Galatians 3:18

18 For if the inheritance **is** of the law, **then** it is no more of promise; but God gave it to Abraham by promise.

19 Wherefore then serveth the law [*what is the purpose of the law of Moses*]? It was added because of transgressions, till the seed should come to whom the promise was made; and it was ordained by angels in the hand of a mediator.

JST Galatians 3:19

19 Wherefore then [*this, then, is the reason that*], **the law was added because of transgressions** [*of the children of Israel*], till the seed should come to whom the promise was made **in the law given to Moses, who was ordained by the hand of angels to be a mediator of this first covenant, (the law** [*meaning the law of Moses*].)

20 Now a mediator is not a mediator of one, but God is one.

JST Galatians 3:20

20 Now **this mediator was not a mediator of the new covenant; but there is one mediator of the new covenant, who is Christ, as it is written in the law concerning the promises made to Abraham and his seed. Now Christ is the mediator of life** [*the one who brings eternal life, exaltation*]; **for this is the promise which God made unto Abraham**.

Next, in verse 21, Paul clarifies that the law of Moses did not work against the promises of God to Abraham. In fact, if properly understood, the law of Moses was designed as a "schoolmaster law" to point the peoples' minds toward Christ and his great last sacrifice in opening the door of exaltation to all.

21 Is the law then against the promises of God [*does the law of Moses work against God's promises of exaltation to Abraham*]? God forbid [*absolutely not!*]: for if there had been a law given which could have given life [*if it had been possible to give a law to the children of Israel, through Moses, which would have brought them to eternal life*], verily righteousness should have been by the law [*such a law would have been given*]. [*In other words, the children of Israel were so far into wickedness that it was impossible to give them a law high enough to bring them exaltation at that point in their lives.*]

22 But the scripture hath concluded all under sin [*the scriptures verify that all are guilty of sinning; see D&C 49:8*], that the promise by faith of Jesus Christ might be given to them that believe [*therefore, all who want to receive the blessings from Christ which come through faith must believe in Him*].

23 But before faith came [*before the gospel of Christ came to us*], we were kept under the law [*we were bound by the law of Moses*], shut up unto the faith [*held back from Christ's full gospel*] which should afterwards be revealed [*which was to be taught to us at a later date*].

Note: This next verse sums up everything Paul has been teaching in this chapter.

24 Wherefore [*therefore*] the law was our schoolmaster [*the law of Moses was our teacher*] to bring us unto Christ, that we might be justified [*saved*] by faith [*in Christ*].

JST Galatians 3:24

24 Wherefore the law was our schoolmaster **until Christ**, that we might be justified by faith.

25 But after that faith is come [*once we have come to the point of having faith in Christ*], we are no longer under a schoolmaster [*we don't need the schoolmaster (law of Moses) any more*].

26 For ye are all the children of God by faith in Christ Jesus [*all of*

you may become saved by faith in Jesus Christ].

JST Galatians 3:26

26 For ye are all the children of God by faith in **Jesus Christ**.

27 For as many of you as have been baptized into Christ have put on Christ [*all of you who have been baptized have taken upon you the name of Christ*].

28 There is neither Jew nor Greek, there is neither bond nor free, there is neither male nor female: for ye are all one in Christ Jesus [*we are all the same in Christ's eyes when we join His Church*].

29 And if ye be Christ's [*if you belong to Christ*], then are ye Abraham's seed [*then you also belong to Abraham*], and heirs according to the promise [*and are entitled to the promises given to him; see Abraham 2:9–11 for these promises*].

GALATIANS 4

Next, Paul will emphasize the fact that all of us are still "children" in comparison to God, and that, even though we can become "heirs" and inherit "all that my Father hath" (D&C 84:38), we still have to be treated as children and servants, governed and tutored along the way to becoming gods. The point is, that the law of Moses was given to the children of Israel to tutor and govern them so that they could progress to the point of receiving the higher laws of Christ's gospel which eventually lead the faithful to exaltation and being gods, in other words, to being "heirs of God, and joint-heirs with Christ" (Romans 8:17), invited to "sit with me in my throne, even as I also overcame, and am set down with my Father in his throne" (Revelation 3:21). Paul teaches very clearly here that we can become gods.

1 NOW I say, That the heir [*the one who will someday inherit the whole estate*], as long as he is a child, differeth nothing from a servant [*is no different than a servant*], though he be lord of all [*even though he will someday own the whole estate*];

2 But is under [*is subject to*] tutors and governors until the time appointed of the father [*until his father gives him his estate*].

3 Even so we, when we were children [*still immature in spiritual things, and thus were given the law of Moses to tutor us and prepare us for Christ's gospel*], were in bondage under the elements of the world [*were in the captivity of sin because we were involved in the ways of the world*]:

4 But when the fulness of the time was come [*when the time was right*], God [*the Father*] sent forth his Son [*Christ*], made of a woman [*born to a mortal woman*], made under the law [*born while the law of Moses was still in effect*],

5 To redeem them that were under the law [*to redeem those who were*

under the bondage of the law of Moses], that we might receive the adoption of sons [*that we might become gods*].

6 And because ye are sons [*because you are heirs*], God [*the Father*] hath sent forth the Spirit of his Son into your hearts, crying, Abba, Father [*you have been inspired in your hearts to feel that Heavenly Father is literally your father and that you have an intimate child to father relationship with Him such that you could feel to call him "Daddy"*].

The term "Abba" is an intimate, familial name for our Father in Heaven. See Bible Dictionary under "Abba." It can be translated as "Daddy" and is the same term the Savior used during His suffering in the Garden of Gethsemane when He asked that, if possible, He might not drink the bitter cup. See Mark 14:36. An explanation of the term "Abba" is given in the Institute of Religion's New Testament student manual, *The Life and Teachings of Jesus and His Apostles*, p. 311, as follows: "Paul suggested that through the atonement of Christ we can be adopted as sons of God, and then the Spirit shall help us cry 'Abba, Father.' Abba is Aramaic (a cognate of Hebrew) and carries more than just the connotation of father. It is the intimate and personal diminutive of the word father used by children in the family circle. The closest equivalent we have is papa or daddy, although neither can really convey fully the impact of the word. The point is that God is not only Father (the formal title and name), but he is also Abba, the parent of love and guidance that knows us intimately and whom we can approach without fear."

7 Wherefore [*therefore*] thou art no more a servant, but a son [*the gospel of Christ elevates you from being a servant under the law of Moses to the level of being a family member*]; and if a son, then an heir of God through Christ [*through Christ's gospel, including the Atonement*].

8 Howbeit [*however*] then [*back then*], when ye knew not God, ye did service unto them which by nature are no gods [*you worshiped idols*].

9 But now, after that ye have known God [*now that you know about the plan of salvation brought by Christ*], or rather are known of God, how turn ye again to the weak and beggarly [*powerless to accomplish the goal;* Strong's *#4434*] elements [*of the law of Moses*], whereunto [*to which*] ye desire again to be in bondage [*how can you possibly turn back to the law of Moses and its accompanying bondage; do you really want to be in bondage again*]?

10 Ye observe days, and months, and times, and years [*you have gone back to the rituals of the law of Moses; see Bible Dictionary under "New Moon"*]. [*Bruce R. McConkie explains "days, and months, and times, and years" as*

"The various feasts, fasting periods, and sabbatical years which were part of the worship of ancient Israel." Doctrinal New Testament Commentary, *Vol. 2, p. 476.*]

11 I am afraid of [*for*] you, lest I have bestowed upon you labour in vain [*for fear that all my work among you has done no good*].

12 Brethren, I beseech [*urge*] you, be as I am; for I am as ye are: ye have not injured me at all.

JST Galatians 4:12

12 Brethren, I beseech you **to be perfect as I am perfect; for I am persuaded as ye have a knowledge of me** [*you have gained knowledge about Christ from me*], ye have not injured me at all **by your sayings**.

13 Ye know how through infirmity of the flesh I preached the gospel unto you at the first [*you know that I was sick when I first arrived among you to teach you the gospel*].

14 And my temptation [*trial*] which was in my flesh [*my illness*] ye despised not, nor rejected; but received me as an angel of God, even as Christ Jesus [*you accepted me as a messenger of God in spite of my being ill when I arrived*].

15 Where is then the blessedness ye spake of [*where is the commitment and spirituality you had back then*]? for I bear you record, that, if it had been possible, ye would have plucked out your own eyes, and have given them to me [*your commitment to the gospel I taught you was so strong that you would have done anything for me*].

16 Am I therefore become your enemy, because I tell you the truth [*have I offended you because I have told you the truth about your status now*]?

17 They [*those who want you to go back to living the law of Moses*] zealously affect you, but not well [*are very energetic but not good for you*]; yea, they would exclude you [*they want to alienate you from us*], that ye might affect them [*in order to make you loyal to them*].

18 But it is good to be zealously affected always in a good thing [*it is good to be enthusiastically involved in a right cause*], and not only when I am present with you.

19 My little children, of whom I travail in birth again until Christ be formed in you [*my dear, immature children in the gospel, I feel like I am having to go through the pains of childbirth again in order to get you "born" or established in the gospel of Christ again*],

20 I desire to be present with you now [*I wish I were with you now*], and to change my voice [*my tone of voice*]; for I stand in doubt of you [*I am worried about you*].

21 Tell me, ye that desire to be under the law, do ye not hear the law [*tell me, you who want to go back to living under the law of Moses again, don't you realize what that law says*]?

22 For it is written [*in Genesis, chapters 16 and 21*], that Abraham had two sons, the one by a bondmaid [*a servant wife, named Hagar*], the other by a freewoman [*Sarah*].

23 But he [*Ishmael; Genesis 16:15*] who was of the bondwoman [*Hagar*] was born after the flesh [*was born normally*]; but he [*Isaac; Genesis 21:3*] of the freewoman [*Sarah*] was by promise [*as a result of a special promise and covenant*].

24 Which things are an allegory [*these things are symbolic*]: for these are the two covenants [*Ishmael and Isaac represent the two covenants (the law of Moses and the higher gospel given to Abraham)*]; the one [*the law of Moses*] from the mount Sinai, which gendereth [*leads*] to bondage, which is Agar [*which came through Hagar*].

25 For this Agar is mount Sinai in Arabia, and answereth to Jerusalem which now is, and is in bondage with her children. [*In other words, the law of Moses came from Mount Sinai, through Moses, and is still going strong in Jerusalem where the Jews hold tightly to it, in spite of Christ's teachings.*]

26 But Jerusalem which is above is free, which is the mother of us all. [*But the New Covenant, which Christ taught in Jerusalem, is the higher, spiritual gospel, which is superior to the law of Moses and is designed to set us free from it. Christ's gospel is our new "mother" and through her, we are born again and set free from the old law of Moses.*]

27 For it is written [*in Isaiah 54:1*], Rejoice, thou barren that bearest not; break forth and cry, thou that travailest not: for the desolate hath many more children than she which hath an husband.

Isaiah 54:1, quoted in verse 27, above, appears in the Old Testament as follows (with notes in brackets added to help with understanding): "Sing, O barren [*one who has not produced children, i.e., Israel who has not produced many righteous children up to now*], thou that didst not bear; break forth into singing, and cry aloud, thou that didst not travail [*go into labor*] with child [*i.e., in former days, you did not succeed in bringing forth righteous children, loyal to Christ*]: for more are the children [*righteous converts*] of the desolate [*perhaps meaning the Gentiles*] than the children of the married wife [*perhaps meaning the Jews who insist on holding on to the law of Moses; in other words, you've got more righteous converts than you ever thought possible, almost all the converts coming from outside the land of Israel*], saith the LORD.

28 Now we, brethren, as Isaac was, are the children of promise [*we are the covenant descendants of Abraham, coming through Isaac*].

29 But as then he [*Ishmael and his descendants*] that was born after the flesh persecuted him [*Isaac and his posterity*] that was born

after the Spirit [*who are children of the covenant*], even so it is now.

30 Nevertheless what saith the scripture [*Genesis 21:10*]? Cast out the bondwoman and her son: for the son of the bondwoman shall not be heir with the son of the freewoman. [*In other words, Paul, speaking symbolically, is saying that just as Hagar and Ishmael, who represent the law of Moses in this discussion, were cast out, so also will God cast out all who adhere to the law of Moses now, rather than being baptized and remaining true to the higher law and spiritual covenants given by Christ, which can make us heirs in heaven with Abraham, Isaac, and Jacob.*]

31 So then, brethren, we are not children of the bondwoman, but of the free. [*Therefore, we are not under the law of Moses, rather, we are made free from it by making and keeping covenants given to us by Christ.*]

GALATIANS 5

Paul continues his skillful and inspired sermon, counseling the Galatian Saints to resist the efforts of some apostates among them to get them to revert back to the law of Moses. He urges them to hold tightly to the freedoms which come with the gospel of Jesus Christ.

A beautiful summary of the whole gospel given us by the Savior is found at the end of verse 14. You will no doubt recognize it.

There are no JST changes for this chapter.

1 STAND fast therefore in the liberty [*the gospel of Christ*] wherewith Christ hath made us free, and be not entangled again with the yoke of bondage [*the law of Moses*].

2 Behold, I Paul say unto you, that if ye be circumcised [*if you live the law of Moses*], Christ shall profit you nothing [*you will not benefit from Jesus Christ*].

3 For I testify again to every man that is circumcised [*who submits to circumcision as required of those who live the law of Moses*], that he is a debtor to do the whole law [*that you are committing yourself to the whole law of Moses*].

4 Christ is become of no effect unto you [*in so-doing, you reject Christ*], whosoever of you are justified by the law [*any of you who go back to the law of Moses in order to be saved*]; *ye are fallen from grace* [*can no longer be saved by Christ's Atonement, thus, you will not be saved.*].

5 For we through the Spirit [*we who believe in Christ*] wait [*patiently wait;* Strong's *#0553*] for the hope of righteousness [*becoming acceptable to God;* Strong's *#1343*] by faith [*exercise faith in Christ toward salvation*].

6 For in Jesus Christ [*for if you are going to follow Christ*] neither circumcision [*being a Jew*] availeth

any thing, nor uncircumcision [*nor being a Gentile*]; [*In other words, in the true gospel, brought by Christ, merely being a Jew or a Gentile does you no good, as far as salvation is concerned.*] but faith which worketh by love [*the only thing that counts is faith in Christ, who came because of the Father's love for us*].

7 Ye did run well [*you were doing well in the gospel I brought to you*]; who did hinder you that ye should not obey the truth [*what happened to take you back to living the law of Moses*]?

8 This persuasion cometh not of him that calleth you [*whoever is persuading you to leave the Church is not from God*].

9 A little leaven leaveneth the whole lump [*a little yeast works its way through the whole lump of dough*]. [*In other words, if you go back to requiring circumcision, you will soon have the law of Moses in every aspect of your life again.*]

10 I have confidence in you through the Lord, that ye will be none otherwise minded [*I have confidence that you will listen to what I am saying and not be led astray*]: but he that troubleth you shall bear his judgment, whosoever he be [*whoever is trying to lead you astray will have to face God and will be held accountable*].

11 And I, brethren, if I yet preach circumcision [*if my preaching included that you should still live the law of Moses*], why do I yet suffer persecution [*why would I continue to be persecuted*]? then is the offence of the cross ceased [*if that were the case, our teachings about Christ would not be offensive to those who continue to live the law of Moses*].

12 I would they were even cut off which trouble you [*I think that you should excommunicate those among you who are trying to lead you astray*].

13 For, brethren, ye have been called unto liberty [*you have been called to come unto Christ and thus be set free of the law of Moses*]; only use not liberty for an occasion to the flesh [*but do not misunderstand this freedom and use it to justify sin*], but by love serve one another.

The word "law" (*Strong's* #3551), as used next in verse 14, is the same word as "law" in Galatians 6:2, which is the "law of Christ," in other words, His whole gospel.

14 For all the law is fulfilled in one word, even in this [*the whole gospel, including all the commandments could be summed up as follows*]; Thou shalt love thy neighbour as thyself.

15 But if ye bite and devour one another [*if you keep picking each other apart, bit by bit*], take heed that ye be not consumed one of another [*watch out or you will eventually destroy each other*].

16 This I say then [*in summary, this is what I'm telling you*], Walk in the Spirit [*follow the Holy Ghost (see Galatians 5:17, footnote a), which teaches you to be loyal to Christ*], and ye shall not fulfil the lust of the flesh [*and you won't get caught up in sin, including sexual immorality*].

17 For the flesh lusteth against the Spirit [*the natural man (Mosiah 3:19) fights against the Holy Ghost*], and the Spirit against the flesh: and these are contrary the one to the other [*the Spirit and the natural man are opposites*]: so that ye cannot do the things that ye would [*you can't just do whatever you want to*].

18 But if ye be led of the Spirit, ye are not under the law [*if you follow the promptings of the Spirit, you will not be under the law of Moses; see Acts 15:5, footnote a*].

19 Now the works of the flesh are manifest, which are these [*now here are some of the worldly sins you must avoid*]; Adultery, fornication, uncleanness, lasciviousness [*lustful thinking and talking and all sexual immorality, including pornography*],

20 Idolatry [*idol worship*], witchcraft, hatred, variance [*disharmony*], emulations [*rivalry, etc., based on jealousy and worldly ambitions*], wrath [*anger, loss of temper*], strife, seditions [*stirring up unrighteous discontent with those in power, including government leaders and church leaders*], heresies [*false doctrines*],

21 Envyings, murders, drunkenness, revellings [*riotous, drunken parties and lifestyles*], and such like: of the which I tell you before [*I forewarn you*], *as I have also told you in time past, that they which do such things shall not inherit the kingdom of God* [*the celestial kingdom*].

Verses 22–23, next, contain one of the most often quoted scriptures in Galatians, by members of the Church.

22 But the fruit of the Spirit [*the result of following the promptings of the Holy Ghost*] is love, joy, peace, longsuffering, gentleness, goodness, faith,

23 Meekness [*mildness, gentleness*], temperance [*self control*]: against such there is no law [*there are no commandments of God against such personal character traits*].

24 And they that are Christ's have crucified the flesh with the affections and lusts [*those who belong to Christ are those who have learned to control the passions and lusts of the body*].

25 If we live in the Spirit, let us also walk in the Spirit. [*In other words, let our actions be in harmony with our beliefs.*]

26 Let us not be desirous of vain glory [*let us not be prideful*], provoking one another, envying one another.

GALATIANS 6

As Paul concludes his letter to the members of the Church in Galatia, he gives clear advice for righteous daily living.

There are no JST changes for this chapter.

1 BRETHREN, if a man be overtaken in a fault, ye which are spiritual, restore such an one in the spirit of meekness [*when you see others' sins, you who are stronger in the gospel should help them in love and kindness so they can also become strong in the gospel*]; considering thyself [*watching yourself*], lest thou also be tempted [*for fear that you might commit sins yourself*].

2 Bear ye one another's burdens [*compare with Mosiah 18:8–9*], and so fulfil the law of Christ.

3 For if a man think himself to be something, when he is nothing, he deceiveth [*fools*] himself.

4 But let every man prove his own work [*consider his own behaviors and deeds carefully and make sure they are in harmony with the gospel*], and then shall he have rejoicing in himself alone, and not in another [*then he will not be dependent on others for status*].

5 For every man shall bear his own burden [*each person is accountable for his own doings*].

6 Let him that is taught in the word communicate unto [*share with*] him that teacheth in all good things.

7 Be not deceived [*fooled*]; God is not mocked [*what God says will happen*]: for whatsoever a man soweth, that shall he also reap [*whatever you plant, you will harvest*]. [*In other words, you will be rewarded on Judgment Day for how you live. This is known as the "law of the harvest."*]

8 For he that soweth to his flesh [*he who plants or lives according to the worldly desires of the flesh*] shall of the flesh reap corruption [*will receive the punishments of God for his corrupt lifestyle*]; but he that soweth to the Spirit shall of the Spirit reap life everlasting [*but those who "plant" righteousness will harvest a reward of exaltation, in other words, eternal life*].

9 And let us not be weary in well doing [*let's not get tired of doing good, thus living the gospel*]: for in due season we shall reap [*when the time comes to be judged, we will harvest a reward of eternal life*], if we faint not [*if we don't give up and quit living the gospel*].

10 As we have therefore opportunity, let us do good unto all men, especially unto them who are of the household of faith [*those who are fellow members of the Church*].

11 Ye see how large a letter I have written unto you with mine own hand.

12 As many as [*those who*] desire to make a fair shew [*a good outward impression among Jews who keep the law of Moses*] in the flesh, they constrain you to be circumcised

[*are trying to make you submit to circumcision*]; only lest they should suffer persecution for the cross of Christ [*the only reason they do this is that they are afraid of being persecuted for following Christ*].

13 For neither they themselves who are circumcised keep the law [*not even those who are circumcised truly understand and keep the law of Moses*]; but desire to have you circumcised, that they may glory in your flesh [*but still they want to convert you back to the law of Moses so they can brag to others about getting you back*].

14 But God forbid that I should glory [*brag*], save [*except*] in the cross [*about the gospel*] of our Lord Jesus Christ, by whom the world is crucified unto me [*through which gospel I overcome my sins*], and I unto the world [*and through which I become unavailable to the sins of the world*].

15 For in Christ Jesus [*in the Savior's gospel*] neither circumcision availeth any thing, nor uncircumcision [*it makes no difference whether one is circumcised or not*], but a new creature [*the only thing that counts is whether or not they have been born again, thus becoming a new "creature" or "creation," in other words, a new person, loyal to Christ and thus freed from sin, kind, pleasant, patient, etc., as mentioned in Galatians 5:22–23*].

16 And as many as walk according to this rule [*what Paul said in verse 15*], peace be on them, and mercy, and upon the Israel [*the covenant people*] of God.

17 From henceforth let no man trouble me [*never let it be said that I am not loyal to Christ*]: for I bear in my body the marks of the Lord Jesus [*because I have many scars from beatings, whippings, stonings, etc., which I received because I was loyal to Him*]. [*Paul could also be saying that his body bears the marks of Jesus in a symbolic sense, meaning that he has exercised self-control over the lusts of the flesh and thus has the effects of the Atonement in his mortal life now.*]

18 Brethren, the grace of our Lord Jesus Christ be with your spirit. Amen.

THE EPISTLE OF PAUL THE APOSTLE TO THE EPHESIANS

According to Ephesians 3:1, 4:1, and 6:20, Paul is in prison when he writes to the members of the Church in Ephesus (on the western coast of what we know as western Turkey today). Most scholars agree that it was during his first imprisonment in Rome when he wrote to these members, and most agree that this letter was written between AD 61 and AD 63. Paul was eventually executed, probably in the spring of AD 65. See Bible Dictionary under "Paul."

Ephesians does not seem to have a particular theme responding to specific false doctrines or apostasy or wickedness as is the case with most of Paul's letters. Rather, it seems to be written to more spiritually mature members of the Church who are living the gospel and are capable of understanding and appreciating doctrines such as premortality, foreordination, the dispensation of the fulness of times, being sealed by the Holy Spirit of Promise (the Holy Ghost), the vital role of Apostles and prophets and other offices in the organization of the true Church, the fact that there is only one true Church, family, family life, and so forth. The letter to the Ephesians is one of the most helpful of Paul's writings for us as we do missionary work among Christians, because it contains so many doctrines which are usually thought of as being distinctive doctrines of The Church of Jesus Christ of Latter-day Saints.

EPHESIANS 1

As Paul begins this letter, among other things, he touches on foreordination, the restoration of the gospel in the last days, the dispensation of the fulness of times, and being sealed by the Holy Spirit of Promise. It is exciting and refreshing to us as Latter-day Saints to realize that these important doctrines were taught in the true church in Paul's day. It is a reminder to us that we indeed belong to the "restored" Church of Jesus Christ.

There are no JST changes for this chapter.

1 PAUL, an apostle of Jesus Christ by the will of God [*called of God*], to the saints which are at Ephesus, and to the faithful in Christ Jesus [*who are being faithful to the gospel of Jesus Christ*]:

2 Grace be to you, and peace, from God our Father, and from the Lord Jesus Christ.

Verse 2, above, is another reminder that the Father and the Son are two distinct, separate personages. As previously noted, one of the exciting things about Ephesians is that Paul teaches so many "LDS" doctrines in it. For instance, the context of verses 3 and 4, next, is our premortal life, our life "before the foundation of the world" (verse 4). With this in mind, we see, in verse 3, that we were blessed with "all spiritual blessings" there, and that these blessings came to us through Christ. In other words, we had the gospel of Jesus Christ there. We know from Moses 4:1–3 and Abraham 3:27–28 that Christ was chosen there to be our Savior. In teaching us that we were blessed with "all spiritual blessings in heavenly places in Christ," Paul teaches that the Atonement of Christ worked for us already in premortality.

While we may not understand how it can be that the Atonement worked for us before it was actually performed here on earth, we do know that the Atonement is "infinite" and that it worked for many who lived before Christ, for instance Alma and the sons of Mosiah. In October 1995 General Conference, Elder Jeffrey R. Holland taught that the Atonement worked for us in premortality when he said, referring to the premortal Jesus Christ, "We could remember that even in the Grand Council of Heaven He loved us and was wonderfully strong, that we triumphed even there by the power of Christ and our faith in the blood of the Lamb."

Another quote reminding us that the Atonement of Christ was already working for us in premortality is found in the Institute of Religion's New Testament student manual, *The Life and Teachings of Jesus and His Apostles*, p. 336, where it says "We were given laws and agency, and commandments to have faith and repent from the wrongs that we could do there." "Man could and did in many instances, sin before he was born."

In summary, one of the marvelous teachings of Paul here is that we were taught the gospel in premortality under the direction of the Father and that the Atonement of Christ worked for us there already, helping us to progress.

3 Blessed [*praised*] be the God and Father of our Lord Jesus Christ, who hath blessed us with all spiritual blessings in heavenly places [*in premortality*] *in Christ* [*through Christ*]:

In verse 4, Paul teaches the doctrine of foreordination, which means that those who were valiant and faithful in the premortal life were chosen and foreordained to perform particular missions and service when they came to earth. We are often told what some aspects of our foreordained missions are in our patriarchal blessings. Joseph Fielding Smith said the following about foreordination and premortal life: "There must be leaders, presiding officers, and those who are worthy and able to take command. During the ages in which we dwelt in the premortal state we not only developed our various characteristics and showed our worthiness and ability, or the lack of it, but we were also where such progress could be observed. It is reasonable to believe that there was a Church organization there. The heavenly beings were living in a perfectly arranged society. Every person knew his place. Priesthood, without any question, had been conferred and the leaders were chosen to officiate. Ordinances pertaining to that pre-existence were required and the love of God prevailed. Under such conditions it was natural for our Father to discern and choose those who were most worthy and evaluate the talents of each individual. He knew not only what each of us could do, but also what each of us would do when put to the test and when responsibility was given us. Then, when the time came for our habitation on mortal earth, all things were prepared and the servants of the Lord chosen and ordained to their respective missions." (Smith, *The Way to Perfection*, pp. 50–51.)

4 According as he [*the Father*] hath chosen [*foreordained*] us in him [*in Christ; in other words, we were foreordained because of our obedience to the gospel of Christ in premortality*] before the foundation of the world [*in premortality*], that we should be holy [*sanctified*] and without blame before him in love [*because of the Father's love for us*]:

5 Having predestinated [*foreordained;* Strong's *#4309*] us unto the adoption of children [*to become sons of God;* Strong's *#5206*] by [*through*] Jesus Christ to himself [*to become "begotten sons and daughters unto God" (in other words, exalted), D&C 76:24*], according to the good pleasure of his will [*according to the kindness of the Father*],

The word "predestinated" as used in verse 5, above, is an incorrect translation. The correct translation from the Greek is "foreordination," which is the word used in most modern translations of the Bible.

6 To the praise of the glory of his [*the Father's*] grace, wherein he [*the Father*] hath made us accepted [*has made it possible for us to return to His presence*] in the beloved [*through His Beloved Son*].

7 In whom we have redemption [*through whom we can be redeemed*] through his [*Christ's*] blood, the forgiveness of sins, according to the riches of his [*the Father's*] grace;

8 Wherein [*in Christ*] he [*the Father*] hath abounded toward us

[*provided us with bounteous blessings*] in all wisdom and prudence [*understanding of our needs*];

9 Having made known unto us the mystery of his will [*the teachings of the gospel which remain a "mystery" to people who will not come unto Christ*], according to his good pleasure [*kindness toward us;* Strong's *#2107*] which he hath purposed [*planned*] in himself [*according to the plan of salvation which the Father has planned for us*]:

10 That in the dispensation of the fulness of times [*in the latter-days, when all things have been restored*] he [*the Father*] might gather together in one all things in Christ [*the restoration of the gospel of Jesus Christ, through Joseph Smith*], both which are in heaven, and which are on earth; even in him [*Christ*]:

Verse 10, above, is the only place in the Bible where the phrase "dispensation of the fulness of times" is used. It is an important doctrinal phrase. The word "dispensation" means "period of time." We know from D&C 27:13 that this dispensation is the last time that the gospel will be restored, and we know from Daniel 2:44 that there will not be another apostasy, rather, the Church, as restored by Joseph Smith, will continue right up to the Second Coming and then, of course, on through the Millennium.

11 In whom [*through Christ*] also we have obtained an inheritance [*we have the opportunity to inherit exaltation; see Romans 8:17*], being predestinated [*foreordained; see verse 5, above*] according to the purpose [*plan*] of him [*the Father*] who worketh all things after the counsel [*plan*] of his own will [*who does all things according to His own will*]: [*In other words, all things are done according to the Father's plan.*]

12 That we should be to the praise of his glory [*in other words, the Father's glory is "to bring to pass the immortality and eternal life of man." Moses 1:39*], who first trusted in Christ [*who trusted Christ to be the Redeemer; see Moses 4:1–3*].

Notice the skillful transition from verse 12, above, to verse 13, next, by which Paul says, in effect, that just as these Ephesian Saints heard and accepted the gospel of Jesus Christ in premortality, so also they have now heard and accepted it here on earth.

13 In whom ye also trusted [*you Ephesian members also trusted in Christ*], after that ye heard the word of truth, the gospel of your salvation [*after the gospel was preached to you*]: in whom also after that ye believed, ye were sealed with that holy Spirit of promise [*the Holy Ghost*],

The phrase "ye were sealed with that holy Spirit of promise" in verse 13, above, is important doctrinally. D&C 132 verses 7 and 19 remind us that all ordinances and covenants between us and God must be sealed by the "Holy Spirit of promise," in other words, by the Holy Ghost. One of the functions of the Holy Ghost is to ratify and approve all such ordinances and covenants. Another way of saying this is that all such covenants and ordinances must be "justified" by the Spirit (see Moses 6:60). Since the Holy Ghost knows all things, if a person lies as he or she seeks approval from the bishop and other authorized priesthood holders to participate in the ordinances of the Church, the Holy Ghost will simply not ratify or approve or seal the ordinance. Thus, the ordinance does the person no good. In fact, the deception can hurt the person spiritually, and if not repented of, can cause eternal damage. On the other hand, if a person, who has been dishonest about qualifying to receive such ordinances, repents, confesses, and gets his or her life in order, the Holy Ghost can then "seal" the ordinance so that it is now valid for that person.

14 Which is the earnest of our inheritance [*the Holy Ghost is the "earnest money" which the Father gives as a "down payment" toward our exaltation*] until the redemption of the purchased possession [*until we are "fully paid for" by our own efforts in combination with the Atonement of Christ; see 2 Nephi 25:23*], unto the praise of his glory [*which brings glory to the Father; see Moses 1:39*].

15 Wherefore I also, after I heard of your faith in the Lord Jesus, and love unto all the saints,

16 Cease not to give thanks for you, making mention of you in my prayers;

17 That the God of our Lord Jesus Christ, the Father of glory, may give unto you the spirit of wisdom and revelation in the knowledge of him [*Christ*]:

18 The eyes of your understanding being enlightened [*your whole being has been enlightened by the gospel*]; that ye may know what is the hope of his calling [*so that you realize the wonderful hope and confidence in salvation which comes through Christ's calling to be our Savior*], and what the riches of the glory of his inheritance in the saints [*and you see the incredibly rich blessings and glory which await the faithful Saints as they inherit exaltation*],

19 And what is the exceeding greatness of his power to us-ward who believe, according to the working of his mighty power, [*In other words, you also see the unbelievably wonderful power of God as it comes into your lives.*]

20 Which he wrought in Christ [*which the Father gave us through Christ*], when he [*the Father*] raised him [*Christ*] from the dead, and set him at his own right hand in the heavenly places [*in heaven; see Acts 7:55–56*],

21 Far above all principality, and

power, and might, and dominion, and every name that is named, not only in this world, but also in that which is to come [*Christ has overcome all things (see D&C 76:106–108) and has power over all things, next to the Father*]:

22 And hath put all things under his feet [*the Father has given Christ power over all things*], and gave him to be the head over all things to the church, [*In other words, Christ is the head of all things in the Church, under the direction of the Father.*]

23 Which is his body [*symbolically, the Church represents the body of Christ*], the fulness of him that filleth all in all [*and thus Christ influences every aspect of the Church*].

An additional explanation of verse 23, above, is given by Bruce R. McConkie as follows: "In the *Lectures on Faith*, Joseph Smith describes the Father and the Son as 'filling all in all' because the Son, having overcome, has 'received a fulness of the glory of the Father,' and possesses 'the same mind with the Father.' Then he announces the conclusion to which Paul here only alludes: 'And all those who keep his commandments shall grow up from grace to grace, and become heirs of the heavenly kingdom, and joint-heirs with Jesus Christ; possessing the same mind, being transformed into the same image or likeness, even the express image of him who fills all in all; being filled with the fulness of his glory, and become one in him, even as the Father, Son and Holy Spirit are one.' (*Lectures on Faith*, pp. 50–51." *Doctrinal New Testament Commentary*, Vol. 2, p. 497.)

EPHESIANS 2

Here, among other things, Paul will address the doctrines of mercy, grace, and faith, coupled with the cleansing blood of Christ and being faithful in the Church, which is built upon the foundation of Apostles and prophets. You may well be familiar with verses 19–21, which are often used in our missionary work.

1 AND you hath he [*Christ*] quickened [*made spiritually alive*], who were dead [*spiritually dead*] in trespasses and sins;

2 Wherein in time past ye walked according to the course of this world [*lived according to the ways of the world*], according to the prince of the power of the air [*Satan; see McConkie,* Doctrinal New Testament Commentary, *Vol. 2, p. 499*], the spirit [*evil spirit;* Strong's *#4151*] that now worketh [*operates*] in the children of disobedience [*in wicked people*]:

The word "conversation," as used in New Testament English, usually means "behavior." An example of this in found in verse 3, next.

3 Among whom also we all had our

conversation [*we behaved like they did*] in times past in the lusts [*sins*] of our flesh, fulfilling the desires of the flesh [*physical desires*] and of the mind; and were by nature the children of wrath [*people facing the punishments of God*], even as others [*just like everyone else*].

4 But God [*the Father*], who is rich in mercy, for his great love wherewith [*with which*] he loved us,

5 Even when we were dead in sins [*even when we were spiritually dead, caught up in sin*], hath quickened us [*has given us new spiritual life*] together with [*through*] Christ, (by grace ye are saved;)

In reference to Paul's parentheses (by grace ye are saved;) in verse 5, above, we know that without God's grace, we could not be saved. In fact, without it, we would eventually be completely subject to the devil and would have become devils. See 2 Nephi 9:7–9. However, we also know that we must do as much as we can in order to qualify for grace, as stated in 2 Nephi 25:23, where it says "For we know that it is by grace that we are saved, after all we can do."

6 And hath raised us up together, and made us sit together in heavenly places in Christ Jesus [*has made it possible for us to enter the celestial kingdom with Christ; see Romans 8:17 and Revelation 3:20–21*]:

7 That in the ages to come [*throughout the eternities*] he might shew [*show*] the exceeding riches of his grace in his kindness toward us through Christ Jesus.

Verses 8 and 9, next, are often used out of context to teach that we do not need works in order to be saved. This is false and Paul himself constantly counsels his people to show by the lives they live that they truly believe in Christ. In fact, in verse 10, he tells them that they should walk in good works. The point is that works alone cannot save us. The law of Moses, as modified and added to by the Jews over many centuries, had led many to believe that works alone could save them. They placed all the emphasis on strictly following the details of their religious laws, and failed to become personally righteous. For example, the Savior scolded them severely in Matthew 23:23 when he said "Woe unto you, scribes and Pharisees, hypocrites! for ye pay tithe of mint and anise and cummin, and have omitted the weightier matters of the law, judgment, mercy, and faith: these ought ye to have done, and not to leave the other undone." In this context, then, Paul teaches the Ephesian members that works alone cannot save them.

8 For by grace are ye saved through faith [*in Christ*]; and that not of yourselves [*you can't save yourselves*]: it is the gift of God [*the Father has given us the gift of his Son and the Atonement*]:

JST Ephesians 2:8

8 For by grace are ye saved through faith; and that not of yourselves; **but** it is the gift of God;

9 Not of works [*works alone can't save us*], lest any man should boast [*lest any people should become prideful, thinking that they can save themselves*].

10 For we are his [*the Father's*] workmanship, created in Christ Jesus [*becoming new people, made spiritually alive, through Jesus Christ*] unto good works [*to do the good works Jesus taught us to do*], which God [*the Father*] hath before ordained that we should walk in them [*which the Father planned in advance for us to do*].

Remember, as previously explained, that "Uncircumcision" means Gentiles, and "Circumcision" means Jews.

11 Wherefore remember, that ye being in time past Gentiles in the flesh [*think back to the time before you joined the Church*], who are called Uncircumcision [*when you were called outsiders, Gentiles*] by that which is called the Circumcision [*by the Jews who kept the law of Moses*] in the flesh made by hands [*because you hadn't been circumcised*];

12 That at that time ye were without Christ, being aliens from the commonwealth of Israel [*not belonging to God's covenant people*], and strangers from the covenants of promise [*and having no knowledge about the covenants which lead to fulfillment of the promises of exaltation*], having no hope [*of attaining exaltation*], and without God in the world [*and living without God's true gospel in your daily lives*]:

13 But now in [*through*] Christ Jesus ye who sometimes were far off [*who were so far away from God*] are made nigh [*are brought near to Him*] by the blood of Christ [*by the Atonement of Christ*].

14 For he is our peace [*He is the source of our peace*], who hath made both one [*who has made both Jews and Gentiles into one covenant people*], and hath broken down the middle wall of partition [*and has broken down the barrier*] between us;

15 Having abolished in his flesh [*by His mortal ministry*] the enmity [*the opposition*], even the law of commandments [*the law of Moses*] contained in ordinances; for to make in himself of twain one new man [*in order to make, through His mission, two peoples (Jews and Gentiles) into one people*], so making peace [*and thus making peace between Jews and Gentiles, as they both join His Church*];

16 And that he [*Christ*] might reconcile [*bring into harmony; atone for*] both [*Jews and Gentiles*] unto God in one body [*uniting them together*] by the cross [*through His Atonement*], having slain the enmity [*destroyed the animosity between Jewish members and Gentile members*] thereby

[*through bringing them into His true church*]:

17 And came and preached peace to you which were afar off [*to you Gentiles*], and to them that were nigh [*and to the Jews*].

18 For through him [*Christ*] we both [*both Jews and Gentiles*] have access by one Spirit [*through the Holy Ghost;* Strong's *#4151*] unto the Father.

19 Now therefore ye are no more strangers [*without knowledge of Christ*] and foreigners [*without citizenship in God's kingdom;* Strong's *#3941*], but fellowcitizens [*equal partners*] with the saints, and of the household of God [*and members of God's family*];

Next, in verse 20, Paul teaches that members are privileged and blessed to build their lives upon the foundation and teachings of Apostles and prophets, which are available only in the Church of Jesus Christ.

20 And are built [*and your lives are built*] upon the foundation of the apostles and prophets, Jesus Christ himself being the chief cornerstone [*with Jesus Himself at the head of the Church*];

21 In whom all the building [*the whole Church*] fitly framed together [*properly put together and guided*] groweth unto an [*becomes a*] holy temple in the Lord [*directed by the Savior*]:

22 In whom ye also are builded together for an habitation of God through the Spirit [*as members of the Church, your lives are put in order so that you become temples (1 Corinthians 3:16) in which the Spirit of God can reside*].

EPHESIANS 3

As you have no doubt sensed already in Paul's sermons and writings, the reluctance of many Jewish converts to accept Gentile converts as being of equal status in the eyes of God is a strong concern. In this chapter, he will speak to Gentile converts, assuring them that they are indeed on equal footing with any other converts.

1 FOR this cause I Paul, the prisoner of Jesus Christ for you Gentiles [*it is because I brought the gospel to you Gentiles that I, Paul, am currently in Prison in Rome*],

JST Ephesians 3:1

For this cause, I, Paul, **am** the prisoner of Jesus Christ among you Gentiles.

2 If ye have heard of the dispensation [*responsibility, stewardship,* Strong's *#3622*] of the grace of God which is given me to you-ward [*which God gave to me to bring you the gospel*]:

JST Ephesians 3:2

2 **For the dispensation** of the grace of God which is given me to you-ward;

Notice that the parenthesis that begins in the middle of verse 3, next, is completed at the end of verse 4.

3 How that by revelation he made known unto me the mystery [*the gospel of Christ, which is a mystery to those who know nothing of Christ*]; (as I wrote afore in few words [*as I wrote previously to you in a brief letter*],

JST Ephesians 3:3

3 **As ye have heard that** by revelation he made known unto me the mystery **of Christ; as I wrote before in few words**;

4 Whereby, when ye read [*so that when you read it*], ye may understand my knowledge in the mystery of Christ)

The brief letter referred to by Paul in verses 3 and 4, above, is missing, and serves to remind us that the Bible is not complete. For more about missing scripture, see Bible Dictionary under "Lost Books."

5 Which in other ages [*in some ages past, the gospel*] was not made known unto the sons of men [*was not revealed to people*], as [*in the way that*] it is now revealed unto his holy apostles and prophets by the Spirit;

6 That the Gentiles should be fellowheirs, and of the same body, and partakers of his promise in Christ by the gospel [*namely, that Gentiles are invited to join the Church and become full partners with the covenant people and become heirs of exaltation through Christ's gospel*]:

7 Whereof I was made a minister [*it was this gospel which I was called to bring to you*], according to the gift of the grace of God given [*by the kindness and mercy of God*] unto me by the effectual working of his power [*which caused the gospel to work effectively in me*].

8 Unto me, who am less than the least of all saints, is this grace [*help and stewardship*] given, that I should preach among the Gentiles the unsearchable riches of Christ [*the infinite blessings of the gospel of Christ*];

9 And to make all men see what is the fellowship of the mystery [*and to plainly teach what some consider to be a mystery, namely that both Jews and Gentiles are to be fellowshipped together as equals in the Church of Jesus Christ*], which from the beginning of the world hath been hid in God [*has not been revealed by the Father because people were not ready to accept it*], who created all things by Jesus Christ: [*Christ created the world under the direction of the Father.*]

10 To the intent that now unto the principalities and powers in heavenly places might be known by the church the manifold wisdom of God, [*In other words, the Father has revealed these things with the intent that members of the Church might now be able to understand the many aspects of God's wisdom as revealed in celestial doctrines.*]

11 According to the eternal purpose [*the plan of salvation*] which he [*the Father*] purposed [*planned for us*] in [*through*] Christ Jesus our Lord:

12 In whom we have boldness and access with confidence by the faith of him [*through faith in Christ we gain confidence to approach the Father*].

13 Wherefore I desire that ye faint not at my tribulations for you [*I hope you don't get too discouraged by what I am now going through in prison because of what I did for you*], which is your glory [*which is for your benefit*].

14 For this cause I bow my knees unto the Father of our Lord Jesus Christ, [*I humbly pray to the Father (this thought is continued in verse 16)*]

15 Of whom the whole family in heaven and earth is named [*who can name every one of His family members, in other words, who knows every one of his children in heaven and earth*],

What Paul says about Heavenly Father in verse 15, above, is similar to what the Lord told Moses in Moses 1:35, wherein He said "All things are numbered unto me, for they are mine and I know them."

16 That he would grant you, according to the riches of his glory, to be strengthened with might by his Spirit in the inner man [*that the Holy Ghost will strengthen your inward self according to the rich blessings available from the Father*];

17 That Christ may dwell in your hearts by faith; that ye, being rooted and grounded [*being solidly based*] in love,

18 May be able to comprehend with all saints what is the breadth [*width*], and length, and depth, and height [*of the Father's plan for us*];

19 And to know [*feel*] the love of Christ, which passeth knowledge [*exceeds our ability to understand*], that ye might be filled with all the fulness of God [*that you might be blessed with all blessings the Father has in store for us*].

20 Now unto him [*the Father*] that is able to do exceeding abundantly above all that we ask or think [*the Father is able to do far more with us than we ask or even think; in other words, he can help us attain exaltation*], according to [*through*] the power [*of God*] that worketh in us,

21 Unto him [*the Father*] be glory in the church by Christ Jesus throughout all ages, world [*worlds; see D&C 76:112*] without end [*in other words, forever*]. Amen.

EPHESIANS 4

This chapter contains strong Biblical evidence that there is one true church. Paul also clearly teaches that the true church will have Apostles, prophets, evangelists, teachers, and so forth, through which the Saints can receive guidance as they progress toward perfection. You may well be familiar with verses 11–14.

1 I THEREFORE, the prisoner of the Lord [*in prison in Rome because of loyalty to Christ*], beseech [*urge*] you that ye walk worthy of the vocation [*responsibilities of membership in the Church*] wherewith [*to which*] ye are called,

2 With all lowliness and meekness [*in humility*], with longsuffering [*patience*], forbearing one another [*being patient with one another*] in love;

3 Endeavouring [*striving*] to keep the unity of the Spirit in the bond of peace [*to live in unity and peace*].

Next, Paul explains that there is just one true church, only one Holy Ghost, only one valid baptism, and only one God. In other words, there can't be more than one true church. If there were more than one, that would mean that there is more than one Holy Ghost and more than one God who are giving conflicting revelations to people everywhere, telling them that their churches are true.

4 There is one body [*there is one true church*], and one Spirit [*and one Holy Ghost*], even as ye are called [*and this is what you have been called by God to participate in*] in one hope [*you only have hope of attaining exaltation in one church, namely the true Church*] of your calling [*to which you have been called to work toward*];

JST Ephesians 4:4

4 **In one body**, and one Spirit, even as ye are called in one hope of your calling;

5 One Lord, one faith, one baptism,

6 One God and Father of all [*we are all His spirit children; Hebrews 12:9*], who is above all, and through all, and in you all.

7 But unto every one of us is given grace according to the measure of the gift of Christ [*the Atonement is available to all of us*].

8 Wherefore [*this is why*] he saith [*in Psalm 68:18*], When he [*Christ*] ascended up on high, he led captivity captive [*overcame the captivity of sin*], and gave gifts unto men [*and gave the gift of resurrection and potential for eternal life to all*].

9 (Now that he [*Christ*] ascended [*to heaven, having finished the Atonement*], what is it but [*isn't it true*] that he also descended first into the lower parts of the earth [*that he had to first descend below all things—see D&C 122:8*]?

10 He that descended is the same also [*the same one*] that ascended up far above all heavens [*rose above all things that stood in His way*], that [*in order that*] he might fill [*fulfil*] all things.)

JST Ephesians 4:10

10 He **who** descended, is the same also **who** ascended up

into heaven, to glorify him who reigneth over all heavens, that he might fill all things.)

Paul has been teaching that there is only one true church. Now he teaches that that Church will have specific priesthood offices in it.

11 And he gave some, apostles; and some, prophets; and some, evangelists [*patriarchs; see Ephesians 4:11, footnote d*]; and some, pastors [*bishops; see Ephesians 4:11, footnote e*] and teachers;

12 For the perfecting of the saints, for the work of the ministry, for the edifying of the body of Christ [*the members of the Church*]:

Next, Paul teaches how long we will need this specific church organization.

13 Till we all come in the unity of the faith, and of the knowledge of the Son of God, unto a perfect man [*until we become perfect*], unto the measure of the stature of the fulness of Christ [*until we measure up to the perfection which Christ has attained*]:

<u>**JST Ephesians 4:13**</u>

13 **Till we, in the unity of the faith, all come to the knowledge of the Son of God,** unto a perfect man, unto the measure of the stature of the fullness of Christ;

Paul next gives us another reason why we need Apostles, prophets, and so forth.

14 That we henceforth be no more children [*immature in the gospel*], tossed to and fro [*thrown all over the place*], and carried about with every wind of doctrine [*all kinds of conflicting teachings*], by the sleight [*deception;* Strong's *#2940*] of men, and cunning craftiness, whereby they lie in wait to deceive [*they try to take us away from Christ by deceiving us*];

15 But speaking the truth in love, may grow up into him [*Christ*] in all things, which [*who*] is the head [*of the Church*], even Christ:

16 From whom the whole body [*Church*] fitly joined together [*properly working together*] and compacted [*helped*] by that which every joint [*office; member*] supplieth, according to the effectual working in the measure of every part [*according to the capacity of each officer and member*], maketh increase of the body [*strengthens the Church*] unto the edifying [*strengthening and building up*] of itself in [*through*] love.

17 This I say therefore [*to teach you these things*], and testify in the Lord, that ye henceforth [*from now on*] walk [*live*] not as other Gentiles walk, in the vanity of their mind [*in pride, arrogance*],

18 Having the understanding darkened [*losing spiritual understanding*], being alienated [*pushed away*] from the life of God through [*because of*] the ignorance that is in them, because of the blindness of their heart [*because they are spiritually blind*]:

19 Who being past feeling have given themselves over unto lasciviousness [*sexual immorality*], to work all uncleanness with greediness [*who are greedy for all kinds of wickedness*].

20 But ye have not so learned Christ [*this is not the way Christ taught you to be*];

21 If so be that ye have heard him [*if it happens that you have listened well to Christ*], and have been taught by him, as the truth is in Jesus [*since Jesus is the source of truth*]:

JST Ephesians 4:21

21 If so be that ye have **learned** him [*if it happens that you have learned the gospel well*], and have been taught by him, as the truth is in Jesus;

In verse 22, next, you will see an important definition. "Conversation," as used here and elsewhere, often means "lifestyle" or "behavior" rather than a discussion or chat between people.

22 That ye put off concerning the former conversation [*lifestyle*] the old man [*that you do away with your old, corrupt lifestyles and associations*], which is corrupt according to the deceitful lusts [*your old lifestyles were corrupt because you were fooled by worldly desires*];

JST Ephesians 4:22

22 **And now I speak unto you concerning the former conversation** [*way of life*], by exhortation, that ye put off the old man, which is corrupt according to the deceitful lusts;

23 And be renewed in the spirit of your mind [*be spiritually renewed in your minds, in other words, be "born again" through following the promptings of the Spirit*];

JST Ephesians 4:23

23 And be renewed **in the mind of the Spirit**;

24 And that ye put on the new man [*become "born again," as new, righteous people*], which after God is created in righteousness and true holiness [*made righteous and truly holy by following Christ*].

25 Wherefore putting away lying [*stop lying*], speak every man truth with his neighbour: for we are members one of another [*for we belong to each other*].

26 Be ye angry, and sin not: let not the sun go down upon your wrath:

JST Ephesians 4:26

26 **Can ye be angry, and not sin?** let not the sun go down upon your wrath;

27 Neither give place to the devil [*don't make room in your lives for the devil*].

28 Let him that stole steal no more: but rather let him labour, working with his hands the thing which is good [*earn his own living*], that he may have to give to him that needeth [*so that he can give to the poor*].

JST Ephesians 4:28

28 Let him that stole steal no more; but rather let him labor, working with his hands **for the things** which **are** good, that he may have to give to him that needeth.

29 Let no corrupt communication [*evil speech*] proceed out of your mouth, but that which is good to the use of edifying [*say only things which strengthen and build up*], that it may minister grace unto the hearers [*so that it strengthens those who hear you*].

30 And grieve not the holy Spirit of God [*don't offend the Holy Ghost*], whereby ye are sealed unto the day of redemption. [*In other words, don't do things that will make it so that the Holy Spirit of Promise (the Holy Ghost) can't seal you to exaltation. See Ephesians 1:13.*]

31 Let all bitterness, and wrath [*rage*], and anger, and clamour [*irreverent noise*], and evil speaking [*slander*], be put away from you, with [*along with*] all malice [*depravity, naughtiness;* Strong's *#2549*]:

32 And be ye kind one to another, tenderhearted, forgiving one another, even as God for Christ's sake [*through Christ's Atonement*] hath forgiven you.

EPHESIANS 5

As Paul continues to encourage the Ephesian Saints to live the gospel in their daily lives, he counsels them to develop Christ like love for one another. He also warns them about specific sins which are all around them in society.

1 BE ye therefore followers of God, as dear children [*like dearly beloved children;* Strong's *#0027*];

2 And walk in love, as Christ also hath loved us, and hath given himself for us an offering [*as an offering*] and a sacrifice to God for a sweetsmelling savour [*as a sacrifice which was pleasing to God;* Strong's *#2175*].

3 But fornication, and all uncleanness, or covetousness, let it not be once named among you [*don't even have a hint of it among you*], as becometh saints; [*In other words, behave like Saints.*]

4 Neither [*nor*] filthiness [*obscenity;* Strong's *#0151*], nor foolish talking, nor jesting [*course joking;* Strong's *#2160*], which are not convenient [*not appropriate;* Strong's *#0433*]: but rather giving of thanks [*gratitude to God*].

Next, Paul teaches against sins which, if not repented of, will lead to telestial glory (see D&C 76:103).

5 For this ye know, that no whoremonger [*one who intentionally seeks sexual immorality as a lifestyle*], nor unclean person, nor covetous man [*one who covets*], who is an idolater [*who worships idols*], hath any inheritance in the kingdom of Christ and of God [*in the celestial kingdom*].

6 Let no man deceive you with vain [*flattering*] words: for because of these things [*these sins*] cometh the wrath [*punishments*] of God upon the children of disobedience [*people who disobey God's commandments*].

7 Be not ye therefore partakers with them [*don't participate in such sins*].

8 For ye were sometimes darkness [*in spiritual darkness*], but now are ye light in the Lord [*you have spiritual light from Christ*]: walk as children of light [*followers of Christ*]:

9 (For the fruit [*product*] of the Spirit is in [*is observed in*] all goodness and righteousness and truth;)

10 Proving [*test, evaluate*] what is acceptable unto the Lord.

11 And have no fellowship with [*do not participate in*] the unfruitful [*unproductive*] works of darkness [*evil*], but rather reprove [*expose;* Strong's #*1651*] them.

12 For it is a shame even to speak of those things which are done of them in secret [*it is a shame to even talk about such secret works of darkness*].

13 But all things that are reproved [*exposed*] are made manifest by the light [*are exposed by the light of the gospel*]: for whatsoever doth make manifest is light [*anything that exposes evil and wickedness is light*].

14 Wherefore [*this is why*] he saith, Awake thou that sleepest, and arise from the dead [*the spiritually dead*], and Christ shall give thee light.

15 See then that ye walk circumspectly [*exercise wisdom in how you live your lives*], not as fools, but as wise,

16 Redeeming the time [*making the best use of your time*], because the days are evil [*because there is plenty of wickedness around*].

17 Wherefore be ye not unwise, but understanding what the will of the Lord is.

<u>JST Ephesians 5:17</u>

17 Wherefore be ye not unwise, but understanding **what is the will of the Lord**.

18 And be not drunk with wine, wherein is excess [*which leads to lustful wickedness*]; but be filled with the Spirit;

19 Speaking to yourselves in psalms and hymns and spiritual songs, singing and making melody in your heart to the Lord;

In verse 20, next, we are reminded that we are to pray to the Father in the name of Jesus Christ. This may seem simple and obvious to us, but there are many in the world who do not know how to pray and wish they did.

20 Giving thanks always for all things unto God and the Father

[*unto God the Father*] in the name of our Lord Jesus Christ;

21 Submitting yourselves one to another [*cooperating with one another;* Strong's *#5293*] in the fear of [*out of respect, reverence for;* Strong's *#5401*] God.

Various translations and explanations of Paul's words in verses 22–24, next, often cause confusion and resentment. When we come to such verses in the Bible, where misinterpretation and misunderstanding is possible, we need to step back and ask ourselves, "What do our current prophets teach us respecting this topic?" In this case, the topic concerns the relationship between husband and wife. There is safety in "following the Brethren." What do the "Brethren" say on the topic of equality of husbands and wives? The answer is clear.

James E. Faust said, "Nowhere does the doctrine of this Church declare that men are superior to women" (In Conference Report, April 1988, p. 43). President Faust also said, "Every father is to his family a patriarch and every mother a matriarch as coequals in their distinctive parental roles" ("The Prophetic Voice," April 1996 General Conference). President Joseph F. Smith said, referring to parents, "They stand as the head of the family, the patriarch, the mother, the rulers" (*Gospel Doctrine*, published by Deseret Book, 1977, p. 161).

Thus, it becomes obvious that there is a difference between how priesthood holders "preside" in the Church and the role of priesthood in the home. In the Proclamation on the Family, given September 23, 1995, the First Presidency and the Quorum of the Twelve said, ". . . fathers and mothers are obligated to help one another as equal partners." Thus, our modern prophets have spoken clearly on the relationship between husbands and wives. President Spencer W. Kimball used the word "cooperate" (see verse 22, below) in describing the relationship between woman and man. (See *Ensign*, March 1976, p. 71.)

22 Wives, submit yourselves unto [*voluntarily cooperate with;* Strong's Exhaustive Concordance of the Bible, *#5293*] your own husbands, as unto the Lord.

Ephesians 5:22, footnote a, in our Bible, suggests that continuing courtship is an important ingredient in correct understanding of verse 22.

23 For the husband is the head of the wife, even as Christ is the head of the church [*see verse 25*]: and he is the saviour of the body [*the marriage*].

24 Therefore as the church is subject unto Christ, so let the wives be to their own husbands in every thing.

We are blessed to be led by inspired prophets of God, members of the First Presidency and the Twelve. We will use their teachings to offer yet additional clarification for these verses.

In "The Family: A Proclamation to the World," the First Presidency and Council of the Twelve Apostles said, "By divine design, fathers are to preside over their families in love and righteousness and are responsible to provide the necessities of life and protection of their families."

Perhaps you are aware that there is a difference between the role of priesthood in the Church as an organization and the role of the priesthood in the family unit. In the Church it provides order, a definite vertical line of government, a hierarchy of leadership, a definite "person in charge." Whereas, in the family, it serves in full partnership and equality with the wife. It is when the role of priesthood in the Church is imposed upon the family, or vice versa, that trouble arises. Elder Boyd K. Packer explained this difference between how the priesthood functions in the Church and in the home. He said, "There is a difference in the way the priesthood functions in the home as compared to the way it functions in the Church . . . . In the Church there is a distinct line of authority . . . . In the home it is a partnership with husband and wife equally yoked together, sharing in decisions, always working together." (See talk entitled, "The Relief Society," April 1998 General Conference.)

25 Husbands, love your wives, even as Christ also loved the church, and gave himself for it [*men should treat their wives as the Savior would treat them*];

26 That he [*Christ*] might sanctify [*make it pure and holy*] and cleanse it [*the Church*] with the washing of water [*through baptism of converts and through the recommitment which should accompany partaking of the sacrament*] by the word [*through His gospel*],

27 That he might present it to himself a glorious church, not having spot, or wrinkle, or any such thing; but that it should be holy and without blemish. [*The Savior works with the members of the Church through His gospel and Atonement, so that He can eventually make them pure and spotless and fit to enter celestial glory.*]

28 So ought men to love their wives as their own bodies. He that loveth his wife loveth himself [*he who loves his wife is doing the very best possible thing for himself*].

29 For no man ever yet hated his own flesh; but nourisheth and cherisheth it, even as the Lord the church [*the same as the Lord treats the Church*]:

30 For we are members of his body, of his flesh, and of his bones [*we are united with Christ through the gospel*].

31 For this cause [*for the purpose of having happy marriages*] shall a man leave his father and mother,

and shall be joined unto his wife [*make his wife top priority*], and they two shall be one flesh [*shall work together in unity and cooperation*].

32 This is a great mystery [*this may sound like a deep mystery*]: but I speak concerning Christ and the church [*but Christ and the Church are symbolic of a good marriage between a man and a woman*].

33 Nevertheless let every one of you in particular so love his wife even as himself; and the wife see that she reverence her husband [*treat her husband with courtesy and respect (see Ephesians 5:33, footnote b, in our Bible)*].

EPHESIANS 6

In this chapter, Paul continues offering counsel that will strengthen families. Also, you will probably recognize verses 11–17 because they are rather famous and often quoted in sermons and lessons.

There are no JST changes for this chapter.

1 CHILDREN, obey your parents in the Lord [*as the Lord would have you do*]: for this is right.

2 Honour thy father and mother; (which is the first commandment with promise [*which is the first of the Ten Commandments with a positive promise attached; see Exodus 20:12*];)

3 That it may be well with thee, and thou mayest live long on the earth [*the promise attached to that commandment*].

4 And, ye fathers, provoke not your children to wrath [*rage*]: but bring them up in the nurture and admonition [*teachings*] of the Lord.

As we move on to verse 5, it helps to know that in Paul's day there was slavery. There were also numerous servants who had sold themselves to owners for a certain number of years in order to satisfy obligations or improve their own status, etc.

5 Servants, be obedient to them that are your masters according to the flesh [*here on earth, even though your ultimate loyalty should be to God*], with fear and trembling [*with respect and humility*], in singleness of your heart [*with pure motives*], as unto Christ;

6 Not with eyeservice [*not only when your masters are watching you*], as menpleasers [*to look good when you have to*]; but as the servants of Christ, doing the will of God from the heart; [*In other words, do a good job of whatever you are asked to do and do it from your heart.*]

7 With good will doing service, as to the Lord, and not to men [*serve with all your heart, as if you were serving God, not men*]:

8 Knowing that whatsoever good thing any man doeth, the same shall he receive of the Lord, whether he be bond or free [*you will be rewarded by God for whatever*

good you do, whether you are a slave, servant, or free citizen].

9 And, ye masters, do the same things unto them [*and you who own slaves or servants should treat them the same as I have told them to treat you*], forbearing threatening [*avoiding threatening them*]: knowing that your Master [*God*] also is in heaven; neither is there respect of persons with him [*God respects each person for who he or she is, not because of social status or position*].

10 Finally, my brethren, be strong in the Lord, and in the power of his might [*in His mighty power*].

Verses 11–17, next, are often quoted and constitute one of Paul's more famous teachings using symbolism. He uses the symbolism of preparing for a serious battle and thus warns us that we need to put on the full gospel of Jesus Christ in order to be protected from the devil and come out triumphant in celestial glory.

11 Put on the whole armour of God, that ye may be able to stand against the wiles [*cunning temptations*] of the devil.

12 For we wrestle not against flesh and blood [*we are not only fighting against evil people*], but against principalities, against powers, against the rulers of the darkness of this world, against spiritual wickedness in high places.

13 Wherefore [*therefore*] take unto you [*put on*] the whole armour of God [*the protection of the whole gospel*], that ye may be able to withstand [*come out the winner*] in the evil day, and having done all, to stand [*to remain standing, as a soldier who survives in battle does when the battle is over*].

"Gird up your loins" is a scriptural phrase which usually means "prepare for action." Or, "don't get caught off guard." We see one form of this used by Paul in verse 14, next.

14 Stand [*win*] therefore, having your loins girt about with truth [*be prepared for action with truth*], and having on the breastplate [*the protection*] of righteousness;

15 And your feet shod with the preparation of the gospel of peace;

16 Above all, taking the shield of faith, wherewith ye shall be able to quench all the fiery darts of the wicked.

Faith is indeed a great and fundamental power in our lives. Joseph Smith, in *Lectures on Faith*, lecture number one, emphasizes that faith is a principle of action as well as a principle of power. In other words, faith compels us to action, to good works, to faithful church attendance, to forgiving others, to repenting, to fleeing evil company, and so on. In Hebrews, chapter 11, Paul teaches the power of faith in the lives of many great people, including Enoch, Noah, Abraham, Sarah, and others, who triumphed over "all the fiery darts of the wicked" spoken of in verse 16 above.

17 And take the helmet of salvation, and the sword of the Spirit, which is the word of God:

The imagery of the "word of God" being like a "sword" is used often in the scriptures. See Topical Guide under "Sword." Thus, the "word of God" cuts through false doctrines and mistaken thinking like a "sword."

For instance, some teach that little children who are not baptized and who die in infancy, are doomed forever. The true "word of God" cuts quickly and completely through this terrible false doctrine and gives comfort by teaching clearly that this is not so (see D&C 137:10 plus Moroni, chapter 8.) Many nowadays, as was the case in the days of Paul, teach that premarital or extramarital sex is just fine. The "word of God" cuts right through this evil falsehood in numerous scriptural passages as well as through modern prophets. Thus, a person who is "armed" with the "word of God" and who uses that mighty "sword" does not fall prey to such evil.

18 Praying always with all prayer [*in all your prayers*] and supplication [*requests to God*] in the Spirit [*as directed by the Holy Ghost*], and watching thereunto [*to that end*] with all perseverance and supplication [*keep praying faithfully*] for all saints;

19 And for me, that utterance may be given unto me [*that I may know what to teach and how to teach it*], that I may open my mouth boldly, to make known the mystery of the gospel [*the simple truths of the gospel which are still a mystery to so many*],

20 For which I am an ambassador in bonds [*I am a messenger of the gospel who is still in prison in Rome*]: that therein I may speak boldly, as I ought to speak [*and I need your faith and prayers for me so that I can write clearly and boldly to teach the gospel*].

21 But that [*so that*] ye also may know my affairs, and how I do, Tychicus [*a faithful member who accompanied Paul on some of his missionary journeys; see* Strong's *#5190*], a beloved brother and faithful minister in the Lord, shall make known to you all things:

22 Whom I have sent unto you for the same purpose, that ye might know our affairs, and that he might comfort your hearts. [*In other words, I've sent Tychicus to visit you, and he will fill you in on everything that is going on with me.*]

23 Peace be to the brethren, and love with faith, from God the Father and the Lord Jesus Christ.

24 Grace be with all them that love our Lord Jesus Christ in sincerity. Amen.

THE EPISTLE OF PAUL THE APOSTLE TO THE PHILIPPIANS

As was the case with Paul's letter to the Ephesian Saints, it seems that the Philippian members of the Church were living the gospel. Thus, there seems to be no real dominant problem among them which Paul addresses. At the time Paul wrote this letter to the Saints at Philippi (in what would be known as northeastern Greece today), Paul was still a prisoner in Rome. Thus, most scholars agree that this letter was written and sent sometime in AD 63. They also believe that this was probably the last letter written by Paul during his first imprisonment in Rome, before he was released. Philippi was the first city on what we now refer to as the European continent to receive the gospel. Paul was told in a vision to go there (Acts 16:9).

PHILIPPIANS 1

In this chapter, Paul compliments and reinforces the good in the lives of the Philippian saints. You will also see him be philosophical and upbeat about the many afflictions he has encountered as he has gone about his ministry.

1 PAUL and Timotheus [*Timothy*], the servants of Jesus Christ, to all the saints in Christ Jesus [*to all the members of the Church*] which are at Philippi, with the bishops and deacons:

2 Grace be unto you, and peace, from God our Father, and from the Lord Jesus Christ.

Verse 2, above, is another reminder that the Father and Son are two separate personages.

3 I thank my God upon every remembrance of you [*I give thanks to God every time I think of you*],

4 Always in every prayer of mine for you all making request [*praying for you*] with joy,

JST Philippians 1:4

4 Always in every prayer of mine, **for the steadfastness of** you all, making request with joy,

5 For your fellowship [*I thank God for your association with me*] in the gospel from the first day until now;

6 Being confident of this very thing, that he [*the Father*] which hath begun a good work in you [*who has introduced the gospel to you*] will perform it [*will continue working with you*] until the day of

Jesus Christ [*until Judgment Day; see McConkie,* Doctrinal New Testament Commentary, *Vol. 2, p. 528*]:

7 Even as it is meet [*necessary*] for me to think this of you all, because I have you in my heart; inasmuch as both in my bonds [*while I am in prison here in Rome*], and in the defence and confirmation of the gospel [*and as I defend and bear testimony of the gospel*], ye all are partakers of my grace [*you are participants with me in the grace of God*].

8 For God is my record [*God is my witness*], how greatly I long after you all [*how my heart yearns for you*] in the bowels [*the tender affection;* Strong's *#4698*] of Jesus Christ.

9 And this I pray, that your love may abound [*increase*] yet more and more in knowledge and in all judgment [*wisdom*];

10 That ye may approve [*recognize:* Strong's *#1381*] things that are excellent; that ye may be sincere and without offence [*and set a good example to others;* Strong's *#0677*] till the day of Christ;

11 Being filled with the fruits [*end results*] of righteousness, which are by Jesus Christ [*which come as a result of following Christ*], unto the glory and praise of God [*and which bring glory and honor to the Father*].

12 But I would ye should understand, brethren, that the things which happened unto me have fallen out rather unto the furtherance of the gospel [*I want you to understand that the seemingly bad things that have happened to me have actually helped further the gospel cause*];

13 So that my bonds in Christ [*so that my being in prison because of my faith in Christ*] are manifest in all the palace, and in all other places [*has called attention to the gospel throughout the Roman emperor's palace and everywhere else*];

14 And many of the brethren in the Lord [*many of the members*], waxing [*growing*] confident by my bonds [*because I am here in prison*], are much more bold to speak the word [*spread the gospel*] without fear. [*In other words, many members are not so afraid anymore to share the gospel because of my being here in prison.*]

Even though much good is being done because Paul is there in Rome under house arrest (he was there for two years under such conditions), there are still some members who do not teach the gospel out of love, but rather because they enjoy stirring up contention. Paul refers to them in the next verses.

15 Some indeed preach Christ [*preach the gospel*] even of envy and strife [*because they enjoy creating contention*]; and some also of good will [*and some preach it with good motives*]:

16 The one preach Christ of contention [*the ones who create contention with the gospel*], not sincerely, supposing to add affliction to my bonds [*are trying to make life more miserable for me*]:

17 But the other of love [*but others preach out of love*], knowing that I am set [*knowing that I am called of God;* Strong's #*2749*] for the defence of the gospel [*to defend the gospel*].

Paul's attitude about the fact that some of his enemies ridicule him and the gospel of Christ, while others teach the gospel with testimony and conviction, is a good lesson for us. His attitude, as seen in verse 18, next, is that either way, people are becoming aware of Christ and His Church. So they also are in our day. Enemies and unknowing people write unkind things in national magazines about the Church. People who don't like the Church make films and videos, write editorials, appear on local or national TV, criticizing us. Paul would probably say, "Don't let it upset you. It is all free advertising!" Indeed, missionaries usually find more success after intense efforts on the part of our enemies and detractors to discredit the Church.

18 What then [*what does it matter*]? notwithstanding [*regardless*], every way [*either way*], whether in pretence [*with evil motives*], or in truth [*or with good motives*], Christ is preached [*Christ and the Church get more public recognition*]; and I therein do rejoice [*and that makes me happy*], yea, and will rejoice.

19 For I know that this shall turn to my salvation through your prayer [*your prayers for me will help all this opposition work toward my salvation*], and the supply of the Spirit of Jesus Christ [*and it will also help the Spirit of Christ, which every person who is born into the world has (see John 1:9) to guide people to the true Church*],

20 According to my earnest [*sincere*] expectation and my hope, that in nothing I shall be ashamed [*that I will not fail in anything*], but that with all boldness, as always, so now also Christ shall be magnified in my body, whether it be by life, or by death. [*I trust that I will not let anyone down, rather that I will continue to represent Christ boldly, whether I live or die.*]

21 For to me to live is Christ, and to die is gain.

22 But if I live in the flesh, this is the fruit of my labour: yet what I shall choose I wot not.

Joseph Smith switched the order of verses 21 and 22, above, and gave them as follows in the JST:

JST Philippians 1:21

21 But if I live in the flesh, **ye are** the fruit of my labor [*if I am not executed, I will have the advantage of being with you whom I brought into the Church*]. Yet what I shall choose [*what will happen to me*] **I know not**.

JST Philippians 1:22

22 For me to live, **is to do the will of Christ; and to die, is my** gain.

23 For I am in a strait betwixt two [*I am caught between two desirable alternatives*], having a desire to depart, and to be with Christ [*I would love to die and thus be with Christ*]; which is far better:

JST Philippians 1:23

23 **Now** I am in a strait betwixt two, having a desire to depart, and to be with Christ; which is far better;

24 Nevertheless to abide in the flesh is more needful for you [*but if I remain here on earth, I can be more helpful to you*].

25 And having this confidence [*and knowing this is true*], I know that I shall abide [*I know that I will not die for a while*] and continue with you all for your furtherance and joy of faith;

26 That your rejoicing may be more abundant in Jesus Christ for me by my coming to you again.

JST Philippians 1:26

26 That your rejoicing **with me** may be more abundant in Jesus Christ, **for** [*because of*] my coming to you again.

27 Only let your conversation [*your behavior, your lives;* Strong's *#4176*] be as it becometh [*be in harmony with*] the gospel of Christ: that whether I come and see you, or else be absent, I may hear of your affairs [*doings*], that ye stand fast in one spirit [*that you are solidly united*], with one mind [*in harmony with each other*] striving [*working*] together for the faith of the gospel;

JST Philippians 1:27

27 **Therefore** let your conversation be as it becometh the gospel of Christ; that whether I come and see you, or else be absent, I may hear of your affairs, that ye stand fast in one spirit, with one mind striving together for the faith of the gospel;

28 And in nothing terrified by your adversaries: which is to them an evident token of perdition, but to you of salvation, and that of God.

JST Philippians 1:28

28 And in nothing terrified by your adversaries, **who reject the gospel,** which bringeth on them destruction; **but you who receive the gospel, salvation**; and that of God.

29 For unto you it is given in the behalf of Christ, not only to believe on him, but also to suffer for his sake; [*In other words, it is a privilege for you to not only believe in Christ, but also to suffer in behalf of Christ just as it is for me to do so.*]

30 Having the same conflict which ye saw in me, and now hear to be in me. [*In other words, you have the privilege of having the same struggles you saw me have in*

times past and know that I am still enduring now.]

JST Philippians 1:30

30 Having the same conflict which ye saw in me, and now **know** to be in me.

PHILIPPIANS 2

Paul is a master teacher, and he starts off this segment of his letter to the Philippians by saying, in effect, "If the gospel has proven beneficial to you in any way, I hope you will make my joy full by being united together in kindness and love for each other."

1 IF there be therefore [*because of the gospel I brought to you*] any consolation [*comfort, solace;* Strong's *#3874*] in Christ, if any comfort of love [*because of His love for you*], if any fellowship of the Spirit [*companionship of the Holy Ghost*], if any bowels [*tender feelings*] and mercies,

2 Fulfil ye my joy [*make my joy complete*], that ye be likeminded [*live in harmony with one another*], having the same love, being of one accord [*united*], of one mind [*united in thought*].

3 Let nothing be done through strife [*contention*] or vainglory [*foolish pride;* Strong's *#2754*]; but in lowliness of mind [*humility*] let each esteem other better than themselves [*consider the needs of others to be more important than their own needs*].

4 Look not every man on his own things [*don't only be concerned about your own needs, in other words, don't be selfish*], but every man also on the things of others [*but be concerned about the needs of others also*].

5 Let this mind [*attitude*] be in you, which was also in Christ Jesus: [*In other words, learn to think like Christ.*]

6 Who, being in the form of God [*who looks just like the Father; see Hebrews 1:3*], thought it not robbery [*not taking anything away from the Father's status*] to be equal with God: [*In other words, even though Christ, during His mortal ministry, constantly taught that the Father was greater than He (example: John 14:28), He now has been resurrected and is equal with the Father in the sense that He has completed what the Father asked Him to do and thus, the Father has given Him "all things" (D&C 76:55). Therefore, He has entered into His exaltation, just as all faithful Saints will when "all that my Father hath shall be given unto (them)." (D&C 84:38.)*]

7 But made himself of no reputation [*did not seek glory for Himself*], and took upon him the form of a servant [*and became the servant of all, providing the Atonement for them*], and was made in the likeness of men [*and took upon Himself a mortal body*]:

8 And being found in fashion as a man [*and having taken upon Himself mortality*], he humbled

himself, and became obedient unto death [*He was humbly obedient to the Father*], even the death of the cross [*even to the point of suffering crucifixion*].

9 Wherefore [*because of that*] God [*the Father*] also hath highly exalted him [*has given Him exaltation*], and given him a name which is above every name [*and given Him power to judge all people; see John 5:22*]:

10 That at the name of Jesus every knee should bow [*everyone will ultimately acknowledge that Jesus is the Christ; see D&C 76:112*], of things in heaven, and things in earth, and things under the earth [*all things have thus become subject to Christ*];

11 And that every tongue should confess [*acknowledge*] that Jesus Christ is Lord, to the glory of God the Father.

12 Wherefore [*therefore*], my beloved, as ye have always obeyed, not as in my presence only, but now much more in my absence, work out your own salvation with fear and trembling [*acute awareness of how important it is to be righteous*].

President David O. McKay explained verse 12, above, as follows: "To work out one's salvation is not to sit idly by dreaming and yearning for God miraculously to thrust bounteous blessings into our laps. It is to perform daily, hourly, momentarily, if necessary, the immediate task or duty at hand, and to continue happily in such performance as the years come and go, leaving the fruits of such labors either for self or for others to be bestowed as a just and beneficent Father may determine." (David O. McKay in Conference Report, Apr. 1957, p. 7.)

13 For it is God which worketh in you both to will and to do of his good pleasure. [*It is God who works with you to help you to want to truly be good as well as to do good.*]

14 Do all things without murmurings [*complaining*] and disputings [*contentions*]:

15 That ye may be [*Greek Bible says "become"*] blameless [*innocent of sin*] and harmless, the sons of God [*followers of God*], without rebuke [*of good reputation*], in the midst of a crooked and perverse [*corrupt;* Strong's *#1294*] nation [*generation;* Strong's *#1074*], among whom ye shine as lights in the world;

16 Holding forth the word of life [*holding up the gospel for all to see*]; that I may rejoice in the day of Christ [*on Judgment Day*], that I have not run in vain, neither laboured in vain [*that my work in bringing you the gospel may not have been without good results*].

17 Yea, and if I be offered upon the sacrifice and service of your faith [*even though I am now in*

prison, being in effect "sacrificed" because of bringing the gospel of Christ to you and others], I joy, and rejoice with you all.

JST Philippians 2:17

17 Yea, and if I be offered **a sacrifice upon the service of your faith**, I joy, and rejoice with you all.

18 For the same cause [*you also have to sacrifice for the gospel*] also do ye joy [*which brings joy to you*], and rejoice with me [*and, thus, you can rejoice with me*].

19 But I trust in the Lord Jesus [*I trust that the Lord will enable me*] to send Timotheus [*Timothy*] shortly [*soon*] unto you, that I also may be of good comfort [*that I may be cheered up*], when I know your state [*when I find out how you are getting along*].

20 For I have no man likeminded, who will naturally care for your state [*there is no one else who cares for you like Timothy does, who will take such a genuine interest in your well-being*].

21 For all seek their own [*most people seek to do as they please*], not the things which are Jesus Christ's [*rather than prioritizing on what Christ taught*].

22 But ye know the proof of him [*you know that Timothy has "passed the test"*], that, as a son with the father [*that, like a son working with his father*], he hath served with me in the gospel.

23 Him therefore I hope to send presently, so soon as I shall see how it will go with me [*as soon as I get an idea of what is going to happen to me here in Rome, I hope to send Timothy to you*].

24 But I trust in the Lord that I also myself shall come shortly [*I hope to visit you myself soon*].

Most scholars think that when Paul was finally released from his two-year house arrest in Rome, he went to Philippi to rest there for a while, then went on from there to visit the members of the Church in Ephesus.

25 Yet I supposed it necessary [*I found it necessary*] to send to you Epaphroditus [*to send Epaphroditus back home to you*], my brother, and companion in labour, and fellowsoldier, but your messenger [*whom you sent to me to help take care of my needs here in Rome*], and he that ministered to my wants [*he performed great service for me while he was here*].

26 For he longed after you all [*because he became very homesick for you*], and was full of heaviness [*and got depressed*], because that ye had heard that he had been sick [*because, as you have heard, he became very sick*].

27 For indeed he was sick nigh unto death [*in fact, he nearly died*]: but God had mercy on him; and not on him only, but on me also, lest I should have sorrow upon sorrow [*because if he had died, it would have been almost more than I could bear*].

28 I sent him therefore the more carefully [*the more quickly*], that, when ye see him again, ye may rejoice, and that I may be the less sorrowful [*less worried about him*].

29 Receive him therefore in the Lord with all gladness; and hold such in reputation [*and hold such men as he in high regard*]:

30 Because for the work of Christ [*because of his work for the Lord*] he was nigh unto death [*he almost died*], not regarding his life [*willing to give his life*], to supply your lack of service toward me [*to do for me what you couldn't do because I am so far away from you*].

PHILIPPIANS 3

The wording here, at the beginning of chapter 3 indicates that Paul is repeating some counsel he has given these members of the Church previously. However, we have no record of when he gave it.

1 FINALLY, my brethren, rejoice in the Lord [*find joy in living the gospel*]. To write the same things to you, to me indeed is not grievous [*I don't mind writing the same things to you again*], but for you it is safe [*and it will help safeguard you against evil*].

JST Philippians 3:1

1 Finally, my brethren, rejoice in the Lord. To write the same things to you, to me indeed is not grievous, **and** for you it is safe.

2 Beware of dogs, beware of evil workers, beware of the concision.

An explanation of verse 2, above, is given in the Institute of Religion's New Testament student manual, *The Life and Teachings of Jesus and His Apostles*, 1979, p. 361, as follows: "Paul was attacking the Judaizers—those Jewish Christians who demanded complete obedience to the Mosaic law as a condition for salvation. He used the word dogs to imply that they were unclean and unholy. His use of the words evil workers indicates those who thought they were righteous and in fact were not. In sarcasm he used the word concision, which means mutilation, instead of circumcision, which is the normal adjective used to define Jews."

3 For we are the circumcision [*we are Jews*], which worship God in the spirit, and rejoice in Christ Jesus, and have no confidence in the flesh [*and have no confidence in being saved by the law of Moses*].

4 Though I might also have confidence in the flesh [*although I am one who could very well have continued to live the law of Moses*]. If any other man thinketh that he hath whereof he might trust in the flesh, I more [*in fact, I probably have more reason to stay with the law of Moses than most men; in other words, I was raised in a very strict Jewish home, where the law of Moses was lived to the letter.*]

5 Circumcised the eighth day, of the stock of Israel [*a descendant of Abraham, Isaac, and Jacob*], of the tribe of Benjamin, an Hebrew of the Hebrews [*I was a "Hebrew's Hebrew," in other words, a model Jew*]; as touching the law, a Pharisee [*as far as the law of Moses was concerned, I was a Pharisee*];

Among the Jews, the Pharisees were the strictest of all in adhering to the law of Moses. See Bible Dictionary under "Pharisees."

6 Concerning zeal, persecuting the church [*I was a most energetic persecutor of this new church started by Jesus*]; touching the righteousness which is in the law, blameless [*I lived the law of Moses down to the very tiniest details*].

7 But what things were gain to me, those I counted loss for Christ [*and that was a big social advantage to me among the Jews, but I gave it all up to follow Christ*].

8 Yea doubtless [*that was absolutely the case*], and I count all things but loss for the excellency of the knowledge of Christ Jesus my Lord [*I would indeed be the loser if I put anything else above the gospel of Christ*]: for whom I have suffered the loss of all things [*I have lost basically everything because of my loyalty to Christ*], and do count them but dung [*and consider what I have lost to be nothing but rubbish;* Strong's *#4657*], that I may win Christ [*that I may win the real prize, which is Christ and His gospel in my life*],

9 And be found in him [*and be found loyal to Christ*], not having mine own righteousness, which is of the law [*not appearing righteous to others, which is often the goal of those who keep the law of Moses*], but that [*true righteousness*] which is [*comes*] through the faith of Christ, the righteousness which is of God [*which comes from the Father*] by faith [*through faith in Christ*]:

10 That I may know him [*Christ*], and the power of his resurrection, and the fellowship of his sufferings, being made conformable unto his death [*conforming to the gospel which lets His Atonement work for me*];

11 If by any means I might attain unto the resurrection of the dead.

JST Philippians 3:11

11 If by any means I might attain unto the resurrection of the **just**.

The change made in the Joseph Smith Translation in verse 11, above, is very significant doctrinally. Some Christians who read verse 11 as it stands in our Bible, claim that this proves that all people will not be resurrected, whereas, what Paul was teaching is that he hopes to be resurrected with those who attain celestial exaltation, in other words, the "resurrection of the just." Thus, some Christians dispute our doctrine that everyone who has ever been born will be resurrected. Of course, Paul taught that all will be resurrected, in 1 Corinthians 15:22.

12 Not as though I had already attained, either were already perfect [*it is not as if I have already attained exaltation or were already perfect*]: but I follow after [*but I am pressing forward in that direction*], if that [*in the hope that*] I may apprehend that [*obtain that*] for which also [*for which purpose*] I am apprehended of Christ Jesus [*Christ has taken me in*].

13 Brethren, I count not myself to have apprehended [*I have not attained this goal yet*]: but this one thing I do, forgetting those things which are behind, and reaching forth unto those things which are before, [*In other words, here is how I plan to attain this goal. I leave the past behind and take advantage of the opportunities to do better which lie before me*].

14 I press toward the mark for the prize of the high calling of God in Christ Jesus [*I continue pressing forward toward the prize of exaltation*].

15 Let us therefore, as many as be perfect [*are mature enough to understand what I am saying;* Strong's *#5046*], be thus minded [*keep this in mind*]: and if in any thing ye be otherwise minded [*and if you think otherwise, with respect to anything I have said*], God shall reveal even this unto you [*God will help you understand*].

16 Nevertheless, whereto we have already attained, let us walk by the same rule, let us mind the same thing [*but let's stick with the progress we have already made in the gospel*].

17 Brethren, be followers together of me [*be united in following me*], and mark them which walk so as ye have us for an ensample [*and take note of those who follow what we taught you and use them for an example*].

18 (For many walk, of whom I have told [*warned*] you often, and now tell you even weeping, that they are the enemies of the cross of Christ [*many are not living exemplary lives and have thus become enemies of Christ's gospel*]:

JST Philippians 3:18

18 (For many walk, of whom I have told you often, and now tell you even weeping, **as the** enemies of the cross of Christ;

19 Whose end is destruction [*they will eventually be destroyed*], whose God is their belly [*who worship the "gods" of physical desires*], and whose glory is in their shame, who mind earthly things [*who think only of worldly things*].)

JST Philippians 3:19

19 Whose end is destruction, whose God is their belly, and **who glory in their shame**, who mind earthly things.)

20 For our conversation is in heaven [*we are governed by heaven;* Strong's *#4175*]; from whence also we look for the Saviour, the Lord Jesus Christ [*and we look to the Savior for guidance*]:

21 Who shall change [*resurrect*] our vile body [*lowly mortal body*],

that it may be fashioned [*become*] like unto his glorious body, according to the working whereby he is able even to subdue all things unto himself [*because of the power He has over all things*].

For Paul to teach that we can have glorious resurrected bodies like the Savior has is marvelous doctrine indeed! In 1 Corinthians 15:40, he spoke of "celestial bodies." In verse 21, above, and in the verses preceding it, he assures the Philippian Saints that they can have celestial bodies. D&C 88:28–32 explains that celestial bodies will be "natural" bodies, whereas, those who go to other kingdoms of glory will have terrestrial bodies or telestial bodies or son of perdition bodies, as the case may be. Joseph Fielding Smith taught about the differences in resurrected bodies as follows: "In the resurrection there will be different kinds of bodies; they will not all be alike. The body a man receives will determine his place hereafter. There will be celestial bodies, terrestrial bodies, and telestial bodies, and these bodies will differ as distinctly as do bodies here. . . Bodies will be quickened (resurrected) according to the kingdom which they are judged worthy to enter. . . Some will gain celestial bodies with all the powers of exaltation and eternal increase. These bodies will shine like the sun as our Savior's does, as described by John. Those who enter the terrestrial kingdom will have terrestrial bodies, and they will not shine like the sun, but they will be more glorious than the bodies of those who receive the telestial glory. In both of these kingdoms there will be changes in the bodies and limitations. They will not have the power of increase, neither the power or nature to live as husbands and wives, for this will be denied them and they cannot increase. Those who receive the exaltation in the celestial kingdom will have the 'continuation of the seeds forever.' They will live in the family relationship. In the terrestrial and in the telestial kingdoms there will be no marriage. Those who enter there will remain 'separately and singly' forever. Some of the functions in the celestial body will not appear in the terrestrial body, neither in the telestial body, and the power of procreation will be removed." (*Doctrines of Salvation*, Vol. 2, pp. 286–88.)

PHILIPPIANS 4

Paul now finishes his letter to the Philippian Saints, reminding them that the things he has written to them are designed to help them remain strong in the gospel. Verse 8 will likely sound familiar to you.

1 THEREFORE, my brethren dearly beloved and longed for, my joy and crown, so stand fast in the Lord [*what I have written above in this letter to you is how to remain firm and faithful in the gospel of*

Christ], my dearly beloved.

2 I beseech [*urge*] Euodias, and beseech Syntyche [*two female members of the Church in Philippi*], that they be of the same mind in the Lord [*that they get along with each other in the gospel*].

3 And I intreat thee also, true yokefellow [*associate; see Philippians 4:3, footnote a*], help those women which laboured [*worked*] with me in the gospel, with Clement [*probably a male member of the Church in Philippi*] also, and with other my fellowlabourers, whose names are in the book of life.

The "book of life" means those whose names are recorded in heaven as being faithful. See Bible Dictionary under "Book of Life."

4 Rejoice in the Lord alway [*always*]: and again I say, Rejoice.

You may recognize the words "again I say, Rejoice" as being part of Hymn #66, "Rejoice, the Lord Is King!," in our current hymn book.

5 Let your moderation [*fairness, mildness, patience;* Strong's *#1933*] be known unto all men. The Lord is at hand [*the Lord is not far from us*].

6 Be careful for nothing; [*In other words, don't worry too much about things of the world.*] but in every thing by prayer and supplication with thanksgiving let your requests be made known unto God [*pray to God with gratitude about all your concerns*].

JST Philippians 4:6

6 Be **afflicted for nothing**; but in everything by prayer and supplication with thanksgiving let your requests be made known unto God.

7 And the peace of God [*which comes from the Father*], which passeth all understanding [*which is beyond comparison to anything else*], shall keep [*guard and protect;* Strong's *#5432*] your hearts and minds through Christ Jesus [*through Christ and His gospel*].

You will immediately see the connection between verse 8, next, and the thirteenth Article of Faith, which says: "We believe in being honest, true, chaste, benevolent, virtuous, and in doing good to all men; indeed, we may say that we follow the admonition of Paul—We believe all things, we hope all things, we have endured many things, and hope to be able to endure all things. If there is anything virtuous, lovely, or of good report or praiseworthy, we seek after these things."

8 Finally, brethren, whatsoever [*whatever*] things are true, whatsoever things are honest, whatsoever things are just [*righteous*], whatsoever things are pure, whatsoever things are lovely, whatsoever things are of good report [*are excellent*]; if there be any virtue, and if there be any praise [*if there is anything that is praiseworthy*], think on these things [*keep such things on your mind constantly*].

9 Those things, which ye have both learned, and received, and heard, and seen in me, do: and the God of peace shall be with you.

10 But I rejoiced in the Lord greatly, that now at the last your care of me hath flourished again; wherein ye were also careful, but ye lacked opportunity. [*In other words, I know you have been worried about me, but you have not had any opportunity to help me.*]

11 Not that I speak in respect of want [*not that I am trying to make you think that I am in any great need*]: for I have learned, in whatsoever state I am, therewith to be content [*because I have learned to be content with whatever conditions I find myself in*].

12 I know both how to be abased [*I know how to live with many unmet needs*], and I know how to abound [*and I can get along fine when surrounded by plenty*]: every where and in all things I am instructed both to be full and to be hungry [*I have experienced having a full stomach and being hungry*], both to abound [*have plenty*] and to suffer need [*and to be in need*].

13 I can do all things through Christ which strengtheneth me.

14 Notwithstanding [*nevertheless*] ye have well done, that ye did communicate with my affliction [*in that you shared with me in my times of need*].

15 Now ye Philippians know also, that in the beginning of the gospel [*in the early days when you were just getting started in the gospel*], when I departed from Macedonia [*when I was leaving your area*], no church [*no other members*] communicated [*worked*] with me as concerning giving and receiving, but ye only.

16 For even in Thessalonica ye sent once and again unto my necessity [*even while I was in Thessalonica, you sent assistance to me time and time again*].

17 Not because I desire a gift [*not that I am looking for assistance from you now*]: but I desire fruit that may abound to your account [*but I want that which is best for you*].

18 But I have all, and abound [*all my needs are now being met*]: I am full, having received of Epaphroditus [*a faithful member of the Church who worked with Paul*] the things which were sent from you [*Epaphroditus brought me the things you sent*], an odour of a sweet smell [*an offering acceptable to God*], a sacrifice acceptable, wellpleasing to God.

19 But my God shall supply all your need according to his riches in glory by Christ Jesus [*God will take care of all your needs as He has mine*].

20 Now unto God and our Father be glory [*praises*] for ever and ever. Amen.

21 Salute [*greet*] every saint in Christ Jesus. The brethren which are with me greet you.

22 All the saints [*members of the Church*] salute [*greet*] you, chiefly they that are of Cæsar's household [*especially those who belong to Caesar's household*].

23 The grace of our Lord Jesus Christ be with you all. Amen.

THE EPISTLE OF PAUL THE APOSTLE TO THE COLOSSIANS

Most Bible scholars agree that Paul's letter to the Colossians in the small city of Colosse (about 11 miles southeast of Laodicea and about 90 to 100 miles east of Ephesus, in what is today western Turkey) was written about AD 62, during Paul's first imprisonment in Rome (see note at the end of Acts 28:31 in this study guide). The church in Colosse was established during Paul's third missionary journey during the three years he spent in Ephesus. It appears that one of Paul's converts named Epaphras (Colossians 1:7, 12, and 13), who was a citizen of Colosse and who was probably converted while visiting Ephesus, was sent by Paul to actually establish the Church in Colosse, although it may be that Paul himself established it there with the help of Epaphras.

In this letter, Paul expresses love and appreciation for the Colossian members and expresses concern that some of them seem to be reverting back to mechanically going through the motions of religion (2:16), rather than internalizing the gospel. He cautions against believing that angels can serve as mediators ("patron saints," etc.) between us and God (2:18.) He repeatedly reminds these members that it is only through Christ and His Atonement that we can attain celestial glory. He also explains that Jesus is the firstborn spirit child of the Father (1:15.)

COLOSSIANS 1

In this chapter, Paul gives one of the most beautiful and powerful testimonies ever given about Jesus Christ. You may want to mark several passages in chapter one in your own scriptures as well as make notes therein. Paul gives much doctrine about Christ which Latter-day Saints are in a position to understand better than any other people on earth. In fact, you may be aware that many Christian churches no longer agree with much of what Paul says here and other places about Christ and His commandments to us. Thus, it is a simple fact that faithful Latter-day Saints actually believe the Bible much more faithfully than any other Christians.

As mentioned above, one of the significant doctrines taught in this chapter is that Jesus Christ was the firstborn spirit child of the Father (verses 13–15). Thus, He is our "Elder Brother," and indeed is our oldest spirit brother.

1 PAUL, an apostle of Jesus Christ by the will of God [*called of God*], and Timotheus [*Timothy, one of Paul's favorite missionary companions who was like a son to Paul*] our brother,

2 To the saints and faithful brethren in Christ which are at Colosse [*a small city in what would be in western Turkey today, about 11 miles south of Laodicea*]: Grace be unto you, and peace, from God our Father and the Lord Jesus Christ.

3 We give thanks to God [*the Father*] and the Father [*who is the Father*] of our Lord Jesus Christ, praying always for you,

4 Since we heard of your faith in Christ Jesus, and of the love which ye have to [*toward*] all the saints [*members of the Church*],

JST Colossians 1:4

4 Since we heard of your faith in Christ Jesus, and **of your love** to all the saints,

The word "Saints" as used often by Paul in referring to members of the Church, means "holy" according to *Strong's* #0040. Thus, when we hear ourselves referred to as "Latter-day Saints," we are reminded that we should be trying to be "holy ones," people who are trying to faithfully follow the Savior and properly represent Him at all times and under all circumstances.

5 For the hope [*the prospect of attaining exaltation*] which is laid up [*which is in store*] for you in heaven, whereof ye heard before [*which you were taught in times past*] in the word of the truth of the gospel [*when you heard the truths of the gospel*];

6 Which is come [*has been brought*] unto you, as it is in all the world; and bringeth forth fruit [*and produces exaltation for the faithful*], as it doth also in you, since the day ye heard of it, and knew the grace of God in truth [*and you knew the truth, that the kindness and mercy of the Father are made available to us through the Atonement of Christ*]:

JST Colossians 1:6

6 Which is come unto you, **as in all generations of the world**; and bringeth forth fruit, as it doth also in you, since the day ye heard of it, and knew the grace of God in truth;

7 As ye also learned of [*as you were taught by*] Epaphras our dear fellowservant, who is for you a faithful minister of Christ [*see note*

about Epaphras at the beginning of Colossians in this study guide];

8 Who also declared unto us [*who told us about*] your love in the Spirit [*because of the Spirit which is with you*].

9 For this cause we also [*this is why we*], since the day we heard it, do not cease to pray for you, and to desire that ye might be filled with the knowledge of his will in all wisdom and spiritual understanding [*understanding which comes through the Holy Ghost*];

10 That ye might walk worthy of the Lord unto all pleasing [*that you might be pleasing to the Lord in all you do*], being fruitful in every good work [*accomplishing good with every aspect of the gospel*], and increasing in the knowledge of God;

11 Strengthened with all might [*with God's power*], according to his glorious power, unto all [*leading you to have*] patience and longsuffering [*endurance;* Strong's *#3115*] with joyfulness;

12 Giving thanks unto the Father, which hath made us meet [*enabled us*] to be partakers of the inheritance of the saints in light [*through the light of the gospel*]:

13 Who hath delivered us [*redeemed us*] from the power of darkness, and hath translated us [*transferred us*] into the kingdom of his dear Son:

14 In whom we have redemption through his blood [*Christ's Atonement*], even the forgiveness of sins:

15 Who is the image of the invisible God [*Christ looks just like His Father; see Hebrews 1:3; also, the Father is invisible in the sense that He can't be seen by people unless He chooses to appear to them; Stephen saw Him in Acts 7:55–56. Joseph Smith saw Him.*], the firstborn of every creature [*the firstborn spirit child of our Heavenly Father*]:

Verse 15, above, has important doctrines. First, the Savior looks just like His Father. Apostle Bruce R. McConkie explained this as follows: "Christ is the image of the Father physically and spiritually, in person and in personality . . . They look alike; in appearance one could pass for the other. Spiritually our Lord is 'in the form of God' (Philip. 2:6); he has acquired all of the attributes of godliness in their perfection; as it is with the Father, so it is with him; he is the embodiment of justice, mercy and truth, of faith, hope and charity, of wisdom, virtue and knowledge, and of every good thing; thus he is in the likeness of and a projection of the personality of the Father." (*Doctrinal New Testament Commentary*, Vol. 3, p. 25.)

Second, the Savior is the firstborn of all Heavenly Father's spirit children. President Joseph F. Smith taught this as follows: "Among the spirit children of Elohim, the first-born was and is Jehovah, or Jesus Christ, to whom all others are juniors." (*Improvement Era*, Vol. 19, p. 940.)

16 For by him [*Christ*] were all things created, that are in heaven, and that are in earth, visible and invisible [*things that we can see with our eyes and things that we can't see with our eyes, such as other worlds in the universe, etc.*], whether they be thrones, or dominions, or principalities, or powers: all things were created by him, and for him [*for the Father; see Moses 1:33*]:

17 And he is before [*above;* Strong's *#4253*] all things, and by him all things consist [*are held together; see D&C 88:40–45*].

18 And he is the head of the body, the church [*Christ stands at the head of the Church*]: who is the beginning [*who has helped us from the beginning in premortal life*], the firstborn from the dead [*the first one resurrected on this earth*]; that in all things he might have the preeminence [*in order that all things might be subject to Him*].

19 For it pleased the Father [*it was the Father's will*] that in him [*Christ*] should all fulness dwell [*the fulness of the gospel would be made available to all people*];

20 And, having made peace through the blood of his cross [*having made it possible for us to be at peace through forgiveness of sin through Christ's Atonement*], by him [*through Christ*] to reconcile [*harmonize*] all things unto himself [*the Father*]; by him [*through Christ*], I say, whether they be things in earth, or things in heaven [*in other words, everything*].

21 And you, that were sometime [*in times past*] alienated [*from God*] and enemies in your mind by wicked works [*because of your wicked deeds*], yet now hath he reconciled [*Christ has atoned for your sins*]

22 In the body of his flesh through death [*by giving His life for you*], to present you holy [*sanctified*] and unblameable [*without sin*] and unreproveable [*no one can accuse you of any wrongdoing*] in his sight:

23 If ye continue in the faith grounded and settled [*on the firm foundation of the gospel*], and be not moved away from the hope of the gospel [*the exaltation which is available to you*], which ye have heard, and which was preached to every creature which is under heaven [*which has been or will be preached to everyone everywhere*]; whereof [*of which gospel*] I Paul am made a minister;

24 Who now rejoice in my sufferings for you [*it is a joy and a privilege to be a prisoner here in Rome because I made the gospel available to you*], and fill up that which is behind of the afflictions of Christ in my flesh [*and to continue to fill my cup with more suffering here in mortality*] for his body's

sake [*for the sake of you members*], which is the church: [*The Church is symbolic of the body of Christ, to which all the "members" belong.*]

25 Whereof [*of which*] I am made a minister, according to the dispensation of God [*calling from God*] which is given to me for you, to fulfil the word of God [*to fulfill the prophecies God made that the gospel would be taken to the Gentiles; see verse 27, below*];

26 Even the mystery [*the gospel of Jesus Christ which replaces the law of Moses*] which hath been hid from ages and from generations, but now is made manifest [*is taught and testified*] to his saints:

27 To whom God [*the Father*] would make known what is the riches of the glory of this mystery [*that which contains the fulness and glory of the gospel*] among the Gentiles; which is Christ in you, the hope of glory [*the hope for celestial glory*]:

28 Whom we preach [*we preach of Christ*], warning every man, and teaching every man in all wisdom; that we may present every man perfect in Christ Jesus [*that everyone may become perfect by following the gospel of Jesus Christ*]:

29 Whereunto I also labour [*I am also striving for perfection*], striving according to his working [*working with God's help*], which worketh in me mightily [*which influences and helps me strongly*].

COLOSSIANS 2

Paul continues by reminding these Saints that the only safety lies in the gospel sent by the Father through His Son Jesus Christ. He counsels them to avoid sin, especially the type that gains acceptance through unrighteous traditions.

1 FOR I would that ye knew what great conflict I have for you [*I hope you know how much I have worried about you*], and for them at Laodicea [*about 11 miles north of Colosse*], and for as many as have not seen my face in the flesh [*and also for all those with whom I have not visited personally*];

2 That their hearts might be comforted, being knit together in love, and unto all riches of the full assurance of understanding, to the acknowledgement of the mystery of God, and of [*from*] the Father, and of Christ;

JST Colossians 2:2

2 That their hearts might be comforted, being knit together in love, and unto all riches of the full assurance of understanding, to the acknowledgment of the mystery of God and of Christ, who is of God, **even the Father**;

3 In whom are hid all the treasures of wisdom and knowledge. [*We can gain all the treasures of wisdom and knowledge which the Father has for us if we follow Christ and His gospel.*]

4 And this I say, lest any man should beguile [*deceive*] you with enticing [*cunning, attractive*] words.

5 For though I be absent in the flesh [*even though I am not physically present with you*], yet am I with you in the spirit, joying and beholding [*seeing and understanding*] your order [*you are trying to put your lives in order*], and the stedfastness [*firmness*] of your faith in Christ.

6 As [*since*] ye have therefore received [*accepted*] Christ Jesus the Lord, so walk ye in him [*live according to His teachings*]:

7 Rooted [*you have put down roots in the gospel*] and built up [*edified*] in him, and stablished [*established*] in the faith [*gospel*], as ye have been taught, abounding therein [*receiving many blessings*] with thanksgiving.

8 Beware lest any man spoil you through philosophy [*the philosophies of men, especially Greek philosophy for these members*] and vain deceit [*worthless deception*], after [*according to*] the tradition of men, after the rudiments [*worldly thinking*] of the world, and not after [*according to*] Christ.

9 For in him dwelleth all the fulness of the Godhead bodily [*in Christ, all the goals and desires of the Godhead are made available to us*].

10 And ye are complete in him [*you can become exalted by following Christ*], which is the head of all principality and power [*who has risen above all things*]:

11 In whom [*through whom*] also ye are circumcised [*dedicated to God; through whom you make covenants with God; see Bible Dictionary under "Circumcision"*] with the circumcision made without hands [*through covenants which come from God, rather than being rooted in man-made philosophies*], in putting off the body of the sins of the flesh [*overcoming sins which tempt us here in mortality*] by the circumcision of [*the covenants we make with*] Christ:

12 Buried with him in baptism [*through proper baptism, we "bury" our old sinful selves; see Romans 6:4–6*], wherein also ye are risen with him [*and come forth "born again," new people*] through the faith of the operation of God [*because of your faith in the Father's plan*], who hath raised him [*Christ*] from the dead.

13 And you, being dead in your sins and the uncircumcision of your flesh [*and you, who were spiritually dead because of your sins*], hath he [*the Father*] quickened [*given new life*] together with him [*along with Christ*], having forgiven you all trespasses [*sins*];

14 Blotting out the handwriting of ordinances that was against us [*doing away with the law of Moses*], which was contrary to us [*which could not save us*], and took it out of the way [*made it so it was no longer an obstacle to us*], nailing it to his cross [*fulfilling the law*

of Moses through His crucifixion and Atonement];

15 And having spoiled [*disarmed;* Strong's *#0554*] principalities and powers [*things that hold us back from salvation*], he made a shew of them openly [*He exposed them to public view*], triumphing over them in it [*through His Atonement*].

16 Let no man therefore judge you in meat, or in drink, or in respect of an holyday, or of the new moon, or of the sabbath days: [*In other words, don't worry if people criticize you for not participating in various aspects of the law of Moses. For instance, there were special rituals and sacrifices required by the law of Moses in conjunction with the new moon; see Bible Dictionary under "New Moon."*]

17 Which are a shadow [*a "type" or symbolic*] of things to come; but the body is of Christ [*the real purpose of the law of Moses was fulfilled by Christ*].

The animal sacrifices and rituals contained in the law of Moses were designed to be "shadows" and "types" or symbols which would point the mind and spirit of the children of Israel toward the coming Messiah. See Bible Dictionary under "Law of Moses."

18 Let no man beguile [*fool, deceive*] you of your reward in a voluntary humility and worshipping of angels [*and strip you of your eternal reward by talking you into worshiping "go-between" angels, "patron saints," and the like*], intruding into those things which he hath not seen [*who supposedly intervene for people between them and God whom they say can't be seen*], vainly puffed up by his fleshly mind [*foolishly caught up in philosophies hatched in their worldly minds*],

Greek philosophy had apparently worked its way into the thinking of some early converts to the Church in Colosse, or else, they still held onto it despite their baptism into Christ's gospel. At any rate, one of these philosophies was that God was totally unapproachable by man. Thus, people needed to contact God by means of angels who were mediators between man and God. This false philosophy is described in the Institute of Religion's New Testament student manual entitled *The Life and Teachings of Jesus and His Apostles*, published in 1979, p. 345, as follows: "The Gnostic philosophy held that God was not directly approachable by man but had to be contacted through a series of angelic mediators or less divine spirits. Paul is here denouncing this idea of worshiping angels, which led the Saints away from allegiance to the true head (Christ), and only true mediator between man and God."

19 And not holding [*sticking with*] the Head [*Christ; see Ephesians 4:15*], from which all the body [*the whole Church, symbolically*] by joints and bands [*sinews*] having

nourishment ministered [*receive nourishment from Christ*], and knit together [*held together*], increaseth [*continues to grow*] with the increase [*nourishment and blessings*] of God.

20 Wherefore [*therefore*] if ye be dead with Christ from the rudiments of the world [*if you have put worldliness out of your lives by joining with Christ's true Church*], why, as though living in the world, are ye subject to ordinances [*why are you behaving as if you did not have the true gospel by submitting to the ordinances of the law of Moses, or to the belief that you need patron saints, etc.*],

21 (Touch not; taste not; handle not; [*don't even touch such things!*]

22 Which all are to perish with the using) [*which will lead to spiritual death and loss of salvation for all who get involved with them*]; after the commandments and doctrines of men?

23 Which things have indeed a shew [*an appearance*] of wisdom in will worship [*in forms of worship which reflect man's will*], and humility [*and have an appearance of promoting humility*], and neglecting of the body [*and sound good to some because they teach to subdue physical needs*]; not in any honour [*which brings no honor to God*] to the satisfying of the flesh.

The JST changes verses 21–23, above, as follows:

JST Colossians 2:21

21 **Which are after the doctrines and commandments of men, who teach you to touch not, taste not, handle not; all those things which are to perish with the using?**

JST Colossians 2:22

22 Which things have indeed a **show** of wisdom in **will-worship**, and humility, and **neglecting the body as to the satisfying the flesh, not in any honor to God**.

COLOSSIANS 3

Basically, what Paul is saying in the following verses is, "How can you even think of returning to the doctrines and philosophies of men after having heard the true gospel of Christ and repenting, being baptized, and coming forth in newness of life, with the happy prospect of living with God forever?" He then counsels them to live the gospel and avoid evil in their daily lives.

There are no JST changes for this chapter.

1 IF ye then be risen [*if you have come out of the waters of baptism*] with Christ [*thus joining Christ's church*], seek those things which are above, where Christ sitteth on the right hand of God [*seek to be guided by Him still, rather than reverting back to false philosophies, ordinances of men, and so forth*].

2 Set your affection [*loyalties and desires*] on things above, not on things on the earth.

3 For ye are dead [*you have buried your old selves and lifestyles through repentance and baptism; see Romans 6:4–6*], and your life is hid [*safe*] with Christ in God [*with Christ who has returned to the Father*].

4 When Christ, who is our life [*who has opened the door for eternal life to us*], shall appear, then shall ye also appear with him in glory [*you will be with Him in celestial glory*].

5 Mortify [*do away with, kill*] therefore your members [*sins; see Romans 6:13 and JST Matthew 5:30*] which are upon the earth [*which tempt you here on earth, such as*]; fornication, uncleanness [*immoral, reckless living;* Strong's *#1067*], inordinate affection [*lust;* Strong's *#3806*], evil concupiscence [*evil, lustful desires;* Strong's *#1939*], and covetousness, which is idolatry [*which are forms of idol worship*]:

6 For which things' sake the wrath of God cometh on the children of disobedience [*which things bring the punishments of God upon those who disobey his commandments*]:

7 In the which ye also walked some time, when ye lived in them. [*You used to be involved in such things.*]

8 But now ye also put off all these [*but now, in addition to the sins mentioned in verse 5, you also avoid*]; anger, wrath [*rage*], malice [*desire to hurt others*], blasphemy [*evil speaking of God or sacred things*], filthy communication out of your mouth [*filthy language*]. [*In other words, you are living a much higher law now.*]

9 Lie not one to another, seeing that ye have put off the old man with his deeds [*you have repented of your previous lifestyle and sins*];

10 And have put on the new man [*you have become new, spiritually reborn*], which is renewed in knowledge after the image of him that created him [*and you are now being helped and shaped to become Christ like*]:

11 Where there is neither Greek nor Jew, circumcision [*Jew*] nor uncircumcision [*Gentile*], Barbarian, Scythian [*rough, rude, ignorant, low in social status;* Strong's *#4658*], bond nor free: but Christ is all, and in all. [*In other words, living the gospel makes us all equal and brings exaltation to all who become worthy, regardless of race, origins, former status, etc.*]

12 Put on therefore, as the elect of God [*as God's chosen people*], holy [*Saints*] and beloved, bowels of mercies [*tender feelings toward others;* Strong's *#4698*], kindness, humbleness of mind, meekness [*not quickly angered*], longsuffering [*patience; endurance in a good cause*];

13 Forbearing [*hold up, sustain;* Strong's *#0430*] one another, and forgiving one another, if any man have a quarrel against any: even

as Christ forgave you, so also do ye [*forgive one another just like Christ forgave you of your former sins*].

14 And above all these things put on charity [*see 1 Corinthians 13*], which is the bond of perfectness [*which leads to perfect, Christ like relationships*].

15 And let the peace of [*from*] God rule in your hearts [*control your hearts*], to the which also ye are called in one body [*as members of the Church*]; and be ye thankful [*have and express gratitude; see D&C 59:21*].

16 Let the word of Christ dwell in you richly [*fill your souls*] in all wisdom; teaching and admonishing [*urging toward righteousness*] one another in psalms and hymns and spiritual songs, singing with grace [*gratitude and God's goodness;* Strong's *#5485*] in your hearts to the Lord.

17 And whatsoever ye do in word or deed, do all in the name of the Lord Jesus, giving thanks to God and the Father by him.

Look again at the last phrase of verse 17, above. There are a number of verses where the Prophet Joseph Smith changed the phrase "to God and the Father" to "to God, the Father" or "unto God, his Father" and such like. For example: Revelation 1:6 is changed from "unto God and his Father" to "unto God, his Father."

18 Wives, submit [*a voluntary attitude of cooperating;* Strong's *#5293*] yourselves unto your own husbands, as it is fit in the Lord [*appropriate in a gospel-centered home*]. [*See notes in Ephesians 5:21–33 in this study guide.*]

19 Husbands, love your wives, and be not bitter against them [*don't make them bitter by your behaviors;* Strong's *#4087*].

20 Children, obey your parents in all things: for this is well pleasing unto the Lord.

21 Fathers, provoke not your children to anger, lest they be discouraged [*for fear that you will break their spirit;* Strong's *#0120*].

22 Servants, obey in all things your masters according to the flesh [*be a good example to your masters, as followers of Christ*]; not with eyeservice [*not just when they are watching you*], as menpleasers [*trying to look good in their eyes*]; but in singleness of heart [*but sincerely*], fearing God [*living the gospel*]:

23 And whatsoever ye do, do it heartily [*energetically, wholeheartedly*], as to the Lord [*as if you were doing it for the Lord*], and not unto men;

24 Knowing that of [*from*] the Lord ye shall receive the reward of the inheritance [*you will inherit exaltation, if faithful*]: for ye serve the Lord Christ [*Christ is your real master*].

25 But he that doeth wrong shall receive for the wrong which he hath done [*if you commit wrongs against your masters, you will be punished by God*]: and there is no respect of persons [*it makes no difference who your are or what you are, God expects personal integrity and righteousness from all members of the Church*].

COLOSSIANS 4

One particularly interesting thing about this chapter is that we discover that Luke, who wrote Luke and Acts is with Paul at the time he wrote this letter. We are also told that Luke is a physician. See verse 14. Perhaps Luke is attending to some of Paul's health needs during Paul's two years of house arrest imprisonment in Rome.

There are no JST changes for this chapter.

1 MASTERS [*you owners of slaves or servants who are members of the Church*], give unto your servants that which is just and equal; knowing that ye also have a Master in heaven [*knowing that God is your Master*].

> It was common in the days of Paul for people to own slaves. It was also common for people to sell themselves to wealthier people for a time in order to pay debts or to improve their status and opportunities in life.

2 Continue in prayer, and watch in the same with thanksgiving [*and express gratitude to God in your prayers*];

3 Withal [*at the same time;* Strong's *#0260*] praying also for us, that God would open unto us a door of utterance [*the opportunity to continue to preach*], to speak the mystery of Christ [*the gospel, which is a mystery to all who do not know about Christ*], for which I am also in bonds [*which is the cause of my being in prison here in Rome*]:

> The phrase "for which I am also in bonds" in verse 3, above, could also mean "to whom I am obligated because of His bounteous blessings to me."

4 That I may make it [*the gospel*] manifest, as I ought to speak [*so that I can preach the gospel as I ought to*].

5 Walk in wisdom toward them that are without [*behave wisely toward those who are not members of the Church*], redeeming the time [*making the best of every opportunity to teach them*].

6 Let your speech [*conversations with nonmembers*] be alway [*always*] with grace [*with the help of God*], seasoned with salt [*making everything go better*], that ye may know [*be inspired as to*] how ye ought to answer every man.

7 All my state shall Tychicus declare unto you [*Tychicus will give you more details about conditions*

here in Rome], who is a beloved brother, and a faithful minister and fellowservant in the Lord:

8 Whom I have sent unto you for the same purpose, that he might know your estate [*that he might see how things are going there in Colosse with you*], and comfort your hearts;

9 With Onesimus [*Tychicus is traveling with Onesimus—see Philemon for information about Onesimus*], a faithful and beloved brother, who is one of you [*who is from your city*]. They shall make known unto you all things which are done here [*they will fill you in with all the details of what is happening here*].

10 Aristarchus my fellowprisoner saluteth [*greets*] you, and Marcus, sister's son to Barnabas, (touching whom ye received commandments [*you already received instructions about him*]: if he come unto you, receive [*welcome*] him;)

In the next verse, Paul mentions a Jewish member of the Church, named Jesus. Jesus was a common name among the Jews at the time. See Bible Dictionary under the second listing for "Jesus."

11 And Jesus, which [*who*] is called Justus, who are of the circumcision [*who are Jewish converts*]. These only are my fellowworkers unto the kingdom of God, which have been a comfort unto me [*these are the only Jewish converts who have been helping me here*].

12 Epaphras, who is one of you [*who is from your city*], a servant of Christ, saluteth [*greets*] you, always labouring fervently for you in prayers [*he constantly prays for you with all his heart*], that ye may stand perfect [*that you will be spiritually mature;* Strong's *#5046*] and complete in all the will of God [*paying attention to all the details of living the gospel*].

13 For I bear him record [*I am his witness*], that he hath a great zeal [*that he works very hard*] for you, and them that are in Laodicea, and them in Hierapolis [*cities a few miles northwest of Colosse*].

14 Luke, the beloved physician, and Demas, greet you.

15 Salute the brethren which are in Laodicea, and Nymphas [*a wealthy and energetic member of the Church in Laodicea;* Strong's *#3564*], and the church which is in his house [*the members in his household*].

16 And when this epistle [*letter*] is read among you [*when you receive this letter*], cause that it be read also in the church of the Laodiceans [*in the Laodicean ward*]; and that ye likewise read the epistle from Laodicea [*and make sure that you read the letter the Laodicean members wrote*].

17 And say to Archippus [*a member of the Church in Colosse, perhaps a member of Philemon's family: see Philemon 1:2;* Strong's *#0751*], Take heed to the ministry [*pay attention to the calling*] which thou

hast received in the Lord, that thou fulfil it.

18 The salutation by the hand of me Paul [*I personally greet you in my own handwriting*]. Remember my bonds [*don't forget me*]. Grace be with you. Amen.

THE FIRST EPISTLE OF PAUL THE APOSTLE TO THE THESSALONIANS

Just a reminder, as mentioned earlier, that Paul's epistles (letters) are arranged in the Bible according to length rather than in chronological order (see Bible Dictionary under "Pauline Epistles"). The exception is his letter to the Hebrews, which was placed at the end of his letters because there was disagreement among scholars as to whether or not Paul wrote it. We know he did write it because the Prophet Joseph Smith informed us that he did (see *Teachings of the Prophet Joseph Smith*, p. 59).

Paul's first and second letters to the Thessalonian members of the Church were written around AD 50–52 from Corinth during Paul's second missionary journey. He and his companion missionaries had recently been driven out of Thessalonica, in what is known today as northeastern Greece, by an angry mob of Jews. See Acts 17:1–15. After they were driven out, they journeyed to Berea, then to Athens and from there to Corinth, in southern Greece, where they were met by Silas and Timothy. Timothy was then sent back to Thessalonica to check on conditions in the ward or branch there and to help them as relatively new members of the Church, most of whom appear to have been Gentile converts rather than Jewish converts. After spending some time among them, Timothy returned to Corinth and reported conditions among the Thessalonian members to Paul. With this information plus Paul's own experience with these Saints, he wrote First and Second Thessalonians to them. These were the first letters written by Paul which are included in our New Testament.

FIRST THESSALONIANS 1

Paul's relief and gratitude upon Timothy's safe return from visiting the Saints in Thessalonica, plus his gratitude for the sincere efforts of the relatively new converts there to live the gospel, are very evident in this chapter.

1 PAUL, and Silvanus [*another form of the name "Silas," see Acts 15:32–34, a missionary companion of Paul on his second missionary journey, Acts 15:40*], and Timotheus [*Timothy*], unto the church [*ward or branch*] of the Thessalonians which is in God the Father and in the Lord Jesus Christ: Grace be unto you, and peace, from God our Father, and the Lord Jesus Christ.

JST 1 Thessalonians 1:1

1 Paul, and Silvanus, and Timotheus, **servants of God the Father and the Lord Jesus Christ**, unto the church of the Thessalonians; **grace unto you,** and peace from God our Father, and the Lord Jesus Christ.

2 We give thanks to God always for you all, making mention of [*remembering*] you in our prayers;

JST 1 Thessalonians 1:2

2 **We give thanks always, making mention of you all, in our prayers to God for you.**

3 Remembering without ceasing your work of faith, and labour of love, and patience of hope in our Lord Jesus Christ, in the sight of God and our Father [*who is our Father*];

4 Knowing, brethren beloved, your election of God. [*In other words, you know that you have been chosen and set apart, because of your baptism, to be a peculiar people and to forsake the world; compare with D&C 53:1–2.*]

5 For our gospel came not unto you in word only [*you didn't just hear the gospel from us with your ears*], but also in power, and in the Holy Ghost, and in much assurance [*but the Holy Ghost bore powerful witness to you*]; as ye know what manner of men we were among you for your sake.

6 And ye became followers of us, and of the Lord, having received the word [*gospel*] in much affliction [*persecution*], with joy of [*from*] the Holy Ghost:

7 So that ye were ensamples [*examples*] to all that believe in Macedonia [*northern Greece today*] and Achaia [*central and southern Greece today*].

8 For from you sounded [*spread*] out the word of the Lord not only in Macedonia and Achaia, but also in every place your faith to God-ward is spread abroad; so that we need not to speak any thing [*we don't have any need to comment on it*].

JST 1 Thessalonians 1:8

8 For from you sounded out the word of the Lord not only in Macedonia and Achaia, but also in every place your faith **toward God** is spread abroad; so that we need not to speak **anything**.

9 For they themselves [*your good example and spreading of the gospel*] shew [*show*] of us what

manner of entering in we had unto you [*what kind of reception you gave us when we came to you*], and how ye turned to God [*Heavenly Father*] from idols to serve the living and true God;

Often, Heavenly Father is referred to in scripture as "the living God." This is obvious to us, but in a culture of idol worship, where people rebelliously or foolishly or unknowingly worship "dead gods" made of wood and stone, the phrase "living God" is a major doctrinal statement.

10 And to wait for his Son from heaven [*and to prepare for the Second Coming; Acts 1:11*], whom he [*the Father*] raised from the dead [*resurrected*], even Jesus, which delivered us from the wrath to come [*whose gospel makes it possible for us to escape the punishments of God which will come upon the wicked*].

It may seem like a bit of a stretch for these Saints to prepare for the Second Coming of Christ, which, for them, is a minimum of approximately 2000 years in the future. But, D&C 88:97–98 reminds us that all the righteous dead, from after Christ's resurrection to the Second Coming, will be privileged to be resurrected and caught up to join Him in His Second Coming, and actually descend to the earth with Him at that time. Thus, these Saints can prepare during their lifetime to be part of that group.

FIRST THESSALONIANS 2

In this chapter, Paul discusses the missionary work he and his companions have done and some of the persecutions they endured in order to do it. Among other things, he discusses how true missionaries go about the work, using himself and his companions as examples.

There are no JST changes for this chapter.

1 FOR yourselves, brethren, know our entrance in unto you [*our coming to you*], that it was not in vain:

2 But even after that we had suffered before [*previously*], and were shamefully entreated [*treated outrageously;* Strong's *#5195*], as ye know, at Philippi [*where Paul and Silas were beaten and placed in prison in stocks; Acts 16:19–24*], we were bold [*we were made bold by our confidence*] in our God to speak unto you the gospel of God with much contention [*in spite of much opposition*].

3 For our exhortation [*teaching*] was not of deceit [*based on deception*], nor of uncleanness [*unworthiness*], nor in guile [*ulterior motives*]:

4 But as we were allowed of God to be put in trust with the gospel [*since we were entrusted by God with the gospel*], even so we speak; not as pleasing men, but God [*we do not teach things pleasing to*

worldly people, rather, we speak the words of God], which trieth our hearts [*who examines our hearts and motives*].

5 For neither at any time used we flattering words [*we didn't use words which would please worldly people*], as ye know, nor a cloke of covetousness [*nor were we secretly covering up greed for gain and power*]; God is witness [*God is our witness*]:

6 Nor of men sought we glory [*neither did we seek for the praise of men*], neither of you, nor yet of others, when we might have been burdensome, as the apostles of Christ [*we could have come across pretty strong as Apostles*].

7 But we were gentle among you, even as a nurse cherisheth her children [*cherishes little children placed in her care*]:

8 So being affectionately desirous of you [*we developed such tender feelings for you*], we were willing to have imparted unto you, not the gospel of God only [*that we didn't just give you the gospel*], but also our own souls, because ye were dear unto us.

9 For ye remember, brethren, our labour and travail [*how hard we worked*]: for labouring night and day, because we would not be chargeable unto any of you [*we worked night and day so we would not be a burden to you*], we preached unto you the gospel of God.

10 Ye are witnesses, and God also, how holily [*holy*] and justly [*living the gospel exactly*] and unblameably [*giving no reason for criticism*] we behaved ourselves among you that believe:

11 As ye know how we exhorted and comforted and charged [*instructed*] every one of you, as a father doth his children,

12 That ye would walk [*live*] worthy of God, who hath called you unto his kingdom and glory.

13 For this cause also thank we God without ceasing, because, when ye received the word of God which ye heard of [*from*] us, ye received [*accepted*] it not as the word of men [*not as the philosophies of men*], but as it is in truth [*as it really is*], the word of God, which effectually worketh also [*which works very effectively*] in you that believe.

14 For ye, brethren, became followers of the churches of God which in Judæa are in Christ Jesus [*you followed in the footsteps of members of the Church in the wards and branches in Judea who follow Jesus Christ*]: for ye also have suffered like things of your own countrymen [*you have suffered similar persecutions by your fellow citizens*], even as they [*the members in Judea*] have of [*through*] the Jews:

15 Who both killed [*who killed both*] the Lord Jesus, and their own prophets, and have persecuted us; and they [*the Jews who persecute Christians*] please not God, and are

contrary [*hostile;* Strong's *#1727*] to all men [*everyone*]:

16 Forbidding us to speak [*teach the gospel*] to the Gentiles that they might be saved, to fill up their sins alway [*the Jews seem to want to constantly add more sins upon their own heads*]: for the wrath [*punishment of God*] is come upon them to the uttermost [*to the extreme*].

17 But we, brethren, being taken from you [*away from you*] for a short time in presence [*in physical presence*], not in heart, endeavoured the more abundantly [*tried all the more*] to see your face with great desire [*to visit you and see you to satisfy the desire of our hearts*].

18 Wherefore we would have come unto you, even I Paul, once and again [*repeatedly*]; but Satan hindered [*stopped*] us.

19 For what is our hope, or joy, or crown of rejoicing [*what is the source of so much joy and happiness for us*]? [*Answer: You are*!] Are not even ye in the presence of our Lord Jesus Christ at his coming? [*We have confidence that you will be with the Savior at His Second Coming.*]

Sometimes people read the last phrase of verse 19, above, and wonder why Paul expected the Second Coming clear back then. But if we correctly understand from Paul's writings in general, that he understood the plan of salvation very well, we might do well to think that he was saying something else. We know from D&C 88:96–98 that the righteous, living and dead, will accompany the Savior as He comes for the Second Coming. Thus, what Paul may well be saying is, in effect, that the righteous members of the Church in Thessalonica should plan on coming with the Savior, at the time when He returns to earth in the last days to preside during the Millennium.

20 For ye are our glory and joy.

FIRST THESSALONIANS 3

Paul is complimentary to these members as he speaks of their faith and charity. He counsels them to strive to increase in love for one another and to get the gospel deep in their hearts.

There are no JST changes for this chapter.

1 WHEREFORE [*so*] when we could no longer forbear [*when we could stand it no longer*], we thought it good [*best*] to be left at Athens alone;

Just a reminder that some angry Jews in Thessalonica assembled a mob to oppose Paul and his companions there (Acts 17:1–9), and, as a result, faithful members quickly helped Paul and Silas escape by sending them to Berea (a few miles south of Thessalonica) that night (Acts 17:10.) However, the Jews in Thessalonica soon found out that Paul and Silas were preaching the gospel successfully in Berea, and so they rushed to that city and stirred up the people there (Acts 17:13). Consequently, worried members quickly sent Paul on his way toward Athens, while Silas and Timothy remained in Berea (Acts 17:14–15). Ultimately, Silas and Timothy caught up with Paul in Corinth, and Paul sent Timothy back to check on conditions among the Saints at Thessalonica.

2 And sent Timotheus, our brother, and minister of God, and our fellowlabourer in the gospel of Christ, to establish you [*to strengthen you in the gospel*], and to comfort you concerning your faith:

3 That no man should be moved [*disturbed or discouraged*] by these afflictions: for yourselves know that we are appointed thereunto. [*In other words, Paul does not want the members in Thessalonica and the surrounding area to lose their testimonies or become discouraged because of the persecutions Paul and his associates are going through.*]

4 For verily, when we were with you, we told you before [*ahead of time*] that we should [*would*] suffer tribulation [*trials and troubles*]; even as it came to pass [*just as it has happened*], and ye know.

5 For this cause [*this is the reason*], when I could no longer forbear [*when I couldn't stand it any longer*], I sent to know your faith [*I sent Timothy to you to find out how your faith was holding up*], lest by some means [*for fear that in some way*] the tempter [*the devil*] have tempted you [*might have succeeded in tempting you to quit the Church*], and our labour be in vain [*and thus our work among you would have been ineffective*].

6 But now when Timotheus came from you unto us [*but now that Timothy has returned from visiting you*], and brought us good tidings [*news*] of your faith and charity, and that ye have good remembrance of us always [*and that you have pleasant memories of us*], desiring greatly to see us [*and that you would love to see us again*], as we also to see you [*as we would love to see you again*]:

7 Therefore, brethren, we were comforted over you in all our affliction and distress by your faith [*we were comforted to the point that we didn't even think of our own troubles when we heard of your faithfulness*]:

8 For now we live, if ye stand fast in the Lord [*you bring new life and energy to us if you remain faithful to the Lord*].

9 For what thanks can we render to God again [*how could we possibly express more gratitude to God*] for you, for all the joy wherewith we joy for your sakes before our God [*because of all the joy you have brought to us*];

10 Night and day praying exceedingly that we might see your face

[*we are constantly praying that we might see you again*], and might perfect that which is lacking in your faith [*and fill in some weak spots in your understanding of the gospel*]?

11 Now God himself and [*who is*] our Father, and our Lord Jesus Christ, direct our way unto you [*guide us toward you*].

12 And the Lord make you to increase and abound [*flourish*] in love one toward another, and toward all men, even as we do toward you:

13 To the end [*for the purpose that*] he may stablish [*establish*] your hearts unblameable [*to become pure and free from sin*] in holiness before God, even our Father, at the coming of our Lord Jesus Christ with all his saints. [*See D&C 88:96–98.*]

FIRST THESSALONIANS 4

In this chapter, as is the case with other letters of Paul to various congregations of the Church in other cities, this great Apostle to the Gentiles will encourage these members to live righteously and will warn them against getting caught up in sins accepted by the culture in which they lived. We face similar threats to our living the gospel today. Among other doctrines he teaches them, he will give some detail about the Second Coming.

1 FURTHERMORE [*in addition*] then we beseech [*ask*] you, brethren, and exhort [*urge*] you by the Lord Jesus, that as ye have received of us how ye ought to walk and to please God [*since you accepted the gospel from us*], so ye would abound more and more [*that you keep increasing in your ability to live it more and more faithfully*].

2 For ye know what commandments we gave you by [*from*] the Lord Jesus.

3 For this is the will of God, even your sanctification [*your salvation depends on this*], that ye should abstain from fornication [*avoid sexual immorality*]:

One of the serious problems among the Thessalonian converts came as a result of the culture in which they lived. Sexual immorality, in many varieties, was commonplace. Thus, many new converts had a difficult time seeing what was so wrong with it. If they had come from a Jewish background, they would have at least had the law of Moses, including the Ten Commandments and would have been trained and warned from the time they were young that any sexual relations, including intercourse, outside of marriage was wrong, being forbidden by God. This would have included homosexuality also (see Leviticus 20:13; Bible Dictionary under "Homosexuality"). Most of the converts in Thessalonica were Gentiles and had no such upbringing or background. Thus,

Paul must often emphasize the law of chastity among them.

4 That every one of you should know how to possess his vessel [*body*] in sanctification and honour; [*In other words, every one of you should know how to keep your body pure and chaste.*]

5 Not in the lust of concupiscence [*not getting involved in sexual immorality*], even as [*like*] the Gentiles which know not God:

6 That no man go beyond [*take advantage of*] and defraud [*wrong*] his brother in any matter: because that the Lord is the avenger of all such [*because the Lord will punish those who do*], as we also have forewarned [*warned*] you and testified.

7 For God hath not called us unto uncleanness [*to remain unclean*], but unto holiness [*but to become holy, to become Saints*].

8 He therefore that despiseth [*rejects this counsel*], despiseth not man, but God [*is not rejecting us but is rejecting God*], who hath also given unto us his holy Spirit.

9 But as touching [*now, speaking of*] brotherly love ye need not that I write unto you [*you don't need me to say anything to you about it*]: for ye yourselves are taught of [*by*] God to love one another.

10 And indeed ye do it toward all the brethren which are in all Macedonia [*northern Greece today*]: but we beseech [*urge*] you, brethren, that ye increase more and more [*develop more and more brotherly love*];

11 And that ye study to be quiet [*learn how to live quiet, peaceful lives*], and to do your own business [*and to mind your own business*], and to work with your own hands [*and to provide for your own living*], as we commanded [*instructed*] you;

12 That ye may walk honestly toward them that are without [*that you may earn the respect of nonmembers*], and that ye may have lack of nothing [*and that you may be self-reliant*].

Paul will now teach these new members more about the resurrection of the righteous.

13 But I would not have you to be ignorant, brethren, concerning them which are asleep [*those who have died*], that ye sorrow not [*don't keep mourning for them*], even as others which have no hope [*like others do who don't believe as we do*].

14 For if we believe that Jesus died and rose again, even so them also which sleep in Jesus [*those who died who were faithful to Jesus*] will God [*the Father*] bring [*to heaven*] with him [*Christ*].

We definitely need the help of the JST to understand verse 15, next. As usual, we will use **bold** to point out the JST changes.

15 For this we say unto you by the word of the Lord [*this is what the Lord says*], that we which are alive

and remain unto the coming of the Lord shall not prevent [*have any advantage over*] them which are asleep [*have died already*].

JST 1 Thessalonians 4:15

15 For this we say unto you by the word of the Lord, that **they** [*the righteous*] **who** are alive **at the coming of the Lord,** shall not prevent them [*have any advantage over those*] **who remain** [*in their graves*] **unto** [*until*] **the coming of the Lord, who** are asleep [*who are dead*].

The word "prevent" in verse 15, above, is key in understanding the verse. "Prevent" is an Old English word which has changed meaning over time. It originally meant "precede" or "to be first" or "to have an advantage over" or "to progress over." See 1 Thessalonians 4:15, footnote c. For another example of how the word "prevent" is used in King James English, see Matthew 17:25, including footnote a, where Peter was coming into the house to ask the Savior a question about paying the temple tax, but Jesus spoke to him first ("Jesus prevented him"), meaning Jesus "preceded" him, in other words, spoke to him before he even had a chance to ask his question.

16 For the Lord [*Christ*] himself shall descend from heaven [*at the Second Coming*] with a shout, with the voice of the archangel, and with the trump of God: and the dead in Christ [*the righteous dead*] shall rise [*be resurrected*] first:

The JST changes made to verse 17, next, are essential for correct understanding. This verse needs to be read along with JST verse 15, above, for correct understanding.

17 Then we which are alive and remain shall be caught up together with them in the clouds, to meet the Lord in the air: and so shall we ever be with the Lord.

JST 1 Thessalonians 4:17

17 Then **they who** are alive, **shall be caught up together into the clouds with them who remain** [*who are dead and in the grave*], to meet the Lord in the air; and so shall we **be ever** with the Lord.

Without the JST, above, it sounds like Paul is teaching that the Second Coming will be in his day. You may wish to read D&C 88:96–98, where the same correct doctrine is taught.

18 Wherefore [*therefore*] comfort one another with these words.

FIRST THESSALONIANS 5

In this chapter, Paul gives a few more details about the Second Coming and counsels the members to live as Saints (meaning "holy ones"). He warns them not to get so comfortable that they start slipping in living the gospel. He counsels them to arm themselves with the gospel as protection against the damaging effects of sin and to strengthen each other.

1 BUT of the times and the seasons [*the signs of the times which will indicate the approximate time of the Second Coming*], brethren, ye have no need that I write unto you.

2 For yourselves know perfectly that the day of the Lord [*the Second Coming which ushers in the Millennium*] so cometh as a thief in the night [*the wicked will be caught off guard, see D&C 106:4, but the righteous will not, see verse 4, below, as well as D&C 106:5*].

3 For when they [*the wicked*] shall say, Peace and safety [*when they claim that there is peace and safety in wickedness*]; then sudden destruction cometh upon them, as travail [*labor pains come*] upon a woman with child [*who is expecting a baby*]; and they shall not escape [*the destruction at the Second Coming*].

The imagery of a woman in labor, which Paul uses to describe the time of the Second Coming is very fitting. A woman who is expecting knows the approximate timing of the birth of her child, because she knows "the times and seasons" or the "signs of the times" that indicate that the birth is close. But she doesn't know exactly when it will occur. So it is with the Second Coming. There are many "signs of the times" which will indicate to the righteous who pay attention to them that the Savior's coming is getting close, but no one knows the exact time. See Matthew 24:36. Also, once the labor pains begin, there is no way in Paul's day to avoid the birth of the baby. So also there is no way for the wicked to escape destruction, once the Second Coming starts.

4 But ye, brethren, are not in darkness [*spiritual darkness, wickedness*], that that day [*the Second Coming*] should overtake you as a thief [*that you would be caught off guard; D&C 106:5*] .

5 Ye are all the children of light [*you are the righteous, who have the light and revelations of the gospel*], and the children of the day: we are not of the night, nor of darkness.

6 Therefore let us not sleep [*fall into a false sense of security*], as do others; but let us watch and be sober [*and be serious about the gospel*].

Next, Paul uses the habits of people as a comparison between the wicked and foolish, and the righteous. In effect, he says that people who don't study about and live the gospel, live in spiritual darkness and are asleep. He also says, in effect, that people who don't take the gospel seriously and choose to "party" instead, do it in the night, symbolic of doing foolish and evil deeds in spiritual darkness.

7 For they that sleep sleep in the night; and they that be drunken are drunken in the night.

8 But let us, who are of the day [*who live in the light of the gospel*], be sober [*be serious-minded*], putting on the breastplate [*spiritual protection; Ephesians 6:11–18*] of faith and love; and for an helmet [*spiritual protection*], the hope [*anticipation*] of salvation.

9 For God hath not appointed us to wrath [*be punished*], but to obtain salvation by [*through*] our Lord Jesus Christ,

10 Who died for us, that, whether we wake or sleep [*live or die*], we should live together with him [*in celestial glory*].

11 Wherefore comfort yourselves together [*comfort one another*], and edify [*strengthen and build up in the gospel*] one another, even as also ye do [*as you have already been doing*].

12 And we beseech [*urge*] you, brethren, to know [*pay attention to;* Strong's #*1492*] them which labour among you, and are over you [*who are your leaders*] in the Lord [*called of God*], and admonish you;

13 And to esteem [*respect*] them very highly in love for their work's sake [*because of the work they do in your behalf*]. And be at peace among yourselves [*avoid contention*].

14 Now we exhort [*warn*] you, brethren, warn them that are unruly [*who refuse to work; see 2 Thessalonians 3:11*], comfort [*encourage*] the feebleminded [*those who are discouraged; see 1 Thessalonians 5:14, footnote d*], support the weak [*those who are spiritually weak; 1 Thessalonians 5:14, footnote f*], be patient toward all men.

15 See that none render evil for evil [*get revenge*] unto any man; but ever follow that which is good, both among yourselves, and to all men.

16 Rejoice evermore.

17 Pray without ceasing.

18 In every thing give thanks [*express gratitude in all things; see D&C 59:21*]: for this is the will of God [*the Father*] in Christ Jesus concerning you.

19 Quench not the Spirit [*don't hold back in following the Holy Ghost*].

20 Despise not [*don't ignore or ridicule;* Strong's #*1848*] prophesyings [*the word of God, including prophecies;* Strong's #*4394*].

Verses 21 and 22, next, are quoted quite often in sermons and classes in the Church.

21 Prove all things [*test everything in comparison to the word of God*]; hold fast that which is good.

22 Abstain [*avoid*] from all appearance of [*kinds of; see 1 Thessalonians 5:22, footnote b*] evil.

23 And the very God of peace sanctify you wholly [*cleanse you from all sin*]; and I pray God your whole spirit and soul and body be preserved blameless unto the

coming of our Lord Jesus Christ [*so that you will be worthy to come with the Savior at His Second Coming; see D&C 88:97–98*].

24 Faithful is he [*Christ*] that calleth you [*to come unto him*], who also will do it [*Christ is capable of making you clean and can and will do it if you live worthily*].

25 Brethren, pray for us.

26 Greet all the brethren with an holy kiss.

JST 1 Thessalonians 5:26

26 Greet all the brethren with a holy **salutation**.

27 I charge [*instruct*] you by the Lord [*in the name of the Lord*] that this epistle be read unto all the holy brethren [*to all the Saints*].

Remember that the word "holy" as used in verse 27, above, is the same as the word "saint" in Greek which essentially means "holy ones." See *Strong's Exhaustive Concordance of the Bible*, #0040.

28 The grace of our Lord Jesus Christ be with you. Amen.

THE SECOND EPISTLE OF PAUL THE APOSTLE TO THE THESSALONIANS

As mentioned in the note at the beginning of First Thessalonians, this letter was written by Paul from Corinth, probably between AD 50–52.

SECOND THESSALONIANS 1

In this chapter, Paul continues teaching these members in Thessalonica about the Second Coming of Jesus Christ. He reminds them that the day of the Savior's coming will not be pleasant for the wicked.

1 PAUL, and Silvanus [*Silas*], and Timotheus [*Timothy*], unto the church [*ward or branch*] of the Thessalonians in God our Father and the Lord Jesus Christ:

JST 2 Thessalonians 1:1

1 Paul, and Sylvanus, and Timotheus, **the servants of God the Father and our Lord Jesus Christ**, unto the church of the Thessalonians;

2 Grace unto you, and peace, from God our Father and the Lord Jesus Christ.

3 We are bound [*obligated*] to thank God always for you, brethren, as it is meet [*appropriate,* Strong's *#0514*], because that your faith groweth exceedingly, and the charity of every one of you all toward each other aboundeth [*is abundant*];

4 So that we ourselves glory in you in the churches of God [*we have bragged about you in many other wards and branches*] for [*because of*] your patience and faith in all your persecutions and tribulations that ye endure:

5 Which is a manifest token of the righteous judgment of God [*which shows obviously that you have God's approval*], that ye may be counted worthy of the kingdom of God [*the celestial kingdom*], for which ye also suffer [*for which you are going through persecutions*]:

6 Seeing it is a righteous thing with God to recompense [*pay back*] tribulation [*punishments*] to them that trouble you; [*In other words, God will punish those who persecute you.*]

7 And to you who are troubled rest with us [*in God's kingdom*], when the Lord Jesus shall be revealed from heaven [*at the Second Coming*] with his mighty angels,

8 In flaming fire [*with His full glory*] taking vengeance on them that know not God [*punishing the wicked*], and that obey not the gospel of our Lord Jesus Christ:

9 Who shall be punished with everlasting destruction from the presence of the Lord, and from the glory of his power [*In other words, the glory of the Lord will destroy the wicked at the Second Coming; see D&C 5:19; 2 Nephi 12:10, 19, 21.*]

JST 2 Thessalonians 1:9

9 Who shall be punished **with destruction** from the presence of the Lord, and from the glory of his **everlasting** power;

10 When he [*Christ*] shall come to be glorified in [*praised and adored by;* Strong's *#1740*] his saints, and to be admired in all them that believe [*because our testimony among you was believed*] in that day [*at the time of the Second Coming and the Millennium*].

11 Wherefore also we pray always for you, that our God would count you worthy of this calling [*being worthy to join with Christ at the time of His Second Coming*], and fulfil all the good pleasure of his goodness [*and give you all the rewards He has in store for you, according to His will*], and the work of faith with power [*because of your faith and the power of God that is in you*]:

12 That the name of our Lord Jesus Christ may be glorified in you [*praised by others because of your*

faithfulness], and ye in him [*and that you might be praised by Him*], according to the grace of our God [*the Father*] and the Lord Jesus Christ.

SECOND THESSALONIANS 2

It appears that some of the Saints in Thessalonica had come to believe that the Second Coming of the Savior was very near and would come in their lifetime. Paul tells them that they should not believe such a thing, no matter what the source of their information. He informs them that there will be an apostasy from the Church before the Second Coming. We often use verses 1–3 in teaching investigators that the Great Apostasy (the falling away from the Church), as it is called, was prophesied by the Apostles in the New Testament. Thus it was necessary that there be a restoration of the gospel, which the Lord accomplished through the Prophet Joseph Smith, beginning with the First Vision in the spring of 1820.

1 NOW we beseech [*urge*] you, brethren, by the coming of our Lord Jesus Christ, and by our gathering together unto him,

2 That ye be not soon shaken in mind [*that you not begin to believe false doctrines*], or be troubled, neither by spirit, nor by word [*no matter what anyone says*], nor by letter as from us, as that the day of Christ is at hand [*that the Second Coming is about to take place*].

JST 2 Thessalonians 2:2

2 That ye be not soon shaken in mind, or be troubled **by letter, except ye receive it from us**; neither by spirit, nor by word, as that the day of Christ is at hand.

3 Let no man deceive you [*don't let anyone fool you*] by any means: for that day [*the Second Coming*] shall not come, except there come a falling away [*apostasy*] first, and that man of sin [*the devil*] be revealed, the son of perdition [*Satan*];

JST 2 Thessalonians 2:3

3 Let no man deceive you by any means; for **there shall come a falling away first**, and that man of sin be revealed, the son of perdition;

4 Who opposeth [*who opposes everything from God*] and exalteth himself [*lifts himself up in pride*] above all that is called God [*that has anything to do with God*], or that is worshipped; so that he as God sitteth in the temple of God [*Satan tries to take over God's position; compare with Isaiah 14:12–14*], shewing himself [*trying to make people believe*] that he is God.

5 Remember ye not, that, when I was yet with you, I told you these things?

6 And now ye know what withholdeth [*what you should beware of;* Strong's #2722] that he [*Satan*] might be revealed in his time [*will*

be exposed for what he is, when the timing is right].

7 For the mystery of iniquity doth already work [*Satan's deception about the timing of the Second Coming is already going around*]: only he who now letteth will let, until he be taken out of the way.

JST 2 Thessalonians 2:7

7 For the mystery of iniquity doth already work, **and he** [*Satan*] **it is who now worketh, and Christ suffereth** [*allows*] him to work, until the time is fulfilled **that he shall be taken** out of the way [*for 1,000 years at the Second Coming, see D&C 101:28, as well as permanently, after the final battle at the end of the Millennium, see D&C 88:11–15*].

8 And then shall that Wicked [*Satan*] be revealed [*exposed*], whom the Lord shall consume [*overpower*] with the spirit of his mouth [*with His authority*], and shall destroy with the brightness of his coming [*with His glory*]:

JST 2 Thessalonians 2:8

8 And then shall that **wicked one** be revealed, whom the Lord shall consume with the spirit of his mouth, and shall destroy with the brightness of his coming.

9 Even him, whose coming is after the working of Satan with all power and signs and lying wonders,

JST 2 Thessalonians 2:9

9 **Yea, the Lord, even Jesus**, whose coming is **not until after there cometh a falling away** [*after the prophesied apostasy*], **by** the working of Satan with all power, and signs and lying wonders,

10 And with all deceivableness of unrighteousness [*with every conceivable form of wickedness*] in them that perish [*in those who will be destroyed at the Second Coming*]; because they received not [*they would not accept*] the love of the truth, that they might be saved.

11 And for this cause [*because they deliberately chose wickedness*] God shall send them strong delusion [*God allows Satan to deceive them*], that they should believe a lie:

12 That they all might be damned [*stopped from progressing toward heaven*] who believed not the truth, but had pleasure in unrighteousness.

13 But we are bound to [*we must*] give thanks alway [*always*] to God for you, brethren beloved of the Lord, because God hath from the beginning [*from the time you were converted and baptized*] chosen you to [*toward*] salvation through sanctification of the Spirit [*has given you the help of the Holy Ghost to lead you toward sanctification (being worthy to dwell in celestial glory)*] and belief of the truth [*because of your accepting the truth of the gospel*]:

14 Whereunto he called you by our gospel [*the Father called you to*

come unto Him through the gospel we preached to you], to the obtaining of the glory of our Lord Jesus Christ [*so that you can obtain exaltation in the celestial kingdom*].

15 Therefore, brethren, stand fast [*be firm and faithful*], and hold the traditions [*of living the gospel*] which ye have been taught, whether by word [*what we have said*], or our epistle [*letter*].

16 Now our Lord Jesus Christ himself, and God, even our Father, which hath loved us, and hath given us everlasting consolation and good hope through grace,

17 Comfort your hearts, and stablish you [*establish; help you to become strong and faithful*] in every good word and work.

SECOND THESSALONIANS 3

There are no JST changes for this chapter. Here, Paul counsels these members of the Church to serve the Lord with all their hearts and emphasizes that work is an important part of the true gospel of Jesus Christ.

1 FINALLY, brethren, pray for us, that the word of the Lord may have free course [*may spread freely and rapidly; see 2 Thessalonians 3:1, footnote a*], and be glorified [*praised by others*], even as it is with you:

2 And that we may be delivered from unreasonable and wicked men [*men who are harmful, way off base,* Strong's *#0824*]: for all men have not faith [*in Christ*].

3 But the Lord is faithful, who shall stablish [*strengthen,* Strong's *#4741*] you, and keep you from evil [*the evil one, the devil; see 2 Thessalonians 3:3, footnote a in our Bible*].

4 And we have confidence in the Lord touching you [*as regarding you*] that ye both do and will do the things which we command you.

5 And the Lord [*may the Lord*] direct your hearts into the love of God [*"to serve him with all your heart and with all your soul" Deuteronomy 11:13*], and into the patient waiting for Christ [*into being steadfast and loyal to Christ;* Strong's *#5281*].

6 Now we command you, brethren, in the name of our Lord Jesus Christ, that ye withdraw yourselves from every brother that walketh disorderly [*who does not try to live the gospel, which includes being lazy and working to provide for his own needs, and who causes contention and divisiveness among you; see Romans 16:17*], and not after the tradition [*teachings; tradition of following Christ*] which he received of [*from*] us.

7 For yourselves know how ye ought to follow us [*you ought to follow our example*]: for we behaved not ourselves disorderly [*we did not neglect our duty; we worked to provide for ourselves;* Strong's *#0812*] among you;

The word "disorderly" as used in verses 7 and 8 above, often means "laziness," "idleness," "unwillingness to work," etc., and thus, Paul is warning his people against the dole, inappropriate use of welfare funds, etc. This is evident when we read verses 10–12, below.

8 Neither did we eat any man's bread for nought; but wrought with labour and travail night and day, that we might not be chargeable to any of you [*we didn't ask for handouts, rather we worked day and night to pay our own way so that we would not be a burden to any of you*]:

9 Not because we have not power [*not that we couldn't justifiably accept donations*], but to make ourselves an ensample [*example*] unto you to follow us.

10 For even when we were with you, this we commanded you, that if any would not work, neither should he eat. [*Compare with D&C 42:42.*]

11 For we hear that there are some which walk [*live*] among you disorderly [*who refuse to work*], working not at all, but are busybodies [*prying into peoples' personal affairs, gossips, etc.*].

12 Now them that are such we command and exhort [*urge*] by our Lord Jesus Christ [*in the name of Jesus Christ*], that with quietness they work [*that they settle down from running around minding everyone else's business and go to work*], and eat their own bread [*provide for themselves*].

13 But ye, brethren, be not weary in well doing [*doing good*].

14 And if any man obey not our word [*instructions*] by this epistle [*given in this letter*], note that man, and have no company with him [*don't associate with him*], that he may be ashamed.

15 Yet count him not as an enemy, but admonish him as a brother [*but don't treat him like an enemy, rather, counsel him and help him understand the importance of work, as you would a brother*].

16 Now the Lord of peace himself give you peace always by all means. The Lord be with you all.

17 The salutation [*greeting*] of Paul with mine own hand [*in my own handwriting*], which is the token in every epistle [*which is something by which you can recognize me in every letter I write*]: so I write.

18 The grace of our Lord Jesus Christ be with you all. Amen.

THE FIRST EPISTLE OF PAUL THE APOSTLE TO TIMOTHY

Paul's letters to Timothy, known as First and Second Timothy, are thought to have been written around AD 64 to AD 65 (see Bible Dictionary under "Pauline Epistles") and, chronologically, are the last of Paul's letters contained in our Bible. First Timothy was written during a brief interval of freedom for Paul after he was set free from his first Roman imprisonment. See Bible Dictionary under "Pauline Epistles," and then keep looking ahead until you find "The Fourth Group." Timothy was a young missionary companion of Paul and was treated tenderly like a son by this great Apostle of the Lord. He was probably Paul's most capable and relied upon companion and assistant. His father was a Greek and his mother (Eunice) was Jewish. See Bible Dictionary under "Timothy." Timothy accompanied Paul on many of his missionary travels, including to Corinth, Macedonia, Troas, Rome, and Ephesus. Paul left Timothy in Ephesus to serve the members of the Church there. In First Timothy, among other things, Paul gives Timothy advice concerning his leadership duties and repeats the Church's stand on many sinful behaviors common in society at that time.

FIRST TIMOTHY 1

In this chapter, Paul counsels Timothy to keep the doctrines of the Church pure and to stand up against some who are trying to get members to return to living the law of Moses. He explains that the law of Moses was designed to pull people away from grievous sins in preparation for accepting the gospel of Jesus Christ. Paul then reviews the doctrines of repentance and mercy.

1 PAUL, an apostle of Jesus Christ by the commandment of God our Saviour, and Lord Jesus Christ [*I have been called of God*], which is our hope [*our hope and optimism comes because of Christ*];

JST 1 Timothy 1:1

1 Paul, an apostle of Jesus Christ by the commandment of God **and the Lord Jesus Christ, our Savior and our hope**;

2 Unto Timothy, my own son [*who is like a son to me*] in the faith [*in the gospel*]: Grace, mercy, and peace, from God our Father and Jesus Christ our Lord.

Verse 2, above, is another reminder that the Father and the

Son are separate personages.

3 As I besought thee to abide still at Ephesus [*I asked you to stay in Ephesus*], when I went into Macedonia [*when I traveled on to northern Greece*], that thou mightest charge some that they teach no other doctrine [*so that you could instruct some members there not to teach false doctrine*],

4 Neither give heed to fables [*falsehoods;* Strong's *#3454*] and endless genealogies, which minister questions [*which generate more questions than they answer*], rather than godly edifying [*rather than building up the Church and its members*] which is in faith [*which comes through faith*]: so do.

The phrase "endless genealogies" in verse 4, above, has been used by some enemies of the Church to attack our emphasis on family history and genealogy work. We understand that Paul was referring to the common practice among some Jews of his day of proving at great lengths that they were descendants of Abraham, claiming that they were thus automatically saved above any Gentiles, no matter what the Gentiles did by way of faithfulness and personal righteousness. In the next verses, Paul will continue his emphasis on the requirement that people are saved individually, through personal righteousness and faithfulness, rather than based on who their ancestors are.

5 Now the end of [*purpose of; end goal of*] the commandment [*the gospel of Christ*] is charity out of a pure heart, and of a good conscience, and of faith unfeigned [*faith which is genuine, not pretended*]:

6 From which some having swerved [*having gone off course*] have turned aside unto vain jangling [*empty talk;* Strong's *#3150*];

7 Desiring to be teachers of the law [*wanting to teach us that we should go back to living the law of Moses; see verse 9, footnote a in our Bible*]; understanding neither what they say, nor whereof they affirm [*they don't know what they are saying nor what they bear witness of*].

8 But we know that the law [*of Moses*] is good, if a man use it lawfully [*according to the purposes for which God gave it to Moses*];

Next, Paul will emphasize that the law of Moses was given as a "schoolmaster" law (see Galatians 3:24), to elevate the children of Israel out of a very corrupt environment of sin and crude behavior, and to prepare them for the higher laws Christ would give during His mortal ministry.

9 Knowing this, that the law [*of Moses*] is not made for a righteous man [*one who is living the higher laws given by Christ*], but for the lawless and disobedient, for the ungodly [*unrighteous*] and

for sinners, for unholy and profane [*irreverent; disrespectful toward sacred things*], for murderers of fathers and murderers of mothers, for manslayers [*murderers*],

10 For whoremongers [*for people whose lives are built around sexual immorality*], for them that defile themselves with mankind [*homosexuals; see Topical Guide, p. 216, under "Homosexuality," for* men-stealers [*kidnappers*], for liars, for perjured persons [*covenant breakers*], and if there be any other thing that is contrary to sound [*correct*] doctrine;

11 According to the glorious gospel of the blessed God, which was committed to my trust [*according to the gospel which God entrusted me to preach*].

12 And I thank Christ Jesus our Lord, who hath enabled me [*made it possible for me to preach and teach*], for that he counted me faithful, putting me into the ministry [*for considering me trustworthy enough to call to this ministry*];

13 Who [*Paul*] was before [*in times past*] a blasphemer [*totally disrespectful of Christ*], and a persecutor [*of Christians; see Acts 9, where Paul, known at that time as Saul, was persecuting early Christians*], and injurious [*doing much damage to Christ's Church*]: but I obtained mercy, because I did it ignorantly in unbelief [*I was forgiven because I didn't know it was wrong*].

14 And the grace [*help, mercy, forgiveness, etc.*] of our Lord [*of the Savior*] was exceeding [*very*] abundant with faith and love which is in Christ Jesus. [*In other words, when I found out that I was wrong in persecuting Christians and repented, I felt the abundant mercy of the Lord.*]

15 This is a faithful saying [*what I say next is absolutely true*], and worthy of all acceptation [*and should be accepted by everyone*], that Christ Jesus came into the world to save sinners; of whom I am chief [*one of the worst*].

16 Howbeit [*however*] for this cause I obtained mercy [*the reason I was forgiven was*], that in me first Jesus Christ might shew forth all longsuffering [*might exhibit incredible patience*], for a pattern [*for an example*] to them which should hereafter believe on him to life everlasting [*to all others who believe in His Atonement, which leads to exalt*ation].

17 Now unto the King eternal [*Christ*], immortal, invisible [*can only be seen by those who are worthy; see JST, 1 Timothy 6:9, 15–16*], the only wise God, be honour and glory for ever and ever. Amen.

Next, Paul gives Timothy a specific charge, to fight against evil. Paul will explain more of this charge, beginning in verse 1 of chapter 2.

18 This charge I commit unto thee [*these instructions I give to you*], son Timothy [*Timothy, my son*], according to the prophecies [*the*

blessings and setting apart; see 1 Timothy 4:14] which went before on thee [*which you were given previously*], that thou by them mightest war a good warfare [*fight a good fight against evil*];

19 Holding faith, and a good conscience; which some having put away concerning faith have made shipwreck [*which some have abandoned and have thus been spiritually shipwrecked*]:

20 Of whom is Hymenæus [*a member who denied the truth of the resurrection; see* Strong's *#5211*] and Alexander; whom I have delivered unto Satan [*turned him over to the buffetings of Satan, which means being turned over to Satan without any of the protective power of God to hold Satan back from tormenting them for a season; see McConkie,* Mormon Doctrine, *p. 108. Compare with D&C 78:12*], that they may learn not to blaspheme [*break covenants and intentionally teach terrible false doctrines*].

FIRST TIMOTHY 2

Paul continues his letter to Timothy by instructing that members of the Church should pray for all people, including leaders of governments and all who have authority over them. He also gives counsel regarding local customs in Ephesus for women and their hairstyles, use of jewelry, etc., some of which we must make sure we leave in local context rather than giving it universal application.

1 I EXHORT [*urge*] therefore, that, first of all, supplications [*requests to God*], prayers, intercessions [*pleadings*], and giving of thanks, be made for all men;

JST 1 Timothy 2:1

1 I exhort therefore, that, first of all, supplications, prayers, intercessions, and **giving thanks**, be made for all men;

2 For kings, and for all that are in authority; that we may lead a quiet and peaceable life in all godliness and honesty [*dignity, respectability; see 1 Timothy 2:2, footnote d, in our Bible*].

For some whose religious beliefs do not permit them to support governments, this teaching from the Apostle Paul to pray for government leaders could serve to inspire them to rethink their position and to give appropriate support and respect, especially in view of verse 3, next.

3 For this is good and acceptable in the sight of God our Saviour [*our Father in Heaven, whose plan of salvation gives all of us the opportunity to be saved*];

4 Who will have all men to be saved, and to come unto the knowledge of the truth.

JST 1 Timothy 2:4

4 **Who is willing to have** all men to be saved, and to come unto the knowledge of the truth **which is in Christ Jesus, who is the Only Begotten Son of God, and ordained to be a**

Mediator between God [*the Father*] and man; who is one God, and hath power over all men.

5 For there is one God [*Heavenly Father*], and one mediator between God and men, the man Christ Jesus;

The word "mediator" as used in verses 4 and 5, above, is very important. By definition, a mediator works out differences between people or groups of people. Christ is the Mediator between us and the Father, meaning that He helps us work out the differences, in other words, our sins, imperfections, shortcomings, etc., which stand between us and the Father. Since the Father is perfect, and thus does not need to change, we are the ones who must change in order to "work out the differences" between us. The Savior is our Mediator, and His Atonement opens the door for us to overcome these differences and to eventually become like our Father.

6 Who gave himself a ransom for all [*who paid the cost of redeeming us from sin*], to be testified in due time.

There are various possible interpretations for the phrase "to be testified in due time" in verse 6, above. One possibility is that everyone who chooses to follow Christ can eventually have a strong testimony of Christ and His Atonement, wherein He ransomed us from sin. Another possibility is that "in due time" everyone will know who Jesus is and that "every knee should bow . . . and every tongue confess that Jesus Christ is Lord," Philippians 2:10–11.

7 Whereunto [*to whom*] I am ordained a preacher, and an apostle, (I speak the truth in Christ, and lie not;) a teacher of the Gentiles in faith and verity [*truth*].

8 I will [*desire*] therefore that men pray every where, lifting up holy hands [*a form used in praying in some cultures*], without wrath [*anger*] and doubting [*contention, arguing;* Strong's *#1261*].

9 In like manner also, that women adorn themselves in modest apparel [*clothing*], with shamefacedness [*reverence and respect for others;* Strong's *#0127*] and sobriety [*a sense of what is appropriate*]; not with broided hair, or gold, or pearls, or costly array [*expensive, showy things*];

JST 1 Timothy 2:9

9 In like manner also, that women adorn themselves in modest apparel, with shamefacedness and sobriety; not with **braided** hair, or gold, or pearls, or costly array;

It is obvious that Paul's counsel regarding women's hairstyles, jewelry, etc., in verse 9, above, is given in the context of local culture. It should not, for instance, be taken out of context and used to demand that women in our culture not be allowed to braid their hair. Perhaps braided hair in the local culture in which the Ephesian Saints lived represented a sinful lifestyle just as a woman with a shaved head represented that she was an adultress in Corinth (see note accompanying 1 Corinthians 11:5–6, in this study guide.)

10 But (which becometh [*is appropriate for*] women professing godliness) [*claiming to be reverent toward God;* Strong's *#2317*] with good works.

Verses 11–15, next, can become a source of contention and hurt if not read in the larger context of the scriptures and the words of the modern prophets. You may wish to review notes accompanying 1 Corinthians 11:1–16 and Ephesians 5:21–33 in this study guide, on the subject of men and women. Specifically, verses 11 and 12 do not reflect the teachings of the modern prophets and Apostles with respect to women and their vital role in our society and the Church, including teaching and leading in many ways. Therefore, we are left to assume that Paul was counseling Timothy with respect to rather drastic local problems where women were being very contentious or exercising unrighteous dominion over men. (The phrase "usurp authority over the man" in verse 12, below, may be a clue to what is going on in the Ephesus Ward.) A possible interpretation for verses 11 and 12 is given by the notes in parentheses. You may well be able to come up with a better one.

11 Let the woman learn in silence [*learn to listen, rather than being contentious and constantly interrupting*] with all subjection [*with proper respect toward local priesthood leaders*].

12 But I [*Paul*] suffer not [*do not allow*] a woman to teach, nor to usurp authority over the man, [*take what properly belongs to another; to domineer; see 1 Timothy 2:12, footnote b*] but to be in silence [*not meddling in the affairs of others;* Strong's *#2271*].

<u>JST 1 Timothy 2:12</u>

12 **For** I suffer not a woman to teach, nor to usurp authority over the man, but to be in silence.

For many centuries in many cultures verses 13–15, below, have sometimes been used by men as the "scriptural justification" for abuse of women. Many cultures and religions criticize and condemn Eve for her role in the fall of Adam and Eve. Our true gospel teaches us great respect for Eve and her role in furthering the purposes of God and making it possible for us to come to earth.

Eve was no doubt deceived in some ways, as indicated in verse 14, below. Perhaps Satan deceived her into believing that mortality and raising children would not ever be difficult. Perhaps he fooled her into believing that it was not that hard to cook for that many people, or to deal with 27 children who had the stomach flu at the same time, or to help Adam prepare a family home evening lesson and activity when she was bone weary from having been up with sick children nightly for two weeks.

Whatever the case, we are taught that Eve was actually not completely deceived when it came to the choice presented to her and Adam in the Garden of Eden. In Moses 4:6, we read that Satan "sought" to deceive Eve. "Sought" means that he "tried to." It implies that Lucifer was not completely successful. Apostle John A. Widtsoe explained this as follows: "Such was the problem before our first parents: to remain forever at selfish ease in the Garden of Eden, or to face unselfishly tribulation and death, in bringing to pass the purposes of the Lord for a host of waiting spirit children. They chose the latter. . . This they did with open eyes and minds as to consequences. The memory of their former estates may have been dimmed, but the gospel had been taught them during their sojourn in the Garden of Eden . . . the choice that they made raises Adam and Eve to preeminence among all who have come on earth." *Evidences and Reconciliations*, pp. 193–194.

In Encyclopedia of Mormonism, under the topic "EVE," we are taught: "Satan was present to tempt Adam and Eve, much as he would try to thwart others in their divine missions: 'and he sought also to beguile Eve, for he knew not the mind of God, wherefore he sought to destroy the world' (Moses 4:6). Eve faced the choice between selfish ease and unselfishly facing tribulation and death (Widtsoe, *Evidences and Reconciliations*, p. 193). As befit her calling, she realized that there was no other way and deliberately chose mortal life so as to further the purpose of God and bring children into the world."

13 For Adam was first formed [*God created Adam first*], then Eve.

14 And Adam was not deceived, but the woman being deceived was in the transgression.

Regarding the word "transgression," as used in connection with the fall of Adam, Joseph Fielding Smith said: "I'm very, very grateful that in the Book of Mormon, and I think elsewhere in our scriptures, the fall of Adam has not been called a sin. It wasn't a sin. . . . What did Adam do? The very thing the Lord wanted him to do; and I hate to hear anybody call it a sin, for it wasn't a sin. Did Adam sin when he partook of the forbidden fruit? I say to you, no, he did not! Now, let me refer to what was written in the book of Moses in regard to the command God gave to Adam. (Moses 3:16–17.) Now this is the way I interpret that: The Lord said to Adam, here is the tree of the knowledge of good and evil. If you want to stay here, then you cannot eat of that fruit. If you want to stay here, then I forbid you to eat it. But you may act for yourself, and you may eat of it if you want to. And if you eat it, you will die. I see a great difference between transgressing the law and committing a sin." (Joseph Fielding Smith, "Fall—Atonement—Resurrection—Sacrament," in Charge to Religious Educators, p. 124.) See Institute of religion *Doctrines of the Gospel Student Manual*, Religion 431 and 432, p. 20.

The JST makes a most significant change in verse 15, next. The Prophet changed the word "she" to "they," thus the verse applies to Adam and Eve, not just to Eve in a subservient role.

15 Notwithstanding she shall be saved in childbearing [*supported and strengthened in their role as parents*], if they continue in faith and charity and holiness with sobriety [*taking their responsibilities seriously; with soberness;* Strong's #*4997*].

JST 1 Timothy 2:15

15 Notwithstanding **they** shall be saved in childbearing, if they continue in faith and charity and holiness with sobriety.

FIRST TIMOTHY 3

Paul now gives Timothy instructions regarding what kind of men he should look for in calling bishops and deacons. He also gives qualifications for the wife of a bishop and the wife of a deacon.

1 THIS is a true saying, If a man desire the office of a bishop, he desireth a good work.

2 A bishop then must be blameless [*must have a good reputation;* Strong's #*0423*], the husband of one wife [*must not be practicing polygamy, which was still done to some extent among the Jews in New Testament times*], vigilant [*temperate;* Strong's #*3524*], sober [*exercising good self-control;* Strong's #*4998*], of good behaviour, given to hospitality, apt to teach [*skilled at teaching;* Strong's #*1317*];

3 Not given to wine [*not a drunkard*], no striker [*not violent or overbearing*], not greedy of filthy lucre [*not greedy where money is involved*]; but patient, not a brawler [*not contentious, not inclined to pick fights;* Strong's #*0269*], not covetous;

4 One that ruleth well his own house [*one who presides appropriately over his own family*], having his children in subjection with all gravity [*one whose children respect and honor him because he earns their respect;* Strong's #*4587*];

5 (or if a man know not how to rule his own house, how shall he take care of the church of God?)

6 Not a novice [*not a very recent convert;* Strong's #*3504*], lest being lifted up with pride [*for fear that he might become prideful and*

exercise unrighteous dominion] he fall into the condemnation of the devil [*and thus becomes a tool in the devil's hand*].

7 Moreover he must have a good report of them which are without [*he must have a good reputation among nonmembers in the community*]; lest he fall into reproach [*be criticized*] and the snare [*trap*] of the devil.

Next, in verse 8, Paul gives counsel concerning deacons. Keep in mind that in the culture of the day, men had to be 30 years old or older in order to be ministers in a church. Thus, deacons would have been mature men at least 30 years old.

8 Likewise must the deacons be grave [*dignified; respected because of their good character;* Strong's *#4586*], not doubletongued [*saying one thing to one person but a different thing to another; deceitful*], not given to much wine [*not given to drunkenness*], not greedy of filthy lucre [*not greedy where money is involved; dishonest in business dealings*];

9 Holding the mystery of the faith [*sticking with the doctrines of the Church*] in a pure conscience.

10 And let these also first be proved [*let them be thoroughly interviewed before calling them to serve as deacons*]; then let them use the office of a deacon, being found blameless [*maintaining a good reputation*].

11 Even so must their wives be grave [*respected because of their good character:* Strong's *#4586*], not slanderers [*not gossipers*], sober [*self-controlled*], faithful [*trustworthy:* Strong's *#4103*] in all things.

12 Let the deacons be the husbands of one wife [*must not be practicing polygamy*], ruling [*presiding over*] their children and their own houses well [*appropriately*].

13 For they that have used the office of a deacon well purchase to themselves a good degree [*earn themselves a reputation of being a good influence in the Church;* Strong's *#0898*], and great boldness in the faith [*and are able to teach the gospel openly and frankly;* Strong's *#3954*] which is [*which exists*] in Christ Jesus.

14 These things write I [*Paul*] unto thee [*Timothy*], hoping to come unto thee shortly [*soon*]:

15 But if I tarry long [*if I end up remaining here for a long time*], that thou mayest know how thou oughtest to behave thyself in the house of God [*in your leadership responsibilities in the Church*], which is the church of the living God [*the God who is actually alive, not an idol carved of wood, made of stone, etc.*], the pillar and ground of the truth.

16 And without controversy [*without a doubt*] great is the mystery of godliness [*this remains a great mystery to unbelievers, namely that*]: God [*Christ*] was manifest in the flesh [*came to earth to live*], justified in the Spirit [*was

testified of by the Holy Ghost], seen of angels [*was pointed out to many mortals by angels*], preached unto the Gentiles [*was preached about to the Gentiles*], believed on in the world [*many now believe in him*], received up into glory [*was received into celestial glory in heaven*].

The JST combines the last phrase of verse 15 into verse 16. This change emphasizes that the Savior is the "pillar" and "ground (foundation) of the truth." Notice that Joseph Smith added a parenthesis to this verse of the JST.

JST 1 Timothy 3:16

16 **The pillar and ground of the truth is**, (and without controversy, great is the mystery of godliness,) God was manifest in the flesh, justified in the Spirit, seen of angels, preached unto the Gentiles, believed on in the world, received up into glory.

FIRST TIMOTHY 4

Paul now will prophesy about conditions in the world in the last days before the Second Coming of the Savior.

1 NOW the Spirit speaketh expressly [*the Spirit tells me specifically*], that in the latter times [*in the last days*] some shall depart from the faith [*some will abandon the gospel of Christ*], giving heed to seducing spirits [*evil spirits who deceive*], and doctrines of devils [*false doctrines and philosophies*];

2 Speaking lies in hypocrisy; having their conscience seared with a hot iron; [*In other words, their consciences will no longer work.*]

JST 1 Timothy 4:2

2 Speaking lies in hypocrisy; having their conscience seared **as with** a hot iron;

3 Forbidding to marry [*see note below*], and commanding to abstain from meats [*and requiring not to eat meat, for religious reasons*], which God hath created to be received with thanksgiving of them which believe and know the truth.

"Forbidding to marry" in verse 3, above, can happen in many ways as described in the following quote: "Celibacy, living together out of wedlock, homosexuality, adultery, abortion, and birth control are but a few of the many methods employed to pervert men's minds and prevent the creation and continuance of this holy union. In the words of President Harold B. Lee, 'Satan's greatest threat today is to destroy the family, and to make mockery of the law of chastity and the sanctity of the marriage covenant' (Church News, 19 Aug. 1972, 3.)" See Institute of Religion's New Testament student manual, *Life and Teachings of Jesus and His Apostles*, p. 363.

Verse 3, above, is also significant in conjunction with our

Word of Wisdom, D&C 89:13–14, regarding the eating of meat. Some members mistakenly believe that faithful members should not eat meat at all, except in times of famine or extreme cold. Paul prophesied that some would teach this as a matter of religious doctrine and would thus lead some astray. In the Word of Wisdom, the key word regarding meat is "sparingly" (D&C 89:12.) That the Word of Wisdom is not a system of vegetarianism is clearly taught in D&C 49:18–19, including footnote 18a. Apostle John A. Widtsoe emphasized this when he said, "The Word of Wisdom is not a system of vegetarianism. Clearly, meat is permitted (see D&C 42:18). Naturally, that includes animal products, less subject than meat to putrefactive and other disturbances, such as eggs, milk, and cheese. These products cannot be excluded simply because they are not mentioned specifically. By that token most of our foodstuffs could not be eaten." (Widtsoe, *Evidences and Reconciliations*, 3:156–57. Quoted in the Institute of Religion *Doctrine and Covenants Student Manual*, p. 210.)

4 For every creature of [*everything created by*] God is good, and nothing to be refused [*rejected; Strong's #0579*], if it be received with thanksgiving [*with gratitude*]:

Under the law of Moses, many foods were to be rejected by faithful Israelites. They had, indeed, a rather strict "Word of Wisdom," including several kinds of meat, fish, poultry, and bugs which were not to be eaten. See Leviticus, chapter 11. In verses 4 and 5, next, Paul reminds Timothy that under the gospel of Christ, these restrictions were done away with.

5 For it is sanctified [*made acceptable*] by the word of God [*the gospel of Jesus Christ*] and prayer.

6 If thou put the brethren in remembrance of [*if you will remind the brethren about*] these things, thou shalt be a good minister of Jesus Christ, nourished up in the words of faith and of good doctrine, whereunto thou hast attained [*of which you have attained a good understanding*].

7 But refuse [*reject*] profane [*the wisdom of men rather than of God*] and old wives' fables [*tales*], and exercise thyself rather unto godliness [*keep learning what God says about such matters*].

8 For bodily exercise profiteth little [*for a little while, in other words, does some good; see 1 Timothy 4:8, footnote a*]: but godliness [*exercising God's word in your life*] is profitable unto all things [*applies to all aspects of living*], having promise of the life that now is [*has benefits during our mortal lives*], and of that which is to come [*and is beneficial into eternity*].

9 This is a faithful saying and worthy of all acceptation [*of being accepted fully*].

10 For therefore [*for the gospel*] we both labour [*work*] and suffer reproach [*endure criticism*], because we trust in the living God, who is the Saviour of all men, specially of those that believe [*who wants to save all people, and will save those who live the gospel*].

11 These things command and teach.

In verse 12, next, we find that Timothy is relatively young. No doubt there were members of the Church in Ephesus who were much older than he, including some of the priesthood leaders.

12 Let no man despise thy youth [*show disrespect for you because of how young you are*]; but be thou an example of the believers, in word, in conversation [*conduct, behavior;* Strong's *#0391*], in charity, in spirit, in faith, in purity.

13 Till I come [*until I can manage to visit you in Ephesus*], give attendance [*apply yourself*] to reading, to exhortation [*to teaching*], to doctrine.

14 Neglect not the gift that is in thee, which was given thee by prophecy, with the laying on of the hands of the presbytery [*do not neglect to use the blessing that was given you under inspiration when you were set apart to your position by the elders*].

15 Meditate upon [*think about*] these things; give thyself wholly [*completely*] to them; that thy profiting [*progress*] may appear to all [*may be easily recognizable by the members there*].

16 Take heed unto thyself, and unto the doctrine [*watch what you do and hold to correct doctrine*]; continue in them: for in doing this thou shalt both save thyself, and them that hear thee.

FIRST TIMOTHY 5

Since Timothy is a relatively young priesthood leader, Paul now counsels him to be careful how he deals with older members under his stewardship.

1 REBUKE not an elder [*don't correct an older man harshly*], but intreat him as a father [*but offer correction gently as if he were your father*]; and the younger men as brethren [*as if they were your brothers*];

2 The elder [*older*] women as mothers; the younger as sisters, with all purity [*with pure motives to help them*].

In the next several verses, Paul will give Timothy instructions concerning welfare assistance to needy members. These principles hold true for us today.

3 Honour widows that are widows indeed [*respond to the welfare needs of widows who are actually in need of assistance because they have no family to help them*].

4 But if any widow have children or nephews [*grandchildren,*

descendants; see 1 Timothy 5:4, footnote b], let them [*her children and relatives*] learn first to shew [*show*] piety [*live their religion*] at home, and to requite [*pay back*] their parents [*for taking care of them when they were growing up*]: for that is good and acceptable before God.

5 Now she that is a widow indeed [*has no one to help her*], and desolate [*and is in need of assistance*], trusteth in God [*has faith in God*], and continueth in supplications [*asking God for help*] and prayers night and day.

6 But she [*the widow*] that liveth in pleasure [*who indulges in worldly pleasures*] is dead [*spiritually dead*] while she [*the widow who humbly relies on God for help*] liveth [*is spiritually alive*].

7 And these things give in charge [*instruct all the members in these matters*], that they may be blameless [*so that they don't make mistakes in the matter of welfare assistance*].

8 But if any provide not for his own, and specially for those of his own house [*if anyone who is capable does not provide for the needs of his own, including his relatives;* Strong's *#3609*], he hath denied the faith [*he has rejected the gospel*], and is worse than an infidel [*one who does not believe in God;* Strong's *#0571*].

9 Let not a widow be taken into the number under threescore years old [*don't put any widow on the list of widows to receive welfare assistance unless she is at least 60 years old*], having been the wife of one man [*and was faithful to her husband while he was alive*],

10 Well reported of for good works [*and has a reputation for doing good deeds*]; if she have brought up children [*such as raising children*], if she have lodged strangers [*providing shelter and food for strangers in need*], if she have washed the saints' feet, if she have relieved the afflicted [*given aid to people in distress*], if she have diligently followed every good work [*and has done all sorts of good deeds*].

JST 1 Timothy 5:10

10 Well reported of for good works; if she have brought up children, if she have lodged strangers, if she have washed the Saints' **clothes**, if she have relieved the afflicted, if she have diligently followed every good work.

Based on what Paul says next about younger widows, there must have been some problems among the members in Ephesus with younger widows desiring sexual relations but not wanting to remarry. It would seem that some things must have been left out of the next verses, so we will make a guess, based on what we know from other scriptures.

11 But the younger widows refuse [*don't put them on welfare assistance*]: for when they have begun to wax wanton [*have become lustful*] against Christ [*against the*

teachings of Christ], they will marry [*they marry for lustful reasons rather than out of desire to raise children, be good homemakers, etc.*];

12 Having damnation, because they have cast off their first faith [*because they have rejected the gospel*].

13 And withal [*at the same time they reject the gospel;* Strong's *#0260*] they learn to be idle, wandering about from house to house; and not only idle, but tattlers [*gossips*] also and busybodies [*minding everybody's business*], speaking things which they ought not.

14 I will [*prefer*] therefore that the younger women [*widows*] marry, bear children, guide the house [*take care of their homes*], give none occasion [*reason*] to the adversary [*enemies of the Church*] to speak reproachfully [*to criticize*].

15 For some are already turned aside after Satan [*some have already left the Church and are following Satan*].

16 If any man or woman that believeth have widows [*if any adult members of the Church have relatives who are widows*], let them relieve them [*render assistance to them*], and let not the church be charged [*don't leave it up to the Church to help them*]; that it may relieve them that are widows indeed [*so that Church funds and resources can be used for those widows who have no other means of support*].

Verses 17 and 18, next, refer to Church leaders and missionaries who are serving full-time and thus need assistance for them and their families while they are serving.

17 Let the elders that rule well [*who serve honorably*] be counted worthy of double honour [*not only respect but also financial and other assistance as needed*], especially they who labour in the word and doctrine [*especially those serving full-time missions*].

18 For the scripture saith [*in Deuteronomy 25:4*], Thou shalt not muzzle the ox that treadeth out the corn [*make sure the ox has plenty to eat while he is working to harvest the grain*]. And, The labourer is worthy of his reward [*Luke 10:7. In other words, the faithful worker deserves to be well taken care of.*]

19 Against an elder receive not an accusation, but before two or three witnesses [*don't take any disciplinary action against a leader unless there are at least two or three witnesses that he has done wrong*].

20 Them that sin rebuke [*correct*] before all [*publicly*], that others also may fear [*will be afraid to commit such sins*]. [*This apparently refers to those who sin openly and, as a result, many know about it. See D&C 42:90–91. D&C 42:92 instructs us to deal privately with people whose sins were done secretly or privately, so that we don't embarrass them unnecessarily*]

21 I charge [*instruct*] thee before God, and the Lord Jesus Christ, and the elect angels, that thou observe these things without preferring one before another, doing nothing by partiality. [*In other words, make sure you are fair and impartial as you deal with such matters.*]

22 Lay hands suddenly on no man [*don't set anyone apart for a church calling or ordain any man to the priesthood without making sure they are prepared and ready for it*], neither be partaker of [*don't participate in*] other men's sins: keep thyself pure.

In verse 23, next, Paul gives Timothy a bit of personal medical advise for stomach problems he apparently has. Some enemies of the Church delight in quoting this verse to us in order to discredit the Word of Wisdom. What they don't realize and what some members today don't remember is that the Word of Wisdom was not given until 1833, and that it was given because of special problems and concerns which would exist in the last days (see D&C 89:4). Therefore, whether the "wine" referred to by Paul was fresh fruit juice or was fermented wine, it is not a problem because the Word of Wisdom had not yet been given.

23 Drink no longer water, but use a little wine for thy stomach's sake and thine often infirmities [*and for your frequent sicknesses*].

Verse 24, next, seems to be a continuation of the counsel given in verse 22, above. It appears that Paul is giving Timothy counsel about interviewing potential priesthood holders or men for particular callings in the Church, before he lays hands on them to set them apart.

24 Some men's sins are open beforehand, going before to judgment [*some men's sins are already well known before they come to an interview*]; and some men they follow after [*and some men's sins show up later*].

25 Likewise also the good works of some are manifest beforehand [*likewise, you will already be familiar with the good works of some men before you interview them*]; and they that are otherwise cannot be hid [*and some will blossom and surprise people after they have been interviewed and called to serve*].

FIRST TIMOTHY 6

In Paul's day, many people had slaves and many had servants. Some of those who were servants or slaves apparently joined the Church. Paul counsels them to be good examples to their masters so that the masters would have a favorable opinion of the gospel of Christ.

1 LET as many servants as are under the yoke [*who are owned by their masters*] count their own masters worthy of all honour

[*show honor and respect toward their masters*], that [*in order that*] the name of God and his doctrine be not blasphemed [*might not be mocked*].

2 And they that have believing masters [*and those who have masters who have joined the Church*], let them not despise them, because they are brethren [*don't become too informal with them because they are members*]; but rather do them service [*serve them well*], because they are faithful and beloved, partakers of the benefit [*partakers of the blessings of the gospel*]. These things teach and exhort [*urge; counsel*].

3 If any man teach otherwise [*if any of your members teach against what I have told you*], and consent not to wholesome words [*and won't accept correction*], even [*according to*] the words of our Lord Jesus Christ, and to the doctrine which is according to godliness [*which leads to godly behavior*];

4 He is proud, knowing nothing [*then you will know that he is prideful and knows nothing*], but doting [*is sick in the head; Strong's #3552*] about questions and strifes of words, whereof cometh envy, strife, railings, evil surmisings [*and will cause doubts and arguments which will lead to envy, contention, vicious criticism, false assumptions*],

5 Perverse disputings [*twisted debates*] of men of corrupt minds, and destitute of the truth [*who do not know the truth*], supposing that gain is godliness [*supposing that dishonest profit in business is righteousness*]: from such withdraw thyself.

6 But godliness with contentment is great gain [*is very profitable*].

7 For we brought nothing into this world, and it is certain we can carry nothing out.

8 And having food and raiment [*clothing*] let us be therewith content.

9 But they that will be rich [*whose top priority is to get rich*] fall into temptation and a snare [*a trap*], and into many foolish and hurtful lusts [*damaging temptations*], which drown men in destruction and perdition [*and lead them to spiritual death*].

Verse 10, next, is one of the most often-quoted verses in the Bible. However, it is very often miss-quoted as follows: "Money is the root of all evil." As you can see, Paul says "**the love of money** is the root of all evil." Many people handle money just fine and remain righteous. It is when people love money more than honesty or integrity or God or covenants or people, and so forth, that they get into trouble.

10 For the love of money is the root of all evil: which while some coveted after, they have erred from the faith [*which has caused some to fall away from the gospel*], and pierced themselves through with many sorrows [*and caused themselves much heartache*].

11 But thou, O man of God [*but if you want to be a true man of God*], flee these things; and follow after righteousness, godliness, faith, love, patience, meekness.

12 Fight the good fight of faith [*remain faithful at all costs*], lay hold on eternal life [*hang on to things which will lead to exaltation*], whereunto [*to which*] thou art also called, and hast professed a good profession before many witnesses [*and of which you have born testimony before many people*].

13 I give thee charge in the sight of God [*I tell you in the strongest possible terms, with God as my witness*], who quickeneth all things [*who gives life to all things*], and before Christ Jesus [*and with Jesus Christ as my witness*], who before Pontius Pilate [*the Roman ruler who turned Jesus over to the crowd to be crucified; see John 18:29–40*] witnessed a good confession [*bore strong testimony of who he was*];

14 That thou keep this commandment without spot [*with absolutely no compromising*], unrebukeable [*allowing no room for being scolded*], until the appearing of our Lord Jesus Christ:

15 Which in his times [*when the time is right*] he shall shew, who is the blessed and only Potentate [*the Supreme Authority*], the King of kings, and Lord of lords;

JST 1 Timothy 6:15

15 Which in his times he shall **show**, who is the blessed and only Potentate, the King of kings, and Lord of lords, **to whom be honor and power everlasting**;

The JST makes very important changes in verse 16, next. Without the Prophet's help on this, a terribly damaging false doctrine might go unchecked, namely, that no one has seen nor can see God, nor can people ever even approach becoming like God. Unfortunately, such tragic false doctrine is taught by many who use this mistranslation in the Bible as their doctrinal foundation.

16 Who only hath immortality, dwelling in the light which no man can approach unto; whom no man hath seen, nor can see: to whom be honour and power everlasting. Amen.

JST 1 Timothy 6:16

16 Whom no man hath seen, nor can see, **unto whom no man can approach, only he who hath the light and the hope of immortality dwelling in him** [*in other words, only those who live the gospel can have such blessings*].

Even honest people who don't believe in the Prophet Joseph Smith but do believe in the Bible would be compelled to conclude that verse 16, as it stands in the Bible, is not correct. All they have to do is read scriptures such as Acts 7:55–56 where Stephen did see both God and Jesus standing on His right side. Also, they can know that

God is approachable by reading such scriptures as Matthew 5:48 where we are told to become perfect like God, or read 1 John 3:2 where we are told in the Bible that the "sons of God," in other words "the righteous" will someday see that they are just like Jesus.

17 Charge [*instruct*] them that are rich in this world, that they be not highminded [*prideful;* Strong's *#5309*], nor trust in uncertain riches [*wealth, which is unreliable*], but in the living God, who giveth us richly all things to enjoy;

18 That they do good, that they be rich in good works, ready to distribute [*share their wealth*], willing to communicate [*be generous with others;* Strong's *#2843*];

19 Laying up in store for themselves a good foundation against the time to come [*storing up for themselves blessings in heaven for the future*], that they may lay hold on eternal life [*so that they can obtain exaltation*].

By the way, the phrase "eternal life," used in verse 19, above, always means "exaltation."

20 O Timothy, keep that which is committed to thy trust [*be faithful in your stewardship, your responsibilities*], avoiding profane and vain babblings [*avoiding commonplace, useless, time-wasting talk*], and oppositions of science falsely so called [*and so-called science which opposes our religion*]:

21 Which some professing have erred concerning the faith [*which have caused some who get caught up in it to not believe the gospel*]. Grace be with thee. Amen.

THE SECOND EPISTLE OF PAUL THE APOSTLE TO TIMOTHY

For background information on Timothy, see note at the beginning of First Timothy in this study guide. Second Timothy was written during Paul's second imprisonment, shortly before he was executed during the extreme persecution of Christians under Nero, Emperor of Rome. Bible Scholars estimate that Paul was killed somewhere between about AD 65 to AD 68 in Rome. As you will sense as you study Second Timothy, Paul knew that his time was short.

SECOND TIMOTHY 1

In the first verse of this chapter, Paul preaches that eternal life is available through Jesus Christ. In this case, "life" means "eternal life." In the scriptures, eternal life always means "exaltation." Exaltation refers to those who attain the highest degree of glory in the celestial kingdom—see D&C 132:19–20.

Later in this chapter, we learn that Paul is rather lonely at this point of his last imprisonment in Rome, not long before his execution (verse 15).

There are no JST changes for this chapter.

1 PAUL, an apostle of Jesus Christ by the will of God [*having been called of God*], according to the promise of life [*eternal life*] which is in [*comes through*] Christ Jesus,

2 To Timothy, my dearly beloved son [*Paul considers Timothy to be like a son to him*]: Grace, mercy, and peace, from God the Father and Christ Jesus our Lord.

3 I thank God, whom I serve from my forefathers [*as my ancestors did*] with pure conscience, that without ceasing I have remembrance of thee in my prayers [*I remember you in my prayers*] night and day;

4 Greatly desiring to see thee, being mindful of thy tears, that I may be filled with joy;

5 When I call to remembrance the unfeigned faith that is in thee [*when I think back on your pure faith*], which dwelt first in thy grandmother Lois, and thy mother Eunice [*which your grandmother and mother had also*]; and I am persuaded that in thee also [*I am convinced that you have that kind of pure faith also*].

6 Wherefore I put thee in remembrance that thou stir up the gift of God, which is in thee by the putting on of my hands [*I want to remind you to be faithful to the spiritual gift which was given to you when I set you apart*].

7 For God hath not given us the spirit of fear; but of power, and of love, and of a sound mind.

8 Be not thou therefore ashamed of [*embarrassed by*] the testimony of our Lord, nor of me his prisoner: but be thou partaker of the afflictions of the gospel according to the power of God [*but endure afflictions, troubles, trials, and so forth, with the help of our Father in Heaven*];

9 Who hath saved us [*from the ways of the world*], and called us with an holy calling [*and called us to serve Him*], not according to our works [*not because we are that worthy or capable*], but according to his own purpose and grace [*according to His plan of salvation*], which was given us in Christ Jesus before the world began [*which the Father gave us through Jesus Christ in premortality*],

As noted above, the last of verse 9, above, contains an important doctrine, namely, that the Savior's Atonement was already working for us in our premortal life. We had agency there (D&C 29:35–36) and could thus make choices. If we made a mistake, we could repent and be forgiven and continue to progress in premortality, because of the infinite Atonement (just as the Atonement also worked before it was performed for Alma, Alma the Younger, and so many others who lived here on earth before the Atonement was done by Jesus.)

Elder Jeffrey R. Holland, of the Quorum of the Twelve, referred to the fact that the Atonement was already working for us in premortality in his General Conference address in October, 1995 when he said, referring to premortality, "We could remember that even in the Grand Council of Heaven He loved us and was wonderfully strong, that we triumphed even there by the power of Christ and our faith in the blood of the Lamb."

10 But [*the Father's plan*] is now made manifest [*made clear to us*] by the appearing of our Saviour Jesus Christ, who hath abolished [*overcome*] death, and hath brought life and immortality to light through the gospel [*and has taught us about eternal life and resurrection through His gospel*]:

11 Whereunto [*for which gospel*] I am appointed [*I have been called to be*] a preacher, and an apostle, and a teacher of the Gentiles.

12 For the which cause I also suffer these things [*and this is the reason I am now in prison in Rome*]: nevertheless I am not ashamed: for I know whom I have believed [*in other words, I believe in Christ*], and am persuaded [*convinced*] that he is able to keep that which I have committed unto him against that day. [*In other words, I am convinced that the sacrifices I have made and continue to make for the gospel will be there on Judgment Day to bless me.*]

13 Hold fast the form of sound words, which thou hast heard of me [*adhere strictly to the words of counsel I have given you*], in faith and love which is in Christ Jesus [*which I gave you in the faith and love which come from the Savior*].

14 That good thing which was committed unto thee keep by the Holy Ghost which dwelleth in us [*use the promptings of the Holy Ghost to help you carry out the responsibilities you were given*].

During Paul's first imprisonment in Rome, which lasted two years, he was under "house arrest," living in a house he rented, and he had many privileges not usually given to prisoners. But now, imprisoned again in Rome and soon to be executed, his conditions are poor. Bible scholars believe that Luke was still with him, but apparently few, if any, others were allowed to visit him or even dared to visit him in prison. His loneliness is felt in verse 15, next.

15 This thou knowest, that all they which are in Asia [*the wards and branches of the Church in what would be western Turkey today*] be turned away from me [*have forgotten me*]; of whom are [*including*] Phygellus and Hermogenes.

16 The Lord give mercy unto the house of Onesiphorus; for he oft refreshed me, and was not ashamed of my chain [*was not afraid to visit me here in prison*]:

17 But, when he was in Rome, he sought me out [*looked for me*] very diligently, and found me.

18 The Lord grant unto him that he may find mercy of the Lord in that day [*on Judgment Day*]: and in how many things he ministered unto me at Ephesus, thou knowest very well.

SECOND TIMOTHY 2

Paul will now compare the work Timothy has before him to the work of a valiant soldier, a well-trained athlete, a skilled farmer who raises fine crops. The imagery is that when we serve the Lord with skill and dedication, we accomplish the work effectively and bring the rewards of the gospel upon ourselves.

1 THOU therefore, my son, be strong in the grace [*merciful kindness;* Strong's *#5485*] that is in [*comes from*] Christ Jesus.

2 And the things [*the words of counsel*] that thou hast heard of [*from*] me among many witnesses, the same commit thou [*teach the same things*] to faithful men, who shall be able to teach others also.

3 Thou therefore endure hardness, as a good soldier of Jesus Christ.

Paul will now compare the work Timothy has to do to the work which a valiant soldier must do to be worthy of his captain's approval.

4 No man that warreth [*no good soldier*] entangleth himself with the affairs of this life [*lets his attention be diverted to other cares*]; that he may please him who hath chosen him to be a soldier [*so that he can remain pleasing to the leader who chose him to join his army*].

The imagery used in verse 5, next, is that of an athlete in training to compete in an event. In the actual competition, the athlete must follow the rules of the game in order to earn the victor's crown.

5 And if a man [*an athlete*] also strive for masteries [*competes in an athletic event; see 2 Timothy 2:5, footnote a, in our Bible*], yet is he not crowned [*he is not given the victor's crown*], except he strive lawfully [*unless he has followed the rules of the game*].

JST 2 Timothy 2:5

5 And if a man also strive for masteries, **he is** not crowned, except he strive lawfully.

Next, in verse 6, Paul uses the imagery of a hardworking farmer who is the first to receive a share of the harvest. In other words, if Timothy continues to labor diligently in the "field," he will enjoy the "harvest" of his own soul.

6 The husbandman [*farmer*] that laboureth [*who works diligently to produce a good harvest*] must be first partaker of the fruits [*harvests salvation for his own soul*].

7 Consider [*think carefully about*] what I say; and the Lord give thee understanding in all things.

8 Remember that Jesus Christ of the seed of David [*who was a descendant of King David*] was raised from the dead according to my gospel [*JST "according to the gospel"*]:

JST 2 Timothy 2:8

8 Remember that Jesus Christ of the seed of David was raised from the dead, according to **the** gospel;

9 Wherein I suffer trouble [*my preaching of the gospel has caused me much trouble*], as an evil doer [*and has made many people think I am an evil man*], even unto bonds [*and is the cause of my being in prison, in chains, here in Rome*]; but the word of God is not bound [*but the gospel can still go forth*].

10 Therefore I endure all things for the elect's sakes [*for the sake of those who are willing to make and keep covenants with God; see D&C 84:34–38*], that they may also obtain the salvation which is in Christ Jesus with eternal glory [*in the celestial kingdom*].

11 It is a faithful saying [*you can trust the following saying completely*]: For if we be dead with him [*if we "bury" our sins through baptism and through his Atonement; see Romans 6:4–6*], we shall also live with him [*we will live with him in celestial glory*]:

JST 2 Timothy 2:11

11 For **this** is a faithful **saying, If** we be dead with him, we shall also live with him;

12 If we suffer [*remain faithful, no matter what*], we shall also reign with him [*we will rule with him during the Millennium; see Revelation 20:4*]: if we deny [*reject*] him, he also will deny us:

13 If we believe not [*whether or not we remain faithful*], yet he abideth faithful [*Christ remains faithful to the Father*]: he cannot deny himself.

14 Of these things put them in remembrance [*teach your people these things*], charging [*instructing*] them before the Lord that they strive not about words to no profit [*don't argue about trivial things*], but to the subverting of the hearers [*which only serves to damage the testimonies of those who hear such arguing*].

15 Study to shew thyself approved unto God [*do all you can to stay in harmony with God*], a workman [*a servant in God's kingdom*] that

needeth not to be ashamed [*who has no need to be ashamed of what he is doing*], rightly dividing [*teaching;* Strong's #*3718*] the word of truth.

16 But shun [*avoid*] profane [*irreverent*] and vain [*worthless*] babblings [*talk*]: for they will increase unto [*lead to*] more ungodliness.

17 And their word will eat as doth a canker [*will spread to others like an infection with gangrene; see* Strong's #*1044*]: of whom is [*for example*] Hymenæus and Philetus;

18 Who concerning the truth have erred [*who are teaching false doctrine*], saying that the resurrection is past already [*has already happened, so it is too late for us*]; and overthrow [*undermine*] the faith of some.

19 Nevertheless the foundation of God standeth sure [*if we build on the sure foundation of Christ, which the Father has given us*], having this seal [*we positively know this*], The Lord knoweth them that are his [*the Lord will reward the faithful*]. And, Let every one that nameth [*who have taken upon them*] the name of Christ depart from iniquity.

20 But in a great [*large*] house there are not only vessels of gold and of silver, but also of wood and of earth; and some to honour, and some to dishonour. [*In other words, even in the Church which is a "big house," there are righteous and unrighteous people, and some will be rewarded by God and some will be punished by him.*]

21 If a man therefore purge himself from these [*the sins, etc., which I have mentioned to you, Timothy*], he shall be a vessel unto honour [*a "container" of righteousness, worthy of being honored by God*], sanctified [*made clean and pure by the Atonement*], and meet [*fit*] for the master's use [*and a worthy instrument in the hand of the Lord*], and prepared unto every good work [*and properly prepared to do much good*].

22 Flee also youthful lusts [*avoid sins and lustful desires which trap many younger people*]: but follow righteousness, faith, charity, peace, with them that call on the Lord out of a pure heart.

23 But foolish and unlearned questions avoid [*avoid getting caught up in foolish, shallow controversies*], knowing that they do gender strifes [*knowing that they lead to contention*].

24 And the servant of the Lord must not strive [*argue with people*]; but be gentle unto all men, apt to teach, patient,

25 In meekness [*slow to anger*] instructing those that oppose themselves [*who argue against them*]; if God peradventure [*perhaps*] will give them repentance to the acknowledging of the truth [*the opportunity to repent and accept the true gospel*];

26 And that they may recover themselves [*so that they can turn their lives around*] out of the snare [*trap*] of the devil, who are taken captive by him at his will [*who are easy for the devil to capture because they don't live the gospel*].

SECOND TIMOTHY 3

In these next verses, Paul describes in considerable detail conditions and evils which will take place in the last days, before the Savior's Second Coming.

1 THIS know also, that in the last days [*before the Savior's Second Coming*] perilous [*dangerous*] times shall come.

2 For men shall be lovers of their own selves [*selfish*], covetous [*wanting what belongs to others*], boasters [*empty pretenders;* Strong's *#0213*], proud, blasphemers [*disrespectful of sacred things*], disobedient to parents, unthankful [*ungrateful*], unholy [*un-religious*],

3 Without natural affection [*involved in homosexuality; see 2 Timothy 3:3, footnotes a and b*], trucebreakers [*breaking their word*], false accusers [*ruining the good reputations of others*], incontinent [*lacking self-control*], fierce [*savage;* Strong's *#0434*], despisers of those that are good,

4 Traitors, heady [*rash, reckless, not thinking ahead*], highminded [*conceited*], lovers of pleasures more than lovers of God;

5 Having a form of godliness [*claiming to be religious*], but denying the power thereof: from such turn away [*avoid such behaviors and people*].

6 For of this sort are they which [*these are the types who*] creep into houses [*who work their way into people's houses and lives*], and lead captive [*gain control over*] silly women laden with sins [*already loaded with sins*], led away with divers [*various*] lusts [*wicked, evil passions*],

7 Ever learning, and never able to come to the knowledge of the truth.

8 Now as Jannes and Jambres [*two Egyptian magicians in Pharaoh's court who, according to Jewish tradition, imitated Aaron's miracles when Moses was trying to get Pharaoh to let the children of Israel go;* Strong's *#2389*] withstood [*opposed*] Moses, so do these also resist the truth: men of corrupt minds, reprobate [*failing the test;* Strong's *#0096*] concerning the faith [*with respect to the gospel*].

9 But they shall proceed no further [*they won't get very far*]: for their folly [*foolishness*] shall be manifest [*exposed*] unto all men, as theirs [*Jannes and Jambres in verse 8*] also was.

10 But thou hast fully known [*you are thoroughly familiar with*] my doctrine, manner of life, purpose, faith, longsuffering [*enduring trials and tribulations*], charity, patience,

11 Persecutions, afflictions, which came unto me at Antioch, at Iconium, at Lystra; what persecutions I endured: but out of them all the Lord delivered [*rescued*] me.

12 Yea, and all that will live godly in Christ Jesus [*everyone who lives the gospel*] shall suffer persecution.

13 But evil men and seducers [*deceivers*] shall wax worse and worse [*will become worse and worse*], deceiving, and being deceived.

JST 2 Timothy 3:13

13 **For** evil men and seducers shall wax worse and worse, deceiving, and being deceived.

14 But continue thou in the things which thou hast learned and hast been assured of, knowing of whom thou hast learned them; [*In other words, but you, Timothy, stay on the "strait and narrow path."*]

15 And that from a child [*and remember that from your youth*] thou hast known the holy scriptures, which are able to make thee wise unto salvation through faith which is in Christ Jesus.

16 All scripture is given by inspiration of God, and is profitable [*beneficial*] , for doctrine, for reproof [*rebuke when needed*], for correction, for instruction in righteousness:

JST 2 Timothy 3:16

16 **And all scripture given by inspiration of God, is profitable** for doctrine, for reproof, for correction, for instruction in righteousness;

17 That the man of God [*the person who wants to be righteous*] may be [*become*] perfect, throughly furnished [*equipped*] unto all good works [*to do all kinds of good works*].

JST 2 timothy 3:17

17 That the man of God may be perfect, **thoroughly** furnished unto all good works.

The only difference in JST verse 17, above, is changing "Throughly" to "thoroughly."

SECOND TIMOTHY 4

You might recognize verse 7. It is often quoted as teaching the importance of our striving to do our best consistently in living the gospel.

1 I CHARGE thee therefore before God, and the Lord Jesus Christ [*I give you instructions, with the Father and the Lord Jesus Christ as my witnesses*], who shall judge the quick [*the living*] and the dead at his appearing and his kingdom; [*In other words, Christ will judge the living and the dead when he comes; see John 5:22 where we are told that the Father has turned all judging over to Christ.*]

2 Preach the word; be instant in season [*be ready to preach the gospel when the opportunity presents itself*], out of season; reprove, rebuke, exhort with all

longsuffering [*patience*] and doctrine.

JST verse 2 is given next with punctuation according to the original JST manuscript research done by Robert J. Matthews as per the Institute of Religion's New Testament student manual, *The Life and Teachings of Jesus and His Apostles*, p. 377. According to Brother Matthews, this is one of very few instances in which the Reorganized Church of Jesus Christ of Latter Day Saints was not absolutely accurate as they published the JST from manuscripts in their possession. (He told us this in a summer class I attended, and stated that none of these instances was doctrinally significant at all.)

JST 2 Timothy 4:2

Preach the word. Be instant in season. **Those who are out of season** [*who are not prepared*], reprove, rebuke, exhort [*urge them to get ready*] with all longsuffering and doctrine.

Next, Paul clearly prophesies the coming apostasy from the Church which the Savior set up during His mortal ministry.

3 For the time will come when they will not endure [*put up with or tolerate*] sound [*correct*] doctrine; but after their own lusts [*according to their own sinful lifestyles*] shall they heap to themselves teachers, having itching ears [*they will select preachers and ministers who will preach what they want to hear, in order to profit by preaching*];

4 And they shall turn away their ears from the truth, and shall be turned unto fables [*and will accept false doctrines and philosophies*].

5 But watch thou in all things [*watch out for such things in everything you do*], endure [*put up with*] afflictions, do the work of an evangelist [*a father or patriarch of a family, in other words, be like a "patriarch" or "father" to the leaders and members under your stewardship*], make full proof of [*complete*] thy ministry.

6 For I am now ready to be offered [*I am ready to be sacrificed, executed, for the gospel*], and the time of my departure is at hand [*my death is getting close*].

7 I have fought a good fight, I have finished my course [*I have finished my work*], I have kept the faith [*I have kept my covenants*]:

8 Henceforth there is laid up for me a crown of righteousness [*I know that I will receive exaltation*], which the Lord, the righteous judge [*Christ*], shall give me at that day: and not to me only, but unto all them also that love his appearing [*not only to me but to all who love his gospel which he gave us when he came to earth to live*].

9 Do thy diligence to come shortly unto me [*finish your duties and come visit me soon*]:

10 For Demas hath forsaken [*deserted*] me [*Demas was a faithful member and companion to Paul during his first imprisonment in*

Rome; see Strong's *#1214*], having loved this present world [*having become worldly*], and is departed [*has gone*] unto Thessalonica; Crescens to Galatia, Titus unto Dalmatia [*northern Albania or southern Yugoslavia today*].

11 Only Luke is with me. Take Mark, and bring him with thee: for he is profitable [*very helpful*] to me for the ministry.

12 And Tychicus have I sent to Ephesus.

13 The cloke [*the long coat used for protection against the weather;* Strong's *#5341*] that I left at Troas with Carpus, when thou comest, bring with thee, and the books [*my small books or scrolls;* Strong's *#0975*], but especially the parchments [*tanned animal skins used to write upon*].

14 Alexander the coppersmith did me much evil [*opposed me much in my work*]: the Lord reward him according to his works:

15 Of whom be thou ware also [*watch out for him*]; for he hath greatly withstood our words [*he is a dangerous enemy to the gospel we have preached*].

JST 2 Timothy 4:15

15 Of whom be thou **ware; for** he hath greatly withstood our words.

16 At my first answer no man stood with me [*no one came with me this time when I went to my first court hearing in conjunction with this second imprisonment*], but all men forsook me [*everyone deserted me*]: I pray God that it may not be laid to their charge [*I hope and pray that God will not hold it against them*].

17 Notwithstanding [*however*] the Lord stood with me [*the Lord was with me*], and strengthened me; that by me the preaching might be fully known [*so that I might complete my mission in preaching the gospel*], and that all the Gentiles might hear [*the gospel*]: and I was delivered out of the mouth of the lion [*I was saved once more*].

18 And the Lord shall deliver me from every evil work, and will preserve me unto his heavenly kingdom [*the Lord will bring me safely to him in his kingdom*]: to whom be glory for ever and ever. Amen.

19 Salute [*greet*] Prisca and Aquila, and the household of Onesiphorus.

20 Erastus abode [*stayed*] at Corinth: but Trophimus have I left at Miletum sick.

21 Do thy diligence to come before winter [*do your best to get here before winter sets in*]. Eubulus greeteth thee, and Pudens, and Linus, and Claudia, and all the brethren.

22 The Lord Jesus Christ be with thy spirit. Grace be with you. Amen.

JST 2 Timothy 4:22

22 The Lord Jesus Christ be with **you, and** grace be with you all. Amen.

Have you noticed the notes at the end of Paul's epistles in your Bible which give information about where and when the letters were written? For instance, in the case of Second Timothy, the note says: "The second epistle unto Timotheus, ordained the first bishop of the church of the Ephesians, was written from Rome, when Paul was brought before Nero the second time."

THE EPISTLE OF PAUL TO TITUS

Most Bible scholars believe that Titus was a Greek who was converted to the Church by Paul, and that he accompanied Paul on his third missionary journey. See Bible Dictionary under "Titus." This letter was probably written sometime between AD 65 and AD 68, between Paul's first and second Roman imprisonments. Sometime before writing this letter, Paul and Titus had visited the Island of Crete in the Mediterranean Sea. When Paul had to leave, he left Titus to help the Church there continue to get established. Sometime later, he wrote this epistle (letter) to him, giving counsel on various organizational and doctrinal matters.

TITUS 1

One of the important doctrines in this chapter is the doctrine of premortality (verse 2). Few, if any, Christian religions in the world today teach that we had a premortal existence before coming to earth. Jeremiah 1:5 teaches this same doctrine.

1 PAUL, a servant of God, and an apostle of Jesus Christ, according to the faith of God's elect [*according to the gospel which those who strive for exaltation follow*], and the acknowledging of the truth which is after [*leads to*] godliness;

2 In hope of eternal life [*exaltation*], which God [*the Father*], that cannot lie, promised before the world began [*promised us in premortality*];

3 But hath in due times [*when the time was right*] manifested his word [*revealed His plan of salvation*] through preaching, which is committed [*assigned*] unto me according to the commandment of God our Saviour;

4 To Titus, mine own son [*who is like a son to me and is my own convert to the gospel*] after the common faith [*in the gospel which is available to all*]: Grace, mercy, and peace, from God the Father and the Lord Jesus Christ our Saviour.

5 For this cause left I thee in Crete

[*this is why I left you in Crete*], that thou shouldest [*so that you can*] set in order the things that are wanting [*that are not as they should be*], and ordain elders in every city, as I had appointed thee [*as I assigned you to do*]:

Next, Paul gives Titus some qualifications which a man should have in order to be called to serve as a bishop. You will note that one of the qualifications is that he must not be practicing polygamy. Polygamy was obviously still being practiced by some people in the Middle East at this time. According to Jacob 2:27 and 30, the Lord controls when plural marriage is to be practiced and when it should not be practiced. Plural marriage is not required for exaltation. See McConkie, *Mormon Doctrine*, p. 578.

6 If any be blameless [*has a good reputation;* Strong's *#0423*], the husband of one wife [*does not practice polygamy*], having faithful children not accused of riot [*wild, partying lifestyle;* Strong's *#0810*] or unruly [*will not submit to authority;* Strong's *#0506*].

7 For a bishop must be blameless [*have a good reputation*], as the steward of God [*as one who takes care of others for God*]; not selfwilled [*stubborn, arrogant;* Strong's *#0829*], not soon angry [*controls his temper*], not given to wine [*not a drunkard*], no striker [*not a bully, not quick to argue with people;* Strong's *#4131*], not given to filthy lucre [*is not greedy for wealth*];

8 But a lover of hospitality [*is pleasant and hospitable*], a lover of good men [*loves that which is good; see Titus 1:8, footnote b*], sober [*temperate; self-controlled;* Strong's *#4998*], just [*lives the gospel with exactness*], holy, temperate [*has self-mastery;* Strong's *#1468*];

9 Holding fast [*holding firmly to*] the faithful word [*the true gospel*] as he hath been taught, that he may be able by sound doctrine both to exhort [*teach*] and to convince [*expose;* Strong's *#1651*] the gainsayers [*those who teach false doctrine or rebel against the Church for their own personal gain*].

10 For there are many unruly [*disobedient;* Strong's *#0506*] and vain talkers [*what they say has nothing of value;* Strong's *#3151*] and deceivers [*apostates, people who are falling away from the Church*], specially they of the circumcision [*especially the Judaizers, Jewish converts to the Church who insist that the law of Moses should still be lived*]:

11 Whose mouths must be stopped [*who must be stopped in their preaching of this false doctrine*], who subvert [*undermine*] whole houses [*whole families*], teaching things which they ought not, for filthy lucre's sake [*preaching what people want to hear in order to get wealthy themselves.*] [*In other words, beware of those who practice "priestcraft," as defined in 2 Nephi 26:29.*]

12 One of themselves, even a prophet of their own said [*even one of these apostates' own false prophets said*], The Cretians [*those who live on the Island of Crete*] are alway liars, evil beasts [*savage and brutal;* Strong's *#2342*], slow bellies [*lazy gluttons;* Strong's *#0692 and #1064*].

13 This witness is true [*what I'm telling you is true*]. Wherefore rebuke them sharply, that they may be sound in the faith [*so that they can repent and be solid in the gospel*];

14 Not giving heed to Jewish fables [*do not give in to Jews or Jewish converts who teach false doctrines; see verse 10, above*], and commandments of men, that turn [*depart*] from the truth.

15 Unto the pure [*in mind and body, including sexual purity*] all things are pure [*all things in the gospel lead to personal purity*]: but unto them that are defiled [*corrupt*] and unbelieving [*don't believe in gospel standards*] is nothing pure [*nothing is sacred*]; but even their mind and conscience is defiled [*they have filthy and corrupt minds and their conscience doesn't work*].

JST Titus 1:15

15 Unto the pure, **let all things be pure**; but unto them **who** are defiled and unbelieving, **nothing is** pure; but even their mind and conscience is defiled.

16 They profess that they know God [*they claim to believe in God*]; but in works they deny him [*their actions prove otherwise*], being abominable [*detestable;* Strong's *#0947*], and disobedient, and unto every good work reprobate [*unfit for doing anything good;* Strong's *#0096*].

TITUS 2

In this chapter Paul continues his counsel to Titus, emphasizing that he should teach the members of the Church under his jurisdiction the importance of personal righteousness in daily living.

1 BUT speak thou the things which become sound doctrine [*you be sure to teach things which are in harmony with correct doctrine*]:

2 That the aged men be [*teach the older men to be*] sober [*serious-minded; can also mean not drinking any wine at all or not drinking too much;* Strong's *#3524*], grave [*worthy of respect;* Strong's *#4586*], temperate [*self-controlled*], sound in faith, in charity, in patience.

3 The aged women likewise, that they be in behaviour as becometh holiness [*that their behavior should be fitting for Saints*], not false accusers [*ruining the reputations of others;* Strong's *#1228*], not given to much wine [*not drunkards*], teachers of good things;

4 That they may teach the young women to be sober, to love their husbands, to love their children,

5 To be discreet [*self-controlled;* Strong's *#4998*], chaste [*keep the*

law of chastity], keepers at home [*good homemakers*], good, obedient to their own husbands [*cooperating with their husbands;* Strong's *#5293; see also notes in this study guide, for Ephesians 5:21–33*], that the word of God be not blasphemed [*so that they do not bring criticism and disrespect to the gospel of Christ*].

6 Young men likewise exhort [*teach young men likewise*] to be sober minded.

7 In all things shewing thyself a pattern of good works [*making sure that you are a good example in all things*]: in doctrine shewing uncorruptness [*preaching uncorrupted, pure doctrine*], gravity [*taking serious things seriously*], sincerity,

8 Sound speech [*teaching that is based on correct doctrine*], that cannot be condemned [*that can't be set aside by honest people*]; that he that is of the contrary part may be ashamed [*so that those who criticize you may realize their mistakes and repent*], having no evil thing to say of you.

9 Exhort [*teach*] servants to be obedient unto their own masters, and to please them well in all things; not answering again; [*In other words, teach servants who are members of the Church to set a good example for their masters.*]

10 Not purloining [*not stealing things for their own use from their masters*], but shewing all good fidelity [*but being trustworthy in all things*]; that they [*servants*] may adorn the doctrine of God our Saviour in all things [*may be a good example for the gospel in everything*].

11 For the grace of God that bringeth salvation hath appeared to all men [*the kindness, mercy, and help from the Father is for everyone*],

JST Titus 2:11

11 For the grace of God **which** bringeth salvation **to all men, hath appeared**;

12 Teaching us that, denying ungodliness and worldly lusts [*that when we avoid wickedness and worldly desires*], we should live soberly, righteously, and godly, in this present world;

13 Looking for that blessed hope [*looking forward to salvation*], and the glorious appearing of the great God and our Saviour Jesus Christ;

14 Who gave [*sacrificed*] himself for us [*who gave us the Atonement*], that he might redeem us [*set us free*] from all iniquity [*from all wickedness*], and purify unto himself a peculiar people [*a people who belong to Him;* Strong's *#4041*], zealous of good works [*eager to do good works;* Strong's *#2207*].

15 These things speak, and exhort [*teach*], and rebuke [*correct*] with all authority. Let no man despise thee [*don't let people who think they know more than you try to exercise authority over you;* Strong's *#4065*].

TITUS 3

On occasions we find Christians who come to believe that if they are truly loyal to God, they must not be loyal to presidents, kings, governments or government entities, and so forth. Some of them base this belief on the first of the Ten Commandments, namely, "Thou shalt have no other gods before me." [See Exodus 20:3.] They believe that any loyalty to government is breaking this commandment. They would do well to take to heart what Paul says in verse 1, next, on this matter.

There are no JST changes for this chapter.

1 PUT them in mind [*teach them*] to be subject to principalities [*governments; see Titus 3:1, footnote b.*] and powers [*the rule of government authorities;* Strong's *#1849*], to obey magistrates [*rulers;* Strong's *#3980*], to be ready to every good work [*to be involved in whatever is good*],

2 To speak evil of no man, to be no brawlers [*to not be quarrelsome or contentious*], but gentle, shewing [*showing; pronounced "showing"*] all meekness [*mildness; slow to anger*] unto all men.

3 For we ourselves also were sometimes [*in times past*] foolish, disobedient, deceived, serving divers lusts and pleasures [*giving in to various passions and pleasures*], living in malice [*with unkind thoughts*] and envy, hateful [*showing hatred, detesting others;* Strong's *#4767*], and hating one another [*detesting others;* Strong's *#3404*]. [*In other words, when you are correcting others, be gentle and meek, keeping in mind that we ourselves are not perfect.*]

4 But after that the kindness and love of God our Saviour toward man appeared [*but then, the kindness and love of the Savior came into our lives as we found out about the gospel*],

5 Not by works of righteousness which we have done, but according to his mercy he saved us [*no matter how many works of righteousness we have done, we still could not be saved if it were not for His mercy*], by the washing of regeneration [*through baptism which allows us to become new people*], and renewing of [*which comes through the Gift of*] the Holy Ghost;

6 Which he [*the Father*] shed on us abundantly [*generously*] through Jesus Christ our Saviour;

7 That being justified by his grace [*through the process of repentance and change made available by the Atonement*], we should be made heirs [*we can inherit exaltation; see Romans 8:17*] according to the hope of eternal life [*as found in God's promises to the righteous*].

8 This is a faithful saying [*these things are true*], and these things I will that thou affirm constantly [*and I want you to teach and bear*

witness of them constantly], that they which have believed in God might be careful to maintain good works [*so that your members there in Crete are encouraged to watch themselves carefully and remain faithful*]. These things are good and profitable unto men.

9 But avoid foolish questions [*foolish controversies*], and genealogies [*many Jews studied their genealogy for the purpose of proving that they were descendants of Abraham and thus were better than Gentiles; compare with Matthew 3:9*], and contentions, and strivings about the law [*arguments about the law of Moses*]; for they are unprofitable and vain [*they do no one any good and are worthless*].

10 A man that is an heretick [*one who is teaching false doctrine intentionally*] after the first and second admonition [*after warning him twice*] reject;

The word "reject" in verse 10, above, could mean "not associate with anymore." It could also mean taking action as severe as excommunication as indicated in Matthew 18:17.

11 Knowing that he that is such is subverted [*knowing that a person who continues to teach false doctrine after repeated warnings is in apostasy*], and sinneth, being condemned of himself [*and is condemning himself*].

Paul now brings this letter to Titus to a close with a few final personal notes and instructions.

12 When I shall send Artemas unto thee, or Tychicus, be diligent [*try your best*] to come unto me to Nicopolis [*most Bible scholars agree that this was a city in what is known as northwestern Greece today; see* Strong's *#3533*]: for I have determined there to winter [*I plan on staying there for the winter*].

13 Bring Zenas the lawyer and Apollos on their journey diligently, that nothing be wanting [*lacking*] unto them [*take good care of them while they are traveling*].

14 And let ours [*let our members*] also learn to maintain [*keep doing*] good works for necessary uses [*for good causes*], that they be not unfruitful [*so that they don't become unproductive; symbolically, "unfruitful" can mean "lose their salvation"*].

15 All that are with me salute [*greet*] thee. Greet them that love us in the faith [*say "hello" to the members of the Church there in Crete for us*]. Grace be with you all. Amen.

THE EPISTLE OF PAUL TO PHILEMON

This brief letter consists of just one chapter and gives us a rather delightful insight into Paul's tenderness, pleasant sense of humor, and spunk. It teaches forgiveness and repentance. It deals with a runaway slave, Onesimus (verse 10,) who stole some things (see Bible Dictionary under "Epistle to Philemon") from his master, Philemon, then ran away to Rome, probably planning on hiding successfully among the crowds there. Somehow, he met Paul in Rome and was converted to the Church. Philemon, his owner, was already a member of the Church and was very well acquainted with this humble and powerful Apostle. Paul was apparently responsible for converting him some time previously when he was in Ephesus (verse 19.) In fact, Philemon was a citizen of Colosse, a city near Ephesus. By the time this letter was written, Paul has convinced Onesimus to return to his owner (verse 12), Philemon, and make restitution. The penalty for a runaway slave was death, but Paul asks Philemon to forgive Onesimus and accept him back as a brother and fellow member of the Church (verses 15–16). Just in case Philemon has difficulty in so doing, Paul asks him to accept Onesimus back as he would Paul himself (verse 17), and if Philemon is too concerned about the financial losses incurred in the whole situation, Paul says "Charge it to my account" (verse 18). Additionally, just in case Philemon still can't bring himself to forgive Onesimus, Paul mentions, in effect, "Remember, you owe me" (verse 19). Paul sends the letter with a trusted member of the Church named Tychicus who accompanies Onesimus back to Colosse to make peace with Philemon.

PHILEMON 1

1 PAUL, a prisoner of Jesus Christ [*a prisoner in Rome because of his preaching the gospel*], and Timothy our brother [*in the gospel*], unto Philemon our dearly beloved, and fellowlabourer [*fellow worker in the Church*],

2 And to our beloved Apphia [*possibly Philemon's wife;* Strong's *#0682*], and Archippus our fellowsoldier, and to the church in thy house [*possibly meaning the members of the Church who meet in Philemon's home, or perhaps other members of Philemon's household who belong to the Church*]:

3 Grace to you, and peace, from God our Father and the Lord Jesus Christ.

4 I thank my God, making mention of thee always in my prayers [*I always remember you in my prayers*],

5 Hearing of thy love and faith, which thou hast toward the Lord Jesus, and toward all saints;

6 [*I pray*] That the communication [*spreading;* Strong's #*2842*] of thy faith [*that your spreading of the gospel*] may become effectual [*powerful;* Strong's #*1756*] by the acknowledging of every good thing which is in you in Christ Jesus [*through others' acknowledging the value of the gospel by seeing your good example*] .

7 For we have great joy and consolation [*comfort*] in thy love, because the bowels [*tender affections;* Strong's #*4698*] of the saints are refreshed by thee, brother.

Next, Paul gets to the main point of his letter to Philemon, namely, asking him to forgive his runaway slave, Onesimus, and take him back.

8 Wherefore, though I might be much bold in Christ to enjoin thee [*even though I could be so bold as to command you;* Strong's #*2004*] that which is convenient [*in the matter at hand*],

9 Yet for love's sake I rather beseech thee [*yet I would rather beg a favor of you, in light of the love we have for each other*], being such an one as Paul the aged [*as one who is getting quite old*], and now also a prisoner of Jesus Christ [*and currently is in prison because I dared to be loyal to Christ*].

10 I beseech thee for my son Onesimus [*I have a big favor to ask for my convert, Onesimus*], whom I have begotten in my bonds [*whom I have converted while here in Rome in prison*]:

11 Which in time past was to thee unprofitable [*who has caused you much trouble in the past*], but now profitable to thee and to me [*but who is now very valuable to both you and me as a new member of the Church*]:

12 Whom I have sent again [*whom I have asked to return to you*]: thou therefore receive him [*I ask you, therefore, to welcome him*], that is, mine own bowels [*for whom I have the deepest affection;* Strong's #*4698*]:

13 Whom I would have retained with me [*I would like to have kept him here with me*], that in thy stead [*in place of you*] he might have ministered unto me in the bonds of the gospel [*he could have helped me here as a brother in the gospel*]:

14 But without thy mind would I do nothing [*but I didn't want to do any such thing without your permission*]; that thy benefit [*so that any help from you*] should not be as it were of necessity, but willingly [*would not come as a matter of obligation but as a matter of choice*].

15 For perhaps he therefore departed for a season [*perhaps the reason he ran away from you*], that thou shouldest receive him for ever [*was so that he could be converted and return to you as a brother in the gospel forever*];

16 Not now as a servant [*he comes back to you not as a servant*], but above a servant [*but much more than a servant*], a brother beloved [*a beloved brother in the gospel*], specially to me, but how much more unto thee [*but even more so to you*], both in the flesh, and in the Lord [*both as your brother here on earth as well as in the gospel*]?

17 If thou count me therefore a partner [*if you consider me worthy to be your partner in this situation*], receive him as myself [*welcome him as you would me*].

18 If he hath wronged thee, or oweth thee ought, put that on mine account [*if he has harmed you or owes you anything, send the bill to me*];

19 I Paul have written it with mine own hand, I will repay it: albeit I do not say to thee how thou owest unto me even thine own self besides [*although I probably don't need to remind you that you owe me for saving your soul*].

20 Yea, brother, let me have joy of thee in the Lord [*bring joy to me by living the gospel in this matter*]: refresh my bowels in the Lord [*reaffirm the tender feelings I have for you*].

21 Having confidence in thy obedience [*knowing that you would do the right thing in this matter*] I wrote unto thee, knowing that thou wilt also do more than I say [*in fact, I know that you will do more even than I am asking*].

22 But withal [*while you are at it*] prepare me also a lodging [*a guest room*]: for I trust that through your prayers I shall be given unto you [*for I trust that your prayers in my behalf will be answered and that I will be freed from prison and come to stay with you for a while*].

23 There salute thee Epaphras, my fellowprisoner in Christ Jesus [*Epaphras sends his greeting to you also*];

24 [*along with greetings from*] Marcus, Aristarchus, Demas, Lucas, my fellowlabourers.

25 The grace of our Lord Jesus Christ be with your spirit. Amen.

JST Philemon 1:25

25 The grace of our Lord Jesus Christ be with **you**. Amen.

THE EPISTLE OF PAUL THE APOSTLE TO THE HEBREWS

There is uncertainty and disagreement among Bible scholars as to who wrote Hebrews. That is why it was placed in the New Testament at the end of Paul's letters. As you can see, Paul is given as the writer of Hebrews in the King James Version of the Bible (the one we use for English speaking areas of the Church). (Look at the beginning of Hebrews in your Bible.) We have the advantage of having a true prophet, Joseph Smith, who told us that Paul is indeed the author of Hebrews. See *Teachings of the Prophet Joseph Smith*, p. 59.

Hebrews is a letter from the Apostle Paul to Jewish members of the Church, who were commonly referred to in his day as "Hebrews," meaning descendants of Abraham, in other words, Israelites. The letter was probably written sometime between AD 62 and AD 65. It is a masterpiece designed to persuade Jewish converts to the Church to accept the fact that Christ fulfilled the law of Moses, and therefore they should no longer practice the law of Moses. So-called "Judaizers," who were Jewish members of the Church, continued to insist that the law of Moses, with all of its detailed requirements, should continue to be lived by both Gentile and Jewish converts. They caused much trouble among members in the early Church as it struggled after Christ's crucifixion.

Paul, who spent most of his ministry tak-ing the gospel to the Gentiles (non-Jews), turns his attention to Jewish members as he writes this magnificent letter pointing out the fallacies of continuing to live the law of Moses. He uses his extensive knowledge of Old Testament writings and prophecies to present his message about Christ, and, as a result, Hebrews becomes one of our best resources for understanding the Old Testament. Hebrews is especially helpful to us in pointing out Old Testament references to the Savior and His Atonement. Hebrews is full of rich doctrine as well as Atonement symbolism.

HEBREWS 1

Paul begins his letter by bearing witness that Jesus is the Son of God and that He is the focus of many Old Testament prophecies and writings. He gives many details as to who Christ actually is.

1 GOD [*the Father*], who at sundry [*various*] times and in divers manners [*different ways*] spake [*spoke*]

in time past unto the fathers [*to our ancestors*] by the prophets,

2 Hath in these last days [*has recently*] spoken unto us by his Son [*Jesus*], whom he hath appointed heir of all things, by whom also he made the worlds [*the Father had Jesus create the worlds*];

Next, Paul teaches us that the Savior has the Father's glory upon Him and that the Father and Son are exact lookalikes.

3 Who being the brightness of his glory, and the express image of his person [*looks just like the Father; compare with John 14:7*], and upholding all things by the word of his power [*and that the Savior used His authority to fulfill everything the Father asked Him to do*], when he had by himself purged our sins [*when He alone had accomplished the Atonement and paid for our sins*], sat down on the right hand of the Majesty on high [*took His rightful place in heaven on the right side of the Father*];

"The right hand" is symbolic of covenants, and the symbolism here includes that Jesus kept all of the covenants He made with the Father.

4 Being made so much better than the angels [*Christ is higher in authority than the angels*], as he hath by inheritance obtained a more excellent name than they. [*In other words, Christ, as the literal Son of the Father, has a name which is superior to any other, namely the "Son of God".*]

5 For unto which of the angels said he at any time, Thou art my Son, this day have I begotten thee [*as prophesied about Christ in Psalm 2:7*]? [*In other words, can you think of any angels to whom the Father said, "You will be my Son?"*] And again [*I repeat, can you think of anyone else to whom God said, as prophesied about Christ in 2 Samuel 7:14 and 1 Chronicles 17:13*], I will be to him a Father, and he shall be to me a Son?

Next, in verse 6, Paul will use the term "firstbegotten." Remember that Jesus was the firstborn spirit child of our Heavenly Father (see Colossians 1:15 and accompanying notes in this study guide.)

6 And again, when he [*the Father*] bringeth in the firstbegotten into the world, he saith, And let all the angels of God worship him. [*In other words, when Jesus was born, all the angels worshiped him, and angels have great glory, which is another reminder of who Jesus was.*]

<u>JST Hebrews 1:6</u>

6 And again, when he bringeth in the first begotten into the world, he saith, And let all the angels of God worship him, **who maketh his ministers as a flame of fire**.

7 And of the angels he saith [*in Psalm 104:4*], Who maketh his angels spirits, and his ministers a flame of fire.

JST Hebrews 1:7

7 And of the angels he saith, **Angels are ministering spirits.**

8 But unto the Son he saith, Thy throne, O God, is for ever and ever: a sceptre of righteousness is the sceptre of thy kingdom. [*In other words, combining verse 7 with verse 8, Paul says, in effect, that the Father uses angels as ministering spirits but the Son is a God with power and authority given only to Gods.*]

Verse 9, next, is a continuation of the first line of verse 8, above, "But unto the Son he [*the Father*] saith . . ." [*As recorded in Psalm 45:7.*]

9 Thou [*Jesus*] hast loved righteousness [*you have been completely faithful to me*], and hated iniquity [*and you are without sin*]; therefore God [*the Father*], even thy God [*thy Father*], hath anointed thee with the oil of gladness above thy fellows [*more than anyone else*].

The phrase "oil of gladness" is a beautiful description of the satisfaction and joy the Savior receives when we accept His gift of the Atonement and repent and come unto the Father through Him. Isaiah 53:11 emphasizes this satisfaction and joy which comes to the Savior as He sees the results of the Atonement in so many lives, as follows: "He [*Christ*] shall see the travail of his soul [*will look back on His Atonement*], and shall be satisfied:"

Paul continues to bear testimony to the Hebrews about Jesus and who He really was, continuing the sentence he used at the beginning of verse 5, "But unto the Son he [*the Father*] saith"

10 And, Thou, Lord [*Christ*], in the beginning hast laid the foundation of the earth [*created the earth*]; and the heavens are the works of thine hands [*created the heavens*]:

11 They [*the heavens and the earth*] shall perish; but thou remainest [*but Christ is eternal*]; and they [*the heavens and the earth*] all shall wax [*grow*] old as doth a garment [*as does a piece of clothing*];

12 And as a vesture [*robe*] shalt thou fold them up, and they shall be changed [*at the time of the Second Coming, and again, at the end of the little season after the end of the Millennium; see D&C 88:26 and 130:6–9*]: but thou art the same [*You will remain the same, exalted as a God; see D&C 76:107–108*], and thy years shall not fail [*Your years will never end*].

13 But to which of the angels said he at any time [*as was written about Christ in Psalm 110:1*], Sit on my right hand, until I make thine enemies thy footstool [*until all Your enemies have been overcome*]?

14 Are they not all ministering spirits, sent forth to minister for them who shall be heirs of salvation [*who receive exaltation*]?

The reference to "angels" in verse 13, above, and the reference to "ministering spirits" in verse 14, above, are references to those who do not earn exaltation, and thus remain "ministering servants" for those who receive exaltation. Compare with D&C 132:16–17.

HEBREWS 2

In this chapter, Paul continues to bear witness to the Jews as to who Christ is. He again uses many Old Testament references to Christ with which the Jews would be familiar.

1 THEREFORE we ought to give the more earnest heed to [*we ought to be all the more careful to pay attention to*] the things which we have heard [*about Christ*], lest at any time we should let them slip [*for fear that we might be disobedient to them*].

2 For if the word spoken by angels was stedfast [*solid, trustworthy*], and every transgression and disobedience received [*has been assigned*] a just recompence of reward [*a fair punishment*];

3 How shall we escape [*how can we escape fair punishment*], if we neglect so great salvation [*if we neglect the opportunity we have been given for salvation*]; which at the first began to be spoken by the Lord [*which Christ Himself taught during His mortal ministry at the first of this dispensation*], and was confirmed [*witnessed*] unto us by them [*including the Apostles*] that heard him;

4 God also bearing them witness [*Christ showed His Apostles and others who He was; see McConkie,* Doctrinal New Testament Commentary, *Vol. 3, p. 143*], both with signs and wonders, and with divers [*various*] miracles, and gifts of the Holy Ghost, according to his own will?

5 For unto the angels hath he not put in subjection the world to come, whereof we speak. [*In other words, "Don't we talk of angels being given responsibilities by Christ in the world to come?" Example: D&C 132:16–17, 19.*]

In the following 3 verses, Paul teaches the wonderful and powerful doctrine that we can actually eventually become gods, with all things "in subjection under [*our*] feet," which means to have power over all things. See verse 8 and also D&C 132:20. For further scriptural evidence that we can indeed become gods, see 1 Corinthians 15:27, where a similar phrase, "all things under his feet" is used to describe Christ.

6 But one [*King David*] in a certain place [*Psalm 8:4–6*] testified, saying, What is man, that thou art mindful of him? or the son of man [*mortal men;* Strong's *#5207*], that thou visitest him?

7 Thou madest him a little lower than the angels [*we were placed here on earth as mortals with mortal weaknesses and limitations*]; thou crownedst him with glory and honour [*the same phrase used in connection with Christ in*

verse 9, below], and didst set him over the works of thy hands:

8 Thou hast put all things in subjection under his feet [*we have the potential to become gods; compare with D&C 132:19–20*]. For in that he put all in subjection under him, he left nothing that is not put under him. But now we see not yet all things put under him [*but we are not gods yet*].

9 But we see Jesus, who was made a little lower than the angels [*Jesus became mortal*] for the suffering of death [*in order to suffer death*], crowned with glory and honour; that he by the grace of God should taste death for every man [*so that every person ever born will be resurrected; see 1 Corinthians 15:22*].

10 For it became him [*it was according to the Father's will*], for whom are all things, and by whom are all things, in bringing many sons unto glory [*in order to bring many to exaltation in celestial glory*], to make the captain of their salvation [*to make Christ*] perfect through sufferings.

11 For both he [*Christ*] that sanctifieth [*who makes it possible for people to become worthy to enter celestial glory*] and they [*faithful Saints*] who are sanctified are all of one [*are united*]: for which cause he is not ashamed to call them brethren [*they are full "brothers" and "sisters," in other words, "joint heirs with Christ" as Paul describes them in Romans 8:17.*]

12 Saying [*as stated in Psalm 22:22*], I will declare thy name unto my brethren, in the midst of the church will I sing praise unto thee. [*In other words, Christ will acknowledge and accept the faithful members into celestial glory.*]

13 And again [*as stated in Psalm 18:2*], I will put my trust in him. And again [*as stated in Isaiah 8:18*], Behold I and the children [*faithful followers*] which God [*the Father*] hath given me [*compare with D&C 27:14*].

14 Forasmuch then as [*since*] the children [*the Father's spirit children*] are partakers of flesh and blood [*are born into mortality*], he [*Christ*] also himself likewise took part of the same [*was born into mortality also*]; that through death he might destroy [*completely overcome*] him that had the power of death, that is, the devil;

15 And deliver [*redeem*] them who through fear of death [*spiritual death*] were all their lifetime subject to bondage [*were subject to sin as mortals*].

16 For verily he took not on him the nature of angels; but he took on him the seed of Abraham. [*In other words, Christ took mortality upon Himself in order to suffer, die, and resurrect for us (see verses 9, 10, 14, and 18), and to fulfill the covenants made to Abraham.*]

JST Hebrews 2:16

16 For verily, he took not on him the **likeness** of angels; but he

took on him the seed of Abraham.

17 Wherefore in all things it behoved him [*it was necessary for Christ*] to be made like unto his brethren [*to become mortal*], that he might be a merciful and faithful high priest in things pertaining to God, to make reconciliation [*to atone*] for the sins of the people.

18 For in that he [*Christ*] himself hath suffered being tempted, he is able to succour [*help*] them that are tempted.

The word "succor," used in verse 18, above, literally means "to rush to the aid of."

HEBREWS 3

Remember that one of Paul's major objectives in writing this letter to the Hebrews (Jewish converts to the Church) was to convince them to accept Christ fully and to discontinue living the law of Moses. Many Jews considered Moses to be the most important prophet of all. Here Paul shows that Moses was indeed a very significant prophet, but that he was Christ's servant.

1 WHEREFORE, holy brethren, partakers of the heavenly calling [*who have been called to hold the holy Melchizedek Priesthood*], consider the Apostle and High Priest of our profession, Christ Jesus [*think about Christ who is the chief High Priest of all high priesthood holders*];

2 Who was faithful to him [*the Father*] that appointed him, as also Moses was faithful in all his house [*just as Moses was faithful in all his responsibilities in God's "house" or Church;* Strong's *#3624; see also verse 6, below, where members of the Church are referred to as Christ's "house"*].

3 For this man was counted worthy of more glory than Moses [*was above Moses in authority*], inasmuch [*since*] as he who hath builded the house hath more honour than the house [*since the one (Christ) who built the house (God's kingdom) is more important than the house itself*].

JST Hebrews 3:3

3 For **he** was counted worthy of more glory than Moses, inasmuch as he who hath builded the house hath more honor than the house.

It is important to remember here that Jesus was the God of the Old Testament, and was known as Jehovah. See Bible Dictionary under "Jehovah." For example, Jesus is the one who gave Moses the Ten Commandments. He did all these things as the God of the Old Testament while He was still a spirit personage, because He had not yet been born and received a mortal body.

4 For every house is builded by some man; but he that built all things is God [*God has power and authority over all things, including His prophets*].

5 And Moses verily was faithful in all his house [*Moses was very faithful in carrying out the responsibilities given him by Christ*], as a servant [*as a servant of Christ*], for a testimony of those things which were to be spoken after [*as a testimony and teaching tool, pointing the peoples' minds toward the coming of Jesus at a later time*];

6 But Christ as a son over his own house [*as the Son of God placed in charge of His own kingdom here on earth*]; whose house are we [*whose church we are*], if we hold fast [*if we are faithful to*] the confidence and the rejoicing of the hope [*which the gospel brings*] firm unto the end [*and remain faithful to the end*].

7 Wherefore [*as the Holy Ghost saith, in Psalm 95:7–11*], To day if ye will hear his voice,

8 Harden not your hearts, as in the provocation, in the day of temptation in the wilderness: [*In other words, don't harden your hearts like the children of Israel did when they provoked God and He caused them to wander 40 years in the wilderness until the older generation died out; see Numbers 14:2–23.*]

9 When your fathers tempted [*provoked; see verse 16, below*] me, proved me [*tried My patience*], and saw my works forty years.

10 Wherefore I was grieved [*made sad*] with that generation, and said, They do alway [*always*] err in their heart [*they do not want to be righteous*]; and they have not known my ways [*they don't try to learn the gospel*].

11 So I sware [*promised them*] in my wrath [*My righteous anger*], They shall not enter into my rest [*they will not enter into the promised land; symbolic of heaven*]. [*This is the end of the quote from Psalms begun in verse 7, above.*]

12 Take heed [*watch out*], brethren, lest there be in any of you an evil heart of unbelief, in departing from the living God [*which would cause you to apostatize and leave the gospel of Christ*].

13 But exhort [*teach*] one another daily, while it is called To day [*while you have the chance*]; lest any of you be hardened [*for fear that your hearts could be hardened*] through the deceitfulness of sin [*through being fooled by sin*].

14 For we are made partakers of Christ [*we can be saved with Christ*], if we hold the beginning of our confidence stedfast unto the end [*if we hold onto the faith we had when we first joined the Church*];

15 While it is said [*as I just said, quoting from Psalm 95:7–8*], To day if ye will hear his voice, harden not your hearts, as in the provocation.

16 For some, when they had heard, did provoke [*disobeyed God and provoked Him to anger*]: howbeit [*however*] not all that came out of Egypt by Moses [*not all who were*

led out of Egypt by Moses provoked God].

17 But with whom was he grieved forty years [*who was it that grieved God and thus caused the children of Israel to wander 40 years in the wilderness*]? was it not with them that had sinned [*wasn't it the sinners among them*], whose carcases [*dead bodies*] fell in the wilderness?

18 And to whom sware he [*to whom did God say*] that they should not enter into his rest [*that they would not enter exaltation; see D&C 84:24, where "rest" is defined*], but to them that believed not [*wasn't He speaking to the unbelievers*]?

19 So we see that they could not enter in because of unbelief [*thus we see that they could not enter into the presence of God because they refused to believe in Him*].

HEBREWS 4

It is very helpful in understanding this chapter to be aware that the word "rest" ultimately means "the fulness of his glory." See D&C 84:24. In other words, "rest" means to return to the presence of God and receive the "fulness" which He has for us, that is, exaltation. Obviously, it also means to have peace of conscience and strength from God in this life. Also, along with other important doctrines about Christ in this chapter, it teaches that Jesus was completely without sin, even though He was tempted in all things (*verse 15.*)

1 LET us therefore fear [*let us be very careful*], lest, a promise being left us of entering into his rest [*since God's promise that we can enter into exaltation with Him still stands*], any of you should seem to come short of it [*for fear any of you would fail to achieve that goal*].

2 For unto us was the gospel preached, as well as unto them: but the word preached did not profit them [*but they did not benefit from it*], not being mixed with faith in them that heard it [*because they did not have faith in it*].

JST Hebrews 4:2

2 For unto us was the **rest** [*the doctrine of exaltation*] preached, as well as unto them; but the word preached did not profit them, not being mixed with faith in them that heard it.

The JST makes very significant changes in verse 3, next. Also, remember that the word "believe" in this context means to live the gospel faithfully.

3 For we which have believed do enter into rest, as he said, As I have sworn in my wrath, if they shall enter into my rest: although the works were finished from the foundation of the world.

JST Hebrews 4:3

3 For we **who** have believed do enter into rest [*exaltation—see D&C 84:24*], as he said,

As I have sworn in my wrath, If they **harden their hearts they shall not enter into my rest; also, I have sworn, If they will not harden their hearts, they shall enter into my rest; although the works of God were prepared, (or finished)**, from the foundation of the world. [*In other words, the Father's plan of salvation for us was planned completely in premortality.*]

4 For he spake in a certain place [*in Genesis 2:2*] of the seventh day on this wise, And God did rest the seventh day from all his works.

5 And in this place again, If they shall enter into my rest.

JST Hebrews 4:5

5 And in this place again, If they **harden not their hearts** they shall enter into my rest.

6 Seeing therefore it remaineth that some must enter therein [*some will enter into exaltation*], and they to whom it was first preached [*many to whom it has been preached in times past, including the children of Israel*] entered not in [*did not enter into God's presence*] because of unbelief:

7 Again, he limiteth a certain day [*he appoints a certain day*], saying in David [*in Psalm 95:7–8*], To day, after so long a time; as it is said, To day if ye will hear his voice, harden not your hearts.

8 For if Jesus [*Joshua; see Acts 7:45, footnote a, in our Bible*] had given them rest [*if the children of Israel had become a righteous people when Joshua was their leader*], then would he [*God*] not afterward have spoken of another day. [*In other words, the majority of the children of Israel were not righteous under Moses or Joshua. Therefore, God prophesied through His prophets that the day would yet come when Israel would become righteous and enter into God's rest. See Isaiah 29:22–24.*]

9 There remaineth therefore a rest to the people of God [*there will come a time when Israel will become righteous and enter into God's rest*].

10 For he that is entered into his rest [*the person who enters into exaltation*], he also hath ceased from his own works [*has finished his labors toward exaltation*], as God did from his [*just as God ceased from His labors when He finished creating the earth; see Genesis 2:2 as referred to in verse 4, above*].

11 Let us labour [*work*] therefore to enter into that rest, lest any man fall after the same example of unbelief [*for fear that we might fall away into unbelief like the children of Israel did*].

12 For the word of God [*the gospel of Jesus Christ*] is quick [*alive; Strong's #2198*], and powerful, and sharper than any two-edged sword, piercing even to the dividing asunder of soul and spirit, and of the joints and marrow, and is

a discerner of [*a revealer of*] the thoughts and intents of the heart.

> **JST Hebrews 4:12**
>
> 12 For the word of God is quick, and powerful, and sharper than any two-edged sword, piercing even to the dividing asunder of **body** and spirit, and of the joints and marrow, and is a discerner of the thoughts and intents of the heart.

13 Neither is there any creature that is not manifest [*revealed*] in his sight [*none of our thoughts and intents are hidden from God*]: but all things are naked [*completely exposed*] and opened unto the eyes of him [*God*] with whom we have to do.

14 Seeing then that we have a great high priest [*Hebrews 3:1*], that is passed into the heavens [*who has gone to heaven*], Jesus the Son of God, let us hold fast our profession [*let us hold firmly to our testimonies and live the gospel we profess to believe*].

> Next, in verse 15, Paul reminds us that the Savior has gone through everything we go through, including temptations, and understands us, and is indeed "touched" with deep feelings and mercy for us.

15 For we have not an high priest [*Christ; see Hebrews 3:1*] which cannot be touched [*can't relate to our mortal weaknesses*] with the feeling of our infirmities; but was in all points tempted like as we are, yet without sin [*Christ was perfect*].

16 Let us therefore come boldly [*with confidence:* Strong's *#3954*] unto the throne of grace [*unto our merciful Father in Heaven*], that we may obtain mercy [*through Christ's Atonement*], and find grace to help in time of need.

HEBREWS 5

This chapter contains one of our most important scripture references used in missionary work, namely, verse 4. It deals with the necessity of having proper priesthood authority in the true Church of Jesus Christ. It emphasizes that we can't just "feel" called to set up a church or whatever; rather, God's kingdom is a kingdom of order and those who hold positions of authority in it must be called by God through the laying on of hands in the same way Aaron was. In this chapter Paul continues to teach the Jewish converts (the Hebrews) about Christ and His role as "the Great High Priest," and begins by comparing Christ with men who are called as high priests.

There are no JST changes for this chapter.

1 FOR every high priest taken from among men [*every mortal man who is called and ordained to be a high priest*] is ordained for men in things pertaining to God [*is called to serve his fellow beings in God's work here on earth*], that he may offer both gifts and sacrifices for sins [*and is authorized to perform priesthood functions for the people*]:

2 Who can have compassion on [*for*] the ignorant, and on them that are out of the way [*those who are going astray*]; for that [*because*] he himself also is compassed with [*surrounded by*] infirmity [*has shortcomings and imperfections*].

3 And by reason hereof [*and because of this*] he ought, as for the people, so also for himself, to offer for sins [*he ought to work on his own salvation as well as on the salvation of the people whom he serves*].

4 And no man taketh this honour unto himself, but he that is called of God, as was Aaron. [*In other words, no one takes this priesthood upon himself without being properly called of God and having it conferred upon him by the laying on of hands as was the case with Aaron. See Numbers 27:18–23.*]

5 So also Christ glorified not himself to be made an high priest [*Christ did not want to bring glory to Himself as a high priest*]; but he [*to the Father*] that said unto him [*in Psalm 2:7*], Thou art my Son, to day have I begotten thee [*you are my Only Begotten Son in the flesh*].

6 As he saith also in another place [*Psalm 110:4*], Thou art a priest for ever after the order of Melchisedec. [*In other words, Christ was a high priest in the Melchizedek Priesthood. Melchizedek was the great prophet and leader to whom Abraham paid tithing (Genesis 14:20.) For more about Melchizedek, see Bible Dictionary under "Melchizedek."*]

Verses 7 and 8, next, refer to Melchizedek. See Hebrews 5:7, footnote a, in our Bible.

7 Who in the days of his flesh, when he [*Melchizedek*] had offered up prayers and supplications with strong crying and tears unto him [*God*] that was able to save him from death [*perhaps referring to the event in JST Genesis 14:26, where Melchizedek, when he was a child, "stopped the mouths of lions, and quenched the violence of fire."*], and was heard in that he feared [*was heard because he had reverence for God;* Strong's *#2124*];

Verse 8 refers to both Melchizedek and Christ. See McConkie, *Doctrinal New Testament Commentary*, Vol. 3, p. 157.

8 Though he were a Son, yet learned he obedience by the things which he suffered;

9 And being made perfect, he [*Christ*] became the author [*provider*] of eternal salvation unto all them that obey him;

10 Called of God an high priest [*called by the Father to be a high priest*] after the order of Melchisedec.

11 Of whom we have many things to say [*we have much to say about this*], and hard to be uttered [*but it is hard to explain*], seeing ye are dull of hearing [*because you are spiritually out of tune and slow to learn*].

12 For when for the time ye ought to be teachers [*considering the time you have already had to learn about this, you should be teaching it to others*], ye have need that one teach you again [*but you have to be taught it again and again yourselves*] which be the first principles [*these are basic principles*] of the oracles of God [*words of God;* Strong's *#3051*]; and are become such as have need of milk, and not of strong meat [*you have become the type of members who have to be fed milk because you are not ready for meat*]. [*In other words, you can't be given the deeper doctrines of the gospel because you have not yet mastered the basics.*]

13 For every one that useth milk [*everyone who can only handle milk*] is unskilful [*inexperienced;* Strong's *#0552*] in the word of righteousness [*in the gospel*]: for he is a babe [*he must be treated as a small child as far as what we can teach him*].

14 But strong meat [*more advanced doctrine and truth*] belongeth to them that are of full age [*mature in the gospel*], even those who by reason of use have their senses exercised [*developed*] to discern both good and evil [*to distinguish between good and evil, true doctrine and false doctrine*].

HEBREWS 6

Paul continues by encouraging these members to go on to perfection, and warns against becoming sons of perdition. Among other things, he describes sons of perdition as those members whose hatred toward Christ is such that they would gladly crucify Him again if they could (verse 6).

The JST for verse one makes an important change. It says "Therefore not leaving. . ." as opposed to "Therefore leaving. . ." in the Bible.

1 THEREFORE leaving the principles of the doctrine of Christ, let us go on unto perfection [*let us continue growing toward exaltation*]; not laying again the foundation of repentance from dead works, and of faith toward God, [*In other words, let's keep growing in the gospel, not having to relearn again and again the basics or the "first principles" of the gospel (Hebrews 5:12) including those things mentioned in verse 2, next.*]

JST Hebrews 6:1

1 Therefore **not** leaving the principles of the doctrine of Christ, let us go on unto perfection; not laying again the foundation of repentance from dead works, and of faith toward God.

2 Of the doctrine of baptisms, and of laying on of hands, and of resurrection of the dead, and of eternal judgment.

JST Hebrews 6:2

2 Of the doctrine of **baptisms, of** laying on of hands, and of **the** resurrection of the dead, and of eternal judgment.

3 And this will we do, if God permit. [*In other words, we will continue advancing until we reach exaltation if God judges us worthy of it.*]

JST Hebrews 6:3

3 **And we will go on unto perfection if God permit.**

Next, in verses 4–6, Paul briefly describes what it takes to become a son of perdition, assigned to perdition (sometimes referred to as "outer darkness") forever. Compare with D&C 76: 31–35.

4 For it is impossible, and have tasted of the heavenly gift [*have participated in temple endowments*], and were made partakers of the Holy Ghost [*who had the Gift of the Holy Ghost and who had strong testimonies*],

JST Hebrews 6:4

4 For **he hath made it impossible for those who were once enlightened,** and have tasted of the heavenly gift, and were made partakers of the Holy Ghost,

5 And have tasted the good word of God, and the powers of the world to come, [*In other words, they have participated fully in the gospel and understand the plan of salvation and the possibility of exaltation in the world to come.*]

6 If they shall fall away, to renew them again unto repentance [*God cannot bring them back again through the process of repentance*]; seeing they crucify to themselves the Son of God afresh, and put him to an open shame [*since they have become just like Satan and would gladly crucify Christ again if they could and would openly condemn Him again in front of the whole world*].

JST Hebrews 6:6

6 If they shall fall away, **to be renewed** again unto repentance; seeing they crucify **unto** themselves the Son of God afresh, and put him to an open shame.

President Joseph F. Smith explained the concepts given in verses 4–6, above, as follows: "And he that believes, is baptized, and receives the light and testimony of Jesus Christ, and walks well for a season, receiving the fulness of the blessings of the gospel in this world, and afterwards turns wholly unto sin, violating his covenants, he will be among those whom the gospel can never reach in the spirit world; and all such go beyond its saving power, they will taste the second death, and be banished from the presence of God eternally." (*Gospel Doctrine*, Deseret Book, 1939, p. 476.)

7 For the earth which drinketh in the rain that cometh oft upon it, and bringeth forth herbs [*plants*] meet [*necessary*] for them by whom it is dressed, receiveth blessing from God:

JST Hebrews 6:7

7 **For the day cometh that the earth** which drinketh in the

rain that cometh oft upon it, and bringeth forth herbs meet for them **who dwelleth thereon,** by whom it is dressed, **who now receiveth blessings from God, shall be cleansed with fire.**

8 But that which beareth thorns and briers is rejected, and is nigh unto cursing; whose end is to be burned.

JST Hebrews 6:8

8 **For** that which beareth thorns and briers is rejected, and is nigh unto cursing; **therefore they who bring not forth good fruits, shall be cast into the fire; for their** end is to be burned.

9 But, beloved, we are persuaded better things of you [*we are convinced that you will be found among the righteous*], and things that accompany salvation [*and doing things that lead to salvation*], though we thus speak [*even though we speak and warn against becoming sons of perdition*].

10 For God is not unrighteous to forget your work and labour of love, which ye have shewed [*showed*] toward his name, in that ye have ministered to the saints, and do minister. [*In other words, God is aware of your righteousness and that you have done many good deeds to the Saints and continue to do so.*]

JST Hebrews 6:10

10 For God is not unrighteous, **therefore he will not** forget your work and labor of love, which ye have showed toward his name, in that ye have ministered to the saints, and do minister.

11 And we desire that every one of you do shew the same diligence to the full assurance of hope [*leading to the full assurance of salvation*] unto the end: [*In other words, we desire that each of you continue faithful to the end so that you make your salvation sure.*]

12 That ye be not slothful [*lazy*], but followers of them who through faith and patience inherit the promises [*inherit salvation*].

13 For when God made promise to Abraham, because he could swear [*make covenants*] by no greater, he sware by himself [*he made promises to Abraham in His own name; see Genesis 22:16*],

14 Saying, Surely blessing I will bless thee [*"I will bless thee above measure"; see Abraham 2:9 (In other words, I will bless you with exaltation)*], and multiplying I will multiply thee [*you will have descendants as numerous "as the sand which is upon the sea shore;" see Genesis 22:17*].

15 And so, after he [*Abraham*] had patiently endured [*after he waited until he was 100 years old; see Genesis 21:5*], he obtained the promise [*he and Sarah had Isaac, through whom the promises made to Abraham would be fulfilled; see Genesis 21:2*].

16 For men verily swear by the greater [*make promises by someone or something greater than themselves*]: and an oath for confirmation is to them an end of all strife [*when men give their word by making an oath, there is no more debating over the matter*].

17 Wherein God, willing more abundantly to shew unto the heirs of promise the immutability of his counsel [*willing to give even more abundant evidence of the unchangeable nature of His plan of salvation for us*], confirmed it by an oath [*God made an unchangeable oath with Abraham to bless his descendants*]:

In verse 18, next, Paul speaks of "two immutable things." They are two unchangeable promises given to Abraham in Genesis 22:17, as follows: (1) "That in blessing I will bless thee [*I will give you innumerable blessings leading to exaltation*], and (2) in multiplying I will multiply thy seed as the stars of the heaven, and as the sand which is upon the sea shore [*I will give you innumerable posterity*]."

18 That by two immutable things, in which it was impossible for God to lie, we might have a strong consolation [*comfort*], who have fled for refuge [*who have fled to God*] to lay hold upon the hope set before us [*to take hold of the promise of exaltation through righteousness and covenant making which He has made available to us*]:

19 Which hope we have as an anchor of the soul [*this hope for exaltation through Jesus Christ is an anchor for our souls*], both sure and stedfast [*absolutely dependable*], and which entereth into that within the veil [*this hope for exaltation penetrates the veil between earth and heaven*];

20 Whither [*to which*] the forerunner [*Christ*] is for us entered, even Jesus, made an high priest for ever after the order of Melchisedec. [*In other words, Christ was the "forerunner" who prepared the way for us to go through the veil into the presence of God. The symbolism is of the high priest serving in the temple in Jerusalem going through the veil into the Holy of Holies, which is symbolic of entering into celestial glory and into the presence of God.*]

HEBREWS 7

Paul will now teach more about Melchizedek, who was the king of Salem, to whom Abraham paid tithing and for whom the high priesthood was named. One of Paul's overall goals in this chapter is to point out to the Jewish (Hebrew) converts to the Church in his day what Christ's position was compared to Abraham (whom the Jew's held in highest esteem as their great ancestor) and Melchizedek. The logic that Paul uses is this: The Levites were under Moses. Moses was under Abraham. Abraham was under Melchizedek. Melchizedek was under Christ. The point is that

Christ is above them all. All of this will lead up to the point that salvation cannot be attained through living the law of Moses. Rather, it is attained through Christ.

1 FOR this Melchisedec, king of Salem [*Jerusalem; see Bible Dictionary under "Salem"*], priest of the most high God, who met Abraham returning from the slaughter of the kings, and blessed him [*see Genesis 14:17–19*];

Verse 2, next, can be used to teach the law of tithing as well as to teach what the name "Melchizedek" means.

2 To whom also Abraham gave a tenth part of all [*to whom Abraham paid tithing; Genesis 14:20*]; first being by interpretation King of righteousness [*first of all, the name, "Melchizedek," means "King of righteousness"*], and after that also King of Salem, which is, King of peace [*secondly, Melchizedek was the King of Salem, which means King of peace*];

The two definitions of the name "Melchizedek," given in verse 2, above, are reminders to all Melchizedek Priesthood holders that they should be righteous and should be peacemakers. Alma 13:17–19 gives us more details about Melchizedek as follows: "Now this Melchizedek was a king over the land of Salem; and his people had waxed strong in iniquity and abomination; yea, they had all gone astray; they were full of all manner of wickedness; But Melchizedek having exercised mighty faith, and received the office of the high priesthood according to the holy order of God, did preach repentance unto his people. And behold, they did repent; and Melchizedek did establish peace in the land in his days; therefore he was called the prince of peace, for he was the king of Salem; and he did reign under his father. Now, there were many before him, and also there were many afterwards, but none were greater; therefore, of him they have more particularly made mention."

Without the help of the JST, verse 3, next, sounds like Melchizedek did not have a father or mother, nor did he have posterity, neither did he die. The JST tells us that this verse refers to the Melchizedek Priesthood, rather than Melchizedek himself.

3 Without father, without mother, without descent, having neither beginning of days, nor end of life; but made like unto the Son of God; abideth a priest continually.

JST Hebrews 7:3

3 **For this Melchizedek was ordained a priest after the order of the Son of God** [*which is the priesthood held by the Savior*], **which order** [*which priesthood*] **was without father, without mother, without descent, having neither beginning of days, nor end of life. And all those who are ordained unto this priesthood are made like unto the Son of**

God, abiding a priest continually [*hold the same priesthood as the Savior, and will hold it forever*].

4 Now consider how great this man [*Melchizedek*] was, unto whom even the patriarch Abraham gave the tenth of the spoils [*unto whom Abraham paid tithing*].

Paul next refers to the Levites who were the men who held the Aaronic Priesthood among the children of Israel under Moses. Among other duties, these "sons of Levi" collected tithing from the Israelites.

5 And verily they that are of the sons of Levi, who receive the office of the priesthood [*the Aaronic Priesthood*], have a commandment to take tithes of the people according to the law [*the law of Moses*], that is, of [*from*] their brethren, though they come out of the loins of Abraham [*even though they are descendants of Abraham*]:

6 But he [*Melchizedek*] whose descent is not counted from them [*who was not an Israelite and did not descend from Abraham*] received tithes of [*from*] Abraham, and blessed him [*Abraham*] that had the promises [*with whom God had made the covenants; see Genesis 12:1–3; 17:1–8; 22:17–18; Abraham 2:9–11*].

The JST, Genesis 14:36–40 expands upon verse 6, above, as follows: "And this Melchizedek, having thus established righteousness, was called the king of heaven by his people, or, in other words, the King of peace. And he lifted up his voice, and he blessed Abram [*Abraham*], being the high priest, and the keeper of the storehouse of God; Him whom God had appointed to receive tithes for the poor. Wherefore, Abram paid unto him tithes of all that he had, of all the riches which he possessed, which God had given him more than that which he had need. And it came to pass, that God blessed Abram, and gave unto him riches, and honor, and lands for an everlasting possession; according to the covenant which he had made, and according to the blessing wherewith Melchizedek had blessed him."

7 And without all contradiction the less [*Abraham*] is blessed of [*by*] the better [*Melchizedek*]. [*In other words, it is not a contradiction that Melchizedek was higher in authority than Abraham, because Abraham paid tithes to him.*]

8 And here men that die receive tithes [*and here, on the one hand, we are dealing with mortal men who receive tithing from other mortals*]; but there [*on the other hand*] he [*Christ*] receiveth them [*receives tithes from all*], of whom it is witnessed that he [*Christ*] liveth [*has been resurrected and is alive*]. [*In other words, Christ is above all, because, ultimately, He is the one to whom all pay tithes. For more on this, see McConkie,* Doctrinal New Testament Commentary, *Vol. 3, p. 169.*]

Verse 9, next, refers back to "the sons of Levi" mentioned in verse 5.

9 And as I may so say [*and if I may stretch your minds a bit*], Levi also, who receiveth tithes, payed tithes in Abraham [*Levi, a descendant of Abraham, was there with Abraham when he paid tithes to Melchizedek*].

10 For he [*Levi*] was yet in the loins of his father [*his ancestor*], when Melchisedec met him [*Abraham*]. [*In other words, in a sense, Levi was still inside Abraham, as a seed, and thus was there when Abraham paid tithes to Melchizedek.*]

Paul will now make the transition from the above doctrines, about Christ's position above all prophets and people, to the fact that the law of Moses is under the gospel of Christ, and that salvation cannot be obtained through the law of Moses. Remember, he is talking to Jews who have joined the Church of Jesus Christ but still think that they should live the law of Moses completely.

11 If therefore perfection were by [*if exaltation came through*] the Levitical [*Aaronic*] priesthood, (for under it the people received the law,) [*in other words, the law of Moses was administered under the Aaronic* Priesthood] what further need was there that another priest [*Christ*] should rise [*come to us*] after the order of Melchisedec [*why would we need someone who held the Melchizedek Priesthood*], and not be called after the order of Aaron? [*In other words, if we could attain exaltation through the ordinances of the Aaronic Priesthood, as had in the law of Moses, why would we need another priest, who was a Melchizedek Priesthood high priest? In other words, why would we need Christ and His gospel if the law of Moses could save us in celestial glory?*]

12 For the priesthood being changed, there is made of necessity a change also of the law. [*Since we have gone from the Aaronic Priesthood to the Melchizedek Priesthood, it means that we have gone from Aaronic Priesthood laws and ordinances (associated with the law of Moses) to the higher laws and ordinances of the Melchizedek Priesthood (Associated with Christ and His gospel) which lead to exaltation.*]

13 For he [*Christ*] of whom these things are spoken pertaineth to another tribe [*comes from a different tribe of Israel (namely, the tribe of Judah)*], of which no man gave attendance at the altar [*and no men from the tribe of Judah held the Aaronic Priesthood and officiated at the altar in the temple under the law of Moses*].

14 For it is evident [*clear*] that our Lord [*Christ*] sprang out of Juda [*came from the tribe of Judah*]; of which tribe Moses spake nothing concerning priesthood [*and Moses did not give the priesthood to the men of the tribe of Judah*].

15 And it is yet far more evident [*clear*]: for that after the similitude of Melchisedec there ariseth another priest [*that we have been given a High Priest (Christ) of whom Melchizedek was symbolic (as "King of righteousness" and "King of peace" in verse 2, above)*],

16 Who is made [*who comes to us*], not after the law of a carnal commandment [*not with the Aaronic Priesthood and the laws and commandments of the law of Moses*], but after the power of an endless life [*but with the higher priesthood power to bring us to exaltation*].

17 For he [*David*] testifieth [*in Psalm 110:4*], Thou [*Christ*] art a priest for ever after the order of Melchisedec.

Are you impressed with Paul's command of the scriptures? As pointed out previously, Paul has an amazing memory for the prophecies about the Messiah contained in the Old Testament, which, of course, was the book of scripture for the Jews. Not only does he recall these passages of scripture, but he has marvelous inspired skill in using them in making convincing arguments as he teaches the gospel of Jesus Christ.

18 For there is verily [*truly*] a disannulling of the commandment going before [*there is a doing away with the law of Moses*] for the weakness and unprofitableness thereof [*because it is weak and unprofitable in the sense that it cannot bring us to exaltation*].

19 For the law [*of Moses*] made nothing perfect [*was not capable of bringing us to perfection in exaltation*], but the bringing in of a better hope did; by the which we draw nigh unto God.

JST Hebrews 7:19

19 For the law **was administered without an oath** [*did not have the oath and covenant of the Melchizedek Priesthood, as explained in D&C 84:33–42*] **and** made nothing perfect [*could not lead us to perfection*], **but was only the bringing in of a better hope** [*rather was only the means of pointing our minds to Jesus Christ*]; by the which we draw nigh unto God [*through whom we can return to the presence of the Father*].

20 And inasmuch as not without an oath he was made priest:

JST Hebrews 7:20

20 **Inasmuch as this high priest** [*Christ*] **was not without an oath** [*did not function without the Melchizedek Priesthood*], **by so much** [*all the more*] **was Jesus made the surety** [*the guarantee*] **of a better testament** [*covenant*]. [*In other words, Jesus Christ as the Great High Priest became the anchor or foundation of a "better" covenant, because the ordinances of the Melchizedek Priesthood involve covenants which guarantee exaltation for the faithful.*]

21 (For those [*Aaronic, Levitical; see verse 11*] priests were made without an oath [*the Levitical priests were not called with an oath*]; but this with an oath [*but Christ was made a high priest*] by him that said unto him, The Lord sware [*promised*] and will not repent [*will not go back on His word*], Thou [*Christ*] art a priest for ever after the order of Melchisedec:)

22 By so much was Jesus made a surety [*the guarantee*] of a better testament [*of the "New Testament," in other words, the "new and everlasting covenant," which, when faithfully kept, leads to exaltation*].

23 And they [*Levitical priests; verse 5*] truly were many priests, because they were not suffered [*allowed*] to continue by reason of death [*because they eventually died*]:

24 But this man [*Christ*], because he continueth ever [*lives forever*], hath an unchangeable priesthood [*will hold His priesthood authority forever*].

25 Wherefore he [*Christ*] is able also to save them to the uttermost [*to and including exaltation*] that come unto God by him [*who come unto the Father through Him*], seeing he ever liveth to make intercession for them [*since His Atonement continues forever with its power to intercede and save them*].

26 For such an high priest became us [*was needed by us*], who is holy, harmless, undefiled, separate from sinners [*sinless*], and made higher than the heavens;

JST Hebrews 7:25

25 For such an high priest became us, who is holy, harmless, undefiled, separate from sinners, and made **ruler over the heavens**;

A little background will help you in understanding the next verses. In Old Testament times, before the Levitical priests went to perform sacrifices for the cleansing of the people of Israel, they were required first to offer sacrifices for their own cleansing and purification. Christ, of course, did not need to cleanse Himself from sin first, before offering Himself as a sacrifice for us whereby we can become clean and pure from our sins.

27 Who needeth not daily, as those high priests, to offer up sacrifice, first for his own sins, and then for the people's: for this he did once, when he offered up himself.

JST Hebrews 7:26

26 **And not as those high priests who offered up sacrifice daily, first for their own sins, and then for the sins of the people; for he needeth not offer sacrifice for his own sins, for he knew no sins; but for the sins of the people. And** this [*atoning for the sins of the people*] he did once, when he offered up himself.

28 For the law [*of Moses*] maketh men high priests which have

infirmity [*who have imperfections*]; but the word of the oath [*the covenants administered by the Melchizedek Priesthood*], which was since the law [*which were given after the law of Moses was given*], maketh the Son [*were given by Christ*], who is consecrated for evermore [*who is our Savior for evermore*].

HEBREWS 8

Paul will now summarize what he has taught in the previous chapters, as he continues to teach the need for the Savior, Jesus Christ.

1 NOW of the things which we have spoken this is the sum [*now, to summarize what I have said in this letter so far*]: We have such an high priest [*Christ*], who is set on the right hand of the throne of the Majesty in the heavens [*who has returned to heaven and sits at the right hand of the Father*];

2 A minister of the sanctuary, and of the true tabernacle, which the Lord pitched, and not man. [*In other words, Christ is our High Priest who serves for us in heaven. He has gone on to prepare a place for us.*]

3 For every high priest is ordained to offer gifts and sacrifices: wherefore it is of necessity that this man [*Christ*] have somewhat also to offer [*something to offer as a sacrifice also*].

4 For if he were on earth, he should not be a priest, seeing that there are priests that offer gifts according to the law:

JST Hebrews 8:4

4 **Therefore while he was on the earth, he offered for a sacrifice his own life for the sins of the people. Now every priest under the law** [*who served under the law of Moses*], **must needs** [*must of necessity*] **offer gifts, or sacrifices,** according to the law.

5 Who serve unto the example and shadow [*whose service is symbolic*] of heavenly things, as Moses was admonished of God [*instructed by God in Exodus 25:40*] when he was about to make the tabernacle: for, See, saith he, that thou make all things according to the pattern shewed to thee in the mount [*while you were on Mount Sinai*].

6 But now hath he [*Christ*] obtained a more excellent [*a superior*] ministry, by how much also he is the mediator of a better [*higher*] covenant, which was established upon better [*higher*] promises. [*In other words, the ministry of Jesus is as superior to the ministry of the priests of the Aaronic Priesthood mentioned in verses 4 and 5, above, as the Melchizedek Priesthood covenants and ordinances are to the ordinances of the law of Moses.*]

7 For if that first covenant [*the law of Moses*] had been faultless [*had been able to lead us to perfection*], then should no place have been sought for the second [*then there*

would have been no need for the new covenant brought by Christ].

8 For finding fault with them [*pointing out that the requirements of the law of Moses were not able to bring us salvation in heaven*], he saith [*God said, in Jeremiah 31:31–34*], Behold, the days come [*the time will come in the future*], saith the Lord, when I will make a new covenant with the house of Israel and with the house of Judah [*and with the Jews*]:

9 Not according to the covenant [*the law of Moses*] that I made with their fathers [*ancestors*] in the day when I took them by the hand to lead them out of the land of Egypt; because they continued not in my covenant [*because they broke the higher gospel laws I had given them*], and I regarded them not [*I had to withdraw some blessings from them*], saith the Lord.

10 For this is the covenant [*I will describe the covenant*] that I will make with the house of Israel after those days [*in a future time*], saith the Lord; I will put my laws into their mind, and write them in their hearts: and I will be to them a God, and they shall be to me a people [*as prophesied in Jeremiah 31:33*]: [*In other words, the new covenant (the gospel of Jesus Christ) which I make with them will involve personal righteousness of heart and mind and testimony, rather than a law of performances and daily ritual and sacrifices, as was the case with the law of Moses.*]

Next, in verse 11, Paul teaches that because of the new covenant brought in the gospel of Jesus Christ, the day will come in which everyone will follow Christ. We understand this to be referring to the Millennium. See D&C 84:98.

11 And they shall not teach every man his neighbour, and every man his brother, saying, Know the Lord: for all shall [*because everyone will*] know me, from the least to the greatest.

Next, Paul explains how such widespread acceptance of and loyalty to Christ can happen. The answer is simple. It will happen because people will take advantage of the gift of the Atonement.

12 For I will be merciful to their unrighteousness, and their sins and their iniquities will I remember no more. [*In other words, I will forgive them when they repent.*]

13 In that he saith, A new covenant, he hath made the first old [*the simple fact that God mentions a "new covenant" tells us that the "old covenant" (law of Moses) will someday become obsolete*]. Now that which decayeth and waxeth old is ready to vanish away. [*In other words, the law of Moses is on its way out because Christ fulfilled it.*]

HEBREWS 9

Paul will continue here with the comparison between the symbolism contained in the rituals and sacrifices required by the law of Moses and the sacrifice given by Christ as He carried out the Atonement. A brief description of the portable tent used by the children of Israel, which was very elaborate and ornate and was known as the "tabernacle," is helpful in understanding this chapter. We will use a description given in the Institute of Religion's New Testament student manual, *The Life and Teachings of Jesus and His Apostles*, 1979 edition, p. 390. It is: "During Israel's wanderings and prior to the building of a temple in Solomon's day (about 970 B.C.), the priests of Israel performed the sacred ordinances in behalf of their people in a portable tent known as the tabernacle. This edifice, constructed in such a way that it could be quickly moved from place to place, was the first item set up in any new place of encampment. The tabernacle was composed of two parts. There was an outer compartment into which the Levites and sons of Aaron might enter daily to perform the sacred ordinances prescribed by the Mosaic law. There was also an inner compartment separated by a veil and considered to be the most holy place, into which the high priest might enter but once a year to perform his sacred duties on the Day of Atonement. As explained by Paul, the outer division of the tabernacle contained the sacred candlestick, twelve loaves of shewbread, and an altar of incense; in the inner chamber known as the Holy of Holies was located the ark of the covenant, a chest somewhat equivalent to a good-sized modern trunk. In the ark were kept the golden censer, the golden pot containing manna, Aaron's rod, and the tablets on which were inscribed the Ten Commandments."

1 THEN verily the first covenant [*the law of Moses; see notes in chapter 8, above*] had also ordinances of divine service, and a worldly sanctuary [*an earthly tabernacle, temple*].

2 For there was a tabernacle made [*by Moses for the children of Israel; see heading to Exodus 26 in our Bible*]; the first [*the first room in the tabernacle*], wherein was the candlestick, and the table, and the shewbread; which is called the sanctuary [*this room in the tabernacle was called "the sanctuary"*].

3 And after the second veil, the tabernacle, [*behind the second veil in the tabernacle made by Moses was the room*] which is called the Holiest of all [*the "Holy of Holies" or the "Most Holy Place"*];

4 Which had the golden censer, and the ark of the covenant overlaid round about with gold, wherein [*in the Ark of the Covenant*] was the golden pot that had manna, and Aaron's rod that budded, and the tables of the covenant [*the stone tablets which had the Ten Commandments on them*];

5 And over it [*above the Ark of the Covenant*] the cherubims of glory shadowing the mercyseat; of which we cannot now speak

particularly [*about which we will not give details at this time*].

6 Now when these things were thus ordained [*when the tabernacle was being used among the Israelites*], the priests went always [*all of the priests could go*] into the first tabernacle [*into the first room*], accomplishing [*performing*] the service of God.

7 But into the second went the high priest alone [*but only the high priest could go into the Holy of Holies*] once every year, not without blood, which he offered for himself, and for the errors of the people [*not without offering a blood sacrifice to atone for his own sins and for the sins of the people*]:

8 The Holy Ghost this signifying, that the way into the holiest of all was not yet made manifest, while as the first tabernacle was yet standing: [*In other words, the Holy Ghost tells us that, under the law of Moses, the way to the "Holy of Holies," (symbolic of the celestial kingdom) was not showN to the people.*]

JST Hebrews 9:8

8 The Holy Ghost **signifying this** that the way into the holiest of all was not yet made manifest, while as **yet** the first tabernacle was standing;

9 Which was a figure [*served as symbolism*] for the time then present [*for that time among the Israelites*], in which were offered both gifts and sacrifices [*when they were following the law of Moses*], that could not make him that did the service perfect [*which could not make the priests who were performing the rituals or the people providing the sacrifices perfect*], as pertaining to the conscience [*with respect to the deep, inner soul*];

10 Which stood only in [*the law of Moses consisted only of*] meats [*foods*] and drinks, and divers [*various*] washings, and carnal [*earthly*] ordinances, imposed on them until the time of reformation [*until the time when Christ would restore the higher laws and ordinances of His gospel*].

JST Hebrews 9:10

10 Which **consisted** only in meats and drinks, and divers washings, and carnal ordinances, imposed on them until the time of reformation.

11 But Christ being come an high priest of good things to come, by a greater and more perfect tabernacle, not made with hands, that is to say, not of this building; [*In other words, Christ has already come and performed the role of a high priest for us, sacrificing Himself as a blood sacrifice for us so that we can enter into a "more perfect tabernacle," in other words, the celestial kingdom.*]

12 Neither by the blood of goats and calves [*as used by the high priests in the tabernacle to symbolically cleanse themselves and their people from sin*], but by his own blood [*by giving His own life for us*] he entered in once into the holy

place [*he entered into the "Holy of Holies," in other words, the celestial kingdom*], having obtained eternal redemption for us [*having made eternal exaltation available to us*].

13 For if the blood of bulls and of goats, and the ashes of an heifer sprinkling the unclean, sanctifieth to the purifying of the flesh: [*If, according to the law of Moses, the blood of sacrificial animals and the ashes of burnt offerings can be ceremonially sprinkled upon a person to make him ritually "clean."*]

14 How much more shall the blood of Christ, who through the eternal Spirit offered himself without spot [*as a perfect sacrifice, without sin or blemish*] to God, purge your conscience from dead works to serve the living God? [*In other words, don't you think that if people can be made outwardly clean through ritual cleansing in the law of Moses, you can become inwardly clean through purging you mind of notions of following the dead works of the law of Moses and following Christ?*]

15 And for this cause [*this is the purpose for which*] he is the mediator [*the one who helps us return to the Father*] of the new testament, that by means of death [*by offering Himself as a sacrifice*], for the redemption of the transgressions that were under the first testament, [*in other words, to redeem us from personal sins which remained upon us when we were living the law of Moses*], they which are called [*the Israelites*] might receive the promise of eternal inheritance [*the promise of exaltation*].

JST Hebrews 9:15

15 And for this cause he is the mediator of the new **covenant**, that by means of death, for the redemption of the transgressions that were under the first **covenant**, they which are called might receive the promise of eternal inheritance.

16 For where a testament is, there must also of necessity be the death of the testator.

JST Hebrews 9:16

16 For where a **covenant** is, there must also of necessity be the death of the **victim**.

The word "testator," as used in the King James Bible, means a person who is making out a will to leave an inheritance to someone else. Thus, the "testator" must die before the heir can inherit the gift. So also, says Paul in effect, the Savior had to die in order for us to be able to inherit His gift to us, which is eternal life, provided we live His gospel.

17 For a testament is of force after men are dead [*the will transfers the gift or inheritance to the heir only after the person who made the will is dead*]: otherwise it is of no strength at all while the testator liveth.

<u>**JST Hebrews 9:17**</u>

17 For a **covenant** is of force after **the victim is dead**; otherwise it is of no strength at all while the **victim** liveth.

The word "victim," used by Joseph Smith in these verses, carries the connotation of one who is innocent suffering for the sins of others.

18 Whereupon neither the first testament was dedicated without blood. [*This is why even the law of Moses was not put into effect without the shedding of blood.*]

<u>**JST Hebrews 9:18**</u>

18 Whereupon neither the first **covenant** was dedicated without blood.

19 For when Moses had spoken every precept [*teaching and commandment*] to all the people according to the law [*see Exodus 24:7–8*], he took the blood of calves and of goats, with water, and scarlet wool, and hyssop, and sprinkled both the book [*scroll*], and all the people,

There is much symbolism in verse 19, above, which relates to Christ's Atonement. Blood, water, scarlet fabric, and hyssop were all present during Christ's atoning sacrifice for us. Blood came from every pore in Gethsemane. Water gushed forth from the wound in His side after He had died upon the cross. The soldiers mocked Him with a scarlet robe upon His back, before He was crucified. Hyssop was used in putting vinegar to Christ's mouth while He was on the cross; see John 19:29.

20 Saying, This is the blood of the testament which God hath enjoined [*commanded;* Strong's *#1781*] unto you.

<u>**JST Hebrews 9:20**</u>

20 Saying, This is the blood of the **covenant** which God hath enjoined unto you.

21 Moreover he [*Moses*] sprinkled with blood both the tabernacle, and all the vessels of the ministry [*containers used in the services and rituals*].

<u>**JST Hebrews 9:21**</u>

21 Moreover he sprinkled likewise with blood both the tabernacle, and all the vessels of the ministry.

Next, Paul points out that virtually everything was cleansed by blood, in the rites and rituals of the law of Moses. This, of course, is symbolic of the cleansing and healing that comes into every aspect of our lives through the cleansing blood of Christ.

22 And almost all things are by the law [*of Moses*] purged [*cleansed*] with blood; and without shedding of blood is no remission [*of sins*].

23 It was therefore necessary that the patterns of [*the "types" or things in the law of Moses that are symbolic of*] things in the heavens should be purified with these [*with the blood of sacrificial animals*]; but the heavenly things themselves

with better sacrifices than these [*but the things which lead to exaltation in the celestial kingdom must be made available to us with a better sacrifice than animal sacrifices, namely, Christ*].

24 For Christ is not entered into the holy places made with hands [*for Christ's sacrifice did not take place in the tabernacle or the temple made by men*], which are the figures of the true [*which are symbolic of the true "holy places," namely, celestial glory*]; but into heaven itself, now to appear in the presence of God for us [*and now He is in the presence of the Father as our Mediator*]:

25 Nor yet that he should offer himself often, as the high priest entereth into the holy place every year with blood of others [*Christ's sacrifice does not have to be repeated every year for us*];

26 For then must he often have suffered since the foundation of the world [*if that were the case, He would have had to have suffered, been crucified and resurrected over and over again ever since the beginning of the world*]: but now once in the end of the world hath he appeared to put away sin by the sacrifice of himself. [*Jesus only had to die once to atone for us.*]

JST Hebrews 9:26

26 For then must he often have suffered since the foundation of the world; but now once in the **meridian of time** hath he appeared to put away sin by the sacrifice of himself.

27 And as it is appointed unto men once to die, but after this the judgment [*men die just once and then will appear before God on Judgment Day*]:

28 So Christ was once offered to bear the sins of many; and unto them that look for him shall he appear the second time without sin unto salvation.

JST Hebrews 9:28

28 So Christ was once offered to bear the sins of many; **and he shall appear the second time**, without sin unto salvation **unto them that look for him**.

There are some important doctrines contained in verses 27 and 28, above. First of all, many people believe in reincarnation, meaning that they believe that we have many lives here on earth. We live one life, for instance as a peasant, then another as a wealthy person, then another life as a soldier, etc., until we overcome evil and are worthy of heaven. This cannot be so, according to verse 27, above, because "it is appointed unto men once to die." In other words, we only have one mortal life here on earth. Another doctrine of interest especially to Latter-day Saints, is taught in verse 28. Occasionally, members of the Church who are aware that the Savior's Atonement works for the inhabitants of other worlds belonging to Heavenly Father (see D&C 76:24), ask whether or not Jesus has to be born, crucified, and die on each of those worlds. The answer is "No." Verse 28, above, informs us that Christ was sacrificed "once," and we know that His sacrifice occurred on our earth.

HEBREWS 10

Paul will continue in this chapter with the theme that the law of Moses cannot make us perfect, but the gospel brought by Christ can.

1 FOR the law [*of Moses*] having a shadow of good things to come [*is symbolic of the complete gospel to come*], and not the very image of the things [*and is not the full gospel*], can never with those sacrifices which they offered year by year continually make the comers thereunto perfect [*the law of Moses cannot bring those who come unto it to exaltation*].

JST Hebrews 10:1

1 For the law having a shadow of good things to come, and not the very image of the things, can never with those sacrifices, which they offered **continually year by year** make the comers thereunto perfect.

2 For then would they not have ceased to be offered [*if it could, wouldn't the sacrifices have ceased to be offered*]? because that the worshippers once purged [*once cleansed and made perfect*] should have had no more conscience of sins [*would have had no more guilty conscience for sins*].

3 But in those sacrifices [*in the sacrifices required by the law of Moses*] there is a remembrance again made of sins every year [*the sacrifices for sins continue to be made year after year*].

4 For it is not possible that the blood of bulls and of goats should take away sins [*animal sacrifices cannot take away sins*].

5 Wherefore when he [*Christ*] cometh into the world, he saith [*as recorded in Psalm 40:6–8*], Sacrifice and offering thou [*God*] wouldest not, but a body [*a mortal body*] hast thou prepared me [*Christ*]:

6 In burnt offerings and sacrifices for sin thou hast had no pleasure [*compare with Isaiah 1:11*].

7 Then said I, Lo, I come (in the volume of the book it is written of me,) to do thy will, O God [*O Father*].

8 Above when he said [*and, more importantly, He said*], Sacrifice and offering and burnt offerings and offering for sin thou [*Father*] wouldest not [*do not like*], neither hadst pleasure therein; which are offered by the law [*which are part of the law of Moses*]; [*In other words, Paul explains that the Savior explained that the Father does not like or enjoy animal sacrifices and burnt offerings. His goal is to have people become truly personally righteous through the Atonement of Christ.*]

9 Then said he [*Christ*], Lo, I come to do thy will, O God [*Father*]. He taketh away the first [*the law of Moses*], that he may establish the second [*the gospel of Christ*].

10 By the which will we are sanctified [*made clean, pure, holy and fit to be in the presence of the Father*] through the offering of the body [*through the sacrifice*] of Jesus Christ once [*only once*] for all.

JST Hebrews 10:10

10 **By which** will we are sanctified through the offering **once** of the body of Jesus Christ.

11 And every priest [*in the law of Moses*] standeth daily ministering and offering oftentimes the same sacrifices, which can never take away sins: [*No matter how many sacrifices are offered by how many priests, they still cannot take away our sins.*]

12 But this man [*Christ*], after he had offered one sacrifice for sins for ever [*after offering just one eternal sacrifice for sin*], sat down on the right hand of God;

13 From henceforth expecting till his enemies be made his footstool [*In other words, until He has overcome all things.*]

JST Hebrews 10:13

13 From henceforth **to reign until** his enemies be made his footstool.

14 For by one offering [*sacrifice*] he [*Christ*] hath perfected for ever them that [*has brought eternal exaltation to those who*] are sanctified [*made worthy to enter celestial glory*].

15 Whereof the Holy Ghost also is a witness to us [*the Holy Ghost bears witness to us of this*]: for after that he [*Christ*] had said before [*in the past, as recorded in Jeremiah 31:33–34*],

16 This is the covenant that I will make with them after those days [*after the law of Moses has done its job*], saith the Lord, I will put my laws into their hearts, and in their minds will I write them; [*In other words, the day will come when I will have a righteous people.*]

17 And their sins and iniquities will I remember no more [*compare to D&C 58:42–43*].

18 Now where remission of these is, there is no more offering for sin [*when sins have been forgiven, there is no more need for additional sacrifices for sin*].

19 Having therefore, brethren, boldness [*confidence*] to enter into the holiest [*to enter into the heavenly "Holy of holies," in other words, the celestial kingdom*] by the blood of Jesus [*because of Christ's Atonement*],

20 By a new and living way [*through the new and living gospel of Christ rather than the old, dead law of Moses*], which he [*Christ*] hath consecrated [*prepared*] for us, through the veil [*so that we can pass through the veil into the celestial kingdom*], that is to say,

his flesh [*because Christ sacrificed His mortal life for us*];

21 And having an high priest over the house [*kingdom*] of God;

JST Hebrews 10:21

21 And having **such** an high priest over the house of God;

22 Let us draw near [*let us approach the Father*] with a true heart [*a pure heart, focused on righteousness*] in full assurance of faith [*with full confidence*], having our hearts sprinkled [*cleansed by the blood of Christ*] from an evil [*guilty*] conscience, and our bodies washed [*baptized*] with pure water.

23 Let us hold fast the profession of our faith [*let us hold firmly to what we profess (claim) to believe*] without wavering; (for he [*God*] is faithful [*is completely reliable*] that promised [*who promised that we could attain exaltation through Christ*];)

24 And let us consider one another to provoke unto love and to good works: [*In other words, let us help one another, reminding each other to show love and to do good works.*]

25 Not forsaking the assembling of ourselves together [*not missing church meetings*], as the manner of some is [*like some are doing*]; but exhorting [*teaching and warning*] one another: and so much the more, as ye see the day [*the Second Coming and final judgment;* Strong's *#2250*] approaching.

Next, Paul warns them not to wait until it is too late to repent and faithfully follow Christ.

26 For if we sin wilfully [*if we refuse to repent*] after that we have received the knowledge of the truth, there remaineth no more sacrifice for sins [*the Savior's sacrifice cannot cleanse us from our sins*],

27 But [*all we will have left will be*] a certain fearful looking for of judgment and fiery indignation, which shall devour the adversaries [*the burning of the wicked at the Second Coming*].

28 He that despised [*rejected, disregarded;* Strong's *#0114*] Moses' law died without mercy under two or three witnesses [*when testified against by two or three witnesses*]:

29 Of how much sorer [*worse*] punishment, suppose ye, shall he be thought worthy, who hath trodden under foot [*who has despised, rejected*] the Son of God, and hath counted [*considered*] the blood of the covenant [*the Savior's blood which he shed for us*], wherewith he was sanctified, an unholy thing [*who has mocked the Savior's sacrifice*], and hath done despite unto the Spirit of grace [*and has despised the Atonement*]?

30 For we know him [*Jehovah*] that hath said [*in Deuteronomy 32:35*], Vengeance belongeth unto me, I will recompense [*repay*], saith the Lord. And again [*in Deuteronomy 32:36*], The Lord shall judge his people.

31 It is a fearful thing to fall into the hands of [*to be punished by*] the living God.

32 But call to remembrance the former days, in which, after ye were illuminated, ye endured a great fight of afflictions [*think back to the days when you were converted and had to endure many persecutions*];

33 Partly, whilst ye were made a gazingstock both by reproaches and afflictions [*sometimes you were insulted and persecuted in public*]; and partly, whilst ye became companions of them that were so used [*and sometimes you accompanied those who were so treated*].

34 For ye had compassion of me in my bonds [*you sympathized with me while I was in prison*], and took joyfully the spoiling of your goods [*and you cheerfully submitted to being plundered and ruined financially*], knowing in yourselves [*because of the inner assurance*] that ye have in heaven a better and an enduring substance [*that a better reward awaits you in heaven*].

35 Cast not away therefore your confidence [*don't set aside your faith in Christ*], which hath great recompence of reward [*through which you have a great reward in store for you*].

36 For ye have need of patience [*you will need to have patience in afflictions*], that, after ye have done the will of God [*that after you have endured faithfully to the end*], ye might receive the promise [*you will receive the promised exaltation*].

37 For yet a little while, and he [*Christ*] that shall come will come, and will not tarry [*when the time is right, Christ will not wait any longer, but will come again to earth; see Habakkuk 2:3*].

38 Now the just shall live by faith [*as written in Habakkuk 2:4*]: but if any man draw back [*if anyone apostatizes*], my soul shall have no pleasure in him.

39 But we are not of them who draw back unto perdition [*but we are not among those who will become sons of perdition*]; but of them that believe to the saving of the soul [*rather, we will remain among those who will stay faithful and thus save our souls*].

HEBREWS 11

This chapter contains one of the most important, most beautiful, and most skillfully taught sermons about faith anywhere in scripture. So far in this letter, the Apostle Paul has prepared the Hebrew Saints with much skill and inspiration to receive the crowning principle which will help them attain exaltation. What is this crowning principle? Answer: Faith. We are taught in the Articles of Faith that faith is indeed the first principle of the gospel (see Fourth Article of Faith). Paul now teaches us why this is so.

1 NOW faith is the substance of things hoped for, the evidence [*the*

proof, conviction; Strong's *#1650*] of things not seen.

JST Hebrews 11:1

1 Now faith is the **assurance** of things hoped for, the evidence of things not seen.

The words "substance," "evidence," and "assurance" (JST) in verse 1, above, are powerful words defining faith. "Substance," as defined in *Strong's Exhaustive Concordance of the Bible*, #5287, means "confidence, foundation." This is in harmony with the Prophet Joseph Smith's word "assurance." When we are "assured" in our hearts and minds that our course of action is in harmony with God's will, our lives are built upon that foundation. Thus, faith is the foundation upon which our whole lives are based.

Joseph Smith defined faith as both a "principle of action" and also a "principle of power." (See *Lectures on Faith*, Lecture First, published by Deseret Book Company, 1985, p. 7.) When we build our lives upon faith as a "principle of action," it influences every aspect of life. It gets us to church on Sunday. It urges us to "action" in doing good, paying tithing, fleeing filth, reading scriptures, praying, even if we don't feel like it, and on and on. It motivates us to attend the temple, to go on missions, to be honest when everyone around us is lying. It compels us to accept callings in the Church, to agree to speak in sacrament meeting when such things frighten us. In short, faith truly becomes the "substance" around which our lives are built. And, when such is the case, we are constantly given "evidence" or "proof" and "conviction," in other words, the Holy Ghost constantly bears testimony to us "assuring" us that the direction of our lives is correct and is leading us on a path which will lead to exaltation.

As mentioned above, Joseph Smith taught that faith is a principle of action and also a principle of power. For our lives, it is primarily a principle of action which will lead to our eventually having the power of gods. However, it gives us power right now to overcome evil and fear. It gives us power, when it is God's will, to have miracles performed in our behalf or in behalf of others. You may wish to pay special attention to the examples of faith given by Paul in the following verses and note which ones are primarily examples of faith as a principle of action and which are primarily examples of faith as a principle of power.

2 For by it [*faith*] the elders [*ancient prophets*] obtained a good report [*obtained strong testimonies;* Strong's *#3140; also see Hebrews 11:39, footnote a, in your Bible*].

3 Through faith we understand that the worlds were framed [*created*] by the word of God, so that things which are seen [*God's creations*] were not made of things which do

appear [*were not created by powers which are visible to common man*].

4 By faith Abel offered unto God a more excellent sacrifice than Cain [*Abel offered an acceptable sacrifice, whereas Cain did not; see Moses 5:16–23*], by which he [*Abel*] obtained witness that he was righteous, God testifying of his gifts: and by it he [*Abel*] being dead yet speaketh.

The Prophet Joseph Smith adds much to our understanding of verse 4, above. He explains that Abel was taught by God concerning the Atonement and the symbolism of blood sacrifices. (See *Teachings of the Prophet Joseph Smith*, p. 58.) Thus, Abel offered one of the firstlings of his flock as a blood sacrifice to God. (See Moses 5:20.) Cain, on the other hand, in a rebellious mood and commanded by Satan, offered a sacrifice of garden produce rather than an animal sacrifice. (See Moses 5:18–19.)

Joseph Smith also explained what Paul meant in verse 4 when he said, referring to Abel, "he being dead yet speaketh," as follows: "How doth he yet speak? Why he magnified the Priesthood which was conferred upon him, and died a righteous man, and therefore has become an angel of God by receiving his body from the dead, holding still the keys of his dispensation; and was sent down from heaven unto Paul to minister consoling words, and to commit unto him a knowledge of the mysteries of godliness. And if this was not the case, I would ask, how did Paul know so much about Abel, and why should he talk about his speaking after he was dead? Hence, that he spoke after he was dead must be by being sent down out of heaven to administer." (*Teachings of the Prophet Joseph Smith*, selected and arranged by Joseph Fielding Smith [Salt Lake City: Deseret Book, 1976], p. 168.)

5 By faith Enoch was translated [*taken up to heaven without dying first*] that he should not see death; and was not found [*on earth*], because God had translated him: for before his translation he had this testimony [*he was given the assurance*], that he pleased God [*he knew that he was acceptable to God*].

Enoch and his entire city were translated (see Bible Dictionary under "Enoch.") He and his people in the City of Enoch were resurrected at the time of the Savior's resurrection (see D&C 133:54–55), and they will return to earth at the time of the Second Coming.

6 But without faith it is impossible to please him [*to become acceptable to God*]: for he that cometh to God must believe that he is, and that he is a rewarder of them that diligently seek him.

7 By faith Noah, being warned of God of things not seen as yet, moved with fear [*motivated by fear because he had faith in*

what God had told him about the coming flood], prepared an ark to the saving of his house [*family*]; by the which he condemned the world [*Noah became a witness that obedience to God saves us, and thus his good example condemned those who disobeyed*], and became heir of the righteousness [*received exaltation*] which is by faith [*which comes through faith*].

8 By faith Abraham, when he was called to go out into a place [*the Land of Canaan; see Abraham 2:3–4*] which he should after receive for an inheritance, obeyed; and he went out, not knowing whither he went [*where he was going*].

9 By faith he sojourned in the land of promise, as in a strange country, dwelling in tabernacles [*tents;* Strong's *#4633*] with Isaac and Jacob, the heirs with him of the same promise [*who had been given the same promises of exaltation through their faithfulness; see Abraham 2:9–11; Genesis 26:1–4; Genesis 28:13–15*]:

10 For he looked for a city [*the "celestial city," the celestial kingdom; Revelation 21:2*] which hath foundations, whose builder and maker is God. [*In other words, Abraham built his life on the sure foundation of faith in God which would lead him to the celestial kingdom and exaltation.*]

11 Through faith also Sara [*Sarah, Abraham's wife*] herself received strength to conceive seed [*see Genesis 18:10–11*], and was delivered of a child [*and had a baby who was named Isaac*] when she was past age [*when she was beyond child-bearing age*], because she judged him [*God*] faithful who had promised.

12 Therefore sprang there even of one [*from Abraham*], and him as good as dead [*he was about 100 years old when Isaac was born; see Genesis 17:1 and 15–16*], so many [*posterity as many*] as the stars of the sky in multitude, and as the sand which is by the sea shore innumerable. [*In other words, through faith, no matter what other obstacles or circumstances get in the way, the promises of God will ultimately be completely fulfilled.*]

JST Hebrews 11:12

12 Therefore sprang there even of one, and him as good as dead, **as** many as the stars of the sky in multitude, and as the sand which is by the seashore innumerable.

13 These all [*all of these great people*] died in faith, not having received the promises [*not having received exaltation yet*], but having seen them afar off [*but knowing the promised blessings were coming far off in the future*], and were persuaded of them [*and were convinced they would receive those blessings*], and embraced them [*and made covenants with God in order to receive them*], and confessed [*acknowledged*] that they were strangers and pilgrims on the earth [*that this earth is not their*

final destination, rather it is just a station en route to exaltation; see verse 16, below].

14 For they [*righteous "strangers" and "pilgrims" in verse 13, above*] that say such things declare plainly that they seek a country [*a final home where they can stay forever; see Hebrews 11:14, footnote a; in other words, they are seeking a permanent home in celestial exaltation*].

15 And truly, if they had been mindful of that country from whence they came out, they might have had opportunity to have returned. [*If they had only thought of this mortal life and what is available to them on earth, they might have been satisfied.*]

16 But now [*because they know about celestial glory and have that for perspective*] they desire a better country, that is, an heavenly [*the celestial kingdom*]: wherefore God is not ashamed to be called their God [*God has accepted them*]: for he hath prepared for them a city [*the celestial kingdom; see Revelation 21, heading plus that whole chapter where the celestial kingdom is described*].

Next, we gain insight into how faith helped Abraham when he was given the commandment to sacrifice Isaac, his only covenant son through Sarah. See Genesis 22:1–19 for more details.

17 By faith Abraham, when he was tried [*tested*], offered up Isaac: and he [*Abraham*] that had received the promises [*who had been promised posterity as numerous as the sands of the sea through his only covenant son, Isaac; see Genesis 21:12*] offered up his only begotten son [*Isaac*],

18 Of whom it was said, That in Isaac shall thy seed be called [*Genesis 21:12*]:

19 Accounting that God was able to raise him up, even from the dead [*knowing that, if necessary, God would bring Isaac back to life after he had been sacrificed*]; from whence also he [*Abraham*] received him [*Isaac*] in a figure [*figuratively or symbolically speaking*].

20 By faith Isaac blessed Jacob and Esau concerning things to come [*prophesying about the future*].

21 By faith Jacob, when he was a dying [*Genesis 48:2*], blessed both the sons of Joseph; and worshipped, leaning upon the top of his staff [*using his staff for support*].

22 By faith Joseph [*who was sold into Egypt*], when he died [*when he was dying*], made mention of the departing of the children of Israel [*prophesied that the children of Israel would be delivered out of Egyptian bondage (see JST Genesis 50:24 in the Joseph Smith Translation section, at the back of your Bible*]; and gave commandment concerning his bones [*and instructed that his bones be carried out of Egypt and that he be buried in the promised land when the time came for the children of*

Israel to be set free from Egyptian bondage; see Genesis 50:24–25].

23 By faith Moses, when he was born, was hid three months of [*by*] his parents, because they saw he was a proper child; [*In other words, Moses' parents knew that he was a special child and it was their faith which preserved his life*] and they were not afraid of the king's [*Pharaoh's*] commandment [*to kill all the male Hebrew babies when they were born*].

JST Hebrews 11:23

23 By faith Moses, when he was born, was hid three months of his parents, because they saw **that** he was a **peculiar** [*special*] child; and they were not afraid of the king's commandment.

Thanks to Stephen, in Acts 7:20–25, we know that Moses actually knew that he was to be the one who would lead the children of Israel out of Egypt. In the next verses here, Paul emphasizes the role of faith in Moses' carrying out his mission.

24 By faith Moses, when he was come to years [*in other words, when he grew up*], refused to be called the son of Pharaoh's daughter [*refused to continue the privileged life of royalty in Pharaoh's court*];

JST Hebrews 11:24

24 By faith Moses, when he was come to years **of discretion**, refused to be called the son of Pharaoh's daughter;

25 Choosing rather to suffer affliction with the people of God [*choosing instead to join with the Hebrew slaves and help them*], than to enjoy the pleasures of sin for a season [*rather than enjoying the pleasures of sin and luxury for a time which was available to him in Pharaoh's palace*];

26 Esteeming the reproach of Christ [*the burden of being loyal to Christ*] greater riches [*to be of greater worth*] than the treasures in Egypt: for he had respect unto the recompence of the reward [*he understood the rewards which come to the righteous*].

27 By faith he forsook [*left*] Egypt, not fearing the wrath of the king [*Pharaoh*]: for he endured, as seeing him who is invisible [*he endured because he saw God, who is not seen by most people*].

28 Through faith he kept the passover [*when the destroying angel "passed over" the firstborn of the Israelites in Egypt*], and the sprinkling of blood [*on the doorposts and lintel (top of the door frame); see Exodus 12:21–23*], lest he [*the destroying angel*] that destroyed the firstborn [*in Egypt*] should touch them [*the children of Israel*].

29 By faith they passed through the Red sea as by dry land: which the Egyptians assaying to do [*attempting to do, as they continued pursuing the Israelites*] were drowned.

30 By faith the walls of Jericho fell down, after they were compassed

about [*marched around*] seven days.

31 By faith the harlot Rahab perished not with them that believed not [*Rahab was not killed with the unbelievers in Jericho when the walls tumbled down (verse 30, above) because of her faith*], when she had received the spies [*who were sent out by Joshua; see Joshua 2:1*] with peace.

Some people are not comfortable with the word "harlot" used in reference to Rahab in verse 31, above. This should not be a problem to those who believe that the Atonement provides forgiveness for such people when they repent. If you read Joshua 2:1–11, you will see that Rahab had apparently gained a testimony of the gospel and acted accordingly. Both Paul, here, and James in James 2:25, use her as a good example of faith. For additional discussion of this, see the Institute of Religion's *Old Testament Student Manual, Genesis–2 Samuel*, pp. 236–237.

32 And what shall I more say [*what more shall I say*]? for the time would fail me to tell of [*I don't have time to tell you about*] Gedeon [*Gideon; see Judges, chapters 6–8*], and of Barak [*Judges, chapter 4*], and of Samson [*Judges, chapters 13–16*], and of Jephthae [*Jephthah; see Judges, chapter 11*]; of David also, and Samuel, and of the prophets:

33 Who through faith subdued [*conquered*] kingdoms, wrought [*caused*] righteousness, obtained promises, stopped the mouths of lions,

34 Quenched the violence of fire, escaped the edge of the sword, out of weakness were made strong, waxed [*grew*] valiant [*mighty;* Strong's *#2478*] in fight, turned to flight the armies of the aliens [*foreigners;* Strong's *#0245*].

35 Women received their dead raised to life again: and others were tortured, not accepting deliverance; that they might obtain a better resurrection:

JST Hebrews 11:35

35 Women received their dead raised to life again; and others were tortured, not accepting deliverance; **that they might obtain the first resurrection** [*meaning those who will go to celestial glory*];

36 And others had trial of cruel mockings and scourgings [*whippings*], yea, moreover of bonds [*captivity*] and imprisonment:

37 They were stoned, they were sawn asunder [*cut in two with saws*], were tempted [*tested;* Strong's *#3985*], were slain [*killed*] with the sword: they wandered about in sheepskins and goatskins [*had insufficient wealth to even afford fabric for clothing*]; being destitute [*in extreme poverty*], afflicted, tormented;

38 (Of whom the world was not worthy:) they wandered in deserts,

and in mountains, and in dens and caves of the earth.

39 And these all, having obtained a good report [*having obtained a strong testimony; see Hebrews 11:39, footnote a*] through faith, received not the promise [*were not given exaltation while they were still on earth*]:

40 God having provided some better thing for us, that they without us should not be made perfect.

JST Hebrews 11:40

40 God having provided some better **things** for **them through their sufferings, for without sufferings they could not be** made perfect.

HEBREWS 12

As Paul continues his letter to the Jewish converts to the Church (the "Hebrew" members of the Church), he counsels them to avoid sin and look to Jesus Christ for salvation, rather than to the law of Moses.

One of the great doctrinal verses of this chapter is verse 9, in which Paul teaches that we are the spirit children of our Father in Heaven.

1 WHEREFORE seeing we also are compassed [*surrounded*] about with so great a cloud [*large dense multitude;* Strong's *#3509*] of witnesses, let us lay aside every weight [*anything which would hold us back;* Strong's *#3591*], and the sin which doth so easily beset [*surround;* Strong's *#2139*] us, and let us run with patience the race that is set before us,

2 Looking unto Jesus the author and finisher of our faith [*the one who helps us complete our quest for exaltation*]; who for [*because of*] the joy that was set before him [*that was available to Him*] endured the cross [*crucifixion*], despising [*not paying attention to*] the shame, and is set down at the right hand of the throne of God [*is now in heaven in a position of authority with the Father*].

3 For consider him [*just think about Christ*] that endured such contradiction [*opposition*] of sinners against himself, lest ye be wearied and faint in your minds [*when you start feeling tired and discouraged because of the opposition you face*].

4 Ye have not yet resisted unto blood [*you have not given your lives yet, as Christ did*], striving [*fighting*] against sin.

5 And ye have forgotten the exhortation [*encouragement;* Strong's *#3874*] which speaketh unto you as unto children [*in Proverbs 3:11–12*], My son, despise not thou the chastening of the Lord [*do not take the Lord's discipline lightly*], nor faint [*become too discouraged*] when thou art rebuked of [*by*] him:

6 For whom the Lord loveth he chasteneth [*disciplines*], and scourgeth [*punishes as needed*] every son whom he receiveth [*whom He accepts into celestial glory*].

7 If ye endure chastening [*put up with discipline*], God dealeth with you as with sons; for what son is he whom the father chasteneth not [*how would a son turn out if his father did not discipline him*]?

8 But if ye be without chastisement [*if you do not accept discipline from the Father*], whereof all are partakers [*which all people get*], then are ye bastards [*then you are not covenant children*], and not sons [*and you cannot return to Him*].

9 Furthermore we have had fathers of our flesh [*we have had our mortal fathers*] which corrected [*disciplined*] us, and we gave them reverence [*respect*]: shall we not much rather [*shouldn't we even more*] be in subjection unto [*in obedience to*] the Father of spirits [*the Father of our spirit bodies*], and live [*receive exaltation*]?

10 For they [*our mortal fathers*] verily for a few days [*for our relatively short mortal lives*] chastened [*disciplined*] us after their own pleasure [*according to what they thought best*]; but he [*the Father of our spirits*] for our profit [*knows exactly what is best for us*], that we might be partakers of his holiness [*so that we can become like Him in exaltation; compare with D&C 88:107 which says, "and the Saints shall be filled with his glory, and receive their inheritance and be made equal with him."*].

11 Now no chastening for the present seemeth to be joyous [*being disciplined is not particularly pleasant while it is going on*], but grievous [*rather, it is miserable*]: nevertheless afterward [*when it is finished*] it yieldeth [*produces*] the peaceable fruit of righteousness unto them which are exercised [*trained, disciplined; see Hebrews 12:11, footnote b*] thereby.

12 Wherefore lift up the hands which hang down, and the feeble knees [*strengthen yourselves and one another*];

JST Hebrews 12:12

12 Wherefore lift up the hands which hang down, and **strengthen** the feeble knees;

13 And make straight paths for your feet [*follow a straight course in the gospel*], lest that which is lame [*for fear that members who are weak*] be turned out of the way [*might lose the way*]; but let it rather be healed [*let weaker members be healed by your good deeds and example*].

14 Follow peace with all men, and holiness, without which no man shall see the Lord:

15 Looking [*watching over one another*] diligently lest any man fail of the grace of God [*so that no one misses out on the help and mercy provided by the Atonement*]; lest any root of bitterness springing up [*for fear that apostasy might come up among you and*] trouble you, and thereby many be defiled [*and thus, many members become unclean*];

16 Lest there be any fornicator [*guilty of sexual immorality*], or profane [*worldly*] person, as [*like*] Esau, who for one morsel of meat sold his birthright [*sold his salvation*].

17 For ye know how that afterward, when he would have inherited the blessing [*when he decided he wanted the birthright blessings after all*], he was rejected [*he was turned down*]: for he found no place of repentance [*because he refused to repent of his wicked lifestyle*], though he sought it [*the birthright*] carefully [*with much emotion*] with tears.

Next, Paul reminds the Hebrews that they should not be like the children of Israel who could not stand the glory of God on Mount Sinai or even the glory which was upon Moses when he came down from talking with the Lord on Sinai.

18 For ye are not come unto the mount [*Mount Sinai; see Exodus 19, starting with verse 12*] that might be touched [*that can be touched, physically*], and that burned with fire, nor unto blackness, and darkness, and tempest,

19 And the sound of a trumpet, and the voice of words; which voice they that heard intreated [*pleaded*] that the word should not be spoken to them any more [*see Exodus 20:19*]:

20 (For they could not endure that which was commanded, And if so much as a beast touch the mountain, it shall be stoned, or thrust through with a dart [*compare with Exodus 19:12–13*]:

21 And so terrible was the sight, that Moses said, I exceedingly fear and quake [*compare with Deuteronomy 9:19*]):

Next, Paul uses several vocabulary words and phrases which mean "celestial glory" and most often mean "exaltation in the presence of God." Compare with D&C 76:66–69. We will put these words and phrases in bold print in order to point them out to you.

22 But ye are come unto **mount Sion**, and unto **the city of the living God**, the **heavenly Jerusalem**, and to **an innumerable company of angels**,

23 To **the general assembly** and **church of the firstborn**, which are written in heaven [*whose names are written in heaven; D&C 76:68*], and to God the Judge of all, and to the spirits of **just men made perfect**,

24 And to Jesus the mediator of the new covenant [*to Jesus, who works with us to help us take advantage of the "new covenant" or gospel of Jesus Christ, which replaces the "old covenant" or the law of Moses*], and to the blood of sprinkling [*the Atonement, which was made available to us by the shedding of the Savior's blood*], that speaketh better things than that of Abel.

The phrase "and to the blood of sprinkling, that speaketh better things than that of Abel" in verse 24, above, needs explaining. Apostle Bruce R. McConkie gave his explanation as follows: "But whatever the then prevailing views of the Hebrews may have been (including the false doctrine that Abel's blood was an atonement for the sins of others), Paul is here teaching: 'The blood of righteous Abel' (Matt. 23–35), together 'with the innocent blood of all the martyrs under the altar that John saw (D&C 135:7; Rev. 6:9–11) cries unto the Lord for vengeance against the wicked; the blood of Christ, on the other hand, was poured out as a propitiation for sins, and through it men are empowered to repent and be reconciled to God. Thus the voice of Abel's blood is one of death and separation and sorrow; the voice of our Lord's blood is one of life and reunion and eternal joy. Truly his blood speaketh better things than that of Abel!" (McConkie, *Doctrinal New Testament Commentary*, Vol. 3, pp. 231–32.)

25 See that ye refuse not him that speaketh [*don't reject the Lord*]. For if they [*the children of Israel*] escaped not who refused him that spake on earth [*who rejected Jehovah (Christ) when He spoke from Sinai*], much more shall not we escape, if we turn away from him [*if we reject Christ*] that speaketh from heaven [*as He speaks to us now from heaven, and including when He comes at the Second Coming*]:

26 Whose voice then shook the earth [*on Sinai; see Exodus 19:18*]: but now he hath promised, saying, Yet once more I shake not the earth only, but also heaven [*the heavens and the earth will shake at the time of the Second Coming*].

27 And this word, Yet once more [*and this phrase, "Yet once more"*], signifieth [*indicates*] the removing of those things that are shaken, as of things that are made, that those things which cannot be shaken may remain. [*In other words, the phrase "Yet once more" points out that all corruptible things which do not belong on earth during the Millennium will be done away with at the time of the Second Coming, when the Lord "shakes" the earth, and cleanses it from all wickedness, so that the things that belong on earth during the Millennium can remain in an environment of peace and righteousness.*]

28 Wherefore we receiving a kingdom which cannot be moved [*we, belonging to the kingdom of Christ, which cannot be done away with*], let us have grace, whereby we may serve God acceptably with reverence and godly fear:

JST Hebrews 12:28

28 Wherefore we receiving a kingdom which cannot be moved, **should** have grace, whereby we may serve God **acceptable** with reverence and godly fear [*we can serve God acceptably because of the Atonement*];

29 For [*as it says in Deuteronomy 4:24*] our God is a consuming fire. [*In other words, when the Savior comes again, all the wicked and all corrupt things will be consumed or burned by his glory. See D&C 5:19.*]

HEBREWS 13

Paul now concludes by counseling these members of the Church to love one another and live the gospel in their daily lives. He reminds them to be constantly aware of Christ and to let their daily sacrifices be those of righteous deeds and kind treatment of others.

1 LET brotherly love continue.

2 Be not forgetful to entertain strangers [*do not forget to be hospitable toward strangers;* Strong's *#5381*]: for thereby [*by so doing*] some have entertained angels unawares [*without being aware of it*].

Bruce R. McConkie suggests that many of these "angels," spoken of in verse 1, above, are righteous mortals who are involved in the service of God. (See *Doctrinal New Testament Commentary*, Vol. 3, p. 235.) In addition, we might consider the words of the Savior in Matthew 25:34–40 wherein the righteous ask, "Lord, when saw we thee an hungred, and fed thee? Or thirsty, and gave thee drink?" The Master answered, "Inasmuch as ye have done it unto one of the least of these my brethren, ye have done it unto me."

3 Remember them that are in bonds [*in prison*], as bound with them [*as if you were in prison with them*]; and them which suffer adversity, as being yourselves also in the body [*as if you were suffering their adversity with them*].

JST Hebrews 13:3

3 Remember them that are in bonds, as bound with them; and them which suffer adversity, as being yourselves also **of** the body.

Next, Paul teaches that marriage is approved by God. This shows that celibacy as a means of showing loyalty to God is wrong. He also teaches that sexual relations between husband and wife do not make them unclean. In other words, such a relationship is clean and righteous, but he warns that such relations between those who are not married are wicked.

4 Marriage is honourable in all, and the bed undefiled: but whoremongers [*those who make sexual immorality a major focus of their lives*] and adulterers [*those who have sexual relations outside of marriage*] God will judge [*punish*].

5 Let your conversation be without covetousness [*give willingly to the Lord's work; in other words, don't "covet" what you are dedicating to the Lord*]; and be content with such things as ye have: for he [*the Lord*] hath said [*in Deuteronomy 31:6;*

Joshua 1:5], I will never leave thee, nor forsake thee.

JST Hebrews 13:5

5 Let your **consecrations** be without covetousness; and be content with **giving** such things as ye have; for he hath said, I will never leave thee, nor forsake thee.

6 So that we may boldly say [*we may say with confidence;* Strong's *#2292; as stated in Psalm 118:6–7*], The Lord is my helper, and I will not fear what man shall do unto me.

7 Remember them which have the rule over you [*remember your leaders in the Church*], who have spoken unto you the word of God: whose faith follow [*follow their example*], considering the end of their conversation [*behavior, way of life;* Strong's *#0391*]. [*In other words, being aware of where their way of life is taking them.*]

8 Jesus Christ the same yesterday, and to day, and for ever. [*The doctrines and ordinances of the gospel, which lead to exaltation, remain the same throughout eternity.*]

9 Be not carried about with divers [*various*] and strange [*false*] doctrines. For it is a good [*meet, necessary;* Strong's *#2570*] thing that the heart [*the center of spiritual life;* Strong's *#2588*] be established [*made firm;* Strong's *#0950*] with grace [*the Atonement of Christ*]; not with meats [*not with the ceremonial foods and rituals of the law of Moses*], which have not profited them that have been occupied therein [*which do not lead to exaltation*].

As he finishes his letter to the Jewish converts to the Church (the Hebrews), Paul will now emphasize once more that the law of Moses does not have the power to bring people to exaltation. The gospel of Jesus Christ does.

10 We have an altar [*in other words, we have the sacrament which commemorates His body and blood sacrificed for us*], whereof they [*the Levitical priests spoken of in Hebrews 9:1–10 and elsewhere, who offer sacrifices in the tabernacle and temple, under the law of Moses*] have no right to eat which serve the tabernacle [*are not authorized to eat because they haven't joined the Church*].

11 For the bodies of those beasts [*sacrificial animals*], whose blood is brought into the sanctuary [*speaking both of the tabernacle while the Israelites traveled in the wilderness etc., and also the temple in Jerusalem*] by the high priest for sin [*as an offering for sin, as required by the law of Moses*], are burned without [*outside of*] the camp [*outside of the camp of the children of Israel, in other words, outside of the city*].

12 Wherefore [*for this reason*] Jesus also, that he might sanctify [*cleanse*] the people with his own blood, suffered without the gate [*Jesus was likewise crucified outside of the city*].

13 Let us go forth therefore unto him without the camp, bearing his reproach. [*Let us depart from the law of Moses and the people who still insist on living it and go forth unto Christ.*]

14 For here have we no continuing city, but we seek one to come. [*In a way, this leaves us without a "home" among men here on earth, but we strive to attain the celestial kingdom in the future.*]

15 By him [*through Christ*] therefore let us offer the sacrifice of praise to God [*the Father*] continually, that is, the fruit of our lips [*the words which come out of our mouths*] giving thanks to his name.

16 But to do good and to communicate [*spread the gospel*] forget not: for with such sacrifices God is well pleased.

17 Obey them [*your church leaders*] that have the rule over you, and submit yourselves: for they watch [*watch out*] for your souls, as they that must give account [*they have that stewardship and are accountable to God*], that they may do it with joy, and not with grief [*when you obey them, it makes their job more pleasant*]: for that [*disobedience which brings them grief*] is unprofitable for you [*is not good for you*].

18 Pray for us: for we trust we have a good conscience, in all things willing to live honestly.

19 But I beseech you the rather to do this [*please pray for me*], that I may be restored to you the sooner [*so that I can come visit you sooner*].

20 Now the God of peace [*Heavenly Father*], that brought again from the dead our Lord Jesus [*who resurrected Jesus Christ*], that great shepherd of the sheep, through the blood of the everlasting covenant,

21 Make you perfect [*prepare you; equip you;* Strong's #*2675*] in every good work to do his will, working in you that which is wellpleasing in his sight, through Jesus Christ; to whom be glory for ever and ever. Amen.

22 And I beseech you, brethren, suffer the word of exhortation [*please accept my counsel to you*]: for I have written a letter unto you in few words.

23 Know ye that our brother Timothy is set at liberty [*has been released*]; with whom, if he come shortly, I will see you.

24 Salute all them that have the rule over you [*greet all your local leaders for me*], and all the saints. They of Italy salute you [*the members here in Italy send their greetings to you*].

25 Grace be with you all. Amen.

THE GENERAL EPISTLE OF JAMES

It is the general belief of many Bible scholars that James is the half brother of Jesus and is the son of Joseph and Mary. See Bible Dictionary under "James," definition #3, and also under "James, Epistle of." This is a "general epistle" or "general letter," so named because it is not written to any specific location, as is the case with most of Paul's letters. It is written to the twelve tribes of Israel (see chapter 1, verse 1) and consists of a series of "mini" sermons and contains valuable counsel for us to follow in our daily lives. It is not known when this letter was written, but a best guess might put the date of writing around AD 50–51, possibly written from Jerusalem.

JAMES 1

This chapter contains one of the best-known verses among members of the Church, namely verse 5. Joseph Smith read this and was thus motivated to go into the Sacred Grove and pray, which led to the First Vision. See Joseph Smith–History 1:11–20.

1 JAMES, a servant of God and of the Lord Jesus Christ, to the twelve tribes which are scattered abroad, greeting.

2 My brethren, count it [*consider it*] all joy when ye fall into divers temptations;

JST James 1:2

2 My brethren, count it all joy when ye fall into **many afflictions**;

3 Knowing this, that the trying [*testing*] of your faith worketh [*builds*] patience.

4 But let patience have [*do*] her perfect work, that ye may be perfect and entire, wanting [*lacking*] nothing.

JST James 1:4

4 But let patience have **its** perfect work, that ye may be perfect and entire, wanting nothing.

5 If any of you lack wisdom, let him ask of God, that giveth to all men liberally, and upbraideth not [*will not scold you for asking*]; and it shall be given him.

6 But let him ask in faith, nothing wavering [*not doubting*]. For he that wavereth is like a wave of the sea driven with the wind and tossed. [*In other words, is unstable.*]

7 For let not that man [*whose faith wavers*] think that he shall receive any thing of the Lord.

8 A double minded [*wavering, uncertain, doubting;* Strong's *#1374*] man is unstable in all his ways [*in all he does*].

9 Let the brother [*member of the Church*] of low degree [*who is in humble circumstances*] rejoice in that he is exalted [*in that the gospel makes him of equal worth with all other members*]:

10 But the rich, in that he is made low [*let the rich member rejoice that he is made humble by the gospel*]: because as the flower of the grass he shall pass away [*because his worldly wealth will pass away like grass and be of no value to him when he dies*].

11 For the sun is no sooner risen with a burning heat, but it withereth the grass, [*In other words, wealth is very temporary.*] and the flower thereof falleth, and the grace of the fashion of it [*its beauty*] perisheth: so also shall the rich man fade away in his ways [*such will be the case with the rich man who lets his wealth corrupt him*].

12 Blessed is the man that endureth temptation: for when he is tried [*proven worthy*], he shall receive the crown of life [*eternal life; he will receive exaltation*], which the Lord hath promised to them that love him.

JST James 1:12

12 Blessed is the man that **resisteth** temptation; for when he is tried, he shall receive the crown of life, which the Lord hath promised to them that love him.

13 Let no man say when he is tempted, I am tempted of God: for God cannot be tempted with evil, neither tempteth he any man: [*In other words, God does not tempt people to do evil.*]

14 But every man is tempted, when he is drawn away of his own lust, and enticed [*when he allows himself to be pulled away by the desire for sexual immorality*].

15 Then when lust hath conceived [*when he allows sexual temptation to remain in his mind and grow*], it bringeth forth sin [*it eventually causes him to commit such sin*]: and sin, when it is finished [*when it has finished its work*], bringeth forth death [*brings spiritual death*].

16 Do not err [*don't be mistaken*], my beloved brethren.

17 Every good gift and every perfect gift is from above, and cometh down from the Father of lights [*from God, who created the stars;* Strong's *#3962*], with whom is no variableness [*who does not change*], neither shadow of turning [*not even the slightest bit*].

18 Of his own will begat he us with the word of truth [*he gave us new life by giving us the gospel of Christ*], that we should be a kind of firstfruits [*superior in excellence;* Strong's *#0536*] of his creatures. [*In other words, so that we could become exalted.*]

19 Wherefore, my beloved brethren, let every man be swift to hear

[*listen*], slow to speak, slow to wrath [*anger*]:

20 For the wrath [*extreme anger*] of man worketh not the righteousness of God [*does not lead to personal righteousness*].

21 Wherefore lay apart [*set aside*] all filthiness and superfluity of naughtiness [*the evil, especially hatred and bitterness toward others, which is so prevalent around you*], and receive with meekness the engrafted word [*the gospel which has been implanted in you;* Strong's *#1721*], which is able to save your souls.

JST James 1:21

21 Wherefore lay **aside** all filthiness and superfluity of naughtiness, and receive with meekness, the engrafted word, which is able to save your souls.

22 But be ye doers of the word [*live the gospel*], and not hearers only [*don't merely listen to it*], deceiving [*fooling*] your own selves.

23 For if any be a hearer of the word [*if anyone hears the gospel*], and not a doer [*but does not live it*], he is like unto a man beholding [*looking at*] his natural face in a glass [*a mirror;* Strong's *#2072*]:

24 For he beholdeth [*sees*] himself, and goeth his way, and straightway [*immediately*] forgetteth what manner of man he was [*what he looked like*].

25 But whoso looketh into the perfect law of liberty [*whoever sees himself reflected in the light of the perfect gospel*], and continueth therein [*and continues to walk in that light*], he being not a forgetful hearer [*not as one who forgets about the gospel*], but a doer of the work [*but one who lives it*], this man shall be blessed in his deed [*in what he does*].

26 If any man among you seem [*appears*] to be religious, and bridleth not [*doesn't control*] his tongue, but deceiveth [*fools*] his own heart, this man's religion is vain [*is worthless to him*].

Next, in verse 27, James gives a rather famous definition of what pure religion is.

27 Pure religion and undefiled before God and the Father is this, To visit the fatherless [*orphans*] and widows in their affliction, and to keep himself unspotted from the world.

JST James 1:27

27 Pure religion and undefiled before God and the Father is this, To visit the fatherless and widows in their affliction, and to keep himself unspotted **from the vices of** the world.

JAMES 2

This chapter is very important doctrinally, because it teaches the necessity of works to go along with faith.

You will see that the Prophet Joseph Smith not only changed wording in some verses, but also rearranged the order of some of them in the JST.

1 MY brethren, have not the faith of our Lord Jesus Christ, the Lord of glory, with respect of persons [*In other words, if you are truly living the gospel, you cannot show prejudice toward others; see verses 2–4, below.*]

JST James 2:1

1 My brethren, **ye cannot** have the faith of our Lord Jesus Christ, the Lord of glory, **and yet have respect to persons.**

2 For if there come unto your assembly a man [*if a man comes into your meetings*] with a gold ring, in goodly apparel [*wearing fine clothes*], and there come in also a poor man in vile raiment [*and a poor man comes in wearing dirty, shabby clothing*];

JST James 2:2

2 **Now** if there come unto your assembly a man with a gold ring, in goodly apparel, and there come in also a poor man in vile raiment;

3 And ye have respect [*show preferential treatment*] to him that weareth the gay [*fine*] clothing, and say unto him, Sit thou here in a good place; and say to the poor, Stand thou there, or sit here under my footstool [*sit on the floor by my chair*]:

4 Are ye not then partial in yourselves, and are become judges of evil thoughts? [*In other words, haven't you just become unrighteous judges?*]

JST James 2:4

4 Are ye not then **in yourselves partial judges, and become evil in your thoughts?**

5 Hearken [*listen to me*], my beloved brethren, Hath not God chosen the poor of this world [*who are*] rich in faith, and heirs of the kingdom which he hath promised to them that love him? [*In other words, doesn't God give righteous poor people exaltation also, who show their love to Him by faithfully living the gospel?*]

6 But ye have despised the poor [*treated them with contempt;* Strong's *#0818*]. Do not rich men oppress you, and draw you before the judgment seats? [*Have you forgotten what it feels like to be treated with contempt yourselves?*]

7 Do not they [*the men of high position in the community who oppress members of the Church*] blaspheme [*mock*] that worthy name [*the name of Christ*] by the which ye are called [*which you have taken upon you*]?

8 If ye fulfil [*obey*] the royal law according to the scripture [*Leviticus 19:18*], Thou shalt love thy neighbour as thyself, ye do well:

9 But if ye have respect to persons [*if you show unrighteous favoritism*], ye commit sin, and are convinced of the law [*convicted by the law of God*] as transgressors.

In the next verses, James teaches a very important gospel doctrine, namely that if we claim to be living the whole gospel, but intentionally disobey a certain obvious part of it, it is as if we were violating the whole gospel. For instance, if a person holds a temple recommend, and is doing well at keeping all the requirements of it, however, he or she decides to drink wine on occasions for social reasons, it voids the recommend and the person's worthiness to attend the temple.

10 For whosoever shall keep the whole law [*keeps all the commandments*], and yet offend in one point [*and intentionally breaks just one of the commandments*], he is guilty of all [*it is as if he broke all the commandments*].

JST James 2:10

10 For whosoever **shall, save in one point**, keep the whole law, he is guilty of all.

11 For he [*the Lord*] that said, Do not commit adultery, said also, Do not kill. Now if thou commit no adultery, yet if thou kill, thou art become a transgressor of the law [*you will still go to the telestial kingdom; see D&C 76:103 and Revelation 22:15*].

12 So speak ye, and so do, as they that shall be judged by the law of liberty. [*In other words, you should speak and act like those who will be shown mercy on Judgment Day.*]

13 For he shall have judgment without mercy, that hath shewed no mercy [*the person who showed no mercy to others will be shown no mercy on Judgment Day, because the law of justice will take over in their case*]; and mercy rejoiceth against judgment [*if you are merciful, you will be able to rejoice on Judgment Day; see Alma 41:14*].

14 What doth it profit, my brethren, though a man say he hath faith, and have not works? can faith save him? [*In other words, what good does it do to claim to have faith but not have good works to go along with it?*]

JST James 2:14

14 What profit is it, my brethren, for a man to say he hath faith, and hath not works? can faith save him?

15 If a brother or sister be naked [*inadequately clothed*], and destitute [*has run out*] of daily food,

16 And one of you [*who claim to have faith in Christ's gospel*] say unto them, Depart in peace, be ye warmed and filled; notwithstanding [*but*] ye give them not those things which are needful to the body; what doth it profit [*what good does it do*]?

JST James 2:16, given next, covers both verses 15 and 16 above.

JST James 2:16

16 **For** if a brother or sister be naked and destitute, **and one of you say, Depart in peace, be warmed and filled;** notwithstanding **he give not** those

things which are needful to the body; **what profit is your faith unto such?**

Verses 17 and 20, next, are much-used in teaching the restored gospel in the mission field.

17 Even so faith, if it hath not works [*if we don't have deeds to go along with it, which demonstrate our faith*], is dead, being alone.

JST James 2:17

17 Even so faith, if it **have** not works is dead, being alone.

18 Yea, a man may say, Thou hast faith, and I have works: shew [*show*] me thy faith without thy works, and I will shew [*demonstrate*] thee my faith by my works.

JST James 2:15

15 Yea, a man may say, **I will show thee I have faith without works; but I say, Show me thy faith without works,** and I will show thee my faith by my works.

19 Thou believest that there is one God; thou doest well: the devils also believe, and tremble. [*In other words, you are just like the evil spirits from the premortal existence who know who Christ is but have no righteous works to go along with it.*]

JST James 2:19

19 Thou **believest there** is one God; thou doest well; the devils also believe, and tremble; **thou hast made thyself like unto them, not being justified** [*not doing the things you must do in order to be saved; see JST 2:18, below*].

20 But wilt thou know, O vain [*foolish, prideful*] man, that faith without works is dead?

JST James 2:18

18 **Therefore** wilt thou know, O vain man, that faith without works is dead **and cannot save you?**

21 Was not Abraham our father justified [*was made acceptable to God*] by works, when he had offered Isaac his son upon the altar?

22 Seest thou how faith wrought [*went along*] with his works, and by works was faith made perfect [*complete;* Strong's *#5048*]?

23 And the scripture [*Genesis 15:6*] was fulfilled which saith, Abraham believed God, and it was imputed [*credited:* Strong's *#3049*] unto him for [*as*] righteousness: and he was called the Friend of God [*Isaiah 41:8*].

24 Ye see then how that by works a man is justified [*lined up in harmony with God*], and not by faith only.

JST James 2:23

23 Ye see **then that** by works a man is justified, and not by faith only.

25 Likewise also was not Rahab the harlot justified [*made right with God*] by works, when she had

received the messengers [*the spies sent out by Joshua in Joshua 2:1*], and had sent them out another way?

JST James 2:24

24 Likewise also **Rahab the harlot was justified** by works, when she had received the messengers and sent them out another way.

For some thoughts about Rahab, see the note which follows Hebrews 11:31 in this study guide.

26 For as the body without the spirit is dead, so faith without works is dead also.

JST James 2:25

25 For, as the body without the spirit is dead, **so faith without works is dead**.

JAMES 3

James continues by urging members to control their tongues. He gives many examples of how much damage an uncontrolled tongue can cause.

1 MY brethren, be not many masters, knowing that we shall receive the greater condemnation. [Strong's *#1320 defines "masters" as "teachers" and "the teachers of the Jewish religion." The Martin Luther edition of the German Bible basically says, "Don't debate and argue among yourselves about what you are teaching. If we, who are supposed to be teaching others the gospel of peace, have contention among ourselves about such things, we will receive the greater condemnation or be judged more harshly by the people."*]

JST James 3:1

1 My brethren, **strive not for the mastery, knowing that in so doing we shall receive the greater condemnation**.

James will now lead up to the importance of controlling our tongues, in other words, controlling the words which come out of our mouths.

2 For in many things we offend all [*we all offend others at one time or another*]. If any man offend not in word [*does not ever offend others in what he says*], the same is a perfect [*complete*] man, [*In other words, he "has his act together."*] and able also to bridle the whole body [*is able to exercise self-control over the whole self*].

3 Behold, we put bits [*bridle bits*] in the horses' mouths, that they may obey us; and we turn about their whole body [*we control the whole horse with just a small bit in its mouth*].

4 Behold [*consider*] also the ships, which though they be so great [*even though they are so large*], and are driven of fierce winds, yet are they turned about [*they are controlled*] with a very small helm [*rudder; Strong's #4079*], whithersoever [*wherever*] the governor listeth [*wherever the captain wants*].

5 Even so the tongue is a little member [*is a small part of the body*], and boasteth great things [*and has great power*]. Behold, how great a matter [*forest;* Strong's *#5208*] a little fire kindleth [*consider how big of a forest fire a small fire can start*]!

6 And the tongue is a fire, a world of iniquity [*the tongue is like a fire and can cause a world of wickedness*]: so is the tongue among our members [*our body parts*], that it defileth [*corrupts*] the whole body [*it can ruin us spiritually*], and setteth on fire the course of nature [*it inflames the passions of the "natural man"; see verse 15, below, as well as Mosiah 3:19 and Moses 6:49*]; and it is set on fire of hell [*and is often inspired by hell*].

7 For every kind of beasts, and of birds, and of serpents, and of things in the sea, is tamed, and hath been tamed of [*by*] mankind:

8 But the tongue can no man tame; it is an unruly [*uncontrollable; see James 3:8, footnote b, in our Bible*] evil, full of deadly poison.

9 Therewith bless we God [*with the tongue, we praise God*], even the Father; and therewith curse we men [*and with it we hurl insults at our fellow men*], which are made after the similitude of God [*which deserve more respect than that because they are God's children*].

10 Out of the same mouth proceedeth blessing and cursing. My brethren, these things ought not so to be. [*In other words, we ought to control our tongues and not use them to make ourselves hypocrites.*]

11 Doth a fountain [*spring of water*] send forth at the same place [*out of the same source*] sweet water and bitter?

12 Can the fig tree, my brethren, bear olive berries [*produce olives*]? either a vine, figs [*or a grape vine produce figs*]? so can no fountain [*spring of water*] both yield salt water and fresh [*produce salt water and fresh water at the same time*].

13 Who is a wise man and endued with knowledge among you [*who wants to be endowed with knowledge (including wisdom—see verse 17) among you*]? let him shew [*show, demonstrate*] out of a good conversation [*by righteous behavior;* Strong's *#0391*] his works with meekness of wisdom [*the self-control produced by wisdom*].

14 But if ye have bitter envying and strife [*contention*] in your hearts, glory not [*don't boast*], and lie not against [*don't deny*] the truth [*which is that this kind of behavior does not come from heaven, rather is as described in verse 15, next*].

15 This wisdom descendeth not from above [*does not come from heaven*], but is earthly, sensual, devilish.

16 For where envying and strife [*contention; selfish ambition;* Strong's *#2052*] is, there is confusion and every evil work [*and*

every form of evil as a result].

17 But the wisdom that is from above [*which comes down to us from heaven*] is first [*above all*] pure, then peaceable, gentle, and easy to be intreated [*humble and teachable*], full of mercy and good fruits, without partiality [*favoritism*], and without hypocrisy.

18 And the fruit of righteousness is sown [*planted*] in peace of [*by*] them that make peace.

JAMES 4

James now explains the root causes of contention and wickedness. There are no JST changes for this chapter.

1 FROM whence come wars [*quarreling;* Strong's *#4171*] and fightings among you [*what causes quarreling and fighting among you*]? come they not hence, even of your lusts that war in your members [*don't they ultimately come from the evil desires that battle for control within each of you*]?

2 Ye [*worldly people*] lust, and have not [*you covet what others have and haven't obtained it*]: ye kill, and desire to have [*and want others' possessions*], and cannot obtain [*and still don't end up getting them*]: ye fight and war, yet ye have not [*you fight and war among yourselves but are never satisfied*], because ye ask not [*because you don't consult God as to how to attain true satisfaction in life*].

3 Ye ask, and receive not [*some of you do pray to God, but still don't get what you want*], because ye ask amiss [*because you are not asking with the right attitude and for the right reasons*], that ye may consume it upon your lusts [*you are asking so that you may satisfy your own evil lusts and ambitions*].

4 Ye adulterers and adulteresses, know ye not that the friendship of the world [*joining in with wicked and lustful people*] is enmity with God [*is antagonism toward God*]? whosoever therefore will be a friend of the world [*participates in worldly wickedness*] is the enemy of God.

5 Do ye think that the scripture saith in vain, The spirit that dwelleth in us lusteth to envy?

Bruce R. McConkie deals with verse 5, above, as follows: "There is no scripture to this effect in our present Old Testament. As here given, the meaning must be that man in this mortal probation is subject to envy and other lusts. (*Doctrinal New Testament Commentary*, 3 Vols. [Salt Lake City: Bookcraft, 1965–1973], Vol. 3, p. 266.)

6 But he giveth more grace [*help; mercy and kindness;* Strong's *#5485*]. Wherefore he saith [*in Proverbs 3:34*], God resisteth [*opposes*] the proud, but giveth grace unto the humble.

7 Submit yourselves therefore to God. Resist the devil, and he will flee from you.

8 Draw nigh [*near*] to God, and

he will draw nigh to you. Cleanse your hands [*repent*], ye sinners; and purify your hearts, ye double minded [*you who cannot decide whether to serve God or the devil*].

9 Be afflicted, and mourn, and weep: let your laughter be turned to mourning, and your joy to heaviness.

It appears that verse 9, above, refers back to verse 8 and the issue of being "double minded." With this in mind, one interpretation of verse 9 might be: "Allow yourselves to feel godly sorrow (2 Corinthians 7:8–11) for your sins, and weep for them; let your riotous living be turned into mourning for your sins, and your shallow happiness to solemn thinking about your sins." Another possible interpretation might be, referring to those who resist the devil in verse 7, above: "You Saints will suffer and mourn and weep because of the wickedness around you; much sadness will replace your laughter, and your joy will turn to depression because of the wickedness in this world."

10 Humble yourselves in the sight of the Lord, and he shall lift you up [*encourage you and eventually exalt you in the celestial kingdom*].

11 Speak not evil one of another [*don't slander or criticize*], brethren. He that speaketh evil of [*slanders*] his brother, and judgeth [*passes judgment against*] his brother, speaketh evil of the law [*is going against the laws of God*], and judgeth the law [*is, in effect, acting as if he had power to be above the law himself*]: but if thou judge the law, thou art not a doer of the law, but a judge. [*In other words, what right have you to be a judge?*]

12 There is one lawgiver [*God*], who is able to save and to destroy: who art thou that judgest another [*who do you think you are, judging one another, in other words, taking over God's job*]?

13 Go to now [*listen carefully*], ye that say, To day or to morrow we will go into such a city, and continue there a year, and buy and sell, and get gain: [*In other words, listen carefully, you who think you are in control of life and can go about your daily affairs without having God in your lives.*]

14 Whereas ye know not what shall be on the morrow [*you don't even know what will happen tomorrow, let alone a year from now*]. For what is your life [*what is your mortal life; how long do your think it will last*]? It is even a vapour [*it is like a bit of mist in the morning*], that appeareth for a little time [*it is there for a moment*], and then vanisheth away [*and then it is gone*].

15 For that ye ought to say [*what you ought to say is*], If the Lord will [*if it is the Lord's will*], we shall live, and do this, or that [*we will do thus and such*].

16 But now ye rejoice in your boastings [*in your prideful living without God*]: all such rejoicing is evil.

Next, James teaches about what we often call "sins of omission," as opposed to "sins of commission," meaning that we need to repent not only of sins we commit, but of things we are not doing (omitting) and should be doing.

17 Therefore to him that knoweth to do good, and doeth it not, to him it is sin.

JAMES 5

This chapter is of particular interest to Latter-day Saints because it contains verse 14, which deals with administering to the sick. First, in verses 1–6, James warns rich people about a miserable future if they keep setting their hearts on wealth rather than on God. He speaks of the future of corrupt rich people as if it had already come upon them. After that, he gives encouragement and counsel to the righteous.

There are no JST changes for this chapter.

1 GO to now [*listen carefully*], ye rich men, weep and howl for your miseries that shall come upon you [*if you don't repent*].

2 Your riches are corrupted [*have become rotten and dissolved away*], and your garments [*luxurious clothes*] are motheaten [*have turned to rags*].

3 Your gold and silver is cankered [*has rusted;* Strong's *#2728; in other words, has lost its value*]; and the rust of them shall be a witness against you, and shall eat your flesh [*will destroy you*] as it were fire [*as if it were fire*]. Ye have heaped treasure together for the last days [*you have foolishly stockpiled your worldly treasures as a means of surviving the last days*].

4 Behold [*look ahead into the future and see*], the hire [*wages*] of the labourers [*workers*] who have reaped down your fields [*whom you hired to harvest your fields*], which is of you kept back by fraud [*which wages you dishonestly refused to pay*], crieth [*shout against you*]: and the cries of them which have reaped are entered into the ears of the Lord of sabaoth [*the Lord has heard the cries of the workers you cheated out of their wages*].

The phrase "the Lord of sabaoth" in verse 4, above, is defined in D&C 95:7 as follows: "Lord of Sabaoth; which is by interpretation, the creator of the first day," in other words, it means "Jesus" or "Jehovah." See also Bible Dictionary under "Sabaoth."

5 Ye have lived in pleasure [*luxury and excess;* Strong's *#5171*] on the earth, and been wanton [*voluptuous; have given in to sensual, lustful pleasures:* Strong's *#4684*]; ye have nourished your hearts, as in a day of slaughter [*you have fattened yourselves up as if in preparation to be slaughtered*].

6 Ye have condemned and killed the just [*murdered the righteous*]; and he doth not resist you [*and he*

was not doing anything against you; Strong's *#0498*].

James now switches his attention from the wicked wealthy to the humble righteous.

7 Be patient therefore, brethren, unto the coming of the Lord [*until the Savior returns*]. Behold [*think about it*], the husbandman [*farmer*] waiteth for the precious fruit of the earth [*waits for the harvest*], and hath long patience for it, until he receive the early and latter rain [*and patiently waits for the spring and fall rains*].

8 Be ye also patient; stablish your hearts [*and stand firm in the gospel*]: for the coming of the Lord draweth nigh [*is getting close*].

9 Grudge not one [*don't hold grudges*] against another, brethren, lest ye be condemned: behold, the judge standeth before the door [*the time when you will be judged is getting close*].

10 Take, my brethren, the prophets [*use the prophets*], who have spoken in the name of the Lord [*who have taught us as authorized servants of the Lord*], for an example of suffering affliction, and of patience.

11 Behold, we count [*consider*] them happy which endure [*remain faithful in the gospel*]. Ye have heard of the patience of Job, and have seen the end [*purposes*] of the Lord; that the Lord is very pitiful [*full of pity;* Strong's *#4184; compassionate*], and of tender mercy.

12 But above all things, my brethren, swear not [*don't make contracts, agreements, and so forth*], neither by heaven, neither by the earth, neither by any other oath [*don't make your agreements with others so complex with legalistic language, etc., that no one can understand it*]: but let your yea be yea [*if you say "Yes," let it mean "Yes,"*] and your nay, nay [*in other words, be honest and simply keep your word when you give it to someone*]; lest ye fall into condemnation [*or you will be punished by God*].

13 Is any among you afflicted [*in trouble*]? let him pray. Is any merry? let him sing psalms.

Next, James gives instructions regarding administering to the sick.

14 Is any sick among you? let him call for the elders of the church [*Melchizedek Priesthood holders*]; and let them pray over him [*administer to him*], anointing him with oil [*pure, consecrated olive oil*] in the name of the Lord [*in the name of Jesus Christ*]:

15 And the prayer of faith shall save the sick, and the Lord shall raise him up [*either literally heal him here on earth or bring him to celestial glory, eventually if he has lived righteously*]; and if he have committed sins, they shall be forgiven him.

The phrase "if he have committed sins, they shall be forgiven him" in verse 15, above, needs to be handled with care. It is very comforting and truly significant just as it stands, when applied to the lives of righteous and faithful Saints. However, there is no such thing as "automatic salvation" or "automatic forgiveness of sins" through merely performing a particular ordinance or having one performed for you. If a member who is administered to is healed, but has not repented of sins nor is trying to do so, he would still need to go through the repentance process in order to be forgiven.

16 Confess your faults one to another, and pray one for another, that ye may be healed. The effectual fervent prayer of a righteous man availeth much [*is very effective*].

The phrase "Confess your faults one to another" in verse 16, above, needs explaining. It obviously does not mean that we should confess all our faults, shortcomings, sins, and so forth, to every member we meet. Spencer W. Kimball said the following regarding this matter: "The confession of . . . major sins to a proper Church authority is one of those requirements made by the Lord. These sins include adultery, fornication, other sexual transgressions, and other sins of comparable seriousness. This procedure of confession assures proper controls and protection for the Church and its people and sets the feet of the transgressor on the path of true repentance. When one has wronged another in deep transgression or in injuries of lesser magnitude, he, the aggressor, who gave the offense, regardless of the attitude of the other party, should immediately make amends by confessing to the injured one and doing all in his power to clear up the matter and again establish good feelings between the two parties." (Kimball, *Miracle of Forgiveness*, pp. 179, 186.)

17 Elias [*Elijah*] was a man subject to like passions [*temptations and imperfections*] as we are [*just like we are*], and he prayed earnestly [*this is referring back to the last half of verse 16, above*] that it might not rain: and it rained not on the earth by the space of [*for*] three years and six months [*see 1 Kings 17:1*].

18 And he prayed again, and the heaven gave rain, and the earth brought forth her fruit [*see 1 Kings 18:41–45*].

19 Brethren, if any of you do err [*stray;* Strong's *#4105*] from the truth, and one convert him [*bring him back;* Strong's *#1994*];

20 Let him know, that he which converteth the sinner from the error of his way shall save a soul from death [*from spiritual death*], and shall hide a multitude of sins.

Regarding the phrase "and shall hide a multitude of sins" in verse 20, above, it is interesting to note that Joseph Smith changed the phrase "cover the multitude of sins" in 1 Peter 4:8, to "preventeth a multitude of sins" in JST 1 Peter 4:8.

This concludes Part 2 of *The New Testament Made Easier*. Part 3 of this set covers the remainder of the New Testament, 1 Peter through Revelation, plus Brother Ridges' book, *The Savior's Life and Mission to Redeem and Give Hope*.

SOURCES

Doctrine and Covenants Student Manual, Religion 324 and 325. Salt Lake City: The Church of Jesus Christ of Latter-day Saints, 2001.

Ensign. March 1976 and November 1995.

Hymns of The Church of Jesus Christ of Latter-day Saints. Salt Lake City: The Church of Jesus Christ of Latter-day Saints, 1985.

Improvement Era. Vol. 19.

Journal of Discourses. Vol 18. London: Latter-day Saints' Book Depot, 1854–86.

Parry, Jay A. and Donald W. *Understanding the Book of Revelation.* Salt Lake City: Deseret Book, 1998.

Kimball, Spencer W. *The Miracle of Forgiveness.* Salt Lake City: Bookcraft, 1969.

Life and Teachings of Jesus and His Apostles, The. New Testament student manual, Religion 211. Salt Lake City: The Church of Jesus Christ of Latter-day Saints, 1979.

McConkie, Bruce R. *Doctrinal New Testament Commentary.* 3 vols. Salt Lake City: Bookcraft, 1965–73.

McConkie, Bruce R. *Mormon Doctrine.* 2d ed. Salt Lake City: Bookcraft, 1966.

Millet, Robert L. *Alive in Christ: The Miracle of Spiritual Rebirth.* Salt Lake City: Deseret Book, 1997.

Pratt, Orson. *Masterful Discourses and Writings of Orson Pratt.* Compiled by N. B. Lundwall. Salt Lake City: Bookcraft, 1962.

Smith, Joseph. *History of The Church of Jesus Christ of Latter-day Saints.* Edited by B. H. Roberts. 2d ed. rev., 7 vols., Salt Lake City: The Church of Jesus Christ of Latter-day Saints, 1932–51.

Smith, Joseph. *Joseph Smith's "New Translation" of the Bible* (JST). Independence, Missouri: Herald Publishing House, 1970.

Smith, Joseph. *Lectures on Faith.* Salt Lake City: Deseret Book, 1985.

Smith, Joseph. *Teachings of the Prophet Joseph Smith.* Selected by Joseph

Fielding Smith. Salt Lake City: Deseret Book, 1976.

Smith, Joseph F. *Gospel Doctrine: Selections from the Sermons and Writings of Joseph F. Smith.* Salt Lake City: Deseret Book, 1971.

Smith, Joseph Fielding. *Doctrines of Salvation.* Compiled by Bruce R. McConkie. 3 vols. Salt Lake City: Bookcraft, 1954–56.

Strong, James. *The Exhaustive Concordance of the Bible.* Nashville: Abingdon, 1890.

Talmage, James E. *Jesus the Christ.* Salt Lake City: Deseret Book, 1982.

Widtsoe, John A. *Evidences and Reconciliations.* Salt Lake City: Bookcraft, 1943.

Various translations of the Bible, including the Martin Luther edition of the German Bible, which Joseph Smith said was the most correct of any then available.

About the Author

David J. Ridges taught for the Church Educational System for thirty-five years and taught for several years at BYU Campus Education Week. He taught adult religion classes, Especially for Youth, and Know Your Religion classes for BYU Continuing Education for many years. He has also served as a curriculum writer for Sunday School, Seminary, and institute of religion manuals.

He has served in many callings in the Church, including Gospel Doctrine teacher, bishop, stake president, and patriarch. He and Sister Ridges have served two full-time eighteen-month CES missions. He has written over 40 books, including study guides for Isaiah, the book of Revelation, the Old Testament, New Testament, Book of Mormon, Doctrine and Covenants and Pearl of Great Price.

Brother Ridges and his wife, Janette, are the parents of six children, have 17 grandchildren, and make their home in Springville, Utah.

Scan to visit

www.davidjridges.com